GLOBAL PROJECT MANAGEMENT HANDBOOK

Planning, Organizing, and
Controlling International Projects

David I. Cleland   Editor

Professor Emeritus, School of Engineering
University of Pittsburgh
Pittsburgh, Pennsylvania

Roland Gareis   Editor

Project Management Group
University of Economics and Business Administration
Vienna, Austria

Second Edition

McGRAW-HILL

New York   Chicago   San Francisco   Lisbon   London   Madrid
Mexico City   Milan   New Delhi   San Juan   Seoul
Singapore   Sydney   Toronto

The **McGraw·Hill** *Companies*

Cataloging-in-Publication Data is on file with the Library of Congress

1 2 3 4 5 6 7 8 9 0   DOC/DOC   0 1 2 1 0 9 8 7 6

ISBN 0-07-146045-4

*The sponsoring editor for this book was Larry S. Hager and the production
supervisor was Pamela A. Pelton. It was set in Times by International Typesetting
and Composition. The art director for the cover was Anthony Landi.*

Printed and bound by RR Donnelley.

McGraw-Hill books are available at special quantity discounts to use as premiums and
sales promotions, or for use in corporate training programs. For more information,
please write to the Director of Special Sales, McGraw-Hill Professional, Two Penn
Plaza, New York, NY 10121-2298. Or contact your local bookstore.

This book is printed on acid-free paper.

CONTENTS

iii

Chapter 4. Total Life-Cycle System Management   *James V. Jones*   4-1

Chapter 5. Developing Multinational Project Teams   *Aaron J. Nurick and Hans J. Thamhain*   5-1

Chapter 6. Risk Identification and Assessment for International Construction Projects   *John A. Walewski, G. Edward Gibson, Jr., and Ellsworth F. Vines*   6-1

Chapter 7. Program Management and Project Portfolio Management   *Roland Gareis*   7-1

Part 2 Competency Factors in Project Management 8-1

Chapter 8. Competencies of Project Managers *Lynn Crawford* 8-3

Chapter 9. Managing Risks and Uncertainty in Major Projects in the New Global Environment *Roger Miller and Brian Hobbs* 9-1

Chapter 10. Managing Human Energy in the Project-Oriented Company *Pernille Eskerod* 10-1

Chapter 11. Managing Project Management Personnel and their Competencies in the Project-Oriented Company *Martina Huemann* 11-1

Chapter 17. Managing Global Projects Over a Collaborative Knowledge Framework   *Suhwe Lee*

Part 4   Management of the Project-Oriented Company   18-1

Chapter 18. Management of the Project-Oriented Company *Roland Gareis*

Chapter 19. Project Portfolio Score Card   *Ernst Jankulik and Roland Piff*

Chapter 20. Partnering in Projects   *J. Rodney Turner*

Chapter 21. Business Process Management in the Project-Oriented Company   *Roland Gareis and Michael Stummer*   **21-1**

Part 5   National Project Management   **22-1**

Chapter 22. Project Management in Austria: Analysis of the Maturity of Austria as a Project-Oriented Nation   *Roland Gareis and Claudia Gruber*   **22-3**

Chapter 23. A Brief Insight of Project Management in the Mainland of China   *Chao Dong, K. B. Chuah, and Li Zhai*   **23-1**

Chapter 24. Project Management in Australia   *Brian R. Kooyman*   **24-1**

Chapter 25. Project Management in Romania
Constanta-Nicoleta Bodea   **25-1**

Chapter 26. Japanese Project Management Practices on
Global Projects *Hiroshi Tanaka*   **26-1**

Index follows Chapter 26

CONTRIBUTORS

Ozlem Arisoy *Department of Industrial Engineering, University of Pittsburgh, Pittsburgh, Pennsylvania* (Chap. 14)

Murat Azim *Katz Graduate School of Business, University of Pittsburgh, Pittsburgh, Pennsylvania* (Chap. 14)

Bopaya Bidanda *Department of Industrial Engineering, University of Pittsburgh, Pittsburgh, Pennsylvania* (Chap. 14)

Constanta-Nicoleta Bodea *Academy of Economic Studies, Bucharest, Romania* (Chap. 25)

Christophe N. Bredillet *ESC Lille, France* (Chap. 3)

K. B. Chuah *Associate Professor, Department of Manufacturing Engineering and Engineering Management, City University of Hong Kong* (Chap. 23)

David I. Cleland *Professor Emeritus, School of Engineering, University of Pittsburgh, Pittsburgh, Pennsylvania* (Chap. 1)

Lynn Crawford *ESC Lille, France, and University of Technology, Sydney, Australia* (Chap. 8)

Chao Dong *Ph.D, Department of Manufacturing Engineering and Engineering Management, City University of Hong Kong* (Chap. 23)

Pernille Eskerod *University of Southern Denmark, Esbjerg, Denmark* (Chap. 10)

Roland Gareis *Vienna University of Economics and Business Administration, Vienna, Austria* (Chaps. 2, 7, 18, 21, 22)

G. Edward Gibson, Jr. *University of Texas at Austin, Austin, Texas* (Chap. 6)

Claudia Gruber *Vienna University of Economics and Business Administration, Vienna, Austria* (Chap. 22)

Brian Hobbs *Université du Québec à Montréal, Montreal, Quebec, Canada* (Chap. 9)

Martina Huemann *Vienna University of Economics and Business Administration, Vienna, Austria* (Chap. 11)

Lewis R. Ireland *President, American Society for the Advancement of Project Management, Clarksville, Tennessee* (Chaps. 1, 15)

Ernst Jankulik *Siemens AG Austria, Building Technologies, 1230 Vienna, Austria* (Chap. 19)

James V. Jones *President, Logistics Management Associates, Irvine, California* (Chap. 4)

Charles W. "Chick" Keller *University of Kansas, Edwards Campus, Overland Park, Kansas* (Chap. 12)

Brian R. Kooyman *Managing Director, Tracey, Brunstrom & Hammond Group, Offices in Sydney, Brisbane, Melbourne, Perth and Canberra, Australia* (Chap. 24)

Suhwe Lee *Singapore* (Chap. 17)

Roger Miller *École Polytechnique de Montréal, Montreal, Quebec, Canada* (Chap. 9)

Dragan Milosevic *Maseeh College of Engineering and Computer Science, Portland State, University, Portland, Oregon* (Chap. 16)

Aaron J. Nurick   *Bentley College, Waltham, Massachusetts* (Chap. 5)

And Ozbay   *Maseeh College of Engineering and Computer Science, Portland State University, Portland, Oregon* (Chap. 16)

Roland Piff   *MCE AG, Vienna, Austria* (Chap. 19)

Jeffrey K. Pinto   *Black School of Business, Pennsylvania State University, Erie, Pennsylvania* (Chap. 13)

Dennis P. Slevin   *Katz Graduate School of Business, University of Pittsburgh, Pittsburgh, Pennsylvania* (Chap. 13)

Sabin Srivannaboon   *Maseeh College of Engineering and Computer Science, Portland State University, Portland, Oregon* (Chap. 16)

Michael Stummer   *Roland Gareis Consulting, Vienna, Austria* (Chap. 21)

Hiroshi Tanaka   *Yokohama, Japan* (Chap. 26)

Hans J. Thamhain   *Bentley College, Waltham, Massachusetts* (Chap. 5)

J. Rodney Turner   *The Lille School of Management, France, and University of Limerick, Ireland* (Chap. 20)

Ellsworth F. Vines   *Dick Corporation, Pittsburgh, Pennsylvania* (Chap. 6)

John A. Walewski   *University of Texas at Austin, Austin, Texas* (Chap. 6)

Li Zhai   *Associate Professor, Fudan University, Shanghai, China* (Chap. 23)

PREFACE

In the last forty years there has been a tidal wave of interest in project management as a management philosophy to use in dealing with the many *ad hoc* activities found in contemporary organizations. Project management is clearly an idea whose time has come. A substantial body of theory exists in the field, reflecting the wide experience gained by practitioners in many different industries and environments. Project management is recognized as a principal strategy and process to deal with the inevitable change facing organizations. The social, political, economic, technological, and competitive changes underway in the global marketplace require that any organization wishing to survive in the face of such change needs to understand how such change can be managed.

Business organizations in particular are facing awesome challenges in the intensely competitive global marketplace. Quality, productivity, costs, faster commercialization of products and services, cooperative research and development, and the dynamic changes being wrought by the "factory of the future" all can be dealt with through the use of project management philosophies and techniques. Add to these changes the continued erosion of quality to products and services that have to be designed, developed, produced, and marketed in global markets—the importance of a management philosophy to deal with such universal changes becomes apparent.

Project management has truly become "boundaryless"—cutting across disciplines, functions, organizations, and countries. The formation of "strategic alliances" to share project risk, resources, and rewards are becoming commonplace in the management of international businesses. Today, a truly domestic market does not exist; enterprise managers the world over must face the unforgiving global marketplace. Not only is the survival of enterprises at stake, the country's national and international competitiveness is at stake as well. In the past two decades the global economy has been transformed; vigorous new companies from countries in the Pacific Rim and elsewhere are challenging many of the traditional industries and the way of managing in these industries. The competitive pathway to be followed in the political, economic, and technological conversion of Eastern Europe and Russia to free market economies will be a pathway characterized by the use of project management strategies. The ability to develop and produce products and services faster, at lower costs, with higher quality, and meeting the criteria for both local and international markets have become key performance factors. To remain competitive in the global markets, companies must develop the ability to make incremental improvements in the technology embodied in the products and services to be offered in the markets, as well as in the organizational processes needed to conceptualize, create, design, develop, and produce value that provide total customer satisfaction.

Successful project-oriented companies today are using project management processes to transfer technology from around the world and integrating those processes effectively into their products, services, and organizational processes. Global project management provides a solid foundation of management technology to create products and services that did not previously exist but are needed to remain competitive in the global marketplace.

In the fast evolving field of global project management, there is a critical need to pull together a practice reference to explain the new techniques of the field, provide understanding of the unique nature of global project management, and instill confidence in the user that truly practical global project management philosophies and strategies are available and can be used. The second edition of this handbook provides that reference source for pragmatic how-to-do-it global project management information, tempered by that bit of theory needed to be consistent with the state-of-the-art of this important discipline. Anyone who wants to learn about global project management is faced with an abundance of published information. The best of this published information, integrated in this handbook and presented in a global and project-oriented perspective, provides a coherent and relevant prescription for the global owner. In a rapidly developing field such as project management, even experienced project "stakeholders" need a source that can help them understand some of the competitive changes in the world that are without precedent.

All project stakeholders—project managers, functional managers, general managers, project team members, support staff, and the many outside organizational units with which the global project manager must deal—will find this handbook useful. Students of project management may use the handbook as a self-study aid, for it has been organized to facilitate an easy and enjoyable learning process. Senior managers can, through a careful perusal of this publication, gain an appreciation, and respect, for what global project management can do to make their enterprises more competitive in the international markets.

This handbook is the result of the cooperative effort of many experts in the field, both in academic and in real world practice. The qualifications of these learned and experienced people are clear from the biographical sketch that is provided on the title page of each chapter. The content of the handbook is broadly designed to be relevant to the general organization contexts in which global project management is found.

Within the global marketplace the time between the creation of inception of a new technology in products and processes is decreasing. Until a few years ago, it took up to ten to twelve years or more for a scientific discovery—even a discovery leading to an incremental advancement of technology in products and processes—to wend its way from the point of origin to commercial use. Today much less time is required; global project management done within the context of concurrent engineering or simultaneous engineering, and though the organizational mechanism of product-process design teams is reducing that time dramatically. Global project management, done within the authority of strategic management, has become a common language for global enterprises to cooperate across organizational, cultural, and national boundaries in seeking mutual objectives and goals. It is to this purpose that the second edition of this *Global Project Management Handbook* is dedicated.

David I. Cleland
Roland Gareis

ACKNOWLEDGMENTS

Many people contributed to this handbook. The authors who provided the chapters are an assemblage of experts in the business of global project management. Their contributions reflect a wide range of expertise and viewpoints in this growing and important field of project management. We thank, and are deeply indebted to, these chapter authors.

We thank our graduate students, who in many indirect yet meaningful ways added to the value created by this handbook. Our classroom discussions with these young scholars surfaced many ideas that became integrated into this publication. We also thank our many friends in the project management professional associations for the opportunity to discuss with them the strategy for the development of the handbook. Each of these friends contributed in some way to the substantive content of the book, as well as the intellectual processes needed to pull together this important publication.

We are deeply indebted to Lisa Bopp, who managed the overall development and administration of the handbook. As was to be expected, her professionalism, dedication, and optimism encouraged us during the long period from the book's concept through to its actual publication. We also thank Rachel Borchardt for her assistance in the preparation of the manuscript.

Special thanks to Dr. Bopaya Bidanda, Chairman of the Industrial Engineering Department and Dr. Gerald D. Holder, Dean of the School of Engineering of the University of Pittsburgh, who provided us with the needed resources and environment to pursue the creation and publication of this handbook.

Finally, we hope that the people who use this handbook will find it a useful and timely source for the development of the knowledge, skills, and attitudes needed to compete in the growing field of global project management.

P · A · R · T · 1

STATE OF THE ART OF GLOBAL PROJECT MANAGEMENT

In Chapter 1, David I. Cleland and Lew Ireland show us how project management has evolved over the centuries as an effective way of dealing with (as well as causing) change, from the beginning of projects in antiquity to the early development of literature and management practices in the 1950's. Cleland and Ireland illustrate the continuing impact projects and project management have had on numerous events throughout history by examining the artifacts and literature associated with these events.

In Chapter 2, Roland Gareis introduces project management as a business process of the project-oriented company. Its sub-processes project start, project controlling, project coordination, and project close-down as well as the resolution of a project discontinuity are described. Methods and communication structures for the performance of project management are defined.

In Chapter 3, Christophe Bredillet introduces the reader to the ongoing need for project management research in a field that is rapidly expanding. Current and future trends in the field of project management are discussed, from categorizing project types to integrating supply chain management with learning and knowledge management to the link between strategy and projects. While Chapter 1 demonstrates how far we have come, Bredillet shows us the many areas in which project management could be developed in the future.

In Chapter 4, Jones takes a look at the life cycle of a project, from conception to evaluation, and analyses the way in which projects are typically evaluated, comparing short-term and long-term approaches to evaluation. Factors such as amount of time, budget constraints, and project results are examined, and show how a long-term approach may be the key to successful project evaluation.

Chapter 5 deals with the growth of project teamwork development around the world as a way to complete projects effectively and with minimal expense. Nurick identifies and analyses the key barriers to overcome in order to ensure that a global project partnership will be successful, as well as the key drivers necessary to achieve success. Nurick also offers tips for keeping project team members motivated and productive in their common endeavor.

Chapter 6 discusses the unique difficulties associated with international construction project ventures. The results of research findings are presented, along with an analysis of *International Project Risk Assessment (IPRA)*, a tool useful in assisting projects with assessing risk factors before beginning a project. Walewski provides recommendations on use of the IPRA for international projects.

In Chapter 7, Roland Gareis introduces program management and project portfolio management as specific management processes of the project-oriented company. A program is defined as a temporary organization that requires a specific organizational structure in addition to the organizations of the single projects belonging to the program. The project portfolio as the set of projects held by a project-oriented company at a given point in time is a new object of consideration of the management of the project-oriented company, requiring specific processes and methods.

CHAPTER 1
THE EVOLUTION OF PROJECT MANAGEMENT

David I. Cleland

Professor Emeritus, School of Engineering,
University of Pittsburgh,
Pittsburgh, Pennsylvania

Lewis R. Ireland

President, American Society for the Advancement of Project Management,
Clarksville, Tennessee

David I. Cleland is the professor emeritus in the School of Engineering at the University of Pittsburgh. He is the author/editor of 36 books in the fields of project management, engineering management, and manufacturing management. An active member of the Project Management Institute (PMI), he has published numerous articles and handbook chapters and has presented many papers at professional meetings in his field. He has served as a consultant for both national and foreign companies and is recognized as one of the best known members of PMI. He has been described as the "Father of Project Management." He has both a national and international reputation in his field and has been honored for his original and continuing contributions to his disciplines. He is a three-time recipient of the Distinguished Contribution to Project Management Award from the PMI. In 1987 he was elected a fellow of PMI. In 1997 he was honored with the establishment of the David I. Cleland Excellent in Project Management Literature Award sponsored by the PMI.

Lewis R. Ireland has more than 30 years of project experience and 16 years of work with quality aspects of projects. He is an executive project management consultant and author of quality and project management books. He served as the 1998 president and chair of the PMI and has served as the president of the American Society for the Advancement of Project Management (*asapm*) since 2003. Dr. Ireland's achievements in volunteer work have been recognized by the PMI through the Distinguished Contribution Award, Person of the Year, and being made a fellow of PMI. He continues to contribute time and energy to the advancement of project management around the world through professional exchanges of information on the practice and theory of project management.

INTRODUCTION

In the early 1970s it was stated in the project management community that "project management is the accidental profession." This statement has been quoted many times since, with all the implications that a discovery had been made and a new profession had been defined in the late twentieth century. Recognition of project management as a discipline and the use of this management approach have varied over several thousands of years.

The treatment of the subject of projects and project management in this chapter encompasses several thousands of years where evidence exists to demonstrate that projects were used to change and advance societies and that some form of project management was needed to ensure favorable conversion of resources to the benefit of these societies. The selection of examples of projects reported in this chapter is made based on available artifacts, literature, and other evidence reflecting a high degree of understanding and sophistication in effecting change through planned actions.

For centuries, project management has been used in some rudimentary form to *create change* or *deal with change* in societies. *Change* in a positive sense is caused by the application of management action that results in the consumption of resources to create a desired product, service, or organizational process. *Change* also may be meeting uncertain situations to identify and implement actions to obtain the most favorable outcome. Project management, in whatever form, has been used for centuries to plan for, implement, and meet change.

The general management discipline, although practiced in some form in antiquity, emerged as an explicit discipline in the twentieth century. It was during this period that concepts, philosophies, principles, processes, tools, and techniques began to appear in literature that reflects the intellectual framework found in the management of contemporary organizations. Yet a form of general management existed in antiquity to deal with the need to lead and organize various elements of society.

General management, often described in the context of leadership, was ubiquitous in the past, being the medium by which changes in societies were accomplished. The great leaders of history were "managers," managing political organizations, countries, explorations, wars, technological and social change, and so forth. The principal challenge to these managers was the need to create change for the better or to deal with the change that affected their societies.

It was the 1950s when project management was formally recognized as a distinct contribution arising from the management discipline. Prior uses of project management had a focus on cost, schedule, and technical performance but lacked the formal definition and embracing of the management concepts and processes in an integrated manner. Since the early 1950s, names and labels have been given to the elements of the project management discipline, helping to facilitate its further development as a profession.

The vocabulary associated with project management has grown from some original definitions The single term *project* has an origin that dates back several hundreds of years. According to the *Oxford English Dictionary,* the word *project* was first used in the sixteenth century. The following list presents some samples from the second edition of the *Oxford English Dictionary* listed in chronological order from the year 1600 through 1916:

Year 1600   "A projecte, conteyninge the State, Order, and Manner of Governments of the University of Cambridge. As it is now to be seen."

Year 1601   Holland Pliny II 335: "Many other plots and projects there doe renaime of his (Parasius') drawing. . . ."

Year 1623   T. Scot Highw: "All our Projects of draining surrounded grounds. . . ."

Year 1863   Geo. Eliot Rhola Proem: "We Florentines were too full of great building projects to carry them all out in stone and marble. . . ."

Year 1916   M. D. Snedden in *School and Society* 2:420, 1916: "Some of us began using the word 'project' to describe a unit of educative work in which the prominent feature was a form of positive and concrete achievement."

From earliest recorded times, people have worked together toward designing and creating projects. Although the term *project management* did not come into wide use until the 1950s, its history is much longer that the term itself.

This chapter is a step toward acknowledgment and a fuller appreciation of the role that project managers and project teams have played throughout history in the evolution of society. A study of projects of the past would include an assessment of the effectiveness in management of the projects—as well as development of an informal "lessons to be learned" profile in the conceptualization and completion of the projects. As an inventory of these profiles is developed, our knowledge of what to do in managing contemporary projects, as well as what to avoid, adds to our understanding of how project management should be carried out in both the present and the future.

An early form of project management was used to plan for and use the resources needed to deal with change. Only through studying the past can we fully perceive how the world has been changed by projects. A study of these projects helps us to understand how institutions have emerged and survived using a form of project management. Having a knowledge and appreciation of past projects binds us to the present and the future. If we do not learn from the past, we are condemned to make the same mistakes and pay for those mistakes again.

TYPES OF EVIDENCE FOR HISTORICAL PROJECTS

A review of the results of projects in antiquity reveals evidence about how several historical projects originated and developed. The evidence takes three primary forms:

1. *Artifacts*—something produced by human workmanship, such as a tool, weapon, structure, or substance of archeological or historical interest. Examples include the Great Pyramids and the printing press.

2. *Cultural strategies*—such as found in the arts, beliefs, institutions, and other products of work and thought typical of a society at a particular time. Examples include the English Magna Carta, the U.S. Emancipation Proclamation, and the U.S. Social Security Program.

3. *Literature and documents*—publications and project-related documents that describe project management and how it was used. Examples include books, articles, and editorials that describe projects and the use of project management.

From the period *circa* 1950 to the present time, there is a growing abundance of articles, books, papers, and miscellaneous documentation that can be used to build a contemporary model of project management. For the period prior to 1950 back through antiquity, there is very limited documentation and literature. To understand how project management emerged requires examination of the artifacts and the social, military, technological, political, industrial, and governmental strategies that existed. From study of these areas, we may reach a judgment concerning the role of supporting projects. Then we can draw conclusions about how the projects were managed and in the process identify any "seeds" of the project management concepts and processes that existed.

PROJECT CHARTER

A *project charter* describes at a high level what is to be accomplished in a project and delegates authority to the project manager to implement actions required for project completion. It typically grants the project manager or project leader the authority to conduct selected actions while planning, implementing, and completing the project. It may contain details on what is to be done and what may not be done. Statements of mission, objectives, or policies also may be included and accompanied by a budget.

An examination of historical documents that recognized the need for new artifacts or strategies can provide initial insight into how and why the artifacts or strategies evolved. These historical documents usually provide the "strategic need" for the action being considered and in most cases provide for a document similar to a "project charter" to guide the design and execution of the initiative. For example:

- The *Spanish Book of Privileges and Prerogatives* granted to Christopher Columbus, April 20, 1492. This document sets forth the compensation promised to Columbus by Queen Isabel and King Fernando, if Columbus discovered land on his first voyage to the New World.

- The *English Charter to Sir Walter Raleigh,* March 25, 1584. This document, executed by Queen Elizabeth I, granted Sir Walter Raleigh authority to explore and claim lands for England. It also defined the compensation that Raleigh would receive.

- The *United States Congress Act authorizing Lewis and Clark Expedition*, February 28, 1803. This act authorized exploration of the Northwest Territory of the United States to find a land passage to the Pacific Ocean.

- The *United States Homestead Act*, May 20, 1862. This document granted an individual, free of charge, 160 acres of public land if within five years a house was built on the land, a well was dug, 10 acres were plowed, a specific amount of land was fenced, and the individual actually lived there. An individual could claim an additional 160 acres of land if 10 acres were planted and cultivated successfully with trees.

- The *United States Tennessee Valley Act,* May 18, 1933. This law established the Tennessee Valley Authority for the purpose of reforestation, marginal land improvement, flood control, and agricultural and industrial development of an area covering seven states.

- The *English Instructions authorizing the voyages of discovery of Captain James Cook,* August 1768, July 1772, and July 1776. Captain Cook was chartered by the United Kingdom Royal Society to conduct three voyages in search of scientific information and various lands; each voyage was about three years in duration.

EARLY LITERATURE ON PROJECTS

In all too many cases it will be impossible to find the original documents that established the need for the artifact or strategy. For example, the Great Pyramids of Egypt, the Great Wall of China, the Grand Canal of China, Roman roads, and Roman aqueducts are without written documentation, but the artifacts remain today in some state. In these cases, descriptions provided in the anthropologic, archeologic, and other historical literature can supply some insight into how and why these projects were accomplished.

Perhaps the earliest publication on the management of projects appeared in 1697, entitled *An Essay Upon Projects,* authored by Daniel Defoe, who had an interesting comment on the building of the Ark:

> The building of the Ark by Noah, so far as you will allow it human work, was the first project I read of; and no question seem'd for it, and had he not been set on work by a very peculiar Direction from Heaven, the Good old Man would certainly have been laugh'd out of it, as a most senseless ridiculous project [p. ii].

Some additional comments Defoe made regarding projects include

- "Every new Voyage the Merchant contrives is a Project" (p. 8).
- "After the Fire on London, the contrivance of an Engine to Quench Fires, was a Project the Author was said to get well by, and we have found to be very useful" (p. 25).
- "The project of the Penny-Post, so well known, and still prais'd . . ." (p. 27).
- "And to Dedicate a Book of Projects to a Person who had never concern'd himself to think that way, would be like Music to one that has no Ear" (p. ii).

Defoe identifies in 1697 the dilemma still facing contemporary managers: how to design and implement project management concepts and philosophies.

Mary Parker Follett, writing in 1920, extolled the benefits of teams and participative management and said that leadership comes from ability rather than hierarchy. She advocated empowerment, drawing on the knowledge of workers, and supported the notion of the formation of teams through cross-functions in which a horizontal rather than a vertical authority would foster a freer exchange of knowledge within organizations.

A 1959 article that caught the attention of the growing project management community was authored by Paul Gaddis, entitled "The Project Manager," and published in the *Harvard Business Review.* It described the role of an individual in an advanced-technology industry who functioned as a focal point for the management of resources being applied to manage ad hoc activities across organizational boundaries.

Another contribution to the emerging theory and practice of project management, entitled "Functional Teamwork," appeared in the *Harvard Business Review* in 1961, authored by Gerald Fish. He described the growing trend in contemporary organizations toward functional-teamwork approaches in organizational design.

Professor John F. Mee, a noted scholar in the history of management theory and practice, published an article in *Business Horizons* in 1964 that described the characteristics of the "matrix organization." He described one of the key characteristics of this approach as an organizational system that created a "web of relationships" rather than a line and staff relationship of work performance.

David I. Cleland and William R. King published *Systems Analysis and Project Management* (New York: McGraw-Hill) in 1968. This book was the first scholarly work on project management cast in the context of the emerging "systems approach" in management theory and practice.

Since these landmark documents were published, a host of publications has appeared each year. Amazon.com lists more than 2300 books for sale in 2005, and this number does not include books that are out of print. It is estimated that more than 500 project management books are published each year in the United States in the English language. This number does not include books on aspects of project management that have other terms in their titles, such as *project manager* and *risk management.*

GOVERNMENT LITERATURE

In 1964, the U.S. Air Force announced publication of a series of manuals and policies to force consistent management processes over the design and acquisition of major weapons systems. The series changed the relationship between the government and private industry, whereby private industry had to adopt and use the defined practices. The manuals and policies selected to effect management change were part of a series of *Air Force Systems Command Manuals* referred to as the *375 Series.* The six most important of these manuals are

AFSCM 375-1, *Configuration Management*

AFSCM 375-3, *System Program Office Manual*

AFSCM 375-4, *System Program Management*

AFSCM 375-5, *System Engineering Management Procedures*

AFSCM 375-6, *Development Engineering*

AFSCM 310-1, *Management of Contractor Data and Reports*

In addition, other policy and procedure guidelines were published in the form of operating instructions, pamphlets, regulations, and other supporting documentation.

The impact of the 375 Series of guidelines was to introduce changes in the government–defense industry relationship. The impact that these guidelines had on the evolving project management literature was significant in terms of shaping project management in the United States and in countries influenced by the manner in which U.S. project management has been conducted. Much of the early literature of the 1960s and 1970s drew on and reflected the philosophies, concepts, processes, and techniques put forth in the 375 Series. Today, as the project management literature continues to emerge, one can see some of the early seeds of the 375 Series and how these seeds matured.

LEADING PROJECTS OF ANTIQUITY

One cannot review the history of civilization without concluding that projects on scales both small and epic have been central to the continued evolution of society. Examples of some of the leading people and projects of antiquity that have created change include the following:

Prince Henry of Portugal (1394–1460)

In the early years of the fifteenth century, Prince Henry the Navigator developed and operated what could be called today a *research and development laboratory* located in Sagres, Portugal. The voyages of the discovery that set forth could be considered to be "projects." These projects of discovery made important conditions to the evolving body of knowledge in cartography, navigation, and shipbuilding. Experiments in shipbuilding produced a new type of ship—the caravel, which made future exploration projects possible.

The caravel, a major improvement over older ships, contributed to the success of Prince Henry's exploration efforts. It was faster and could sail well into the wind with both square sails and a triangular one. At about 65 feet long with a capacity of roughly 130 tons of cargo or supplies, the caravel was more perfectly sized for the type of exploration conducted by Prince Henry.

Each voyage documented discoveries, and each following voyage built on prior work. Each new "project" was a continuation of the process for exploring and assessing the lands of Africa. Ship captains were sent on voyages with questions to be answered, which gave them a specific set of objectives—as with all good projects.

The Great Pyramids of Egypt (*circa* 2700 to 2500 B.C.)

Outside Cairo, Egypt, stand the Great Pyramids at Giza. Some of the characteristics of these projects are as follows:

- The pyramids were national projects.
- The workers were organized into competing teams.
- The workers were motivated through their deep religious belief, and they believed that by building a tomb for their king, they were ensuring his rebirth.
- The workforce was highly organized. Each group of workers was responsible for one part of the pyramid complex.
- A highly developed support force was needed, including a place to feed and house all the workers, as well as the bakers, brewers, butchers, and so on.
- The workers were well treated and well fed and had access to medical care.

The workforce had all the evidence of a highly organized team of motivated individuals—not the typical depiction of slaves being whipped to work. There is little doubt that the project team for each pyramid had a mixture of technical skills and knowledge that represented a sophisticated approach to building the structure.

The Great Cathedrals of Europe

Between 1050 and 1350 in France alone, more than 500 large churches were built, as well as 1000 parish churches, so that there was a church or chapel for every 200 people. In Germany, the Cologne Cathedral, considered by some to be the most perfect specimen of Gothic architecture in the world, undoubtedly took the longest to build. The foundation alone was laid in 1248. By 1417, one of the towers was finished to one-third its present height, but at the time of the Reformation, its roof was still covered with boards. Finally, the cathedral was completed in 1880, more than 630 years after construction first began.

Each church and chapel was a project that relied on the technology of the day. These artifacts of projects suggest that an early form of project management had to be used to organize the workforce and construct these houses of worship. The positive impact on society because of the churches cannot be estimated in any comparative analysis.

The Grand Canal of China (486 B.C. to the present)

This is the world's oldest and longest canal, far surpassing the next two grand canals of the world: the Suez and Panama Canals. The building of the canal began in 486 B.C. during the

Wu Dynasty. It was extended during the Qi Dynasty and later by Emperor Yangdi during the Sui Dynasty. The canal is 1114 miles long with 24 locks and some 60 bridges. A project is currently underway to extend the Grand Canal to Ningbo—or more than twice it present length to 3100 miles.

This canal has served China for nearly 2500 years and continues to be used as a means of commerce through waterborne transport of goods. The project to construct the canal and its supporting bridges and locks could have been accomplished only through dedicated planning and work effort to achieve its objectives.

Noah's Ark

The designer of the Ark was God Himself. The shape of the ark was that of a rectangular barge with a low draft. Some other specifications include

- Make a roof and finish it to within 18 inches at the top.
- Coat inside and out with pitch.
- The Ark was to be about 437 to 512 feet in length, with a beam of 75 feet.
- The Ark would have an internal volume of 1,515,750 cubic feet.
- There would be only one door to enter and exit.

Historians have speculated that it took 120 years to build the Ark. The size of the project and its end product—the Ark—leave much to the imagination as to how the "project team" acquired the materials and the technology needed to shape and assemble the parts.

St. Petersburg, Russia (1703–1713)

In 1703, Emperor Peter began construction of a new city in the north of Russia, where the Neva River drains Lake Ladoga. The city was built on a myriad of islands, canals, and swamps. Construction conditions were brutal. Nearly 100,000 workers perished in the first year. Within 10 years, St. Petersburg was a city of 35,000 buildings of granite and stone and the capital of the Russian Empire. Today, the city is valued for its historic buildings and contribution to Russian history. Although no longer capital of Russia, it plays an important role in industrial and cultural activities of the people.

Tower of Babel

According to Genesis 11:1-9, a structure was erected in the plain or valley of Shinar. The builders presumed to build an edifice that reached the heavens—symbolizing human self-sufficiency and pride. Historians believe that the myth on which the building of the tower rests may have developed as an attempt to account for the diversity of human language—in the modern thought, an inability to communicate or to fail to understand one another's communication. One might ask if there have been any modern construction projects where a lack of communication among the project stakeholders was a cause for delay or cancellation of the project.

Signing of the Magna Carta (1215)

The Magna Carta is a document that states the basic liberties guaranteed to the English people. The Magna Carta proclaims rights that have become a part of English law and are now the foundation of the constitution of every English-speaking nation. The Magna Carta, which means "great charter" in Latin, was drawn up by English barons and churchmen, who forced the tyrannical King John to set his seal on it on June 15, 1215. King John's cruelty and greed united the powerful feudal nobles, the churchmen, and the townspeople against him. While he was waging a disastrous war in France, the leading nobles met secretly and swore to compel him to respect the rights of his subjects. When King John returned from the war, they presented him with a series of demands. King John tried to gather support, but almost all his followers deserted him. At last he met with the nobles and bishops along the south bank of the Thames in a meadow called Runnymede and affixed his seal to the Magna Carta.

Empress Catherine the Great of Russia (1729–1796)

Catherine assumed power in Russia in 1762 after a coup d'état in which she led officers of the Royal Guard. Unlike her husband, she was well loved by the country's elite and received good press in Europe thanks to her contacts with many figures of the French Enlightenment. Catherine's court was extremely luxurious. She was the first to move into the newly built Winter Palace. Catherine started a royal art collection, which later was housed in the world-famous Hermitage. Several additional buildings (the Small Hermitage and the Old Hermitage) were commissioned for the growing royal collection of art. The Hermitage Theater was built, and the area around the palace was put in order and built up with the finest houses and palaces.

MILITARY CAMPAIGNS

Most, if not all, military campaigns have taken on the characteristics of projects. Military battles and campaigns have objectives and consume resources through planned activities in most cases. The introduction of new weapons that have been developed in a structured form typically gives military leaders some advantage over their adversaries by exploiting a weakness.

These new weapons frequently represent a response to an adversary's weakness, such as the introduction of body armor on the battlefield to counter sword, knife, and club weapons. The opposition countered with weapons that exploited the openings in the armor, such as under the armpits when a knight would raise a sword to strike. One response was to provide armor under the armpits. Armor was discarded as an advantage when weapons such as guns were able to penetrate the material. Interestingly enough, the modern-day helmet and bulletproof vest have been adopted as a means to stop opposing gunfire.

The Battle of Grecy (August 26, 1346)

Fought on Saturday, August 26, 1346, the Battle of Grecy, France, was the first of several significant battles during which the longbow triumphed over crossbows and armored knights. The French forces in the battle numbered approximately 30,000; English forces numbered 12,000, of which 7000 were archers. The battle line was about 2000 yards wide. The English army occupied the top of a gentle ridge near the town. Each English archer carried two sheaves of arrows into battle. The arrows could be shot at 250 to 300 yards. The French made 14 to 16 charges against the English lines from the start of the battle at 4:00 P.M. until the end of the battle at midnight. Casualties were estimated to be 5000 for the French knights and Genoese crossbowmen and about 100 for the English.

The Battle of Grecy had political consequences in Europe. From a military hardware perspective, the use of the longbow by the English forces proved superior to the traditional crossbow and mounted-knight strategy of the French. Tactically, the Battle of Grecy established the supremacy of the longbow on the battlefield and gave England standing as a great military power. The longbow was responsible for vast changes in the nature of medieval warfare. It made England the foremost power in Europe during the fourteenth and fifteenth centuries. England won almost every battle fought through a skillful and tactical use of massed archers and men-at-arms. On many occasions, the English troops were outnumbered but still were able to win the battle. It was during King Edward's victory at Caen, on the way to Grecy, that a "mooning" incident occurred. Several hundred Norman soldiers "mooned" the English archers; many of these soldiers paid a painful price for their display!

Some Significant Projects of the World

A few other projects that have changed the world include

- The Great Wall of China, built in segments over 2000 years, from 221 B.C. to A.D. 1644. It was constructed to keep out foreign invaders.
- The first Trans-Atlantic cable, constructed in three attempts from Valencia Harbor, Ireland, to Trinity Bay, Newfoundland, starting in June 1857 and completed on July 27, 1866.
- Ancient Roman roads, a planned system of public roads around Rome constructed and maintained by the state. The roads were constructed from different materials layered to provide for durability. The roads ranged in width from 8 to 40 feet with ditches for good drainage.
- The first steam engine (1704), built to pump water from mines. This engine used atmospheric pressure to power the thrust of the piston (by cooling the steam to create a vacuum). Later versions used steam to power the thrust of the piston.
- The Coliseum of Rome, constructed in the first century. The Coliseum was constructed to a height of 160 feet and could seat about 50,000 spectators. Its purpose was for games of entertainment.
- The catacombs of Alexandria, Egypt (second century A.D.), are the graves of a single family. These catacombs, opposite of the Great Pyramids of Egypt, are more than 100 feet below ground at their lowest point.
- The dikes of Holland, started in the thirteenth century. The dikes of Holland are a form of water management system that recovers land. The levees and dams retain the water while windmills pump excess water out. This represents recovery and use of more than 160,000 hectares of land.
- The Siberian Transcontinental Railroad (1891–1905). This railroad was built to link Moscow with Vladivostok in the east—a distance of some 6000 miles. This commercial link aided in transporting materials in both directions.
- The railroad from Buenos Aires to Valparaiso, (1910–1982). This 156-mile railroad rose to a height of 10,500 feet in the Andes Mountain Range to transport passengers

and freight over winding tracks and through long tunnels between Argentina and Chile.

- The exploratory journeys of Ponce de Leon (1540–1621) resulted in the discovery and claiming of Florida for Spain. Ponce de Leon accompanied Columbus on his second voyage to America in 1593 and stayed in the Dominican Republic as its governor.

SUMMARY OF THE RESULTS OF HISTORICAL PROJECTS

Projects of the past have been challenging and have contributed to the well-being of millions of people by creating changes that advanced society. In some instances, the project was a response to a situation such as a natural disaster that threatened lives. Change through making the best use of resources is project management. The resulting benefits throughout history have been delivered in the form of new or enhanced projects, valuable services, and improved organizational processes.

Projects have ranged in length throughout antiquity from perhaps a single day to hundreds of years. A battle fought in a single day could change the future of generations. Some of the effects of projects include

- Change or reactions to change
- New or enhanced products, services, or organizational processes
- Varied degrees of risk and uncertainty
- Benefits and/or destructive results
- Modest to spectacular results
- Creation of something that did not exist previously
- Integrated results into the strategic or operational initiatives of the owner
- Social progress (or lack of progress)

MORE MODERN PROJECTS

Lewis and Clark Expedition (1803–1806)

In 1801, President Jefferson long had an interest in exploration of the western area of America leading to the Pacific. What helped to prompt Jefferson to dispatch the first American exploration to the Pacific was the publication of a small book detailing the first British expedition to reach the Pacific from Canada in the late eighteenth century. Rival Canadian competitors in the fur trade, the Hudson Bay Company and the Northwest Company were striving to dominate the fur trade in what now is western Canada and the western United States. In one of the trading posts in what is now Alberta, Canada, Alexander Mackenzie, a member of the Northwest Company began to consider how far it might be to the Pacific coast, which had been explored by James Cook, George Vancouver, and other English seamen. Mackenzie followed the river named for him, and the river took him to the shores of the Arctic Ocean. In a journey in 1792, he had better success by following the Peace River and its tributaries, reaching the Continental Divide. From the western slope of the Rockies, he struck the upper reaches of the Fraser River, hoping that it would lead him to the coast. He found that the canyons of the Fraser River were impossible to traverse. Following some suggestions made by a group of Indians, he set out on an overland journey and reached the coast of British Columbia in July 1793. It was another eight years before he published a full account of the journey. A year later, Thomas Jefferson received a copy in the United States.

An American captain, Robert Gray, had already found the Columbia River. It was a massive river that Jefferson believed must reach inland to the Rockies. He believed that if Americans could travel up the Missouri River and reach the Columbia from the east, they might find what MacKenzie had missed: an effective water route from the American heartland to the Pacific coast and the markets of Asia. Apparently the fact that the Missouri River flowed through territory not belonging to America did not bother Jefferson.

The prize that Jefferson sought was a practical route to the Pacific. The U.S. Congress could sponsor such a journey. The earliest assessment of cost for the journey was $2500 for equipment and provisions, including gifts for the Indians. During the spring and summer of 1803, Jefferson and Lewis worked feverishly to get the expedition under way.

In the charter given to Lewis, Jefferson stated that the mission was to find "the most direct and practicable water communication across the continent for the purposes of commerce" and to ensure that the U.S. Government received accurate information about it. Jefferson also instructed Lewis and Clark to take careful note of the latitude and longitude of all remarkable points between them from the Missouri River and the coast of the Pacific Ocean. Jefferson had another assignment for Lewis and Clark—to be Jefferson's roving ambassador to the western Indians. Lewis and Clark were to compile as much information as they could about the Indian nations through the lands in which they passed. They were instructed to meet with Indian leaders and make them acquainted with our wish to be friendly and useful to them.

It is widely known by the project management community that a project has to have a strong sponsor—an individual or organization that justifies the project, sets a time schedule, establishes the technical objectives, and provides resources is essential. This is what was done in the planning for the Lewis and Clark expedition.

The Suez Canal (1859–1869)

The Suez Canal is one of the wonders of the nineteenth century. It was a French initiative, designed by a Frenchman, financed by Frenchmen, and opened up by a French symbol of power. French entrepreneur Ferdinand de Lesseps led the Suez Canal effort. The canal ended up being one of the strengths of British imperial power.

During the campaign of Napoleon in Egypt in the late eighteenth century, the French had seen the commercial and military possibilities of linking the Mediterranean and Red seas. One man, a diplomat in the French Foreign Service, saw his career eroding in the diplomatic service. His personal life was saddened by the loss of his wife and one of his children. He dedicated himself to a one-man canal-building campaign from 1853 until 1869 and was obsessed with the building of the Suez Canal.

He convinced the Egyptians that the building of the canal would prove that they still had the potential to be a powerful force in world affairs. To the French he said that the canal would offer a grand example of their national capability more than wars and revolutions. Rich Frenchmen invested in his company. Unfortunately, he was considered to be somewhat of a crackpot in other countries. In England, British leaders trashed his plans. A spokesman in England called it "among the many bubble schemes that from time to time have been put on gullible capitalists." Whether this trashing was a reflection of British stupidity, a lack of foresight by British leaders, or a subtle cunning on the part of the British leaders is not known.

The Franco-Egyptian feat of engineering was advantageous to the British, who were the most skeptical. Britain's ocean links to India would benefit most from a canal. Before the canal opened, it had taken at least 113 days for a steamship to sail the 6000 miles from London to Calcutta via the Cape of Good Hope. The canal cut the distance by a third under the terms of the concession obtained by Lesseps, whose company had the clearance to dig a channel across the arid Suez Isthmus, a distance of 100 miles, and to operate it for 99 years. The Egyptian government would receive 15 percent of the profits, the founders 10 percent, and the shareholders the rest.

Experience with modern major construction projects indicates that they cost at least twice the amount stated in the prospectus and that the expected revenues usually are about half of what is projected. In the Suez Canal there were additional reasons for cost overruns. A huge labor force would have to be obtained from the Egyptian peasantry. In addition, there were major problems in cutting the canal through its pathway in arid land.

The Panama Canal (1870–1914)

The Panama Canal, often called the "big ditch," was started by a French company in 1870. The company ultimately went into bankruptcy. The technical challenges were part of the problems faced by the French company, but perhaps the greatest problem was one of health. Malaria plagued the workers and many died within weeks of arriving in Panama. The French company sold its interest in the Panama Canal to the United States in 1903. The United States, under the political leadership of President Teddy Roosevelt, started working on the Panama Canal and finally finished it in 1914. The canal was the biggest and most costly venture that Americans had ever tried outside their borders.

The Panama Canal was a vast, unprecedented feat of engineering, political intrigue, and logistic challenge. Apart from wars, it represented the largest, most costly single effort ever before mounted and held the world's attention over a span of 40 years.

Transcontinental Railroad, Omaha, Nebraska, to Sacramento, California (1862–1869)

In the United States in the mid-1800s, a project was initiated to join the continent of North America by railroad. The two biggest corporations in America, the Central Pacific and the Union Pacific railroads, had armies of men at work building separate railroad lines. This project was an epic of logistics, organization, and endurance. When the two railroads were joined in Promontory, Utah, a single transportation system became operational from the east coast to the west coast of the United States.

Completion of this project linked the east and west coasts of the United States through a rail system to conduct commerce. Between Omaha and Sacramento, there were few towns on the path to benefit from the commerce. The railroad, however, provided the incentive to build communities both to service the system and to use it.

The Pennsylvania Turnpike (1935–1940)

Building the Pennsylvania Turnpike in the late 1930s is an example of the early use of project management in the United States. The Pennsylvania Turnpike opened on October 1, 1940, and was completed on time and within budget. Moreover, it attained its objective as an innovative means for improving highway systems.

The initial turnpike was envisioned as a four-lane road extending from just east of Pittsburgh to Carlisle—a distance of 160 miles—using the right of way for a planned railroad. The turnpike incorporated the latest is design features to accommodate modern travel, such as no road or rail crossings, gentle curves and slopes, and 10 service plazas for travelers. This turnpike set the example for roadways in the future and subsequently was incorporated into the overall system of major highways.

The Manhattan Project (1942–1945)

The Manhattan Project for the development and delivery of the atomic bomb had a major impact on the strategy for winning World War II by the United States and its allies. General Leslie R. Groves was appointed as the project manager for the development, production, and delivery of the atomic bomb, which, although devastating to Japan, is credited with saving the lives of thousands of American military personnel.

The Manhattan Project was a complex arrangement of participants in Chicago, Illinois, Oak Ridge, Tennessee, and Los Alamos, New Mexico. The technical challenge to harness the atom required the work of many scientists working under the direction of a military man, General Groves. In addition, the requirement for security and administration of the various participants posed an additional burden on the project manager.

The Normandy Invasion (June 6, 1944)

Operation Overlord was the largest military seaborne and airborne invasion of World War II. Planning for the invasion began in the summer of 1942, with detailed planning nearly completed by late 1943. Revision and updating of the plan continued until June 1944, when the invasion took place. This planning encompassed a massive assembly of human resources, war materials, air and sea transport, and logistic support. Significant Allied (Britain, Canada, France, Greece, The Netherlands, Norway, Poland, and the United States) military forces and resources were gathered in Britain. The initial sea assault from landing ships and craft was on a five-division front between the French Orne River and the Cotentin Peninsula. Airborne forces parachuted behind German lines to capture critical lines of communication and resupply routes.

The seaborne region was divided into five landing beaches (code named from west to east Utah, Omaha, Gold, Juno, and Sword). The overall battle itself, however, would be decided by the abilities of the Allies to reinforce their initially weak beachhead by sea as compared with the easier movement of German reinforcements by land.

On June 5, 1944, thousands of ships and craft from the Allies put to sea and gathered in assembly areas southeast of the Isle of Wight. Airborne forces assembled at key airfields in anticipation of parachuting into France. After overrunning the German beach defense, the Allies rapidly expanded the individual beachheads and reinforced the beach assault forces with new troops, munitions, and supplies. By July 25, the Allies were strong enough to launch Operation Cobra to begin the liberation of France.

In a larger sense, the successful Allied landing in France was a psychological blow to the German occupation of Europe. The invasion challenged the ability of the German to control western Europe, dramatically increased partisan activity and heartened the morale of all the people in Europe fighting against Nazi tyranny. The balance of power on the continent, already weakened by a Soviet offensive into Poland, was tipped in favor of the Allies. From the breakout at Normandy, the Allies would begin the drive into Germany, leading to surrender of the Nazi regime on May 7, 1945.

The Internet (August 1962)

The creation and building of the Internet was not a monolithic project. Rather, it was a patchwork of individual and organizational contributions pieced together through the years. It was an immense integration of much solitary effort and cooperative work. It came into being where knowledge and competency resided in thousands of uncelebrated places—laboratories, classrooms, offices, social gatherings, and so forth—where people knowledgeable in computers and telephone lines got together and tried to improve communication among themselves.

Professor and innovator J. C. R. Lickrider played a role much akin to a "virtual project manager," throwing out ideas and concepts to fertile minds that worked informally together to create a means of communication that led to the World Wide Web and other supporting technologies and protocols that are known today as the Internet. [A fascinating summary description of the evolution of the Internet can be found in James Tobin, "The Internet," Chapter 8 in *Great Project* (New York: Free Press, 2001).]

MODERN PROJECT MANAGEMENT PRACTICES

Project Management Today

Project management has evolved over the centuries from a rudimentary form of managing projects to a sophisticated process that has been defined in literature as well as being promoted by major professional associations around the world—namely, the Project Management Institute (PMI) and its chapters, the International Project Management Association (IPMA) with its national associations, the Japanese Project Management Forum, and the Australian Institute of Project Management. These organizations have defined project management for their members in bodies of knowledge and competence baselines.

The PMI, for example, has nine areas of focus for project management that define the categories of its recognized body of knowledge. These categories are shown in Table 1.1.

These areas have been developed over time and through the experiences of project practitioners. The PMI has been developing and evolving its body of knowledge since 1983—nearly 25 years—for use by its members.

The IPMA, headquartered in Zurich, Switzerland, and its national associations have a body of knowledge (referred to as a *competence baseline*) that describes the topics that are important for their planning and implementation of project management. Table 1.2 lists topics that the IPMA uses to define and describe its body of knowledge.

TABLE 1.1   PMI Categories of Project Management

Project time management
Project cost management
Project quality management
Project scope management
Project risk management
Project procurement management
Project quality management
Project human resources management
Project integration management

TABLE 1.2   IPMA Competence Elements

1. Technical competences	2. Behavioral competences	3. Contextual competences
1.1 Project management success	2.1 Leadership	3.1 Project orientation
1.2 Interested parties	2.2 Engagement	3.2 Program orientation
1.3 Project requirements & objectives	2.3 Self-control	3.3 Portfolio orientation
1.4 Risk & opportunity	2.4 Assertiveness	3.4 Project, program, & portfolio implementation
1.5 Quality	2.5 Relaxation	
1.6 Project organization	2.6 Openness	3.5 Permanent organization
1.7 Teamwork	2.7 Creativity	3.6 Business
1.8 Problem resolutions	2.8 Results orientation	3.7 Systems, products & technology
1.9 Project structures	2.9 Efficiency	
1.10 Scope & deliverables	2.10 Consultation	3.8 Personnel management
1.11 Time & product phases	2.11 Negotiation	3.9 Health, security, safety & environment
1.12 Resources	2.12 Conflict & crisis	
1.13 Cost & finance	2.13 Reliability	3.10 Finance
1.14 Procurement & contract	2.14 Values appreciations	3.11 Legal
1.15 Changes	2.15 Ethics	
1.16 Control & reports		
1.17 Information & documentation		
1.18 Communication		
1.19 Start-up		
1.20 Close-out		

SUMMARY

Project management has evolved over many centuries of use. It was not until the 1950s that the literature began to reflect the evolving theory and practice of this discipline. An early rudimentary form of project management was used over the centuries in the creation of artifacts and cultural enhancements in world societies.

This chapter makes a contribution to the literature on how project management has evolved to become the principal means for dealing with change in modern organizations. Project management has a rich heritage throughout its development of artifacts and cultural enhancements in the world of antiquity.

This chapter will be a landmark contribution to the birth and growth of project management discipline. It will raise a greater awareness of the project management profession and its place in history.

BIBLIOGRAPHY

Boorstin DJ. *The Discoverers*. New York: Vintage Books, 1983.

Cleland DI, King WR. *Systems Analysis and Project Management*. New York: McGraw-Hill, 1968.

Defoe D. *An Essay upon Projects* (1697). Menston, England: Scholar Press, Ltd., 1969.

Department of the Navy. Washington, DC: Naval Historic Center, 20374; www.history.navy.mil.

Fish G. Functional teamwork. *Harvard Business Review* Vol 39: 5, Sep/Oct 1961, pp. 67–79 [see Linden].

Gaddis P. The project manager. *Harvard Business Review* Vol 37: 13, pp. 89–97, 1959 [see Strickland].

Linden DW. The mother of them all. *Forbes*, January 16, 1988, pp. 75–76.

McCullough D. *The Path Between the Seas.* New York: Simon & Schuster, 1977.

Mee JF. Matrix organization". *Business Horizons,* Summer 1964, Vol 7: 12, pp. 70–72.

Strickland M, Hardy R. The *Great Warbow.* London: Sutton Publishing Company, 2005.

Tobin J. The Internet. *Great Projects.* New York: Free Press, 2001, Chap. 8.

US Air Force. *USAF Systems Command Manuals,* nos. 375–1 through 375–6 and 310–1. Washington: US Government Printing Office, 1964–1966.

CHAPTER 2
PROJECT MANAGEMENT: A BUSINESS PROCESS OF THE PROJECT-ORIENTED COMPANY*

Roland Gareis

*Vienna University of Economics and Business Administration,
Vienna, Austria*

Roland Gareis holds an M.B.A. and a Ph.D. He was a Fullbright scholar at the University of California, Los Angeles, in 1976, professor for construction management at the Georgia Institute of Technology, and visiting professor at the Georgia State University, ETH in Zürich, Switzerland, and the University of Quebec in Montreal, Canada. Since 1983, he has been director of the postgraduate program "International Project Management" at the Vienna University of Business Administration. For 15 years he was president of Project Management Austria, the Austrian project management association. He was project manager of the 10th Internet World Congress on Project Management and manager of the research program "Crisis Management." Currently, he is professor of project management at the Vienna University of Economics and Business Administration, manager of the global research program "Project Orientation," and owner of Roland Gareis Consulting. He has published several books and papers on management of the project-oriented company.

ABSTRACT

Projects are temporary organizations that are used for the performance of relatively unique short- to medium-term strategically important business processes with medium to large scope. Project management is a business process of the project-oriented company that includes the subprocesses project start, continuous project coordination, project controlling, project close-down, and possibly, resolution of a project discontinuity. In the project management process, project objectives, objects of consideration, project schedules, project costs and project income, project resources, and project risks, as well as the project organization, the project culture, and the project context, are considered.

*Parts of this chapter are based on the book *Happy Projects!* by Roland Gareis (Vienna: Manz, 2005).

THE PROJECT: A SOCIAL CONSTRUCT

In project management research, as well as in the practice of project-oriented companies, various project definitions are used. This is important inasmuch as different perceptions of projects lead to different project management approaches.

The definition of projects as tasks rather than as temporary organizations and as social systems results in a different understanding of the objectives of project management, of the project management tasks, of the objects of consideration of project management, and of the project management methods used.

Perception of Projects as Tasks with Special Characteristics

Traditionally, projects are defined as tasks with special characteristics. The special characteristics of projects are the "complexity" of the content, the relative uniqueness, the high risk, and the high strategic importance for the project-oriented company. Projects are understood as goal-oriented tasks because the objectives in terms of the scope, the schedule, the required resources, and the costs are planned, agreed on, and controlled.

Typical representatives of this project understanding are, for example, the Project Management Institute (PMI), the American Project Management Institute (APMI), and the German Society for Project Management (GPM), whose project definitions are cited below. The GPM defines a *project* as ". . . an undertaking which is basically characterized by the uniqueness of conditions, e.g., objective, temporal, financial, personnel and other limitations, boundaries against other undertakings, project specific organization." *Project management* is ". . . the entirety of management tasks, management organization, management techniques and tools for the performance of a project."[1]

The PMI defines a *project* as "a temporary endeavor undertaken to create a unique product or service. . . . Projects are undertaken at all levels of the organization. They may involve a single person or many thousands. Their duration ranges from a few weeks to more than five years."[2] *Project management* is "the application of knowledge, skills, tools and techniques to project activities to meet project requirements."[3]

Perception of Projects as Temporary Organizations

According to organizational theory, projects can be perceived as temporary organizations for the performance of business processes that are limited in time. As with other organizations, a project has a specific identity that is characterized by its specific project objectives, project organization, project values, and project environment relationships.

A project is a temporary organization. Through this temporary character, the establishment of the project in the project start process, as well as the dissolution of the project in the project close-down process, attains a special meaning.

Perception of Projects as Social Systems

The perception of projects as temporary organizations also makes it possible to view them as social systems. According to social systems theory, organizations, and therefore also projects, can be viewed as social systems that have clear boundaries to differentiate themselves from their environments. However, they are also related to those environments. The specific characteristics of social systems, such as their social complexity, dynamics, and self-reference, are management topics in projects as well.

Therefore, projects are understood as temporary organizations and social systems. This understanding of projects results in a systemic project management approach that matches the complexity and dynamics of projects.

Definition of Project

A *project* is a temporary organization of a project-oriented company for the performance of a relatively unique short- to medium-term strategically important business process of medium or large scope. Projects are used for the performance of relatively unique processes. The more unique the objectives and deliverables to be fulfilled, the higher is the associated risk. Information from past experiences that can be used as reference often is available only to a limited extent.

Projects are used for the performance of business processes with short to medium duration. These projects should be performed as quickly as possible—in other words, in several months. One exception is the performance of infrastructure projects (construction or engineering projects), which can have a longer duration.

Business processes for which projects are used have a medium to high strategic importance for the company performing them. The performance of contracts contributes to, for example, the short- to medium-term survival of the company. The development of new products and the establishment of a new strategic alliance, however, have long-term consequences and therefore are strategically more important.

Projects are used for business processes of medium to large scope. The scope of a business process can be described by the tasks and resources required, the costs occurring, and the organizations involved. To operationalize the definition of *project,* the characteristics of business processes are used, that is, the strategic importance, duration, organizations involved, resources required, and costs occurring. The scaling of these characteristics is to be defined by each organization. Table 2.1 gives an example of the definitions from an Austrian bank. In other organizations, some aspects (e.g., costs) will be higher or lower.

The table shows that there is a possibility for organizational differentiation in project-oriented companies to differentiate between projects and small projects. Projects with a lower level of complexity, such as the performance of an event, the development of a brochure, or the completion of a small contract, can be defined as *small projects.* Fewer

TABLE 2.1 Operationalizing the Definitions of Projects and Programs by a Bank

Criteria	Small Project	Project	Program
Strategic importance	Net present value: At least 50,000	Net present value: At least 50,000	Net present value: At least 250,000
Duration	At least 2 months	At least 3 months	At least 12 months
Organizations involved	At least 3 organizations	At least 5 organizations	At least 7 organizations
Resources	At least 100 person-days	At least 200 person-days	At least 500 person-days
Costs	At least 0.1 million	At least 0.5 million	At least 1 million

project management methods are used for small projects than for projects, and there is less detail in the project plans than there is with projects. It is usually sufficient to segment the work breakdown structure only to the third level.

For small projects a less differentiated design of the project organization will suffice than for projects. The role of the "project owner" will be filled by one person instead of a team. Subteams probably will not be necessary. Project marketing is less extensive for small projects than for projects.

In order to ensure the organizational advantage of projects, business processes that are fulfilled as projects should be differentiated from business processes that are not project-worthy. The fulfillment of routine business processes is accomplished by the permanent organization, as well as by work groups.

Relationships among Projects, Business Processes, Investments, and Objects

To clarify the definition of what a project is, differentiation between projects, business processes, investments, and objects is helpful. The relationships among projects, business processes, investments, and objects then can be analyzed.

Several business processes are combined in an investment process. The investment in an industrial plant, for example, combines the business processes of developing a feasibility study, planning the plant, constructing and commissioning the plant, use, maintenance, and decommissioning of the plant.

Investments can be initialized by a project and/or a program (Fig. 2.1). Projects can segment the investment process.

Objects are both the objects of consideration and the results of an investment. They can be divided into material and immaterial objects. The material object of the investment in an industrial plant is the industrial plant. All the business processes to be fulfilled in the framework of this investment are related to this object.

A project is to be differentiated from the object that results from the project. Projects are to be labeled not only with the object name (e.g., "Product XY") but also with their function (e.g., "Development of Product XY").

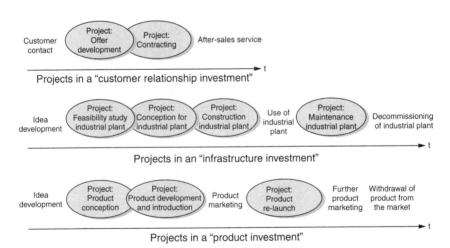

FIGURE 2.1   Segmentation of investment processes through projects.

PROJECT MANAGEMENT APPROACHES

Project management approaches can be differentiated by the way in which projects are perceived. Traditional method-oriented project management approaches are based on the perception of projects as tasks with special characteristics. The systemic and process-oriented project management approach of Roland Gareis' *Project and Program Management* is based on the perception of projects as temporary organizations and as social systems.

Traditional Project Management

The traditional perception of projects as tasks with special characteristics promotes the planning orientation in project management.[4] The main focus is on how an assignment is to be performed. Methods for work planning and work organization, such as the REFA methods,[5] or methods of operations research[6] represent the theoretical basis of traditional project management.

For decades, project management was understood as the use of project scheduling methods, such as Critical Path Method (CPM) and Program Evaluation and Review Technique (PERT), for scheduling projects, as well as for supporting resource and cost planning. Because of the CPM-based risks tied to unique tasks, traditional project management uses methods for risk management as well as for controlling the project progress, project schedule, project resources, and project costs.

Only through the definition of nontechnical projects, such as marketing and organizational development projects, and the consideration of additional disciplines, such as organization, marketing, and controlling, have methods been introduced that are easy to use and to communicate, such as the work breakdown structure. Organizationally, it appears that the most important element in traditional project management is the division of formal authorities between the project manager, the immediate supervisor of the project team member, and the team member. As possible solutions to this, the pure project organization, the matrix project organization, and the influence project organization are offered as standards.[7]

The project management tasks are defined as the planning, controlling, and organizing of projects. In traditional project management, the objects of consideration of project management are the scope, the schedule, and the costs. The relationships among these objects of consideration are depicted as the "magic triangle" (Fig. 2.2).

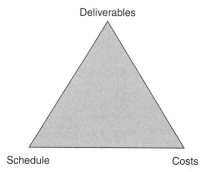

FIGURE 2.2 Traditional objects of consideration of project management ("magic triangle").

Roland Gareis' Project and Program Management

Influences of Organization Theory.   The perception of projects as temporary organizations promotes the awareness that every project requires a specific organizational design that goes beyond the definition of the formal authority of the project manager. In addition to project planning, a situational design of the project organization should contribute to the success of the project.

The organizational design of projects includes the definition of project-specific roles, the development of project organizational charts, the definition of project-specific communication structures, and the agreement on project-specific rules. Through the temporary character of projects, the design of the project start and the project close-down obtains a special importance.

Relatively new management approaches, such as customer orientation, empowerment, flat organizational structures, team work, organizational learning, process orientation, and networking, can be implemented in projects to contribute to project success. The management approaches "learning organization," "lean management," "process management," and "total quality management" therefore are to be seen as an additional, new theoretical basis for project management.

The perception of projects as temporary organizations also promotes the development of a project-specific culture. Such project management methods are, for example, the choice of the project name and the formulation of the project mission statement and project-specific slogans.

Influences of Social Systems Theory.   The perception of projects as social systems enables the use of views and models of social systems theory for project management. A "systemic" project management builds not on traditional project management but rather puts its methods into a new framework, interprets them, and promotes the development of new project management methods.

Because of the need to manage the boundaries and the context as well as the complexity and the dynamics of projects, new potential avenues and challenges arise for project management. A new understanding of the project management tasks to be fulfilled is enabled. Instead of planning, controlling, and organizing the project, the tasks of constructing the project boundaries and the project context, building up and reducing the project complexity, and managing the dynamics of the project become relevant.

Construction of the Project Boundaries and the Project Context.   Construction of the project boundaries and the project context ensures a holistic view of the project (Fig. 2.3). Definition of the project boundaries should enable an integrated consideration of technical, organizational, personnel, and marketing objectives in the project.

For detailed management of the project boundaries, the following project management methods are available: project objectives plan, objects of consideration plan and work breakdown structure, project schedule and project resource plan, project costs and project income plan, project organization, and so on. For an analysis of the project context and

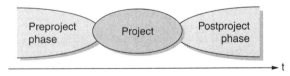

FIGURE 2.3   Project boundaries and project context (time dimension).

the design of project context relationships, project environment analysis, analysis of the pre- and post-project phases, business case analysis, and analysis of the relationship of the project to other projects and to the company strategies can be used.

Building Up and Reducing Project Complexity. Projects require a certain amount of complexity in order to be able to relate to the (infinitely) complex environment. The building up and reducing of complexity is a project management task.

A holistic project view, creativity in the project, and acceptance of project-related decisions can be ensured through adequate communication structures. The performance of project workshops at the project start process, at milestones, and at the close-down process of the project, as well as the performance of project team and project owner meetings, promotes the building up of complexity in a project. The differentiation of project roles, the definition of the relationships among the roles, and the inclusion of different specialist disciplines and hierarchical levels in the project team are further organizational possibilities for the building up of complexity in a project (Fig. 2.4).

By using different project management methods, different perspectives for designing a project are chosen. Only the linking up of these different views in a "multimethods approach" enables appropriate consideration of the project complexity.

To ensure continuity in a project, redundant structures should be created. A reduction of project complexity is achieved through agreement on the project objectives within the project team. Furthermore, the use of project management standards, the establishment of project-specific rules and norms, the development of project plans, and the performance of integrative project team meetings gives repeated orientation to the work of the project.

Management of the Project Dynamics. The dynamics of a project result from the interventions of relevant environments, as well as through the self-reference of the project. Examples of interventions from relevant project environments are new legal requirements

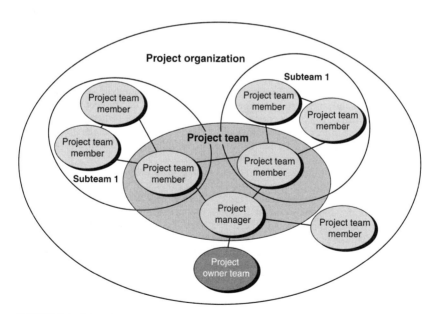

FIGURE 2.4 Roles of the project organization and their relationships (project organization chart).

from public authorities, a change in scope by the customer, cancellations from suppliers, an unexpected media response, a demotivated project team, and so on.

The formal communication structures of a project enable its self-reference. Project management methods, such as the work breakdown structure, the milestone plan, and the project environment analysis, can support the communication in the project. The possibility of change in a project depends on its relationship to relevant environments. Only when the functionality of the (relative) project autonomy is recognized and therefore the interventions of the permanent organization of the project-oriented organization are limited is there a possibility of self-reference.

In order to promote change in a project, reflections and metacommunications, that is, communications about communications, are necessary. Time, space, and the corresponding know-how are all necessary for reflection. In a cyclic process, the structures necessary for the performance of a project are formed, questioned, and possibly adapted according to the new requirements.

Self-referencing processes in a project or interventions from project environments can lead to continuous or discontinuous changes in a project. Continuous changes in projects are considered in project controlling. Continuous changes in projects take the form of adaptations in the project structures, such as new project slogans, new formations of relationships to relevant environments, new definitions of project roles, new demands on the project team members, new planning of the scope and the project schedule, and so on.

A discontinuous development in a project comes about when a change in the project identity takes place. This can result from a substantial deviation from the project objectives. A project discontinuity can take the form of a project crisis, a project change, or a structurally determined change in the project identity.

Process-Oriented Project Management.   Method-oriented project management focuses on the project management methods. The use of methods for planning and controlling project scope, project schedule, project resources, and project costs is understood as project management. The success of project management is assessed on the basis of the method application. Competence for the application of the project management methods is achieved through training. There is a supposition that good knowledge of methods ensures good project management.

Roland Gareis' *Project and Program Management* defines project management as a business process of the project-oriented company and focuses on its subprocesses. The project management personnel require competencies for managing the subprocesses project start, continuous project coordination, project controlling, and project close-down and possibly resolving a project discontinuity. The success of project management is assessed on the basis of the professional performance of these processes, not on the basis of a project handbook that meets all formal demands. In so doing, the relationships among the subprocesses also must be considered and optimized.

For performance of the individual project management subprocesses, the corresponding project management methods are used. The importance of the methods does not get lost. Definition of the subprocesses of project management adds an integration level for ensuring the professional application of project management methods. Producing an optimal project schedule cannot be an objective in itself, but it must be an overall integrative objective to start the project in an optimal way.

Management of project objectives, management of the project schedule, management of the project cost planning, and so on cannot be accepted as project management processes[8] because only an integrated consideration of all methods of project management can lead to optimal results. The management of project plans as "processes" cannot ensure a holistic management.

THE PROJECT MANAGEMENT PROCESS: AN OVERVIEW

Project management is a business process of the project-oriented company that is fulfilled in projects. The methods of process management can be used to describe the project management process. At a macro level, the project management process is to be given boundaries and differentiated from other processes. At the micro level, the objectives, tasks, responsibilities, and results of the project management process and its subprocesses are to be described.

Documentation of the project management process promotes communication about the objectives, tasks, responsibilities, and results of project management. Definition of the results of the project management subprocesses makes it possible to measure and evaluate the performance of project management and the quality of project management. Description of the project management process also provides the basis for a targeted further development of individual and organizational project management competencies in the project-oriented company.

Description of the Project Management Process

The objective of the business process of project management is the professional management of projects. A prerequisite for the realization of project objectives is the professional fulfillment of the subprocesses of project start, project coordination, project controlling, (possibly) resolving of a project discontinuity, and project close-down.

The objects of consideration in project management are the project objectives, the project scope, the project schedule, the project resources, the project costs and project income, and the project risks, as well as the project organization, the project culture, and the project context (Fig. 2.5). The dimensions of the project context are the pre- and postproject phases, relevant project environments, other projects, the company strategies, and the business case for the investment that is initiated by a project.

The structure of the project management process is shown in Fig. 2.6, and the objectives and and time boundaries are listed in Table 2.2.

From a systemic point of view, it is the objective of the project start to establish the project as a social system. The objective of project control is to promote the evolution of the project, and the objective of project close-down is to dissolve the project as a social system. The objective of resolving a project discontinuity is to develop a new project

FIGURE 2.5 Objects of consideration in project management.

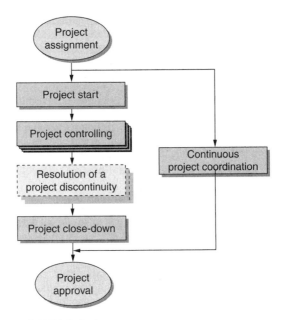

FIGURE 2.6   Project management process.

identity in order to resolve the discontinuity. The objective of continuous project coordination is to ensure the progress of the project.

The project coordination process is performed continuously. The performances of the other project management subprocesses are limited in time.

By definition, the project start and the project close-down are each performed only once. Project control is performed several times in a project and takes place either periodically or at project milestones. The need to resolve a project discontinuity depends on the occurrence of a project crisis or a project chance (Fig. 2.7).

TABLE 2.2   Objectives and Time Boundaries of the Project Management Process

Objectives of the project management process
- Providing the structural prerequisites for the realization of the project objectives
- Efficient performance of the project start, project controlling, project close-down, and continuous project coordination
- Possibly: Efficient resolution of a project discontinuity
- Management of the social-, time- and content-related project boundaries
- Management of the relationships of the project to the project context
- Building up and reducing of project complexity
- Management of the project dynamics
- Nonobjective: Realization of the content work of the project (*Note*: This is an objective of the project and not of project management)

Time boundaries of the project management process
- Start: Project assigned
- End: Project approved

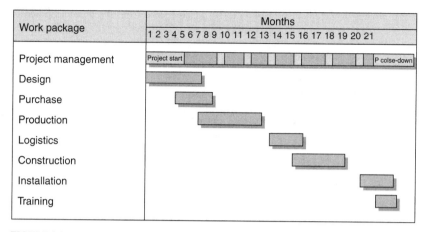

FIGURE 2.7   Project management subprocesses in an engineering project.

The benefit of a common view of the project management subprocesses lies, on the one hand, in ensuring the uniformity of the project management approach used and, on the other hand, in considering the relationships between the subprocesses. The application of a uniform project management approach ensures that uniform terminology and methods are used in all subprocesses. Professional project management considers the relationships among the subprocesses in order to optimize the project management results. The following relationships exist among the project management subprocesses:

- At the project start, the structures for project control and project close-down are planned.

- The criteria for evaluating project success at project close-down are determined at the project start by defining the project objectives.

- At the project start, the working methods to be applied during project control and project close-down are established (e.g., project meetings, project workshops, developing minutes, and reflections).

- Through application of the scenario technique and development of alternative plans at the project start, potential measures for the resolution of a project discontinuity are provided.

- Management of any structurally determined change of identity of the project is planned at project start.

- In project control, the project plans developed at the project start will be controlled and possibly adapted.

- When managing a project discontinuity, the alternative plans developed at the project start and/or the current project plans from the latest project control can be used.

- At project close-down, the plans developed at the project start and adapted during project control form the basis for evaluating project success and for ensuring organizational learning.

- Project marketing is performed in all subprocesses of project management based on an overall project marketing strategy.

The project management process is to be differentiated from the business processes for the fulfillment of project deliverables. Therefore, project content-related processes such as procurement, engineering of components, and testing of software, for example, are not management processes.

Context of the Project Management Process

The context in terms of time of the project management process is the project assignment and the investment controlling processes. In terms of content, these processes are the content-related business processes.

The content-related business processes depend on the project type. For an information and communications technology (ICT) project, the following content-related business processes have to be performed according to the project phase structure: gathering information, analysis of the current situation, definition and description of alternative solutions, implementation plan for each alternative, and decision making. For a contracting project, the engineering, the procurement, the production and the logistics, the construction and the installation, and the training and the commissioning make up the content-related business processes.

Content-related business processes are performed during a project parallel with the project management process. The relationship between the project management process and the business processes for the performance of a project contents is immediate because it is an objective of the project management process to develop appropriate structures for the fulfillment of the project contents.

The project assignment process is performed before the project start, whereas that of the investment controlling process is performed during the project and after the project closedown. The project assignment process is especially important for project management because in it the basic structures for the project are determined. The definition of the project objectives, the planning of the project organization, and the drafts of the project plans are roughly worked out. Project management is important for the investment controlling process because the project documentation constitutes an essential foundation for control.

PROJECT MANAGEMENT SUBPROCESSES

Project Start Process

The project start process can be described with regard to its objectives, time boundaries, tasks and responsibilities, and the tools to be used. Figure 2.8 illustrates the project start process, and Table 2.3 lists the objectives and time boundaries.

Owing to the time pressure of projects, once they are assigned, it is tempting to start the content-related business processes immediately without having performed the corresponding project start process. This lack of willingness to perform project planning and design of the project organization together with the project team often results in

- Unrealistic project objectives and unclear definitions of roles
- Project plans that are inadequate and not binding
- Unclear agreements regarding the design of project environment relationships and missing organizational rules

A professional project start is to be performed in order to ensure adequate project management quality.

Tasks / Responsibilities	Project owner team	Project manager	Project team	Project team members	Project management consultant	Expert pool manager	Representatives of relevant project environments	Documents
Planning the project start								
• Checking the project assignment and the results of the pre-project phase		P						
• Selecting start communication form		P						
• Selecting project team members (and a PM consultant)		C				P		
• Selecting PM methods and PM templates to be used		P						
• Agreeing with project owner	C	P						1)
Preparing the project start communications								
• Hiring of a project coach (possible)		P			(C)			
• Preparing start communications I, II, etc.		P			(C)			
• Inviting participants		P				C		2)
• Documenting the results of the pre-project phase		P	C		(C)		C	
• Developing drafts for planning, organizing and marketing the project		P	C		(C)		C	
• Developing information material for start communication		P	C		(C)			3)
Performing the project start communications								
• Distributing information material to participants		P						
• Performing start communication I	C		P		(C)		C	
• Developing draft of PM documentation "Project start"		P			(C)			
• Performing start communication II, etc.	C		P		(C)		C	
Follow-up to the project start communications								
• Completing draft of PM documentation "Project start"		P			(C)			
• Agreeing with project owner	C	P						4)
• Project marketing: Initial information	C			P	(C)		C	
• Distributing PM documentation "Project start"		P				I		
• Filing of PM documentation "Project start"	C			P			C	
Performing first work packages (parallel)				P			P	

Legend:	Documents:
P ... Performance	5) List of project management methods to be used
C ... Contribution	6) Invitation of participants to the project start workshop
I ... Information	7) Information material for the project start workshop
	8) Project management documentation "Project start"

FIGURE 2.8 Description of the project start process.

Project Control Process

Since changes occur in a project, such as changes in the objectives, changes in the availability of resources, and so on, and since the level of information improves during the performance of the project, it is necessary to perform a project control periodically. Project control is to be planned subject to project duration. In a product-development project of six months duration, it is recommended to perform a formal project control

TABLE 2.3   Objectives and Time Boundaries of the Project Start Process

Objectives of the project start process
- Information transfer from the preproject phase into the project
- Definition of expectations regarding the postproject phase
- Development of adequate project plans for managing the project objectives, scope, schedule, resources, costs, income, and risks
- Design of the project organization, adequate integration of the project into the permanent organizations
- Development of the project culture
- Establishment of communication relationships between the project and other projects and relevant project environments, initial project marketing
- Communicating the "big project picture" to all members of the project organization
- Planning of measures for discontinuity management
- Definition of the structures for the following project management subprocesses
- Developing the documentation "project start"
- Efficient design of the project start process

Time boundaries of the project start process
- Start:Project assigned
- End: Documentation "project start" filed
- Duration: 2–3 weeks

every two to three weeks. In an engineering construction project with a duration of, for example, 24 months, formal project control meetings with the project owner team will be necessary every two months, and short project progress reports should be issued once a month. It is recommended to perform project control on reaching project milestones.

The evolution of the project, which results from the dynamics of the project itself and from the dynamics in project environment relationships, must be followed. Possible deviations of the actual data from the planned data are to be identified, and directive measures for using new potentials and/or for correcting undesirable deviations are to be set. Opportunities for organizational learning on the project are to be used.

Project control refers to all objects of consideration of project management, not just the project scope, the project schedule, and the project costs. Within the framework of "social" control, above all, the project organization, the project culture, and the relationships to the relevant project environments are to be controlled.

For preparing project control communications, the following tasks must be fulfilled by the project manager and project team members:

- *Project control*—determining actual data, performing planned versus actual analyses, performing deviation analyses
- *Project direction*—planning directive measures
- *Adaptation of the project plans*—updating project plans
- *Development of the project control reports*—developing project progress reports, project score cards, and deviation trend analyses

Figure 2.9 illustrates the project control process.

The performance of project control communications usually includes a project team meeting and a project owner team meeting. In these meetings, a common project reality

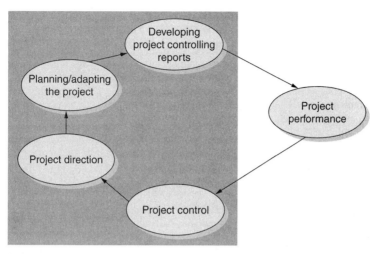

FIGURE 2.9   Project control cycle.

should be constructed that forms the basis for agreeing on directive measures. The follow-up to project control communications includes completing the project control reports, possibly initializing adaptations to the project portfolio database, project marketing based on new intermediary results of the project, and distributing the project control reports.

An adequate project control quality is ensured only by applying project management methods and communication forms in the project control process. The project plans that were developed in the project start are to be controlled and adapted, if required.

Project Coordination Process

In contrast to periodically performed project control, project coordination is performed continuously. Project coordination is the ongoing task of the project manager. Beside the supply of continuous information to members of the project organization and to representatives of relevant project environments, the objectives of project coordination are continuous project marketing, coordination of project resources, ensuring project progress, and ensuring the quality of the work package. Project progress is ensured by the project manager controlling the progress of individual work packages, coordinating the relationships between the work packages, and accepting the results of individual work packages.

The quality of the project coordination process depends on the quality of the communication between the project manager and the other members of the project organization and representatives of relevant project environments. On the one hand, this requires appropriate social competence and, on the other hand, appropriate communication tools. These are, above all, the project management documents developed in the project start process, such as the project objectives plan, the work breakdown structure, and the project environment analysis, but they also include specific tools of project coordination, that is, to-do lists, meeting minutes, and work package acceptance certificates. The commitment established in these communications determines the quality of the project coordination process.

Managing Project Discontinuities

Tasks involved in managing discontinuities are, on the one hand, the resolution of project discontinuities and, on the other, the avoidance of project crises, the provision of project opportunities, and the management of project discontinuities (Fig. 2.10).

The objectives are to plan and implement strategies and measures that avoid crises, that promote project opportunities, and that manage discontinuities in an efficient manner in the case of their occurrence. Avoiding project crises, promoting project opportunities, and providing for project discontinuities are not subprocesses of project management in their own right but are tasks to be fulfilled in both the project start process and the project control process. Therefore, in the following, only the resolution of a project discontinuity will be described.

Owing to their complexity and dynamics, projects have a high potential for discontinuities. In order to be able to complete a project successfully, the competence to resolve a project discontinuity professionally is needed in the project-oriented company.

The definition of a discontinuity is a central task in the process of resolving a project discontinuity. The existence of a project discontinuity cannot be measured by means of objective criteria, such as project ratios, but must be constructed in a communication process. A loss in a contracting project amounting to 50,000 may or may not lead to a project crisis. This depends on the size of the project and the structures and cultures of the project-performing organization. If the loss is defined as a crisis, this leads to the use of crisis management; otherwise, "normal" project management is practiced.

The resolution of a project discontinuity thus requires a conscious construction of the discontinuity as a new project reality. Watzlawik assumes that no objective reality exists but only a subjective construction of reality.[9] Only the conscious definition of a discontinuity gives the situation a specific sense and clarifies its social meaning. By defining a discontinuity, the "crisis" or the "chance occurrence" are differentiated from normality. A difference is made "that makes a difference." On the one hand, identification of a situation as a crisis or a chance occurrence serves as a "label" that aims at securing special management attention, and on the other hand, it legitimizes the use of (radical) measures for resolving the discontinuity.

The process of resolving a project discontinuity consists of the phases of planning and performing immediate measures, cause analysis, planning alternative resolution strategies, and planning and performing additional measures. General strategies for resolving a project discontinuity include

- Redesigning the project
- Stopping the project
- Interrupting the project

Redesigning the project may lead to appointing a new project owner team, a new project manager, or new individual project team members; may require redefining the project objectives and project content; may necessitate a new design of the project environment relationships; and may include creating a new project culture. By redesigning the project, a new project identity is created. This "revolution" in the project serves as the basis for a successful continuation of the project.

The resolution of a discontinuity is characterized by a high demand for creativity and discipline. Central weaknesses are to be identified and eliminated, strengths are to be preserved and expanded, important existing environment relationships are to be secured, and new ones are to be developed. The necessary strategies and measures are to be operationalized to enable traceability and measurement of success.

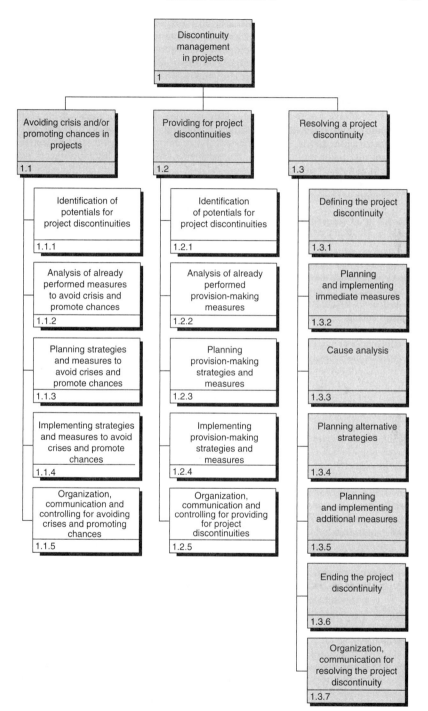

FIGURE 2.10   Managing project discontinuities.

Stopping a project poses a catastrophe in the development of the social system "project"—its survival is no longer guaranteed. From the point of view of the project-performing company, however, the decision to stop a project may be reasonable. Interrupting a project is a further strategic alternative. It presupposes that the project can be continued successfully after the period of interruption.

The objectives and the processes for stopping or interrupting a project correspond to those of the project close-down. In stopping a project, the project environment relationships are dissolved, the results achieved are secured, and the members of the project organization are given feedback and a new orientation for their work. In the event of a project interruption, the relevant environments are informed about the project interruption, the results achieved are secured, the members of the project organization are given feedback, and a new start for the project is planned. The availability of important members of the project organization at the new start of the project must be ensured.

As with project definition, the resolution of a project discontinuity is also an act of symbolic management. The resolution of the discontinuity should take place as early as possible and as late as necessary for establishing a new project identity. In the course of the resolution it should be agreed which new project rules and values apply after the discontinuity.

Generally, in addition to members of the project organization, external experts are required for resolving a project discontinuity so as to provide the know-how required at short notice. When the members of the project owner team and the project manager are not the cause of the project discontinuity, they should retain their roles in the resolution of the project discontinuity. The extent and intensity of the project communication increases during the resolution of a project discontinuity.

Crises and chance occurrences are seen often in projects but are rarely resolved professionally in practice. The process of resolving a project discontinuity is formalized only in a few companies; organizational competencies that address this process generally do not exist. The quality of the resolution of project discontinuities depends exclusively on the individual competencies of members of the project organization. The effort of avoiding crises and providing for chance occurrences in projects is also rarely practiced.

Project Close-Down Process

When the objectives of a project are achieved, the project as a social system is no longer needed. This contradicts the general objective of social systems to secure their viability. Therefore, as with the project start, the close-down of a project requires much effort.

The project close-down process is characterized by the fact that often unattractive work packages remain to be performed, some project environments (e.g., the project owner team, the customer, and individual project team members) may be interested in the persistence of the project, and some former project team members already may be working on new projects. The formal ending of the project serves to release resources and energy for new tasks. Know-how gained in the project should be transferred to the project-performing companies and to other projects by the project documentation and by exchange of experiences. A contribution to the knowledge management of the project-oriented companies is made.

Project close-down communications consist of the documentation of remaining work and drafts for planning the tasks and responsibilities in the postproject phase, evaluating project success, dissolving and establishing environment relationships, and creating drafts of project close-down reports and the final project management documentation. In the project close-down process, several closing communications are to be performed: a close-down workshop with the project team, a close-down meeting with the project owner team, a closing "social event," and possibly an exchange-of-experience workshop.

The objectives of the team's internal close-down are to evaluate project success, to assess the performance of the members of the project organization, and to provide information on the disposition of personnel after the project end. The close-down meeting with the project owner team deals with assessment of the project by the project owner team, reflection of the fulfillment of the project owner team's role, and formal project approval.

In practice, a formal project close-down is rarely performed. The right of the members of the project organization to adequate feedback and an emotional close-down, as well as the learning potentials for the project-oriented companies concerned, conflicts with the dynamics of everyday business and results in a lack of professionalism in project management.

Similar to the project control process, the quality of the project close-down process is ensured by the continuity of the project management methods used. For example, the project objectives plan, the business case analysis, and the project environment analysis are central methods of the project close-down process. On the basis of the business case analysis and the project objectives agreed to at the project start and adapted during project control, project success can be evaluated in project close-down. A "retrograde" sense-making through a redefinition of the project objectives in the project close-down process is often useful.

The project environment analysis enables dissolution of existing project environment relationships in an appropriate way and allows establishment of new relationships of the project-oriented company with relevant environments for the postproject phase. It also forms the basis for the final project marketing.

In order to enable a social project close-down—and not only a close-down on paper—adequate social competencies are required. Giving and taking feedback as an individual and as an organization, addressing positive and negative points, requires adequate competencies and experience.

PROJECT MARKETING: A PROJECT MANAGEMENT TASK

Many projects are characterized by a high degree of content orientation but a low degree of marketing orientation. The members of the project organizations concentrate mainly on fulfilling the work packages. They do not realize that an appropriate communication of the objectives, the content, and the organization of a project to the relevant project environments is also necessary to ensure the project success.

When there is not enough project marketing, there is a risk that the project is not getting enough management attention and is provided with inadequate resources. Not only is the quality of the results of a project ensured by adequate communication but also their acceptance. The success (S) of a project can be defined as the product of the quality (Q) of the results of a project and its acceptance (A):

$$S = Q \times A$$

If, in the extreme case, acceptance of the project results is zero despite good quality, the project success is also zero.

Project marketing is a success factor in projects. It supports the management of the project environment relationships. Objectives of project marketing include

- Ensuring appropriate management attention
- Ensuring adequate resources for the project
- Ensuring acceptance of the (intermediary) results of the project
- Minimizing conflicts in the project
- Promoting identification of the members of the project organization with the project

By means of adequate project information, conflicts in the project and in the relationships to relevant environments are minimized, and adequate expectations regarding project results are developed. Feedback for the project is ensured, and a dialog with the relevant environments is established.

Project information projected to the outside creates constructive pressure on the inside. The project organization must satisfy the expectations developed. Thus project marketing promotes identification of the members of the project organization with the project. Project marketing also aligns with the personal interests of self-marketing of the members of the project organization.

Project marketing can be defined as project-related communication with relevant project environments. Project marketing is a project management task, and it is pointed out here because of its importance to the success of a project. Project marketing focuses on communication.

Project marketing is a project management task to be fulfilled in all subprocesses of project management. Project marketing therefore is rarely considered a work package in its own right in projects.

Project marketing starts with the project assignment. The definition of a project for fulfilling a business process of a medium to large scope represents an important marketing measure. Project marketing is especially important in the project start process. Initial information about the project and the project identity can be communicated.

Subsequently, project marketing measures should be sustained at a relatively even level of intensity over the whole duration of the project and according to specific requirements. During ongoing project coordination, it is possible to perform informal project marketing at lunch, over a cup of coffee, in the elevator, and so on with all those interested in the project. During project control, the intermediary results of the project and changes in project structures can be communicated.

In resolving a project discontinuity, communication of the project discontinuity is a work package in its own right because communication is of special importance in the resolution of a project discontinuity. In the project close-down, not only the project results but also the process of the project work and the contribution of the members of the project organization are communicated.

Project environment analysis and development of the project culture form the basis for project marketing. Project environment analysis enables the differentiation of project-specific marketing strategies and concrete measures by environments (target groups of marketing). (Objectives of project environment analysis, however, are not only the planning of marketing measures but also the planning of organizational, contract-designing, and personnel measures.)

In developing the project culture, the project name, a project logo, project slogans, and project-specific values are defined that can be used in developing the instruments for project marketing. To ensure consistent use, the font to be used, the font sizes, the project colors, and so on must to be clearly defined.

Instruments of project marketing include

- *Print media*—project folder, project information sheet, project newsletter, project wall newspaper, project report (in the company newspaper)
- *Project-related events*—project finishing touches, project presentation, project meeting, project-related competition, project start event, project end event, press conference
- *Give-aways*—project stickers, project T-shirts, etc.
- *Online*—project homepage, etc.
- *Visits*—visiting a construction site, visiting a project room, etc.
- *Project management documentation*—project handbook, project progress report, project score card, etc.

All members of the project organization are responsible for project marketing. Not only the project manager but also the project owner team and the project team members are responsible for adequate communication of the project. Project contributors, who only work on the project selectively, do not bear responsibility for project marketing.

The members of the project organization need marketing competence. Project marketing therefore is not only an instrument but also a matter of attitude; it is part of self-understanding and is especially important for the project manager. This self-understanding requires adequate ethical standards that rule out misinformation and manipulation in project marketing.

The costs of project marketing must be addressed in the project management budget. Personnel costs and material costs for various project marketing instruments (e.g., project folder, project newsletter, project finishing touches, etc.) must be accommodated.

DESIGN OF THE BUSINESS PROCESS "PROJECT MANAGEMENT"

The business process "project management" must be designed in accordance with the specific requirements of a project. The use of project management methods and standard project plans, of project communication forms, of the project infrastructure, and of project consultants and project management coaches must be managed.

Use of Project Management Methods

The use of project management methods in projects should be laid down in the organizational guidelines of project-oriented companies. In accordance with the structure of the project management process, the project management methods to be used in the project start, in project coordination, in project control, in resolving project discontinuities, and in the project close-down must be differentiated. With regard to the use these methods, a distinction must be made between *must* and *can* use. Decisions regarding the use of *can* methods and the degree of detail in the use of such methods must be made based on to the project. Further, the use of project management methods must be differentiated for projects and for small projects (Table 2.4).

Each new project plan resulting from the use of a project management method is a model of the project and serves to construct the project reality. The use of several different project management methods enables the development of a management complexity that matches the complexity of the project.

The quality of the project plans must be ensured by applying multiple methods. The completeness of the project plans can only be ensured by relating the project management methods with each other and by cyclic revisions of the project plans. For example, insights from project environment analysis can be incorporated into the work breakdown structure and/or in the project cost plan. The degree of detail of project plans must be determined in relation to the complexity of the project.

Project plans should be developed jointly by the project team in a project start workshop. Thus the creativity of the team can be engaged, and identification of project team members with the results is promoted. The initial development can be prepared by a small group of selected project team members. The use of moderation techniques ensures target-oriented and efficient teamwork. Visualization techniques promote communication in the project management process and support the documentation of results.

Project plans often are understood to be instruments used exclusively for documentation. In fact, however, project plans are also instruments for decision making (decisions on alternative strategies), for leadership (basis for agreements on objectives, establishing commitment), and for communication. Adequate information technology (IT) support

TABLE 2.4   Checklist: Use of Project Management Methods (to be Adapted for Each Company)

Methods for the Project Start	Small Project	Project
Project planning		
Project scope planning		
• Project objectives plan	Must	Must
• Objects of considerations plan	Can	Must
• Work breakdown structure	Must	Must
• Work package specifications	Can	Must
Project scheduling		
• Project milestone plan	Must	Must
• Project bar chart	Can	Must
• CPM schedule	Can	Can
Project resources, project costs, project income		
• Project resource plan	Can	Can
• Project cost plan	Must	Must
• Project income plan	Can	Can
Designing the project context relationships		
• Project environment analysis	Must	Must
• Business case analysis	Can	Must
• Project–other projects' analysis	Can	Must
• Pre- and postproject phase analysis	Can	Must
• Project presentations, project vernissage	Can	Can
Designing the project organization		
• Project assignment	Must	Must
• Subproject assignment	Can	Can
• Project organization chart	Must	Must
• Project role descriptions	Must	Must
• Project responsibility matrix	Can	Can
• Project communication plan	Must	Must
• Project rules	Can	Must
Developing the project culture		
• Project name	Must	Must
• Project logo	Can	Can
• Project-specific "social" events	Can	Can
Project risk management and project discontinuity management		
• Project risk analysis	Must	Must
• Project scenario analysis and alternative planning	Can	Can
Methods for Project Coordination	Small Project	Project
• To-do lists	Must	Must
• Meeting minutes	Must	Must
• Work package approval certificate	Must	Must

TABLE 2.4   Checklist: Use of Project Management Methods (to be Adapted for Each Company) (*Continued*)

Methods for Project Controlling	Small Project	Project
Project controlling reports		
• Project progress reports	Must	Must
• Earned value analysis	Can	Can
• Project trend analyses	Can	Can
• Project score card (plus interpretations)	Must	Must
Project controlling		
• To-do lists	Must	Must
Adaptation of the project documentation		
• Adaptation of the project management documentation	Must	Must

Methods for Resolving a Project Discontinuity	Small Project	Project
• Definition of the project discontinuity	Must	Must
• Planning immediate measures	Must	Must
• Cause analysis	Must	Must
• Planning alternative resolution strategies	Must	Must
• Planning additional measures	Must	Must
• Ending the project discontinuity	Must	Must

Methods for the Project Close-Down	Small Project	Project
Planning of measures		
• To-do list: Remaining work	Must	Must
• Designing the environment relationships	Must	Must
• To-do list: Postproject phase	Must	Must
• Adaptation business case analysis	Can	Must
Know-how transfer		
• Project close-down report	Must	Must
• Special reports	Can	Can
• Actual project management documentation	Must	Must
• Project presentation	Can	Can
• Articles in newsletters, on homepage, in journals	Can	Can
• Exchange of experience workshop	Can	Can
Assessment of performance		
• Evaluation of project success	Must	Must
• Assessment of the members of the project organization	Can	Must
Symbolic actions in the project close-down		
• "Social" end event	Can	Must
• Closing project cost center	Must	Must
• Project acceptance certificate	Must	Must

Designing the Project Management Process	Small Project	Project
Project communication		
• Kick-off meeting	Must	Can
• Project workshop	Can	Must
• Project team meetings	Must	Must
IT support		
• Project management software	Must	Must

(project management and graphics software) serves to facilitate the design and communication of recipient-specific information.

Use of Standard Project Plans

Standard project plans can be used for managing repetitive projects. If a project-oriented company repeatedly performs certain types of projects (e.g., contracting projects of an IT company or product-development projects of a pharmaceutical company), standard project plans can be developed for these types of projects. This kind of standardization represents an instrument of organizational learning and knowledge management in the project-oriented company. Project plans that can be standardized are, for example, work breakdown structures, work package specifications, objects-of-consideration plans, milestone lists, project organization charts, and project responsibility matrices.

The efficiency of the project management processes can be increased considerably by the adequate use of standard project plans. Standard project plans should be adapted based on the respective project conditions.

Use of Adequate Project Communication Forms

In the project management process, the communication forms for meetings between the project manager and individual project team members, team meetings, and workshops can be combined (Fig. 2.11). Project workshops should be performed to ensure appropriate project management quality.

The objective of a meeting between the project manager and individual project team members in the project start process is to exchange information regarding the project and mutual expectations regarding cooperation in the project. This general orientation forms the basis for participation in project team meetings and in the project start workshop.

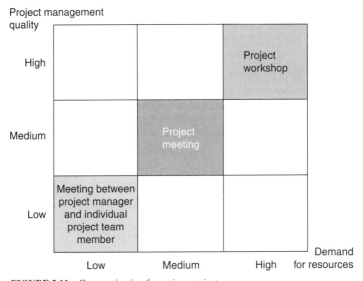

FIGURE 2.11   Communication forms in a project.

The objective of a kick-off meeting is for the project owner team and the project manager to inform the project team about the project. It usually takes place as a one-way communication of two to three hours with little opportunity for interaction.

The objective of a project workshop is to jointly develop a "big picture" of the project for the project team. As a result of interaction bewteen team members in the workshop an important contribution to the development of the project culture is made. A project start workshop lasts one to three days, is moderated, and generally takes place outside the usual workplace, possibly in a hotel.

The objectives of regular control meetings of the project team are to provide information about the status of the project and to achieve the agreement on ways to proceed. The objectives of regular meetings of the project owner team are to receive information from the project manager on the status of the project and to make strategic decisions concerning the project.

Design of the Project-Related Infrastructure

Professional project management requires the use of an appropriate information and communications technology (ICT) infrastructure, as well as of an appropriate spatial infrastructure. Especially in virtual project organizations with project team members working at different locations, the planning of the software and telecommunications to be used in the project poses a challenge. The use of a uniform project management and office software is necessary, and appropriate hardware should be provided. Decisions have to be made regarding the use of new communication tools, such as project management portals, collaboration software, telephone conferences, and video conferences. A spatial infrastructure must be planned and provided for holding meetings, for performing project presentations, and for creating a workspace for a project office.

Use of Project Management Consultants and Project Management Coaches

Projects, project managers, and project teams represent new "objects" for consulting. *Project management consulting* can be defined as management consulting on a project. *Project management coaching* is management consulting on the part of the project manager and/or the project team. Project management consulting and/or project management coaching serve to ensure and increase the quality of project management.

Given the social complexity of projects, the use of a project management consultant or a project management coach is recommended, especially in the project start process. In the resolution of a project discontinuity, external project support also may be useful.

The decision regarding the use of a project management consultant or a project management coach should be made jointly by the project team. In an external project support position, the role of a project management consultant or project management coach can be assumed either by an adequately qualified employee of the project oriented company or by an external consultant.

REFERENCES

1. Motzel E. *Projektmanagement Kanon—der deutsche Zugang zum Project management Body of Knowledge.* Cologne: TÜV, 1998, p. 12.

2. Duncan WR. *A Guide to the Project Management Body of Knowledge*: Automated Graphic Systems, North Carolina: Charlotte, 2000, p. 6.

3. *Ibid.*, pp. 6*ff.*
4. Steinle H. *Projektmanagement: Instrument moderner Dienstleistung.* Frankfurt: Blickbuch Wirtschaft, 1995, p. 354.
5. Čamra JJ. *REFA-Lexikon.* Berlin: Beuth, 1976.
6. Hillier FS, Liebermann GJ. *Introduction to Operations Research.* New York: McGraw-Hill, 2001.
7. Reschke H. *Formen der Aufbauorganisation in Projekten.* Cologne: TÜV Rheinland, 1989, pp. 874*ff.*
8. Duncan WR. *A Guide to the Project Management Body of Knowledge*: Automated Graphic Systems, North Carolina: Charlotte, 2000, pp. 47*ff.*
9. Watzlawick P. *Wie wirklich ist die Wirklichkeit?* Munich: Piper & Co., 1976, p. 69.

BIBLIOGRAPHY

Gareis R, Huemann M. Maturity-models for the project-oriented company, in J. R.Turner (ed.), *The Gower Handbook of Project Management*, 4th ed. Aldershot: Gower, 2006.

Gareis R (ed.). *Handbook of Management by Projects.* Vienna: Manz, 1990.

Gareis R. *Happy Projects!*, Vienna: Manz, 2005.

Gareis R. Management of the project-oriented company, in J. K. Pinto and P. W. G. Morris (eds.), The Wiley Guide to Managing Projects. New York: Wiley, 2004.

CHAPTER 3

THE FUTURE OF PROJECT MANAGEMENT: MAPPING THE DYNAMICS OF PROJECT MANAGEMENT FIELD IN ACTION

Christophe N. Bredillet

ESC Lille, France

Professor Christophe N. Bredillet holds a Ph.D., a D.Sc., an MBA, and engineering degree from Ecole Centrale Lille. He is a certified project director level A (IPMA), PRINCE2 practitioner, and certified cost engineer. He has been working at ESC Lille since 1992, where he is currently professor of strategy, program and project management and associate dean, director of postgraduate programmes at ESC Lille. He is strongly involved in project management research networks (IRNOP, EPSRC, and PMI®). His main interests and research activities are in the field of program/project management (principles and theories of program/project management, knowledge management, bodies of knowledge, standards, use of system dynamics modeling to design life-long learning structures in project management) and business dynamics (use of systems thinking and system dynamics in both program/project and strategic management). In both the research and professional domains, he is strongly involved with professional project management associations [PMI®, IPMA, and PMCC (Japan)]. These commitments enable him to be strongly aware of project management research and cutting-edge professional practice.

ABSTRACT

If project management is a well-accepted mode of managing organizations, more and more organizations are adopting project management in order to satisfy the diversified needs of application areas within a variety of industries and organizations. Concurrently, the number of project management practitioners and people involved at various level of qualification is rising vigorously. Thus the importance of characterizing, defining, and understanding this field and its underlying strengths, bases, and development is paramount. For this purpose, this chapter will refer to the sociology of actor networks and qualitative scientometrics leading to choice of the coword-analysis method in enabling capture of the the project management field and its dynamics. Results of a study based on an analysis of the EBSCO Business Source Premier Database will be presented and some future trends and scenarios proposed.

The main following trends are confirmed, in alignment with previous studies: continuous interest in the "cost engineering" aspects, ongoing interest in the economic aspects and contracts, how to deal with various project types (categorizations), integration with supply-chain management, and learning and knowledge management. Furthermore, besides these continuous trends, we can note new areas of interest: the link between strategy and project, governance, the importance of maturity (organizational performance and metrics, control), and change management.

We see the actors (professional bodies) reinforcing their competing/cooperative strategies in the development of standards and certifications and moving to more business-oriented relationships with their members and main stakeholders (governments, institutions such as the European Community, industries, agencies, and nongovernment organizations) at least at a central level.

According to a prospective study (PMI, 2001), the estimated population dealing to a certain extent with projects is of 16.5 million worldwide. The number of project management practitioners is around 2 million, with an increase of about 20 percent per year. About 220,000 people are members of a project management association, and 105,088 people hold the PMP certification (PMI Fact Sheet, January 2005), 18,416 hold an International Project Management Association (IPMA) 4 level certification (IPMA, retrieved February 26, 2005, from www.ipma.ch/managers/). The growth rate of PMI membership is around 24 percent per year. In the meantime, project management has to satisfy the diversified needs of application areas with a variety of industries or organizations, and US $10 trillion are spent globally on projects. Thus the importance of projects and the number of people involved in various projects keep on rising.

This leads us to question the evolution of the project management field. Indeed, the project management discipline and the scientific field should be the basis for the development and use of bodies of knowledge, standards, certification programs, education, and competencies and, beyond this, as a source of value for people and of competitive advantage for organizations and society. Thus the need to characterize, define, and understand this field and its underlying strengths, bases, and development is paramount.

For this purpose, we propose to provide some insights on the current situation. We will refer to the sociology of actor networks and qualitative and quantitative scientometrics leading to choice of the coword-analysis method in enabling us to capture the project management field and its dynamics. Results of a study based on analysis of the EBSCO Business Source Premier Database will be presented and some future trends and scenarios proposed.

PROJECT MANAGEMENT: A KNOWLEDGE FIELD NOT THAT CLEAR

First, hypothetically, it might be useful to assume that the project management knowledge field does exist. Consider Audet's definition (1986) with respect to the behavior of professional bodies, authors, and academics:

> A knowledge field is the space occupied by the whole of the people who claim to produce knowledge in this field, and this space is at the same time a system of relationships between these people. Those persons are competitors to gain control of the definition of the conditions and the rules of the production of knowledge.

The relationships between established professional bodies [PMI, IPMA, Project Management Professionals Certification Center (PMCC), and the APM Group] and their methods of development through individualism and collaboration [PMI through the PMBOK Guide; IPMA through a shared-competence baseline (ICB-IPMA Competence Baseline); the APM Group through "PRojects IN a Controlled Environment" (PRINCE2™), Managing Successful Programmes (MSP), and Management of Risk (M_o_R)®; PMCC through *A Guidebook of Project and Program Management for Enterprise Innovation* (P2M)] are contextualized according to the needs of the national and international associations.

For example, the PMI, the IPMA, the Association for Project Management (APM), and the Australian Institute of Project Management (AIPM) headquarters draw from the Global Project Management Forum (GPMF)—a kind of suprainstitutional body and think tank—the desire to create global standards, and in addition, the PMI is very active in supporting research in areas such as establishing a theory of project management, demonstrating project management value for executives, and achievement of corporate strategy through successful projects.

The evolution of bodies of knowledge (e.g., the PMBOK Guide, ICB, APM BOK, and P2M) and methodologies [e.g., the Organizational Project Management Maturity Model (OPM3), PRINCE2™, and MSP] is evidenced further by themes in papers and books citing techniques of psychosociology of temporary groups through to knowledge creation and organizational learning.

In addition, the field is currently characterized by this abundance of initiatives:

- *Research*—for example, the Engineering and Physical Sciences Research Council (EPRSC) Network in the United Kingdom "Rethinking Project Management" Web site (www.rethinkingpm.org.uk)
- *Development of standards*—for example, the current development of "Global Performance-Based Standards for Project Management Personnel" (GPBSPMP) under the direction of Prof. Lynn Crawford and involving industries, professional bodies, institutions and organizations, and universities from all over the world
- *Increasing use of project management methods and techniques*—in a preparadigmatic phase according to Kuhn's (1983) sense

This phase is the place of revolution, inaugurated by a growing but still narrow subdivision within the project management community that believes that the existing positivist paradigm has ceased to function adequately in the exploration of the nature of project management. A second and more profound aspect on which the significance of the former belief depends is that the success of the revolution necessitates full or partial relinquishment of one set of institutions in favor of another. Is this the intention of the creation, in the United States, of an alternative professional body [American Society for the Advancement of Project Management (ASAPM)] to the PMI? Is this PMI's purpose in creating regional service centers in Europe, the Middle East, and Africa (EMEA) and the Asia-Pacific, with others to come?

In order to develop bodies of knowledge, standards, certification programs, education, and competencies, a knowledge field is needed. Yet, in both the academic and business worlds, the field of project management is not clearly established and defined. In addition, the field is still evolving in breadth and depth.

- In breadth, it is embracing information systems, human resources management, change management, strategic management, economic value management, psychology, management of technology, quality, sociology, multicultural management, systems thinking, knowledge management, organizational learning, team management, temporary group, and systems engineering.

- In depth, it is going further into cost engineering, finance, specific aspects of risk management, earned-value management, scheduling methods, resources allocation, project life cycle, processes, studying phases, types of projects, project portfolio management, and maturity.

In addition, a number of books and papers explore issues that contribute both depth and breadth in several technical, methodologic, and managerial dimensions. They aim to fill a long-standing need for a comprehensive, unified, and practical description of the field. Over the last 20 years, the profession has been working on its recognition. Both standards and certifications have been addressed by professionals associations working on both definition of the field and recognition of project management as a profession. This demonstrates that the positivist perspective, if valid in a specific area, cannot produce answers to every type of problem and raises the need for a historical and contextual/situational perspective.

Moving beyond a "one best way" to describe the field, Tanaka (2004), in the presentation of his historical view of project management models over four generations, offers views on project management opportunities and challenges into the future. Project management models can be drawn from such attributes as project management structure and methods, socioeconomic drivers that prompt the buildup of the model in question, typical project management techniques offered by the model, primary application areas, and mechanisms for popularizing the model. Tanaka classified project management models into seven distinct models over the four generations (Fig. 3.1).

From the original "classical" model, project management has developed into the "modern" model, which is divided into three submodels bearing characteristics particular to relevant areas of applications, and then into the "neoclassical" model, which is a global operation adaptation of the classical model, and then into the "strategic" model expected as a project management model of this century. A hypothesis is that the "versatile" model is forthcoming in which traditional general management will have been replaced by or merged into project management.

One should be aware that the evolution of project management models does not necessarily represent the incremental sophistication of project management methods and that the value of project management models should be relative to the practicing industry branch, organization, or individual rather than absolute. Thus incoming new models do not necessarily replace existing ones.

These considerations lead us to define the method we propose in mapping the dynamics of the project management field.

PROJECT MANAGEMENT FIELD IN ACTION

Theoretical Foundation

The analysis of the dynamics of science has attracted much interest. A qualitative concern with scientific change can be found in a range of disciplines such as philosophy (Popper, 1959), social science (MacKenzie, 1978), history of science (Kuhn, 1983), and science policy (Weingart, 1982). Although these many writers have advocated a wide variety of theoretical perspectives, they all have one thing in common: They do not make use of quantitative indicators in order to handle aggregated data. Quantitativists have worked in a quite different way, using large databases to count publications, citations, and patents (Garfield et al., 1978). And they share a common interest in the dynamics of science.

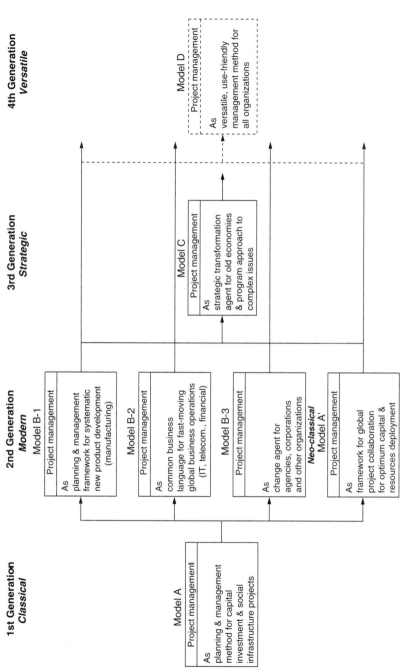

FIGURE 3.1 Development of project management models. (*From Tanaka, 2004.*)

However, it is necessary to build on this convergence. The reluctance of the qualitativists to use statistical analysis must be overcome, and on the other hand, the materials collected and their application must contribute to a theoretically defensible concept of science (Callon et al., 1986b).

Built on the actor-network theory, and as a consequence of interaction between actor networks, resulting structure of problems, and networks of problematization (Callon et al., 1986a), the coword-analysis technique was first proposed to map the dynamics of science. The most feasible way to understand the dynamics of science is to take the force of science in present-day societies into account. *Actor network* is the theoretical foundation for coword analysis to map the dynamics of science. Laboratories and the literature are considered as two powerful tools for scientists to change the world. They build complex worlds in laboratories and enforce them on paper (Latour, 1987). This implies that scientists attach particular importance to texts. They use texts not only to publish their world built in the laboratory but also as a way to build a world and enroll others. Even though science cannot be reduced to texts alone, texts are still a prime source for studies on how worlds are created and transformed in the laboratory. Therefore, instead of following the actors to see how they change the world, following the texts is another way to map the dynamics of science.

Based on the co-occurrence of pairs of words, coword analysis seeks to extract the themes of science and detect the linkages among these themes directly from the subject content of the texts. It does not rely on any *a priori* definition of themes in science. This enables us to follow actors objectively and detect the dynamics of science without reducing them to the extremes of either internalism or externalism (Callon et al., 1986b). Overall, coword analysis considers the dynamics of science as a result of actor strategies. Changes in the content of a subject area are the combined effect of a large number of individual strategies. This technique should allow us in principle to identify the actors and explain the global dynamics (Callon et al., 1991).

Coword Analysis Method

Coword analysis is a content-analysis technique that uses patterns of co-occurrence of pairs of items (i.e., words or noun phrases) in the corpus of texts to identify the relationships between ideas within the subject areas as presented in these texts. Indexes based on the co-occurrence frequency of items, such as an inclusion index and a proximity index, are used to measure the strength of relationships between items. Based on these indexes, items are clustered into groups and displayed in network maps. Some other indexes, such as those based on density and centrality, are employed to evaluate the shape of each map, showing the degree to which each area is centrally structured and the extent to which each area is central to the others. By comparing the network maps for different time periods, the scientific dynamic can be detected. For about 25 years, this technique has been employed to map the dynamic development of several research fields.

Many examples (Turner and Callon, 1986; Callon, 1986; Courtial and Law, 1989; Law and Whittaker, 1992; Coulter et al., 1998) reveal that coword analysis is a promising method for discovering associations among research areas in science and for revealing significant linkages that otherwise may be difficult to detect. It is a powerful tool that makes it possible to trace the structure and evolution of a sociocognitive network (Bauin, 1986). As such, it offers a significant approach to knowledge discovery.

The following paragraphs introduce the main metrics used in this study. A more detailed presentation of the metrics employed in coword analysis can be found in He (1999).

Metrics. The basis of a coword-analysis study is calculation of the *equivalence* or *link coefficient:*

$$[E.ij] = ([C.ij]/[C.i]) \times ([C.ij]/([C.j]) = [([C.ij]).2]/([C.i] \times [C.j]) \tag{1}$$

where $[C.ij]$ is the co-occurrence frequency of the keyword pair ($[M.i]$ and $[M.j]$) in the set of articles, $[C.i]$ is the occurrence frequency of keyword $[M.i]$ in the set of articles, $[C.j]$ is the occurrence frequency of keyword $[M.j]$ in the set of articles, and $[E.ij]$ has a value between 0 and 1.

This coefficient is used to define the clusters and draw the *strategic diagram*. A cluster is a lexical structured set built from a co-occurrence analysis. It is constituted by a set of words strongly associated or in strong co-occurrence in the documents. The co-occurrence analysis is conducted through the index (list of words to take into consideration) associated with the corpus of documents.

Density, Centrality, and Strategic Diagram.

A strategic diagram is used to illustrate the "local" and "global" contexts of themes. This diagram is created by putting the strength of global context on the x axis (called *centrality*) and the strength of local context on the y axis (called *density*). This diagram is used in many coword studies. Two kinds of indexes (i.e., density and centrality) are used to measure the strengths of local context and global context, respectively.

Density. Density is used to measure the strength of the links (*equivalence* or *link coefficient*) that tie together the words making up the cluster. This is the internal strength of a cluster and provides a good representation of the cluster's capacity to maintain itself and to develop over the course of time in the field under consideration (Callon et al., 1991). Ranking subject areas (clusters) in terms of their internal coherence (density) is designed to provide information for systematic discussion of a major policy alternative. Further, sorting the keywords by decreasing order of density can provide a precise description of the areas (Bauin et al., 1991). The value of the density of a given cluster can be measured in several ways. Generally, the index value for links between each word pair is calculated first. Then the density value can be the average value (mean) of internal links (e.g., Turner et al., 1988; Coulter et al., 1998), the median value of internal links (e.g., Courtial et al., 1993), or the sum of the squares of the value of internal links (e.g., Bauin et al., 1991). An internal link means that both the words linked by it are within the cluster. Here we consider the average value (mean) of internal links.

Centrality. Centrality is used to measure the strength of a subject area's interaction with other subject areas. Ranking subject areas (clusters) with respect to their centrality shows the extent to which each area is central within a global network. The greater the number and strength of a subject area's connections with other subject areas, the more central this subject area will be in the network (Bauin et al., 1991). For a given cluster (area), its centrality can be the sum of all external link values (e.g., Turner et al., 1988; Courtial et al., 1993) or the square root of the sum of the squares of all external link values (e.g., Coulter et al., 1998). More simply, it can be the mean of the values of the first six external links (e.g., Callon et al., 1991). An external link is one that goes from a word belonging to a cluster to a word external to the cluster. Here we consider the mean of the values of the first six external links.

Strategic Diagram. A strategic diagram that offers a global representation of the structure of any field or subfield can be created by plotting centrality and density into a two-dimensional diagram (Law et al., 1988). Typically, the horizontal axis represents centrality, the vertical axis represents density, and the origin of the graph is at the median of the respective axis values. This map locates each subject area within a two-dimensional space divided into four quadrants. The strategic diagram is used in many coword-analysis studies (e.g., Turner et al., 1988; Courtial and Law, 1989; Turner and Rojouan, 1991; Callon et al., 1991; Coulter et al., 1998). and the analysis based on it is similar among these studies. All the characteristics of a strategic diagram can be summarized in Fig. 3.2.

Dynamics of Networks. A striking feature of some strategic diagrams is the radical change in the configuration of the network at two periods. This reflects the dynamics of science. Based on the strategic diagram, we can analyze the stability of the networks and foresee their changes in the future. This issue is addressed in many studies, and the methods used in these studies fall into two categories: the study of strategic diagrams and the ratio of centrality to density. Here we use the former one. This method is used to study the stability of networks and is based directly on the strategic diagrams (e.g., Callon et al., 1991; Turner and Rojouan, 1991). The findings can be summarized as showing that the probability for the content of themes situated in quadrants 2 and 3 to change over time is significantly higher than it is for themes that are situated in quadrant 1. With a low density, the unstructured themes in quadrant 2 tend to undergo an internal restructuring to improve their cohesiveness. With a low centrality, the scope of themes in quadrant 3 is likely to be extended in order to better articulate what is being done in the rest of the network. The reason, as well as the goal, for all these changes is to place their work at the heart of their field (quadrant 1). This can be done either by enlarging its scope or by improving its visibility through conceptual developments in the definition of the field.

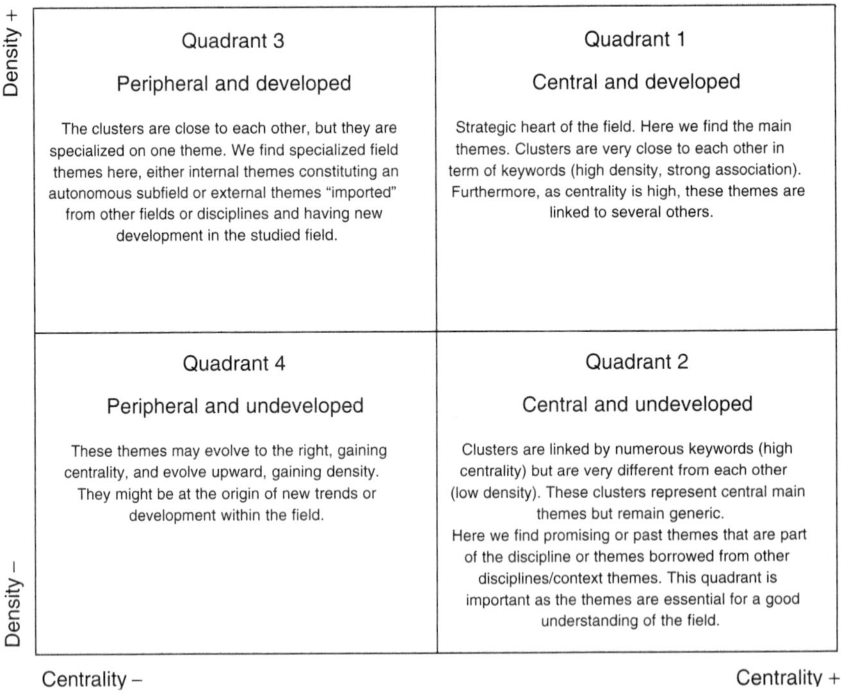

Density +		
Quadrant 3 Peripheral and developed The clusters are close to each other, but they are specialized on one theme. We find specialized field themes here, either internal themes constituting an autonomous subfield or external themes "imported" from other fields or disciplines and having new development in the studied field.	**Quadrant 1** Central and developed Strategic heart of the field. Here we find the main themes. Clusters are very close to each other in term of keywords (high density, strong association). Furthermore, as centrality is high, these themes are linked to several others.	
Quadrant 4 Peripheral and undeveloped These themes may evolve to the right, gaining centrality, and evolve upward, gaining density. They might be at the origin of new trends or development within the field.	**Quadrant 2** Central and undeveloped Clusters are linked by numerous keywords (high centrality) but are very different from each other (low density). These clusters represent central main themes but remain generic. Here we find promising or past themes that are part of the discipline or themes borrowed from other disciplines/context themes. This quadrant is important as the themes are essential for a good understanding of the field.	
Density –		

Centrality –   Centrality +

FIGURE 3.2 Strategic diagram.

Network Comparison. In coword-analysis studies, several subnetworks (clusters) can be constructed concurrently, even though each network changes over time. To detect the difference among subnetworks simultaneously or subnetworks at different times has been a long-standing research issue. The transformation of networks and their intersections with other networks across time periods provides insights into theme emergence. The similarity of networks in different time periods also has been studied by Coulter et al. (1998). In this study, the authors employ the *similarity index (SI)*, which comes from Callon's *dissimilarity* (or *transformation*) *index (T)* (Callon et al., 1991).

Index of Influence and Provenance. Another comparative analysis is done by Law and Whittaker (1992) to highlight the overlap between themes on similar subjects in succeeding time periods. Two indexes, the *index of influence (I)* and the *index of provenance (P)*, are employed to measure the degree of continuity between themes in generations. The index [*I.ij*] shows the proportion of the words within a theme in one generation attached to any given theme in the next generation. A high [*I.ij*] means that the "influence" of a first-generation theme on one of the second-generation themes is high. The [*P.ij*] index shows the proportion of words within a second-generation theme that come from any given theme in the preceding generation. A high [*P.ij*] means that the "provenance" of a second-generation theme primarily lies in a single theme of the first generation.

Some Key Issues in Coword Analysis. The maps obtained by coword analysis generally are considered very difficult to understand in isolation. They have to be interpreted with caution. It is suggested that the interpretation must be active and based on the comparison of maps (Callon et al., 1986a). Given that the goal of coword analysis is not just to photograph a field of knowledge but to reveal the strategies by which actors mutually define one another, Callon et al. (1991) suggest that the maps cannot be considered in statistical isolation; they must be interpreted dynamically.

The choice of the words (keywords, descriptors) is another issue to be considered carefully and has led to many discussions (Leydesdorff, 1997; Whittaker, 1989). A literature review shows that the words used in coword analysis are expanding from keywords in a lexicon to words in the full text (Bauin, 1986; Callon et al., 1991; Rotto and Morgan, 1997; Kostoff et al., 1997). The "normalization" of words must be considered as well (e.g., many words for which British and American spellings differ have been standardized to the American spelling by the Institute for Scientific Information when they are put into the citation-index databases). This has been addressed in several studies (Turner et al., 1988; Courtial et al., 1993; Nederhof and van Wijk, 1997).

Questions of meaning or change of word meaning at different levels (e.g., during a period of time or from one author to another) also are addressed (Leydesdorff, 1997, 1998). Words are not used as linguistic items to mean something in coword analysis but are used as indicators of links between texts, whatever they mean. They are chain indexes, allowing one to compute translation networks. What is important for coword analysis is not the exact meaning or definition of a word but the fact that this word is linked to word *x* in one case and word *y* in another case (Courtial, 1998).

Research Process

Figure 3.3 describes the research process. Three key aspects of this process are (1) the use of the keywords *project management* and *program management* to extract from the ABI Inform database the articles we wish to analyse as reflecting the project management scientific field, (2) the combination of different glossaries (Max Wideman, PMBoK Guide, IPMA Competence Baseline, OPM3™, PRINCE2™, and P2M) to

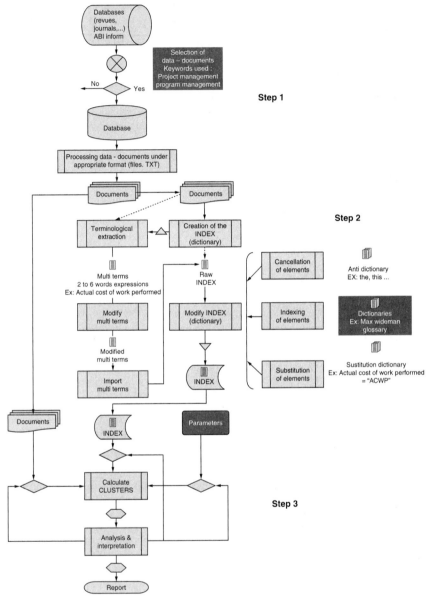

FIGURE 3.3 Research process.

define the descriptors (index) and constitute the dictionary we are using for this research, and (3) the choice of the parameters for the analysis (use of SAMPLER, developed by Cisi, Groupe Compagnie des Signaux).

Resulting Data: Overview and First Findings

The research is based on study of the EBSCO Business Source Premier Database abstracts, using the keyword *project management,* from 1985 to 2004. The distribution of the documents by year is given in Fig. 3.4.

Note that the number or articles from 1985 to 2004 is 7289. This simple count of papers reveals four distinct time periods: From 1985 to 1991, the growth rate (number of papers) averaged 11 percent per year; from 1992 to 1996, 32 percent per year (showing an increasing interest for project management); then from 1997 to 2001, 28 percent per year (this led many people to think that project management was reaching a level of maturity); and then from 2002 to 2004, 36 percent per year (demonstrating that interest in project management is still growing and that the field is everything but mature).

For the purpose of this study, the data were grouped into four time periods: 1985–1991, 1992–1996, 1997–2001, and 2002–2004. The first three time periods were chosen in a previous study (Bredillet, 1998, 1999, 2002). We wish to update the previous results by taking into consideration new developments and adding the new time period.

Table 3.1 shows the numbers of documents and descriptors per period. This gives a first indication of the expanding nature of project management given that the descriptors/documents ratio and coverage of the field descriptors/words are decreasing at first and then increase in the last period (but we are considering here a three-year period of time). This means that the field encompasses new concepts (i.e., new words) during the first three periods and then tends to stabilize in terms of development of new concepts. At the same time, the evolution of centrality and density shows that from 1985–1991 to 1997–2001, the field is in development (from 10 clusters to 49) and that themes are changing (lower density); then there is a slight increase in 2002–2004 (but much lower than for 1992–1996). It also shows that new themes are part of the field (lower centrality). From 1997–2001 to 2002–2004, the change and arrival of new themes occurring in the previous period became more integrated within the field (higher density and centrality), and the number of clusters declined from 49 to 36. This demonstrates the recomposition

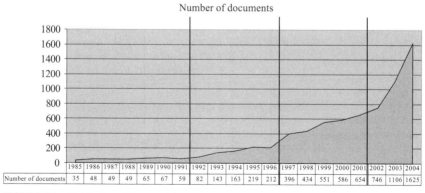

FIGURE 3.4   Distribution of documents by year.

TABLE 3.1 Documents and Descriptors per Period

Time Period	Documents	Descriptors (Index)	Descriptor/ Document Ratio	Words	Percent Coverage Index/Words	Centrality	Density
1985–1991	504	18474	36,65	90059	20,51%	c.m = 0.065931	d.m = 0.219080
1992–1996	3276	91288	27,87	520661	17,53%	c.m = 0.020814	d.m = 0.076533
1997–2001	19756	481375	24,37	2775827	17,34%	c.m = 0.004941	d.m = 0.044454
2002–2004	9315	231633	24,87	1312140	17,65%	c.m = 0.009138	d.m = 0.058869

of the field, still in development, as correlated with the evolution of the number of papers (see Table 3.1), around new concepts shows more focus around diversified themes, indicating perhaps more maturity with possibly a paradigm shift.

Strategic Diagram Analysis

After an overview on the first findings, it is appropriate to study the strategic diagrams generated and their evolution. A wealth of information emerges from these maps, but sometimes it is difficult to translate. We are using a combination of qualitative and quantitative approaches in analyzing them. The four strategic diagrams are presented in Fig. 3.5.

Note: In the following development, we refer to the *names* of clusters; the names (in parentheses) are the main content of the clusters mentioned. They give sense to the clusters.

We can note the general structure of the field and its evolution by period.

Quadrant 1: "Strategic Heart" of the Field. Here we find the main themes. Clusters are very close to each other in term of keywords (high density, strong association). From a 1985–1991 period focused on *building* (construction, engineering, contacting) and *project type,* we then moved to a period (1992–1996) where the strategic issues were *cost, information, engineering, development* (team, behavior, change, organization, education), and *system* (companies, business, industry, management, project). Then we moved to a period (1997–2001) where the main themes were *power* (investment, finance, bank), *computer, budget, manager* (learning, education, training), *building, service* (sharing, collaborating, user), *end* (coordination, implementation, communication), *technology* (team, quality, performance), and *company* (development, system, management, project, business, type, industry, need). Finally, we move to the 2002–2004 period, where the "strategic heart" of the field is consists of *training* (education, learning knowledge, leader, staff, mentoring coaching, organization), *financial* (investment, bank, partner), *director* (executive, CEO), *cost* (economic, contract, developing, contracting, general, construction, building, engineering, design), *information,* and *business* (company, management, need, type, industry, project). As a first remark, note that the cluster *business* is very consistent (made up of similar concepts such as company, management, need, type, industry, and project) through the various time periods, coming from *type* in 1985–1991, *system* in 1992–1996, and then *company* in 1997–2001. Furthermore, it is of interest to note that the clusters *manager* (1997–2001) and *training* (2002–2004), consisting of concepts such as education, learning knowledge, leader, staff, mentoring coaching, and organization, are gaining in density and centrality, becoming really hot topics within the field.

Quadrant 3. We find specialized field themes here, either internal themes constituting an autonomous subfield or external themes "imported" from other fields or disciplines and having new development in the studied field. During the period 1985–1991, the theme is *written* (content, item, express, permission). Then in 1992–1996 the theme is *method* (Pert, CPM, Gantt, critical path, WBS, estimating, standard, estimate), showing the focus of most of the authors at that time. Then in 1997–2001 several themes emerged: *acquisition* (DOD, earned value, IPT, performance), *member* (PMI, IPMA, APM, committee, body of knowledge), *institute* (written, content, express, permission, item), *component* (quality assurance, Juran, inspection, defect), *request* (RFP, law, legal), *infrastructure,* and *managing* (change, impact, value, assessment, risk, environmental, mitigation, contingency). Then we move in 2002–2004 to

1985–1991 c.m = 0.065931 d.m = 0.219080

	centrality	density
building	0.079580	0.229412
type	0.096035	0.629865

1992–1996 c.m = 0.020814 d.m = 0.076533

	centrality	density
cost	0.034097	0.131418
information	0.029669	0.250531
engineering	0.025494	0.106422
development	0.030698	0.123505
system	0.048416	0.389269

1997–2001 c.m = 0.004941 d.m = 0.044454

	centrality	density
power	0.006664	0.070964
computer	0.006510	0.073994
budget	0.018087	0.061675
manager	0.011352	0.045008
building	0.010015	0.105722
service	0.005437	0.045429
end	0.006666	0.045078
technology	0.008709	0.056114
company	0.009816	0.304099

2002–2004 c.m = 0.009138 d.m = 0.058869

	centrality	density
training	0.014941	0.066938
financial	0.011054	0.069814
director	0.011329	0.063660
cost	0.013007	0.136661
information	0.025058	0.094600
business	0.029816	0.468515

quadrant 1 (d | c)

1992–1996 (quadrant 2)

	centrality	density
group	0.072755	0.160994
company	0.068383	0.076049
it	0.081639	0.163655
research	0.089011	0.070828

production	0.023011	0.058539
market	0.021773	0.074337
level	0.022693	0.057516
schedule	0.033787	0.066979
quality	0.032323	0.063441
strategic	0.021666	0.075002
target	0.021677	0.010823

phase	0.006114	0.024465
safety	0.005781	0.040455
community	0.004959	0.015334
capacity	0.006106	0.022195
leadership	0.005383	0.024681
theory	0.006125	0.032893
total	0.006358	0.026074
volume	0.004948	0.004205
review	0.005290	0.029645
professional	0.005817	0.023542

collaboration	0.009203	0.037007
planning	0.016436	0.050876
change	0.011048	0.056321
metrics	0.010762	0.039453
team	0.009676	0.053227
infrastructure	0.009703	0.029257
experience	0.011336	0.024064
capability	0.012976	0.006020

---

quadrant 3

written	0.010204	0.559469
method	0.016213	0.086731

acquisition	0.003635	0.112418
member	0.003943	0.079053
institute	0.004042	0.270601
component	0.001493	0.090053
request	0.003715	0.091053
infrastructure	0.003149	0.044638
managing	0.004378	0.045472

electronic	0.002765	0.301687
budget	0.007676	0.059511

---

quadrant 4

	centrality	density
cash	0.058039	0.168802
training	0.057361	0.085310
application	0.046304	0.046417

department	0.014133	0.061161
function	0.012724	0.020134
training	0.019191	0.069255
managing	0.013911	0.041735
field	0.016839	0.040481
review	0.016105	0.034787
accounting	0.006593	0.072493
ability	0.015408	0.017723
complete	0.011961	0.026506
percent	0.014835	0.037190
client	0.019168	0.064798
contractor	0.012763	0.030642
division	0.006799	0.016946
group	0.020026	0.038027

programme	0.002579	0.014799
asset	0.001567	0.006366
ensure	0.004640	0.026075
integrated	0.004939	0.031752
purchase	0.003458	0.008926
interpersonal	0.001057	0.004916
factor	0.003556	0.011508
proposed	0.004664	0.020137
programming	0.004604	0.023740
framework	0.003618	0.027038
vendor	0.003747	0.009253
cycle	0.003350	0.010410
environment	0.003798	0.029372
far	0.001867	0.011355
vision	0.001738	0.007175
office	0.004247	0.029284
electronic	0.004120	0.037916
field	0.002768	0.004802
methodology	0.003102	0.018963
corp	0.004086	0.031887
priority	0.001865	0.007115
department	0.004768	0.014800
recovery	0.003475	0.005798

improving	0.004740	0.021349
percent	0.005636	0.021700
agreement	0.006617	0.023262
phase	0.005708	0.018311
contractor	0.006813	0.056622
effort	0.005821	0.042254
environmental	0.004571	0.028936
center	0.005628	0.027079
market	0.007422	0.024402
did	0.005375	0.015447
lead	0.005278	0.015103
department	0.007833	0.041151
association	0.007418	0.054761
maintenance	0.005538	0.013069
making	0.008033	0.042764
provider	0.005804	0.041997
value	0.007632	0.028878
influence	0.004172	0.014693
community	0.004166	0.013819
responsible	0.007986	0.016059

FIGURE 3.5 Strategic diagrams.

electronic (content, written, express, permission, item, publishing) and *budget* (scheduling, CPM, critical path, Gantt, Pert). Here we can see that the management of information has been a constant: from the cluster written in 1985–1991 to the cluster *electronic* in 2002–2004 through the cluster *information* (quadrant 1, "strategic heart" of the field, in 1992–1996) and the cluster *institute* in 1996–2001. Furthermore, the aspects of *methods* (scheduling, CPM, critical path, Gantt, Pert, budget) have been an autonomous subfield since 1992–1996, coming from the cluster *cash* (quadrant 4 in 1985–1991) and having gained density to move upward.

Quadrant 4. These themes may evolve to the right, gaining centrality, and evolve upward, gaining density. They may be at the origin of new trends or development within the field. In this quadrant it is easy to see that we find a number of clusters, and thus we are not going to consider all of them here. Let us give three notable examples. The first one, already mentioned, is the cluster *cash* (1985–1991), which has been moving upward, and the cluster *method* (quadrant 3, 1992–1996) at the origin of the cluster *budget* (quadrant 1, 1997–2001, and quadrant 3, 2002–2004). The second one is the cluster *training* (education, learning, knowledge, leader, staff, mentoring, coaching, organization). This cluster has been part of the quadrant in 1985–1991 and 1992–1996 before moving into the "strategic heart" of the field in 1997–2001 and 2002–2004, showing that from the periphery of the field, these topics have become of central importance and have gained in density, becoming well defined and accepted within the field. The last example concerns the cluster *phase* (2002–2004), which integrates the notion of accountability, one dimension of governance.

Promising Themes within the Project Management Field and Cluster Analysis

Quadrant 2. Here we find promising or past themes that are part of the discipline or themes borrowed from other disciplines (context themes). This quadrant is important because the themes are essential for a good understanding of the field. If we consider the period 2002–2004, the cluster *collaboration* (broadband, user, LAN, collaborative tool) shows the development of collaborative approaches. The cluster *planning* (model, strategic, assess, chaos, performance, variation, vision, uncertainty, control, managerial) exemplifies the focus on how to manage and control performance strategically in chaotic and uncertain environments. The cluster *infrastructure* focuses on supply-chain management, ERP projects, connectivity, deployment, platform management, and integration, themes that are becoming more and more crucial. The cluster *experience* is self-explanatory. The need for *experience* (consultant, team, third party, sponsor, expertise, project manager) is of primary importance. The cluster *change* (practice, organization, organizational theory, behavior, partnership, thinking, social, commitment, escalation, psychological, responsibility) is in development, which is not a surprise. The cluster *team* is connected to the cluster *change* (team as change agent and factor for success) and demonstrates the importance of this theme within the field. The cluster *metrics* is a good indicator of themes borrowed from the quality management and control disciplines; it consists of concepts such as functional analysis, quality, quality control, measurement, benchmarking, best practice, total quality, and performance measurement. The position of this cluster has to be related to the growing importance of the strategic control (cluster *planning*) of performance. The last cluster, *capability,* is linked to the development of all aspects of maturity within organizations.

Once we have analyzed the general dynamic of the field, we can focus on specific and interesting clusters. Here we propose an analysis of the cluster *training* because it is part of quadrant 1 for the four periods under study and the emergence of the cluster *planning* in period 2002–2004 (quadrant 2) because it reflects the strategic role of project. Table 3.2 gives the content of the cluster *training* according to the periods considered.

From this table it is possible to study the indepth evolution of the cluster during the various time periods. Table 3.3 summarizes the main information needed to analyze each cluster.

We can see that the cluster *training* is neither complex through the various time periods (complexity = number of internal links/number of words), nor it is strongly connected (low percentage of connectivity). This indicates that the theme is not well defined and still moving, as indicates the transformation index. The transformation index is high (36 between 1985–1991 and 1992–1996), showing an almost complete transformation of the content of this cluster (just one word is in common), and then decreases to 5.71 (from 1992–1996 to 1997–2001), showing more consistency; it then increases to 8 between 1997–2001 and 2002–2004, which means that this theme is still moving in terms of content but is starting to gain in consistency. This indicates that there is still a need for clarification, although the cluster is in quadrant 1 during the various periods under consideration, as well as for further research or study.

Let's now consider the emergence of the cluster *planning* between 1996–2001 and 2002–2004. Table 3.4 shows the provenance of this cluster.

The cluster *planning* (2002–2004) comes from 22 clusters of the preceding period (1996–2001). Of 25 words constituting the cluster *planning,* 24 come from clusters of the preceding period. Four clusters have a special importance in this genesis: *budget* (quadrant 1, provenance index 0.31), *managing* (quadrant 3, provenance index 0.31), *phase*

TABLE 3.2   Content of the Cluster *Training* According the Different Periods of Time

	1985–1991	1992–1996	1997–2001	2002–2004
1	education	contract	designer	visual
2	training	supply	education	leadership
3	knowledge	personnel	training	classroom
4	course	program	curriculum	knowledge
5	communication	training	teaching	mentoring
6	manager	learning	classroom	customized
7	sense	teaching	instructional	interactive
8	completion	evaluation	instructor	training
9	end	summative	lecture	learning
10	human	proposal	program	leader
11	executive	writing	learning	ca
12	chief	instructional	manager	booth
13	success	instruction	course	coaching
14		interactive	faculty	staff
15		multimedia	student	education
16		classroom	capstone	knowledge management
17		designer	undergraduate	organizational learning
18		bid		course
19		developer		multimedia
20		assembly		object
21		collaborative		occupational
22		funding		vocational
23		evaluating		boundary

TABLE 3.3 Cluster *Training* Summary Data

Cluster	training			
Period (p)	1985–1991	1992–1996	1997–2001	2002–2004
NMOT (N)	13	23	17	23
LINT (L)	12	25	20	25
Complexity L/N	0,92	1,09	1,18	1,09
Percentage of connectivity $2L/(N*(N-1))$	15%	10%	15%	10%
N Commons for both periods p-1 and p $N(p\text{-}1 \cap p)$		1	7	5
Transformation Index $T = (N(p\text{-}1) + N(p))/N(p\text{-}1 \cap p)$		36,00	5,71	8,00
Similarity index $SI = 2*N(p\text{-}1 \cap p)/(N(p\text{-}1) + N(p))$		0,06	0,35	0,25

(quadrant 2, provenance index 0.27), and *computer* (quadrant 1, provenance index 0.23), contributing 12 words (48 percent) to the cluster *planning*. Furthermore, 10 clusters from quadrant 4, 4 clusters from quadrant 3, 4 clusters from quadrant 2, and 4 clusters from quadrant 1 contribute to the emergence of the cluster *planning*. This indicates a recomposition of "old" themes to give a new promising one and demonstrates the dynamic of evolution of the domain.

We cannot go any further within the scope of this chapter. Many other theme transformations are suggested by the clusters and strategic diagrams and have been studied.

SOME NOTICEABLE TRENDS FOR THE PROJECT MANAGEMENT FIELD

At this stage we may formulate a few possible trends for the project management field. Some of the results are aligned with the results of our former studies, based on analysis of the ABI Inform (ProQuest) database between 1985 and 2001 (Bredillet, 1998, 1999, 2002):

- At the operational level (quadrant 3), the continuous interest in the "cost engineering" aspects
- At the strategic level (quadrant 1), the interest in
  - Economic aspects and contracts
  - How to deal with various project types (categorizations)
  - The integration with supply-chain management
  - Learning and knowledge management

At the operational level, from the study of quadrant 3, we note a continuous interest in and focus on management of information and optimization techniques (Pert, Gantt, scheduling) (cluster *budget*).

At a more strategic level (quadrant 1), we note a continuous interest in the financial, investment, and economic aspects, including contracts. The cluster *business* (very consistent thoughout the various time periods) indicates a permanent trend in how to deal with specific types of projects. It appears to justify the new interest in and the importance of this theme and the growth of research dealing with project categorizations (Crawford et al., 2005; Archibald, 2003; current categorization project; see www.projectcategories.org/).

TABLE 3.4 Provenance of the Cluster *Planning* between 1996–2001 and 2002–2004

Cluster Source (= Theme i) 1996–2001	Quadrant 1996–2001	Cluster Planning (= Theme j) 2002–2004 (Common Words to Theme j and Preceding Theme i)	M_{ij}	Ln_{ij}	N_j	$[P.ij] = (2*[M.ij] + [Ln.ij])/[N.j]$
budget	1	control plan planning strategic	4		26	0.31
managing	3	analysis assess plan planning	4		26	0.31
phase	2	monitoring planned progress	3	1	26	0.27
computer	1	based model analysis	3		26	0.23
member	3	wbs work breakdown structure planning	3		26	0.23
cycle	4	assess plan strategic	3		26	0.23
factor	4	managerial styles	2	1	26	0.19
framework	4	conceptual framework	2	1	26	0.19
component	3	variation control	2		26	0.15
environment	4	production	1	1	26	0.12
leadership	2	improve	1		26	0.12
office	4	strategy	1	1	26	0.12
recovery	4	chaos	1		26	0.12
theory	2	uncertainty	1	1	26	0.12
acquisition	3	performance	1		26	0.08
ensure	4	plan	1		26	0.08
far	4	control	1		26	0.08
integrated	4	planning	1		26	0.08
methodology	4	performance	1		26	0.08
power	1	analysis	1		26	0.08
professional	2	strategic	1		26	0.08
technology	N/A	performance	1		26	0.08
		management styles	0		26	0.00

[M.ij] is the number of words in both theme j and (preceding) theme i
[Ln.ij] is the number of words in both theme j and linked to preceding theme i but belonging to no other theme in this generation
[N.j] is the number of words in theme j

Information systems applications and projects (ERP, BPR) are still an area of interest, and this is reinforced by the cluster *infrastructure* in quadrant 2, demonstrating a growing importance of the issues of integration, connectivity, supply-chain management, and platform management. A confirming trend since 1996–2001 is the stronger importance of the cluster *training* and the attached concepts (education, organizational learning, knowledge management, leading, coaching) as of strategic importance.

Besides these continuous trends, we can note new possible areas of interest while considering quadrant 2:

• The link between strategy and project
• Governance
• The importance of maturity (organizational performance and metrics, control)
• Change management

The link between strategy and project becomes clear within the field through the cluster *planning,* and there is here a strong connection with the development of an interest in maturity (cluster *capability*). The importance of organizational performance is reinforced by the cluster *metrics* and the integration of concepts coming from the quality management and control discipline. On the softer side, *change* and the role of teams as change agents and keys for success are also clearly new concerns within the field.

The field seems to be gaining in maturity, although it is very dynamic and focused around the role of project in such strategic issues as management, organizational issues, effective management, and/or use of resources and cost. The contextualization of the applications and the creation of value for the stakeholders seem to be another main trend. Furthermore, clarification of the theme *professional* seems to be a major issue. As part of the weak signal detected, the threat of having project management become a part of general management may be considered. It reinforces the need to clarify the former theme. Another trend is that the more "technical" aspects of project management are no longer appearing as strategic for the field. Project management is becoming more focused on implementation of organization strategy.

There are some important consequences regarding the strategies of the actors (professional bodies). Generally speaking, the field is growing rapidly (number of papers written), is in a process of construction/deconstruction, and is very dynamic, demonstrating its preparadigmatic nature. This reinforces the former analysis of the games of the actors and their competing/cooperative strategies in the development of standards and certifications.

Comparisons with Other Studies

It is interesting at this point to briefly compare our factual findings with the main results of some other recent studies addressing in one way or another some predictions about the future of project management. These results derive from different approaches and different methods: research based on literature review since 1960 (Kloppenborg and Opfer, 2002), expert questioning (Archibald, 2003), and longitudinal case study and personal experience (Tanaka, 2004). The conclusion is that the main trends appear to be identical whatever the approach and the method are, even if the proposed conclusions and views offered by the various authors are presented from different perspectives. The main (selected) findings are summarized below:

Kloppenborg and Opfer, 2002. The most important trend commonly observed is the increase in literature on project management issues. The dominant application areas described in the project management literature are the construction, information systems, and utilities industries. The authors found numerous articles about the government in the different knowledge areas. Regarding the processes of project management, the trend was toward planning and control.

Based on the identified trends, a few of the predictions are (selected) as follows:

- Standardization of processes and tools, as well as standardization of terminology, is expected to contribute to project management success.

- There will be greater use by practitioners of Web technologies for enterprise communication and collaboration.

- Major companies will engage in more outsourcing of project management.

- The project manager's role will evolve to demonstrate more leadership than project management. Advanced training for project managers will be offered through companies, universities, and professional organizations.

- There will be a movement away from "superprojects."

- Refinements will occur in how project scope is defined and related to business requirements and measurable benefits.

- Selection and prioritization of projects will continue to evolve as a large issue for both government and industry.

- Increased emphasis will be placed on formal project management training and certification and verification of what training really works.

- More emphasis will be placed on risk management in general and specific training for project managers on risk identification, contingency planning, risk mitigation, and managing risk events.

- There will be increased focus on communications and communications planning, particularly as it relates to stakeholder management and communications in times of project crisis.

Archibald, 2003.   Here are a few of Archibald's conclusions and predictions about where the discipline of project management will be in the year 2008:

- *Characteristics of project management.* The basic characteristics of project management have not changed appreciably in the past 10 years and are not expected to change much within the foreseeable future.

- *Major project management trends.* Three major project management trends are observed that will continue: (1) linking strategic and project management through project portfolio management practices, (2) broadening the application of project management to include the total project life cycle from concept through to full realization of project benefits, and (3) continued discovery of new application areas for the project management discipline.

- *Organization capabilities and maturity in project management.* Rather than continue to be developed as a separate specialty within organizational management disciplines, the principles and practices of project management will merge gradually with other areas of management and be an important part of every manager's responsibilities, much like financial management is today.

- *Project management maturity models.* There will be at least three major models competing in the global marketplace: PMI's OPM3™, Japan's P2M, and outgrowths from the United Kingdom's OGC PRINCE2™ approach.

- *Individual capabilities in project management.* Certification of individuals in project management will be much more heavily based on proven capabilities, almost entirely focused on specific areas of application and/or specific categories of projects, awarded at several levels: program manager, project manager, and several project specialist categories (cost, estimating, scheduling, risk, and others).

- *Projects, programs, and project portfolios.* Project portfolio management will be in widespread use; a global project classification system based on the characteristics of project results will be accepted by the major project management associations and used by most practitioners.

- *Project life-cycle models.* The postproject phase of "realization of project benefits" will become increasingly recognized as a proper part of the total project life cycle.

- *Areas of application of project management.* Within the next five years, formalized project management will be in use in essentially all areas of human endeavor.

- *Project management planning and control systems and tools.* Project management software and the information it produces will be fully integrated with all corporate information systems.

- *Project teams.* Most project managers will understand the importance of and be proficient in team building and team leadership.

- *The profession of project management.* Project management disciplines and practices will be known and used widely by managers at many levels in essentially all industries and human agencies in the developed world.

Tanaka, 2004. This author offers an "opportunities/challenges" approach to the development of project management. The following opportunities are identified:

- *Tooling the strategic project management model.* The strategic project management model pioneered by P2M of Japan and OPM3™ released by the PMI should be supported by techniques and tools ready for use by organizations and validated by successful application cases that will have delivered innovation and other strategic value to organizations.

- *Verification of value delivered by project management.* Emergence of a strategic project management model.

- *Global project management.* Take profit from the experience of the engineering and construction industry.

- *Project management in public sectors.* Promotion of project management by all professional bodies toward governments and public agencies.

- *Social project management.* One of the most prospective application area of project management is societal management and activities.

  The main challenges are

- Establishment of project management as a firm, testable academic and professional discipline

- Harmonization of project management bodies of knowledge, competency standards, and certifications systems

- Corporate support

CONCLUSION

The project management field is still in a preparadigmatic stage. Among the main trends, we can note the focus around the role of project management in such strategic issues as management, organizational issues, maturity, performance management, and/or use of resources and cost. The contextualization of the applications and the creation of value for the stakeholders seem to be another main trend. As part of the weak signal detected, the threat of having project management become a part of general management may be considered. This reinforces the need to clarify the former theme. Another trend is that the more "technical" aspects of project management are still appearing along with softer issues (change management and the role of the teams). But it seems that project panagement is becoming more focused on implementation of organization strategy.

Methodologic limitations were addressed earlier. This study is based exclusively on the EBSCO Business Source Premier Database. It is too far away to reflect on the entire project management field, and it would be very interesting to add proceedings of congresses, in-company publications, and other publications, books, theses, and unpublished works.

However, this study demonstrates the interest of coword analysis in extracting patterns of form, structure, and dynamics in the field and in identifying trends within the discipline represented by a corpus of publications. It shows clearly that the analysis of a discipline must combine both quantitative and qualitative methods and integrate both synchronic and diachronic perspectives.

We hope that this brief study has shown an innovative way to gain indepth knowledge and perception of the evolution of the project management field. Further work is underway to integrate this approach as part of an "International Observatory of Project Management Practices." This method is used as well to study the interactions between the project management field and others disciplines and to link concepts together in the design of educational programs and curricula.

REFERENCES

Archibald R. 2003. State of the Art of Project Management: 2003. Project Management Conference, Escuela Colombiana de Ingeniera, Bogota, Colombia, December 5–6, 2003.

Audet M. 1986. Le procès des connaissances de l'administration dans *La production des connaissances de l'administration* sous la direction de Audet et Malouin. Quebec: Les Presses de l'Université Laval.

Bauin S. 1986. Aquaculture: A field by bureaucratic fiat, in M Callon, J Law, A Rip (eds.), *Mapping the Dynamics of Science and Technology: Sociology of Science in the Real World*. London: Macmillan, pp. 124–141.

Bauin S, Michelet B, Schweighoffer MG, Vermeulin P. 1991. Using bibliometrics in strategic analysis: Understanding chemical reactions at the CNRS. *Scientometrics* 22(1):113–137.

Bredillet C. 1998. Essai de définition du champ disciplinaire du management de projet et de sa dynamique d'évolution. Mémoire de DEA, USTL–IAE de Lille.

Bredillet C. 1999. Essai de définition du champ disciplinaire du management de projet et de sa dynamique d'évolution. *Rev Int Gest Manag Projets* 4(2):6–29.

Bredillet C. 2002. Mapping the dynamics of project management field: Project management in action, in *Proceedings of PMI Research Conference* Project Management Institute, Newton Square, Pennsylvania, *2002*, pp. 157–169.

Callon M. 1986. Pinpointing industrial invention: An exploration of quantitative methods for the analysis of patents, in M Callon, J Law, A Rip (eds.), *Mapping the Dynamics of Science and Technology: Sociology of Science in the Real World*. London: Macmillan, pp. 163–188.

Callon M, Courtial J-P, Turner W. 1986a. Future developments, in M Callon, J Law, A Rip (eds.), *Mapping the Dynamics of Science and Technology: Sociology of Science in the Real World*. London: Macmillan, pp. 211–217.

Callon M, Law J, Rip A. 1986b. How to study the force of science, in M Callon, J Law, A Rip (eds.), *Mapping the Dynamics of Science and Technology: Sociology of Science in the Real World.* London: Macmillan, pp. 3–15.

Callon M, Courtial J-P, Laville F. 1991. Coword analysis as a tool for describing the network of interactions between basic and technological research: The case of polymer chemistry. *Scientometrics* 22(1):155–205.

Coulter N, Monarch I, Konda S. 1998. Software engineering as seen through its research literature: A study in coword analysis. *J Am Soc Inform Sci* 49(13):1206–1223.

Courtial J-P, Law J. 1989. A coword study of artificial intelligence. *Soc Stud Sci (Lond)* 19:301–311.

Courtial J-P. 1998. Comments on Leydesdorff's article. *J Am Soc Inform Sci* 49(1):98.

Courtial J-P, Callon M, Sigogneau A. 1993. The use of patent titles for identifying the topics of invention and forecasting trends. *Scientometrics* 26(2):231–242.

Crawford L, Hobbs B, Turner JR. 2005. *Project Categorizations Systems.* Project Management Institute, Pennsylvania.

E. Garfield, M. V. Malin, and H. Small. Citation data as science indicators. In Y. Elkana, J. Lederberg, R. K. Merton, A. Thackray, and H. Zuckerman, editors, *Toward a Metric of Science: The Advent of Science Indicators.* John Wiley and Sons, 1978.

He Q. 1999. Knowledge discovery through coword analysis. *Library Trends* 48(1):133–159.

Kloppenborg T, Opfer W. 2002. The current state of project management research: Trends, interpretations, and predications. *Project Manag J* 33(2):5–18.

Kostoff RN, Eberhart HJ, Toothman DR, Pellenbarg R. 1997. Database tomography for technical intelligence: Comparative roadmaps of the research impact assessment literature and the *Journal of the American Chemical Society. Scientiometrics* 40(1):103–138.

Kuhn TS. 1983. *La structure des révolutions scientifiques.* Paris: Flammarion.

Latour B. 1987. *Science in Action: How to Follow Scientists and Engineers Through Society.* Cambridge, MA: Harvard University Press.

Law J, Whittaker J. 1992. Mapping acidification research: A test of the coword method. *Scientometrics* 23(3):417–461.

Law J, Bauin S, Courtial J-P, Whittaker J. 1988. Policy and the mapping of scientific change: A coword analysis of research into environmental acidification. *Scientometrics* 14(3–4):251–264.

Leydesdorff L. 1997. Why words and cowords cannot map the development of the science. *J Am Soc Inform Sci* 48(5):418–427.

Leydesdorff L. 1998. Reply about using cowords. *J Am Soc Inform Sci* 49(1):98–99.

MacKenzie D. 1978. Statistical theory and social interests: A case study. *Soc Stud Sci* 8:35–83.

Nederhof AJ, van Wijk E. 1997. Mapping the social and behavioral sciences worldwide: Use of maps in portfolio analysis of national research efforts. *Scientometrics* 40(2):237–276.

Project Management Institute (PMI). 2001. *PMI Project Management Fact Book,* 2d ed. Project Management Institute, Pennsylvania.

Popper K. 1959. *The Logic of Scientific Discovery* (trans. by Logik der Forschung). London: Hutchinson.

Rotto E, Morgan RP. 1997. An exploration of expert-based text analysis techniques for assessing industrial relevance in US engineering dissertation abstracts. *Scientometrics* 40(1):83–102.

Tanaka H. 2004. The changing landscape of project management. 4th International Project Management Workshop, ESC Lille, August 16–20, 2004.

Turner WA, Callon M. 1986. State intervention in academic and industrial research: The case of macromolecular chemistry in France, in M Callon, J Law, A Rip (eds.), *Mapping the Dynamics of Science and Technology: Sociology of Science in the Real World.* London: Macmillan, pp. 142–162.

Turner WA, Rojouan F. 1991. Evaluating input/output relationships in a regional research network using coword analysis. *Scientometrics* 22(1):139–154.

Turner WA, Chartron G, Laville E, Michelet B. 1988. Packaging information for peer review: New coword analysis techniques, in AFJ Van Raan (ed.), *Handbook of Quantitative Studies of Science and Technology*. Amsterdam: Elsevier Science, pp. 291–323.

Weingart, P. 1982. The scientific power elite—a chimera: the de-institutionalization and politicization of science, in: N. Elias, H. Martins, R. Whitley (eds.), *Scientific Establishments and Hierarchies, Sociology of the Sciences, Yearbook*. Dordrecht: Reidel, pp. 71–87.

Whittaker, J. 1989. Creativity and conformity in science: Titles, keywords and co-word analysis. *Soc Stud Sci* 19:473–496.

CHAPTER 4
TOTAL LIFE-CYCLE SYSTEM MANAGEMENT

James V. Jones

President, Logistics Management Associates,
Irvine, California

James V. Jones is an internationally recognized authority on integrated logistics support and has an indepth experience in program management, business processes, and development of logistics support systems. He is an internationally sought-after consultant, lecturer, and educator and has authored several technical reference books, including *Integrated Logistics Support Handbook* (3rd ed., McGraw-Hill, 2006), *Engineering Design: Reliability, Maintainability, and Testability* (McGraw-Hill, 1988), and *Logistic Support Analysis Handbook* (McGraw-Hill, 1989). Mr. Jones has participated as a member of several U.S. Department of Defense committees that produced key policies and standards. His involvement with U.S. logistics policy continues to this date. Mr. Jones is currently president of Logistics Management Associates (LMA), Irvine, CA, a consulting firm with emphasis on systems engineering, supportability engineering, and logistics management. LMA enjoys an international array of clients in both the military and civilian sectors.

The success or failure of a project typically is measured against established budget and schedule requirements. If a project is completed on schedule and within budget, then it is considered to have been completed successfully, and if the project exceeds either its budget or its schedule, then it is probably deemed to have been unsuccessful. However, this traditional method may not be the most appropriate in all cases. It may be better to assess success or failure based on the long-term results of the project output. Situations where a project has resulted in a capital expenditure of a company or organization, such as building a new manufacturing facility or purchasing a new fleet of aircraft, should be gauged based on the financial viability and utility of the manufacturing facility or aircraft fleet rather than on the adherence to schedule and budget by the project that managed their development and acquisition.

The most common measures for long-term success are

Operational effectiveness (O_E), which is a measure of how well a system performs assigned performance functions

Operational availability (A_O), which determines how often the system is available to perform assigned functions

Cost of ownership (C_O), which is the annualized representation of resources consumed directly in the procurement, operation, training, support, and maintenance of a system at all stages of its life

TABLE 4.1   Reasons for TLCSM

- Link everything into one "big picture"
- Provide better management information
- Increase capability
- Improve availability
- Make better use of critical resources
- Minimize cost of ownership
- Recognize relationships between distributed organizations

Total life-cycle system management (TLCSM) is a technique that takes the long-term view of projects to guide decision making toward solutions that provide lifetime success rather than short-term limits of schedule and budget. TLSCM can be defined as

- The implementation, integration, and management of all activities associated with the acquisition, development, production, introduction, sustainment, and disposal of a system across its life cycle.
- Establishment of a single point of management responsibility and accountability for system acquisition and sustainment.
- Emphasis on early and continuing translation of performance objectives into operationally available and affordable increments of capability over the system life cycle. The result of this sustainment planning is encompassed in the product support solution describing post-introduction support of the operational system.

The reasons justifying application of TLCSM to a project are listed in Table 4.1. Most notably, TLCSM focuses on the results of decisions made by the project team during acquisition of a system and their effect on long-term goals for the system being procured. The key issues are having the "big picture" view rather than short-term limitations so that the end result of an acquisition project minimizes the total cost of ownership of a system. The goals of TLCSM are to produce benefits in terms of revenue and profitability by focusing on optimizing system operational effectiveness and operational availability while at the same time minimizing cost of ownership.

PRODUCT LIFE CYCLE

Any discussion of TLSCM must start with a description of the product life cycle. Figure 4.1 shows the six typical stages over the life of any item, which are concept, assessment, development, manufacture or build, operation, and disposal. A system begins its life when a need is identified. This occurs in the concept phase, where the organization's current and future requirements are continually reviewed to identify needs before they start to impede productivity or capability. Once identified as a requirement, it is studied to define the parameters that must be achieved to meet the need. Sufficient justification of the need should receive management approval to initiate a formal project to procure or develop a system to meet the need. During the assessment phase, the project team identifies and investigates alternatives to determine the best approach to meet the need. The project moves into the development phase when management accepts the project's recommendation for the most reasonable alternative to meet the need. This move to the development phase equires funding for development, manufacture, and delivery of the system. The development phase consists of all system architecting, systems engineering,

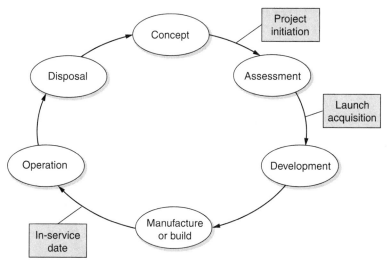

FIGURE 4.1   Product life cycle.

design engineering, and purchasing activities necessary to produce the final system. All activities point toward the in-service date when the system commences operation to meet the need. The system remains in service until replaced or retired, when it is disposed to complete its life cycle. The key point in understanding the system life cycle is to understand when decisions must be made to achieve the desired project result of minimizing cost of ownership.

The expenditure of funds over the life of a system typically can be categorized by product life-cycle phase. Figure 4.2 shows that the concept and assessment phases account for an estimated 2 percent of the total cost of ownership. Expenditures during development and manufacturing are probably around 12 percent of the total. The majority of expenditures occur when the system is being operated and sustained—a whopping 85 percent in most cases. The thrust of TLSCM is to attempt to reduce the total outlay of funds over the system life. However, there is a very significant point that is often overlooked and misunderstood by many project managers. This is the cause and effect of decisions versus when the effect of the decision is realized. Figure 4.3 indicates that 70 percent of the cost-of-ownership decisions are made during the concept phase of the product life cycle. These are obviously very significant to realize. Early decisions dictate the ultimate cost of ownership of a system. By the end of system development, probably more than 85 percent of the cost-of-ownership decisions have been made. The actual expenditure of funds probably will occur several years in the future, but the decision that causes the requirement for expenditure has been made.

When project managers make a short-term decision to stay within an acquisition budget or to cut a project schedule, they may be increasing the overall system cost of ownership inadvertently by making a decision that causes long-term expenditure to rise. One of the obvious ways that this occurs is when poor-quality systems or subsystems are procured to limit acquisition budget expenditures. Eventually, poor quality induces increases in maintenance problems, long system downtime, and lost productivity. The short-term solution creates long-term increases in the cost of ownership.

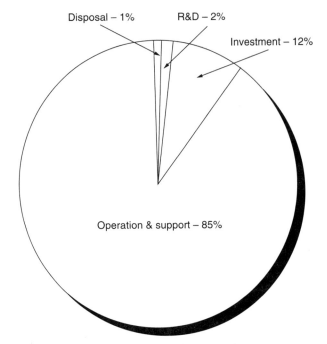

FIGURE 4.2   Life-cycle costs.

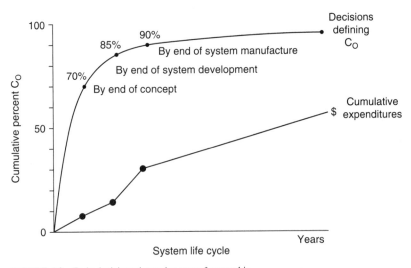

FIGURE 4.3   Early decisions determine cost of ownership.

AN EXAMPLE OF THE TLCSM CONCEPT

The following is a description of how TLCSM concepts should be applied by a project team. The example presents a series of decision-making process that should be applied by any acquisition project team to achieve the best long-term success possible as an outcome of their activities.

Situation.   A project team has been constituted to acquire a fleet of 20 helicopters for use in the logging industry. The helicopters will be used to ferry supplies to remote locations and also may be used for medical evacuation or other emergency situations. The team must assess a range of possible models from several manufacturers to determine the specific model and configuration that best fits the company's requirements. Upper management requires detailed justification before any helicopters will be purchased. The project team must evaluate all candidates to identify the best balance between operational effectiveness, operational availability, and cost of ownership. Additionally, the project team must develop a cost-effective solution to logistically support the fleet over its operational life.

OPERATIONAL EFFECTIVENESS (O_E)

It is essential that the helicopter selected for purchase be capable of performing all the activities needed by the logging company, so the first task for the project team is to identify all the missions and roles for the fleet. This should be a comprehensive list of scenarios, including flying time, distance traveled, possible maximum load, and minimum performance requirements. Second, the team should analyze the geographic region where the scenarios will be performed to determine any environmental considerations that would have a negative effect on performance, such as altitude, obstructions, weather conditions, and anything else that must be considered as significant possible limits on helicopter safe operation. The combination of the mission and usage environment identifies the range of performance functions that any selected helicopter must perform to meet the company's requirements successfully. Next, the project team must construct an evaluation methodology to be used in assessment of the possible helicopters to be purchased. Figure 4.4 shows how O_E forms the core of a cost-effectiveness analysis. The O_E portion of the diagram identifies all necessary system functions required to meet its requirements successfully. The numerical weighting of each function represent the team's concept of relative importance between the functional requirements. In this example, the project team has divided system requirements into five major categories: inherent performance characteristics, operational suitability, mission specifics, health and safety, and risk. Four of these categories have been divided further to identify specific issues that must be considered. This diagram then is used to assess each helicopter to determine its potential to meet the O_E requirements. Some of the mandatory characteristics are more important that others, so possible points are assigned to reflect this. Each helicopter is then assessed and provided point values against each block. If any block rating received a 0 score, the helicopter is eliminated from further consideration because it does not meet the minimum functional requirements. The total of all possible points added up to a score of 98 points. The 2 final points are reserved for intrinsic or aesthetic award owing to intangibles such as reputation, good will, etc. Thus the maximum point value that any helicopter can receive is 100.

OPERATIONAL AVAILABILITY (A_O)

Any helicopter selected for purchase must be available to perform assigned missions that may be scheduled at any random time. Operational availability provides a statistical

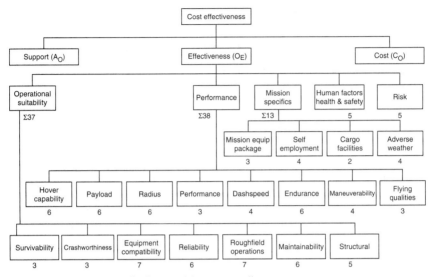

FIGURE 4.4   Operational effectiveness (O_E) assessment diagram.

estimate of the probability that a helicopter will be capable of responding to a mission requirement. It includes the design characteristics of the system plus the responsiveness of the support infrastructure into an overall estimate of system availability. Figure 4.5 shows the concept of calculating A_O by dividing the amount of time a system is operationally available by the total time being measured.

Typically, A_O is calculated on an annual basis. If a system has the possibility of being required anytime day or night, then its maximum total time per year is (365 days × 24 hours) 8760 hours. If a system never breaks, is never removed from service for maintenance, and never has to wait for support resources, then it would be available 100 percent of the time. However, this is not possible because systems do break, they do require maintenance, and they do sometimes wait for support resources. Figure 4.6 presents an alternate concept for calculating A_O that highlights non-mission-capable time as being the reason for a system not being operationally available. The project team should address the issues that would cause the helicopter to be non-mission-capable to determine its potential A_O if selected for purchase.

Figure 4.7 shows that there are three different reasons for a system to be non-mission-capable (NMC). These reasons include the time a system is undergoing repair, being serviced, or waiting for support resources. Each of the reasons must be addressed separately and then combined to determine total time that the system will not be available over a year. Figure 4.8 shows the formula for calculating total corrective maintenance downtime (TCM) and then illustrates how TCM is calculated for one of the helicopters

$$A_O = \frac{\text{mission-capable time}}{\text{total time}}$$

FIGURE 4.5   Operational availability (A_O).

$$MCT = \text{total time} - NMCT$$
$$\text{Therefore,}$$
$$A_O = \frac{\text{total time} - NMCT}{\text{total time}}$$

where MCT = mission-capable time
NMCT = non-mission-capable time

FIGURE 4.6 Operational Availability.

$$NMCT = TCM + TPM + ALDT$$

NMCT consists of

TCM = total corrective maintenance downtime when the system is
undergoing repair because it failed
TPM = total preventive maintenance downtime when the system is
undergoing scheduled maintenance which renders it NMC
ALDT = administrative or logistics delay time when the system is NMC
because it is awaiting logistics support resources (spares,
personnel, etc.)

FIGURE 4.7 Non-mission-capable time.

$$TCM = \left(\frac{\text{number of systems} \times \text{number of annual missions} \times \text{mission time}}{MTBF} \right) \times M_{CMT}$$

Number of systems = the total number of systems the user can task perform a mission
Number of annual missions = the total number of times that a mission is performed
Mission time = the average time required to perform the mission once

Example: Number of systems (aircraft) = 20 (total number in the operational inventory)
Number of annual missions = 180 (total sorties per year per system)
Mission time = 8 hours
MTBF = 200 hours
M_{CMT} = 4 hours

$$TCM = \left(\frac{20 \times 180 \times 8}{200} \right) \times 4 = 576 \text{ hours}$$

FIGURE 4.8 Calculating TCM.

Example: Number of systems = 20
          Average annual mission per aircraft = 180
          Average mission time = 8 hours

PM Tasks	Task Frequency	Task Time
Preflight	Once per mission	0.5 hour
Postflight	Once per mission	1.0 hour
Periodic inspection	Once per month	6.0 hours
Overhaul	1200 flying hours	40.0 hours

Calculations (for one aircraft, then the fleet of 20)

M_{PT} (preflight) = 180 missions x 0.5 hour = 90 hours
M_{PT} (postflight) = 180 missions x 1.0 hour = 180 hours
M_{PT} (periodic inspection) = 12 months x 6.0 hours = 72 hours
M_{PT} (overhaul) = (180 missions x 8 hours)/1200 x 40 = 48 hours

Total TPM (for 1 aircraft)   390 hours
Total TPM (for 20 aircraft)   7800 hours

FIGURE 4.9   Calculating TPM.

being considered for purchase by the project team. Calculating TCM involves projecting total fleet usage for a year by multiplying the number of systems times the number of missions per year times the mission duration. Then the result is divided by the average rate that the system experiences a failure that requires maintenance [mean time between failures (MTBF)] and then multiplying that by the mean corrective maintenance time required to fix the failure. This results in the total time per year that the systems will not be available to respond to a mission requirement. Figure 4.9 shows how total preventive maintenance downtime (TPM) is calculated by determining scheduled maintenance requirements for a system and then projecting the total number of hours per year that the system will be nonavailable owing to scheduled maintenance. Table 4.2 shows that administrative and logistics delay time (ALDT) can consist of several different types of support resources needed to sustain system capability. A shortage of any of these resource types will negatively affect A_O. The formula in Fig. 4.10 shows that the combination of the delay times for each resource type determines the total ALDT for a system. Example input values for each resource type are listed in Table 4.3, and the calculation of ALDT for the example helicopter project is provided in Fig. 4.11. The final calculation of A_O for one of the possible helicopters that the project team could select for procurement is provided in Fig. 4.12, which shows that the predicted A_O for this helicopter is 94 percent.

TABLE 4.2   Administrative and Logistics Delay Time

ALDT includes
• Logistics support infrastructure
• Spares availability
• Support equipment availability
• Personnel availability
• Facility capacity limitations
• Transportation responsiveness

TABLE 4.3   Input Values for Calculating ALDT

Percent of spares available at system location	95%
Time required to obtain spare at system location	2 hours
Time required to obtain spare from other location	72 hours
Operational availability for required support equipment	98%
Delay time when support equipment is not available	48 hours
Average time for personnel to arrive to start maintenance	1 hours
Average time waiting to enter maintenance facility	2 hours
Average time waiting for transport to maintenance facility	0.5 hour
Average ADT while non-mission-capable	4 hours

$$ALDT = D_{TS} + D_{TE} + D_{TP} + D_{TF} + D_{TT} + ADT$$

where D_{TS} = delay time spares
D_{TE} = delay time support equipment
D_{TP} = delay time personnel
D_{TF} = delay time facilities
D_{TT} = delay time transportation
ADT = administrative delay Time

FIGURE 4.10   Calculating ALDT.

$D_{TS} = (144 \times 0.95 \times 2) + (144 \times 0.05 \times 72) =$	792.0 hours
$D_{TE} = 144 \times (1-.98) \times 48 =$	230.4 hours
$D_{TP} = 144 \times 1 =$	144.0 hours
$D_{TF} = 144 \times 2 =$	288.0 hours
$D_{TT} = 144 \times 0.5 =$	72.0 hours
$ADT = 144 \times 4 =$	576.0 hours
Total ALDT =	2102.4 hours

Calculating the number of NMC
demands placed on the support
infrastructure

$(20 \times 180 \times 8)/200 = 144$

FIGURE 4.11   Calculating ALDT.

Total time = 20 aircraft × 8760 possible operating hours per year = 175,200

NMCT = 576 hours + 7800 hours + 2102.4 hours = 10,478.4
         (TCM)   (TPM)   (ALDT)

$$A_O = \frac{175,200 - 10,478.4}{175,200} = 0.94 = 94\%$$

FIGURE 4.12   Calculating A_O.

TABLE 4.4   Targets and Measurements to Improve A_O

- Reliability—MTBF
- Maintainability—M_{CMT}
- Scheduled maintenance requirements
- Logistics support infrastructure
- Spares availability
- Support equipment availability
- Personnel availability
- Facility capacity and utilization rate
- Transportation responsiveness
- Administration requirements

It is important to point out that the inputs for the calculations come from many different sources. The reliability (MTBF) and maintainability (M_{CMT}) statistics must be provided by the helicopter manufacturer. Identification of scheduled maintenance requirements and time for performance of the tasks must come from the helicopter manufacturer. The ALDT inputs may come from either the manufacture, the organization that the logging company may contract for maintenance services, or internally within the logging company. However, the most significant inputs (mission descriptions, mission time, and annual number of missions) must be developed by the project team. As the project team studies each helicopter to determine the one preferred for procurement, they must analyze the possible options for improving A_O. The possible options for improvement are listed in Table 4.4. Each of these factors must be studied to ensure that every possible option has been considered before making the final purchase decision.

OPERATION AND MAINTENANCE SUPPORT REQUIREMENTS

As seen earlier, achieving a desirable A_O for a system requires having the necessary support resources to sustain operations. Additionally, Fig. 4.2 shows that most of costs incurred for system ownership happen during the operational phase of the product life cycle. Therefore, it is very important that the project team quantify the possible physical resource package that will be required to operate and maintain the system over its operational life. Figure 4.13 illustrates that the combination of both operation and maintenance functions required to support a system constitute the physical support package. Operational support resources tend to be fairly easy to quantify because they consist mainly of operators, fuel, operator training, and operational facilities. Maintenance support resources are far more difficult to quantify because a detailed knowledge of the design and construction of the system is needed to identify specific requirements accurately.

Figure 4.14 shows the normal process for identification of maintenance support resource requirements for any system. The process starts with identification of every item within the system architecture that potentially will require any type of maintenance over its life cycle. This identification should be based on the results of two engineering analyses. These are a *failure modes effects criticality analysis* (FMECA) and a *reliability-centered maintenance analysis* (RCM analysis). The FMECA identifies every way that the system can fail. Every failure will require maintenance and therefore is the basis for identification of total corrective maintenance (TCM) discussed earlier. RCM analysis is used to develop the scheduled maintenance for a system to avoid or prevent unwanted catastrophic failures while the system is being used. The results of RCM analysis are realized in the total preventive maintenance (TPM), also discussed earlier. Both corrective and preventive maintenance require support resources for accomplishment. The maintenance significant items resulting from the FMECA and RCM analysis represent

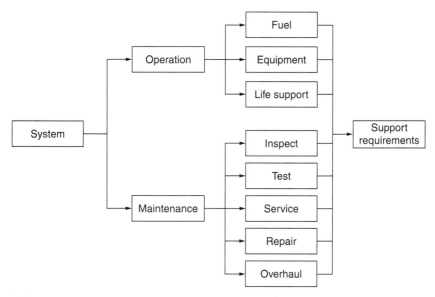

FIGURE 4.13   Identifying support requirements.

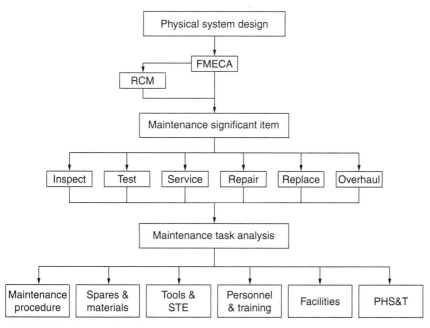

FIGURE 4.14   Resource identification process.

TABLE 4.5   Support Resource Categories

- Operation and maintenance manuals
- Spares and support materials list
- Tools and support and test equipment list
- Maintenance personnel requirements and work loading
- Training courses for operators and maintainers
- Operation, maintenance, supply, and training facilities
- Requirements for packing, handling, storage, and transportation

the liability to support the system throughout its operational life. If sufficient resources are not available, administrative and logistics delay time (ALDT), discussed earlier will increase, and A_O will decrease accordingly.

The process continues by identification of each maintenance task that will be applicable to support each maintenance significant item. Then a maintenance task analysis is performed that identifies the total number and quantity of resources required to perform the task. The results of all task analyses are consolidated to determine the full range and depth of the required support resource package, which includes the things listed at Table 4.5. The complete package includes all maintenance procedures (both corrective and preventive) that then will be contained in the operation and maintenance manuals for the system; the range of spares and other materials required for maintenance; the complete set of tools and test equipment required for maintenance; the number of personnel required for maintenance and their work loading; training course needs for operators and maintainers; facility requirements for operation, maintenance, training, and storage; and finally, requirements for packaging, handling, storage, and transportation of resources.

COST OF OWNERSHIP (C_O)

The third and possibly most important factor in decision making is the ultimate long-term cost of ownership that may result from the final decisions made by the project team during acquisition. As illustrated by Fig. 4.3, most of the cost-of-ownership decisions are made early in the acquisition of a system. Therefore, it is extremely important that the project team make every effort to determine the possible costs of each option being considered prior to making the final decision. The most common technique for estimating C_O during acquisition is *life-cycle costing* (LCC). The definition and typical purposes of LCC are provided at Table 4.6. LCC is an attempt to identify and quantify the total costs that may be incurred over the product life cycle.

TABLE 4.6   Life-Cycle Cost (LCC)

LCC: A cost-estimation process that compares the costs of the relative merits of two or more options. Results in an estimate of the relative costs of the options so that the total of differences can be compared as a single cost figure.

This includes the evaluation of
- Alternative operation/maintenance concepts
- Alternative design configurations
- Alternative systems/products
- Alternative logistics support policies
- Alternative suppliers

$$C_T = C_R + C_I + C_O + C_D$$

where C_T = Total cost of ownership
C_R = Research and development costs
C_I = Investment costs
C_O = Operation and support costs
C_D = Disposal costs

FIGURE 4.15   Total cost-of-ownership stages.

These costs are divided into four distinct stages of the product life (Fig. 4.15): research and development (R&D), investment, operation and support (O&S), and disposal. These four stages do cross over several of the product life-cycle phases discussed earlier. The R&D stage consist of all the initial studies conducted at the beginning of a project prior to any procurement decision. The investment stage is where the organization purchases everything necessary to meet the mission requirement. The investment stage ends with delivery of the system and all necessary support resources. The O&S stage is the operational life of the system, when it is being used to perform assigned tasks and is being maintained using the support resource package. The disposal stage is when the system and all support resources are removed from service and either disposed of or sold to another organization. Calculation of the estimated C_O using LCC requires identification of an extensive number of statistics that are then combined in a computer model based on the cost-estimation model architecture shown at Fig. 4.16.

As seen in this figure, LCC is an all-encompassing estimate of all direct and indirect costs associated with owning a system. Each of the subelements of this cost-model architecture represents between three and seven submodels needed to calculate each identifiable cost. Normally, the project team must gather the required model input data from many sources, including internal project data, design data from the system manufacturer, and information from the possible future users of the system being purchased. Producing the estimated LCC for a system is not an exact science because the project team can never obtain all the input data that it would like to have before using the computer model. Thus some degree of expertise is needed to make the appropriate assumptions to fill in the knowledge gaps where required input data cannot be found. The resulting LCC estimate should be the total cost of owning a system for its entire life cycle.

The resulting LCC figure may be many millions of dollars, especially if the system being purchased itself costs millions. The investment costs are combined with the operation and support costs and disposal costs to determine the total costs of ownership. This may be such a large figure that it is difficult to use it as a significant factor in deciding which option is more attractive in terms of cost of ownership, so it may be desirable to reduce the total to a more understandable and usable number. Typically, the project team will calculate the total number of operational hours for the system over its life and then divide the estimated LCC by this number to produce an average cost per operating hour. In the case of the example of the helicopter purchase, the total number of operating hours calculated in Fig. 4.17 is 576,000 hours. If the total estimated LCC for one of the helicopters that could be purchased for the fleet were $365 million, then the estimate of operating costs would be approximately $634 per flying hour. A similar estimate for all other helicopters under consideration also would be made so that each could be compared on equal terms.

$$C_T = C_{RP} + C_{RM} + C_{REN} + C_{REV} + C_{REQ} + C_{RF} + C_{IPR} + C_{IPN} + C_{IM} + C_{IS} + C_{ISE} + C_{IM} + C_{IE} + C_{IF} + C_{IP} + C_{ODP} + C_{OC} + C_{ORS} + C_{OSE} + C_{ODF} + C_{ODM} + C_{OP} + C_{OTD} + C_{OSM} + C_{OM} + C_{OIP} + C_{OIF} + C_{OIT} + C_{DI} + C_{DP} + C_{DDM} + C_{DR} + C_{DD} + C_{DW}$$

where

C_T	=	total life cycle cost
C_{RP}	=	R&D planning costs
C_{RM}	=	R&D management costs
C_{REN}	=	R&D engineering costs
C_{REV}	=	R&D evaluation costs
C_{REQ}	=	R&D equipment costs
C_{RF}	=	R&D facilities costs
C_{IPR}	=	investment production costs
C_{IPN}	=	investment planning costs
C_{IM}	=	investment management costs
C_{IS}	=	initial spares cost
C_{ISE}	=	initial support equip. costs
C_{IM}	=	technical manual costs
C_{IE}	=	investment engineering costs
C_{IF}	=	investment facilities costs
C_{IP}	=	initial PHS&T costs
C_{ODP}	=	O&S direct personnel costs
C_{OC}	=	O&S consumables cost
C_{ORS}	=	O&S replacement spares costs
C_{OSE}	=	O&S support equipment costs
C_{ODF}	=	O&S direct facilities costs
C_{ODM}	=	O&S maintenance costs
C_{OP}	=	O&S PHS&T costs
C_{OTD}	=	O&S technical data costs
C_{OSM}	=	O&S supply management costs
C_{OM}	=	O&S modification costs
C_{OIP}	=	O&S indirect personnel costs
C_{OIF}	=	O&S indirect facilities costs
C_{OIT}	=	O&S indirect training costs
C_{DI}	=	disposal inventory closeout costs
C_{DP}	=	disposal PHS&T
C_{DDM}	=	disposal data management costs
C_{DR}	=	disposal refurbishment costs
C_{DD}	=	disposal demilitarization costs
C_{DW}	=	disposal waste management costs

FIGURE 4.16 Cost model architecture.

• Number of helicopters	20 helicopters
• Missions per year	180 missions
• Mission duration	8 hours
• Operational life	20 years
20 × 180 × 820 = 576,000 life operating hours	

FIGURE 4.17   Estimate of life usage.

MAKING THE FINAL DECISION

The final project team decision as to which helicopter to purchase must consider all three factors O_E, A_O, and C_O as significant indicators of the potential results for each option under consideration. Table 4.7 presents an example of the results for the helicopter purchase. Using these data as the basis for a final decision, it appears that the helicopter that provides the best balance between operational effectiveness, operational availability, and cost of ownership is helicopter 1. This helicopter does not have the highest operational effectiveness rating, but it does provide a reasonably high capability for a far less cost per operating hour. The helicopter with the highest operational effectiveness rating, helicopter 2, has a much lower operational availability rating and a much higher cost-of-ownership estimate. Helicopters 3 and 4 both have two of three ratings that are lower than helicopter 1, so they are obviously not desirable options for purchase.

ESTABLISHING THE CAPABILITY

TLCSM does not stop with the project team decision about which option to select for procurement. TLCSM includes putting into place the complete capability to support the system selected for procurement and the capability to support it throughout its operational life. The statistics (see Table 4.7) used to select the preferred option for procurement become the in-service measurement criteria. It is important that the project team initiate the processes necessary to collect and analyze the in-service operation and support data to ensure that the system attains the O_E, A_O, and C_O estimated during procurement. All resources required to support operation and maintenance of the system must be purchased and positioned so that they will be available when required. It is only when the complete package of systems and necessary support infrastructure has been delivered and positioned that the capability to perform the required mission will be realized.

TABLE 4.7   **Decision-Making Statistics**

Helicopters being considered	#1	#2	#3	#4
Operational effectiveness (O_E)	91	94	89	86
Operational availability (A_O)	94	89	92	94
Cost per operating hour (C_O)	$634	$841	$572	$756

THROUGH-LIFE COST

The project team is responsible for projecting budgetary requirements for the new system and then ensuring that the necessary funding is available to support the system. This type of cost estimation is different from the LCC technique used as a key element of the decision-making process. To estimate the actual expenditure of money required to operate and support the system, the project team should use *through-life cost* (TLC). The concept of TLC is illustrated in Table 4.8. The TLC cost-estimation technique differs from LCC because it identifies direct costs that must be funded specifically for system operation and maintenance. TLC can be performed only after the preferred system to be purchased has been selected because it requires detailed information that typically is not available until after the purchase decision has been completed. Detailed design information, final repair processes, and support-infrastructure costs are used to project the budgetary requirements for the system by financial accounting period and by budget category.

TLCSM AND SUSTAINMENT

The TLCSM concept can be successful only if it is perpetuated throughout the operational life of the system. The project team must transition with the system into the operational phase and continue its management of the system. This focused responsibility is the core of success for TLCSM. The goals, thresholds, and constraints developed during acquisition of a system now must be used to continually evaluate the success of the system and its support infrastructure to ensure that it is meeting its requirements. Every statistic used to make the purchase decision should be used to assess its success. Therefore, the project team must be capable of monitoring and tracking all system activities. This typically is accomplished through use of a facilities management system that includes an operation and maintenance support data collection and information tracking system. The data collection should be as focused as possible on the key indicators needed to identify shortcomings of the system or support infrastructure. Table 4.9 provides a list of the statistics that are normally collected and analyzed as an integral part of the TLCSM process. This range of information provides the project

TABLE 4.8   Through-Life Cost (TLC)

TLC: A budget-estimation process that estimates the costs of a single option over its intended life. Estimate results in costs calculated by financial year and budget category.

Establish budgets for:
- Operational resources
  - Fuel
  - Personnel
  - Training
- Support resources
  - Spares and materials
  - Maintenance
  - Personnel
  - Facilities
  - Transportation and storage

TABLE 4.9   Measurable Supportability Goals, Thresholds, and Objectives

Maintenance
- Mean time between failure (MTBF)
- Mean time to repair (MTTR)
- Mean restoration time (MRT)
- Mean active maintennce time (MAMT)
- Max time to repair (MAX_{TTR})
- Repair cycle time
- Annual maintenance man-hours
- O&S cost per operating hour
- Maintenance downtime
- Waiting time—NMCM (non-mission-capable maintenance)

Manpower and personnel
- Crew performance
- Maintenance cost per operating hour
- Skill-level limit
- Maintenance hours by person
- Personnel costs as percent of O&S costs

Technical data
- Technical document accuracy
- TM correction rate

Supply support
- Spares availability
- Backorder rate
- Backorder duration
- Failure factor accuracy
- Order-ship time
- Spares costs to TLC ratio

Support eqipment and testing
- On-system diagnostics
- Operational support equipment
- Diagnostics effectiveness
- Tools effectiveness
- Support equipment availability

Facilities
- Facility utilization rate
- Facilities cost as percent of LCC

Training
- Time to achieve proficiency
- Training costs per student
- Maintenance-induced error rate
- Training equipment availability

team with the detailed information required to identify and quantify specific problems so that they can be resolved expeditiously and effectively.

The TLCSM process is a continuous evaluation and assessment of the system success through its life cycle. As issues are identified that might improve the performance of the system, improve support of the system, or lower cost of ownership, the project team should initiate the actions necessary to incorporate these as efficiently as possible. Figure 4.18 illustrates this process of continuous improvement. Typically, the company management that established the project team will require periodic updates on the status of the system to achieve and maintain the desired levels of O_E and A_O while not exceeding the C_O baseline.

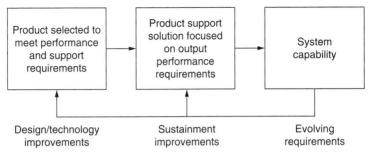

FIGURE 4.18   The continuous TLCSM process.

BENEFITS OF TLCSM

Table 4.1 listed the following reasons for implementing the TLCSM process:

- *Link everything into one "big picture."* The TLCSM concept integrates the concerns and issues of all organizational groups into a single decision-making process that provides traceability of all resulting decisions to the initial requirements established in the project team's charter.
- *Provide better management information.* The TLCSM concept provides significant and focused information with detailed backup so that management has a far better understanding of the situation and the possible results of all decisions that other methods do not provide.
- *Increase capability.* The sequence of activities used to first determine the new system need and use and then identify the functional requirements necessary to maximize capability are pivotal points of the TLCSM process.
- *Improve availability.* Identification, development, and delivery of a support resource package linked to operational availability requirements ensures that the system will be supported adequately and effectively throughout its operational life.
- *Make better use of critical resources.* The centralized and focused TLCSM approach to managing resources throughout the system's operational life ensures that critical items, specifically personnel and money are not wasted.
- *Minimize cost of ownership.* One of the basic premises of the TLCSM process is that long-term solutions tend to lower the cost of owning systems by avoiding short-term decisions, to achieve artificial goals that do no contribute to overall success.
- *Recognize relationships between distributed organizations.* It is imperative that the project team have representatives from every group within the organization so that all views can be considered throughout the decision-making process. This ensures that the final result of the TLCSM process meets the requirements of the total organization.

The points presented and discussed in this chapter have substantiated that the TLCSM process is a valid undertaking that has merit for application by any organization that makes critical decisions about capital equipment or long-term investment in systems and support infrastructures. The benefits of the TLCSM process have been demonstrated repeatedly by highly successful and profitable organizations as potentially the most effective and efficient method to purchase and sustain systems and capital equipment.

CHAPTER 5
DEVELOPING MULTINATIONAL PROJECT TEAMS

Aaron J. Nurick
Bentley College, Waltham, Massachusetts

Hans J. Thamhain
Bentley College, Waltham, Massachusetts

Aaron J. Nurick is Wilder Professor of Management and Psychology at Bentley College. He received a B.S. in business administration from the University of North Carolina at Chapel Hill and a Ph.D. in organizational psychology from the University of Tennessee. He holds a postdoctoral certificate from the Boston Institute for Psychotherapy, as well as certifications in mediation and emotional intelligence assessment. Dr. Nurick's teaching and scholarship have been devoted to the application of psychology to management and organizations. His published work includes articles in the *Journal of Management Inquiry, Psychological Bulletin, Human Relations, Human Resource Management, Organizational Behavior Teaching Review, Journal of Management Education, Business Horizons,* and *Human Resource Planning,* among others. He is also the author of the book, *Participation in Organizational Change: The TVA Experiment* (Praeger, 1985) that documents a long-term organizational change project.

Hans Thamhain specializes in research and development (R&D) and technology-based project management. He is a professor of management and director of MOT and project management programs at Bentley College. His industrial experience includes 20 years of management positions with high-technology companies: GTE/Verizon, General Electric, and ITT. Dr. Thamhain has written over 70 research papers and five professional reference books in project and technology management. His latest book is *Management of Technology* (Wiley, 2005). He is the recipient of the Distinguished Contribution Award from the Project Management Institute in 1998 and the IEEE Engineering Manager of the Year 2000–2001 Award. He is certified as New Product Development Professional and Project Management Professional, and profiled in *Marquis Who's Who in America.*

To succeed in our rapidly changing, interactive, and interconnected business environment, companies are continuously searching for ways to improve effectiveness. They look for partners that can perform the needed work better, cheaper, and faster. This results in alliances across the globe, ranging from research and development (R&D) to manufacturing and from customer relations to field services. Estimates suggest that within the United States alone, over 8 million employees are part of such distributed teams.[23] These geographically dispersed workgroups have become an important competitive tool in a business environment characterized by highly mobile resources, skill sets, and technology transfers across global regions and multinational borders. Companies that survive and prosper in today's amalgamated global marketplace continuously find new and innovative ways to integrate their resources and to develop, produce, and market products and services more cost-effectively, more timely, and at higher value to their customers.[1,3,5,6,14,16,26] However, all this also represents great managerial challenges.

MANAGERIAL CHALLENGES IN MULTINATIONAL TEAM ENVIRONMENTS

Managing teamwork is challenging, even in its most basic form. It involves intricately connected organizational systems, behavioral issues, and work processes.[9,18,25,38,62,65] It also has been changing over the years with increasing project complexities and team efforts that span organizational lines, including an intricate functional spectrum of assigned personnel, support groups, subcontractors, vendors, partners, government agencies, and customer organizations.[33,43] Uncertainties and risks introduced by technological, economic, political, social, and regulatory factors are always present and can be an enormous challenge to organizing and managing project teams. All this has led to new concepts, managerial principles, and practices that have changed the organizational landscape. This changed landscape has been labeled *teamwork as a new managerial frontier* and is summarized in the following box. Additional challenges are yet created by focusing on geographically distributed teams.[1,22,29] While for conventional projects the direction toward project objectives, technology transfer, project integration, and business strategy comes mostly from one central location, for globally dispersed teams, these directions are shared and distributed geographically.[10,13,19,26,30,41] Furthermore, the linkages among individual work components need to be developed and effectively "managed" across countries and organizational cultures, as shown graphically in Fig. 5.1. Multinational projects not only need to be integrated across the miles, but they also must be unified among different business processes, management styles, operational support systems, and organizational cultures.[13,16,22,29,33,44] As a result, organizations that manage projects across international borders often find it highly challenging and frustrating to implement their project plans, even with carefully prepared and mutually agreed-on contracts. In addition, company management itself, including its top executives, are often distributed geographically, separated by distance, time zones, and organizational cultures.[58] As companies engage in more multinational joint developments, outsourcing, and global expansion,[46,57] virtual teams promise the flexibility, responsiveness, cost advantage, and improved resource utilization necessary to survive and prosper in our ultracompetitive environment.[38,55]

Technology: A New Paradigm

Technology in both the work and its support systems creates additional challenges reflected in the complexities of the work and its processes. It affects the people, their skill

---

Teamwork: A New Managerial Frontier

Teamwork is not a new idea. The basic concepts go back to biblical times, and managers have recognized the critical importance of effective teamwork for a long time. More formal concepts evolved with the *human relations movement* that followed the classic Hawthorne studies by Roethlingsberger and Dickinson.[49] Visionaries such as McGregor (Theory Y, 1960), Likert (participating group management, system 4, 1961), Dyer, (cohesion in the workplace 1977), and more recently Tichy and Urlich (1984), Walton (1985), Dumaine (1991), and Oderwald (1996) have further broadened the understanding of the teamwork process. However, with declining bureaucratic hierarchies and more complex and geographically dispersed projects, the increased complexity of teamwork required more conceptual refinement and higher levels of management sophistication.

Redefining the Process. In today's more complex multinational and technologically sophisticated environment, the group has reemerged with a broader definition.

> *Teambuilding* can be defined as the process of taking a collection of individuals with different needs, backgrounds, and expertise and transforming them into an integrated, effective work unit.

In this transformation process, the goals and energies of individual contributors merge and focus on specific objectives and desired results that ultimately reflect project performance which is graphically shown in Fig. 5.1 below.

This may sound straightforward, but today's project complexities introduce many subtle variables. Not too long ago, project leaders *could* ensure successful integration for most of their projects by focusing on properly defining the work, timing, and resources and by following established procedures for project tracking and control. Today, these factors are still crucial. However, they have become threshold competencies, critically important but unlikely to guaranty by themselves project success. Today's complex business world requires *project teams* who are fast and flexible and can dynamically and creatively work toward established objectives in a changing environment.[9,28,61] This requires effective networking and cooperation among people from different organizations, support groups, subcontractors, vendors, government agencies, and customer communities. It also requires the ability to deal with uncertainties and risks caused by technological, economic, political, social, and regulatory factors. In addition, project leaders have to organize and manage their teams across organizational lines and international borders. Dealing with resource sharing, multiple reporting relationships, and broadly based alliances is as common in today's business environment as e-mail, flextime, and home offices.

In addition, managers in these environments must have the human and interpersonal skills, known collectively as *emotional intelligence*,[7,12,24,42] to meet the complex demands.

Team building is an ongoing process that requires strong leadership skills and an understanding of the organization, its interfaces, authority, power structures, and motivational factors. This process is particularly crucial in environments where complex multidisciplinary or transnational activities require the skillful integration of many functional specialties and support groups with diverse organizational cultures, values, and intricacies.

---

requirements, leadership, and ultimately overall project performance. While these technology challenges exist in general, they are further amplified in geographically dispersed project environments because of the less unified nature of the team and its communication, decision, and control channels.[54,62,77]

On the positive side, advances in collaborative and enabling technology, such as groupware and general telecommunications, have made geographically dispersed work groups more feasible and effective, arguing that today people can work together as virtual teams from anywhere in the world. Whether an organization has 100,000 employees or

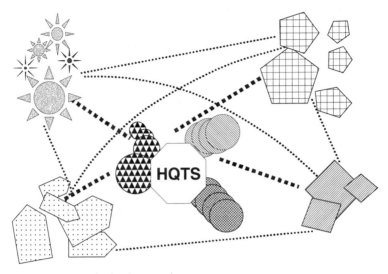

FIGURE 5.1 Multinational team environment.

just 10 people, it is interconnected with the rest of the world and can work with any person from any enterprise in any place at any time. This opens up great opportunities and flexibilities of conducting business, including codevelopments, partnering, joint ventures, strategic alliances, and outsourcing, as well as customer and supplier relations management. However, even the best technology cannot solve all problems. Nor can it by itself ensure unified teamwork, cooperation, decision making, and task integration. Effectively handling these challenges requires a great deal of cross-cultural and interpersonal sensitivity, special management skills, and administrative support systems.[62]

Taken together, five organizational subsystems make globally dispersed project teams unique and influence the situational leadership style most appropriate: (1) business environment, (2) project work, (3) team culture, (4) work process, and (5) managerial tools and techniques, as shown graphically in Fig. 5.2 and summarized below.

Multinational Business Environment

Businesses that extend globally operate in a highly dynamic environment regarding market structure, suppliers, and regulations. Local operations are highly intricate and enormously diverse regarding organizational culture, structure, and management philosophy. Managers have to deal with *differences* in languages, time zones, organizational and personal cultures, policies, regulations, business processes, and political climate.[2,11,33,45] These complexities call for specialized work processes, new concepts of technology and knowledge transfer, and more sophisticated management skills and project leadership.

Project Work

The complexity of project work, as well as its scope and risks, represents yet another dimension of multinational management challenges. Large and technologically complex

FIGURE 5.2 Business sub-systems that need to be integrated for global teams.

projects appear to benefit most from joint-venturing and a broad talent search. Therefore, these situations are most likely to produce global teams. Typical examples are R&D or product development, such as for avionics, automobiles, computers, software, and pharmaceuticals, as well as large service programs ranging from airline ticketing to medical diagnostics. When describing their complexities, multinational project managers point to specific indicators, such as the high degree of technical difficulties,[15] evolving solutions,[4,13] high levels of innovation and creativity, complex decision processes and uncertainty, intricate technology-transfer networks,[31,63] complex support systems, intricate multicompany support,[13,20] and highly complex forms of work integration.[56]

Team Culture

By their very nature, multinational project teams are highly diverse in their culture and value system, as well as in their team leadership. Work integration relies to a considerable extent on member-generated performance norms and evaluations rather than on top-down hierarchical guidelines, policies, and procedures.[50] As a result, self-directed team processes have become very common and are gradually replacing traditional, more hierarchically structured project teams for orchestrating and controlling multinational projects.[72] Effective role performance in such a contemporary work environment requires a more sophisticated management style that relies strongly on group interaction at local levels, as well as resource and power sharing, individual accountability, commitment, conflict handling, cooperation, and top-management involvement.

Work Process

Because of the distributed nature of multinational projects, work processes are also distributed, less sequential, and less centrally administered. They are more team-based and self-directed and often are structured for parallel, concurrent execution of the work. As a result, traditional project management tools, designed for managing teams in one location via a conventional matrix or projectized organization with clearly defined horizontal and vertical lines of communication and control and centralized "command system," are no longer effective in these contemporary situations and are being replaced by more team-based management processes. New organizational models and management methods such as *stage-gate, concurrent engineering,* and *design-build processes* evolved together with refinements of long-time conventional concepts such as the *matrix, project,* and *product management.* All these work processes also affect the behavior of the people, management style, and organizational culture.

Managerial Tools and Techniques

While many of the managerial tools and techniques form a common operational platform throughout the global team, many local subteams have their own unique tools and application or deploy conventional tools in a unique way. Spiral planning, stakeholder mapping, concurrent engineering, and integrated product developments are just a few examples of the specialized, diversified nature of tools used in the global project environment. Matching organizational culture with any of these tools is a great challenge for the overall management of a project and its integration. Stakeholder involvement during the tool platform selection, development, and implementation, as well as tradeoffs among efficiency, speed, control, flexibility, creativity, and risk, is critical to the effective use of these tools and techniques throughout the global project team organization.

Emotional Intelligence Defined:

"An array of non-cognitive personal, emotional, and social capabilities, competencies and skills that influence one's ability to succeed in coping with environmental demands and pressures. (Ref: Bar-On, 1997)

A MODEL FOR TEAM BUILDING

Team characteristics drive project performance. However, this relationship is frequently lost in practice. Companies trying to enhance their project performance often focus on the individual or a subgroup of the whole team. This is reflected in hiring practices, performance incentives, outsourcing, and joint ventures, just to name a view. Moreover, project performance is not "linear" and is influenced by many "external" factors such as technology, socioeconomic factors, and market behavior, making it difficult to determine exactly how much each individual or task group contributes to project performance. However, many of these relationships are known. Lessons from field research[62] strongly suggest that specific factors such as (1) work and its structure, (2) business processes, (3) managerial tools and techniques, and (4) the "emotional intelligence" of team leaders and members significantly influence individual behavior, including attitudes and values. Ultimately, these factors contribute to the overall team culture and project team performance, which is a derivative of many factors, as shown graphically in Fig. 5.3. The broad set of performance influences and their linkages is listed below:

FIGURE 5.3   Traits of a high-performing team.

On the Local Level

1. *Influences of external business environment.* The external business environment influences the internal organizational environment, including its (a) work and organizational processes, (b) tools and techniques, and (c) management style and leadership.

2. *Drivers and barriers toward team characteristics.* The three organizational variables of (a) work and organizational processes, (b) tools and techniques, and (c) management style and leadership create certain *conditions* that influence the team characteristics at the local level.

3. *Influences on team performance.* The organizational conditions created in step 2 influence team performance at the local level.

On the Global Level

4. *Work and performance integration.* Project subteam performance integrates into global team performance. The process is intricate and often nonlinear.

5. *Feedback loop.* Global team performance influences the organizational variables at the local level that create the conditions for local team performance.

Although all variables and influences are intricately interrelated, using the systems approach allows researchers and management practitioners to break down the complexity of the process to create a framework for monitoring and analyzing team performance in global environments and for fine-tuning the enterprise toward high overall team performance. It also provides the basis for monitoring and managing early warning signs and compound indicators, such as drivers and barriers to global team performance.

DRIVERS AND BARRIERS OF HIGH TEAM PERFORMANCE

Management tools such as benchmarking and root-cause analysis can be helpful in identifying the drivers and barriers to effective teamwork. *Drivers* are factors that influence the project environment favorably, such as interesting work and good project leadership. These factors are perceived as enhancing team effectiveness and therefore correlate positively with team performance. *Barriers* are factors that have an unfavorable influence, such as unclear objectives and insufficient resources, therefore impeding team performance. Based on field research,[61,62] the strongest drivers and barriers are listed in Table 5.1. All these factors have been listed alphabetically to avoid too narrowly drawn conclusions. However, the factors in Table 5.1 represent the strongest association observed in the field studies, explaining over 85 percent of the variance in project team performance, such as characterized in Fig. 5.3. It is further interesting to note that many of the factors in Table 5.1 are, to a large degree, based on the perception of team members. That is, team members *perceive* "good personal relations" or "communication problems." Since this perception is the reality that influences the team behavior, management must deal with the conditions as seen by the people and foster a project environment that is conducive to the needs of the team. Table 5.1 also can be used for examining the organizational environment via benchmarking, as discussed in Table 5.2, hence providing an important reference point for team self-assessment, managerial audit, or organizational development.

TABLE 5.1   Strongest Drivers and Barriers to Project Team Performance (Listed Alphabetically)

Drivers
- Clear project plans and objectives
- Emotional intelligence of team members
- Good interpersonal relations and shared values
- Good project leadership and credibility
- Management involvement and support
- Professional growth potential
- Professionally interesting and stimulating work
- Project visibility, high priority
- Proper technical direction and team leadership
- Qualified, competent team personnel
- Recognition of sense of accomplishment

Barriers
- Communication problems
- Conflict among team members or between team and support organizations
- Different outlooks, objectives, and priorities perceived by team members
- Poor qualification of team/project leader
- Poor trust, respect, and credibility of team leader
- Insufficient resources
- Insufficient rewards
- Lack of project challenge and interest
- Lack of senior management support, interest, and involvement
- Lack of team definition, role conflict, and confusion
- Lack of team member commitment
- Poor project team/personnel selection
- Shifting goals and priorities
- Unclear team leadership, power struggle
- Unstable project environment, poor job security, anxieties

TABLE 5.2 Benchmarking the Project Team

Table 5.1 can provide an important reference point for defining *specific metrics*, desirable for high-performing teams and their organizational environments. Then this metrics can be used for benchmarking teams or their task groups as part of a team self-assessment, managerial audit, or organizational development. In this context, Table 5.1 can be used as a startup database for a *force-field analysis,*[34] where team members diagnose what helps or hinders them in attaining desired performance. It is a simple yet powerful technique that can help a project manager and team to identify those forces which drive their projects toward success. The techniques also can help to identify the barriers or restraining forces that may keep a team from attaining its goal, hence causing project failure.

Furthermore, Table 5.1 can be used for benchmarking the project environment and its leadership. That is, the typology of Table 5.1 can assist in comparing established management practices with those of other operations, including global experiences. As such, Table 5.1 can become the focus of a five-step continuous improvement process that involves: (1) defining *what* should be benchmarked and *how* it should be compared, (2) analyzing team performance and establishing operational norms and performance targets, (3) communicating these targets to all organizational levels and developing action plans, (4) implementing these action plans, and (5) fine-tuning and integrating the new practices with the total business process.

If used properly, either the force-field analysis or the benchmarking process, or any combination of the two, can be powerful tools for diagnosing the need for change and implementing it. The personal involvement of the team members during the situational assessment and action plan development is critical for buy-in and ultimate commitment to the necessary change process.

Minimizing Barriers to Team Performance

As functioning groups, project teams are subject to all the phenomena known as *group dynamics.* As a highly visible and focused work group, the project team often takes on a special significance and is accorded high status with commensurate expectations of performance. Although these groups bring significant energy and perspective to a task, the possibilities of malfunctions are great.[42,62]

A myth is that the assembly of talented and committed individuals automatically makes the team immune to many of the barriers commonly found in the project team environment.[57,62,75] These barriers, while natural and predictable, take on additional facets in *global* project situations, which are exposed to the many challenges discussed earlier. Understanding these barriers, their potential causes, and their influences on performance is an important prerequisite for managing them effectively and hence facilitating a work environment where team members can focus their energy on desired results. The most common barriers to effective team performance are discussed in the context of multinational project environments.

Different Points of View. The purpose of a project team is to harness divergent skills and talents to accomplish project objectives. Having drawn on various departments or perhaps even different organizations, there is the strong likelihood that team members naturally will see the world from their own unique point of view. There is a tendency to stereotype and devalue other views. Such tendencies are heightened when projects involve work groups from different countries with different work cultures, norms, needs, and interests. Further, these barriers are particularly strong in highly technical project situations where members speak in their own codes and languages. In addition, there may be historical conflict among organizational units. In such a case, representatives from these units more than likely will carry their prejudices into the team and potentially subvert attempts to create common objectives. Often these judgments are not readily known until the team actually begins to work and conflict starts developing.

Role Conflict.   Project or matrix organizations are not only the product of ambiguity; they create ambiguity as well. Team members are actually in multiple roles and often report to different leaders, possibly creating conflicting loyalties. As "boundary role persons," they often do not know which constituency to satisfy. The "home" group or department has a set of expectations that might be at variance with the local project organization. For example, a "home office" may be run in a very mechanistic, hierarchical fashion, whereas the local project team may be more democratic and participatory. Team members also may experience time conflicts owing to multiple task assignments that overlie and compete with traditional job responsibilities. The pull from these conflicting forces either can be exhilarating or can be a source of considerable tension for individual team members. It is here that the emotional intelligence of team members becomes important because a key component is the ability to tolerate the demands and pressures of such ambiguity.

Implicit Power Struggles.   While role conflict often occurs in a horizontal dimension (i.e., across units within the same division or across geographic and culture regions), conflict also can occur vertically because different authority levels are represented on the team. Individuals who occupy powerful positions elsewhere can try to recreate—or be expected to exercise—that influence in the group. Often such attempts to impose ideas or to exert leadership over the group are met with resistance, especially from others in similar positions. There can be subtle attempts to undermine potentially productive ideas with the implicit goal of winning the day rather than looking for what is best for the team. There is also the possibility that lower-status individuals are being ignored, thus eliminating a potentially valuable resource.

An example of such power struggles occurred in a *quality of work life project team* in an engineering organization.[9,17,29,28,36] The team was set up as a collaborative contributor-management group designed to devise ways to improve the quality of work life in one division of a utility company. The membership of this representative group was changed halfway through the project to include more top managers. When the managers came aboard, they continued in the role of "manager" rather than "team member." Subsequently, the weekly meetings became more like typical staff meetings rather than creative problem-solving sessions. Although there was considerable resistance, the differences were pushed under the table because the staff people did not wish to confront their superiors. There also was considerable posturing among the top managers in all effort to demonstrate their influence, although none would directly attempt to take the leadership position. While some struggle for power is inevitable in a diverse group, it must be managed to minimize potentially destructive consequences.

Group Think.   This phenomenon of groups was identified by Irving Janis[27] in 1972 as a detriment to the decision-making process. It refers to the tendency for a highly cohesive group to develop a sense of detachment and elitism. It can particularly afflict groups that work on special projects. In an effort to maintain cohesion, the group creates shared illusions of invulnerability and unanimity. Since cohesion "feels better," there is a reluctance to examine different points of view because these are seen as dangerous to the group's existence. Members of the group seek to avoid the perceived emotional pitfalls of such conflict. As a result, group members may censor their opinions as the group rationalizes the inherent quality and morality of its decisions. Because many project teams typically are labeled as special and often work under time pressure, they are particularly prone to the dangers of group think.

KEEPING THE TEAM FOCUSED

The key to continuous team development and effective project management is to keep the team focused. Field studies on multidisciplinary work groups show consistently and measurably that, to be effective, the project leader not only must recognize the potential drivers of and barriers to high team performance but also must know when in the life cycle of the project they are most likely to occur.[61,62] Team leaders can take preventive actions early in the project life cycle and foster a work environment that is conducive to team building as an ongoing process. A crucial component of such a process is the sense of ownership and commitment of the team members. Team members must become stakeholders in the project, buying into the goals and objectives of the project, and they must be willing to focus their efforts on the desired results.

Specific management insight has been gained from studies by Thamhain and Wilemon[66] into the work group dynamics of project teams. These studies clearly show significant correlations[61,66] and interdependencies among work environmental factors and team performance. They indicate that high team performance involves four primary factors: (1) managerial leadership, (2) job content, (3) personal goals and objectives, and (4) work environment and organizational support. The actual correlation of 60 influence factors with project team characteristics and performance provided some interesting insight into the strength and effect of these factors. One of the important findings was that only 12 of the 60 influence factors that were examined were found to be statistically significant. Other factors seem to be much less important to high team performance. Listed below are the 12 factors, classified as drivers, that associate with project team performance most strongly:

1. Professionally interesting and stimulating work
2. Recognition of accomplishment
3. Clear project objectives and directions
4. Adequate resources
5. Experienced management personnel
6. Proper technical direction and leadership
7. Mutual trust, respect, low conflict
8. Qualified project team personnel
9. Involved, supportive upper management
10. Professional growth potential
11. Job security
12. Stable goals and priorities

It is interesting to note that these factors not only correlated favorably with the direct measures of high project team performance, such as technical success and on-time/on-budget performance, but also were positively associated with other indirect measures of team performance, such as commitment, effective communications, creativity, quality, change orientation, and need for achievement. These are especially important characteristics for high team performance in a multicultural, multinational environment where management control is weak through traditional chain-of-command channels but relies more on the norms and desires established by local teams and their individual members. What we find consistently is that successful project leaders pay attention to the human side. They seem to be effective in fostering a work environment that is conducive to innovative creative work, where people find the assignments challenging, leading to recognition and professional growth. Such a professionally stimulating environment also seems to lower communication barriers and conflict and enhances the desire of personnel to succeed. Further, this seems to increase organizational awareness as well as the ability to respond to changing project requirements.

In addition, an effective team has good leadership. Team managers understand the task, the people, the organization, and all the factors crucial to success. They are action-oriented, provide the needed resources, properly direct implementation of the project plan, and help in the identification and resolution of problems in their early stages.

Management and team leaders can help a great deal in keeping the project team focused. They must communicate and update organizational objectives and relate them to the project and its specific activities in various functional areas and geographic regions. Management can help in developing priorities by communicating the project parameters and organizational needs and by establishing a clear project focus. While operationally the project might have to be fine-tuned to changing environments and evolving solutions, the top-down mission and project objectives should remain stable. Project team members need this stability to plan and organize their work toward unified results. This focus is also necessary for establishing benchmarks and integrating innovative activities across all disciplines. Moreover, establishing this clear goal focus stimulates interest in the project and unifies the team, ultimately helping to refuel the commitment to established project objectives in such crucial areas as technical performance, timing, and budgets. Effective team leaders monitor their team environments for early warning signs of potential problems and changing performance levels.

BUILDING HIGH-PERFORMING GLOBAL TEAMS

As more companies compete on a global scale and transfer knowledge across multinational boundaries, their project operations have become vastly more complex. The recommendations advanced here reflect the realities of this new environment where project managers have to cross organizational, national, and cultural boundaries and work with people over whom they have little or no formal control. Alliances and collaborative ventures have forced project managers to focus more on cross-boundary relationships, negotiations, delegation, and commitment rather than on establishing formal command and control systems.

In fact, global teams rarely can be managed top-down. Given the realities of multinational project environments—with their cultural diversities, organizational complexities, decision processes distributed throughout the world, and solutions often evolving incrementally and iteratively—project leaders have to rely on information and judgments by their local team leaders. Power and responsibility are shifting from managers to local project team leaders and their members who take higher levels of responsibility, authority, and control for project results. That is, these teams become *self-directed*, gradually replacing the more traditional, hierarchically structured project team. These processes rely strongly on group interaction, resource and power sharing, group decision making, accountability, and self-direction and control. Leading such self-directed teams also requires a great deal of emotional intelligence, team management skills, and overall guidance by senior management.

Taken together, no work group comes fully integrated and unified in its values and skill sets but needs to be nurtured and developed skillfully. Leaders must recognize the professional interests, anxieties, communication needs, and challenges facing their team members and anticipate them as the team goes through the various stages of integration. That is, project leaders must foster an environment where team members can work together across organizational and national boundaries in a flatter and leaner company that is more flexible and responsive to quality and time-to-market pressures. To be effective in such a team environment, the leader must create an ambience where people are professionally satisfied, are involved, have mutual trust, and can communicate well with each other. The more effective the project leader is in stimulating the drivers of effective team performance (see Table 5.1), the more effective the manager can be in developing team membership and the higher can be the quality and candor in sharing ideas and approaches and in effectively transferring knowledge and integrating work among global partners.

The effective team leader is a social architect who understands the interaction of organizational and behavioral variables and can foster a climate of active participation and minimal dysfunctional conflict. This requires carefully developed skills in leadership, administration, organization, and technical expertise. It further requires the project leader's ability to involve top management and to ensure organizational visibility, resource availability, and overall support for the new project throughout its life cycle.

RECOMMENDATIONS

Managing global project teams is not for the weak or faint of heart. However, observations from best practices show that specific working conditions and managerial processes appear most favorably associated with teamwork despite the complexities, organizational dynamics, and cultural differences among global companies. These conditions serve as bridging mechanisms that enhance team performance. A number of specific recommendations may help managers to facilitate working conditions conducive to organizing and developing high-performing global project teams. The sequence of recommendations follows to some degree the chronology of a typical project life cycle.

Early Project Life-Cycle Team Involvement

As for any project, effective project planning and early team involvement are crucial to successful project team performance. This is especially important for product developments where parallel task execution depends on continuous cross-functional cooperation for dealing with incremental work flow and partial-result transfers. Team involvement early in the project life cycle also will have a favorable impact on the team environment, building enthusiasm toward the assignment, team morale, and ultimately, team effectiveness. Because project leaders have to integrate various tasks across many functional lines, proper planning requires the participation of all stakeholders, including support departments, subcontractors, and management. Modern project management techniques, such as phased project planning and stage-gate concepts, as well as established standards, such as Project Management Book of Knowledge (PMBOK), provide the conceptual framework and tools for effective cross-functional planning and for organizing the work toward effective execution.

Define Work Process and Team Structure

Successful project team management requires an infrastructure conducive to cross-functional teamwork and technology transfer. This includes properly defined interfaces, task responsibilities, reporting relations, communication channels, and work-transfer protocols. The tools for systematically describing the work process and team structure come from the conventional project management system; they include (1) *a project charter* defining the mission and overall responsibilities of the project organization and including performance measures and key interfaces, (2) *a project organization chart* defining the major reporting and authority relationships, (3) *a responsibility matrix* or *task roster,* (4) *a project interface chart,* such as the N-squared chart, and (5) *job descriptions.*

Ensure Uniform Procedures for Technology and Knowledge Transfer

As part of the work process definition, management must ensure that the procedures for technology and knowledge transfer are clear and workable for all parties across the global team. English is not spoken the same the world over, and concepts such as "deadline" and "way over budget" may be interpreted differently in different locations. Working with local leaders one on one and allowing local and regional management to establish their own procedures and managerial controls is recommended for effective local project execution and subsequent integration.

Develop Organizational Interfaces

Overall success of a project team depends on effective cross-functional integration. Each task team should clearly understand its task inputs and outputs, interface personnel, and work-transfer mechanism. Team-based reward systems can help to facilitate cooperation with cross-functional partners. Team members should be encouraged to check out early feasibility and system integration. Quality function deployment (QFD) concepts, N-squared charting, and well-defined phase-gate criteria can be useful tools for developing cross-functional linkages and promoting interdisciplinary cooperation and alliances. It is critically important to include into these interfaces all the support organizations, such as purchasing, product assurance, and legal services, as well as outside contractors and suppliers.

Staff and Organize the Project Team

Leadership positions should be defined and staffed carefully at the beginning of a new project. At the local level, key project personnel selection is the joint responsibility of the local project leader and functional management. The credibility of project leaders among team members, with senior management, and with the project headquarters or program sponsor is crucial to the leader's ability to manage and integrate the project activities effectively. One-on-one interviews are recommended for explaining the scope and project requirements, as well as the management philosophy, organizational structure, and rewards.

Communicate Organizational Goals and Objectives

Management must communicate and update the organizational goals and project objectives. The relationship and contribution of individual work to the overall product development, the business plans, and the importance to the organizational mission must be clear to all team personnel. Senior management can help in unifying the team behind the project objectives by developing a "priority image" through their personal involvement, visible support, and emphasis of project goals and mission objectives.

Build a High-Performance Image

Building a favorable image for an ongoing project in terms of high priority, interesting work, importance to the organization, high visibility, and potential for professional rewards is crucial for attracting and holding high-quality people. Senior management can help to develop a priority image and communicate the key parameters and management guidelines for specific projects. Such a priority image, combined with the visibility of the work and management attention and support, fosters a climate of active participation at all levels throughout the global team. It also helps to improve communications, increase commitment, unify the team, and minimize dysfunctional conflict.

Define Effective Communication Channels

Poor communication is a major barrier to teamwork and effective project performance, especially in global team environments with their different time zones, languages, cultures, and work processes. Management can facilitate the free flow of information, both horizontally and vertically, by workspace design and regular meetings, reviews, and information sessions. In addition, collaborative, enabling technology, such as groupware, voice mail, e-mail, electronic bulletin boards, and conferencing, can greatly enhance communications, especially in geographically dispersed organizational settings.

Ensure Senior Management Support

It is critically important that senior management provides the proper environment for the project team to function effectively. An understanding and agreement on the project scope and resource and time requirements at all levels are crucial prerequisites for establishing and maintaining top-management support. Further, the project manager's ability to maintain upper-management support involvement is critically important to the local leaders' credibility and the priority image of the project.

Build Commitment

Managers should ensure commitment from team leaders and team members to project plans and specific objectives and results. Anxieties and fear of the unknown are often major reasons for low commitment. Managers should investigate the potential for insecurities, determine the cause, and then work with the team to reduce these negative perceptions.

Manage Conflict and Problems

Multinational projects are loaded with opportunities for conflict. Conflict is inevitable. Project managers should focus their efforts on problem avoidance. That is, managers should recognize potential problems and conflicts at their onset and deal with them before they become big and their resolutions consume a large amount of time and effort.

Conduct Team-Building Sessions

A mixture of *focus-team* sessions, *brainstorming, experience exchanges*, and *social gatherings* can be a powerful tool for developing the work group into an effective, fully integrated, and unified project team. Such organized team-building efforts should be conducted at the local team level, as well as with the local leaders at the project headquarters. Intensive team-building efforts may be especially needed during the formation stage of a new project team; however, they should be continued in some form throughout the project life cycle. Although formally organized, these team-building sessions often are conducted in a very informal and relaxed atmosphere to discuss critical questions such as (1) How are we working as a team? (2) What is our strength? (3) How can we improve? (4) What support do we need? (5) What challenges and problems are we likely to face? (6) What actions should we take? and (7) What process or procedural changes would be beneficial? Once these issues are diagnosed and discussed properly, specific training or coaching in such critical emotional intelligence skills such as developing empathy, active listening, and conflict management can be vital to the overall performance of the team.

Provide Proper Direction and Leadership

Project managers and local team leaders can influence the attitude and commitment of their people to the project objectives by their own actions. Concern for project team members and enthusiasm for the project can foster a climate of high motivation, involvement with the project and its management, open communications, and willingness to cooperate with the new requirements and to use them effectively.

Reduce the Complexity of the Management System

Complex projects require robust management systems. While management guidelines and procedures must be clear and uniform throughout the global project organization, they also must be simple and robust to allow flexibility to cope with contingencies and cultural nuances. The management system also must be flexible enough for local management to establish its own work processes, procedures, and management controls.

Foster a Culture of Continuous Support and Improvement

Successful project management focuses on people behavior and their roles within the project itself. Companies that manage complex projects effectively have cultures and support systems that demand broad participation in their organization developments. Encouraging team members throughout the project organization to be proactive and aggressive toward change is not an easy task. Yet such organizational developments must be undertaken on an ongoing basis to ensure relevancy to today's global project management challenges. It is important to establish support systems—such as discussion groups, action teams, and suggestion systems—to capture and leverage the lessons learned and to identify problems as part of a continuous improvement process. Tools such as the *project maturity model* and the Six Sigma project management process can provide the framework and toolset for analyzing and fine-tuning team development and its management process.

A FINAL NOTE

In conclusion, building effective global project teams involves the whole spectrum of management skills and company resources and is the shared responsibility of headquarters management and local project leaders. Managerial leadership at all project levels has a significant impact on the team environment that ultimately affects team and project performance. Effective project managers understand the interaction of organizational and behavioral variables. They can foster a climate of active participation and minimal dysfunctional conflict. This requires carefully developed skills in leadership, administration, organization, and technical expertise. It further requires the ability to involve top management and ensure organizational visibility, resource availability, and overall support for the project throughout its life cycle and across the enterprise, its support functions, suppliers, sponsors, and partners.

REFERENCES

1. Armstrong D. Building teams across boarders. *Exec Excell* 17(3):10, 2000.

2. Asakawa K. External-internal linkages and overseas autonomy control Tension. *IEEE Trans Eng Manag* 43(1):24–32, 1996.

3. Bahrami H. The emerging flexible organization: Perspectives from Silicon Valley. *Calif Manag Rev* 34(4):33–52, 1992.

4. Bailetti A, Callahan J, and DiPietro P. A coordination structure approach to the management of projects. *IEEE Trans Eng Manag* 4l(4):394–403, 1994.

5. Barkema H, Baum J, Mannix E. Management challenges in a new time. *Acad Manag J* 45(5):916–930, 2002.

6. Barner R. The new millennium workplace. *Eng Manag Rev (IEEE)* 25(3):114–119, 1997.

7. Bar-On R. *Bar-On Emotional Quotient Inventory Technical Manual.* Toronto: Multi-Health Systems, 1997.

8. Belassi W, Tukel O. A new framework for determining critical success/failure factors in projects. *Int J Project Manag* 14(3):141–151, 1996.

9. Bhatnager A. Great teams. *Acad Manag Exec* 13(3):50–63, 1999.

10. Bond E, Walker B, Hutt M, Reigen P. Reputational effectiveness in cross-functional working relationships. *J Prod Innov Manag* 21(1):44–60, 2004.

11. Brockhoff K, Schmaul B. Organization, autonomy, and success of internationally dispersed R&D facilities. *IEEE Trans Eng Manag* 43(1):33–40, 1996.

12. Caruso D, Salovey P. *The Emotionally Intelligent Manager.* San Franscisco: Jose-Bass, 2004.

13. DeMaio A, et al. A multi-project management framework for new product development. *Eur J Operat Manag* 78(2):178–191, 1994.

14. Deschamps J, Nayak R. Implementing world-class process, in *Product Juggernauts.* Cambridge, MA: Harvard University Press, 1995, Chap. 5.

15. DeSanctis G, Jackson B. Coordination of information technology management: Team-based structures and computer-based communication systems. *J Manag Inform Syst* 10(4):85–110, 1994.

16. Dillon P. A global challenge. *Forbes Magazine* 168:73ff, 2001.

17. Druskat V, Wheeler J. How to lead a self-managing team. *Sloan Manag Rev* 45(2):65–71, 2004.

18. Dumaine B. The trouble with teams, *Fortune* 130(5):86–92, 1994.

19. Dyer W. *Team Building: Issues and Alternatives.* Reading, MA: Addison-Wesley, 1977.

20. Earl M. The risks of outsourcing IT. *Sloan Manag Rev* 37(3):26–33, 1996.

21. English K. The changing landscape of leadership. *Res Technol Manag* 45(4):9, 2004.

22. Fink G, Holden N. Global transfer of management knowledge. *Acad Manag Exec* 19(2):5–8, 2005.

23. Furst S, Reeves M, Rosen B. Managing the lifecycle of virtual teams. *Acad Manag Exec* 18(2):6–20, 2004.

24. Goleman D. *Working with Emotional Intelligence.* New York: Bantam Books, 1998.

25. Hardaker M, Ward B. How to make a team work. *Harvard Bus Rev* 65(6):112–120, 1987.

26. Hartman F, Ashrafi R. Project management in the information systems and technologies industries. *Proj Manag J* 33(3):5–15, 2002.

27. Janis I. *Victims of Groupthink.* Boston: Houghton Mifflin, 1972.

28. Jassawalla A, Sashittal H. Building collaborate cross-functional new product teams. *Acad Manag Exec* 13(3):50–63, 1999.

29. Javidan M, Stahl G, Brodbeck F, Wilderon C. Cross-border transfer of knowledge: Cultural lessons from project GLOBE. *Acad Manag Exec* 19(2), pp. 59–76.

30. Karlsen J, Gottschalk P. Factors affecting knowledge transfer in IT projects. *Eng Manag J* 16(1):3–11, 2004.

31. Keller R. Cross-functional project groups in research and new product development. *Acad Manag J* 44(3):547–556, 2001.

32. Kostner J. *Bionic eTeamwork: How to Build Collaborative Virtual Teams at Hyperspeed.* Dearborn, MI: A Kaplan Professional Company, 2001.

33. Kruglianskas I, Thamhain H. Managing technology-based projects in multinational environments. *IEEE Trans Eng Manag* 47(1):55–64, 2000.

34. Lewin K. Frontiers in group dynamics. In D. Cartwright (Ed.) (1952). *Field theory in social sciences: Selected theoretical papers by Kurt Lewin* (pp. 188–237). London: Tavistock.; also see Levin K. *Field Theory in Social Sciences.* New York: Harper, 1951.

35. Likert R. *New Patterns of Management.* New York: McGraw-Hill, 1961.

36. Lunnan R, Lervik, J. Traavik, L., Nilsen, S., Amdam, R., Hennestad, B. Global transfer of management practices across nations and MNC subcultures. *Acad Manag Exec* 19(2):77–80, 2005.

37. McGregor D. *The Human Side of Enterprise.* New York: McGraw-Hill, 1960.

38. Mowshowitz A. Virtual organization. *Commun ACM* 40(9):30–37, 1997.

39. Nellore R, Balachandra R. Factors influencing success in integrated product development (IPD) projects. *IEEE Trans Eng Manag* 48(2):164–173, 2001.

40. Newell F, Rogers M. *Loyalty.com: Relationship Management in the Era of Internet Marketing,* New York: McGraw-Hill, 2002.

41. Nurick A. *Participation in Organizational Change.* New York: Praeger, 1985.

42. Nurick A. Facilitating effective work teams. *SAM Adv Manag J* 58(1):22–27, 1993.

43. Nurick A, Kamm J, Shuman J, Seeger J. Entrepreneurial teams in new venture creation: A research agenda. *Entrepreneurship Theory and Practice* 14(4):7–17, 1990.

44. Oderwald S. Global work teams. *Train Dev* 5(2):32–42, 1996.

45. Ohba S. Critical issues related to international R&D programs. *IEEE Trans Eng Manag* 43(1):78–87, 1996.

46. Peters TJ. *The Circle of Innovation.* New York: Knopf, 1997.

47. Pillai A, Joshi A, Raoi K. Performance measurement of R&D projects in a multi-project, concurrent engineering environment. *Int J Project Manag* 20(2):165–172, 2002.

48. Prasad B. Toward life-cycle measures and metrics for concurrent product development. *Int J Comput Appl Technol* 15(1/3):1–8, 2002.

49. Roethlisberger F, Dickerson W. *Management and the Worker.* Cambridge, MA: Harvard University Press, 1939.

50. Sawhney M, Prandelli E. Communities of creation: Managing distributed innovation in turbulent markets. *Calif Manag Rev* 42(4):45–69, 2000.

51. Senge P. *The Fifth Discipline: The Art and Practice of the Learning Organization.* New York: Doubleday/Currency, 1994.

52. Senge P, Carstedt G. Innovating our way to the next industrial revolution. *Sloan Manag Rev* 42(2):24–38, 2001.

53. Shenhar A, Thamhain H. A new mixture of project management skills: Meeting the high-technology challenge. *Hum Sys Manag J* 13(1):27–40, 1994.

54. Shim D, Lee M. Upward influence styles of R&D project leaders. *IEEE Trans Eng Manag* 48(4):394–413, 2001.

55. Snow C, Snell S, Davison S. Use transnational teams to globalize your company. *Organ Dyn* 24(4):50–67, 1996.

56. Solomond J. International high technology cooperation: Lessons learned. *IEEE Trans Eng Manag* 43(1):69–77, 1996.

57. Stewart GL, Barick MR. Team structure and performance: Assessing the mediating role of intrateam process and the moderating role of task type. *Acad Manag J* 43(2):135–148, 2000.

58. Stoddard D, Donnellon A. *Verifone, a Harvard Business School Case Study*, 9–398–030. Boston, MA: Harvard Business School Publishing, 1997.

59. Stum D. Maslow revisited: Building the employee commitment pyramid. *Strategy and Leadership* 29(4):4–9, 2001.

60. Thamhain H. *Management of Technology: Managing Effectively in Technology-based organizations.* New York: Wiley, 2005.

61. Thamhain H. Leading technology teams. *Project Manag J* 35(4):35–47, 2004.

62. Thamhain H. Linkages of project environment to performance: Lessons for team leadership. *Int J Project Manag* 22(7):90–102, 2004.

63. Thamhain H. Managing innovative R&D teams. *R&D Manag* 33(3):297–312, 2003.

64. Thamhain H. Criteria for effective leadership in technology-oriented project teams, in DP Slevin, DI Cleland, and JK Pinto (eds.), *The Frontiers of Project Management Research.* Newton Square, PA: Project Management Institute, 2002, Chap. 16.

65. Thamhain H. Working with project teams," in DI Cleland, L Ireland (eds.), *Project Management: Strategic Design and Implementation* New York: McGraw-Hill, 2001, Chap. 18.

66. Thamhain H. Managing self-directed teams toward innovative results. *Eng Manag J* 8(3):31–39, 1996.

67. Thamhain H, Wilemon D. Building effective teams in complex project environments. *Technol Manag* 5(2):203–212, 1998.

68. Thamhain H. Effective leadership style for managing project teams, in P Dinsmore (ed.), *Handbook of Program and Project Management.* New York: AMACOM, 1992, Chap. 22.

69. Thamhain H. Skill developments for project managers. *Project Manag J* 22(3):39–45, 1991.

70. Thamhain H. Building high performing engineering project teams. *IEEE Trans Eng Manag* 34(3):130–142, 1987.

71. Tichy N, Ulrich D. The leadership challenge: Call for the transformational leader. *Sloan Manag Rev* 35(3):59–69, 1984.

72. Tomkovich C, Miller C. Riding the wind: Managing new product development in the age of change. *Product Innov Manag* 17(6):413–423, 2000.

73. Walton R. From control to commitment in the workplace. *Harvard Business Rev* 61(2):65–79, 1985.

74. Whitten N. *Managing Software Development Projects,* 2d ed. New York: Wiley, 1995.

75. Williams J. *Team Development for High-Tech Project Managers.* Norwood, MA: Artech House, 2002.

76. Zanoni R, Audy J. Project management model for physically distributed software development environment. *Eng Manag J* 16(1):28–34, 2004.

77. Zhang P, Keil M, Rai A, Mann J. Predicting information technology project escalation. *J Operat Res* 146(1):115–129, 2003.

CHAPTER 6
RISK IDENTIFICATION AND ASSESSMENT FOR INTERNATIONAL CONSTRUCTION PROJECTS

John A. Walewski

University of Texas at Austin, Austin, Texas

G. Edward Gibson, Jr.

University of Texas at Austin, Austin, Texas

Ellsworth F. Vines

Dick Corporation, Pittsburgh, Pennsylvania

Dr. John Walewski is currently a postdoctoral fellow with the Center for Transportation Research at the University of Texas at Austin. He has worked in and as a consultant to the construction management profession for both owners and contractors. His research interests include risk management, project planning, and environmental impact assessment.

Dr. G. Edward Gibson, Jr., is a professor of civil, architectural, and environmental engineering at the University of Texas at Austin and is the current W. R. Woolrich Professor in Engineering. He is the author of numerous articles on project management, and his teaching and research interests include front-end planning, risk management, dispute resolution, computer-integrated construction, and organizational change.

Ellsworth F. Vines, is senior vice president of the Dick Corporation and has more than 39 years of experience in the engineering, management, and construction of large and small lump-sum turnkey projects. He has successfully led startup and mature operations in both domestic and international environments. His work has included all phases of the management of projects and operations for his firm's industrial and highway groups. He has worked in the minerals processing, steel, nonferrous, transportation, water-wastewater, and hospitality sectors.

Construction is a major worldwide industry accounting for approximately US$3.5 trillion, or almost ten percent of global gross domestic product. New markets, domestic competition, and trade liberalization have impelled owners, contractors, and investors to aggressively pursue business opportunities and projects outside their home jurisdictions. While international projects may appear to be attractive investments, such projects usually involve elevated levels of risk and uncertainty. International work requires owners to assess a diverse set of political, geographic, economic, environmental, regulatory, and cultural risk factors. Moreover, contractors must consider a similar set of risk factors in determining whether to take on such projects and how to price and schedule the work once they have engaged in it. A limited amount of research has been undertaken to address these unique issues, and most efforts to assess and evaluate the risks associated with international construction are fragmented and fail to provide adequate assistance to project managers. In short, poor cost and schedule performance of international construction projects is more often the rule than the exception, and the successful delivery of such projects has proven to be difficult for the parties involved.

Industry practices and the academic literature are in agreement that risks should be allocated to the party in the best position to manage them. However, evidence shows that there is a gap between existing risk management techniques and their application and use by contractors and owners (Han and Diekmann, 2001). The research suggests that this gap is due in large part to the complexity of the ventures and the extensive resource commitment necessary to perform good risk management. Complicating the situation is the fact that no easy-to-use management tool is available to identify and assess the risks specific to international construction.

The purpose and need for such a tool were identified initially and championed by the Construction Industry Institute's (CII) Globalization Committee. In 2001, the CII, with additional support from the Center for Construction Industry Studies (CCIS) and the Design, Procurement, and Construction Specific Interest Group (DPC SIG) of the Project Management Institute (PMI), commissioned a research effort [Project Team 181, Risk Assessment for International Projects (PT 181)] to assist with the development of a tool that could help owners and contractors to improve the performance of international projects. Along with the authors, a research team composed of representatives from CII owner and contractor organizations and the DPC SIG participated in this effort.

Completed in December 2003, PT 181 produced the *International Project Risk Assessment* (IPRA) *Tool* (CII Implementation Resource 181-2; CII, 2003a). The tool and its supporting documentation provides a systematic method to identify, assess, and determine the relative importance of the international-specific risks across a project's life cycle and of the spectrum of participants needed to allow for subsequent mitigation. The reports generated from this study describe in detail the research performed, including the methodology, data analysis, and value of the research to the industry (CII Research Report 181-11; CII, 2003b).

The IPRA tool is unique because its baseline relative impact values were developed using empirical data from industry experts reporting on actual projects. Subsequently, the IPRA tool assists in identifying the risk factors of highest importance to a project team. The IPRA tool also fits within the project risk management area of the project management body of knowledge (PMBOK), specifically with regard to risk identification and risk quantification and, to a lesser extent, risk response development and control (PMI, 2000).

In order to improve international construction project performance, it is critical that consideration be given to the portfolio of risks that fall to all participants across the life cycle of a project. Many of these risks are jurisdiction-specific. Because no common and overarching methodology to assess and manage these risks exists, owners, investors, designers, and constructors do not fully recognize and realize the value of a systematic risk management process. Differing objectives and the adversarial relationships these differences generate between the parties are also common. Consequently, the overall inability of project participants to understand the risks associated with international project constitutes an industry blind spot that particularly plagues contractors and owners. This chapter provides an overview of the IPRA tool development and research findings, a brief explanation of how the tool is used, and recommendations for its use on international projects.

RESEARCH OBJECTIVES

The primary objectives of this research investigation were (1) to develop a user-friendly, systematic management tool and process to identify and assess the risks specific to international construction, with the ultimate goal of improving project performance, (2) to quantify and prioritize the relative importance of the identified risks in order to gauge which risks have the highest impact, and (3) to provide guidance when risk impacts are unknown or when uncertainty is high.

DEVELOPMENT OF THE IPRA TOOL

The research investigation began with an extensive literature review on the topics of risk identification, assessment, and management, as well as on issues related to international construction. To gain additional insight into these issues, information also was gleaned from a review of industry practices for international project risk assessments and from CII's globalization forums.

To further evaluate the approaches that organizations use to manage the risks incurred on international projects, 26 structured interviews were conducted with middle- to upper-level management personnel. Eight were contractors, eight were owner organizations, and the remaining 10 were distributed among legal, professional service, financial, and insurance experts. Construction industry experience of interviewees ranged from 20 to over 50 years, and all participants had at least 10 years of working experience with international projects of various types and sizes (Walewski and Gibson, 2003a).

The literature review and structured interviews showed that a number of techniques and practices exist to identify and assess risks that occur on international projects, but there was no standard technique or practice specifically tailored to such projects (CII, 1989: Walewski et al., 2002). Decisions on country-specific risks often are made by top management and separated from other business, technical, and operational risks of the project. Few project participants have a complete understanding of the portfolio of risks that happen on such projects, and a life-cycle view of the risks is uncommon. Given these limits of perspective, compartmentalization of the risks occurs, and international projects often are organized and managed in ways that create information and communication disconnects.

A detailed list of the risk elements that affect the project's life cycle (i.e., planning, design, construction, and operations) of international facilities was developed from five primary sources: the expertise of the research team, literature-review results, the structured interviews, input from members of CII's Globalization Committee, and further review by industry representatives. Initial topic categories were gathered from previous research and from the structured interviews and then screened using the research team's expertise. The resulting list of international risks was further refined, and an agreement was reached regarding exact terms and nomenclature of element definitions. Once this effort was completed, separate reviews were performed by Globalization Committee members and vetted again by participants during a series of workshops.

The final list consists of 82 elements grouped into 14 categories and further grouped into four main sections that reflect the project's life cycle. Presented in Table 6.1, this list forms the basis of the IPRA tool and can be considered comprehensive for pursuing capital projects outside of one's home jurisdiction. Each section, category, and element of the IPRA tool has a corresponding detailed description to assist project participants in gaining an understanding of the issues related to that component of the risk being considered. The IPRA assessment sheets and element descriptions are to be used together by a project team to identify and assess specific risk factors, including the likelihood of occurrence and relative impact for each element. The development, format, and use of the assessment sheets and associated output documents are discussed in detail in the application section of this chapter.

RISK ASSESSMENT WORKSHOPS

The research team hypothesized that all elements are not equally important with respect to their relative impact on overall project success. Their importance varies depending on the project type and location as well. The research team believed that there would be a significant benefit if a standard baseline (impact) risk value could be determined for each element. A standard guidance value of a risk's effect on a project would be of assistance when the risk is unknown by project participants and also could provide a framework to rank order risk elements on the project for subsequent mitigation.

We determined that the best way to develop reasonable and credible relative impact values for each element was to rely on the expertise of a broad range of construction industry experts. The research team hosted four risk assessment workshops in which a total of 44 industry executives were involved. These executives reported results on approximately US$23 billion worth of international projects from 20 different countries. Participants represented 25 organizations and were made up of 26 contractor and 18 owner representatives. In addition to having an owner-contractor balance, a fairly equitable distribution of project types and locations was achieved. Each participant completed a series of documents at the workshops; in addition to personal history, participants were asked to consider and document a typical international project that they had completed recently for the organization they represented. The details regarding the workshops and the projects used for this effort are provided in CII Research Report 181-11 (CII, 2003b) and are beyond the scope of this chapter.

The element rankings obtained from the workshops were developed statistically and yielded the relative impact value for each element. The *relative impact* value of each element is its rank, the calculation of which is based on its potential impact to the project within its category, section, and the overall IPRA tool. Definitions were developed for each of the five values based on a review of the literature and industry practices. The overall rankings were broken into five levels of corresponding relative impact that were given letter designations ranging from A to E, with A = negligible, B = minor, C = moderate, D = significant, and E = extreme, corresponding to degrees of impact as defined in Table 6.2. The baseline relative impact values of the significant (D) and extreme (E) elements are given in Appendix 6A.

TABLE 6.1   IPRA Structure

SECTION I – COMMERCIAL
I.A. Business Plan
  I.A1. Business case
  I.A2. Economic model/feasibility
  I.A3. Economic incentives/barriers
  I.A4. Market/product
  I.A5. Standards and practices
  I.A6. Operations
  I.A7. Tax and tariff
I.B. Finance/funding
  I.B1. Sources & form of funding
  I.B2. Currency
  I.B3. Estimate uncertainty
  I.B4. Insurance

SECTION II – COUNTRY
II.A. Tax/tariff
  II.A1. Tariffs/duties
  II.A2. Value added tax
  II.A3. Legal entity establishment
  II.A4. Application of tax laws
      and potential changes
  II.A5. Technology tax
  II.A6. Personal income tax
  II.A7. Corporate income tax
  II.A8. Miscellaneous taxes
II.B. Political
  II.B1. Expropriation and nationalism
  II.B2. Political stability
  II.B3. Social unrest/violence
  II.B4. Repudiation
  II.B5. Government participation and
      control
  II.B6. Relationship with government/
      owner
  II.B7. Intellectual property
II.C. Culture
  II.C1. Traditions and business practices
  II.C2. Public opinion
  II.C3. Religious differences
II.D. Legal
  II.D1. Legal basis
  II.D2. Legal standing
  II.D3. Governing law/contract formalities
      and language
  II.D4. Contract type and procedures
  II.D5. Environmental permitting
  II.D6. Corrupt business practices

SECTION III – FACILITIES
III.A. Project scope
  III.A1. Scope development process
  III.A2. Technology
  III.A3. Hazardous material requirements
  III.A4. Environmental, health, and safety
  III.A5. Utilities and basic infrastructure
  III.A6. Site selection and clear title
  III.A7. Approvals, permits, and licensing

III.B. Sourcing and supply
  III.B1. Engineered equipment/
      material/tools
  III.B2. Bulk materials
  III.B3. Subcontractors
  III.B4. Importing and customs
  III.B5. Logistics
III.C. Design/engineering
  III.C1. Design/engineering process
  III.C2. Liability
  III.C3. Local design services
  III.C4. Constructability
III.D. Construction
  III.D1. Workforce availability and skill
  III.D2. Workforce logistics and support
  III.D3. Climate
  III.D4. Construction delivery method
  III.D5. Construction permitting
  III.D6. General contractor availability
  III.D7. Contractor payment
  III.D8. Schedule
  III.D9. Insurance
  III.D10. Safety during construction
  III.D11. Communication and data
      transfer
  III.D12. Quality
III.E. Start-up
  III.E1. Trained workforce
  III.E2. Facility turnover
  III.E3. Feedstock and utilities reliability

SECTION IV – PRODUCTION/ OPERATIONS
IV.A. People
  IV.A1. Operational safety
  IV.A2. Security
  IV.A3. Language
  IV.A4. Hiring/training/retaining
  IV.A5. Localizing operational workforce
IV.B. Legal
  IV.B1. Governing law/operational
      liability
  IV.B2. Permitting
  IV.B3. Insurance
  IV.B4. Expatriates
  IV.B5. Environmental compliance
IV.C. Technical
  IV.C1. Logistics and warehousing
  IV.C2. Facilities management and
      maintenance
  IV.C3. Infrastructure support
  IV.C4. Technical support
  IV.C5. Quality assurance and control
  IV.C6. Operational shutdowns and
      startup

TABLE 6.2   Relative Impact Definitions

A	Negligible consequence that routine procedure would be sufficient to deal with the consequences.
B	Minor consequence that would threaten an element of the project. Normal control and monitoring measures are sufficient.
C	Moderate consequence would necessitate significant adjustment to the project. Requires identification and control of all contributing factors by monitoring conditions and reassessment at project milestones.
D	Significant consequence that would threaten goals and objectives; requires close management. Could substantially delay the project schedule or significantly affect technical performance or costs, and requires a plan to handle.
E	Extreme consequence would stop achievement of project or organizational goals and objectives. Most likely to occur and prevent achievement of objectives, causing unacceptable cost overruns, schedule slippage, or project failure.

Likelihood of occurrence values also were developed by dividing the probability that the identified risk will occur into the following five designations (with numerical range from 1 to 5): 1 = very low (<10 percent), 2 = low (10 to less than 35 percent), 3 = medium (35 to less than 65 percent), 4 = high (65 to less than 90 percent), and 5 = very high (90 percent or greater). These designations are based on the research team's review and assessment of the literature and industry practices for determining and assigning risk probabilities. Table 6.3 gives the probability division for the likelihood of occurrence used in the IPRA tool.

As a supplement to the workshops, the October 2002 CII Emerging Markets Forum in Baltimore, MD, provided an opportunity for 29 industry representatives to test the mechanics of using the IPRA tool and element descriptions on a case study of a cement production facility located in Bulgaria. Forum participants were asked to assess and comment on the theory, structure, and usefulness of the research team's work. Introducing the IPRA tool to forum participants and having them participate in this case-study evaluation proved valuable. The case-study issues and expectations of forum participants were well defined during an introduction to the IPRA tool. This exploration of the group's mind-set, combined with a subsequent interactive group discussion on assessing the project risks and then reporting the results, helped to (1) create

TABLE 6.3   Division for Likelihood of Occurrence in the IPRA

Occurrence	Probability
NA = not applicable to this project.	Zero
1 = very low chance of occurrence, rare, and occurs only in exceptional circumstances.	(<10% chance)
2 = low chance and unlikely to occur in most circumstances.	(10% chance of occurrence <35%)
3 = medium chance and possible to occur in most circumstances.	(35% chance of occurrence <65%)
4 = high chance of happening and will probably occur in most circumstances.	(65% chance of occurrence <90%)
5 = very high chance of occurrence and almost certain and expected in most circumstances.	(90% or greater chance of occurrence)

a high level of interest in the IPRA tool, (2) check the thoroughness of the tool, and (3) provide an excellent opportunity to observe the personal interaction of participants when using the tool. In the concluding discussion session at the forum, participants made it clear that the IPRA tool should provide separate assessment scales for likelihood of occurrence and relative impact for each element.

CONSISTENCY TEST

In order to verify its completeness and to assess the relationship to actual performance, the IPRA tool was used on 25 recently completed and ongoing projects representing greater than US$4.6 billion in project value. Project performance data were collected on 16 of these 25 completed test projects in order to identify the relationship between risk and project performance. More than a third of these projects reported that at least one risk not identified at contract formation occurred and had a significant impact on project performance. These issues are identified in Table 6.4.

The respondents also were asked to identify the unforeseen severe and extreme risks that existed at the contract-formation phase of their projects, to estimate the impacts of those issues on the project's ultimate performance, and to describe the mitigation steps taken. A selected subsample of these unforeseen issues is given in Table 6.5.

The IPRA tool also was used on nine ongoing projects to observe its effectiveness in helping project teams assess international risks. On seven of these projects, the authors facilitated an IPRA assessment session with project team members. In each case, the IPRA tool gave the project team a comprehensive mechanism to identify and assess project risks and to determine which risks had the highest relative importance at the time of the assessment.

The IPRA results from the nine ongoing projects demonstrate the tool's ability to assist in proactively identifying issues that can have a significant impact on project performance. It also can assist in the identification and preclusion of issues not typically considered at contract formation. The results to date show that early and consistent application of the IPRA tool is an effective risk management approach.

Detailed risk status reports were generated from the full IPRA assessments of the ongoing projects used in the sample. These assessment sessions took from one to four hours each and proved that the tool was an effective mechanism for identifying and evaluating a wide spectrum of risks on real international projects whether used by a team or an individual project participant. In each case, the IPRA tool gave project participants a viable platform for discussing project-specific issues and helped to

TABLE 6.4   Frequency of IPRA Elements Identified during Testing Having a Significant Project Impact Not Addressed at the Time of Contract Formation ($N = 16$)

IPRA Risk Elements		Frequency of Occurrence (Percent)
III.A1.	Scope development process	33
III.A2.	Technology	33
III.D8.	Schedule	27
I.B3.	Estimate uncertainty	20
II.C1.	Traditions and business practices	20
III.D10.	Safety during construction	20
III.E1.	Trained workforce	20

TABLE 6.5   Selected Examples of Unforeseen Project Risk Issues Impacting Performance

Project ID No.	IPRA Risk Element	Performance Issues
1	III.A1. Scope development process III.D8. Schedule	The initial agreement to stay within scope was not followed by the owner, who spent $3 million more than budget without increasing the project schedule. The follow-on schedule compression had severe impacts on the contractor and resulted in increased labor workloads, costs, and availability on other projects.
2	II.A2. VAT II.B6. Relationship with government III.D8. Schedule	The government sold the project to private investors and the sale impacted the contractor's financing, cash flow, and schedule. To maintain schedule, the contractor had to use $3 million of its own funds, a contingency that resulted in VAT and other tax issues.
5	III. C3. Local design service III.D8. Schedule	The requirement to have a local architect and engineer approve plans and specifications was not taken into consideration, and project contingency was used to pay for the added cost of additional design services and schedule delays.
9	II.C3. Religious differences III.D8. Schedule	The observance of holidays, daily prayer times, and work schedules (local work week was Saturday to Thursday) decreased productivity. The religious and cultural differences required the contractor to provide more on-site management than originally planned.
9	III.A2. Technology III.D8. Schedule III.E2. Facility turnover	The use of experimental technology by the process technology supplier increased plant capacity and process water system specifications for this remote project. However there were unforeseen problems with the technology that occurred during start-up and this adversely affected both cost and schedule. The contractor's site staff was required to work with the client and technology provider to resolve the problems.
12	II. C1. Traditions and business practices III.D12. Quality	In-country building practices made it difficult to achieve plans and specifications. As a result the owner required the construction manager to increase the number of supervisors to monitor project performance.

identify critical risk issues. Members of the research team were involved directly in observing the use of the tool on most of these projects. Their observations were useful for modifying the assessment sheets slightly and helped them in writing instructions on its application for field use.

The research indicates that many of the highest-impact risks occur in the first two sections of the IPRA tool and relate to jurisdictional and financial issues. Organizations that have been in a country performing projects appear to have the ability to identify and better manage these risks, indicating that the issue of jurisdictional experience is important.

TABLE 6.6   Summary of PT 181 Activities and Industry Input

Activity	Number of Participants[*]
PT 181 meetings and deliberations	12
Globalization committee review and assessments	10
Structured interviews	22
Risk scoring workshops	38
CII Globalization committee emerging market forum	20
Consistency test—completed projects	12
Consistency—ongoing projects	28
Total	119

[*]Participation is only counted once as some contributed to more than one activity.

Using the IPRA risk register and a lessons-learned database system could allow companies to shorten the learning curve for becoming successful on international projects. Use of these tools in association with proactive and repeated use of the IPRA tool can improve the chances that organizations with little or no experience in a jurisdiction will be able to avoid or mitigate the risks. This research also illustrated that there is no single "blueprint" for assessing the risks associated with international projects and that use of the IPRA tool must be tailored to adjust for country, user, and business-sector concerns.

In addition to recognizing these limitations of the IPRA tool, the researchers acknowledge the reduced scope that comes from their generalization of the sample characteristics to a larger population. In this study, relatively small samples were used for the both development of baseline relative impact values and the consistency test investigation. Furthermore, because the sample project selection was based on organizations volunteering projects and not on a random selection process, organizations may have selected projects with a bias toward success, which may have influenced the results.

As summarized in Table 6.6, the research team performed a variety of activities and received input from 119 different industry experts from 52 different firms to develop and test the IPRA tool. Although the consistency test used a relatively small nonrandom sample of 25 projects and is susceptible to bias, the collective results from it show that the tool is a sound, comprehensive method to identify and assess the relative impact of the majority of risk issues encountered on international capital facilities (CII, 2004).

APPLICATION AND USE OF THE IPRA TOOL

Because risks can arise throughout the project life cycle, effective risk management is an iterative process and not limited to a one-time analysis. Given the evolving nature of risk, the primary value of the tool is highest during the program decision and preproject planning phases. To be most effective, we recommend that the IPRA tool should be deployed at three points on the project timeline: (1) program decision, (2) validation of project feasibility, and (3) decision to proceed with detailed engineering and construction. Further use of the tool could occur during project execution and operations. In addition, the tool can be used as a checklist at any time. Figure 6.1 illustrates where the tool is most applicable during the project life cycle.

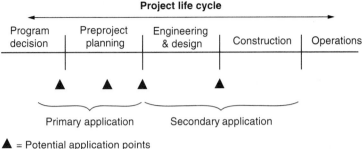

FIGURE 6.1   Application of the IPRA tool during the project life cycle.

Individuals involved with the project should become familiar with the format of the IPRA tool and use the IPRA project assessment worksheets when evaluating a project. Two types of worksheets are available—the difference between them being that participants have the option of selecting their own relative impact level or using the baseline relative impact for each element. Table 6.7 gives an example of one of the 14 categories within the worksheets, showing the structure of the IPRA tool with the baseline values. The baseline is intended for use when specific values are unavailable or when project participants have little knowledge of the potential consequences. (Users of the nonbaseline assessment sheets determine their own level of relative impact, and no baseline is provided.) The mechanics of this process and of completing an assessment are outlined in succeeding sections.

HOW TO ASSESS A PROJECT

To assess the project, each of the 82 elements must be addressed. Individual elements must be evaluated by using either of the detailed assessment worksheets in conjunction with the IPRA risk elements descriptions document, where detailed descriptions and checklists of concern are provided for each element. Project team members should refer to these definitions and go through the checklist before they rate likelihood of occurrence and relative impact. This initial evaluation ultimately facilitates a greater understanding of the risk.

Using the element descriptions and associated checklists as guides, the team evaluates the project based on the issues raised by the assessment process. This process requires common sense and reasonable judgment. The IPRA tool is a process tool to help identify and assess risks associated with international projects, but it does not provide solutions to these jurisdiction-specific issues. It should be noted that one of the key requirements for performing an adequate assessment is to make sure that knowledgeable participants are included, including business, project management, and operations representatives.

The likelihood of occurrence combined with the relative impact at the time of the assessment determines the relative importance of the risk. The difference between the perceived and actual risks of any IPRA element depends on the knowledge levels of the project participants and includes such things as

- Availability of information
- Experience and expertise of project participants

TABLE 6.7 Example IPRA Assessment Sheet, Category I.A. Business Plan, with Baseline Values

Category	Likelihood of occurrence (L)						Relative impact (I)					Baseline	L, I	Comments
	NA	Very low → Very High					Negligible → Extreme							
		1	2	3	4	5	A	B	C	D	E			
I.A. Business plan														
I.A1. Business case												E		
I.A2. Economic model/ feasibility												D		
I.A3. Economic incentives/ barriers												E		
I.A4. Market/product												D		
I.A5. Standards and practices												D		
I.A6. Operations												D		
I.A7. Tax and tariff												D		

Likelihood of occurrence
NA = Not applicable to this project
1 = Very low probability and occurs in only exceptional circumstances (<10% chance)
2 = Low chance and unlikely to occur in most circumstances (10% chance <35%)
3 = Medium chance and will probably occur in most circumstances (35% chance <65%)
4 = High chance and will occur in most circumstances (65% chance <90%)
5 = Very high chance, almost certain and expected to occur (90% or greater chance of occurrence)

Relative impact
A = Negligible impact and a routine procedures sufficient to deal with the consequences
B = Minor impact and would threaten an element of the function
C = Moderate impact and would necessitate significant adjustment to the overall function
D = Significant impact and would threaten goals and objectives; requires close management
E = Extreme impact and would stop achievement of functional goals and objectives

6-11

- Understanding of the issues creating the risk
- Extent to which the risks are stable or subject to change
- Reliability of assumptions

The team evaluates each IPRA element based on the perception of the known or perceived risk at the time of the assessment. Although these variables, likelihood of occurrence and relative impact, may be challenging to judge, the project participants should reach consensus for each element, given the knowledge available at the time of the assessment.

The assessment worksheet has fields for evaluation of likelihood of occurrence and includes six preassigned values ranging from 1 (very low) to 5 (very high) and an NA value corresponding to "not applicable" for the given element. All the elements should be evaluated, except for items that are truly not applicable to the project. If the individual element is not applicable, the corresponding (NA) box is checked.

Depending on the nature of the element and the specifics of a project, likelihood of occurrence can be expressed as a probability that an event can happen or the chance that an element's existing status will change and require risk-mitigation steps. The likelihood is determined by identifying all the possible risks that may have a significant impact on a project's success. The project team should consider the description and then ask the question, "Will this issue necessitate mitigation methods because (1) events are likely to occur and/or (2) information is not known?" Elements that have a very high, high, or medium level of probability of occurrence generally require the project team's attention.

Assessment participants should recognize that the likelihood of occurrence can be anticipated for certain IPRA elements, whereas for others the likelihood is uncertain and the probability of their occurrence is not well-defined or is even unknown. Often not enough information exists to determine or assess the likelihood of occurrence. In these cases, it is recommended that participants be conservative in their assessment and rate the likelihood as having a higher chance. These elements obviously need to be investigated further. Once the likelihood of occurrence for the element has been determined, the corresponding box is checked.

For the relative impact section of the assessment worksheet, the project team has the choice of using either the preassigned baseline relative impact or the project-specific relative impact. These values are in response to the perceived or actual impact that may occur if the given risk materializes. As with likelihood of occurrence, assessment session participants should recognize that the relative impact may be known for certain IPRA elements, but for others the consequences of the element occurring and how it influences the project can be ill defined or even unknown. Situations will exist where not enough information exists to determine or assess relative impact. In these cases, it is recommended that participants use the baseline relative impact rating. When the baseline rating is not used, the project team chooses a project-specific relative impact level. For this decision, the project team should consider the IPRA description and then ask the question, "If the issue occurs, how will it affect cost, schedule, and the relative success of the project?"

As discussed earlier, these steps are repeated for each of the 82 IPRA elements. The combination of these two values (likelihood of occurrence and relative impact) will help to determine the relative importance of risk for a given element on a project. This combination is shown in Fig. 6.2. The appropriate relative importance risk level can be found by locating the coordinates of the likelihood of occurrence (L) and relative impact (I). Once the relative importance for the element has been determined, it is plotted at its specific location on the risk matrix. Risk items that plot in the upper right-hand corner of the risk matrix represent the greatest risk to the project, whereas those in the lower left are of lesser concern. Obviously, elements with higher relative

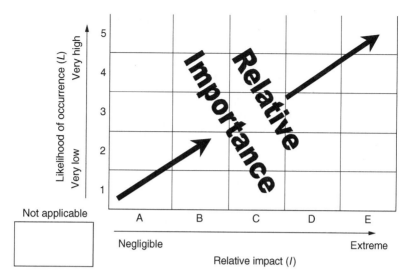

FIGURE 6.2   IPRA risk matrix.

importance need to be mitigated by the project team. Major project dangers and/or irregularities should become apparent to the project team as the assessment proceeds, and this prospective view should prove to be useful in the project's risk monitoring, control, and mitigation measures.

The IPRA gives the assessment team a process to gauge the relative importance of the project's risk. It should be noted that the relative importance of a specific risk may change during the life cycle of the project, and therefore, mitigation methods may need to be adjusted accordingly. Using this guidance, the assessment team determines the type and level of mitigation for the individual elements. Elements with high relative importance need to be further addressed.

A risk register can be used to track and ensure that mitigation occurs. The intent of using the risk register is to systematically identify and track specific high-priority risks that result from an IPRA assessment. A high-level methodology to identify and track individual risk issues was undertaken by the research team, and further details are provided in CII Implementation Resource 181-2 (CII, 2003a).

PHILOSOPHY OF USE

Ideally, the project team conducts an IPRA evaluation at strategic points in the project. Engaging a neutral facilitator familiar with the process, along with appropriate members of the project team, improves the assessment and limits in-house biases. The facilitator also provides objective feedback to the team and controls the pace of the assessment meeting. When this arrangement is not feasible, the alternative approach is to have key individuals evaluate the project separately and then come together for consensus. Although personal reviews can be biased, using the

IPRA tool from an individual point of view can be of merit in situations where an expedited review is necessary or very early on in project development.

The IPRA tool is best used to help project participants arrive at a studied understanding of risk. The team should strive for consensus around each IPRA element before moving to the next. If action needs to be taken on an element, possible remedies should be captured on a flip chart or by another method of recording action items. Using the IPRA tool early in the project life cycle will identify many areas of risk and gives the project team a roadmap for control and mitigation. In this early phase, several important issues typically affect the overall viability of the project, such as scope development and the alignment of project participants. The IPRA tool is a mechanism that can be used to identify or discover risks specific to international ventures and to organize the work to diffuse future risks. It also can provide an effective means of "handing off" the project to other entities or helping to maintain continuity as new project participants are added to the project.

The IPRA assessment worksheet serves as a basis for risk mitigation by the project team. The IPRA risk matrix can be used as a summary roll-up for senior management, in effect, helping to bridge any communication gaps concerning project understanding. In addition to the risk matrix, the summary also should contain a brief write-up addressing the specific areas of concern, and it should summarize the IPRA analysis. In particular, the assessment can focus attention on the elements that show higher relative impact (levels D and E), as well as higher likelihood of occurrence (levels 3 through 5), on the risk matrix.

CONCLUSIONS

In the course of this research it became clear that participants valued the identification and management of overarching project risks and recognized the dangers of exclusive attention to only risks within their areas of influence. Although the need for comprehensive risk identification, assessment, and management was acknowledged by all, it was practiced by few. Project participants are often segmented into project phases and disciplines that create information and communication disconnects. Complicated by the historically adversarial owner-contractor relationship, new risks go unnoticed or are not addressed, exacerbating disconnects between the project team and executive management. As a result, few project participants have an understanding of all the risks involved. Many of the risks that influence international projects fall outside those typically found on domestic projects. Acknowledging this reality, almost all the participants in this research agreed that an improved process is needed to identify and assess international risks and that there would be a benefit to having a structured tool/process. Effective risk management improves project performance on international projects in terms of cost, schedule, and market viability.

This chapter details the research and development of the IPRA tool, a project management tool that allows for the identification and assessment of the life-cycle risk issues specific to international construction for both owners and contractors. As summarized in Table 6.6, the development of the IPRA tool involved a variety of data collection activities based on input from 119 different industry experts. Data were analyzed using standard statistical and qualitative analysis techniques, and the fundamental conclusions are as follows:

1. The collective results from this research shows that the IPRA tool is a comprehensive and sound method for identifying and assessing the relative impact of the majority of risk issues encountered on international capital facilities.

2. The IPRA tool and the baseline relative impact values help the project team to identify the risk factors of highest importance to the project team.

This research was an exploratory effort that has expanded the body of knowledge and research regarding international construction risk management. It offers a systematic and integrated risk identification, assessment, and management method for international projects; this method addresses both the full project life cycle and the portfolio of risks encountered by both owners and contractors. Other efforts to date within the construction industry have been fragmented and have tended to focus on country-specific issues or on concerns unique to a given participant. The IPRA tool is a management tool applicable to all project participants because it focuses on the life-cycle risk issues proper to international projects.

The development of 82 discrete IPRA risk elements and associated descriptions and the worksheets that generate a ranking of them provides a unifying process to organizations involved with international projects; it gives them a common point of departure as well as a project touchstone once work is underway. No industry-wide process to evaluate the risks specific to international projects existed previous to the IPRA tool. Because its structured risk identification and assessment process can rank the relative importance of a project's risk, this work also contributes an additional precursive analytical method to the more vexed process of detailed analysis, quantification, and modeling of risk issues that are more elaborate than necessary.

Unique to this effort was the development of baseline relative impact values for individual risk elements based on data collected from industry experts who were reporting on recently completed projects. Because few organizations collect and track information related to risk severity, the baseline values fill a knowledge gap and can provide some guidance when risk impacts are unknown or when uncertainty is high. This is especially critical during the business and preproject planning phases because failure to identify risks early in the project life cycle can cause serious ramifications.

RISK MANAGEMENT TO IMPROVE PROJECT PERFORMANCE

Based on the wisdom collected and organized by this research, we recommend the following risk response actions as a critical phase of a project's overarching risk management process:

1. *Organize and formalize a risk management process and keep it as simple as possible.* The project manager for an international construction project must create the proper context and environment for the risk assessment and management process to occur.

2. *Begin early to be most effective.* Most successful projects take the time and allocate resources to collectively identify, analyze, and develop risk mitigation and control approaches during the early, formative stages of the project.

3. *Keep a broad perspective to get the diversified input required.* It may be necessary to bring in special expertise from outside the project to get fresh insights and perspectives into the risks. Brainstorming sessions guided by a person trained in conducting such sessions may be beneficial.

4. *Undertake adequate preproject planning, analysis, and engineering.* Preproject planning facilitates a better understanding of the project's scope of work, thus leading to a better knowledge of risk. Preproject planning tools such as the CII's PDRI (project development rating index) are complementary to the IPRA tool (CII, 1996; CII, 1999).

5. *Partner with owner and contractor management.* In too many international construction projects the relationships between the investor, the project sponsor/owner, the project management contractor, the designer, and the construction contractor are not optimal for effective risk management.

6. *Recognize that certain projects are more prone to risk and that experience in a jurisdiction is important.* Projects having one or more of the following factors are significantly more likely to need a comprehensive, detailed risk management process:

- Substantial resources
- Significant novelty
- Long planning horizons
- Large size
- Complexity
- Several organizations
- New jurisdiction for one or more major project participants
- Significant political issues

Many international construction projects have several of these characteristics, and in general, the more experience an organization has within a jurisdiction, the better its ability to manage risks.

7. *Document project risks effectively.* Owners and contractors can profit by keeping records of their risk management results on various projects. These results are of much more value if they are shared. Given this shared knowledge, the result is more efficient project implementation and lower overall costs.

REFERENCES

Construction Industry Institute. 2004. *International Project Risk Assessment: A Management Approach* (Research Summary 181-1). Austin, TX: CII.

Construction Industry Institute. 2003a. *International Project Risk Assessment (IPRA) Tool* (Implementation Resource 181-2). Austin, TX: CII.

Construction Industry Institute. 2003b. *Risk Assessment for International Projects* (Research Report 181-11). Austin, TX: CII.

Construction Industry Institute. 1999. *Development of the Project Definition Rating Index (PDRI) for Building Projects* (Research Report 155-11). Austin, TX: CII.

Construction Industry Institute. 1996. *Project Definition Rating Index (PDRI)* (Research Report 113-11). Austin, TX: CII.

Construction Industry Institute. 1989. *Management of Project Risks and Uncertainties* (Publication 6-8). Austin, TX: CII.

Han S, Diekmann J. 2001. Approaches for making risk-based go/no-go decision for international projects. *ASCE J Construct Eng Manag* 127(4):300–308.

Project Management Institute. 2000. *A Guide to the Project Management Body of Knowledge.* Newton Square, PA, PMI.

Walewski J, Gibson G, Vines E. 2002. Improving international capital project risk analysis and management, in *Proceedings of the Project Management Institute Research Conference 2002, Seattle, WA,* pp. 493–501.

Walewski J, Gibson G. 2003a. *International Project Risk Assessment: Methods, Procedures, and Critical Factors.* Austin, TX: Center for Construction Industry Studies, University of Texas at Austin, Report 31.

Walewski J, Gibson GE. 2003b. *International Project Risk Assessment: Methods, Procedures, and Critical Factors* (Center for Construction Industry Studies Report 31). Austin, TX: University of Texas at Austin.

Walewski J, Gibson G, Jackson Y, Vines E. 2004. Risk assessment on international projects: a management approach, in *Proceedings of 2004 PMI Research Conference, July 2004, London.*

Walewski J. 2005. International project risk assessment. Doctoral dissertation, University of Texas at Austin.

APPENDIX 6A

TABLE 6A.1   Rank Order of IPRA Risk Elements by Relative Impact, Extreme and Severe Elements

Rank	IPRA Element	Element Description	Baseline Relative Impact*
1	I.B1	Source and form of funding	E
2	I.B3	Estimate uncertainty	E
3	I.A1	Business case	E
4	I.B4	Insurance	E
5	I.A2	Economic model/feasibility	E
6	I.B2	Currency	E
7	II.B6	Relationship with government/owner	E
8	I.A4	Market/Product	E
9	II.C1	Traditions and business practices	E
10	II.D4	Contract type and procedures	E
11	II.B2	Political stability	D
12	II.B3	Social unrest/violence	D
13	III.E1	Trained workforce	D
14	I.A6	Operations	D
15	III.A1	Scope development process	D
16	I.A5	Standards and practices	D
17	IV.A1	Operational safety	D
18	III.C1	Design/engineering process	D
19	I.A3	Economic Incentives/barriers	D
20	I.A7	Tax and tariff	D
21	II.C2	Public opinion	D
22	II.B5	Government participation and control	D
23	IV.A4	Hiring/training /retaining	D
24	II.D3	Governing law/contract formalities and language	D
25	III.C3	Local design services	D
26	III.B3	Subcontractors	D
27	II.D5	Environmental permitting	D

* Levels of Relative Impact:
E = Extreme and would stop achievement of functional goals and objectives
D = Significant and would threaten goals and objectives

CHAPTER 7
PROGRAM MANAGEMENT AND PROJECT PORTFOLIO MANAGEMENT*

Roland Gareis

Vienna University of Economics and Business Administration, Vienna, Austria

Roland Gareis holds an M.B.A. and a Ph.D. He was a Fullbright scholar at the University of California, Los Angeles, in 1976, professor for construction management at the Georgia Institute of Technology, Atlanta, and visiting professor at the Georgia State University, ETH in Zürich, Switzerland, and the University of Quebec in Montreal, Canada. Since 1983, he has been the director of the postgraduate program "International Project Management" at the Vienna University of Business Administration. For 15 years he was president of Project Management Austria, the Austrian project management association; he was project manager of the 10th Internet World Congress on Project Management; and he was manager of the research program "Crisis Management." Currently, he is professor of project management at the Vienna University of Economics and Business Administration, manager of the global research program "Project Orientation [international]," and owner of Roland Gareis Consulting. He has published several books and papers on management of the project-oriented company.

ABSTRACT

A program is a temporary organization for the fulfillment of a unique business process of large scope. The projects that are part of a program serve to realize common program objectives. Program management is a business process of the project-oriented company, which includes the subprocesses program start, program coordination, program control, possibly resolution of a program discontinuity, and program close-down.

The clustering of projects and programs into project portfolios, networks of projects, and chains of projects can create synergies for management of a project-oriented company. The assigning of a project or a program, the coordination of a project portfolio, and the networking of projects are project portfolio management processes. Important methods for fulfilling these business processes are the investment and the project proposal, the

---

*Parts of this chapter are based on selections from the book *Happy Projects!* by Roland Gareis (Vienna: Manz, 2005).

investment portfolio score card, the business case analysis, the project assignment, the project portfolio database, the project portfolio score card, and the network-of-projects graph.

THE PROGRAM: A SOCIAL CONSTRUCT

A *program* is a temporary organization to fulfill a unique business process of large scope. It is of great strategic importance for the company performing the program, and it is limited in time. The projects that are part of the program serve to realize common program objectives (Fig. 7.1).

Objectives of a program can be the performance of a contract (contracting program), the establishment of a new infrastructure (a construction program or an IT program), or the development of a new organization (reorganization program). The yearly investment program or the strategic priorities of a company are not programs in an organizational sense. The term *program* is used every day in different ways. The organizational meaning of the word must still make its mark.

Programs are a new possibility for the organizational differentiation of the project-oriented company. In practice, the term *project* is often used for temporary organizations that should be managed as programs. In order to communicate the difference in scope and complexity of such organizations, some companies refer to these as "total projects" or "large projects." In doing so, however, the following organizational potentials are lost, which result from the differentiation between projects and programs:

- Differentiation between the program owner team and the owner teams of the projects of the program
- Use of different project owner teams for different projects in the program
- Promotion of the autonomy of the individual projects in a program, such as the development of a project-specific culture and the design of project-specific environment relationships
- Substitution of the hierarchical organizational structure of a complex project with several subprojects (Fig. 7.2) with a flat program organization (Fig. 7.3)

Characteristic of business process	Scale		
Frequency	Continuous	Unique	Unique
Duration	Short-term	Short-term – medium-term	Medium-term – long-term
Importance	Low	Medium – high	High
Scope	Small	Medium – large	Large
Resource demand	Low	Medium	High
Cost	Low-medium	Medium – high	High
Organizations involved	Few	Several – many	Many
Organizational form	Permanent organization or working group	Project	Programme

FIGURE 7.1   Characteristics of business processes that are organized as programs.

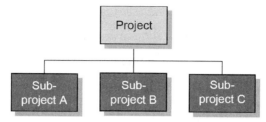

FIGURE 7.2   Hierarchical organizational structure of "large projects" (project and subprojects).

- Ensuring clear terminology and discarding the unpopular name *subproject manager*
- Reduction of the complexity of "large projects" through the establishment of smaller, easy-to-survey project organizations
- Development of several easy-to-read project documents and one lean integrated program documentation instead of a "large project" documentation

The use of program management in the project-oriented company ensures better quality, lower costs, shorter durations, and lower risks of the programs.

THE PROGRAM MANAGEMENT PROCESS

Program management is a business process of the project-oriented company that includes the subprocesses program start, program coordination, program control, possibly resolution of a program discontinuity, and program close-down. The program management process corresponds to the project management process. Programs also must be started,

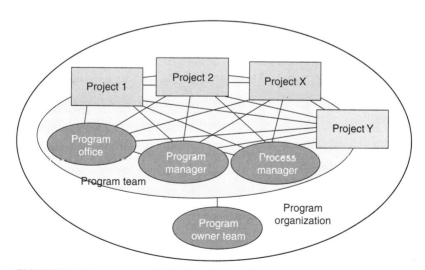

FIGURE 7.3   Flat program organization (standard organization chart).

controlled, and closed down. Because of its great importance, program marketing should be seen as its own subprocess of program management and not—as in project management—as a part of the start, control and close-down processes.

The assignment of a program to a program manager by the program owner team is the starting event of a program. Program approval by the program owner team is the formal program close-down (Fig. 7.4).

Program management is to be performed in addition to management of the individual projects that make up the program. Instruments for integrating projects into a program are the planning and control of program objectives, the program schedule, the program budget and the program risk, the design of the program environment relationships, and the design of the program organization and of the program culture. It is to be ensured that the projects follow the program standards. The projects of a program are closely coupled by fulfilling program management functions.

Program Management Subprocesses

The program start and program close-down processes are limited in time and are performed only once in a program, but the program control process in a program is performed several times. Program coordination and program marketing are continuous processes.

As an example of the description of the subprocesses of program management, the objectives and time boundaries of the program start process are listed in Table 7.1, and the tasks and responsibilities are described in Fig. 7.5.

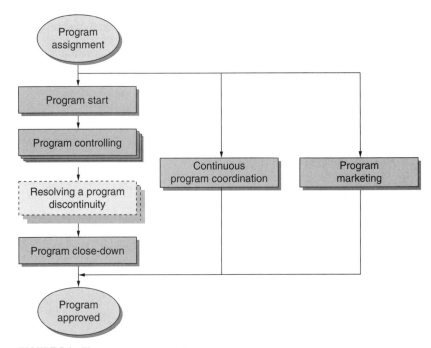

FIGURE 7.4 The program management process.

TABLE 7.1   Objectives and Time Boundaries of the Program Start Process

Objectives of the program start process
- Information transfer from the preprogram phase into the program
- Definition of expectations regarding the postprogram phase
- Developing adequate program plans for managing the program objectives, deliverables, schedule, resources, costs, income, risks, and financing
- Designing the program organization, adequate integration of the program into the permanent organization
- Developing the program culture
- Establishing communication relationships between the program and other programs and relevant program environments, initial program marketing
- Communicating the "big program picture" to all members of the program organization
- Planning of measures for discontinuity management
- Definition of the structures for the program management subprocesses to follow
- Developing the program management documentation "Program start"
- Efficient design of the program start process

Time boundaries of the program start process
- Start: Program assigned
- End: Documentation "Programme start" filed
- Duration: 3–4 weeks

Design of the Program Management Process

The design of the program management process centers on the use of program management methods, standard program plans, program communication forms, Information and Communication Technology (ICT) instruments, project management consultants, and project management coaches, as well as program management checklists (see Chapter 2). The methods of program management correspond to the project management methods; that is, a program objectives plan, an objects-of-consideration plan, a program workbreakdown structure, a program bar chart, a program environment analysis, etc. are all used.

Competencies for Program Management

For professional program management, individual and organizational competencies are required in the project-oriented company. Specific requirements for the performance of program management roles are dealing with program complexity and fulfilling the integrative functions in the program. Both require experience in project management and a high level of social competence.

SPECIFIC FEATURES OF PROGRAM MANAGEMENT

Conception Projects as the Basis for Programs

Because of the complexity of programs, it is advisable to perform a conception project as the basis for the investment decision and program assignment. The objectives of such a conception project are to describe the need for investment, to analyze the current situation,

Responsibilities / Tasks	Program owner team	Program manager	Program office	Program team member	Program team	Representatives of relevant program environments	External	Documents
Planing the program start								
• Checking the program assignment and the results of the preprogram phase		P						
• Selecting start communication form		P	C					
• Selecting program team members (and a PM consultant)		C				P		
• Selecting PM methods and PM templates to be used		P	C					
• Agreeing with program owner team	E	P						1)
Preparing the program start communication								
• Hiring of a PM consultant (possible)	E	P	C					
• Preparing start communications I, II, etc.		P	C					
• Inviting participants	I	P	C				C	2)
• Documenting the results of the preprogram phase		C	P	C			C	
• Developing drafts for planning, organizing, and marketing the program		C	P	C			C	
• Developing information material for start communication		C	P	C			C	3)
Performing the program start communication								
• Distributing information material to participants	I	C	P					
• Performing start communication I	C	C1				P	C	
• Developing draft of PM documentation "program start"		C	P					
• Performing start communication II, etc.	C	C1				P	C	
Follow-up to the program start communication								
• Completing draft of PM documentation "program start"		C	P					
• Agreeing with program owner team	E	P	C					4)
• Program marketing: Initial information	C	P	C	C			C	
• Distributing PM documentation "program start"		C	P			I		
• Filing of PM documentation "program start"	C	C1		P			C	
Performing first work packages (parallel)		C1		P			C	

Legend:	Results/documents:
P ... Performance	5) List of program management methods to be used
C ... Contribution	6) Invitation of participants to program start workshop
I ... Information	7) Information material for program start workshop
C1 ... Coordination	8) Program management documentation "program start"
D ... Decision	

FIGURE 7.5 Description of the program start process.

and to analyze the costs and benefits of the investment. Other objectives are planning the content, the organization, the budget, and the schedule of the planned program in order to initialize the investment.

The sequence of a conception project and a program for initializing an investment becomes a chain of a project and a program (Fig. 7.6). In the conception project, the structures for realizing the program to follow are planned. In the program start process,

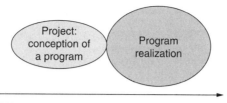

FIGURE 7.6 Chain of a conception project and a program.

these structures are detailed and concretized. To ensure continuity in this chain, members of the project organization of the conception project also can take on roles in the program organization.

Definition of Program Objectives

Because of the large scope and long duration of programs, the objectives of programs are more dynamic than those of projects. During program assignment, the global program strategy and program objectives are defined, and these will become adapted and more detailed during performance of the program start process.

Conception projects in programs are a central instrument for planning the objectives of follow-up projects and also for adapting the program objectives. The medium- to long-term durations and the dynamics of programs can make it necessary to plan alternative program objectives with different end events and schedules. The boundaries of the program should, however, always be defined. Programs should not have an open end.

Program Organization Chart and Program Roles

The main difference between projects and programs lies in their organizational design. This differentiation requires that projects and programs are perceived as temporary organizations.

Elements of the organizational structures of programs are the projects of the program and the program-specific roles, that is, program owner team, program manager, possibly program process experts, program team, and a program office. The program roles and their relationships to each other can be visualized in a program organization chart (see Fig. 7.3).

The program owner team assigns the program manager and the program office with performance of the program. Strategic decisions of program management, such as selection of projects to be started, changing of program priorities, and definition of program strategies toward relevant program environments, are made by the program owner team. The program owner team also decides about project-related issues that are beyond the decision-making authority of the program team or the relevant project owner and project manager.

The program owner team should consist of managers of those areas of the company that will be affected most by the program. There should not be more than four persons in the program owner team. A speaker for the program owner team is to be nominated who will act as the first contact person for the program manager. An expanded program owner team also can include as members representatives of partners and important suppliers. The role of the program owner team is described in Fig. 7.7.

The program manager is responsible for realization of the program objectives, together with program process experts and the program office. The program manager ensures the

Role: Program owner team
Objectives
• Coordinate program and company interests
• Assign a program manager to perform the program
• Perform strategic program controlling
• Lead the program manager
Position in the organization
• Part of the program organization
• Program manager reports to the program owner team
Tasks
Tasks in the program start
• Assign the program
• Provide support in the selection of the program team members
• Establish the program context
• Ensure the availability of program resources
• Contribute to the initial program marketing
• Participate in the initial program team meeting
• Hold program owner team meeting
Tasks in program controlling
• Hold program owner team meetings
• Coordinate the program with other programs, projects and company objectives
• Analyze the program progress report
• Select the project owner team and project managers
• Ensure the availability of program resources
• Continually contribute to program marketing
Tasks in resolving a program discontinuity
• Define a program discontinuity
• Collaborate in the development of and decisions about immediate measures
• Collaborate in the cause analysis of the program crisis
• Decide about alternative strategies
• Collaborate on the performance of corrective measures and checks on their success
• End a program discontinuity
Tasks in program close-down
• Hold program owner team meeting
• Participate in the closing program team meeting
• Formal program approval
Formal authority
• Selecting the program manager
• Providing the program budget
• Changing the program objectives
• Definition of a program discontinuity
• Program stopping
• Program close-down

FIGURE 7.7   Role description: Program owner team.

professional fulfillment of the program management processes. The role of the program manager is described in Fig. 7.8.

Because of the extensive management and marketing effort in programs, it is recommended that a program office be established for operational support of the program manager. This is a major contribution to securing success in the program. The integrative program management tasks are institutionalized in the program office. It establishes

Role: Program manager
Objectives
• Realize program interests
• Ensure the realization of the program objectives
• Lead the program team
• Represent the program toward representatives of relevant environments
Position in the organization
• Member of the program team
• Reports to the program owner team
• Gets organizational support from the program office
• Leads the project owner team and the project managers
Tasks
Tasks in the program start
• Design the program start process (together with the program team)
• Hold program team meetings
• Design adequate program plans and the program organization (together with the program team)
• Risk management and development of a specific program culture (together with the program team)
• Design program context relationships and perform program marketing
• Develop program management documentation "Program start" (with support from the program office)
Tasks in program controlling
• Design the program controlling process (together with the program team)
• Hold program team meetings and participate in program owner team meetings
• Coordinate all resources required in the program
• Agree on or perform controlling measures (together with the program team)
• Set project priorities within the program
• Adapt program plans (with support from the program office)
• Develop program progress reports (with support from the program office)
• Perform program marketing tasks (with support from the program office)
• Start new projects (together with the relevant project owner team and project manager)
• Perform strategic control of the current projects together with the respective project owner team; networks between current projects and the program
• Define a project discontinuity (together with the respective project owner team)
• Contribute to project close-downs, transfer of know-how into other projects of the program
Tasks in resolving a program discontinuity
• Work out immediate measures (together with the program team)
• Perform cause analysis (together with the program team)
• Work out alternative strategies (together with the program team)
• Perform measures to resolve the crisis and check for success (together with the program team)
• End the program discontinuity (together with the program owner team and the program team)
Tasks in program close-down
• Design the program close-down process (together with the program team)
• Hold the program close-down meetings (together with the program team) and participate in the closing program owner team meeting
• Develop the program close-down report
• Transfer know-how into permanent organization and make agreements for the postprogram phase
• Perform closing program marketing
Formal authority
• Decisions about coordinating the program (together with the program team)
• Decisions on the project priorities within the program
• Responsibility for the program budget
• Calling program owner team meetings
• Coordination of resources required in the program
• Starting projects (together with the respective project owner team and project manager)
• Changes to project objectives, definition of a program discontinuity, and closing down projects (together with the respective project owner team)

FIGURE 7.8   Role description: Program manager.

a "home base" for the program. Program management experts are available in the program office for the individual projects and for representatives of the relevant environments.

The program team is made up of the program manager, representatives of the program office, and possibly, program process experts. The active projects of a program or those that are due to start soon are represented in the program team by the respective project managers. The composition of the program team changes over time because different projects are active at different times. The tasks of the program team are to ensure synergies in the program and to set priorities among the projects of the program.

Program Work-Breakdown Structure

The objectives to be realized in a program require the performance of projects. The projects of the program therefore are to be depicted in a program work-breakdown structure. Programs also have tasks to be fulfilled, such as training tasks or program management tasks that do not require a project organization but can be performed as work packages of the program.

It is recommended that the objects of consideration of the program be used as a basis for development of the program work-breakdown structure. Objects of consideration can be, for example, services and products, regions and markets, objects (e.g., buildings, IT infrastructure), organizations, and personnel groups. When structuring a program into projects, a rough process orientation must be ensured. Given the high complexity of programs, there is a stronger object orientation (such as structuring by location) than in projects.

The projects of a program are performed in parallel as well as sequentially. The sequential performance of projects in a program leads to chains of projects.

Organizational learning in programs can be ensured through definition of pilot projects within the program. Pilot projects should have available to them time and room for reflection and documentation of the experiences gained. The experiences gained in pilot projects are to be made available to follow-on projects.

During program control, it may become apparent that the dynamics of programs require the splitting or merging of projects. Splitting projects into several projects and merging two or more projects into one pose discontinuities for the affected projects. Their structures must be redesigned.

Program Risk Management

Given that the size, complexity, and novelty of a program, risks are high. There is a danger of failure or of stopping before completion. The object of consideration in program risk management is the program, in addition to the risks of the individual projects of the program.

In programs, too, risk analysis, measures to avoid or promote risk, and provisions for risks and risk control are management tasks to be performed. In programs, a global as well as a detailed risk management can be performed.

In global risk management, the risks for the program are analyzed without taking into account the risks for the individual projects and their relationships to one another. The program is viewed as an individual project.

Detailed risk management for programs accounts for the risks of the individual projects and the relationships between the risks of the projects of the program. Because of the relationships between the projects, the program risk is not equal to the sum of the project risks. The risks of several projects together can have positive or negative correlations, or they can have a neutral effect on each other.

Only when there is no correlation between the risks of the projects of a program is the program risk equal to the sum of all the project risks. In the case of a positive correlation of project risks, the program risk is increased; in the case of a negative correlation, the program risk is decreased.

The basis of the program risk analysis is an analysis of the risks of the individual projects of a program. Then the correlation between the project risks can be analyzed. Positive correlation between project risks occurs, for example,

- In a chain of projects between the pilot and follow-on projects or a conception and a realization project
- In cooperations with the same suppliers or partners in several projects of the program
- In the use of the same technologies in several projects of the program
- In the performance of several projects for the same customer
- In the performance of several projects of the program in the same country

By deploying the same supplier or the same technology for several projects, "economies of scale" and learning potential can be used, which are reflected in lower project costs. On the other hand, a higher level of dependence, that is, risk, on the chosen supplier or on the technology is created. With loss of the supplier or if the technology is not yet ready for implementation, not only one project suffers, but several projects of the program are damaged. Here one has to strike a balance between lower program costs and the risk of an even higher loss for the program.

A negative correlation between projects occurs when a risk in one project becomes acute and in doing so excludes a risk in another project. Such relationships between projects are rare. Risk management in programs therefore must concentrate on reduction of the positive correlation between the project risks. By adapting the correlations of the risks between projects, the program risk can be influenced.

Program Standards

In programs, there are often repetitive projects. For the performance of repetitive projects in a program, it is recommended that program standards be developed. For the management of projects, standard project plans (e.g., standard work-breakdown structures, standard work-package specifications, or standard milestone plans) can be developed and used.

The objective in the use of program standards is to develop a uniform way of working in the projects of a program. Through the application of standards, the projects are more closely coupled in the program. The relative autonomy of the projects therefore is less than in projects that are not part of a program. The development and use of program standards ensure quality in the projects of programs and promote organizational learning in programs.

Program Marketing

Because of the high strategic importance and uniqueness of a program, the professional communication of the program objectives and the program structures plays a large part in the success of the program. Professional marketing therefore is especially important in programs. Only through professional marketing can an understanding of the meaning of the program be communicated to the relevant program environments and the availability of management attention, know-how, and resources for the performance of the program ensured.

CLUSTERS OF PROJECTS AND PROGRAMS IN THE PROJECT-ORIENTED COMPANY

Project-oriented companies simultaneously perform a multitude of projects and programs. They are therefore highly differentiated organizations. To comply with integration tasks, projects and programs can be clustered into project portfolios, networks of projects, and chains of projects. Synergies can be created by means of clustering several projects and considering relationships between those projects. Furthermore, this clustering can promote the realization of the strategies and objectives of the project-oriented company. Considering relationships between the projects in a relevant cluster of projects provides optimization opportunities.

The project portfolio is the set of all projects of a project-oriented company. A project portfolio takes into consideration all the current (and planned) projects and programs at a given point in time. If a project-oriented company holds many projects in its portfolio (e.g., more than 50 to 60 projects), it is sensible to define several project portfolios for different types of projects (e.g., contracting projects, product-development projects, etc.). A project portfolio presents a point-in-time analysis.

A network of projects is a set of closely coupled projects held within the project portfolio. Various criteria can be used for coupling projects into networks of projects, such as the use of a joint technology, performance in the same geographic region, or performance for a common customer.

A chain of projects is a set of sequential projects for the performance of several related business processes. It represents a specific form of a network of projects. A chain of projects is analyzed over a period of time. Chains of a project and a program are also possible (e.g., a conception project followed by a realization program).

Compared with projects and programs, project portfolios, networks of projects, and chains of projects are not organizations but rather are clusters of organizations. As such, they are objects of management consideration (Fig. 7.9).

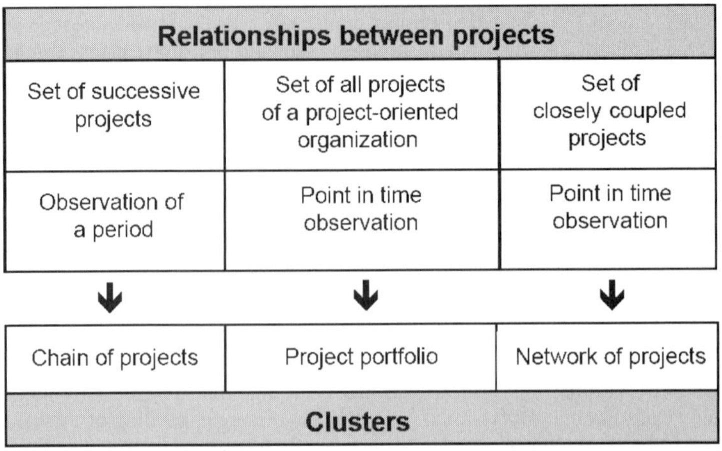

Relationships between projects		
Set of successive projects	Set of all projects of a project-oriented organization	Set of closely coupled projects
Observation of a period	Point in time observation	Point in time observation
⬇	⬇	⬇
Chain of projects	Project portfolio	Network of projects
Clusters		

FIGURE 7.9   Clusters of projects.

PROJECT PORTFOLIO MANAGEMENT: OVERVIEW

The general objective of project portfolio management is optimization of project portfolio results. From the project-oriented company's point of view, the goal is not optimization of the results of individual projects or programs but rather optimization of the results of the project portfolio. This objective can conflict with optimization of the objectives of individual projects.

Different objectives are pursued in the various business processes of project portfolio management. The central objectives of assigning a project or a program are selection of a favorable investment and definition of an adequate organizational form for initializing the investment. The objectives of project portfolio coordination are coordination of the objectives of the projects of the portfolio, coordination of the internal and external resources used in these projects, organization of learning from and between the projects, and determination of the projects' priorities. The objective of project networking is the creation of synergies between the projects of a network of projects.

The assigning of a project or a program, the coordination of a project portfolio, and the networking of projects are business processes for project portfolio management. The managing of a chain of projects is to be seen as a specific form of project networking.

The assigning of a project or a program is to be seen as a business process for project portfolio management because a decision to start a new project or program ought not to be taken in isolation but rather in the context of the newly created project portfolio.

The methods for the different business processes of project portfolio management are listed in Table 7.2 and are described in the following.

The tasks involved in integrating projects and programs in project portfolios, networks, and chains are fulfilled by specific, permanent organizational units of the project-oriented organization, that is, the project portfolio group, the PM office, and expert pools (see Chapter 18).

TABLE 7.2   Methods of Project Portfolio Management

Methods for assigning a project or a program	
• Investment proposal	Must
• Investment portfolio score card	Can
• Business case analysis or cost-benefit analysis	Must
• Project definition	Must
• Project proposal	Must
• Project assignment	Must
Methods of project portfolio coordination	
• Project portfolio database	Must
• Project portfolio score card	Must
• Other project portfolio reports	Can
• Project proposals	Must
• Project progress reports	Must
Methods for networking of projects	
• Networking workshop	Can
• Network of projects graphics	Can
• Project portfolio reports	Can
• Project progress reports	Can

ASSIGNING A PROJECT OR A PROGRAM

Assigning a project or a program is a project portfolio management process. The assigning process considers those investments whose initialization probably requires a project or a program. It is the objective of the assigning process to decide on the realization of an investment and the organization of the initialization of that investment. The consequences of a proposed investment for the investment portfolio of the project-oriented company must be considered. Investments that make an optimal contribution to realization of the strategic objectives of the project-oriented company should be selected.

Possible organizational alternatives for the initialization of an investment are the project organization, the program organization, and the permanent organization. By defining the assigning of a project or a program as a business process, its tasks and the necessary decisions are formalized. The clear differentiation between the investment decision and the organization decision contributes to ensuring the quality of decision making. It reduces the risk of bad investments and inadequate organization forms for the initialization of investments.

Tasks in Assigning a Project or a Program

The business process of assigning a project or a program starts with formulation of a reason for an investment and ends with assignment of a project or a program. The phases of the assignment process are

- Developing the investment idea
- Developing an investment proposal and a project proposal
- Investment decision making
- Organization decision making
- Formal assignment of the project or program

Methods for assigning a project or a program are

- Investment proposal
- Investment portfolio score card
- Business case analysis or cost-benefit analysis
- Project proposal
- Project assignment

The decision regarding the realization of an investment and the decision regarding the adequate organizational form for its initialization can be taken by the project portfolio group. Many project-oriented organizations employ an investment-decision committee for investment decision-making purposes and use the project portfolio group only for project portfolio coordination.

Investment Proposal and Investment Portfolio Score Card

The investment proposal serves the purpose of describing an investment to be proposed. The investment proposal summarizes the problem formulation and the reason for the investment, the investment objectives, a description of the investment object, the required first payments for the investment, the contributions of the investment for realizing the financial objectives, the contributions to realization of other objectives of the project-oriented company, and the organizational form for the initialization of the investment (Fig. 7.10).

INVESTMENT PROPOSAL
Name of the investment: _____
Type of investment: ☐ Services   ☐ Organization ☐ Marketing   ☐ Personnel ☐ Infrastructure   ☐ Environment relationships
Problem formulation, reasons for the investment:
Investment objectives:
Description of the investment objects:
First payments for the investment:
Contribution for realizing financial objectives:
• Net present value:
• ROI:
• Benefit-cost ratio:
• Amortization period:
• Risks:
Contribution for realizing customers' objectives:
Contribution for realizing environment-related objectives:
Contribution for realizing innovation objectives:
Contribution for realizing business process and resource objectives:
Organization form for initializing the investment: ☐ Small project   ☐ Project   ☐ Program   ☐ Permanent organization
Appendices: • Business case analysis or cost-benefit analysis • Project proposal
_____   _____ **Promoter of the investment**   **Investment proposal team**
Version: Date: Name: Page1 of 1

FIGURE 7.10 Investment proposal form.

A crucial criterion for the investment decision is its financial success. The business case analysis or the cost-benefit analysis thus are to be enclosed within the investment proposal. The investment proposal is to be supplemented by a project or program proposal for initialization of the investment. The investment proposal therefore must be differentiated from the project proposal.

The decision to perform an investment can be taken either by an isolated analysis of the investment or by an integrated analysis of the investment portfolio. In the case of an isolated analysis of the investment, the contribution of the investment toward realization of the strategic objectives of the project-oriented company is assessed. If you are considering several investments, the results of the individual investments are compared with each other, and the "best" investments are selected. As a tool for this, a scoring table such as that from the ABN AMRO bank can be used (Fig. 7.11).

In the case of an analysis of an investment portfolio, the investments and their relationships to each other are analyzed. Complementary and competing relationships between investments are analyzed and integrated into the overall assessment of the portfolio. Alternative investment portfolios can be compared with the aid of investment portfolio score cards. Considering the strategic objectives of the project-oriented company, the selection of investments is made as a decision for the optimal investment portfolio.

In accordance with the balanced score-card model, various criteria can be used to analyze the investment portfolio. Basically, the realization of financial objectives, objectives concerning relevant environments, innovation objectives, and business process and resource objectives are considered. These criteria must be operationalized to enable analysis of the compliance with individual objectives. This is done in the investment portfolio score card depicted in Fig. 7.12.

Project Proposal and Project Assignment

A project proposal presents the basis for the decision to initialize an investment by a project (or a program). The project proposal is developed by defining the boundaries and the context of a project. The results of this project definition are documented in the project proposal form. This project definition is performed by roughly planning the project objectives, the project phases, the project start and end dates, and the project costs and project income, as well as central project roles. In order to enable a holistic project point of view, a project must be considered from these various perspectives. The compatibility of the defined project boundaries must be guaranteed by coordinating the results achieved.

The project context is defined by a rough representation of the relationships between the project and the company strategies, a rough description of the activities of the pre- and

Investment	Financial perspective	Customer perspective	Internal processes	Innovation	Score	Approved/ denied
A					90	Approved
B					86	Approved
C					81	Approved
D					70	Denied
E					65	Denied

FIGURE 7.11   Table for selecting investments (example from ABN AMRO bank).

Financial ratios	
NPV/ROI	2
Amortization period	2
Risks	1
Financing	3

Innovation	
New products	2
New processes	3
Further development	2
Optimization of the value-added chain	2

Investment
score card
as at 17.09.2003

Customer relationships	
Customer relations	1
New customer segments	3
Cooperation with customers	2

Processes and resources	
Existing process know-how	2
Available internal resources	3
Available external resources	2
Project/program to be implemented	1

Legend	
Very poor	5
Poor	4
Average	3
Good	2
Very good	1

FIGURE 7.12   Investment portfolio score card.

post-project phases, a list of relevant project environments, and a list of those projects in the project portfolio that have relationships with the project.

In order to provide these crucial project informations, it is necessary to develop rough project plans (e.g., work-breakdown structure, bar chart, cost plan, project environment analysis, etc.). These project plans form the basis for a detailed project planning during the project start process.

For developing a project proposal, a project proposal form should be used. The project proposal form is designed based on the project assignment form (to be used later). An example of a project proposal form is given in Fig. 7.13. Appendices to the project proposal form should represent the first drafts of the project management documentation.

The basis for assignment of the project by the project owner team to the project manager and project team is the decision taken by the project portfolio group to initialize an investment in a project form. A formal project assignment is made in writing and is signed by the project manager and the project owner team.

PROJECT PORTFOLIO COORDINATION

Structures of Project Portfolios

The set of all projects and programs that are managed simultaneously in a project-oriented company can be perceived as the project portfolio. Either all the projects of an organization or subsets of the projects can be clustered in project portfolios. Subsets of projects can lead to project portfolios, such as the portfolio of offer development projects, of contracting projects, of product-development projects, etc.

The start of new projects and the close-down of projects result in high dynamics of project portfolios. The structures of project portfolios—that is, the types of projects

PROJECT PROPOSAL		
Name of the investment:		
Project start date:	**Project end date:**	
Project objectives:	**Nonobjectives of the project:**	
Project phases:	**Project costs:**	**Project income:**
Project owner team:	**Project manager:**	
Project team members:		
Decisions and documents from the pre-project phase:		
Expectations regarding the post-project phase:		
Business case information:		
Relationships to other projects:		
Relevant project environments:		
Appendices: • Project objectives plan • Work breakdown structure • Project milestone plan • Project cost plan • Project environment analysis		
_____ **Promoter of the investment**	_____ **Investment proposal team**	
Version: Date:	Name: Page 1 of 1	

FIGURE 7.13 Project proposal form.

contained, the types of relationships between projects, the environment-related relationships of the projects, and the durations, costs and, risks of the projects, etc.—remain relatively constant, however.

Since project-oriented companies continually perform projects, project portfolios are not limited in time but rather extend over the lifetime of the project-oriented company. The project portfolio is a central integration instrument of project-oriented companies. The organizational differentiation resulting from the performance of projects and programs is complemented by an integrative point of view.

Objectives of Project Portfolio Coordination

Objects of consideration in the project portfolio coordination process are the projects and programs and their relationships to each other at a certain point in time. Objectives of the coordination of the project portfolio are to coordinate projects with regard to the strategic objectives of the project-oriented company and to optimize project portfolio results. However, the objectives of project portfolio coordination can conflict with the objectives of individual projects.

Various projects performed for the same customer should be coordinated with regard to long-term customer strategies and behavior patterns toward the customer. Purchases and services from various projects by the same supplier can be optimized with regard to the purchasing conditions. The internal and external resources used in the projects should be coordinated, and project priorities regarding access to scarce resources should be established.

Control of the structure of the project portfolio, the project portfolio risk, and the organization of the learning process for and between projects is a further objective. The potential to stop or interrupt projects for strategic reasons is also an objective of project portfolio coordination.

Tasks in Project Portfolio Coordination

The business process of project portfolio coordination encompasses the phases of preparation, performance, and follow-up of the periodic coordination meetings by the project portfolio group. Depending on the size and dynamics of the project portfolio to be coordinated by a project portfolio group, it may be necessary to hold a coordination meeting each week or every two weeks. Such meetings may last two to four hours.

In order to prepare the coordination meeting, the project portfolio database is updated, project portfolio reports are developed, new investment and project proposals are collected and checked for completeness. Then project progress reports of selected projects are compiled.

The necessary decisions regarding optimization of the project portfolio are taken by the project portfolio group. Preparation of the decision-making process is performed by the project management office through maintenance of the project portfolio database, analysis of the project portfolio, and compilation of project portfolio reports.

Results of Project Portfolio Coordination

The documents resulting from project portfolio coordination are project portfolio reports, investment and project proposals, project progress reports, and the minutes of the coordination meetings held by the project portfolio group. Typical project portfolio reports are, for example, a project portfolio bar chart, a project portfolio budget, a project portfolio personnel timetable, or a profit-risk matrix.

With regard to design of the project portfolio of a project-oriented organization, various quality criteria can be applied, such as the ideal number of projects per type of project, the minimum/maximum project portfolio budget, the maximum use of scarce resources in the project portfolio, the maximum number of cooperation projects with one supplier, the maximum number of projects with the same person as project manager, etc. The results of project portfolio coordination are, on the one hand, optimized structures of the project portfolio regarding these quality criteria and an optimized project portfolio risk.

On the other hand, overall optimization of the relationships to the project and program environments; optimization of the project and program results with regard to progress, costs, and income; assurance of the realization of the investment strategies of the project-oriented organization; and optimization of the implementation of organizational and personnel strategies in project portfolio coordination constitute the results of project portfolio coordination.

Measures for implementing organization and personnel strategies are, for example, the assignment of multirole performers to several projects, the application of guidelines for project and program management, the use of project management consulting and project management auditing for quality assurance purposes in projects and programs, and the targeted development of project management personnel. The current status of a project portfolio considering these different criteria can be visualized in a project portfolio score card (Fig. 7.14).

Project Portfolio Database

The project portfolio database forms the basis for project portfolio management. A project portfolio database is a database of information accumulated from past projects and

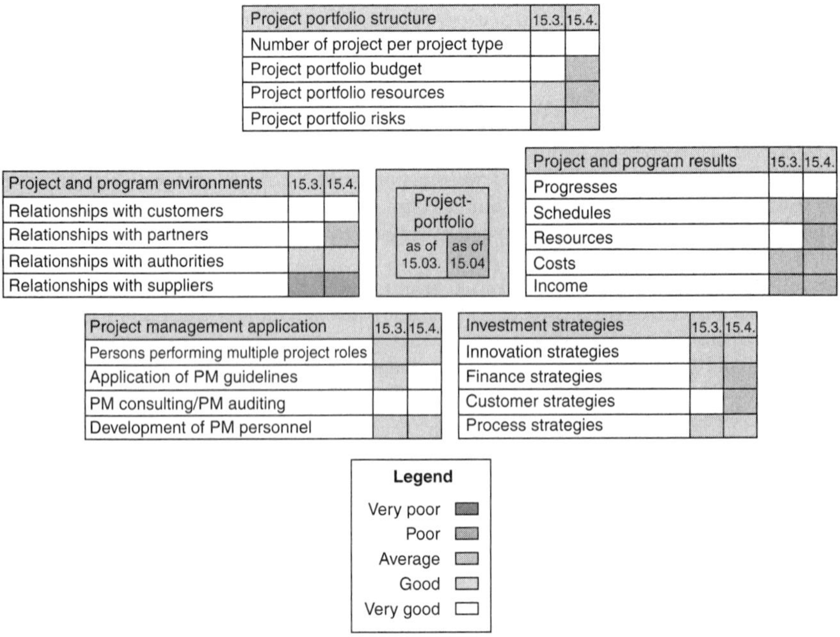

FIGURE 7.14   Project portfolio score card.

programs. It is not a project information system that contains detailed information about all projects. The project portfolio database relies on data on individual projects. In order to compare and accumulate data from projects, standardized minimum requirements should be established for documentation of projects. The project portfolio database should include the following information:

- Information regarding project organization, such as project owner team, project manager, and selected project team members
- Information regarding relevant project environments, such as customers, suppliers, and partners
- Information regarding products and markets, such as type of product, technology, and region
- Information regarding the type of project and relationships between the project and other projects, such as type of project and affiliation with a program
- Information regarding project ratios, such as project start date, project end date, net present value of the investment initialized by the project, project profit, project risk, project progress, and level of criticalness of the project

The project portfolio database can encompass data concerning current, planned, interrupted, stopped, and completed projects. The project portfolio database is the basis for analysis of the project portfolio, development of project portfolio reports, and networking of projects. Hence the project portfolio database is not only an instrument of the project portfolio group and the project management office but also contributes benefits to project managers of project-oriented organizations. The "big picture" of all the organization's projects is communicated to project managers. They are empowered by the availability of the relevant information, and they have an opportunity to optimize the results of their projects by applying synergies.

The current status of a project portfolio should be viewed in its temporal context. Changes to the project portfolio over time can be analyzed. For two or several control dates, the following applies:

- The number of newly started projects and the number of closed-down/stopped projects can be determined.
- The progress of various stages in the project portfolio can be compared.
- Changes in the contribution risk matrix can be observed.

PROJECT NETWORKING

Objectives of Project Networking

Networks of projects are social networks of closely coupled projects. Coupling of projects into networks of projects can result from cooperation among individual projects with the same partners or suppliers, performance of services for the same customer, performance of projects in the same region, use of the same technology by the projects, etc. Networks of projects do not have clear boundaries; that is, any project, as well as projects from customers, partners, or suppliers, that can contribute to the creation of synergies can be considered in the network.

The partners in project networks are temporary organizations, that is, projects and programs, that can communicate with each other. The joint intentions of the network partners are the creation of synergies in the network of projects and the organization of learning. Networking comes about by means of communication of network partners in workshops, meetings, and discussions. This communication can be supported by means of joint databases, chatrooms, and links.

The need for project networking can be determined by project managers, by the project portfolio group, and by the project management office. Because leaders and team members focus on project objectives and deliverables, the potential for networking with other projects is not always clear to the members of project organizations. It is therefore also the task of the project portfolio group and the project management office to promote project networking.

Project networking can be performed for a specific reason only or be established as a periodic form of communication in a project-oriented company. One reason for the ad hoc networking of projects is, for example, project discontinuities. The consequences of a project crisis for other projects should be analyzed, and any necessary preventive measures should be implemented.

Even if project networking is established as a periodic form of communication in a project-oriented company, the criteria for coupling projects into networks of projects should be defined ad hoc. Communication can take place either via existing communication structures, for example, profit-center meetings, or in networking workshops and meetings to be arranged.

Project networking requires a cooperative organizational culture. An active information policy, the chance for horizontal communication, and mutual trust are central values for project networking.

Tasks in Project Networking

Project networking commences with definition of the requirement for networking. As a preparatory measure for project networking, the networking requirement should be concretized, members of the individual project organizations should be invited to meet, and relevant information regarding the projects to be networked should be supplied.

It is recommended that a networking workshop be carried out for the purpose of project networking. As a form of communication, the workshop enables direct interaction between the members of various project organizations. Based on an appropriate exchange of information, the relationships between the projects that make up the network of projects can be analyzed. A project network graph can be used to show these relationships among projects.

Participants of a networking workshop are, on the one hand, members of the networking project organizations and, on the other hand, representatives of relevant project environments. A networking workshop lasts between half a day and a full day. Only one workshop usually is required for project networking. If needed, networking workshops can be supplemented by periodic networking meetings.

Based on analysis of conflicting and complementary relationships among projects, strategies and measures for management of the project network can be determined. The arrangement of agreed-on measures is the responsibility of the project managers of the projects to be networked.

Results of the Project Networking

The results of project networking are, on the one hand, an analysis of the relationships among the projects of a project network (possibly visualized in a project network graph) and, on the other hand, a list of measures for employing the synergies in the project network. The following basic measures are possible:

- Redefinition of project objectives based on conflicts of objectives among projects
- Rearrangement of personnel based on resource conflicts among projects and potential changes to project priorities
- Redesign of project environment relationships based on a more holistic point of view by considering several projects
- Balancing-out of risks among projects by changing contractual relationships with customers, partners, and suppliers
- Transfer of know-how among projects of the project network
- Establishment of communication structures for periodic coordination between two or more projects

In an extreme case, the information generated in an analysis of the relationships in a project network can result in the stopping or interruption of projects.

Network-of-Projects Graph

The relationships among the projects of a project network can be visualized in the form of a network-of-projects graph. This diagram depicts, on the one hand, the networking projects and, on the other hand, the relationships among those projects. Circles of varying sizes and colors can be used to depict the projects. The symbols used should be described in the form of a legend.

Several projects with common features can be grouped together by using various frames. Lines between the projects can be used to depict the relationships. Objects to be considered in networking are, above all, the relationships among the projects. For example, the relationships among individual projects can be described in the form of qualitative statements (Fig. 7.15).

MANAGEMENT OF PROJECT CHAINS

The projects within a chain of projects are closely linked by their affiliation with the same investment. Therefore, the business case analysis of the investment is an important integrative instrument in a chain of projects. Typical chains of projects are the chains of a conception and a realization project, of an offer and a contracting project, and of a pilot and a follow-up project.

The objective of the management of chains of projects is to ensure the continuity of the management of two or several successive projects or of a project and a program. The management of chains of projects does not present a business process on its own but rather a special case of networking among (successive) projects. The management of relationships among the projects of a chain of projects should be performed in the project management processes of the individual projects.

For the management of chains of projects, personnel policy and organizational measures must be fulfilled. An essential measure with regard to personnel is the inclusion of members of the project organization of the current project into the project organization of a follow-up project, for example, overlap among the members of project owner teams and project teams. The project portfolio group takes the decision regarding composition of the project owner team as part of project portfolio coordination.

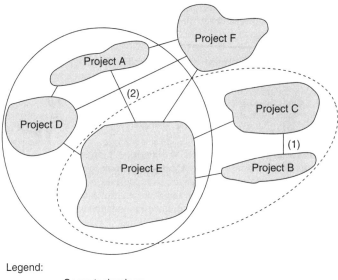

Legend:
- - - - - - - - -   Same technology
——————————   Same customer

Interpretation:
(3) There is the danger of bottlenecks in capacity occurring at the supplier used in projects B and C.
(4) Milestone 3 must have been reached for project A in order to be able to close down project E.

FIGURE 7.15   Symbolism and interpretations in a network-of-projects graph.

The objective of integrating two successive projects into a chain of projects can be realized in the project close-down process of the current project and in the project start process of the follow-up project. Planning of the structures of the follow-up project and their documentation in a draft of a project manual present a central content of the project performed beforehand. Potential members of the project organization of the follow-up project should be included in the project close-down process in order to participate in the structuring of the follow-up project and to get to know representatives of relevant project environments. In order to ensure the transfer of know-how into the follow-up project, members of the project organization and representatives of relevant project environments of the project performed beforehand should be invited to participate in the new project start process.

No specific methods are required for the management of chains of projects. The (organizational) measures for integrating two projects are depicted in the project management documents, in particular, in the documents of the project organization.

BIBLIOGRAPHY

Aarto K, Martinsuo M, Aalto T. 2001. *Strategic Management through Projects,* 1st ed. Helsinki: PMA Finland.

Enzenhofer D, Semper W. 1995 Controlling von Projekte-Netzwerken in projektorientierten Unternehmen. *Projekt Journal*

Lipnack J, Stamps J. 1982. *Networking: The First Report and Directory.* New York: Doubleday.

COMPETENCY FACTORS IN PROJECT MANAGEMENT

In Chapter 8, Crawford examines what competency means as a project manager, as well as how to identify and measure competency in managers. Core personality traits and characteristics are discussed, as well as how to apply effective competency models to the decision-making process for choosing a project manager.

In Chapter 9, the risks and uncertainties involved with the undertaking of any major global project are discussed. Miller and Hobbs show how changing global factors are affecting projects, analyze the development and delivery cycle of contemporary major global projects through an emerging framework, and discuss strategies to deal with global project risks and uncertainties.

In Chapter 10, Eskerod shows us what factors motivate project-oriented employees, how human energy affects individual motivation, and how to effectively use these factors to build productivity and morale. Motivation theories are presented and compared, as well as continuing themes that can be applied when analyzing motivation theories.

Chapter 11 introduces the reader to the project-oriented company, as defined by Gareis. The role of the project manager, needed competencies, and the career path of a successful project manager are examined by Huemann, along with ways to develop the skills and competencies necessary to develop as a project manager. Finally, one model used for analyzing management personnel is discussed.

In Chapter 12, Keller outlines the design, implementation, reporting, and results of the myriad projects taking place to restore conditions in Iraq. Keller's intimate involvement with the process in Iraq is reflected in the great detail he gives, providing structure to the programs currently underway, and shows the unique challenges present in the rebuilding effort.

Chapter 13 analyzes the project success factors present in any given project. Pinto and Slevin demonstrate not only how to pinpoint success factors, but also how to measure them using the Project Implementation Profile (PIP). The reader is taken through each step of the four-step process, and is shown how PIP can be utilized for any given project.

CHAPTER 8
COMPETENCIES OF PROJECT MANAGERS

Lynn Crawford

ESC Lille, France, and
University of Technology, Sydney, Australia

Lynn Crawford holds a DBA and has qualifications in human resource management, town planning, and architecture. She was director of the postgraduate Project Management Program at the University of Technology, Sydney, for six years and has been project director for several major research projects funded by the Australian Research Council in collaboration with industry in areas of project management competence and the management of multiple interdependent and soft projects. She continues to conduct research in these areas with support of industry partners.

Dr. Crawford has been involved in development of competency standards since the early 1990s and was a member of the steering committee for the development of Australian National Competency Standards in Project Management. She is currently leading initiatives aimed at the development of global standards for project management. These initiatives involve project management professional associations, recognized leaders in project management, and representatives of global corporations.

Currently, Dr. Crawford is professor of project management at ESC Lille in France, directs a project management research group at the University of Technology, Sydney, and is managing director of Human Systems Asia Pacific, which is part of a global network that facilitates knowledge sharing, benchmarking, and enhancement of delivery capability between major corporations.

Competent project managers are vital to the effective management of projects, and the successful delivery of projects is a major contributor to corporate performance. An increasing focus on governance means that shareholders, clients, governments, and the public are demanding evidence of corporate delivery capability, which includes the competence of project managers. It is therefore not surprising that there is considerable interest in assessing and developing project management competence. As globally mobile project managers contemplate their careers and global corporations consider how to assess the competence of their workforce to deliver projects and develop programs for development and ways of demonstrating that competence to stakeholders, they are faced with decisions concerning choice of standards and qualifications that will provide guidelines for development and provide transferability and mutual recognition across national boundaries. This chapter is intended to assist individuals and organizations faced with these decisions.

Although we all have a general idea of what we mean by *competence,* it is helpful to be able to break it down into component parts as a basis for assessment and development, so the chapter begins with a discussion of what constitutes competence. The next section of the chapter presents the components of generic project management competence, identifying standards, guides, and qualifications that are available for use, both globally and locally. Finally, guidelines are given for comprehensive assessment and development of project management competence that satisfies both local and global requirements.

UNDERSTANDING COMPETENCE

When we say that someone is *competent,* we generally mean that he or she has the ability to do a job or task, and our opinion is often based on evidence such as qualifications or observation of the person over a period of time. Competency tends to cover anything that might contribute to job performance.

Traditionally, in selection and promotion, employers have looked for the "right" technical qualifications and a proven track record of doing the same job in a similar organization. This does not always work for a number of reasons, including the following:

- Demand for such people may exceed supply.
- The new environment may differ from that which fostered past successes.
- There may be factors in the individual's private life—health, family, or other commitments—that have an impact on performance.

A number of factors have driven the search for a new way of selecting and developing people. With downsizing and pressure on organizations to do more with fewer resources, the link between business performance and the skills of employees has been emphasized. Changing demands in the marketplace and new ways of working often require changes in behavior. Technological changes mean that there are many jobs that have not been done before and for which there are no qualifications, so traditional methods of selection are not applicable. In developing countries, there may be very few people who have the qualifications and experience to fill the jobs that are being created.

In response to these pressures, competence over time has acquired new layers of meaning through use for specific purposes. It has come to mean different things to different people and has different purposes in different parts of the world. When people in North America and human resources managers talk about competence, they are generally thinking in terms of *competency models* and the attributes and behaviors that lead to superior performance in the workplace. In the United Kingdom, South Africa, Australia, and New Zealand, discussion of competence often refers to *competency standards* that are the basis for national qualifications frameworks in these countries. The competency standards approach involves the inference of competence based on evidence of performance in the workplace and is concerned primarily with threshold rather than superior performance.

The Competency Model Approach

The competency model approach is based on the work of McClelland and McBer in the United States beginning in the 1970s and reported by Boyatzis[1] in the early 1980s. Followers of this approach define a competency as an "underlying characteristic of an individual that is causally related to criterion-referenced effective and/or superior performance in a job or situation."[2]

Spencer and Spencer[3] define five competency characteristics that they consider to be causally related to criterion-referenced effective and/or superior performance in a job or situation. Two of these competency characteristics are knowledge, the information a person has in specific content areas, and skill, the ability to perform a certain physical or mental task. These are considered to be surface competencies and the most readily developed and assessed through training and experience.

In addition to these surface competencies, there are three core personality characteristics that are considered to be difficult to assess and develop. These are

Motives. The things a person consistently thinks about or wants that cause action; for example, achievement-motivated people consistently set challenging goals, take personal responsibility for accomplishing them, and use feedback to do better.

Traits. Physical characteristics and consistent responses to situations or information; for example, emotional self-control and initiative.

Self-concept. A person's attitudes, values, or self-image.

This can be referred to an *attribute-based approach to competence.* According to this approach, competence can be inferred from an analysis of personal characteristics and knowledge that lead to behaviors and skills.

Inherent in the competency model approach is the concept of threshold and high performance or differentiating competencies. A *high-performance competency* can be defined as "a relatively stable set of behaviors which produces significantly superior workgroup performance in more complex organizational environments."[4]

For this approach to be used effectively in selection, promotion, and development, employers need to know what personal characteristics, knowledge, behaviors, and skills are causally related to superior job performance in their organization. Many organizations have competency models that have been developed specifically for their environment and which are used across all job families in the organization.

The competency model approach is used in numerous organizational competency development programs worldwide usually across all job families within an organization. Competencies are seen as inputs, consisting of clusters of knowledge, attitudes, skills, and in some cases, personality traits, values, and styles that affect an individual's ability to perform.

The Competency Standards Approach

While the competency model or attribute-based approach assumes that identifiable personal attributes will translate into competent performance in the workplace, the competency standards approach assumes that competence can be inferred from demonstrated performance at a predefined acceptable standard.[5] The competency standards approach has not attracted the same degree of support and interest in the United States as it has in the United Kingdom, where it is the basis for National Vocational Qualifications (NVQs), and in Australia, New Zealand, and South Africa, where it underpins the national qualifications frameworks. Competency standards have a specific format, which includes

Units and elements of competency. Describe what is done in the workplace, profession, or role.

Performance criteria. The required standard of performance.

Range indicators. The context of performance.

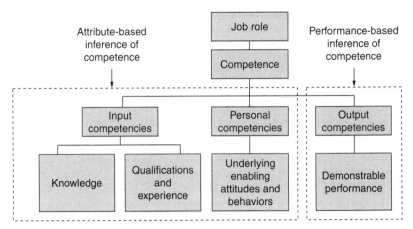

FIGURE 8.1   Components of competence.

This approach has been particularly attractive from an equity viewpoint and in recognition of prior learning. It provides a basis for recognition of the competence of those who can demonstrate ability to perform but have not had the opportunity to gain qualifications required for entry to particular jobs, occupations, or professions. This makes it particularly attractive in areas such as project management, for which qualifications have not been available previously, and in developing economies such as South Africa, where many jobholders do not have formal qualifications relating directly to the work that they do.

An Integrated Approach to Competence

Each of the approaches outlined earlier involves assessment of a different aspect of competence. Ideally, all aspects should be considered. The framework shown in Fig. 8.1 combines the competency model (attribute-based) and competency standards (performance-based) approaches to competence described earlier.

Input (knowledge and experience) and *personal* (attitude and behavior) *competencies* are both *aspects of attribute-based inference of competence.* Demonstrable performance is represented by *performance-based competency standards* that essentially describe *output competencies. Input* and *output competencies* generally relate to *threshold* performance, whereas *personal competencies* distinguish *superior* performance.

PROJECT MANAGEMENT COMPETENCIES

Job Role

The first step in considering competencies of project managers is to define the role. This is extremely difficult because the role varies considerably within and between industries and organizations. A useful approach to defining project management roles is to consider the types of projects undertaken and their organizational context. An initiative working on development of global performance-based standards for project management personnel

TABLE 8.1   Crawford-Ishikura Factor Table for Evaluating Roles (CIFTER)

Project Management Complexity Factor	Rating			
	1	2	3	4
1. Stability of the overall project context	Very high	High	Moderate	Low
2. Number of distinct methods and approaches involved in performing the project	Low	Moderate	High	Very high
3. Magnitude of legal, social, or environmental implications from performing the project	Low	Moderate	High	Very high
4. Overall expected financial impact (positive or negative) on the project's stakeholders	Low	Moderate	High	Very high
5. Strategic importance of the project to the organization or organizations involved	Very low	Low	Moderate	High
6. Stakeholder cohesion regarding the characteristics of the product of the project	High	Moderate	Low	Very low
7. Number and variety of interfaces between the project and other organizational entities	Very low	Low	Moderate	High

Source: GPBSPMP Initiative. 2005. *Performance-Based Competency Standards for Global Levels 1 and 2 Project Managers: Exposure Draft for Public Review, July 8, 2005* (Version 0.9). Sydney: Global Performance-Based Standards for Project Management Personnel.

(GPBSPMP Initiative, 2005[6]; now known as the Global Alliance for Project Performance Standards (GAPPS); www.globalPMstandards.org) has created a framework for differentiating projects based on their management complexity (Table 8.1).

The CIFTER table provides a useful starting point for thinking about competencies of project managers. Using this table, the global standards initiative has developed performance-based competency standards for two levels of project manager, Global level 1 and Global level 2, using the following ranges:

- *Below level 1*. Total score is 11 or lower.
- *Global level 1*. Total score is from 12 to 18.
- *Global level 2*. Total score is from 19 to 25.
- *Above level 2*. Total score is 26 or higher.

Many organizations develop similar frameworks as a basis for assessment and development of competencies and assignment of project personnel.

Knowledge

Over the last 20 years, project management professional associations have devoted considerable effort to identifying knowledge that is relevant to project management practice. The Project Management Institute's (PMI's) *Guide to the Project Management Body of Knowledge* (*PMBOK Guide*) is the most widely distributed of these guides and has been approved as an American National Standard (ANSI/PMI 99-001-1999). With reference to this document, the PMI offers a project management professional certification based on evidence of qualifications and experience and a multiple-choice knowledge test.

The structure of the *PMBOK Guide* includes nine project management knowledge areas: integration, scope, time, cost, quality, human resources, communications, risk, and procurement. There is a section dealing with project management context and processes that identifies five process groups: initiating, planning, executing, monitoring and controlling, and closing.

The Association for Project Management (APM) in the United Kingdom produces the *APM Body of Knowledge,* which is different in structure from the *PMBOK Guide* and somewhat wider in scope. It presents those "topics in which practitioners and experts consider professionals in project management should be knowledgeable and competent" (Dixon, 2000, p. 9).[7] The fifth edition of the *APM Body of Knowledge,* released in January 2006, has 52 topics listed under seven headings: project management in context, planning the strategy, executing the strategy, techniques, business and commercial, organisation and governance, people and the profession. A separate syllabus for the APMP examination has been published by APM, based on the *APM Body of Knowledge* (fourth edition). It defines the topics that candidates for the APM examination (APM's baseline professional qualification) are expected to know and provides learning objectives and a glossary of key terms.

The International Project Management Association (IPMA) has developed the IPMA Competence Baseline (ICB). The ICB has 28 core elements and 14 additional elements of project management knowledge and experience (a total of 42 elements), similar to those of the *APM Body of Knowledge,* which is one of the four national documents on which it was based. The primary purpose of the ICB is to provide a basis for its four-level certification program for project managers. The IPMA is a federation of national project management professional associations, and it encourages the national associations to develop their own national competence baselines (NCBs), consistent with the ICB. Each NCB is required by IPMA to include all 28 of the ICB core elements and at least six additional elements chosen by the nation. This allows each nation, in developing its NCB, to take into account local requirements or emerging developments in project management. The NCB is used as the basis for national certification programs validated by the IPMA Certification Validation Management Board.

Most NCBs have been developed by European countries. An Egyptian competence baseline was published in 1999, and an Arabic version was in preparation in 2002. The Chinese NCB, also referred to as the C-PMBOK, was published in Standard Modern Chinese in 2001. An Indian NCB was in preparation in 2002.

P2M, "A Guidebook for Project and Program Management for Enterprise Innovation" was released, in Japanese, in November 2001. An English-language version has since been developed. The Project Management Professionals' Certification Center (PMCC) of Japan, a nonprofit organization established in May 2002, is responsible for maintenance of the P2M, for promotion of project management, and for the certification system for project professionals. The P2M is intended to provide a capability building baseline (CBB) for project management, with capability being developed and expanded through professional experience as well as related disciplines of science and technology in the context of continuing professional development. The PMCC offers three levels of project management certification on an international basis.

The P2M has four parts:

Part I: Entry. Describes how to make a first step as a professional.

Part II: Project Management. Explains the basic definitions and framework of project management.

Part III: Program Management. Introduces management of programs of multiple projects.

Part IV: Project Segment Management. Presents 11 "segments" or knowledge areas of project management. These 11 knowledge areas are strategy, systems, objectives, risk, relationships, finance, organization, resources, technology, value, and communications.

Qualifications and Experience

The usual reference for qualifications and experience is a résumé or curriculum vitae. As mentioned earlier, employers, in recruiting project managers, generally will look for experience on similar projects in similar organizations and will be interested in evidence of successful completion of projects similar to those that will be covered by the proposed job role.

Studies indicate that most project managers have a bachelor's degree or higher and, on average, over 10 years of experience.[8,9] The first degrees of most project managers are not in project management because undergraduate degrees in project management are uncommon but rather in a range of disciplines including business, law, social sciences, computer sciences, teaching, and education.[10] Most, however, have degrees in engineering, primarily civil and mechanical engineering, or in design and construction. Postgraduate qualifications are similarly varied, including postgraduate diplomas and MBAs. An increasing number of academic institutions now offer postgraduate project management qualifications. Originally, these qualifications were focused primarily on engineering and construction, but an increasing number of project management academic programs are now generic in nature, and many are based in business schools. Several academic institutions now offer professional doctorates in project management that are intended for senior practitioners. A number of organizations work with academic institutions to develop specific academic qualifications for their personnel. One of the earliest sources of education in project management was the Defense Systems Management College in the United States. A number of academic institutions, primarily in North America, offer masters certificates that are based on programs that are more akin to industry short courses than to full academic programs. It is therefore becoming more common for project managers to have postgraduate qualifications in the field.

Although there are relatively few project managers with directly relevant academic qualifications, there are an increasing number with project management qualifications awarded by professional associations such as the PMI, the APM, the IPMA, and the Project Management Professionals Certifications Center, as discussed earlier. Other qualifications are offered by professional institutions such as the Australian Institute of Project Management and relate to national qualifications frameworks, which will be discussed in more detail below. Organizations such as the British Computer Society and the Singapore Computer Society offer information technology (IT)–based project management qualifications.

The range of expertise covered by nonacademic project management qualifications varies among associations/organizations, with some encompassing project team members to program managers (such as IPMA), whereas the offerings of others are not as broad, and some focus on a single-level qualification (such as PMI's PMP). For the majority of qualifications there is a requirement of project management experience as well as equivalencies for experience against formal education. Only the APM's foundation qualification, the APMP, and its equivalent, IPMA's Level D, do not specify a need for project management experience, although a curriculum vitae is required as a basis for determining "suitability" to sit for the APMP examination.

Another form of project management qualification is the one based on a project management methodology. The best known and most common of these are the foundation and practitioner examinations and qualifications based on PRINCE2. PRINCE, which stands for "Projects in Controlled Environments," is a project management methodology or approach to management of projects that was first developed in 1989 by the Central Computer and Telecommunications Agency (CCTA), now part of the U.K. Office of Government Commerce (OGC). When first developed, it was intended as a U.K. government standard for IT project management. PRINCE2 is a development of the original methodology that is intended as a generic approach applicable to management of all types of projects [Office of Government Commerce (OGC), 2004].[11] Training in use of PRINCE2 is available in many parts of the world through accredited training organizations, and there is a quality-assured process of assessment and certification in use of the methodology. PRINCE2 qualifications often are specified as a requirement for positions in organizations that use the PRINCE2 methodology, particularly in the United Kingdom. The methodology, often customized for local use, has been adopted by many organizations throughout the world.

Personality Characteristics, Attitudes, and Behaviors

Although there is strong guidance on what project managers need to know and to do in order to be considered competent, there is far less guidance available in terms of personality characteristics, attitudes, and behaviors. There are a number of reasons for this. One reason is that different people with different personality characteristics can use knowledge and practices differently but still achieve satisfactory results. Another is that it is ethically questionable to establish standards for personality characteristics, attitudes, and behaviors. Competency models are designed specifically for identifying the personality characteristics, attitudes, and behaviors that are found to be causally related to superior performance in particular organizations, but there is no expectation that there is one competency model that will be applicable to all organizations. Further, studies of personality characteristics of project managers have found only weak correlations between personality characteristics and successful performance. This can be explained in part by the difficulties surrounding judgments concerning success. However, although inconclusive and in most cases based on assumptions rather than research, there is some information available concerning the personality characteristics, attitudes, and behaviors that are expected to be associated with competent performance as a project manager.

The IPMA Competence Baseline includes a section on the expected personality characteristics for a certificated project manager. These are the same as appeared in the *APM Body of Knowledge* (version 3.0). They were developed in a series of practitioner workshops or meetings conducted by the APM. It is understood that they have no basis in research. These characteristics are

- Attitude
- Common sense
- Open-mindedness
- Adaptability
- Inventiveness
- Prudent risk taker
- Fairness
- Commitment

The 1996 version of the Australian National Competency Standards for Project Management suggested, in describing the nature of the project manager, that "technical know-how alone is not sufficient to bring a project to successful completion" and that "desirable attributes of a project manager include"

- Leadership ability
- The ability to anticipate problems
- Operational flexibility
- Ability to get things done
- An ability to negotiate and persuade
- An understanding of the environment within which the project is being managed
- The ability to review, monitor, and control
- The ability to manage within an environment of constant change

The need for *operational flexibility* identified in this list and *adaptability* identified in the ICB is supported by research reported by Mullaly and Thomas,[12] who found that the most effective projects managers are flexible in their style.

The most significant research on behavioral characteristics of project managers remains that conducted by Gadeken,[13] who, based on critical incident interviews with 60 U.S. and 15 U.K. project managers from Army, Navy, and Air Force acquisition commands, identified six behavioral competencies that distinguished outstanding project managers from their peers:

Sense of ownership/mission. Seeing oneself as the one responsible for the overall success of the program.

Political awareness. Understanding who the influential players are, what they want, and how best to work with them.

Relationship development. Spending time and energy getting to know program sponsors, contractors, or other influential people.

Strategic influence. Building coalitions with influential others and orchestrating situations to overcome obstacles and obtain support.

Interpersonal assessment. Identifying the specific abilities, interests, motivations, characteristics, or style of others.

Action orientation. Reacting to issues and problems energetically and with a sense of urgency.

A further five behavioral competencies were demonstrated, but with no significant differences indicated between outstanding and average performers:

Assertiveness. Stating one's own position forcefully or aggressively in the face of opposition from influential others.

Critical inquiry. Exploring critical issues that are not explicitly addressed or recognized by others.

Long-term perspective. Taking the time needed to think through future issues and problems.

Focus on excellence. Striving to achieve the highest standards regardless of circumstances.

Innovativeness/initiative. Championing or initiating new ways of meeting project requirements.

Analysis of findings of a number of studies concerning the personal attributes of project managers highlights the following as important characteristics[14]:

- Leadership
- Team development
- Communication
- Strategic direction
- Stakeholder management

An individual's personality characteristics, attitudes, and behaviors are the most difficult aspects of competence to change and develop. Characteristics associated with effective performance in project management roles will vary considerably according to the specific responsibilities of the role and its context. A characteristic that is strongly associated with competent performance is the ability to reflect on one's own performance. Behavioral and personality assessment instruments can be extremely useful as a basis for reflection and enhanced understanding of one's own performance. Some organizations, notably NASA, encourage their project personnel to use such instruments for this purpose.

Demonstrable Performance

Performance-based competency standards describe what people can be expected to do in their working roles, as well as the knowledge and understanding of their occupation that are needed to underpin those roles at a specific level of competence. A valuable aspect of such standards is that they are specifically designed for assessment purposes and are developmental in their approach, with assessment being undertaken by registered workplace assessors within a well-defined quality-assurance process. Such standards have been developed within the context of government-endorsed standards and qualifications frameworks in Australia, New Zealand, South Africa, and the United Kingdom. Performance-based inference of competence is concerned with demonstration of the ability to do something at a standard considered acceptable in the workplace.

> Performance based models are concerned with results, or outcomes in the workplace rather than with potential competence as indicated by tests of attributes, such as knowledge. Even when the underlying competence being tested is not itself readily observable, such as the ability to solve problems, performance and results in the workplace are still observable and the underlying competence they reflect can be inferred readily. Performance based models of competence should specify what people have to be able to do, the level of performance required and the circumstances in which that level of performance is to be demonstrated [Heywood L., et al., 1992, p. 23].[15]

The definition of competency, within the context of performance-based or occupational competency standards, is considered as addressing two questions:

1. What is usually done in the workplace in this particular occupation/profession/role?
2. What standard of performance is normally required?

The answers to these questions are written in a particular format.

Units of competency. A unit of competency describes a broad area of professional or occupational performance that is meaningful to practitioners and which is demonstrated in the workplace. Units may represent particular work roles, work functions, processes, or product outcomes.

Elements of competency. Elements of competency define the critical components that reflect the scope of work covered in each unit of competency. The elements are the building blocks of each unit. A single unit generally will have three to five elements.

Performance criteria. Performance criteria set out the standard of performance that is required for each element. Performance criteria specify the type and/or level of performance required that would constitute adequate demonstration of competence. They describe what a competent practitioner would do, expressed in terms of observable results and/or actions in the workplace from which competent performance would be inferred.

Range statements. Range statements add definition to the performance criteria by elaborating critical or significant aspects of the criteria and enabling application in different contexts. Where the range statements contain lists, the lists generally are illustrative and not exhaustive.

PERFORMANCE-BASED COMPETENCY STANDARDS FOR PROJECT MANAGEMENT

There are performance-based standards for project management in Australia, South Africa, and the United Kingdom. The Australian National Competency Standards for Project Management were first endorsed by the Australian government on July 1, 1996, and then revised in 2004. They are the responsibility of an industry training advisory board, Innovation and Business Skills Australia (IBSA). Although New Zealand does not have its own performance-based standards for project management, it has reciprocal agreements for use of the Australian standards. In the United Kingdom, performance-based standards for project management were first endorsed by the government in early 1997. Reviewed and revised standards were endorsed in 2002 and are the responsibility of the Engineering Construction Industry Training Board (ECITB). There are also global performance-based standards for project managers developed by the Global Alliance for Project Performance Standards (formerly Global Performance Based Standards for Project Personnel [www.globalPMstandards.org]), an initiative that involves professional associations, standards and qualifications organizations, academic institutions, and industry. Available performance-based standards for project management are

- National Competency Standards for Project Management, Australia (Certificate IV, Diploma, and Advanced Diploma)
- The National Occupational Standards for Project Management, United Kingdom (NVQ Levels 4 and 5)
- National Certificate in Generic Project Management, South Africa (NQF Level 4)

All these standards are formally recognized and provide the basis for the award of qualifications within national qualifications frameworks. The National Competency Standards for Project Management also form the basis for award of professional qualifications by the Australian Institute of Project Management. In addition to these standards, there are global standards for project managers that have been developed with reference to existing standards and with the intent of providing a basis for transferability and mutual recognition of qualifications. These are

- Global Alliance for Project Performance Standards (Global Levels 1 and 2) (www.globalPMstandards.org)

National Competency Standards for Project Management, Australia

There are 12 levels in the Australian Qualifications Framework (AQF), from school level to doctorate, and the National Competency Standards for Project Management have been developed at levels of Certificate IV, Diploma, and Advanced Diploma. The standards have been adopted by the Australian Institute of Project Management as the basis for its professional registration process (Table 8.2).

There are nine units in the standards, which reflect the nine knowledge areas of the *PMBOK Guide* (Table 8.3).

The Australian performance-based standards, through both the AQF qualifications (Certificate IV, Diploma, and Advanced Diploma) and the Australian Institute of Project Management's Registered Project Manager program, are very strongly supported in Australia, with a number of organizations, including the Defence Materiel Organisation (DMO), requiring project staff to achieve these qualifications. A number of other organizations support staff in gaining the qualifications. As of January 10, 2006, 945 people had been awarded the Australian Institute of Project Management's Master Project Director certification, and 1813 had received the Registered Project Manager qualification.[16]

National Occupational Standards for Project Management, United Kingdom

The U.K. standards, which are the responsibility of the ECITB, are intended to be generic and applicable:

- *At Level 4.* To all those who take responsibility for managing projects at the operational level.
- *At Level 5.* To those with a strategic role in project management.

TABLE 8.2 AIPM Registered Project Manager Program Levels Related to Australian Qualifications Framework

AQF Level		AIPM Recognition Descriptors	Level of Experience Required for Assessment of Competence at This Level
Certificate IV	QPP	Qualified Project Professional	• Specialist or team member
Diploma	RegPM	Registered Project Manager	• Project manager of well-defined or less-complex projects • Section leader of complex-projects
Advanced diploma	MPD	Master Project Director	• Project manager of complex projects • Project manager or director of multiple projects

TABLE 8.3 Units in the Australian National Competency Standards for Project Management

	Certificate IV	Diploma	Advanced Diploma
Unit 1	Apply scope management techniques	Manage application of project integrative processes	Direct the integration of multiple projects/programs
Unit 2	Apply time management techniques	Manage project scope	Direct the scope of multiple projects/programs
Unit 3	Apply cost management techniques	Manage project time	Direct time management of multiple projects/programs
Unit 4	Apply quality management techniques	Manage project costs	Direct cost management of multiple projects/programs
Unit 5	Apply human resources management approaches	Manage project quality	Direct quality management of multiple projects/programs
Unit 6	Apply communications management techniques	Manage project human resources	Direct human resources management of multiple projects/programs
Unit 7	Apply risk management techniques	Manage project communications	Direct communications management of multiple projects/programs
Unit 8	Apply contract and procurement techniques	Manage project risk	Direct risk management of multiple projects/programs
Unit 9		Manage project procurement	Direct procurement and contracts of multiple projects/programs

Note: Level 4 of the standards does not include the unit relating to integrative processes.

The U.K. NVQ Levels 4 and 5 equate to the Australian AQF diploma and advanced diploma. The standards have been written as 51 separate units of competence, each relating to a distinct functional area covering both strategic and operational project management functions. Revision of the standards is claimed to incorporate content of the fourth edition of the *APM Body of Knowledge* (Dixon, 2000). Definition of terms within the document is taken from the *Guide to Project Management: British Standards BS6079.* Each of the two qualifications based on the standard (Levels 4 and 5) consists of a total of 20 units that must be completed, of which 11 are mandatory and 9 can be drawn from a selection of options. This allows for variation in the context (range indicators) in which the profession/occupation is performed.

National Certificate in Generic Project Management (Project Administration and Coordination) at NQF Level 4 (PMSGB/SAQA), South Africa

The South African NQF Level 4 standards are the first set of performance-based standards and associated qualifications to be produced for project management in South Africa, and work is proceeding on development of standards at other levels. The NQF Level 4 standards are at approximately the same level as the Australian AQF Certificate IV.

The National Certificate in Generic Project Management (Project Administration and Coordination) at NQF Level 4 is available with electives offering specialization in one of the following:

• Supervising a project team of a developmental project to deliver project objectives
• Supervising a project team of a technical project to deliver project objectives
• Supervising a project team of a business project to deliver project objectives
• Supporting project environment and activities to deliver project objectives

The qualification is intended to provide recognition of basic project management skills in the execution of small, simple projects or providing assistance to a project manager of large projects. The focus is primarily on skills as a project team member but includes working as a leader on a small project/subproject involving few resources and having a limited impact on stakeholders.

There are 15 core titles or units and 4 elective titles that relate to differing contexts or specializations, as indicated earlier (e.g., developmental or technical projects). The structure and number of units bear more similarity to the revised U.K. standards (ECITB, 2002) than to the Australian standards.

GLOBAL PERFORMANCE-BASED STANDARDS FOR PROJECT MANAGERS

Since the mid-1990s, there has been considerable interest in the development of global standards for project management to assist both mobile practitioners and global corporations faced with a range of different project management standards, guides, and qualifications offered by professional associations and other organizations throughout the world. Following from a global working group on standards initiated by the international project management associations, global performance-based standards for two levels of project manager have been developed. This initiative is known as the Global Alliance for Project Performance Standards (GAPPS) and formerly as the Global Performance Based Standards for Project Management Personnel (GPBSPMP).

In the course of this initiative, research was undertaken to review and compare existing project management standards and guides for knowledge and practice. Knowledge guides selected for review were

• *APMBoK: APM Body of Knowledge,* 2000 edition
• *ICB: IPMA Competency Baseline,* 1999 edition
• *P2M: A Guidebook to Project and Program Management for Enterprise Innovation,* 2001 (PMCC, Japan)
• *PMBOK Guide,* 2000 edition, PMI

Performance-based competency standards reviewed were

• *NCSPM: National Competency Standards for Project Management* (revised draft version 1.1, February 2003, BSTA, now IBSA) (Australia)
• *ECITB: National Occupational Standards for Project Management* (prelaunch version, September 2002) (United Kingdom)

- *PMSGB/SAQA: National Certificate in Generic Project Management (Project Administration and Coordination) at NQF Level 4* (South Africa)
- *PMI PMCDF: Project Manager Competency Development Framework* (2002) (PMI)

The primary focus in selecting performance-based competency standards was on those standards and/or guidelines that were developed in the context of nationally endorsed qualifications frameworks. Such standards have been developed as a basis for criterion-based assessment of workplace performance, and those available at the time the research was conducted were those of Australia, South Africa, and the United Kingdom. The PMI's *Project Manager Competency Development Framework* was also included because its format is similar to that of the government-endorsed performance-based standards.

Review and comparison of these standards[17] identified 48 concepts or topics, of which 18 were represented at the topic level in all eight of the documents reviewed. These may be considered core topics:

- Change control
- Cost management
- Document management
- Information/communication management
- Procurement
- Project closeout/finalization
- Project context/environment
- Project initiation/startup
- Project planning
- Project monitoring and control
- Quality management
- Reporting
- Resource management
- Risk management
- Time management/scheduling/planning
- Stakeholder/relationship management
- Team building/development/teamwork
- Work content and scope management

In developing the performance-based standards, the underlying assumption was that regardless of the range of responsibilities, project managers at the threshold level of competence are expected to produce essentially the same result—outputs and outcomes that are acceptable to relevant stakeholders. However, they will be required to do this in differing contexts. The CIFTER table (see Table 8.1) was developed as a basis for identifying roles based on the nature and context of projects. From this it was determined that there should be two levels of project manager standards, Global Level 1 and Global Level 2, where the Global Level 2 project manager would be operating in a more senior role and a more complex environment.

Through a series of working sessions, issue of exposure drafts, and review and response to feedback over a two-year period, performance-based standards were developed for these two levels of project manager, Global Level 1 and Global Level 2, and ready for public release in March 2006. There are six units in the standards:

PM01   Manage Stakeholder Relationships

PM02   Manage Development of the Plan for the Project

PM03   Manage Project Progress

PM04   Manage Product Acceptance

PM05   Manage Project Transitions

PM06   Evaluate and Improve Project Performance

The standards are the same for each level except that Global Level 1 is required only to demonstrate competence against the first six of the units, and Global Level 2, against all seven. The other major difference is that in order to be assessed at Global Level 1, an individual must have managed projects where the complexity factor ratings put it into the established range for Global Level 1 in accordance with the CIFTER table. In similar fashion, an individual wishing to be assessed at Global Level 2 must have managed a project whose complexity factor ratings put it into the established range for Global Level 2 in the CIFTER table (see Table 8.1).

The intent of this framework is to provide a basis for mapping of existing standards and guidance for development of new standards that will facilitate transferability across national boundaries. In developing these standards, it was explicitly recognized that there are many different approaches to the management of projects to achieve satisfactory results and that there are many different ways for project managers to develop their competence. The global standards are intentionally generic because they are written to complement other project management standards, including those of professional associations (e.g., *PMBOK Guide,* IPMA Competence Baseline, and associated national competence baselines, *APMBoK, P2M*). All these documents can be used in association with the GAPPS standards to provide further detail or specific applications.

The GAPPS initiative encourages professional associations to consider adopting these standards to support their existing standards and qualifications processes by adding and/or strengthening the performance-based dimension. Additions and modifications can be made to suit specific local and regulatory requirements. Standards and qualifications bodies are similarly encouraged to consider adopting the global performance-based standards to facilitate transferability and mutual recognition of qualifications. Professional associations that do not have their own standards or qualifications processes are encouraged to adopt the standards.

Public and private organizations also may adopt the global standards as a basis for internal development and accreditation systems that will facilitate consistency across their global operations. Even organizations that only operate locally are required to operate, source, and assess their project management personnel in an increasingly global marketplace where assurance of global relevance is of value.

ASSESSING AND DEVELOPING COMPETENCIES OF PROJECT MANAGERS

The foregoing sections of this chapter have addressed the components of project management competence, including development of standards, guides, and qualifications for project management knowledge and demonstrable performance in the form of performance-based standards and qualifications. This final section provides brief guidelines on how project management competence may be effectively assessed and developed in a manner that is relevant both locally and globally.

Project managers need competence in a number of areas. They need generic project management competence as well as competence in project management as it is practiced in particular organizations. This may include understanding and ability to manage projects in accordance with particular project governance structures and methodologies, such as the U.K.'s PRINCE2.

Figure 8.2 indicates the range of competencies likely to be relevant for a particular project management job role. The CIFTER table (see Table 8.1) suggests one way in which the job role might be categorized.

As a guide for individual self-development or for an organization wishing to design an internal accreditation process and/or program for the competency development of the project managers, it is useful to consider all the items indicated in Fig. 8.2. For project management–specific competence, it would make sense, in a global organization, to address project management knowledge by having project managers undertake the PMP examination. This is effective for use in global organizations because it is available in a number of languages. Alternatively, it would be possible to adopt the IPMA certification process, which enables reference to national competence baselines such as the *APMBoK* (United Kingdom) and the APMP examination. This then can be complemented by use of the GAPPS global performance-based standards (www.globalPMstandards.org), which can provide for the assessment and development of the use of practices or demonstrable performance. This is particularly useful in recognizing current competence and encouraging development through reflection and work experience. These standards are also designed to complement the existing knowledge guides and standards and to provide a process for transferability and mutual recognition with nationally based performance-based standards

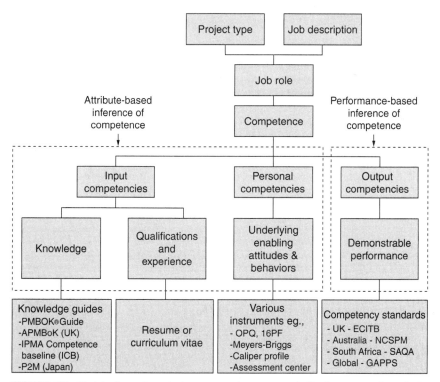

FIGURE 8.2   Model of generic project management competence indicating suggested standards, guides, qualifications, and assessment instruments.

such as those of Australia, South Africa, and the United Kingdom. These approaches will provide guidance for threshold performance and can be extremely useful as a basis for benchmarking and further development of project management competence for an individual or an organization both nationally and globally.

Development of superior performance requires that underlying enabling attitudes and behaviors be addressed. A useful approach is to design and operate a development center (also commonly referred to as an *assessment center*) that could include use of a number of personality instruments to provide individuals with a better understanding of themselves and a sound basis for reflection and development. Development/assessment centers also provide opportunities for observation and feedback given by trained assessors as a basis for personal development.

REFERENCES

1. Boyatzis RE. 1982. *The Competent Manager: A Model for Effective Performance*. New York: Wiley.

2. Spencer LMJ, Spencer SM. 1993. *Competence at Work: Models for Superior Performance*, 1st ed. New York: Wiley, p. 9.

3. *Ibid.*

4. Schroder HM. 1989. *Managerial Competence and Style*. London: Routledge, p. 67.

5. Gonczi A, Hager P, Athanasou J. 1993. *The Development of Competency-Based Assessment Strategies for the Professions* (NOOSR Research Paper No. 8). Canberra: Australian Government Publishing Service.

6. GPBSPMP Initiative. 2005. *Performance-Based Competency Standards for Global Level 1 and 2 Project Managers: Exposure Draft for Public Review, July 8, 2005*, version 0.9. Sydney: Global Performance Based Standards for Project Management Personnel.

7. Dixon, M. 2000. *APM Project Management Body of Knowledge* (4th ed.). Peterborough, England: Association for Project Management

8. Crawford LH. 2001. Project management competence: The value of standards. DBA thesis, Henley Management College/Brunel University.

9. Project Management Institute. 1999. *The PMI Project Management Fact Book*. Newtown Square, PA: Project Management Institute.

10. Crawford L. 2000. Project management competence for the new millennium, in *Proceedings of 15th World Congress on Project Management, London, England*. IPMA. London.

11. OGC, 2005, *Introduction to OGC's Project Management Method–PRINCE2*; www.ogc.gov.uk/prince2/; accessed March 14, 2006.

12. Mullaly ME, Thomas J. 2004. Linking personality and project success: Exploring the interrelationship of psychological type and project manager competency, in K Wikström, K Artto (eds.), *Proceedings of the IRNOP VI Conference in Turku, Finland, 2004*. Turku, Finland: Abo Akademi University and Helsinki University of Technology, Abo Akademi University Press.

13. Gadeken DOC. 1994. Project managers as leaders: Competencies of top performers, in *12th INTERNET (IPMA) World Congress on Project Management, Oslo, Norway*, Vol. 1. IPMA, Oslo, pp. 14–25.

14. Crawford LH. 2001. Project management competence: The value of standards. Doctoral thesis, Henley Management College/Brunel University.

15. Heywood, L., Gonczi, A., & Hager, P. 1992. *A Guide to Development of Competency Standards for Professions* (NOOSR Research Paper No. 7. Canberra: Australian Government Publishing Service.

16. AIPM. 2006. *AIPM Membership Statistics;* www.aipm.com.au/html/membership_statistics.cfm; accessed March 14, 2006.

17. Crawford LH. 2004. Global body of project management knowledge and standards, in PWG Morris, JK Pinto (eds.), *The Wiley Guide to Managing Projects*. Hoboken, NJ: Wiley.

CHAPTER 9
MANAGING RISKS AND UNCERTAINTY IN MAJOR PROJECTS IN THE NEW GLOBAL ENVIRONMENT

Roger Miller
École Polytechnique de Montréal, Montreal, Quebec, Canada

Brian Hobbs
Université du Québec à Montréal, Montreal, Quebec, Canada

Roger Miller is Jarislowsky Professor of Innovation and Project Management at École Polytechnique in Montreal and a founding partner of SECOR, a strategy consulting firm with offices in Montreal, Toronto, and Paris. His work has focused on (1) strategy and industry dynamics, (2) public policies in science and technology, and (3) project management. He was the director of the International Program in the Management of Engineering and Construction (IMEC) sponsored by 10 large international project developers. IMEC results were published by MIT Press as *The Strategic Management of Large Engineering Projects: Shaping Risks, Institutions and Governance*.

Dr. Miller is presently the director of the MINE Programme, the purpose of which is to understand the management of innovation in the context of the new economy. The data for this research consist in 240 case studies and a worldwide survey of 1500 chief technology officers. The research is being conducted by a core team located in École Polytechnique with partners at the University of Sussex, Torino, MIT, Stanford, and Toronto.

Brian Hobbs holds a degree in industrial engineering, an MBA, and a Ph.D. in management. He has been a professor at the University of Quebec at Montreal in the master's program in project management for 20-some years. This program, of which he is a past director, is accredited by PMI's Global Accreditation Center. Dr. Hobbs is very active internationally in both the project management professional and research communities. He filled a three-year mandate on PMI's Standards Members Advisory Group (MAG) ending in 2002. He is a reviewer for both the *Project Management Journal* and the *International Journal of Project Management*. He has presented several papers at both research and professional conferences organized by PMI and other project management organizations worldwide. In recent years, he has been a member of three teams of researchers that have been awarded competitively bid research grants by PMI.

The global environment for large, complex projects has changed significantly in recent years. The changes in context have produced important challenges and new approaches to the development and delivery of major projects throughout the world. The roles of the different players involved in the development and delivery of large projects have been redefined during a period of intense experimentation and innovation. New development strategies and delivery mechanisms have redefined and modified the distribution of risk among project participants. The traditional risk management approaches and tools are somewhat paradoxically more important than ever, whereas at the same time they are showing their limits and the need to be supplemented with alternative strategies to cope with uncertainty.

The first section of this chapter examines the nature of the forces behind the changing environment and their impact on the management of major projects. The second section of the chapter develops a framework for describing and analyzing the development and delivery cycle of major projects in the new global context. The framework is focused on the critical roles of the project sponsor/developer and the interaction with the institutional context. The final sections examine the nature of risks in this context and the strategies used to manage them.

THE NEW GLOBAL ENVIRONMENT FOR LARGE, COMPLEX PROJECTS

Changes in the environment of large projects have been multifaceted and systemic. Since the late 1980s and early 1990s, several forces have come into play. Over time, the interactions among them have radically altered the way large, complex projects are managed. In reality, the context of projects moved from institutional frameworks built on the assumptions of rational management to ones based on shared governance (Miller and Lessard, 2000).

As is always the case with systemic changes, there are many forces in play and many interaction effects among them. The most evident manifestations of the changing environment are globalization; the prominence of new models for project development and delivery, such as design-built, build-operate-and-transfer (BOT), and concessions; a larger role for private financing of public infrastructure; and more collaborative project structures. Many forces are at play to produce these more evident manifestations, each of which, in turn, is among the forces participating in the systemic change. Several of these forces are identified in Fig. 9.1 and are discussed below.

Ideological Shifts Favoring Privatization

Ideas are important if many people share them. Beginning with the era of Margaret Thatcher and Ronald Reagan, emphasis was put on private competition, market economies, reduced role of government, and privatization in the 1980s.

During the late 1980s and early 1990s, worldwide, most governments—national, regional, and local—were very deeply in debt. Financial markets and international agencies became more sensitive to the issue of public debt. Governments and publicly owned organizations started searching for ways to finance public infrastructure without increasing their debt load. A period of experimentation started with privatization as a significant part of this trend. The search for new means of delivering new or revamped public infrastructure with off-the-balance-sheet financing has had a very significant effect of the way many major projects are delivered.

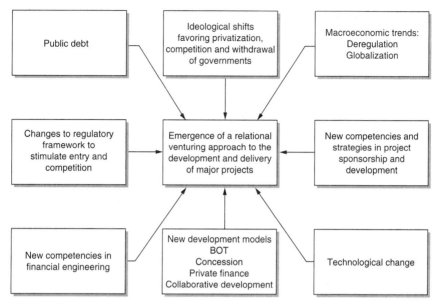

FIGURE 9.1   The new global environment.

Deregulation and Globalization of Markets

Since the late 1980s, a global trend toward deregulation and a reduction in barriers to international trade has affected the world economy. Many industries have been deregulated, and many public monopolies have been broken up or reduced in scope. Many markets worldwide have become more accessible to foreign firms. Bilateral or multilateral trade negotiations have been a major part of this trend to globalization. The result has been tremendous increases in both international commerce and investment.

Regulatory regimes encourage investments. In addition to participating in trade negotiations, some countries also have taken initiatives to stimulate interest in particular types of projects by creating or modifying the country's regulatory regimes. Conditions that apply to foreign investment and regulatory regimes were modified to allow private investment in what were previously areas reserved for state monopolies. Many countries have set up regulatory regimes to facilitate particular types of projects, BOT projects in particular.

Development of New Competencies

Responding to these initiatives, operators, concessionaires, and entrepreneurial companies from around the world became more active in many more markets than before. Over the last two decades, many firms involved in major projects in different capacities have been exploring new markets and new modes of project delivery. Many of these firms have built competencies in the initiation, organization, development, financing, design, execution, operation, or ownership of major projects.

Increased Project Scrutiny

During the 1990s, many governments promoted concession and BOT projects as a means of building new public infrastructure without increasing public debt. Many projects were financed through project finance, that is to say, financed by private financial markets based on the forecasted revenue stream of the project and without significant guarantees by either private or public participants in the project. Developing financing for projects has become a major part of project development. The nominal placement of ownership in private hands is insufficient for the financing of a project to be considered as being off the balance sheet and thus not be counted as a part of public debt.

In order to be considered as being off the balance sheet, significant control and risk must be assumed by the private party. The increased role of financial analysts subjects projects to more scrutiny and places more emphasis on the analysis and allocation of risk. The development of financial packages has increased in complexity, and financial engineering has become a key competency in project development.

Collaborative Contracting

The new modes of project development and delivery typically involve many more organizations in more interdependent roles than traditional projects organized by a dominant owner and coordinated through rigid contracts. Many of the projects in the newer modes of organization involve many specialized firms and public participants in situations of mutual interdependence. Joint ventures, consortiums, and alliances of different kinds are more often the basis for participation in major projects.

The ideal of collaborative involvement and working with alliances has been a powerful trend in organizations in all areas, not just in project management. The trend has been manifest both within and between organizations. An example that is particularly relevant to project management is concurrent engineering. This organizational arrangement has replaced sequential development in isolated departments with the creation of multidepartmental teams bringing resources specialized in manufacturing and operations into the early design of projects. Examples of collaborative and interdependent relationships among organizations include alliances, joint ventures, partnering, and outsourcing.

Cospecialization

The trend toward more specialization among organizations is not restricted to the realm of major projects. The dominant idea in the field of business strategy for more than a decade has been the division of labor in areas where organizations have distinctive core competencies and of allocating nonstrategic activities to other organizations with distinctive competencies in these areas. The ideals of the vertically integrated or widely diversified firm are challenged by the value of outsourcing and cospecialization (Chesbrough, 2003).

These major trends in organization and in strategy are part of the general context in which experimentation with new development and delivery modes were tested in the field of major projects. The fact that these practices were popular in both private and public administration legitimated and facilitated their adoption on major projects.

Technology

Some projects are in fact high-technology ventures. However, many projects implement technologies that are less high-tech. Technology has played a less dramatic and subtler role in such projects. Information and telecommunication technologies have facilitated the interdependent involvement of more players in project design and execution, often at a distance. In many cases technology facilitates the adoption of alternate modes of project development and delivery but is not a major driving force.

Experimentation and Innovation

Concessions and project finance are not new ideas. However, they had not been in widespread use prior to the 1980s. Few organizations, therefore, had significant expertise in these types of projects. This lack of expertise, combined with the ideological conviction of the natural superiority of private over public organizations, led to private firms, investors, and financial institutions assuming considerable risk and to spectacular losses on projects that failed.

This period of relatively intense experimentation, with its collection of both very successful and very unsuccessful projects, facilitated leaning by individual organizations and the development of their distinctive competencies. It also facilitated institutional learning as organizational fields became better structured and as regulatory regimes became more refined. Alternative modes of project development and delivery, such as BOT, concessions, and project finance, have become part of the repertoire of available alternatives for those initiating major projects and for those seeking to participate in them.

UNDERSTANDING THE DYNAMICS OF MAJOR PROJECTS

This second section presents a framework that describes the organization of major projects in this new environment. This framework is based on a reexamination and a further elaboration of the results of a major research program, the International Research Program on the Management of Large Engineering and Construction Projects (IMEC) (Miller and Lessard, 2000; Miller and Hobbs, 2002) and on more recent investigations by the authors.

The aim of the IMEC was to better understand the dynamic patterns that were emerging in the ways projects are structured and managed and in the approaches that are associated with successful or less successful projects. The program produced and analyzed 60 case studies of large engineering projects in both developed and developing countries on four continents that were using an approach based on grounded theorizing.

The case studies documented the evolutionary dynamics of projects from the earliest phase of inception through to commissioning and the start of operations. The average duration of these projects was 10 years, of which 6 to 7 years were devoted to front-end development phases and only 3 to 4 years to design and construction phases. Figure 9.2 sketches an archetypal representation of the dynamics of projects over the main periods of their life cycle.

The Beginning of the Project: The Search Period

Search refers to the original efforts to match needs, solutions, and opportunities. A private or public owner may signal interest in or receptivity to proposals for a project either by a policy statement or a call for proposals. Often the original show of interest is the result of a long preproject process of discussion and lobbying by different interest groups. Private sponsors/developers also initiate proposals for projects in their search for project opportunities.

Projects go through a long period during which both the problem and some elements of its solution are sorted out. The process is a search for solutions to poorly defined

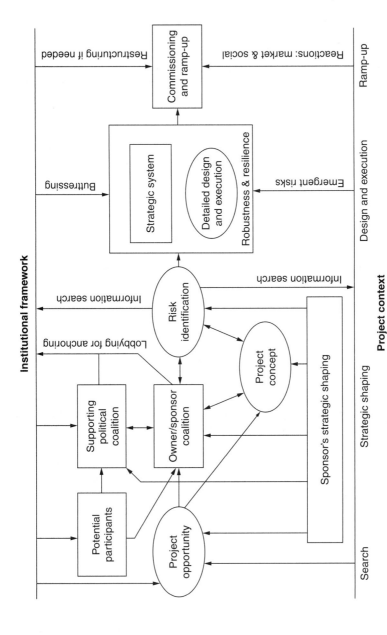

FIGURE 9.2 The life cycle of large complex projects. *(Adapted from Miller and Hobbs, 2002, p. 209; printed with permission of PMI.)*

problems that become better defined as the process unfolds. Politicians may be searching for political opportunities, whereas contractors may be searching for business opportunities. Potential sponsors from diverse fields are also searching for opportunities at the same time. This early project phase therefore has been called the *search period.*

It is often difficult to know when exactly a project starts. In retrospective, it is possible to trace the project back to its beings, the time when serious effort was first put into what would become the project concept. The search process is very nonlinear and episodic. Often the project will have been considered on different occasions over a long period of time. For example, many transportation infrastructure projects and facility development projects are in the air for decades before the timing is right to move to some form of concrete proposal for action. After all, Napoleon did start work on a tunnel under the English Channel.

The existing institutional framework or a proposed new institutional framework will define to a large extent who the main project actors can be. Regulations typically set out who can undertake particular types of projects, particularly in areas such as transportation infrastructure. Many examples have been seen over the last 20 years of governments signaling their interest in alternative project-delivery methods by indicating changes to be made to the institutional framework.

The project sponsor brings closure to the process of searching for a preliminary concept and for the organizations that could play a part in developing and delivering the project by signaling a choice. The sponsor identifies the critical issues that must be addressed, the general strategies for addressing them, and the participant organizations that can contribute to their resolution.

The Strategic Shaping Period

In order for a project to be viable, many pieces of the puzzle must come together. A project concept must be developed. A sponsor/owner coalition must be formed and structured. Political support must be mustered. The project must be anchored into the institutional framework. And project risks must be identified and a mechanism put in place for their management. The project sponsor plays a key role in moving the project opportunity forward.

A preliminary concept is developed, and a preliminary coalition is formed. The sponsor often will initiate a small number of alternative concepts in a search for a viable project. The project concept or concepts are tested in different arenas and found to be wanting in many respects. The concepts and the coalition therefore must be modified and retested. Negotiations take place with many stakeholder groups and particularly with regulator agencies and political representatives in an effort to modify and stabilize the regulatory regime or institutional framework. The project concepts, the environment, and the institutional framework are subjected to intense scrutiny from many different points of view. The sponsor plays a critical role in identifying the relevant points of view and in setting up a structure that will make certain that the relevant issues are addressed. As the issues are addressed, the concept again must be modified and retested.

Not only are the problem or opportunity and the solution being sorted out, coalitions of players are also taking form. The rhythm is broken and sporadic. Projects often go into limbo after periods of considerable exploratory activity. Exploratory processes often lead to dead ends and are abandoned, at least temporarily. Major setbacks are not uncommon because this protracted process is vulnerable to significant and unforeseen changes in the project environment. Timing is key.

This iterative process, called *strategic shaping,* molds not only the project concept but also the project organization and the way it is anchored into the institutional framework to produce a viable project (Miller and Olleros, 2000). The results of the IMEC clearly indicate that the strategic shaping process is the most critical aspect of the management of major projects. If this process produces a satisfactory result, the project has considerable chance of success.

The Design and Execution Period

In most major projects, a time can be identified when most, if not all, the pieces come into place and when significant and irreversible commitments are made. This is typically the time when major contracts are signed and financing is secured. This point marks the end of the strategic structuring phase and the beginning of the *design and execution phase*.

From this point, the management of the project is more in line with conventional project management theory and practice, which does not mean that it is issue-free but that the issues and their management are more in line with well-established project management practice.

Commissioning and Ramp-up Period

Ramp-up is the moment when assumptions become reality and revenues flow in as expected or not. At the time the artifact is put into service, many projects face severe crises because revenues are unable to cover capital and interest payments. By assuming more responsibility for the operational success of their projects, many have discovered that building the artifact is only part of the task to be mastered and that other, sometimes more challenging tasks are associated with early operation after delivery.

Under traditional procurement practices, the functioning of the artifact after commissioning has been of little or no concern to those responsible for design and delivery. However, more and more often, those executing major projects are taking on the responsibility for the effective operation of the projects in service. In concession and BOT projects, the project developer and builder also have the role of owner and operator, at least for several years. In these types of projects, the financial viability relies on early positive market reaction. Transportation infrastructure projects that rely on toll revenues and projects that depend on demand in a market that has historically been cyclical or unstable, such as the energy and natural resource sectors, are examples of capital-intensive projects that are vulnerable to low demand in the period immediately following commissioning.

In many transportation concession projects built over the last 15 years, usage levels have been lower than forecasted, particularly during the first few years of operations. Users often take time to adopt the new service. Early market responses to this type of service in areas where tolls have not been an established practice are very hard to predict. In extreme cases, the shortfall in early revenues has lead to insolvency. Many times the state has had to step in because of the bankruptcy of the concessionaire and the obvious social value of operating the artifact.

In many infrastructure projects, problems have come from adjacent systems. In some instances, the feeder systems that other parties were committed to install were not finished as planned. In other situations, a competing system was built alongside the concession. In yet other situations, governments have reneged on their commitments because of protests by pressure groups. In some cases projects have been taken over by the state because the project was too successful and the concessionaire was seen as making unreasonable profits from a public service.

MANAGEMENT OF RISK AND UNCERTAINTY

In order to fully grasp the reality of risk management in this context, a distinction needs to be made between two broad types of risks. First, there are risks that can be anticipated, and second, there are risks that merge over time and cannot be easily anticipated. The expressions *known-unknown* and *unknown-unknown* can be used to describe each. Risk management as it is practiced in the project management community is a methodology for dealing with anticipated risks. However, the specific dynamics of projects in this new global environment require different and more explicit methods for managing both antici-pated and emergent risk.

Economists have made the distinction between these two types of risk for some time. (Knight, 1921; Keynes, 1973; Adams, 1995, all quoted in Froud, 2003) For these authors, a *risk* is a future event or state that, if it materializes, will have a negative or positive impact on the project. The future event is not completely known but at least can be identi-fied or modeled. With enough effort, the probability of occurrence and the potential impact on the project can be forecasted. This definition and treatment of risk are identical to those found in the field of project management.

Uncertainty refers to the possibility of emergent indeterminate events. Under condi-tions of low uncertainty, approximate forecasts still can be made. High uncertainty entails conditions of indeterminacy where future events are neither identifiable nor amenable to calculation. The strategies for managing risks and uncertainty are quite different. Traditionally, the project management community has focused on what economists have called risk and has tended not to deal explicitly with uncertain emergent and unforeseen events.

The results of the IMEC show that large, complex projects face an average of four major unexpected and potentially catastrophic risk events despite the systematic application of very good risk management practice. Examples of emergent events are (1) a partner's bankruptcy, (2) a radical drop in demand triggered by a distant cause, (3) a noncoopera-tive attitude by ministerial officials, and (4) a political turnaround.

The emergent risks can be both *endogenous,* or internal to the project, and *exogenous,* coming from the project environment. The significant exposure to emergent risk has many causes: (1) duration and scope of projects, (2) large number of stakeholders with diverse and often conflicting interests, (3) their visibility, (4) the irreversibility of many decisions, and (5) the systemic effects found in such large complex projects.

For instance, concession and BOT projects have even more exposure because their financial viability depends on a revenue stream going out as much as 35 years. It is not possible to anticipate all the major events over a 10-year period and even less so for a 35-year period. The scope of these projects includes many different dimensions in terms of both their technical content and the areas of responsibility that must be managed.

The management of risk and uncertainty in the face of this dynamic unfolding has to go much beyond risk management as it is traditionally conceptualized and practiced in the field of project management. Risks and opportunities appear over the 10-year period during which the dynamics of projects unfold. Risks and uncertainties can be regrouped under such categories as (1) market, (2) institutional, and (3) design and construction. Risk can emerge endogenously or crop up exogenously.

Sociopolitical Impacts

Large projects tend to produce large economic, environmental, and sociopolitical impacts, both positive and negative. These impacts will affect a wide variety of stakeholders with varying and often conflicting interests. Infrastructure projects are particularly vulnerable to emergent risks from stakeholder groups because of both their physical and social visibility. Physical infrastructure projects attract a great deal of media and public attention because of their size, impact, and visibility. In addition, infrastructure projects provide services to which many constituents feel they have a right and can become the subject of political debate and claims from diverse stakeholder groups. Major projects are particularly vulnerable to being held hostage by pressure groups because beyond a certain point the decision to invest in the creation of the artifact becomes irreversible. It is difficult to halt or downsize the construction because when it is partially completed, it is worth very little. Once it is completed, it can be used for little else than its intended purpose. For all these reasons, large projects are vulnerable to both anticipated and emergent claims from stakeholders, and infrastructure projects are particularly vulnerable.

Redefinition of Roles

Projects that redefine the role of the state and participants from the private sector, both national and foreign, are even more vulnerable because they can provoke debates, claims, and protests on a very wide number of issues. These projects can be the object of debates and protests about privatization and globalization. It is difficult to anticipate all the issues that the different stakeholders might evoke when logging a claim against the project. Unforeseen claims are likely to emerge from the project environment despite the best efforts toward stakeholder and risk management.

Opportunism

Project structures such as those that have been described in this chapter involve many participants in networks of interdependent relations. Thus they are more vulnerable to endemic emergent risks related to participant behavior. Multiple interdependencies are both a cause and an effect of emergent risk. Interdependency and the increased number of relations obviously increase vulnerability to endemic emergent events related to participant behavior. On the other hand, because of higher levels of emergent risk, it is not possible to specify everything in advance, and participants are forced to accept some degree of indeterminacy and interdependency in order to maintain the flexibility that response to emergent risk requires. Overall, large projects are vulnerable to exogenous emergent risks related to stakeholder behavior. Projects that are organized as relational ventures are more vulnerable to both endogenous and exogenous emergent risks related to stakeholder behavior.

Interdependencies

A complex system is a system with many interdependent components. Large projects are certainly complex systems. Projects organized as relational ventures are more complex because they have more components that are more interdependent. All the project characteristics described earlier contribute to complexity. Because of nonlinear interaction effects, it is very difficult, if not impossible, to predict the behavior of complex systems. The more complex the system, the more emergent events are likely to manifest themselves. In complex systems it is also more difficult to predict the chain of events that any emergent event will produce. There is thus a nonlinear increase in emergent properties as systems become more complex. Because of the large number of interdependencies, complex systems are more likely to "unravel." Relatively small disturbances can provoke chain reactions that can cause substantial damage and even cause the system to collapse. Because unraveling is the result of complex interactions that are difficult to apprehend or predict, the appearance of symptoms of unraveling are perceived as emergent events. Complex systems in general and relational venturing projects in particular therefore are considerably more exposed to emergent risk. Their management must introduce mechanisms for dealing with emergent risk.

MANAGEMENT OF ANTICIPATED RISKS

Risk management is an integral part of project management; witness the risk management knowledge area in recent versions of the Project Management Institute's (PMI's) *Project Management Body of Knowledge* (PMI, 2004). Risk management as it exists in the field of project management involves identifying future probable events, analyzing the events to determine their probability of occurrence and potential impact on the project, and elaborating strategies for managing the risks. Good management of projects, therefore, requires good risk management. The best sponsors show an ability to manage risks more effectively, which, in turn, contributes to making projects more successful.

Anticipated risks are amenable to analysis, both qualitative and quantitative. The disciplines of management science and scenario building form the backbone (Miller and Lessard, 2000). The keys to effective risk management are the identification of risks, their analysis, and the elaboration of effective strategies for managing them. Rigor and discipline also are necessary to act on this information. Effective risk management relies on the identification of risks particularly in the early phases before the project concept has been elaborated. In the early phases, it is more important to identify all the potential types and sources of risk than to actually identify individual risk events.

Competent sponsors are very good at identifying the issues that will need to be resolved, and putting in place mechanisms to resolve them. Effective sponsor organizations rely a great deal on their own experience for this, but they also know who to involve in the risk management process. A wider variety of points of view is likely to be better at identifying more areas that should be of concern and will have more information and competency to draw on in all the steps of the risk management process. Having a rich coalition of project participants and a large network external to the project that the sponsor can draw on in the search for information and solutions are keys to effective identification and management of risks.

As a project gets closer to the point were commitments will be made, sponsors often organize risk management workshops where risks, risk management strategies, and the allocation of risks are reviewed for completeness and acceptability prior to commitment. Many points of view are brought to these workshops.

Effective management of risks requires the courage to withhold commitment until risks have been dealt with adequately. In the enthusiasm and drive to move projects forward, some sponsors and other participants tend to neglect downside risks, that is, risks with low probabilities but large impacts. People with a background in finance tend to be very sensitive to these types of risk and often will withhold their approval and commitment until they are dealt with. The presence of people with this type of background and this attitude is often associated with project success. It is the sponsor's role to identify the need for such scrutiny and to engage the right people.

In general, successful projects undergo more scrutiny than less successful projects. They are scrutinized from more points of view, in more detail, and more rigorously than less successful projects. Scrutiny is applied throughout the project development process and the project execution process. It is the sponsor's role to identify the issues that need scrutiny and the points of view that are relevant to each issue and to put a project organization in place that will ensure that issues are addresses as completely and as rigorously as possible.

Risk management is more than applying a method to identify and analyze risks. Project organization is an important risk management tool in large, complex projects. Effective risk management requires that the project organization include the right combination of participants and that it structures them to ensure that risks are identified and dealt with effectively. Establishing an effective project structure means identifying the issues that need to be resolved, as well as the participants with the competence and resources to deal with them, and setting up a structure that forces issues to resolution. Aligning participant roles with their particular competencies and interests in the project is a key element of the design of the project structure and of risk management. As can be seen from this description, the effective management of anticipated risks in large, complex projects in general and in relational venturing in particular goes much beyond the steps in the risk management methodology of traditional project management.

MANAGEMENT OF POTENTIAL EMERGENT RISKS

The effective management of anticipated risks actually reduces the number of risks that will be perceived as being emergent events or surprises. However, despite best efforts, emergent risks still are likely, and the project organization must be designed to manage them.

Design to withstand and manage emergent risks must be done from a complex systems perspective. The objective is to build in institutional, organizational, or governance properties that will increase the chances that responses or reactions will allow survival in the face of unforeseen events and situations. Control of emergent risks is usually indirect. In a nutshell, project design must build on the ability to imagine emergent risks early and to create a stable and supportive project environment, as well as a project governance framework that can withstand and respond to emergent risk. Several strategies for building governance properties are discussed below.

ANCHORING THE PROJECT INTO ITS INSTITUTIONAL ENVIRONMENT

The environment of a large, complex project and the interrelationships and interdependencies between the project and its institutional context are molded over a long period of time. Effective sponsors invest considerable time and effort into shaping the project and its context. There are two important aspect of the relationship between the project and its context. First, the project is developed, delivered, and eventually operated in an institutional framework composed of laws and regulations. Second, the project interacts with a wide array of external stakeholders. Each of these must be managed so as to stabilize the context and make it as supportive of the project as possible.

The results of the IMEC showed very clearly that the anchoring of a project into its institutional context is one of the most critical aspects of managing a large, complex project. This is a very active process in which the sponsors are very highly involved. The process is often very drawn out, taking several years to put in place. The process involves educating and lobbying legislators and regulatory authorities and possibly bringing pressure to bear on them. At the same time, the project concept is being elaborated and tested. There is a coevolution of the project concept and the laws and regulations that make it viable.

The level of development, stability, and specific content of regulatory regimes vary enormously from one country to the next. In countries with very weak regulatory regimes, anchoring the project and stabilizing the regulatory context may require actions that are very proactive and that would seem exceptional in other countries. Even in countries with highly developed regulatory regimes and where the rule of law is well established, anchoring of the project and stabilization of the context often require modification of existing laws and regulations or the creation of new laws and regulations. Laws and regulations provide guarantees for certain rights and privileges or can place limits on the future actions of certain parties, including the government itself. In countries where the rule of law is well established, they are enforceable in the courts.

Beyond their strictly legal implications, supporting legislation, laws, and regulations provide a great deal of legitimacy to projects. Once the supporting laws have been passed and the regulations have been put into place, stakeholders are much less likely to contest the project. By passing legislation, the government publicly commits itself to supporting the project and is more likely to come to the project's rescue in case of severe unforeseen difficulty. There are many examples of governments stepping up to save projects from collapse. This is more likely if the government's support for the project has been clearly signaled at some earlier stage and if the project provides significant public service or economic or political benefit. Anchoring to the institutional framework, therefore, has the effect of reducing the likelihood of unforeseen risk events but also increases the project's legitimacy and the likelihood of its receiving support if faced with unforeseen difficulties.

Sponsors that venture into areas previously reserved for government monopolies can evoke such a wide variety of issues over such a long period of time that it is not possible to identify all the potential stakeholders and their actions that could pose threats to the project. Successful projects show exceptional stakeholder management. However, the management of unknown stakeholders and their unforeseen actions requires measures in addition to good stakeholder management. Instilling legitimacy and momentum to the complex system that is the project can render it less likely to be attached and can increase its chances of survival.

Anchoring the project into the institutional framework confers considerable legitimacy. An effective communication plan also will be an essential ingredient in building the project's legitimacy and in creating momentum. Effective sponsors often go beyond these actions by deploying proactive cooptation strategies with potential opponents and/or opinion leaders. Early in the life of the project, before stakeholders have taken a public position with respect to the project, it is often possible to identify stakeholders that are only partially antagonistic to the project and are potential opinion leaders. If a group of affected parties or a pressure group is brought into the project development and approval process and eventually supports the project, their presence and actions confer significant legitimacy to the project. This not only virtually removes the possibility of opposition from these groups but also provides sufficient legitimacy and momentum to reduce the likelihood of other groups being mobilized in opposition to the project.

CREATING A PROJECT CONCEPT AND ORGANIZATION TO ENHANCE GOVERNABILTY

Creating a project organization that will be able to face unforeseen difficulties and capture yet unknown opportunities can be likened to building a team to do the same. In building the team, the sponsor must choose and motivate the members, establish the network of interdependent relationships among them, and allocate roles, responsibilities, and risks. The team will need to remain cohesive and to attack emergent issues as problems to be solved. To solve the future problems, they will need to have the incentive and motivation to work together. To be able to solve the yet unidentified problems, they will need to make creative use of the diverse and rich set of skills and resources they bring collectively to the project. In solving the emergent problems, both the project concept and the project organization may need to be modified or adapted. Flexibility in the organization and the concept will facilitate the necessary adaptation.

Inversely, a project organization in which the members have no real incentive to solve collective problems but are motivated to exit the project or escalate internal conflicts is more likely to unravel in the face of an emergent crisis. Project teams and project plans that have been optimized in terms of material resources and competencies to meet the anticipated project requirements and risks are likely to fall short in attempts to solve emergent problems. Likewise, rigid project organizations and concepts are less likely to be adaptable to unforeseen situations.

Projects as complex systems need to be instilled with the properties of cohesion and resilience in order to perform well in unforeseeable situations. As complex systems, they must have the requisite variety to deal with the situations they will face. In other words, their repertoire of possible responses must be at least as rich as the set of situations they will face. In practical terms, this means that the project organization must have a rich set of competencies and resources at its disposal if it is to be able to solve future problems. This is best accomplished by having an organization whose members have diverse competencies and backgrounds and also have surplus professional and material resources that they can draw on if needed.

Having the professional and material resources to solve problems is insufficient. Team members must have the motivation and incentive to do so. This is best accomplished through ownership in both the psychological sense of commitment and in the sense that the team members have a material incentive to make the project a success. In structuring the project, the sponsor must establish a project organization in which all the key players have the motivation and the incentive to solve problems creatively and make extra efforts if the project gets into difficulty. Creating a project organization whose members have the incentives and the means to solve problems will instill flexibility and responsiveness into the system.

Effective sponsors take additional measures to instill flexibility into their projects. The project front-end development takes several years, and it is not possible to foresee the exact situation that will prevail when the final concept is chosen. Developing alternate scenarios and concepts and delaying commitment to the final concept give the project more flexibility. In some projects, it is possible to use modular designs that allow partial execution or more flexibility, but this is only possible on certain projects. Instilling flexibility gives a project more resilience in the face of emergent risks, but there is a cost to flexibility. Developing alternate scenarios and delaying concept selection generate costs and delays and can lead to suboptimal design.

Creating a project concept and organization to deal with emergent risk is a very active and very lengthy process. The project sponsor exercises influence on the project context and anchors the project into this context. The sponsor also conceptualizes the project as a complex system and builds a cohesive, resilient, and responsive organization. In so doing, the sponsor goes much beyond the management methods that are effective for the management of anticipated risks.

COPING WITH TRADEOFFS IN THE MANAGEMENT OF ANTICIPATED AND EMERGENT RISK

The approaches used by effective sponsors to manage anticipated and emergent risks are often complementary, but in some cases they create paradoxes. Tradeoffs are necessary.

The management of both anticipated and emergent risks relies on rigorous and continuous scrutiny of the project and its environment, which, in turn, relies on the competencies and incentives of both the project participants and the networks to which they have access. Being able to draw on diverse points of view and skill sets in the analysis of a risk and in the elaboration of a response will be of great value whether the risk is anticipated or not. A project structure that allocates risks to those parties with the means to control and respond will be more effective in dealing with risks, whether they are anticipated or not.

However, there are two important paradoxes in attempting to establish a project concept and organization that will anticipate risks and manage them effectively and at the same time be resilient and responsive in the face of unforeseen events. First, an organization that does a very good job of anticipating risks must realize that its job is only partly done and that no amount of anticipatory risk management will prepare it well to deal with emergent risk. Somewhat paradoxically, the organization must plan for the future while knowing that the future will be different from that which it plans.

Second, the most efficient and effective means for dealing with anticipated risks can introduce rigidities that reduce cohesion and responsiveness in the face of emergent events. A rigid allocation of risks may create a situation in which project participants have no motivation or incentive and limited possibilities to solve problems collectively. Rigid contracts may be very efficient for the management of anticipated risks, but their highly specified nature introduces rigidities that may hamper efforts to modify a project and adapt to an emerging situation. There is a paradox between contractual efficiency in the management of anticipated events and the provision of flexibility to respond to emergent situations, often through contingent contracts. Striking a balance between the two requires considerable judgment on the part of the project sponsor and participants.

CONCLUSION

Project sponsors and owners must create a project system that will effectively identify and manage risks, applying excellent risk management as it is conceived and practiced in the project management community to a very wide array of risks. However, the indeterminate nature of this complex system requires that the project organization also be designed to face unanticipated or emergent risk as effectively. Infusing the project organization with the properties of cohesion and resilience requires an approach that goes beyond the risk management approach currently practiced in the field of project management. To face uncertainty, successful sponsors and owners must expend much greater resources on imagining and creating futures than a traditional model would suggest. Good sponsors and owners become project champions that

> *Dream big but willingly submit to discipline and due diligence.* Good project champions make daring acts of faith and sketch utopias as wonderful, compelling possibilities. During the front-end period, creative ideas need to predominate. Nevertheless, projects must be submitted to tests periodically. Without discipline, erroneous commitments may be made or projects may be abandoned prematurely. Worse, the wrong projects may be built efficiently.
>
> *Avoid locking in too early or too late.* Good sponsors and owners are cautious in making irreversible commitments, but they recognize that eventually they must make such commitments. Sponsors must avoid making irreversible commitments until they gain enough knowledge to make reasoned choices. Effective sponsors cannot remain flexible indefinitely; eventually, bold actions and large investments are necessary. By contrast, during the engineering and construction period, committing as fast as possible to

build and operate the project will generate flows of revenue early. Flexibility at this stage usually will not make sense; full commitment is necessary.

Shaping the future rather than planning in detail. If the future could be predicted adequately, contracts could be designed to lock in on the most rational options. Unfortunately, the future is often unknowable in advance. The longer the development time, the higher is the likelihood that projects will be affected by turbulence. If events go unchecked by the timely actions of sponsors, degenerative processes may ensue.

Effective sponsors recognize explicitly that projects are not once-and-for-all decisions but rather journeys characterized by multiple decision episodes. During the front-end period, the role of the sponsor is first to foster multiple perspectives by enlarging the boundaries of groups participating in the project and shaping moves to break indeterminate situations. As uncertainty reveals itself, leverage can be applied to make desired futures happen. Reasoned commitments thus are made in the face of uncertainty.

REFERENCES

Chesbrough H. 2003. *Open Innovation: The New Imperative for Creating and Profiting from Technology.* Boston: Harvard Business School Press.

Froud J. 2003. The private finance initiative: Risk, uncertainty and the state. *Account Organ Soc* 28:567–589.

Miller R, Hobbs B. 2002. A framework for analyzing the development and delivery of large capital projects, in D Slevin, D Cleland, J Pinto (eds.), *The Frontiers of Project Management Research.* Newtown Square, PA: Project Management Institute, pp. 201–210.

Miller R, Lessard DR. 2000. *The Strategic Management of Large Engineering Projects: Shaping Institutions, Risks and Governance.* Cambridge, MA: MIT Press.

Miller R, Olleros X. 2000. Project shaping as a competitive advantage, in R Miller, DR Lessard (eds.), *The Strategic Management of Large Engineering Projects: Shaping Institutions, Risks and Governance.* Cambridge, MA: MIT Press, pp. 93–112.

Projevt Mmanagement Institute (PMI). 2004. *A Guide to the Project Management Body of Knowledge (PMBOK Guide),* 3d ed. Newtown Square, PA: Project Management Institute.

CHAPTER 10
MANAGING HUMAN ENERGY IN THE PROJECT-ORIENTED COMPANY

Pernille Eskerod

University of Southern Denmark, Esbjerg, Denmark

Pernille Eskerod holds a M.Sc. in business administration (1192) and a Ph.D. (1996). In 1990 she completed, among other courses, an MBA-course in project management at Oregon State University. She was a visiting researcher in 1997 at the Umea School of Business, Umea University, Sweden, and in 2001 at the Vienna University of Economics and Business Administration, Austria. In 2005 she taught project management at the Vienna International Summer University at the Vienna University of Economics and Business Administration.

Since 1993, she has been a member of the Danish Project Management Association. Since 2001, she has been chairman of a research and education group in the association and conducts three annual seminars for teachers and researchers in project management. Further, she was involved in developing the Danish Project Management Competence Baseline in 2002 and the Scandinavian Project Management Competence Baseline in 2004.

Currently, she is an associate professor of project management at the University of Southern Denmark. There she conducts research and teaches in the field of project management and organizational behavior. She has published a number of papers on project management and participates in international conferences every year.

A project-oriented company is an organization that uses projects as its main structural element. The projects are expected to ensure the necessary level of renewal and learning in the organization and enable the organization to accommodate the many demands and possibilities it is confronted with in the form of prompt shifts in customer preferences, technology, competition, legislation, supplier structure, composition of personnel, etc. However, it is not unproblematic to manage a project-oriented company. Research (e.g., Eskerod, 1997, 1998; Eskerod et al., 2004) has shown that actors in many project-oriented companies experience the situation that there are many projects to accomplish but only few resources available. Both managers and employees report that they feel they have lost overview of the portfolio of projects owing to the high number of projects. At the same time, distressed and suffering projects can be observed. Some are never accomplished, while others end up with time and budget overruns, specifications and quality requirements not met, dissatisfied stakeholders, and/or failure to achieve the purpose of the project. On top of this, some employees display symptoms of stress and burnout. It seems very difficult for company management to balance ideas, wishes, and demands with the resource capacity of the organization. Since it may be difficult to choose among promising project proposals and running projects, many managers (at all levels) are constantly seeking more efficient ways to make use of the resources, not least the human resources the employees posses. The purpose of this chapter is to discuss how it is possible to influence employees in a project-oriented company in ways that make them, at the same time, perform well and enjoy working for the company, thus taking care of and supporting the human resources over the short and long term.

In the project management literature, human resources are understood and conceptualized as calendar time booked for the projects. The underlying assumption is that a formal agreement on providing a certain number of personnel hours to the project in question will provide the project with sufficient contributions in form of work effort, knowledge, attention, etc. This assumption seems to be too simple because many projects are not accomplished in a satisfying manner even though project plans are worked out and staffing of the project with competent team members is done. Instead of discussing project performance by means of having sufficient human resources in form of calendar time, performance by means of having enough human energy will be discussed in this chapter.

Human energy is difficult to define and measure. It is intangible and impossible to quantify in the same manner as calendar time can be quantified. It has to do with enthusiasm, attention, competencies, motivation, commitment, and capacity. However, being energetic/full of energy is not a stable state. The level changes from one person to another, but it certainly also changes over time for a single individual. It may change during the day, the week, the month, or the year. Even though it is hard to conceptualize, it is easy to feel whether a person is energized or not in his or her work on a specific task or project. The same holds true for a team as a whole.

Human energy relates a lot to motivation. Motivation is not an easy concept either. It can be defined as "an invisible inner force that drives a person to act" (Andersen, 2005, p. 293; author's translation). In the project management literature, motivation of a team member is not discussed very thoroughly. The reason may be that the mere act of being assigned to a project is assumed to be motivational in itself. Projects are assumed to be attractive owing to the fact that they are very goal-oriented, task- and action-oriented, and unique when it comes to process and/or result. Relating a job as a project team member or project manager to a very well-known model, the job-characteristic model, offered by Hackman and Oldham (1975), a project participant provides high scores on all the job core dimensions mentioned in the model (i.e., autonomy, skill variety, task identity, task significance, work feedback, friendship opportunities, and initiated task interdependence). Therefore, project work is supposed to lead to fulfilment of critical psychological states and thereby be motivational in itself. Another reason why motivation is not a significant part of the project management literature may be that the theoretical roots are grounded in engineering science (Packendorff, 1995; Söderlund, 2002) and a planning perspective (Eskerod, 1997, 1998) or a task perspective (Andersen, 2005) and thereby not emphasizing the humans involved (very much).

This chapter rests on the assumption that both employees and managers in a project-oriented company would gain from a deeper understanding on how certain ways of managing the project portfolio and the single projects influence the energy of the people involved in the projects and thereby also accomplishment of the projects. Of course, management is only one of many internal and external factors influencing the accomplishment of projects. However, discussing other factors is outside the scope of this chapter.

The structure of this chapter is as follows: In the second section, a research project, "The Project Effective Company," on which the chapter is based is presented. The research project included empirical studies in 30 companies. Based on the study, two new concepts, "energy killers" and "energy creators," are offered to describe the impact of various actions or lack thereof on human energy. The energy killers and energy creators identified in the organizations involved are presented. In the third section, the empirical findings are related to theoretical concepts, and three themes especially valuable for interpreting the data are offered. These themes are conception of time, conception of pressure, and conception of importance. In the fourth section, concluding remarks are made.

THE RESEARCH PROJECT

To be able to understand how the energy possessed by employees is influenced by the way projects and project portfolios are managed, it is important to notice that the project is not the proper unit of analysis. Even though the single project manager is assumed to have a significant potential influence on the motivation and commitment of individual team members, focus in this chapter is broader owing to the fact that the person in question (whether this person is a team member or a project manager) is affected by all the projects and tasks he or she is engaged in. Therefore, the single person is chosen as the unit of analysis, and human energy is studied from the perspective of the individual and his or her whole situation at work. (Of course, human energy may be affected a lot of things besides work-related issues, for example, health, family situation, leisure activities, age, etc. However, discussing these issues is beyond the scope of this chapter.)

I have undertaken a number of empirical studies to investigate the effects on the individual of being in a multiproject environment [studies and findings are presented in Eskerod and Darmer (1994); Eskerod (1995, 1996, 1997, 1998); Eskerod et al. (2004); Blichfeldt and Eskerod (2005); and Eskerod and Jepsen (2005); Eskerod et al. (2005)]. However, one of the empirical studies seems to qualify as especially valuable when it comes to discussing issues that may promote or impede energy of the employees. This study is presented in the following section.

Research Method

In order to investigate how project portfolios are managed in companies, I was involved in a research project, "The Project Effective Company". Over a period of two years (2002–2004), a multimember researcher team[1] worked with 30 Danish companies while applying a qualitative research strategy. The primary goal of the research project was to get a deeper understanding of how top management, middle management, and project team members in the companies perceived how the "sum" of projects is managed. What are the challenges related to managing and coordinating the activities/projects? Which decisions, dilemmas, and possibilities does the portfolio of projects impose on the companies? It should be noticed that the portfolio of projects on which the project focuses was not solely composed of product-development projects, which are the most common project type in the project portfolio management literature. On the contrary, the project focused on the entire spectrum of projects and project-like tasks in the individual companies,

---

[1]The research team was composed of four senior researchers and five research assistants. The institutions involved were the Centre for Industrial Production, Aalborg University; the Department of Environmental and Business Economics, University of Southern Denmark; and the Department of Operations Management, Copenhagen Business School.

including, for example, renewal projects, strategic projects, information technology (IT) projects, department-specific projects, and production-based projects.

The primary source of evidence employed by the group of researchers was interviews. In total, the research project draws on 128 interviews. However, quantitative data were obtained from additional sources, including project handbooks, project lists, computer systems and databases, and other company-specific documents. Furthermore, additional data were obtained as the group of researchers engaged in a series of workshops with the companies—workshops at which the researchers' preliminary interpretations, findings, and conclusions were discussed with the group of participants upon which the empirical study draws.

Findings

Findings presented in this chapter represent only a small fraction of all the findings generated in the research project. However, statements and discussions about (the lack of) human energy took up a big portion of the time in the interviews, especially in the interviews with team members and project managers, because the energy theme was especially prominent in the minds of these groups. Therefore, the issues are mainly derived from the discussions with team members and project managers and are as seen from the perspective of the employees. However, the issues were brought to top management by the research team, and therefore, their comments are also included in the following presentation of the energy killers and energy creators.

Energy Killers.   The following issues were identified as reasons for a decrease in the feeling of being enthusiastic, motivated, and committed to the project work:

- High pressure because of many simultaneous projects
- Lack of attention from top management
- Incomprehensible interventions in the projects
- Unclear roles
- Too little pressure owing to a long project course and/or a slow startup
- Lack of sufficient follow-up

High Pressure Because of Many Simultaneous Projects.   Many of the employees interviewed found that the number of projects was too high in relation to the number of people involved. Many employees are engaged in several projects simultaneously, and they have to split their work on the projects and shift quite often. The employees claim that they loose a lot of energy from changing from one project to the other. At the same time, they feel that they never accomplish anything. Even though they work very hard every day, only a small fraction of the work gets finished. This feels like an extra burden/ pressure and drains the energy level. One employee described[2] it this way:

> . . . You run around from one project to another in the organization, and you don't get into the depth, because you are happy just to get through with your current meeting and be able to head on to the next.

---

[2]The interviews were carried out in Danish. Statements from the interviews offered in this chapter are translated by the author.

According to the literature (Cooper et al., 1999, 2000), an important part of project portfolio management is to select among project proposals in such a way that the resource requirements match the resource capacity. Therefore, it may seem surprising that employees in the majority of the companies involved in the research project feel that the organization runs too many projects simultaneously. The empirical data revealed a lot of explanations for this.

The most striking finding is that many top managers believe that a healthy company is an organization that runs many projects and has many projects in the pipeline. The mere number of projects is seen as a way for the company/top management to signal healthiness. Therefore, they claim, the motivation to cut down the number of projects is not very high.

Another issue influencing the number of projects is that it is not easy for top managers to select between the various projects and project proposals because it is difficult to determine the benefits of each project. Top managers are afraid of missing a good option if they don't run for the various opportunities. Therefore, they are very reluctant to say no.

A third issue is that nobody in the companies seems to have an overview of the (full) resource requirements and capacity. Projects are initiated both locally in the departments and centrally in the organization, and nobody feels responsible for collecting information about all initiatives.

Further, it is difficult to estimate resource requirements because many of the project tasks are new, and therefore, the estimates cannot be based on earlier experience. In combination with this, the employees claim that it is difficult to estimate resource capacity. As mentioned earlier, it may be possible to calculate the calendar time available but not the energy/working capacity: "On a good day I can accomplish this task in two hours; on a bad day it takes me eight hours."

Not only are there difficulties in terms of determining the list of projects and the resource requirements and capacity, but some top managers also point out that they do not want an overview to exist. They are afraid that the organization will loose flexibility and dynamics if they emphasize planning very much. Further, they are afraid that employees will feel overwhelmed if they become more conscious of the amount of work they are supposed to do. They prefer a "muddling through" way of working. These thoughts are illustrated by the following statements offered by three top managers:

> I truly believe that a better resource management would have the effect that we didn't start up so many projects. On the other hand, we would not be that dynamic.
>
> I am a little against that you organize [the projects] in lists and plans— "This project goes from here to there and require these and these resources." Quite soon [all] the resources have been spent. Our customers don't care about this. They don't give a damn whether we have resources or not. They just want to get the products to the right price and the right quality.
>
> To allocate resources [for a list of projects] would give a picture to which people would say, "Pooh!" . . . So if you [make the resource requirements visible by calculating estimates on project outlines], people almost say, "Pooh, we cannot do it, because we don't have all these resources." By not [making the resource requirements visible] we have motivated a lot of people to speed up because they were forced to get the work done in the time [available].

These statements relate to the amount of pressure on employees. Many top managers feel that performance will be higher if their employees are challenged very hard at all times. Running several projects simultaneously is a way of creating a sense of urgency. Two statements illustrate this:

> We try all the time to place the bar a little higher than last time to see whether it is possible to accomplish something extra.
>
> I guess we have more things running than we should if you would calculate. But taken together, I think it is good. All the time we have a little more on the plate than you can eat.

To conclude, the empirical study shows that employees (including project managers) and top managers do not (fully) agree on whether the high number of simultaneous projects is an issue or not. Employees feel that their performance and their work satisfaction would be much better if the number of projects they had to work on at the same time was smaller, whereas many top managers only pay lip service to the wish for a lower number of projects because they have many reasons to keep the number high.

Lacking Attention from Top Management. An energy-draining issue often referred to by the employees interviewed is insufficient or unstable attention from top management. A typical scenario is that top management is very interested in the project in the project initiation phase, but when the project proposal has been approved and the project manager and project team have been assigned, many top managers more or less forget about the project and turn their attention to other duties and new project proposals. A top manager says:

> When starting new projects up, a risk is that top management gets fed up with the [old] project. Then you don't feel like engaging in this project anymore because something else is more fun. I must admit that this is a bit as it is here . . . [concerning] the "Quality on Time Project." We assume that it flickers around somewhere out there, but we [top management] are not interested in this project anymore. . . . Now it is the "Lean Project" that occupies [our minds].

Incomprehensible Interventions in the Projects. Project team members and project managers fully understand that new internal and external conditions may lead to changed priorities in the portfolio of projects. This may be caused by, for example, changes in customer preferences, technology options, workforce, legislation, etc. Furthermore, they accept that this may lead to changes in the content and objectives of some of the projects. However, a true energy drainer arises if top management intervenes and requires changes in the project course based on the fact that they did not involve themselves (in time and according to the project plan) and thus did not contribute to defining the scope, objectives, and concepts of solutions at the time the project team worked with these issues. Further, the employees do not understand why some top managers suddenly dictate solutions that are not better than the ones proposed by the project teams but only pop up (it seems) because the top manager has not understood or accepted the concept of solutions developed by the project team. These interventions may be caused by lack of top management attention, as mentioned earlier, or may be caused by the fluctuating attention of top managers owing to the fact that they are having an "on-again, off-again" interest in the project.

Unclear Roles. Both project team members and project managers state that they wish to work on profitable projects and they want to do it in an efficient way. Most of them prefer well-defined and well-organized projects, and they want top management to take part in formulating objectives and determining the scope of the project. Ambiguity and unclear expectations concerning the roles of different project participants (including the project owner) drain the individuals for energy. Furthermore, if doubt arises about whether the person in question or another team member has the necessary competence, frustration will be created, and frustration invariably consumes energy.

Too Little Pressure Owing to a Long Project Course and/or a Slow Startup.   Project participants want to see and show results. The energy disappears if the project course is too long. One team member stated:

> A renewal project . . . must not take a long time. If it lasts a whole year, it will be forgotten. In any case, [the project team] has to deliver some very quick results, part results. . . . otherwise the energy disappears.

One problem with a long project course is that in the beginning the project participants feel that they have plenty of time. Therefore, they are disinclined to start. This becomes especially problematic when team members work "on and off" on the project, and the project is put on hold because of other more urgent and/or exciting tasks.

Another issue that may create an energy loss is the time span of the preparation phase and/or the startup phase. A quick start, in which you almost jump directly to the execution phase, may take advantage of the energy, enthusiasm, and optimism that often exists when an idea arises. If enthusiasm and commitment are present, the project may be able to run very long on the energy created. However, it is important to notice that this energy disappears immediately if it is shown that the project is on a wrong track.

Lack of Sufficient Follow-up.   Many team members and project managers claim that a big energy drain is caused by insufficient follow-up on plans and promises. No one seems to care if a milestone is not reached. Often it is very easy to convince top management that new information indicates that the original plans were not good enough and/or that other tasks and projects have become more important. A top manager recognizes this scenario. About the consequences of being very tolerant with overruns in the plans, he says:

> The projects typically flatten out, and at last they flicker, if you don't take care. In the beginning, an immense amount of energy is present, but then [the project manager and the team members] find out that when they overrun a milestone, almost nothing happens. And this may be a problem that we don't do anything—respond more vigorously—when the milestone is not reached. If you just allow the milestones not to be met [according to the plan], as we tend to, because new projects are born and we focus on them, then it all starts to flicker.

Another top manager claims that he does not want to follow up:

> I don't . . . follow up. In this house we operate this way: When you get a project task, and you have presented your time schedule, then you [are expected] to follow the plan. . . . I don't have copies of the time schedules of the employees, and I don't walk around and check up. It is not my task. It is their own task. If they get behind schedule, they must tell. If [one of the employees] cannot [cope with this way], then he [or she] is in the wrong place. Otherwise, I do not have the time to do anything else [than spending time on checking up].

Energy killers derived from the empirical study have now been presented. In the next section energy creators are presented.

Energy Creators.   Based on the empirical data, a number of issues were identified as ways to increase attention, motivation, and commitment to the project work. The following list presents suggestions given by those interviewed to avoid the energy killers mentioned in the preceding section:

- Accomplish fewer projects simultaneously
- Close down projects that are not assigned a high priority
- Make a clear prioritization among projects
- Provide persistent top-management attention
- Involve top management in status reviews
- Communicate reasons for changes/interference initiated by top management
- Work out and communicate role expectations
- Provide help to the single employee on how to prioritize his/her tasks and projects
- Create a sense of urgency by defining many milestones
- Demand frequent results/subdeliveries from the project team
- Make frequent status reports concerning accomplishments
- Celebrate accomplishments

Besides the list of energy creators designed to prevent the emergence of energy killers, the employees interviewed in the empirical study pointed to other ways to create energy in the project-oriented company. These issues were not mentioned as frequently as the ones in the preceding list, but the data cannot reveal which ones were conceived as the most important in terms of improving the level of human energy:

- Staff the project with fiery souls
- Initiate/engage in dialogues with individual project team members
- Create individual and personal objectives as supplements to project objectives
- Acknowledge high performance and learning and give feedback on this
- Make the project visible in the organization
- Speak about the project and emphasize its importance
- Conduct short and efficient meetings instead of long ones

Since these energy creators are more or less self-explanatory, elaborations will not be offered. Instead, the energy killers and energy creators are related to existing theory in the next section.

EMPIRICAL FINDINGS RELATED TO EXISTING THEORY

The preceding section offered a close look at the empirical data. The purpose of this section is to take one step back and discuss the empirical data in further depth by introducing three themes of specific interest: conception of time, conception of pressure, and conception of importance. The thorough study and huge amount of data generated in "The Project Effective Company" offer opportunities for analyzing the data from many different perspectives. However, the themes mentioned earlier seem especially valuable when it comes to understanding the impact on human energy in relation to how management of projects and portfolios takes place. The three themes should not be seen as complementary; instead, they supplement each other.

Conception of Time

The very notion of applying projects as the main structural element in a company points to time as an important issue. A project is a temporary organization, and conception of time is one of the four concepts that differentiate a temporary organization from a permanent organization according to Lundin and Söderholm (1995). (The other concepts are team, task, and transition.) Temporary and permanent organizations differ in two fundamentally different aspects relevant for time conception. The aspects are the length of sight applied and the types of tasks associated with the type of organization. A temporary organization has a limited predefined life span, and in this lifetime, the more or less unique objectives of the project must be reached. The project team has only one chance to accomplish the project successfully. A permanent organization, of course, also has deadlines. But termination of the organization is not given in advance, as it is in a temporary organization. The permanent organization is expected to have eternal life, and at the same time, certain tasks and obligations must be taken care of again and again (making a yearly statement, annual plans and follow-ups, etc.). These different conditions in the two types of organizations influence the conception of time. Roughly speaking, time can be conceived of as linear in a temporary organization, whereas it can be conceived of as cyclic in a permanent organization. [New project management trends, for example, agile movement, suggest incorporation of cyclic thinking in projects (Highsmith, 2004). Furthermore, time can be conceived of as a spiral in a permanent organization (Burell, 1992). However, these nuances are not relevant to the topic discussed in this chapter.]

Lundin et al. (2001) offer two distinct categories of how to conceive of time in that they introduce the concept "master clock" and "countdown clock." The master clock is the overall clock, which runs for everyone. It "runs from infinity to eternity" (Lundin et al., 2001, p. 2). The countdown clock, on the other hand, runs from the defined start to zero. When a temporary organization (i.e., a project) starts, the organization starts to "consume" time in a countdown manner. This time cannot be replaced.

The reason why time is such an important issue in projects is that time conception can be seen as a way to motivate project participants and to help them make sense of their way of working and prioritizing among different tasks. The countdown time imposes a sense of urgency with regard to task completion. A project plan communicates (agreed on) expectations of the project team. Setting challenging goals related to time by defining milestones and deadlines is assumed to stimulate effort and commitment (Shawn et al., 1995). The reason is that it guides the attention of project participants because time-specific objectives produce a kind of competition within the individual: "Is it possible to reach the milestones or not?"—and maybe thoughts such as: "I perceive myself as a responsible and reliable person. A responsible and reliable person meets deadlines. It is therefore of utmost importance that I meet the deadlines in the project."

At the same time, the project work is more or less well defined because the scope of the project is explicitly defined. This is another way of focusing the attention of the project participants.

Conception of time and explicitly defined objectives and tasks help project participants to concentrate on accomplishing the project work. However, as the empirical data have shown, if an individual employee is assigned to more than one project at the same time, a lot of unwanted disturbance might appear. Instead of focusing on the single project, the individual has to slice time and use only a fraction of the work time on each project (or other task) before shifting to another project. According to the empirical data, this time slicing causes severe mental startup costs in every shift because most project work requires mental absorption, and absorption takes time. Therefore, many shifts place big requirements on the cognitive capacity of the person in question.

The mere idea of being confronted with several countdown clocks ticking at the same time creates a large amount of pressure on the individual. (Conception of pressure will be discussed in the next section.)

However, data from the interviews point to the fact that everyone is not affected in the same way by being assigned to several projects simultaneously. Some people thrive on the opportunity to shift from one task to the other. They become bored if they have to work on only one project at a time. Others claim that sometimes they prefer to be absorbed in the same task for a longer time and at other times enjoy the speed and excitement of rapid shifts.

An approach to discussing different reactions to a work situation that requires accomplishing several tasks simultaneously is presented by Hall (1977), who offers the concepts "monochrone" and "polychrone" cultures. A "monochrone culture" (according to Andersen, 2005) is characterized by valuing the members doing one task at a time, observance of the time schedule, strict prioritization of the degree of importance of the various tasks, etc. Such cultures are dominant in northern Europe, England, the United States, and Japan. A "polychrone culture," on the other hand, is characterized by the fact that members value doing more things at the same time and let the work take the time necessary to be accomplished. These cultures are dominant in southern Europe, South America, the Arabic countries, and Southeast Asia (Andersen, 2005). The interesting part is that the concept also can be applied to individuals. Andersen (2005) points to two different methods to measure the "polychronicity" of an individual. One is called the "modified polychronic attitude index" (Lindquist et al., 2001), and the other is called the "inventory of polychronic values" (Bluedorn et al., 1992, 1999). Several research projects have been carried out (Andersen, 2005) to determine who are the most "polychone" individuals. No relations have been found to age and gender. However, it has been shown that a long formal education is positively correlated with a higher degree of "polychronism" (Kaufmann et al., 1991).

Related to the empirical data this chapter rests on, combined with the concepts of "polychronic" and "monochromic" individuals, a conclusion is that top management may benefit from trying to figure out how the individuals in the workforce of the company cope with doing many tasks simultaneously.

Conception of Pressure

As presented previously, employees and top management do not agree when it comes to assessing the right amount of pressure caused by project work. Many employees claim that many deadlines and many projects running at the same time drain their energy because they don't get sufficient time for absorption in the work of a single project. Top management, on the other hand, believes that high pressure leads to better performance and more project work accomplished.

Research (Friend, 1982) has shown that a high number of stress-related stages (i.e., anxiety, arousal, and activation) impairs performance of the individual. An interesting point is that even high motivation may impair performance. A commonly held assumption is that the relation between stress or pressure and performance can be illustrated by an inverse U (Fig. 10.1) (Archer, 1991; Bloisi et al., 2003; Andersen, 2005). This relation is called the *Yerkes-Dodsons law* (Andersen, 2005).

This model can be used to understand the disagreement between employees and top management. Employees feel that they are situated at the right side of the optimum. This means that they are not able to perform at their highest level because the pressure resulting from too many simultaneous projects makes them perform less than optimally. Top managers, on the other hand, are afraid that employees are situated to the left side of the

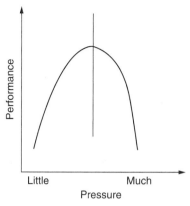

FIGURE 10.1 Relation between pressure and performance.

optimum. Therefore, they want to put a bit more pressure on the organization. Parkinson's law offers an explanation to what is going on in the minds of the top managers. Parkinson (1957, p. 2), referred to in Andersen (2005, p. 168), says: "Work expands so as to fill the time available for its completion." If top managers think that Parkinson's law is working, then employees always will feel that they have not got any extra time for new tasks. Therefore, a certain pressure is the only way to make sure that employees use their time efficiently.

Determination of when work pressure is too high and when it is appropriate, of course, can only be done in the empirical setting. However, the concepts offered in this section may give top managers and employees a tool to reflect on and discuss in relation to their conception of pressure.

Conception of Importance

In the empirical study, many of the employees interviewed did point to the fact that a big problem in the project-oriented company is that it is difficult to determine what is important and what is not. The employees do not know which tasks they should focus on, and top management does not know which projects and project proposals to pick from the many possibilities.

Ambiguity and unclear expectations are mentioned as energy killers. Further, data from the interviews show that many top managers prefer to delegate the project to the project team. This is in line with McGregor's (1966) Theory Y view of human behavior, in which it is assumed that people seek responsibility and have the capacity to take care of their own work if they just get the right opportunities. However, the extreme form of delegation, such as, "I give this to you—and expect you to come back and present the results when the project is finished!" does not function well. Even though it could be expected that well-educated, experienced, and knowledgeable employees should be motivated by intrinsic rewards such as the possibility for self-realization by accomplishing the project, the empirical study shows that lack of sufficient attention from top management through all project phases drains the energy.

Furthermore, employees try to make sense of the lack of attention: "This project may not be that important any more because top management never talks or asks about it." A conclusion that can be drawn from the preceding is that "sensemaking" (Weick, 1995) is also an important task in managing the project-oriented company.

CONCLUDING REMARKS

The purpose of this chapter was to discuss how it is possible to influence employees in a project-oriented company in ways that make them perform well and enjoy working in the company at the same time. Traditionally, human resources in projects have been understood and conceptualized as calendar time booked for the projects. However, research has shown that (a formal) agreement on a certain number of personnel hours in a project may not be the significant human factor behind successful accomplishment of the project. In this chapter the concepts of human energy and energy killers and energy creators were introduced. Human energy is difficult to define and measure, but it relates to such concepts as attention, motivation, commitment, devotion, competencies, and mental capacity.

A big challenge for top management in the project-oriented company is to balance resource requirements and resource capacity. Sometimes this does not turn out very well. The result may be that what was meant to be a stimulating pressure (in terms of amount of projects and tightness of deadlines) turns out to lead to a situation of project constipation—with frustrated employees and few accomplished projects.

This chapter presented several energy killers and energy creators. The lists are not exhaustive. Other companies, employees, and top managers may be able to pinpoint other issues that influence the energy of employees. However, the concepts of killers and creators are supposed to inspire to a reflection and discussion on how to create energy in the company in question. An example drawn from the empirical study is that a sense of urgency concerning task accomplishment can be created by other means than having many simultaneous projects. Milestones, subdeliveries, frequent follow-ups, and celebrations of accomplishments (even the small ones) may create a more energetic project team and thus, hopefully, fewer overruns of the project schedule and dissatisfied and stressed employees. Top management's timely involvement and persistent attention may be another way of creating energy.

The empirical study has shown that employees react differently to the issues mentioned in this chapter. Some need a lot of top-management attention and only a few tasks simultaneously, whereas others are happier when they are working in a environment with a lot of different inputs and shifts. The challenge is to figure out how to manage with respect to the specific people involved and with respect to the conditions facing the company. No "cookbook" can be of any help here. However, a reflection on and a discussion of how the conception of time, the conception of pressure, and the conception of importance influence the people involved may be a way to stimulate the level of energy desired.

REFERENCES

Andersen ES. 2005. *Prosjektledelse—et organisasjonsperspektiv. NKI Forlaget* (in Norwegian).

Archer JA Jr. 1991. *Managing Anxiety and Stress.* Muncie, IN: Accelerated Development, Inc.

Blichfeldt BS, Eskerod P. 2005. Project portfolios: There's more to it than what management enacts, in Christiansen JK (ed.) *Proceedings for the 12th International Product Development Management Conference, June, Copenhagen Business School, Copenhagen, Denmark.*

Bloisi W, Cook CW, Hunsaker PL. 2003. *Management and Organizational Behavior.* New York: McGraw-Hill.

Bluedorn AC, Kalliath TJ, Strube MJ, Martin GD. 1999. Polychronicity and the inventory of polychronic values (IPV): The development of an instrument to measure a fundamental dimension of organizational culture. *J Manag Psychol* 14(3–4):205–230.

Bluedorn AC, Kaufman CF, Lane PM. 1992. How many things do you like to do at once? An introduction to monochromic and polychronic time. *Acad Manag Exec* 6(4):17–26.

Burrell G. 1992. Back to the future: Time and organization, in M Reed, M Hughes (eds.), *Rethinking Organization: New Directions in Organization Theory and Analysis.* London: Sage.

Cooper RG, Edgett SJ, Kleinschmidt EJ. 1999. New product portfolio management: Practices and performance. *J Prod Innov Manag* 16:333–351.

Cooper RG, Edgett SJ, Kleinschmidt EJ. 2000. New problems, new solutions: Making portfolio management more effective. *Res Technol Manag* 43:18–33.

Eskerod P. 1995. Fleksibilitet og forankring i den projektorganiserede virksomhed. *Ledelse & Erhvervsøkonomi* 3 (in Danish).

Eskerod P. 1996. Meaning and action in a multiproject environment: Understanding a multiproject environment by means of metaphors and basic assumptions. *Int J Project Manag* 14(2), pp. 61–65.

Eskerod P. 1997. *Nye perspektiver på fordeling af menneskelige ressourcer i et projektorganiseret multiprojekt-miljø.* Ph.D. dissertation, Southern Denmark Business School (in Danish).

Eskerod P. 1998. The human resource allocation process when organizing by projects, in RA Lundin, C Midler (eds.), *Projects as Arenas for Renewal and Learning Processes.* London: Kluwer Academic Publishers.

Eskerod P, Blichfeldt BS, Toft AS. 2004. Too many good projects: Managing emotions regarding "Project Overload," in R Gareis, M Huemann (eds.), *Proceedings of the Conference Project Management Days 2004, Projects and Emotional Intelligence, November.* Vienna: Vienna University of Economics and Business Administration.

Eskerod P, Darmer P. 1994. Oticon: Spaghetti for the ears, in D Adam-Smith, A Peacock (eds.), *Cases in Organizational Behaviour.* London: Pitman.

Eskerod P, Jepsen AL. 2005. Staffing renewal projects by voluntary enrolment. *Int J Project Manag* 23(6), pp. 445–453.

Eskerod P, Toft AS, Mikkelsen H. 2005. Energi–drivkraft og formåen, in H Mikkelsen (ed.) Ledelse af projektmylderet, Børsens forlag (in Danish).

Friend KE. 1982. Stress and performance: Effects of subjective work load and time urgency. *Personnel Psychol* 35:623–633.

Hackman JR, Oldham GR. 1975. Development of the job diagnostic survey. *J Appl Psychol* 60(2):159–170.

Hall ET. 1977. *Beyond Culture.* Garden City, NJ: Anchor Press.

Highsmith J. 2004. *Agile Project Management. Reading,* MA: Addison-Wesley.

Kaufman CF, Lane PM, Lindquist JD. 1991. Exploring more than 24 hours a day: A preliminary investigation of polychronic time use. *J Consum Res* 18(3):392–401.

Lindquist JD, Knieling J, Kaufman-Scarborough C. 2001. Polychronicity and consumer behavior outcomes among Japanese and U.S. students: A study of response to culture in a U.S. university setting. Presented at the Tenth Biennial World Marketing Congress, Cardiff, Wales.

Lundin RA, Söderholm A. 1995. A theory of the temporary organization. *Scand J Manag* 11:437–455.

Lundin RA, Söderholm A, Wilson T. 2001. On the conceptualization of time in projects, in *Proceedings for the 16th Nordic Conference, August, Uppsala University, Uppsala, Sweden.*

McGregor D. 1966. *Leadership and Motivation.* Boston: MIT Press.

Packendorff J. 1995. Inquiring into the temporary organization: New directions for project management. *Scand J Manag* 11(4):319–333.

Parkinson CN. 1957. *Parkinson's Law and Other Studies in Administration.* Boston: Houghton Mifflin.

Shawn KY, Maitlis S, Briner RB. 1995. An exploratory study of goal setting in theory and practice: a motivational technique that works? *J Occup Organ Psychol* 68:237*ff.*

Söderlund J. 2002. On the development of project management research: Schools of thought and critique. *Int Project Manag J* 6(1):20–31.

Weick KE. 1995. *Sensemaking in Organizations.* Thousand Oaks, CA: Sage.

CHAPTER 11
MANAGING PROJECT MANAGEMENT PERSONNEL AND THEIR COMPETENCIES IN THE PROJECT-ORIENTED COMPANY

Martina Huemann

Vienna University of Economics and Business Administration, Vienna, Austria

Martina Huemann holds a Ph.D. in project management and a master's degree in business administration from the Vienna University of Economics and Business Administration. She also studied business administration and economics at the University Lund, Sweden, and the Economic University Prague, Czech Republic.

Currently she is assistant professor in the Project Management Group of the Vienna University of Economics and Business Administration and since 2003 a visiting fellow of the University of Technology Sydney. She is a board member of Project Management Austria and the IPMA Research Board and the IIPMA Award Board. Dr. Huemann is also a trainer and consultant at Roland Gareis Consulting.

In her research she concentrates on human resources management in project-oriented organizations, management auditing of projects and programs, and maturity of project-oriented individuals, organizations, and nations. Martina has project management experience in organizational development, research, and marketing projects.

In any organization, personnel and their professional management are of strategic importance and contribute to the organizational success (Huselid, 1995). Human resources management is considered to create competitive advantage in organizations (Amit and Belcourt, 1999).

To perceive an organization as a project-oriented company or project-oriented business unit is a social construction. Project-oriented organizations are organizations that, according to Gareis (1990, 2005), perceive themselves as being project-oriented, define "management by projects" as their organizational strategy, apply projects and programs for the performance of complex processes, manage a project portfolio of different internal and external project types, and have specific permanent organizations such as a project portfolio group or a project management office to provide integrative functions. The ideal project-oriented organization is considered a flat organization with a specific project management culture (Gareis, 2004). Use of the organization, whether a line organization to carry out a business process or a project or program, creates competitive advantage. The development from a classic managed organization to a project-oriented organization can be considered to be a paradigm shift.

While traditional human resources management processes and practices (Wright and Boswell, 2002) are designed for the classically managed organization—for the organization that mass produces routine products or services and where the job requirements are well defined and stable (Keegan and Turner, 2003)—the project-oriented company is confronted with specific challenges:

- *Temporarity.* Projects and programs are temporary organizations (Turner and Müller, 2003; Gareis, 2005). Thus every time a new project or program is started, the human resources configuration of the organization must change.

- *More dynamic.* Project-oriented companies have dynamic boundaries and contexts. The number and size of the projects performed are constantly changing, permanent and temporary resources are employed, and cooperation with clients, partners, and suppliers is organized in teams, some of them are virtual (Gareis, 2004). Projects are considered as temporary organizations to bring change (Turner and Müller, 2003). Thus projects and programs entail greater uncertainty, creating a more dynamic environment with more discontinuity.

- *Project portfolio.* At a certain point in time a project-oriented organization holds a project portfolio of different internal and external project types (PMI, 2004; Gareis, 2005). This means that more or fewer projects and programs are carried out at the same time. A person has multiple roles. A person can work on different projects at the same time, maybe even in different project roles. In one project, he or she is a project manager; in another project, he or she is a project team member. Or a person can carry a role in a project and at the same time carry another role in the permanent organization, for example, in the project management office. Consequences are challenges in the multiple resource allocation (Eskerod, 1998).

- *Specific project management culture and management paradigm.* The ideal project-oriented company has a specific project management culture expressed in the empowerment of employees, process orientation and teamwork, continuous and discontinuous organizational change, customer orientation, and networking with clients and suppliers (Gareis, 2004). Therefore, specific competencies and skills are needed by the project management personnel to work together successfully in projects.

Thus human resource management needs to be designed to meet the needs of the project-oriented organization (Huemann et al., 2005). This has not yet been widely acknowledged, except from the multiproject resource-allocation perspective (Eskerod, 1998; Hendriks et al., 1999). While the organizational project management maturity model (OPM3), developed by the Project Management Insitute (PMI, 2003), does not consider managing project management personnel, the maturity model for the project-oriented company (mm-poc) developed by the Projektmanagement Group of the Vienna University of Economics and Business Administration does (Gareis, 2004). The mm-poc recognizes the importance of personnel management in the project-oriented company as one of the dimensions in the spider-web presentation of the model (Fig. 11.1). Based on this model, the Projektmanagement Group of the Vienna University of Economics and Business Administration has analyzed and benchmarked 60 project-oriented organizations from different industries (see Chap. 22).

In the maturity model for the project-oriented company (mm-poc), the dimension "personnel management in the project-oriented company" includes

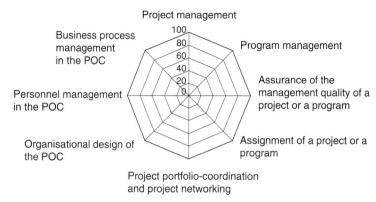

FIGURE 11.1   The maturity model mm-poc based on Roland Gareis' *Management of the Project-Oriented Company®*.

- The existence of the profession project manager in the organization, expressed, for instance, in role descriptions for project manager and other project management personnel, in a project management career path, and in competency profiles for project management personnel.

- Recruiting and release of project and program management personnel and application of adequate methods such as, for instance, analysis of individual project management competencies, assessment centers for project managers, and provision of temporary and permanent contract relationships.

- Leadership of project and program management personnel, including performance of permanent leadership functions such as manager of an expert pool or temporary leadership functions such as project manger or program manager. Specific for the project-oriented company is that a person often has multiple role functions.

- Specific project incentive systems, for instance, individual project incentives and team incentives.

- Development of project and program management personnel, including planning of development, training, and evaluation of project management training.

- Project management competencies of project and program management personnel and other managers in the project-oriented company.

- Organizational design and responsibility for personnel management.

THE PROFESSION OF PROJECT MANAGER AS A BASIS FOR COMPETENT PROJECT MANAGEMENT PERSONNEL

The Profession Project Manager

The demand for establishment of the profession of project manager is based on the demand for professional project managers in project-oriented companies. Not only have construction, engineering, and information technology (IT) companies that perform external projects for customers established the role of project manager, but nowadays insurance companies, banks, hospitals, and research institutes also have a demand for competent project managers who manage internal projects professionally. Thus the profession of project manager is established to formalize the status of project managers and to promote project management.

In a society or an organization, a profession is based on a common body of knowledge, defined entrance barriers, a code of ethics, and professional associations (Kuwan and Waschbüsch, 1996). Professional associations such as the International Project Management Association (IPMA) and the Project Management Institute (PMI) exist and also issue common bodies of knowledge, such as the *PMBOK® Guide* issued by PMI, and competency baselines, such as the International Competence Baseline issued by IPMA. Entrance barriers are defined by certification programs offered by these professional associations.

Whether an organization considers project management to be a profession can be observed. The profession of project manager is expressed, for instance, in role descriptions. Project-oriented organizations that consider project management to be a profession define a project management career path and competence profiles for the different career steps.

Role Descriptions Lay Down the Project Management Competencies Needed

In project-oriented companies, different persons need project management competencies to fulfill their roles. Project roles performed by individuals are project owner, project manager, project management assistant, project team member, and project contributor. This also means that not only the project manager needs project management competence but also, for instance, the project owner needs to understand the project management methods; otherwise, the project owner cannot communicate with the project manager and the project team.

Further, managers who perform roles in permanent functions in a project-oriented company must have the competencies to carry out their roles. Obviously, a member of a project portfolio group needs to have knowledge and experience to carry out the assignment of a project or a program, project portfolio coordination, and project networking.

The project management competence of a project manager is the capability to fulfill all functions specified in the role description (Gareis and Huemann, 2006). An example of a role description of a project manager can be found in Table 11.1 What are considered to be the functions of a project manager very much depend on the project management approach applied in the particular company—whether they are the traditional ones that only emphasize costs, schedule, and scope or a systemic approach that also considers the context of the project, the project organization, and the project culture.

Competency Profile of a Project Manager

Besides having project management knowledge and experience and a certain self-understanding (attitude), a project manager needs product, company, and industry knowledge. In international projects, cultural awareness and language knowledge are also prerequisites. Depending on the project type and the culture of the organization, the project manager also may need technical competence to get acknowledged by the project team, the customer, and the organization (Huemann, 2002). The more project management is considered a profession in the organization, the fewer technical/content competencies will be asked for.

The competency profile shown in Table 11.2 illustrates the minimum competency requirements of a senior project manager of an engineering company as an example.

TABLE 11.1   Part of the Role Description "Project Manager"

Objectives
• Representation of the project interests
• Contribution to the realization of the project objectives and to the optimization of the business case
• Leading the project team and the project contributors
• Representation of the project towards relevant environments
Organizational position
• Member of the project team
• Reports to the project owner team
Tasks
During the project assignment process
• Defining the project assignment together with project owner team
• Nominating the project team members
During the project start process
• Know-how transfer from the preproject phase into the project
• Development of adequate project plans
• Design of an adequate project organization
• Performance of risk management
• Design of project context relations
• etc.
During the project control process
• Determination of the project status
• Redefinition of project objectives
• Development of project progress reports
• etc.
During the resolution of a project discontinuity
• Analysis of the situation and definition of ad hoc measures
• Development of project scenarios
• Definition of strategies and further measures
• Communication of the project discontinuity to relevant project environments
• etc.
During the project close-down process
• Coordination of the final contents work
• Transfer of know-how into the base organization
• Dissolution of project environment relations
• etc.

Project Management Career Path to Further Develop Competencies

A career traditionally means climbing up the ladder within a particular organization or across organizations. Thus, traditionally, the way to measure up is by the number of people managed and the budget of the individual's department. However, project-oriented companies are different from classic companies. The application of projects allows them to become more flat, and therefore, hierarchical climbing up the ladder is not feasible. More modern concepts not only concentrate on vertical hierarchical career movements but also consider horizontal and centripetal career movements that are applicable for flat organizations (Schein, 1978). An example of centripetal movement, which is a move toward the

TABLE 11.2   Competency Profile of a Senior Management Project

Competences	Knowledge					Experience				
	5 Very much	4 Much	3 Average	2 Low	1 None	1 None	2 Low	3 Average	4 Much	5 Very much
Project and program management	■								■	
Management of the project-oriented company		■						■		
Project contents processes				■		■				
Business and product		■								■

more important core of an organization, is becoming a member of a strategically important project portfolio group.

Keegan and Turner (2003) have used the term *spiral staircase career* to describe the project management career. The phrase suggests that people will move through a series of varied and wide-ranging jobs and that each project can be a learning opportunity that contributes to a career. Thus career can be understood as a process that allows further development of one's own individual competencies.

Many project-oriented companies differentiate management career, expert career, and project management career. These career paths need to be positioned equally and need to be flexible to a certain degree. Expert competencies are often core competencies of the organizations that ensure competitive advantage. Thus technical expert careers need to be considered to be as important as project management careers. Figure 11.2 illustrates a project management career path in an engineering company. It is structured with the career steps junior project manager, project manager, senior project manager, and project management executive.

According to this career path, a person can have different roles. A typical project management career may start with the role of project management assistant in a project. Gradually, the responsibility the person takes on will grow. First, the person may take over the role of a project manager for small projects of less complexity, and then the projects assigned will become more and more complex. Further roles a project manager can take are, for instance, program manager or manager of a project management office. Further possibilities are job enlargements such as, for example, becoming a project management consultant, a project management auditor, or a member of the project

FIGURE 11.2   Project management career path in an engineering company.

TABLE 11.3 Relationship between Project Management Career Levels and Possible Roles

Project Management Career Levels	Possible Roles
Junior project manager	PM assistant
	Project controller
	Project manager of less complex projects
Project manager	Project manager
	Member of the PM office
Senior project manager	Project manager of complex projects
	PM coach
	PM consultant of projects
	PM auditor of projects
Project management-executive	Program manager
	Manager of the PM office
	Member of the portfolio group

management office. Table 11.3 shows the relationship between project management career levels and possible roles in a project-oriented company.

Often the project management career path is structured according to project management certification programs. Figure 11.3 shows the project management career path in an international IT company. The career levels are consultant, project manager, senior

Career progression	Consultant	PM Level 3 Project manager	PM Level 2 Senior project manager	PM Level 1 Project director
Total years	2–5	4–9	6–14	
Training & testing	12 Courses	9 Courses	3 Courses	
Experience	2–5 years project team experience lead small teams	2–4 years managing L3 projects participate L2 project	2–5 years managing L2 projects participate L1 projects	
External certification	- IPMA Level D	-IPMA Level C -PMI PMP	-IPMA Level B	Continuing professional development

FIGURE 11.3   Project management career path in an international IT company.

project manager, and project director. The consultant has two to five years of experience and leads small teams. The project manager manages projects of lesser complexity. The senior project manager manages complex projects. The highest career level is project director, who acts as program manager and takes on the responsibility of developing project management further. The number of years shown in the career path derive from the U.S. headquarters. In European parts of the organization, these years are shortened. For each of the career levels, a certain amount of training is required. Training is mainly organized internally according to company internal project management standards and process descriptions. The career path is structured according to IPMA certification levels. In this organization, the project management professional is seen as equivalent to the IPMA certification Level C. External certification programs offered by IPMA and PMI are used to ensure the quality of the project managers.

PROCESSES TO MANAGE PROJECT MANAGEMENT PERSONNEL

Business processes for personnel management in the project-oriented company are recruiting, development, and release. These processes may be fulfilled as general processes independent of the requirements of a specific project. For instance, project managers may be recruited without having a particular project in mind. Also, the further development of project management personnel can be organized independent of single projects. For example, a project management training initiative for all project managers, project team members, and project owners can be organized. Project mangers may be released from the project-oriented company if there is no demand for them in the organization. These processes can be considered to be general personnel management processes.

As shown in Figure 11.4, there exist specific project-related processes based on the fact that every time a new project is started, the human resource configuration of the organization changes. Thus the project-oriented organization needs additional processes for personnel management, particular assignment to projects, personnel development within projects, and dispersion after projects (Huemann et al., 2005).

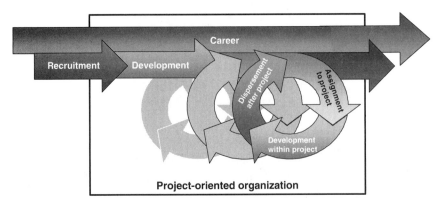

FIGURE 11.4   Personnel management processes in a project-oriented company.

By the process of assigning project personnel, program managers, project managers, and project team members are assigned to new projects and programs. Such methods as assessment centers are being used for this process (Crawford, 2003).

Within a project, a lot of development of personnel takes place. It is strongly linked to the leadership function of the project manager. Project managers may have additional duties, such as project appraisals and support for career development. However, the project owner also has a responsibility to care for the development of the project manager, for instance. Methods used are on-the-job training, feedback, etc.

The need for a dispersion process is not widely recognized. It has similarities to but also is substantial differences from release from the parent organization. It is at the end of a project that core workers are most vulnerable to leaving the organization. At the end of the project, project personnel should be debriefed about their experiences and counseled about the future.

ANALYSIS OF PROJECT MANAGEMENT COMPETENCIES TO FURTHER DEVELOP PROJECT MANAGEMENT PERSONNEL

A Maturity Model for Analyzing Competencies of Project Management Personnel

Recently, there is a lot of discussion regarding the maturity of organizations (Cooke-Davies, 2005; Ibbs et al., 2005). Moreover, maturity of persons is becoming a new buzz word. Project management maturity of a person may be explained as the degree of competence and self-understanding (attitude) of a person to fulfill the functions of a particular project management–related role.

The maturity model for analyzing of the project management competencies of project managers (mm–project manager model) is shown in Figure 11.5. It supports the analysis of knowledge and experience of a project manager in applying adequate methods for project start, project coordination, project control, resolution of a project discontinuity

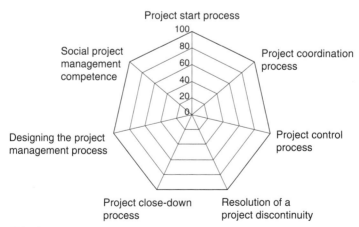

FIGURE 11.5 The maturity model mm–project manager based on Roland Gareis' *Project and Programme Management®*.

(such as a project crisis or chance occurrence), and project close-down. Further dimensions are design of the project management process and social project management competence.

The project manager requires knowledge and experience not only to apply project management methods but also to design the project management process creatively. The dimension designing the project management process includes

- Selection of the appropriate communication structures, such as single meetings or project workshops.
- Appropriate design of the communications, for example, invitation of representatives of external organizations to a project workshop or decision to involve a project management consultant.
- Selection of the appropriate IT and telecom infrastructure.
- Definition of the appropriate project management methods and form for the project management documentation.

The social project management competence is made visible as one dimension to show its importance. It includes methods for presentation and facilitation and team methods, for example, for team building, conflict management, feedback and reflection, negotiating, and management of one's own emotions and the emotions of others.

Beyond considering the dimensions of the mm–project manager, an analysis of the self-understanding (attitude) of the project manager is considered. This self-understanding is analyzed by considering the attitude to apply project management methods, to perceive a holistic project responsibility, to ensure project progress, and to gain agreements in the project team.

Process of the Project Management Competency Analysis

This analysis is based on a self-analysis questionnaire that consists of questions regarding

- *Project management education.* For example, which project management courses the project manager has attended.
- *Project management experience.* For example, in which projects the project manager has gained experience so far.
- *All dimensions of the mm–project manager model described earlier.* Table 11.4 shows an example question.
- *The self-understanding of the person as a project manager.*

TABLE 11.4   Example Question mm-Project Manager Questionnaire

Project start: Methods to design project context relations		
1 = none, 2 = low, 3 = average, 4 = much, 5 = very much	Knowledge	Experience
Project environment analysis Description: Pre- and post-project phase Analysis: Relation to other projects Analysis: Relation to the company strategies Project marketing Business case analysis		

Further, an external analysis is performed by an assessor. The assessor undertakes one to two hours of interviews with the project manager and analyzes the project management documents of a real project of the project manager. In the interviews, the results of the self-analysis are reflected and interpreted. Here, the assessor provides feedback on whether the candidate has done a realistic, too optimistic, or too critical self-analysis.

Example: Result of the Analysis

The result can be shown for a single individual or for a group of project managers. Figure 11.6 shows the result for a group of 12 project managers of a business unit. The result is one spider web for the project management knowledge and another one for project management experience. The shaded areas shown the degree of the maturity of the project management knowledge of the particular group of project managers and the degree of the maturity of the project management experience of the particular group of project managers.

The area for project management knowledge is homogeneous. In this group of project managers, there exists much knowledge in the application of methods for project start, project coordination, and design of the project management process and social project management competence. There is average knowledge of project control, management of a discontinuity, and project close-down. Analysis of the project management knowledge of this group of project managers indicates that there is limited experience in most of the dimensions.

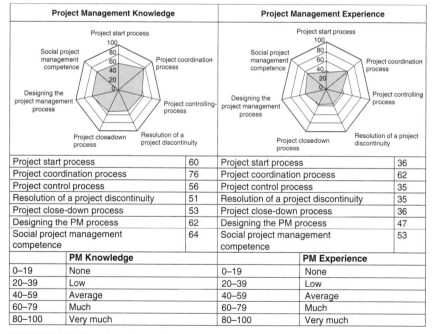

Project start process	60	Project start process	36
Project coordination process	76	Project coordination process	62
Project control process	56	Project control process	35
Resolution of a project discontinuity	51	Resolution of a project discontinuity	35
Project close-down process	53	Project close-down process	36
Designing the PM process	62	Designing the PM process	47
Social project management competence	64	Social project management competence	53

	PM Knowledge		**PM Experience**
0–19	None	0–19	None
20–39	Low	20–39	Low
40–59	Average	40–59	Average
60–79	Much	60–79	Much
80–100	Very much	80–100	Very much

FIGURE 11.6   Example result: Project management knowledge and experience of a group of project managers.

	P1	P2	P3	P4	P5	P6	P7	P8	P9	P10	P11	P12	Ø
Professional application of methods													
Holistic perception of project responsibility													
Assurance of project progress													
Agreements in project team													

None	Low degree	Average degree	Strong degree	Very strong degree
1	2	3	4	5

FIGURE 11.7   Example result: Self-understanding of the group of project managers.

Project Management Knowledge		Project Management Experience	

Project start process	61	Project start process	38
Project coordination process	62	Project coordination process	50
Project control process	56	Project control process	31
Resolution of a project discontinuity	33	Resolution of a project discontinuity	12
Project close-down process	36	Project close down process	14
Designing the PM process	51	Designing the PM process	44
Social project management competence	66	Social project management competence	37

	PM Knowledge		PM Experience
0–19	None	0–19	None
20–39	Low	20–39	Low
40–59	Average	40–59	Average
60–79	Much	60–79	Much
80–100	Very much	80–100	Very much

Self-understanding in the role as project manager	4,25
Professional application of methods	
Holistic perception of project responsibility	
Assurance of project progress	
Agreements in project team	

None	Low degree	Average degree	Strong degree	Very strong degree
1	2	3	4	5

FIGURE 11.8   Example result: Project management knowledge and experience of a particular project manager.

Figure 11.7 shows the self-understanding to fulfill the role of project managers of each project manager analyzed. In this particular case, the result shows that the project managers have relatively strong self-understanding to fulfill the role of a project manager, but there is particularly opportunity for improvement in professional application of methods.

Figure 11.8 shows the analysis result for a single project manager. A particular objective in this analysis was to examine the minimum knowledge and experience required to be certified as project manager (IPMA Level C) by Project Management Austria, the Austrian project management association. As one can see from the spider webs shown in the figure, this project manager has more project management knowledge than experience. The figure shows that the person does not fulfill the minimum requirements set out for certification. The person needs more knowledge in design of the project management process, managing project discontinuities, and project close-down, as well as more experience in project control, managing a discontinuity, and project close-down, to fulfill the minimum requirements.

POTENTIAL APPLICATIONS OF THE MM–PROJECT MANAGER MODEL

There are different possibilities for application of the maturity model to analyze project management personnel. For instance:

- Establishing the status of the project management maturity of a group of project mangers or a single project manager to plan further development actions for the personnel as such or for the single person

- Selecting project personnel for a particular project

- Analyzing the project management competence of a project manager or project owner within a management audit of a project (Huemann, 2006)

REFERENCES

Amit R, Belcourt M. 1999, Human resource management processes: A value-creating source of competitive advantage. *Eur Manag J* 17(2):174–181.

Cooke-Davies T. 2005. Measurement of organizational maturity: Questions for future research, in *Innovations: Project Management Research 2004*. Newtown Square, PA: Project Management Institute.

Crawford L. 2003. Assessing and developing the project management competence of individuals, in JR Turner (ed.), *People in Project Management*, Aldershot: Gower.

Eskerod P. 1998. The human resource allocation process when organizing by projects, in RA Lundin, C Midler (eds.), *Projects as Arenas for Renewal and Learning Processes*. Boston: Kluwer Academic.

Gareis R (ed.). 1990. *Handbook of Management by Projects*. Vienna: Manz.

Gareis R. 2005. *Happy Projects!* Vienna: Manz.

Gareis R. 2004. Management of the project-oriented company, in JK Pinto, PWG Morris (eds.), *The Wiley Guide to Managing Projects*. New York: Wiley.

Gareis R, Huemann M. 2006. Maturity-models for the project-oriented company, in JR Turner (ed.), *The Gower Handbook of Project Management*, 4th ed. Aldershot: Gower.

Hendriks MHA, Voeten B, Kroep L. 1999. Human resource allocation in a multi-project R&D environment: Resource capacity allocation and project portfolio planning in practice. *Int J Project Manag* 17(3):181–188.

Huemann, M., 2002., *Individuelle Projektmanagement Kompetenzen in projektorientierten Unternehmen.*, Europäische Hochschulschriften. Frankfurt-am-Main: Peter Lang.

Huemann M. 2006. Management audits of projects and programmes, in JR Turner (ed.), *The Gower Handbook of Project Management*, 4th ed. Aldershot: Gower.

Huemann M, Turner JR, Keegan AE. 2004. Human resource management in the project oriented company, in JK Pinto, PWG Morris (eds.), *The Wiley Guide to Managing Projects*. New York: Wiley.

Huemann M, Turner JR, Keegan AE. 2005. Human resources management in the project-oriented company: Questions for future research, in DI Cleland, J Pinto (eds.), *Innovations: Project Management Research 2004*. Newtown Square, PA: Project Management Institute.

Huselid MA. 1995. The impact of human resource management practices on turnover, productivity, and corporate financial performance. *Acad Manag Rev* 38:635–672.

Ibbs CW, Reginato JM, Kwak YH. 2005. Developing project management capability: Benchmarking, maturity, modelling, gap analyses, and ROI studies, in JK Pinto, PWG Morris (eds.), *The Wiley Guide to Managing Projects*. New York: Wiley.

Keegan AE, Turner JR. 2003. Managing human resources in the project-based organization, in JR Turner (ed.), *People in Project Management*. Aldershot: Gower.

Kuwan H, Waschbüsch E. 1996. *Zertifizierung und Qualitätssicherung in der beruflichen Weiterentwicklung*. Berlin: Bundesinsitut für Berufsbildung.

Project Management Institute (PMI). 2003. *Organizational Project Management Maturity Model*, Newtown Square, PA: Project Management Institute.

Project Management Institute (PMI). 2004. *A Guide to the Project Management Body of Knowledge*, 3d ed. Newtown Square, PA: Project Management Institute.

Schein E. 1978. *Career Dynamics: Matching Individual and Organizational Needs*. Reading, MA: Addison-Wesley.

Turner JR, Müller R. 2003. On the nature of the project as a temporary organization. *Int J Project Manag* 21(1). 1–8

Wright PW, Boswell WR. 2002. Desegregating HRM: A review and synthesis of micro and macro human resource management research. *J Manag* 28(3):247–276.

CHAPTER 12
LESSONS LEARNED: REBUILDING IRAQ IN 2004

Charles W. "Chick" Keller

University of Kansas, Edwards Campus, Overland Park, Kansas

Charles "Chick" Keller was director of program management for the reconstruction program in Iraq during the second half of 2004. Professor Keller has now returned to his regular job as a professor in the master of engineering management program at the University of Kansas. Prior to joining the University of Kansas, he worked for 15 years in executive positions at Black and Veatch, a global design/build firm, and United Telecom (now Sprint). He has extensive experience in project management, strategic marketing, strategic planning, and capital budgeting.

In 2003, Congress passed two separate funding bills totaling approximately $20 billion to rebuild Iraq. The Iraq rebuilding program consisted of 2500 projects spread across six different sectors: electrical; oil; public works and water; buildings, health, and education; security and justice; and transportation and communications. This chapter will document the following relating to the Iraq reconstruction program in the year 2004:

- Design of the original program
- Implementation of the program
- Program management systems and program reporting
- Lessons learned and conclusion

DESIGN OF THE ORIGINAL PROGRAM

The first bill funding the reconstruction of Iraq was passed by Congress in June 2003. The bill provided $2.4 billion in emergency funding to repair and reconstruct Iraq's oil and electrical infrastructure. In November 2003, Congress passed Public Law 108-106, which provided an additional $18.4 billion of funding for reconstruction in six different sectors: electrical; oil; public works and water; building, health, and education; security and justice; and transportation and communications. The bills were commonly know as the Iraq Relief and Reconstruction Funds (IRRFs) and were referred to as IRRF I and IRRF II.

The bills had two important commonalities that drove the definition of the program. First, the rebuilding of Iraq was to be driven and implemented by the private sector, and second, program implementation was to be as fast as possible. To accomplish these two objectives, contracts were awarded to private-sector firms on a cost-plus basis. Using the cost-plus approach accelerated implementation two ways: (1) Contractors could mobilize to Iraq immediately, and (2) projects could be started before detailed project scopes were defined.

IRRF I

Cost-plus contracts to implement IRRF I were quickly awarded to two major internationally known design-build (DB) contractors. One contractor was to focus on rebuilding Iraqi oil (RIO) and the other contractor on rebuilding Iraqi electricity (RIE). Implementation of RIO and RIE began in the summer of 2003.

IRRF II

Characteristics of IRRF II funding and program implementation were as follows:

- Funding was directed to specific sectors. In the IRRF II appropriation, 10 sectors were defined, and to implement the program, the 10 sectors were regrouped into 6 sectors. Thus, while project funding by law is specific to 10 sectors, this chapter will discuss the program in terms of the 6 sectors defined and used in project implementation. The funding by sector was as shown in Table 12.1.

- The law provided the implementers of the program some flexibility to move money between sectors as the need to rebudget or adjust the programs occurred. Specifically, the implementers of the program were provided the flexibility to move up to 10 percent of the funding out of any given sector, and the funding for any given sector could be increased a maximum of 20 percent. Reprogramming amounts greater than 10 percent out of a sector or 20 percent into a sector required Congressional approval.

- The $18.4 billion funding was further broken down into $12.4 billion for reconstruction projects and $6.0 billion for nonconstruction items. The largest nonconstruction budget was approximately $4 billion for equipment, vehicles, supplies, weapons, and ammunition for the Iraqi army. Examples of other nonconstruction budget items included lab equipment for hospitals and trucks and other vehicles for various programs.

TABLE 12.1   IRRF II Funding by Sector

Sector	IRRF II Funding
Buildings, health, and education (BHE)	$1.05B
Electricity	$5.50B
Oil	$1.70B
Public works and water (PWW)	$4.20B
Security and justice (S&J)	$4.70B
Transportation and communication (T&C)	$0.87
Administration and other	$0.39B
Total	$18.40B

- The law established a new entity, the Coalition Provisional Authority (CPA), to implement the program. Within the CPA was the Program Management Office (PMO). The mission of the PMO was as follows:

  - Build infrastructure.
  - Bolster and enhance the construction industry.
  - Employ Iraqis.
  - Leave so that local people would develop the skills and knowledge to operate, maintain, and grow the infrastructure. An assumption tied to this one is that Iraq will have substantial oil money in the future to continue growing the economy and rebuilding the infrastructure.

- To implement the program, the following types of private-sector firms were retained:

  - *Six engineering firms, one for each sector.* The role of the engineering firms was to define the projects for the sector, task the projects to preselected DB firms, review project designs, monitor project progress, manage the budget for the sector, and drive a capacity-building program (defined in detail later) whereby the Iraqis would be trained to operate and maintain the facilities. These six engineering firms were called *sector program management office contractors* (SPMOCs).
  - *Thirteen DB contractors.* One to three DB contractors were selected to perform work in a given sector. These firms were referred to as *sector program management office design build contractors* (SPMODBs).
  - *One security firm, to provide security for the PMO and armed escorts and convoys to project sites.* Separately, each DB contractor was required to have its own security operation and provide its own security at both its camps and its project sites.
  - *Two information technology (IT) contractors.* Contractors were hired to provide help-desk support, to set up and maintain a network of personal computers, and to provide, implement, and support the project tracking and project database software.
  - *One program manager.* One contractor was to manage integration of the preceding contractors and implementation of the overall program. this contractor was referred to as the *program management office contractor* (PMOC).

- With the program being implemented by the private sector, the role of the government was to be limited to fiduciary or "owner-related" activities. In essence, the entire rebuilding program was outsourced to over 20 private-sector contractors. Figure 12.1 illustrates the program structure as originally conceived.

- The Army Corp of Engineers was designated to be responsible for the construction management function on all projects.

- As noted earlier, to facilitate speed of implementation, all contracts were awarded on a cost-plus basis, and contractors were paid on a cost-plus basis to mobilize their teams in Iraq before the projects were defined.

- To further facilitate speed of implementation, certain selected projects were to be implemented by other execution agencies such as USAID and the contracting sections of the Air Force, Army, and Navy While the implementation of these projects was the responsibility of the executing body; budget and program management functions remained with PMO. This latter created some problems because at times some of these agencies did not have the people on the ground in Iraq with the right skill sets to manage construction projects.

Overarching Goals

The coalition lead by the United States defined the four-step program shown in Table 12.2 to achieve freedom in Iraq.

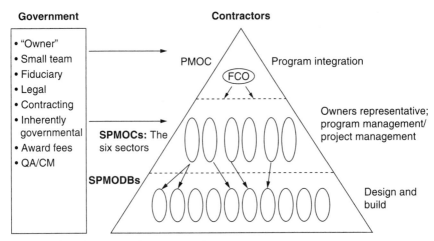

FIGURE 12.1   Contractor and government roles.

During the second phase, when the United States occupied Iraq, Paul Bremer served as the de facto President of Iraq. During this phase, the goal of the CPA was to complete the rebuilding process and then to exit Iraq.

The third phase of the march to Iraqi freedom was to partner with Iraq. During this phase, which began on June 30, 2004, the U.S. State Department, lead by Ambassador Negroponte, was in a partnering relationship with the appointed provisional government of Iraq lead by Prime Minister Allawi. The mission of the coalition and therefore the mission of the CPA in this phase was "nation building." The three pillars of nation building are illustrated in Figure 12.2.

In March 2004, Colin Powell defined the goals of nation building as follows:

> Our goal is to give the Iraqis a country based on democracy, freedom, individual rights of men and women, a free market system; an Iraq that will live in peace with its neighbors and with the world community.

Thus, on July 1, 2004, the role of the CPA transitioned from "rebuild Iraq" to "support the nation building mission." And the exit strategy was redefined from exit Iraq when rebuilding is complete to when there is (1) a secure environment, (2) economic stability, and (3) democratic processes in place.

TABLE 12.2   Four-Step Program to Achieve Freedom in Iraq

Step	Mission
Overthrown	Oust Saddam
Occupy	Rebuild Iraq
Partner	Nation building
Exit	Diplomacy

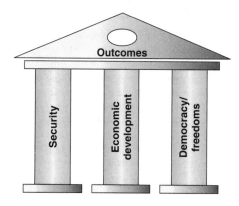

"Our goal is to give the Iraqis a country based on democracy, freedom, individual rights of men and women, a free market system; an Iraq that will live in peace with its neighbors and with the world community." Colin Powell, March 2004

FIGURE 12.2   The three pillars of nation building.

Capacity Building

Part of Public Law 108-106 required that the CPA implement a capacity-building program. The goal of capacity building is to ensure that Iraqis will have the capability not only to operate and maintain the facilities but also to ensure that appropriate systems and policies are in place at both the national and local levels to allow for the continued effective and efficient operations of the rebuilt and newly built infrastructure. Table 12.3 presents the five-level model that was used to define and design the capacity-building program.

A brief example follows to clarify what each level of the capacity-building model means. Suppose that in a given city in Iraq there was a municipal water utility. Further suppose that the utility had two facilities: a water-purification plant and an administration building. Below is an explanation of the activities that would need to occur at each level of capacity building so that the water utility would operate effectively.

- *Level 1.* For a municipal water utility to exist, there would need to be a national policy directive stating that water utilities are to be owned and operated by cities as

TABLE 12.3   Capacity-Building Model

Level	Title	Functions
1	Enabling environment	Iraq policy, strategy, program direction
2	Legal, regulatory, and policy frameworks	Drivers (e.g., regulations, oversite functions, national, governate/state, and municipal roles)
3	Organizational coordination	Liaison and coordination of stakeholders
4	Organizational development	Institutional development such as missions, business systems/processes, HR, and organizational structures
5	Training and skills transfer	Training and skill transfer

opposed to being owned and operated by the national government or private industry. Setting these policies would be part of implementing level 1 capacity building.

- *Level 2.* Once the level 1 policies were set, then national laws and regulatory framework would need to be set in place that all municipal water utilities would follow.

- *Level 3.* Stakeholders in the municipal water utility would include the management of the water utility, the employees, the municipal government, the citizens or customers, and the national-level function that managed water resources for Iraq. Establishing the functions of each group and how they would interrelate would be a level 3 function.

- *Level 4.* Within the administration building, such functions as payroll, customer billing, customer service, engineering, and other administrative functions would occur. Planning, designing, and training personnel to implement these systems would be level 4 training.

- *Level 5.* Conducting training so that the city workers could effectively and efficiently operate the water plant.

IMPLEMENTATION OF THE PROGRAM

IRRF I

Implementation of the IRRF I program began in the summer of 2003 with two internationally renowned DB firms beginning the RIO and RIE programs. All contracts were cost-plus, and the focus was on speed. Many projects were started simultaneously, and virtually every project ran substantially over budget. Unfortunately, the budgeted money ran out before all the projects were completed. In fact, many projects were left in partial-completion mode. Funding the completion of theses projects with alternative funding was a continuing challenge in 2004. Further, the performance on these programs did not meet the expectations of key stakeholders in Iraq; thus IRRF I created an initial negative image of the rebuilding effort.

Mobilization for IRRF II

Contracts with the SPMOCs and the DB firms were signed on March 9, 2004. The contractors began to mobilize their teams to Baghdad in April of 2004. By May 2004, critical mass to manage the program was in place in Baghdad. At this point, the state of the program organization within PMO was as follows:

- Each of the six sectors had three to six government people.

- Further, for each sector, there was a sector contractor (SPMOC) team in place consisting of typically 10 to 30 people. By the end of the summer of 2004, each SPMOC had staffs of about 50 people in Baghdad.

- In the spring of 2004, the staffing in each sector to plan and begin implementation of the work was inadequate, and determination to get the work done was high. Thus the sector government teams and the SPMOC teams worked long hours and worked closely together, and roles blurred because the focus was on getting the job done, not on worrying about whose role was what. In this time period and throughout all of 2004, 7-day workweeks with 12-hour work days were standard.

During the same time period, the DB contractors began to mobilize to Iraq. Mobilization for the DB contractors was more difficult than for the SPMOCs. For each of the SPMOCs, the government provided life support and office facilities in the Green

Zone (later renamed the International Zone, or IZ) in Baghdad. Life support in the Green Zone consisted of such things as sleeping facilities in small trailers or tents, dining facilities providing four meals per day (their was a midnight meal to support late workers), laundry service, and security provided by the coalition Multi-National Forces (MFN). On the other hand, the DB contractors were required to create their own compounds, often outside the Green Zone, with their own life-support facilities and their own security.

Project Definition

While Congress identified how the appropriated funds were to be spent in identified sectors, Congress did not identify specific projects. Thus the first job of the PMO was to define and estimate the cost of potential projects.

In October 2003, the United Nations and the World Bank completed a Joint Iraq Needs Assessment Study. The study concluded that to rebuild Iraq to prewar conditions of 1990 would require $56.1 billion. Given that IRRF II funding was $18.4 billion, it was obvious that many needed projects would not be funded. Figure 12.3 illustrates the comparison of estimated required funding by sector with the actual funding.

From approximately December 2003 until March 2004, the PMO focused all its efforts on creating project definitions and related project cost estimates. Because at this time the PMO staff had yet to fully mobilize and the SPMOCs had not yet signed contracts, much less mobilized to Iraq, it was necessary to bring in a contractor whose mission was to assist the PMO with project definition and project cost estimates.

Initially, 5500 potential projects were defined. PMO leaders and management then worked closely with the Iraqi ministries to select projects to be funded. For example, PMO

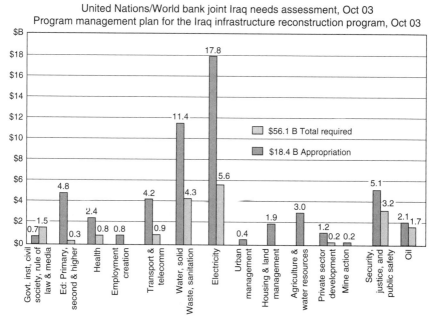

FIGURE 12.3   Iraq reconstruction requirements.

personnel worked closely with the Iraqi Minister of Education to identify which school projects would be funded. Final selection of projects to be implemented was left to the Iraqi ministers. Eventually, 2500 projects estimated to cost $12.4 billion were selected.

Table 12.4 shows the number of funded projects and the project values by sector and subsector.

Baghdad-centric

All the Iraqi ministers were located in Baghdad, as were all the SPMOCs, whose function it was to document and guide implementation of the selected projects. Thus the system to identify and select projects for implementation was Baghdad-centric,

TABLE 12.4   Funded Projects and Project Values

Sector/Subsector	No. of Projects	Value (Millions)
Electrical		
Generation	20	$1760
Transmission	77	1500
Distribution	300	957
Control	15	150
Oil	109	$1701
Public works and water		
Potable water	84	$2,735
Sewers	10	678
Water resources	31	441
Irrigation and drainage	8	279
Buildings, health, and education		
Ministry buildings	4	$12
Hospitals	18	308
Primary health care centers	150	182
School rehabs	1200	118
Security and justice		
Military installations	24	$580
Border forts	178	78
Police training	8	109
Facilities protection	14	8
Rebuild court system	90	105
Fire and police stations	203	101
Detention facilities	3	180
Transportation and communications		
Village roads	15	$42
Carriageways and major roads	6	143
Railroad station rehabs	108	40
Bridges	8	65
Aviation	6	115
Communications	4	57
Ports	3	11
Totals	2587	$12,431

minister-driven. This later proved to be a problem, and the solution is discussed below in the section entitled, "Community-Based Programs"

Get the Money

Once the projects were defined and approved by the Iraqi ministers, the next step was to go back the Office of Management and Budget (OMB) to get the money. First, a little background. When Congress passed Public Law 106-108 that funded the $18 billion Iraq rebuilding effort, the money was placed with OMB, which manages the U.S. government's money. Also, the CPA organization functioned under the Department of Army (DOA), which functioned under the Department of Defense (DOD). To get money released from OMB, the CPA wrote task orders that described the projects to be done and the estimated project costs. The task orders where then sent electronically to the DOA in Washington, where they were approved and forwarded to the DOD, which also approved each task order and then sent it along to OMB. OMB would review the task orders, and if the task orders supported using the money in accordance with the law passed by Congress, then OBM would release the funds to the DOD, which would move the money to the DOA, and then the funds would move to the CPA. During the program, it became a critical success factor to track the status of budgeted funds. Various terms to do this are as follows:

- *Appropriated.* Congress has passed a law and the President has signed the law making money available.
- *Apportioned.* OMB has approved specific task orders and moved the money to implemented the approved task orders to CPA.
- *Committed.* The CPA has committed the funds to a specific project.
- *Obligated.* The CPA has signed a contract with a DB firm to build the project, thus "obligating" the money. Note that often while we say $10 million might be "committed" to a specific project, the CPA would "obligate" a lesser amount, say, $3 million, to a contractor to begin the project. The remaining $7 million would not be obligated until a detailed project scope, schedule, and budget were defined.
- *Definitized.* Once a detailed scope, schedule, and budget were in place, the project was said to be definitized.
- *Disbursed.* Finally, once work had been completed, approved, and invoiced, funds would be disbursed to the contractor.

In general, in the summer of 2004, the financial status was as follows: Project definitions were completed in the spring, and task orders (requests for money to be apportioned for the projects) were rapidly being developed and sent back to Washington. Only a few projects, about 30 or 40, had started. In the mean time, the press was publishing reports that while $18 billion had been allocated to rebuild Iraq, less than $1 billion had been spent or disbursed. While this was true, it was a misrepresentation of the situation.

In response to the negative press reports indicating the slow progress of the rebuilding program, the PMO began to obligate money faster, which was a mistake. For example, if money for a $10 million water-treatment facility had been apportioned, we would obligate the entire $10 million to the DB contractor to do the project as opposed to obligating, say, $3 million and waiting to obligate the remaining $7 million once the scope, schedule, and budget of the project had been finalized. However, doing this allowed the PMO to report to Congress, the DOA, the DOD, and the press that money was being obligated faster.

Creating Community-Based Programs

The fact that all project-selection decisions were being made by the Iraqi ministers in Baghdad created a problem. Local officials, such as mayors and governors, felt left out of the process, and further, they did not trust that any decision being made out of Baghdad would be in their best interest.

Fortunately, in the spring of 2004, Iraqi oil money was becoming available. Since at the time the CPA was occupying Iraq, that is, running the country, the CPA was free to spend the Iraqi oil money as the CPA determined best. A fund called the Defense Funds for Iraq (DFI) was established and was designated to fund community-based programs. A nice characteristic of DFI funds was that unlike the IRRF funds, they came without any strings attached. For example, (1) funding was not tied to a certain sector, (2) implementation did not have to be done by a coalition DB contractor, and (3) the bureaucratic reporting was substantially reduced.

In April of 2004, the insurgency began to flare up in Fallajuh. In an effort to create peace in Fallajuh and to build good relationships with the local leaders and citizens of Fallajuh, the PMO sent representatives to Fallajuh to meet with local leaders to define and designate projects to be funded with DFI money and implemented by local contractors.

This was the start of community-based programs where (1) local leaders selected the projects, and (2) local contractors implemented the program.

The program in Fallajuh was successful and was expanded quickly to 6 additional cites and then to a total of 10 cities. The program at this time was named the Accelerated Iraq Reconstruction Program (AIRP). AIRP was considered a success for several reasons:

- Being community-based, it engaged the local politicians and power brokers.

- Projects were considerably more cost-effective because going direct to local contractors avoided the administrative costs associated with the DB contractors.

- Speed of implementation was faster because there was no need to wait on the coalition DBs to mobilize.

- The projects were being done totally by the Iraqis. With an Iraqi face on the projects, the projects were safer. That is, the insurgents would tend to leave Iraqi-run projects alone.

To support the rapid expansion of AIRP to several cities, a new organization was started within the CPA that consisted of a program leader and regional program managers.

Amazingly, the AIRP program was conceived, staffed, and implemented in a matter of months. By August 2004, over 300 AIRP projects had started.

Concurrently with the implementation of AIRP, another community-based local program was enacted, that is, the Commanders Emergency Relief Program (CERP). CERP was identical to AIRP, except CERP was lead and administered by the Multi-National Forces (MFNs) in Iraq, whereas AIRP was lead and administered by the PMO.

A key issue with both the CERP and AIRP programs was the payment of local contractors. The banking system in Iraq was weak, and there was no capability to complete electronic transfers of funds. This forced both the military and the PMO to make cash payments to the local Iraqi contractors. It was not unusual to move large quantities of cash, $10 million, for example, from Baghdad to a given city to pay the local contractors.

The Starting Point

In general, the condition of infrastructure in Iraq was worst than we expected. While Saddam had spent heavily to build palaces throughout the country and to build a few spectacular projects, he tended to not allocate monies for maintenance of the current infrastructure. It was not uncommon to find pumping stations that had not had annual maintenance in a decade.

The collective impacts of lack of maintenance for several decades, the war, and looting created a dilapidated infrastructure with many needs. In fact, the looting was worse than anticipated, which caused many rehabilitation projects to become rebuilds.

Only 40 percent of the nation had access to potable water, and 90 percent of the sewerage went untreated. The lack of potable water was the main cause of the infant and child mortality rate exceeding 10 percent. Further, the Sweet Water Canal that moved water to the city of Basrah on the southern tip of Iraq failed on occasion, leaving the more than 1 million residents of Basrah without water for a period of five or six days. And 1 million people without water on a 120°F summer day become somewhat hostile.

Five million of Iraq's 25 million citizens were without electricity. And the 20 million who did have access to electricity would experience rolling blackouts, with electricity typically being available four to six hours per day. As one citizen said, "When it is over 100 degrees at night and you have no electricity and no air-conditioning, it is hard to think about the benefits of democracy; show me electricity, and I will show you democracy."

Lastly, many existing facilities were primitive in nature. For example, many rural schools did not have bathroom facilities or electrical lighting. Thus school rehab projects focused on adding the basics such as bathrooms and electricity.

Stakeholder Management

When the program began, PMOs key stakeholders were the Iraqi ministers in Baghdad. This quickly changed, and the following other stakeholders emerged:

- *Local politicians.* The governors of the governates and the mayors of the cities all wanted to know what would happen when in their locality. They were very supportive of the rebuilding effort and had some specific goals, such as (1) to attract as many projects as possible in their locale, (2) to drive some of the construction subcontracts to businesses in their locale, and (3) to be part of the process.

- *The Multi-National Forces (MNFs).* For military purposes, Iraqi was divided into six geographic segments with an MNF led by a general in charge of each segment. The MNFs believed that the quickest way to win the peace and the hearts and minds of the Iraqi people was to build projects as fast as possible. Thus each general was vitally interested in what projects would be done in his area and when the project would start.

- *Army Corp of Engineers.* The corp was in charge of construction management on all 2500 projects, and as such, it was imperative for the PMO to create and maintain good communications with corp offices throughout Iraq.

- *Local contractors.* Local contractors throughout Iraq wanted to be involved in the rebuilding effort, and questions continuously arose relating to how a local contractor could be awarded work. While the DB contractors were the only groups that could subcontract work, the questions from the local contractors usually would come to the PMO. It then became an ongoing effort to link local contractors and the collation DB contractors together. To support the local contractors, the civil affairs function of the MNFs often would set up business centers in cities to create a place for the DB contractors to come and meet with local contractors.

Building a Regional Organization

When started in late 2003, the CPA was located in Baghdad only. As the program was implemented in the spring of 2004, it was necessary to build a regional or outreach program

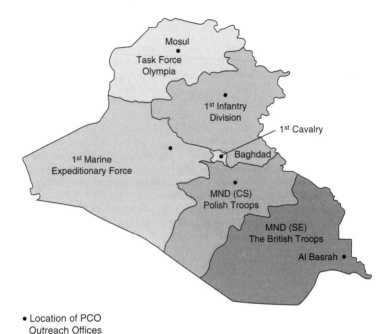

• Location of PCO
  Outreach Offices

FIGURE 12.4   Regional organization, Project and Contracting Office (PCO) outreach offices, and the MNFs.

to improve communications with the key stakeholders listed earlier. Figure 12.4 illustrates the locations of the MNFs and members of the outreach program.

Working in a War Zone

Several adjustments to the program were made to facilitate working in a war zone:

- The goal was to put an Iraqi face on all projects. In the community-based programs such as AIRP, projects were awarded directly to Iraqi firms. In the IRRF II program, all work was subcontracted to Iraqi firms. Thus there was no need to have Americans located at project sites. The insurgents were continually looking for coalition projects and sometimes would come to a project site, such as a school rehab project, and ask the Iraqi contractor who he was working for. To avoid these problems, all the school contractors were provided with letters from the Iraq Minister of Education indicating the school rehab was being done for Iraq not for the Americans.

- On the larger oil, water, and electric sites, a secure camp complete with a secure perimeter and armed guards would be set up at each project site. Americans at the project site would live at the project site and leave the site only as required.

- To help the DB contractors have secure camps, a program was established to assist the DB contractors to colocate camps with the MNFs.

It is important to understand that the goal of the insurgents was to disrupt the reconstruction, not to destroy the infrastructure. While the insurgents might blow up a pipe line that could be repaired in a few days, they did not blow up major oil facilities. Further, for the most part, none of the projects was attacked by the insurgents, A couple of exceptions being a military training facility that was attacked and a school that was attacked just prior to the election in January 2005. But the school was attacked because it was a polling place, not because it was a school.

The Transition

The original mission of the PMO was to rebuild Iraq, and the PMO was both a policy/ strategy-setting organization and a project-implementation organization. The PMO was a policy/strategy-setting organization in that leaders of the PMO worked closely with the Iraqi ministers to create the rebuilding strategy. This all changed on June 30, 2004.

During the first half of 2004, the CPA occupied and ran Iraq. The leader of both Iraq and the CPA at this time was Paul Bremer. On July 1, 2004, the coalition running Iraq switched from a mode of "occupying Iraq" to a mode of partnering with Iraq to run Iraq. At this time, Allawi was appointed president of Iraq, the CPA as an organization ceased to exist, and the U.S. State Department moved into Iraq. At this time, the State Department began to lead the U.S. operations in Iraq, and the PMO was renamed the Project and Contracting Office (PCO).

For the PMO, now the PCO, the significance of this change was that PCO became a project-implementation organization only. Strategy and policy formulation and managing the relationships with the Iraqi ministers became a U.S. State Department responsibility. The State Department created the Iraq Reconstruction and Management Office (IRMO) to lead the Iraq reconstruction effort. Figure 12.5 illustrates the relationship of IRMO, the PCO, and other key stakeholders.

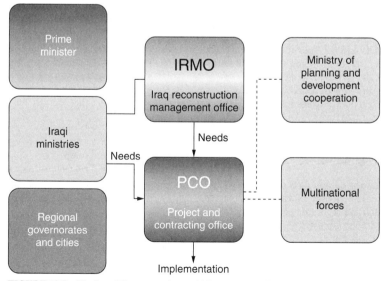

FIGURE 12.5 The Iraqui Reconstruction and Management Office (IRMO) is established.

Strategic Cities Program

In the late summer and early fall of 2004, the insurgency was increasing, particularly in the Sunni triangle area of central Iraq. The MNFs, the U.S. Department of State, and the Iraqi government directed a focused effort to win the peace in these cities. The Strategic Cities Program (SCP) was created to accomplish this. The program plan was simple; first, the MNFs would defeat the insurgency, and then, immediately following the end of hostilities, various groups, including the PCO, would move in to start rebuilding the city, and the IRMO would coordinate the stabilization process.

Program Contractor Role Adjusted

As mentioned earlier, a contractor called the Program and Contracting Office Contractor (PCOC) was retained on a cost-plus basis to manage the IRRF II program. This created a situation where one government contractor was managing other government contractors. In the summer of 2004, it became clear that this arrangement would not work for two reasons. First, the contractor was slow to mobilize the right people to Iraq, and second, the government moved strong leaders into Iraq early on. With the PCOC short of the right people to manage the program, government leaders stepped in to run the program. This illustrated one advantage to cost-plus contracts. That is, when something is not working, you can quickly adjust a contractor's scope to correct the situation.

A DB Contractor Fails

A total of 13 cost-plus contracts were awarded to DB contractors. All the contractors mobilized to Iraq in the second quarter of 2004 and began work immediately. All but one contractor was able to subcontract work to local Iraqi subcontractors and make positive progress on projects.

It became apparent in late summer of 2004 that this one contractor was not going to do any actual on-site project work. At that time, the PCO had two options. One option was to fire the contractor and potentially sue the contractor for not fulfilling the contract, and the second option was to negotiate a "termination for convenience." In the end, the PCO negotiated a termination for convenience with the contractor because it was the quickest thing to do, and the entire focus of the program was speed, that is, to get projects started. It was later reported in the press that the contractor left Iraq because it was unsafe to work in Iraq, but the press missed the fact that all the other 12 contractors were still working in Iraq.

Contracting Office

Regulatory compliance is a big deal when awarding and executing government contracts. And if the contracts are cost-plus, which all the contracts in Iraq were, the bureaucratic regulatory compliance effort becomes a bigger effort. Because of this, the government contracting officers and the contracting office were very important. In fact, it was not unusual that the contracting officer thought that he or she was the project manager because he or she was responsible for making sure that funds were only disbursed for work that was completed in compliance with the contract and within the intent of the law.

Audits and Auditors

Because of the cost-plus contracting approach and the common requirement to pay Iraqi subcontractors in cash, numerous audits were required. It was not unusual to have three to five different audit agencies working on several different audits at any given point in time. For example, as of August 8, 2004, there were 8 audits in progress, 6 audits scheduled to start in fourth quarter 2004, and an additional 12 audits scheduled to start in 2005. The Department of Army Audit Agency and the Department of Defense Audit Agency seemed to have a permanent presence in Baghdad. Since audits were common, the PCO had its own auditor on staff to provide advice as to how to best meet later audit requirements and to also advise PCO staff as to how to respond to audit requests.

Employee Turnover and Quality

There were three types of employees working in the PCO office: military, civilian government employees hired on a part-time status for this rebuilding effort, and contractors. In general, the quality of all employees was exceptional. Not only were the people involved bright, but they also had good, applicable experience, and everyone maintained a positive attitude on a daily basis. While personnel quality was high, employee turnover was a problem. Following is a brief discussion of the employee turnover by type of employee:

- *Military.* The military was concerned with stress experienced while working in a war zone. The military's goal was to minimize the cases of posttraumatic stress while maximizing the length of the tour of duty in the war zone. The Navy had done a study on the occurrence of posttraumatic stress and determined that the optimal tour length was seven months. Each service set its length of tours differently. The tour lengths by service were as follows:

  - Army: 12 months
  - Air Force: Originally 3 months; then moved to 4 months in August 2004
  - Marines: 7 months
  - Navy: 6 months

While the military tours of duty were short, the quality and capability of military personnel working on the rebuilding program were excellent. Most had had 10 to 20 years of experience as "base engineers" or "base facilities managers," and their familiarity with the government procurement process was a big plus.

- *Civilian government employees.* A federal law allows the government to hire employees on a temporary status with full benefits. Since the number of the law was 3161, these temporary government employees were referred to as "3161 employees." The federal government also has an absolute pay cap of approximately $175,000 per year. While working in a war zone, it was common for these employees to work and bill seven 12-hour days per week, receive a 25 percent pay bump for working overseas, and receive a second 25 percent pay bump for working in a war zone. The combination of 84-hour work weeks with the two 25 percent pay bumps caused most, if not all, government employees to hit the pay cap in six to eight months. Once the employee hit the pay cap, he or she usually would quit and go home. Also, government policy allowed for only one R&R trip per year.

- *Contractors.* As mentioned, the actual work was subcontracted by the government to 6 private-sector engineering firms, 13 DB firms, and 2 IT contracting firms. Generally, the pay package for these employees provided for a substantial bonus after the employee had worked one year on the project. Thus most contractors would stay on at least a year. To make staying on the job a year more tolerable, most contractor benefits package allowed for two to three weeks of R&R every two to three months.

Construction Management

There were pluses and minus to having the U.S. Army Corp of Engineers (USACE) provide the construction management services. On the plus side was the USACE experience with the government contracting processes, USACE's capability to mobilize rather quickly, and USACE's familiarity working with the U.S. military. On the minus side, USACE personnel were primarily experienced at doing water and other civil engineering types of contracts and lacked the skills to manage large electrical and oil projects.

PROGRAM MANAGEMENT SYSTEMS AND PROGRAM REPORTING

The government outsourced the responsibility to develop, implement, and maintain an integrated program and project management system that would interface with existing government systems. The plan was to create an integrated system using the following major components all interconnected via an Oracle database:

- P3ec from Primavera for project scheduling
- Maximo, a requirements and life-cycle management system
- The Corp of Engineers Financial Management System (CEFMS)
- RMS, the Corp of Engineers construction management system

    The other key element of the plan was that the PCOC was to develop the policies and procedures for all six sectors to use the preceding systems in a uniform way that integrated program reporting. Further the PCOC was responsible for the program reporting.
    Some key issues developed early on relating to the integrated systems include

- The PCO was slow to define and implement policy and procedures for use of the system, and the IT contractor was slow to develop the automated interfaces between the systems. This meant that the reports showing planned and actual project start dates by city or by governorate were difficult to generate for the first nine months of 2004. This created a big problem in that mayors, governors, and other local officials were continually asking for project lists for their geographic area, and the PCO was not able to produce accurate reports.
- The Corp of Engineers had retained a firm to provide program and project reporting for the corps construction management function. It turned out that there was overlap in the scope of work called for by the PCO and Corp's reporting firm. In the end, the program management responsibility was removed from the PCO's scope of work, and the Corp of Engineers program management contractor preformed the program reporting function for both the corp and the PCO.

- All the sector engineering firms and all the DB firms already had good working project and program reporting systems in place. An issue quickly arose relating to whether to allow each firm to use its own existing system and write interfaces to the government's system or to require each firm to use the system provided by the government. In the end, all the sector engineering firms were required to use the government-provided P3ec system for schedule management.

- Another issue was what common scheduled events to require for all projects so that a rolled-up program management report could be generated? In the end, 10 standard events were defined and required in the schedule for every project. With 2500 projects being planned, this meant that the program management system contained 25,000 events.

Program Reporting

Program reporting went through four distinct phases. In each phase there was a distinct focus so that in each phase a different report was the key report. The four phases and the key reports were as shown in Table 12.5.

Paperless Reporting

All reports were generated electronically using Excel, PowerPoint, or the reporting system within RMS and P3ec. Few, if any, reports were printed. When small project meetings were held, a computer monitor was used to display the report for all to see. This worked well for meetings with up to four or five attendees. When larger meetings were held, a projector was used to display a larger version of the computer monitor on the wall or a screen. Paper copies of reports were rarely generated or stored. Instead, everyone carried a memory stick. Since everyone was required to have an identification badge over his or her neck, the memory stick generally was worn around the neck in combination with the ID badge. When anyone wanted a copy of a report, he or she simply plugged his or her memory stick into the computer in use and downloaded the report to the memory stick. Note that the reports generally were too large to e-mail because the file size limit for e-mail attachments is 5 megabytes.

Further supporting the paperless environment was the fact that everyone had a large-capacity networked desktop computer with the latest versions of Microsoft Outlook and Microsoft Office.

TABLE 12.5 Program Reporting Phases

Phase	Time Frame	Report
1. Project definition	December 2003 to May 2004	Completed and approved project information sheets
2. Get the money	May 2004 to September 2004	Dollars apportioned, committed, and obligated
3. Start projects	September 2004 to January 2005	Projects started
4. Complete projects	January 2005 until December 2008 (estimate)	Earned value and percent complete coupled with project costs

Digital Photos and E-mail

Since travel to site locations was difficult, it was common for project managers to get project status reports via e-mail with digital up-to-date project photos attached. This worked well, was simple, and led to the easy creation of digitized project records.

Stoplight Codes

A paperless environment made possible the full use of color. That is, there was no need to worry about losing color when reports were copied, and all computer monitors were color. This allowed the extensive use of stoplight codes in all reports, that is, red shading or color to indicate a problem, yellow to indicate a potential issue, and green to indicate that things are progressing per plan.

The following sample reports illustrate the use of stoplight codes:

- *Figure 12.6, Sample Project Chart.* For every major project, a project chart was maintained to report on progress versus plan for scope, schedule, and budget.

- *Figure 12.7, Sample Construction Project Started/Planed Summary.* This was a report that was used heavily in executive meetings held during the last part of 2004.

- *Figure 12.8, Sample Project Status Summary Report.* Using mostly this chart coupled with some project charts (see Fig. 12.6), it was possible to review the status of over 100 projects in a given sector in one hour with management. This report was developed by Joe Riccio and was referred to as a "Riccio chart."

- This book is a great example of the downside to paper based reports; that is, with paper, you are often limited to black and white. Thus Figs. 12.6, 12.7 and 12.8 really do not illustrate color based stoplight codes.

BH-003 Design & construct primary healthcare centers

Sector = buildings, health & education   D/B Cont = parsons   As of= 6 December 04
SPCO program manager   SPCOC project manager

Scope - Design and build 150 PHC's distributed across 18 governorates with one basic design.

Schedule:
Construction start = 23 October 04
Estimated const. finish = 30 December 05

Budget/costs:
Program cost = $236 Mil
Project cost = $161 Mil

Current activity:
- 34 sites under construction
- 148 sites identified, 2 unidentified
- 200+ personnel employed

Current issues:
- Working with MoH to confirm 44 sites with legal and site issues
- Labor/material cost increases may reduce program to 135 **PHC's**

Looking ahead:
- 46 sites to start in December

Al Basrah site

FIGURE 12.6   Sample project chart.

Reporting Cycle and Meetings

Reporting systems were developed on the fly in the summer of 2004. We quickly put together the following three-level reporting/meeting system:

- Level 1 reporting called *directors' update briefs* (DUBs) was the highest-level briefing and was held every two weeks and lasted 60 to 90 minutes. The audience for these briefs included the head of PCO, the general in charge of the Army Corp of Engineers, and the ambassador in charge of the rebuilding effort. Each sector was given 10 minutes to provide and overview of their efforts. Standard slides included
  - Top news stories for the week
  - Summary of funding status, that is, funds apportioned, committed, obligated, and disbursed
  - Projects started by month and projects forecast to start for the next three months using a chart such as Fig. 12.6 that featured stoplight codes
  - Presentation of two or three selected projects using a standard project chart such as Fig. 12.7
  - Issues to address

Construction starts summary		25-Oct-04 (Actual)	30-Sep-04	31-Oct-04	30-Nov-04	31-Dec-04
B, H&E	No. of projects	199	256	361	563	863	981
	Value		85	95	257	288	288
Electricity	No. of projects	29	25	28	49	82	84
	Value		625	645	689	1,170	1,170
Oil	No. of projects	9	9	25	34	36	35
	Value		35	73	110	113	113
P W&W	No. of projects	20	7	9	14	21	22
	Value		75	461	567	697	697
S&J	No. of projects	102	108	257	322	329	326
	Value		280	620	848	882	882
T&C	No. of projects	37	55	75	101	122	119
	Value		75	118	151	258	258
AIRP	No. of projects	348	343	345	357	357	357
	Value	313	311	313	328	328	328
Total projects		744	803	1,100	1,440	1,810	1,924
Total value		313	1,486	2,325	2,950	3,736	3,736

■ Forecast on target ■ Forecast within 10% of target

□ Forecast less then 90% of target □ Forecast □ Actual data

FIGURE 12.7 Construction projects started/planned summary.

Sub-sector: Public buildings program status
As of 11 August 2004

Task order	Scope	Schedule	Budget Value = $M Prog/ETC	Tasking Pin/Act	Obligation Pin/Act	Definalization Date	Design % Pin/Act	Construction % Pin/Act	Commissioning Pin/Act	Acceptance Pin/Act
BP-001 Ministry of environment	G	G	G 4.8/4.8	G	G	G	38/38	5/10		
BP-001 Opt 1 ministry of trade	Gy	⇑	G 8.2/8.2	G	G	3/18/04	90/95	35/30		
BP-001 Opt 2 ministry of industry & minerals	G	G	G 13.7/13.7	G	G	G	65/70	05/05		
BP-001 Opt 3 ministry of Education & Hi Ed	G	Gy	⇑ 12.3/25.0	G	G	8/25/04	35/30	03/04		
BP-002 Independent electoral commission	G	G	G 3.5/3.5	G	G	G	55/55	40/40		

ETC: Estimate to complete
Pin/Act: Planned vs. actual

FIGURE 12.8   Sample project status summary report.

- Level 2 reporting called *sector consolidated report and update for management* (SCRUMs) were held every two weeks at first and then moved to ever three weeks. These sessions typically lasted one to two hours. Contents were similar to those in the DUBs; in fact, there were many duplicate slides, but discussion was more in-depth, and more projects were reviewed. Using a project status report chart such as the one in Figure 12.8 allowed a sector to report project status on all projects within the sector in about one hour.
- Level 3 reporting was standard project meetings between the SPCOC (the engineer) and the DB contractor. Meetings covered project details and would last from one to four hours depending on the current situation.

LESSONS LEARNED

The lessons learned listed below are not in a priority order but instead are grouped by topic.

Outsourcing

Outsourcing all functions, for example, engineering, design build, computer services, support systems, etc., creates some issues.

- Scope becomes difficult to manage because scope overlaps occur. This was most evident in the project management systems when initially each of the following groups hired project control personnel: the government, the SPCOCs (the engineers), the design build contractors, and the Army Corp of Engineers. This resulted in duplicate work, inconsistent data, and lengthy discussions about who should do what and how with regard to project tracking.
- When you outsource everything, the management function does not go away. This was particularly apparent in the IRRF I program when many projects were started quickly and the scope management function was left to contractors rather than to the U.S. government, which was the bill payer.

Cost-Plus Contracting

The major focus of the reconstruction program was speed so as to get projects started, employee Iraqis, and thereby win the hearts and minds of the Iraqi people. While facilitating speed, cost-plus contracting created some other issues.

- The PCO was under pressure to obligate as much money as possible to contractors because money obligated was a measure of progress. However, when starting projects with undefined scopes, budgets, and schedules, it is prudent to obligate, say, 20 percent of the project funds. This initial funding would be used to definitize the project scope, schedule, and budget. Only at such time that the project is fully definitized should the remainder of the project funds be obligated or released. Also, by coupling an award fee to meeting the defined project scope, budget, and schedule, the project can be turned into a pseudo-fixed-price contract.

- With cost-plus contracts, the role of the contracting officer because more important, and this could and sometimes did have a negative impact on the authority and effectiveness of the project manager.

- Cost-plus contracts bring the baggage of many audits and many reports.

- Cost-plus contracting tends to place all the project risk on the owner, in this case the government. Ideally, once a project is definitized, some project risk should shift to the DB contractor.

Personnel

Personnel turnover was a problem. The contractor's model of signing people to one-year agreements with liberal R&R benefits and a substantial completion bonus at the end of the year was a more effective model than the government's approach of limited R&R and average tour lengths of about six months.

Program Definition

As designed by Congress in Public Law 106-08, the reconstruction program was to be implemented by large coalition engineering and DB firms, and the Iraqi ministers were to select and approve all projects. This created some issues.

- In hindsight, two programs should have been defined: (1) a program of large-scale infrastructure projects that were defined in Baghdad and (2) a program of smaller projects where the project selection was done on a city-by-city basis by local city officials

- Working through large DB firms to execute small projects such as fire or police station rehab projects is not cost-effective. In fact, most likely every city in the world will hire smaller, local contractors to do small, local projects.

- All programs must be flexible. Day one when any program or project starts, things change, and adjustments must be made. In the case of Iraq, the absence of community-based programs was quickly apparent, but using the same organizational structure and using Iraqi oil money for funding, a community-based program was quickly built to supplement the IRRF II program.

Contractor Failures

Contractor failures occur, and you must be ready to backfill the failed contractor's role. In Iraq, one contractor exited early before doing any construction work, and the contractor hired to manage the entire program, the PCOC, mobilized late and was unable to fulfill its entire roll. In both cases, enterprising, energized people were able to implement alternatives to keep the program moving on schedule.

Paperless

The capabilities of networked computers and the ability of white-collar workers to operate the desktop computers have reached the point were paperless program and project management reporting is possible. Some related points here are as follows:

- Paper reports generally limited reports to black and white. On the other hand, all computer monitors today have color capability. Color can be used to enhance reporting effectiveness. For example, using red, yellow, and green stoplight codes in program reporting facilitated the ability to review 100 projects with management in one hour.
- Digital photos and e-mail have greatly enhanced the ability to manage projects remotely.

Program Management

A few well-known paradigms of program management were reinforced.

- The cardinal error in program management is to start all the projects and then not finish many of the projects because budget runs out before project completion. Best practice, of course, is to only start projects that you can finish. For example, it is better to finish 70 projects than it is to start 100 projects and only complete about 40, which is what happened in the RIO program.
- Stakeholder management is important. In this case, the program was not set up to regularly communicate with several key stakeholders, such as mayors, governors, and military officers within the MNFs. It was necessary to create a regional program to support this effort.
- You get what you measure, and what you measure needs to change with time. For PCO, there were four distinct project phases, and in each phase the key measurement changed. In phase 1, the key measures were the number of projects defined, approved by the Iraqi minister, and documented in a written task order. In phase 2, the key measures were how much money had been apportioned and how much had been obligated to projects. In phase 3, the key measure was projects started. And finally, in phase 4, the key measurements were classic project progress measures such as earned value, schedule variance, and budget variance.
- Adaptability is important. On day one of any program, you quickly realize that some of the assumptions used in the program design are inappropriate and that the project plan must be adapted to the current real-world situation. Some examples of necessary program modifications that were made are as follows: the creation of the Accelerated Iraqi Reconstruction Program (AIRP) to implement community-based projects, the implementation of a regional program to better communicate with key stakeholders, changing

project approaches to facilitate working in a war zone, and taking over the scope of failed efforts by select contractors.

- Accurate reporting to all stakeholders is a must. In this case, the failure of the project reporting systems to operate effectively in the summer of 2004 caused the PMO to look as if it were not managing the program properly.

Press Reporting Often Inaccurate

While the American press does an excellent job of accurately reporting the news in the United States, the American press often misses on international stories. Two examples of this are as follows: First, the press reported that a contractor left Iraq in December 2004 because it was unsafe to work in Iraq. In fact, that one contractor failed to be able to complete work in Iraq, whereas about 20 other contractors continued to work in Iraq successfully. Second, the press reported regularly on the slow progress of the program in the summer of 2004 without even trying to understand what was happening.

CONCLUSION: IRAQIS NEED TO REBUILD IRAQ

At the time of this writing, the reconstruction program is moving on at a rapid pace. As of December 31, 2004, approximately 1400 AIRP and IRRF II projects were started, and as of March 21, 2005, over 2000 projects were underway. However, Americans or other coalition participants will never be able to rebuild Iraq, just as a group of Arabs would not be able to rebuild the Gulf Coast after the recent hurricanes.

The good news is that Iraq has the money to rebuild Iraq. Currently, Iraqi oil money is running about $18 to $20 billion per year. There is widespread agreement that oil revenue would run $50 or $60 billion per year if Iraq's oil infrastructure were expanded and modernized. The estimated cost to bring the oil infrastructure up to date is $15 billion. Iraq does not have the money today to do this, but Iraq does have over $500 billion dollars of proven oil assets in the ground, so financing a $15 billion investment in the oil infrastructure is quite possible. Before this investment can be made, several things need to happen: (1) Iraq needs to have a stable government in place, (2) the laws to facilitate foreign investments need to be put in place, and (3) a national energy policy needs to be developed.

Thus, while we cannot rebuild Iraq, we can help Iraq create a secure environment, create economic stability, and establish democratic processes with basic freedoms for the people of Iraq so that in the end Iraqis can rebuild Iraq. And the reconstruction program will help to do this.

CHAPTER 13

PROJECT CRITICAL SUCCESS FACTORS: THE PROJECT-IMPLEMENTATION PROFILE

Jeffrey K. Pinto

Black School of Business, Pennsylvania State University,
Erie, Pennsylvania

Dennis P. Slevin

Katz Graduate School of Business, University of Pittsburgh,
Pittsburgh, Pennsylvania

Dr. Pinto holds the Andrew Morrow and Elizabeth Lee Black Chair in Management of Technology at the Black School of Business at Pennsylvania State University. He is also adjunct professor at the University of Technology, Sydney. He received both a Ph.D. and an MBA from the University of Pittsburgh and holds a B.A. in history and a B.S. in business administration from the University of Maryland. His research interests include the study of project management and the processes by which organizations implement innovations and advanced technologies. He is a member of the Project Management Institute, the Association of Project Management, and the Engineering Management Society.

Dr. Slevin is professor of business administration at the Joseph M. Katz Graduate School of Business at the University of Pittsburgh. Dr. Slevin holds a B.A. from St. Vincent College, a B.S. from M.I.T., an M.S. from Carnegie-Mellon University, and a Ph.D. from Stanford University. He is the author of numerous refereed journal articles, book chapters, and books. He is a member of the Project Management Institute and the Academy of Management. His research and consulting interests focus on project management, the implementation of organizational innovation, and entrepreneurship.

Many examples of project management tools used for tracking the "harder" technical aspects of projects throughout their development and implementation exist today. While there are great advantages to the use of these techniques, they have some potential drawbacks for successful project implementation. Often some of the longer-run fundamental, strategic, and more subjective factors are overlooked. The Project-Implementation Profile (PIP) was developed with two purposes in mind. First, it allows the project manager to assess the "softer" behavioral side of the project management process to determine the status of the project in relation to its human elements. Second, the PIP gives project managers the opportunity to focus some of their attention on the strategic issues of project development. This chapter discusses the project-implementation process, focusing on 10 critical project success factors identified in a recent study. It further outlines the ways in which the PIP can be used by project managers. An illustrative example of a project that used the PIP to assess the success of implementation is given.

The study of those factors that are critical to project-implementation success has remained an area of tremendous interest within the project management field. These factors, typically referred to as *critical success factors* (CSFs) are, by definition, considered to be the structural and process-related constructs that can positively influence the likelihood of project success. As a result, both practitioners and researchers continue to work to better understand and define the set of CSFs for projects that can demonstrate strong predictive power yet which are also sufficiently "managerial" in nature that they can be materially addressed by personnel involved in the project. Put another way, it does little good to identify CSFs that are beyond the ability of project managers to address (e.g., a healthy national economy).

A number of important papers have been published in recent years in order to reconceptualize the study of project CSFs and their role both in understanding project success and in the formation of current project management theory. Soderlund (2002) highlighted the "critical success factor school" as an example of a normative, planning-based model that focuses on the management and organization of single projects. Other researchers have taken a more directed approach in studying the impact of individual factors as opposed to a collective set of CSFs. For example, Belout and Gauvreau (2004) examined the direct impact of human resources policies and the personnel employed on a project and their effect on project success. Turner and Muller (2005) argued that current CSF research tends to underemphasize the critical leadership role of the project manager as a key contributor to project success. Thus, both collectively and individually, project CSFs continue to serve as a fertile source of research and conceptual thought for furthering project management theory development.

Another way in which researchers have sharpened the focus on studying project CSFs has been to define specific classes of projects in order to identify, compare, and contrast factors critical to success across project categories. For example, Wateridge (1998) examined information technology (IT) projects and contrasted their key CSFs with other project types. Pinto and Covin (1989) contrasted the CSFs across the project life cycle for construction versus research and development (R&D) projects. Amplifying this "one size does not fit all" philosophy, Shenhar (2001) has long argued for the need to clearly, identify, and classify project types as a first means for conducting research.

A recent study articulated this nature of the CSF challenge by distinguishing between three questions that must be answered in identifying the success factors for a project (Cooke-Davies, 2002). These three questions included

1. What factors are critical to project management success?
2. What factors are critical to success of an individual project?
3. What factors lead to consistently successful projects?

Cooke-Davies found that a number of factors, actions, and attitudes contribute to what he termed "the real" project success factors, including adequacy of company-wide training on risk management, adequate documentation of organizational responsibilities, allowing changes to scope only through a mature scope-change-control process, and so forth. In fact, he noted that although his factors were not, of themselves, human factors, "the people side of the success factors is woven into their very fabric"

(Cooke-Davies, 2002, p. 189). This observation echoes a similar theme postulated by Lechler (1998), who put the message more plainly, stating, "When it comes to project management, it's the people that matter." The PIP described here focuses more on managerial factors than on purely behavioral issues, although there is no question that research on project management continues to move in a behavioral direction (Slevin and Pinto, 2004).

THE 10-FACTOR MODEL: THE PROJECT-IMPLEMENTATION PROFILE

Project monitoring and control are difficult and often inexact processes. A number of different cues and a large amount of information are constantly confronting project managers as they attempt to track their projects throughout the various implementation stages. Further, the more complex the project, the more likely it is that project managers are faced with making sense of the wide variety of technical, human, and budgetary issues (or project critical factors) with which they must contend. As a result of the complexity involved in project management and the demands on the project manager's time, the project management process has seen the rise and increasing acceptance and use of a wide variety of tracking systems. These systems are both computer-driven and manual and are intended to aid the project manager in keeping track of the myriad of variables that must be accounted for to help ensure project success.

Well-established project monitoring aids have been in existence for some time. Systems such as the project evaluation and review technique (PERT), Gantt charts, and critical-path methodologies can be extremely useful in helping project managers untangle the various project activities with which they must contend, including the careful tracking of costs, schedules, performance of project subassemblies and subcontractors, and so forth. However, project managers, in focusing on this minute level of detail, may be drawn away from some important "larger picture" aspects of project management necessary for success. In other words, overattention to the specific, tactical "firefighting" and detailed management activities related to project management often prevents the project manager from developing clear, periodic assessments of the overall project strategy. The project manager must constantly ask such questions as

- Is this project solving the right problem?
- Will the project be used by the clients?
- Is top management truly supportive of this project?
- Are the client's needs adequately understood?
- Is the basic project mission still on target?
- Does the company have the necessary project team personnel to succeed?

Questions of this sort emphasize another aspect of project management. Although the project manager may possess numerous detailed reports that provide careful tracking of the "hard" project numbers, there is another major component of project management that should not be overlooked. The so-called soft side of project management involves key behavioral variables that are crucial to project success. Issues for project success such as quality of project team personnel, top-management support, and client acceptance are as equally important as the harder technical detail management and must be attended to by both project managers and upper management.

What has been needed is a project management tool to allow project managers to sort through the information they receive, to more accurately and systematically monitor and assess the current state of those factors that have been shown to be critical for project implementation success. Further, a tool that would allow project managers to gain an overall strategic sense of the project-implementation process would be of great benefit in efforts to exert successful comprehensive project control. It was in order to address these points that the PIP was created. The PIP provides two important resources: a 10-factor model of project implementation and a measurement instrument for assessing those factors.

DEVELOPMENT OF THE 10-FACTOR MODEL

In developing the PIP, projective information was obtained from 54 managers who had experience with a variety of projects. Participants of this study were asked to consider a successful project with which they had been involved recently. Assuming the role of project manager, they were asked to indicate activities in which they could engage or important issues they could address that would increase the likelihood of project success significantly. This process was repeated until a set of critical activities or criteria was uncovered (Pinto and Slevin, 1987). These identified activities resulted in the creation of a set of 10 critical success factors for project implementation and resulted in a 50-item instrument that can be used to measure project-implementation performance in relation to the critical factors.

These 10 critical success factors were validated subsequently and found to be generalizable to a wide variety of project types in a study of over 400 projects (Slevin and Pinto, 1986, 1988). Further, the PIP allows project managers to systematically monitor these 10 critical success factors in relation to their specific projects. On both an individual and collective basis, the following factors are strongly correlated with project success.

Project Mission

Mission refers to the initial clarity of goals and general directions for the project. In a sense, the first step in the project development process is to know what it is one wishes to develop, what the project's capabilities are, why the project is needed, and how it will benefit those who use it. The decision to develop and implement a new project often signals the commitment by the organization of a large amount of time, money, and human and material resources. Before such a commitment occurs, it is vital to have a clear, well-acknowledged vision of the goals or mission underlying the project. Projects often fail because of the need to redefine the mission after substantial resources have been spent on "mission creep" as the project proceeds.

Top-Management Support

An important question to be asked once the mission of the project is determined is whether there exists a willingness on the part of top management to truly support the project. It may be easy for top management to pay lip service to the "importance" of the new project, but often this support can be reduced or not provided over time. Is top management committed to providing the necessary resources throughout the development and implementation process? Will top managers use their authority to help the project? Will top management support the project team in the event of a crisis? Answers to these and similar questions frequently indicate the true degree of support the project manager can expect to receive from top management. Top-management support is more than budget authority. It also implies access to decisions and decision makers.

Project Schedule/Plans

In order for a project to proceed successfully, it requires a well-laid-out and detailed specification of the individual action steps required. All necessary activities must be scheduled. Further, there must be plans in place to determine when vital resources (human, budgetary, and material) will be required. Finally, it is important that a measurement tool be in place to assess the actual progress of the implementation against schedule projections. It is essential to measure actual progress (such as earned-value analysis) rather than simply resources spent.

Client Consultation

The *client* refers to anyone who is the ultimate intended user of the project. Clients can be the firm's customers but also may be internal to the organization. Because a project is intended for the client's benefit, it is vital that communication and consultation with the clients occur not only at the beginning of the development process but also throughout the project's implementation. Projects are often subject to a variety of changes throughout their development; as a result, clients must be kept apprised of the status of the project and its capabilities rather than surprised at the end when the project is transferred to them. The project team must remain aware of the client's needs.

Personnel

The parent organization's people represent a very important ingredient for successful project implementation. Simply put, does the organization have the necessary personnel to staff the project team? Is it necessary for the company to recruit or provide additional training to personnel in order for them to function effectively on the project team? Too often organizations ignore the importance of this factor, sometimes assigning individuals to project teams on the basis of convenience or their nonusefulness to other, current organizational activities. As a result, the project team may be staffed with the castoffs of other departments, a formula sure to result in potential future project difficulties and possible failure.

Technical Tasks

This factor refers to assessment of the availability of the required technology or technological resources to aid in the project's development. Does the organization possess the technological resources to develop the project? Further, it requires a determination of whether or not those individuals who are developing the project understand it from the technological standpoint. For successful project development, skilled people and adequate technology are equally important. Often senior management underestimates the importance and difficulty of the technical tasks performed by these skilled people.

Client Acceptance

The penultimate question that must be asked as the result of any project development is, "Is the client satisfied with the project and making use of it?" One finding that has come through time and again is that it is not enough to simply create a project, transfer it to a client, and assume that it will be accepted and used. In reality, client acceptance is a critical factor that must be handled just like any other criterion for project success. In addition to performing the technical and administrative activities necessary to develop the project, the project team also must function in a marketing/selling role in working to gain client acceptance.

Monitoring and Feedback

It is important that at each step in the implementation process key project team members receive feedback on how the project is progressing. These control mechanisms allow the project manager to be on top of any real or potential problems, to oversee corrective measures, and to prevent deficiencies from being overlooked. The better the control processes, the more likely it is that the final project will retain high quality.

Communication

Communication is a key component for project success throughout the development process. Project teams routinely engage in a three-way pattern of communications with clients and the parent organization. It is vital that these communication channels remain open to ensure the transfer and exchange of relevant information among these three major players in the project-implementation process. Consequently, the project manager needs to ensure that there is an appropriate network to transmit all necessary data concerning the project to each project stakeholder.

Troubleshooting

It is safe to say that few projects are developed without problems occurring along the way. Projects require constant fine-tuning and readjustment throughout their creation in order to address these trouble spots. As a result, the final critical success factor refers to the availability of contingency plans, systems, or procedures that are in place to handle unexpected crises and deviations from plan (Table 13.1).

TABLE 13.1   Ten Project-Critical Success Factors

1. *Mission*—initial clarity of goals and general directions
2. *Top-management support*—willingness of top management to provide the necessary resources and authority/power for project success
3. *Project schedule/plans*—a detailed specification of the individual action steps required for project implementation
4. *Client consultation*—communication, consultation, and active listening to all affected parties
5. *Personnel*—selection, recruitment, and training of the necessary personnel for the project team
6. *Technical tasks*—availability of the required technology and expertise to accomplish the specific technical actions
7. *Client acceptance*—the effect of "selling" the final project to its ultimate intended users
8. *Monitoring and feedback*—timely provision of comprehensive control information at each stage in the implementation process
9. *Communication*—the provision of an appropriate network and necessary data to all key actors in the project implementation
10. *Troubleshooting*—the ability to handle unexpected crises and deviations from plan

HOW THE PROJECT-IMPLEMENTATION PROFILE WORKS

Since its development, the PIP has been completed by thousands of project managers world-wide, responsible for a wide variety of projects from construction to high-technology R&D. Use of the PIP suggests that project managers should engage in regular periodic reviews of their projects throughout the project's entire life. Both the project manager and members of the project team perform an audit of the current status of the project based on an assessment of the project's health as measured by the 10 critical success factors. Each critical factor is composed of a set of five subitems, making a total of 50 questions to which the project manager must respond. Based on a national sample of over 400 projects, percentile scores have been developed so that the project manager can monitor and track project performance in comparison with a database of other successful projects.

The reason for periodic reviews of project status should be readily apparent. Project development and implementation are a dynamic, ongoing process requiring constant review and reassessment in order to gain an accurate picture of the project at any point in time. In terms of deciding when best to reassess project status, our experience has been to employ a combination of two methods: elapsed time and critical incidents. For example, in a project expected to have a one-year duration, we have found that project reviews should take place at regular intervals of not longer than one month. Not only does this method provide regular project assessments, but it also puts the project manager and team members in the habit of performing regular strategic implementation-monitoring activities.

The second assessment method concerns using the PIP following specific critical incidents. Examples of critical incidents may include the achievement of important target dates, the entrance into a new state of the project life cycle, or the development and/or resolution of a crisis situation. These incidents do not neatly follow a one-month project-monitoring program but signal that important changes are taking place in the project that require an updated project status audit.

FOUR-STEP PROCESS

In addition to a discussion of the theory underlying the development and inclusion of each of the 10 critical success factors, Appendix 13A contains an abbreviated copy of the PIP. As a result, project managers can make practical use of this instrument by following a simple four-step process that is outlined below.

Periodically Monitor the 10 Factors over Time

At each project monitoring point, the project manager and significant members of the project team each fill out the PIP. Collecting data from as many people on the project team as possible provides a wide range of perspectives of the status of the project. It also eliminates the possibility that one or two key members of the team may be overly optimistic about the project's progress.

Use Consensus to Develop a Collective Picture of the Project

After everyone has filled out the profile, indicating their perception of the current status of the project, review the results and discuss the likely causes of disagreements among project team members in the scores on the critical success factors of the PIP. Perhaps administrative and technical personnel disagree in their assessments of project status because of their more specifically focused backgrounds. Use consensus to establish as accurate an assessment of project status as possible. The PIP provides a shared vocabulary for reaching this consensus.

Pay Close Attention to Low Factors

"Low" scores are those that have a ranking below the 50th percentile. These low scores indicate likely future problem areas that may have an adverse effect on successful project implementation. Project managers should start developing action plans for improving these factor scores. For example, if the factor score of personnel is rated as low, it is sensible to critically examine the project team to see if present team members have the necessary skills to perform their tasks. This low score may signal the need to locate and enlist additional project team personnel.

Visually Emphasize the Critical Success Factors

Putting the current profile on the bulletin board or in memos can be a powerful tool for indicating to members of the project team and upper management both the current status of the project and where problem areas exist. These problem areas would suggest the obvious "pressure points" that require extra consideration. In one instance, a project manager would attach a copy of the project profile scores to the office doors of members of his project team overnight so that this status report was the first thing they saw when they arrived in the morning. These profile scores represent an excellent visual reinforcement and an alternative feedback mechanism to the reams of budget and schedule data that are generated on a daily basis.

ILLUSTRATIVE EXAMPLE

A major engineering corporation was recently involved in the development, testing, and commercialization of a nuclear reactor monitoring and diagnostic system. The goals of this project were to develop and install a diagnostic system in reactor coolant pumps in order to identify problems before potentially dangerous leakages occur.

Figure 13.1 shows a sample copy of the PIP for this particular project, as filled out by the project manager, indicating the 10 critical factor scores. The raw scores obtained from answering the 50 questions covering the 10 critical factors of the PIP have been converted to percentile scores through use of the database of over 400 projects.

Interpreting this profile would suggest that 6 of the 10 critical factors for the project can be rated as strong or well handled. One of the factors could be considered marginal, and the other three critical success factors can be interpreted as being weak, representing potentially serious problem areas.

The six strong factors include project mission, project scheduling/plans, client consultation, client acceptance, monitoring and feedback, and communication. Each of these critical factors has a percentile ranking of over 60 percent. The practical interpretation of these scores for the project manager would be that these are critical areas that are currently being handled well; that is, there are no problems with these aspects of the

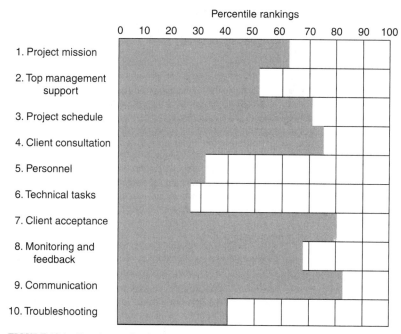

FIGURE 13.1   Sample completed PIP.

implementation process that are being exhibited at the present time. As a result, project managers can turn their attention to other, more immediate problem areas.

The marginal factor is top-management support, with a percentile score hovering near 50 percent. This score would suggest the potential for future difficulties. In this case, a signal should be sent to the project team that they may not have the backing of top management to the degree that is sufficient to implement the project successfully. It would be advisable to look for possible causes or reasons for this potential lack of support because it could be the likely source of future problems.

Finally, the three weak factors are those of personnel, technical tasks, and troubleshooting. These three factors scored below the 50th percentile. While the marginal score discussed earlier suggests future potential for trouble, weak factors such as these indicate present difficulties. Left unattended or unresolved, these factors can have a seriously debilitating effect on implementation of the project. In this case it seems apparent that this project has suffered from a lack of trained personnel, supported by the adequate technology, to successfully develop and install the monitoring and diagnostic system. Further, perhaps as a result of the lack of adequate technology, the troubleshooting mechanisms needed to deal with deviations from plan and unexpected difficulties with developing and installing the system are inadequate. As a result of thorough analysis of the profile shown in Fig. 13.1, action plans were developed by the project team that stressed (1) the need to maintain better linkages with top management, (2) the recruitment of additional project team personnel to ensure greater technical expertise, and (3) the acquisition of state-of-the-art technical equipment to aid project team members in the system development.

IMPLICATIONS OF USE OF THE PIP

The PIP is a managerially useful tool for tracking and controlling a wide variety of human factors and activities that can have a dramatic impact on the likely success of a project. While other tracking devices exist and are popularly used (e.g., earned-value management), they may not communicate "actionable" information in a manner that allows a project manager to immediately target problematic areas and begin formulating means to resolve potential danger points as the project moves forward. Thus the PIP should be used to supplement existing tracking metrics and devices if the project organization wishes to gain the widest possible perspective on how its projects are performing, where problems are likely to occur, and what concrete steps the project manager and team can begin taking to alleviate or resolve these critical "choke points" before they become a serious budgetary and/or schedule drain on the project.

The PIP has proven highly useful in another arena, namely, that of project management research. Offering a series of empirically derived critical success factors and project performance assessment, it is being used increasingly in university settings as a means for investigating a variety of projects and their causes of success and failure. Currently, it has been employed to study projects in settings as diverse as Australia, China, Argentina, Nigeria, Europe, and South Africa. It is also being used to compare and contrast critical success factors in public- versus private-sector firms, Department of Defense projects, NASA-sponsored pure research projects, Air Force systems development projects, and so forth. In fact, the literature on and use of the PIP since its development demonstrate clearly the broad acceptance of both the PIP and its efficacy in studying critical success factors.

Research and theory on project critical success factors has continued to grow apace for the past two decades since the seminal work of Baker, Murphy, and Fisher (1988) first brought the subject to our general attention. Through the general acceptance and use of the PIP, critical success factor research has made tremendous empirical and conceptual strides, shedding important new light on those factors which can improve the likelihood of project success, a goal toward which we are all working.

REFERENCES

Baker BN, Murphy DC, Fisher D. 1998. Factors affecting project success, in D Cleland, W. King (eds.), *The Project Management Handbook,* 2d ed. New York: Van Nostrand Reinhold.

Belout A, Gauvreau C. 2004. Factors affecting project success: The impact of human resource management. *Int J Project Manag* 22:1–12.

Cooke-Davies T. 2002. The "real" success factors on projects. *Int J Project Manag* 20:185–190.

Lechler T. 1998. When it comes to project management, it's the people that matter: An empirical analysis of project management in Germany, in F Hartman, G Jergeas, J Thomas (eds.), *IRNOP III: The Nature and Role of Projects in the Next 20 Years: Research Issues and Problems.* Calgary, Alberta, Canada: University of Calgary, pp. 205–215.

Pinto JK, Covin JG. 1989. Critical factors in project implementation: A comparison of construction and R&D projects. *Technovation* 9(1):49–62.

Pinto JK, Slevin DP. 1987. Critical factors in successful project implementation. *IEEE Trans Eng Manag* 34(1):22–27.

Pinto JK, Slevin DP. 1992. *Project Implementation Profile.* Pittsburgh: Innodyne, Inc.

Shenhar A. 2001. One size does not fit all projects: Exploring classical contingency domains. *Manag Sci* 47:394–414.

Slevin DP, Pinto JK. 1986. The Project Implementation Profile: New tool for project managers. *Project Manag J* 18(4):57–71.

Slevin DP, Pinto JK. 1988. Balancing strategy and tactics in a process model of project implementation. *Sloan Manag Rev* 29(1):33–41.

Slevin DP, Pinto JK. 2004. An overview of behavioral issues in project management, in PWG Morris, JK Pinto (eds.), *The Wiley Guide to Managing Projects*. New York: Wiley, pp. 67–85.

Soderlund J. 2004. On the broadening scope of the research on projects: A review and a model for analysis. *Int J Project Manag* 22:655–667.

Soderlund J. 2002. On the development of project management research: Schools of thought and critique. *Int J Project Manag* 8(1):20–31.

Turner JR, Muller R. 2005. The project manager's leadership style as a success factor on projects: A literature review. *Project Manag J* 36(2):49–61.

Wateridge, J., (1998), How can IS/IT projects be measured for success? *International Journal of Project Management*, vol. 16 (1), pp. 59–63.

MANAGEMENT OF GLOBAL PROGRAMS AND PROJECTS

Chapter 14 shows how good project management is key to successful outsourcing in a company. Bidanda, Arisoy and Azim show how outsourcing can change the dynamics of a company, what the key stages are when managing outsourcing as a major project, and how this technique has been used in recent examples. Success and risk factors associated with the management of outsourcing are also discussed.

Chapter 15 broaches the topic of quality monitoring when engaging in international project management. Ireland discusses how international and cultural differences can lead to different quality expectations, and what approaches can be utilized to ensure that a high quality outcome is achieved by all members of the project team.

In Chapter 16, the unique characteristics and accompanying difficulties associated with virtual global projects in the software industry are discussed. Milosevic, Osbay and Srivannaboon introduce a system of success factors for identifying project factors that lead to success, and how to use these factors to create a successful global software project.

Chapter 17 emphasizes the need to build a collaborative knowledge framework when managing international projects. Lee outlines the key challenges involved in a global project, and offers ways to overcome these barriers using a collaborative knowledge framework, which provides a manageable way to locally operate a global system.

CHAPTER 14
PROJECT MANAGEMENT FOR OUTSOURCING DECISIONS

Bopaya Bidanda

Department of Industrial Engineering, University of Pittsburgh, Pittsburgh, Pennsylvania

Ozlem Arisoy

Department of Industrial Engineering, University of Pittsburgh, Pittsburgh, Pennsylvania

Murat Azim

Katz Graduate School of Business, University of Pittsburgh, Pittsburgh, Pennsylvania

Bopaya Bidanda is the Ernest E. Roth Professor and Chairman of the Department of Industrial Engineering at the University of Pittsburgh. He works actively with regional and national corporations in the area of manufacturing systems improvement within a global environment. He has copublished two books with McGraw-Hill (*Automated Factor Handbook* and *Shared Manufacturing*), in addition to over 100 papers in international journals and conference proceedings.

Ozlem Arisoy has a master's degree in industrial engineering from the University of Pittsburgh and is currently a doctoral candidate there. Her research interests include strategic multicriteria decision making, outsourcing logistics, and global supply networks. Her work has appeared in a number of international conference proceedings and journals.

Murat Azim is a MBA student in the Katz Graduate School of Business at the University of Pittsburgh. He has several years of experience in the energy industry and has worked as an electrical engineer in a group of companies that operate internationally.

The growing outsourcing trend forces companies to transfer their high-cost activities to low-labor-rate countries. Outsourcing stands out as an attractive option to reduce cost. However, such an initiative can give a competitive acceleration to a company only if careful analyses are performed and sound projections are constructed. A systematic project management approach during the process of outsourcing decisions is always the key driver behind the success.

Outsourcing decision-making processes can be considered as large size projects that affect a company's strategies and future operations. Although these projects can be managed based on classic project management principles, modifications and extensions are inevitable to support the wide scope of the globalization movement. This chapter starts by explaining how these outsourcing projects change the entire direction of the company. The next sections analyze the project life cycle of outsourcing decisions by reviewing recent projects from various industries. A modification of general project life-cycle phases is proposed, and the phase procedures are detailed, including critical activities, managerial challenges, and milestones, as well as cost, schedule, and technical performance factors. Methodologies specifically related to outsourcing projects such as risk management, stakeholder management, and contract management are also highlighted, along with their practical applications. As a conclusion, the multiple outcomes of these projects are discussed. Failure and success indicators of outsourcing projects and their implications are justified.

Outsourcing is a rising trend that has been subject to many controversial discussions. For some people, it is a globalization effort that creates opportunities for future innovations, contributing to the world economy. For others, outsourcing has a destructive effect on the U.S. economy, increasing unemployment rates and weakening the industrial power of the country. Above all, outsourcing is a consequence of several reasons. Globalization is a result of the unification of world cultures lead by the media and through the rise of communication technologies. Political and economic developments around the world, such as privatization of public-sector organizations and formation of European Union, also increased the speed of globalization. On the other hand, the U.S. consumption market continued expanding. The development of manufacturing processes and technological enhancements and rising demand caused a reduction in product life cycles. More companies started to provide several versions of consumption goods, leaving fewer features for differentiation between products. The power shift from manufacturers to the big retailers such as Wal-Mart and Home Depot gave the incentive to the retailers for tougher price negotiations, forcing the manufacturers toward lower-cost alternatives.[1] As a result, lower-price offers became the main factor for a larger percentage of market share. Globalization and cost pressures forced U.S. companies to the outside world that already had the basis to accept such a shift.

Today, outsourcing stands out as an attractive option for a growing number of companies to reduce costs of their operational activities by either engaging in direct investment in or having strategic alliances with low-labor-rate countries. From a financial point of view, by such moves, companies also anticipate a remarkable reduction in their capital requirements, which gives top management the opportunity to get a higher return on equity (ROE). Therefore, outsourcing is a credible alternative way for managers to make shareholders happy.

The existence of highly educated youth, government subsidies, tax reductions, and infrastructural improvements in developing countries also motivates senior managers toward offshoring their high-cost activities. However, the outsourcing initiative can give a competitive acceleration to a company only if careful analyses are performed and sound projections are constructed. A systematic project management approach during the process of outsourcing decisions is the key driver behind the success.

Outsourcing decisions are based in large part on organizational strategies. A small shift from the optimal decision will have disastrous effects on the competitiveness of the company. Therefore, outsourcing decision processes should be considered in a structured discipline. Many companies have support from outside consultants for their outsourcing decision process. There are also ways to outsource safely using internal staff and expertise. In both cases, the decision process goes through several phases that have defined beginning and end time points. By its intrinsic properties, an outsourcing decision process fits into the definition of a project: a combination of organizational resources pulled together to create something that did not exist previously and that will provide a performance capability in the design and execution of organizational strategies.[2]

Outsourcing decisions are among the top-management responsibilities; therefore, basic management processes, namely, planning, organizing, motivating, controlling, and directing, should be applied during their execution. Outsourcing projects have significant cost, resource, quality, and schedule considerations that may have a huge impact on the entire organization. Riskiness, multitasking, extensive documentation, and complexity are inevitable. Along with these and their strategic importance to business practices, outsourcing projects often get the highest priority in comparison with other projects. These projects should be seriously managed based on project management principles, with modifications and extensions to support their wider scopes.

PROJECT LIFE CYLE

The model in Fig. 14.1, proposed by the authors, describes a typical outsourcing project within the context of a project life cycle. The durations of life-cycle phases are often long, and the processes within each phase require large cuts across organizational boundaries that need extensive and thorough analyses.

The *conceptual phase* calls for alignment with company strategies. The role and involvement of senior management are very critical for the desired achievement. The *design phase* involves investigation of alternatives, detailed financial analyses, and numerous negotiations. During the *implementation phase,* the appropriate outsourcing practice is brought to life. In this period, contractual meetings, cross-border distribution, and training are among the challenges the company faces. The *divestment stage* of an outsourcing project requires a flexible timeline. It consists of two phases, finalization and control. The *finalization phase* includes alteration of the organization, relocation of idle

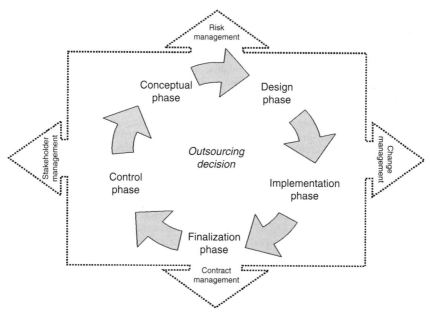

FIGURE 14.1   Project life cycle.

resources, and final documentation, whereas *control phase* is the continuous monitoring of the outsourced activities.

Conceptual Phase

The starting point is to decide whether or not to outsource. Company management must recognize that outsourcing is not the only choice. Although outsourcing is attractive for cost-reduction purposes, there are also many advantages of staying in-house. Control and quality assurance are much easier for in-house operations. Concurrent teams and interdisciplinary projects can be performed more efficiently. One does not have to be concerned about intellectual property protection either. On the other side, outsourcing may help a company to gain competitive advantage by focusing on its core businesses and allowing access to world-class capabilities. It also reduces the capital expenditures and overhead, increasing the value of the company, which in most cases makes the company attractive in the stock market. Charles Gibbons of PricewaterhouseCoopers explains it with the following statement[3]: "If I have a dollar to invest and can manage not to spend any portion of that investment dollar on my back office costs and put it instead in my real core business, that gives me a tenfold return. If my supplier partner will make investments in my back office, then I have that advantage as well. Then I have increased shareholder value."

A company should not decide on moving offshore just because other companies in the industry are outsourcing. The advantages and disadvantages of global outsourcing must be evaluated in detail to ensure its appropriateness with the company's strategic direction. An outsourcing decision project must be consistent with the company's mission statement and strategic objectives.

Case: To Outsource or Not to Outsource.   Two opposite cases involving an outsourcing decision are the dilemmas faced by Huntington National Bank and Sears, Roebuck & Co.[4]

Huntington National Bank Case.   In 2000, outsourcer CSC offered a business process outsourcing (BPO) agreement that promised increased revenue streams in the future. The CIO, Joe Gottron, viewed the proposal with suspicion but could not reject it without further analysis. Huntington began its exploration of CSC's BPO offer by bringing in outsourcing adviser TPI to assess it. The company requested other proposals from different outsourcers in order to compare the economics of what CSC was offering. Gottron also hired Anderson Consulting to benchmark internal information technology (IT) performance and costs. The results showed that the internal IT department had particular flaws, but given built-in administrative and transaction costs, an outsourcer could not provide large cost savings either. Gottran explained his concerns: "Can outsourcing help us get better aligned with the business? We're a midsize company with one data center that's very limited in scope, and just saying, 'Hey, let's go do outsourcing because some company argues that their economies of scale are better,' didn't make sense for us." Cultural issues also were important. Huntington was positioning itself as an "essential partner" with external customers, and with the same spirit, the IT department had to stay as an "essential partner" to its internal customers. Thus the bank chose to keep IT in-house and support its enhancement.

Sears, Roebuck & Co. Case.   Gerald F. Kelly, Jr., was the CIO when outsourcing came up for Sears. The company had not been investing appropriately in the IT infrastructure for many years. Urgent improvement was needed for a more technically reliable infrastructure that would support company objectives. Kelly first asked, "Is this something my team could do?" And the major considerations, in his words, were "time, talent, and treasure." How long would it take? Who would do it? And what would it cost? Another consideration was Sears' mission. After all, it was a retail company, and expecting a technological perfection would not be reasonable. Outsourcing IT infrastructure stood up as a good alternative that would give maximum value in a short period of time without the need for additional investment. Kelly brought in Transitions Partners, an IT outsourcing consultancy, to make a more thorough analysis. The consultants helped Sears to see the major factors in an outsourcing decision and guided the company through all possible choices. For nine months, they analyzed possibilities for transferring the business process. At the same time, they included probable impacts of outsourcing on such stakeholders as employees, customers, and investors. As a result, Sears decided that outsourcing its IT operations would let the company achieve its goal of a stable infrastructure faster and avoid high expenditures.

Conclusion. Among the plausible operations, determining the right application to outsource is also essential. The products or functions that have already reached maturity are less risky choices. These applications do not need big changes and can be managed without the need for direct control. Complexity is important as well. More effort is needed to outsource complex functions since the possibility of failure escalates as the complexity of the job intensifies. Operations will need close monitoring, which, in turn, will add to the transaction and communication costs. Moreover, most companies do not outsource their critical and strategically important applications to prevent the risk of losing intellectual property. This is why call centers and mass-production operations are the most popular processes that U.S. companies outsource.

Long-Range Planning for the Outsourcing Decision.

Outsourcing is a long-range decision. Structured long-range planning mitigates against unnecessary ad hoc decisions and gives common objectives to an organization.[5] Steiner divides the conceptual long-range planning into four stages. Outsourcing decisions also may be conceptualized in the same framework.

Strategic Conceptualization. Management should assess if an outsourcing initiative will be appropriate for the firm's future strategies. The market share, cost structure, product quality, goodwill, and challenges in the organizational structure must be considered. Therefore, multidisciplinary teams are needed to identify and analyze the strategic issues and report their consequences to senior management. To support the managerial make-or-buy decision on outsourcing, management can apply mathematical methods, such as linear programming, that will provide preliminary results on the financial consequences.[6] Subsequently, management must assess the outsourcing decision in terms of its strategic relevance, actionability, criticality, and urgency.

Many organizations have very little experience with outsourcing decisions. Internal assessment never should be neglected, but if enough expertise is lacking, it is advisable to assign a consultancy along with the project team. An outsider can see the real costs, threats, and opportunities more objectively and perform unbiased examination by applying prior experience. Expert opinion is a wise contribution, especially while deciding whether or not to outsource.

Medium-Range Conceptualization. Once the strategic fit of the outsourcing decision is reviewed, a preliminary analysis of the alternatives is necessary. A company can choose to invest in a low-cost country or continue its processes on a local basis. Some companies need close correspondence and reliance in operations owing to the nature of their business. These companies prefer to invest rather than choosing a contract partner. The investment can be in the form either of acquiring an existing local company or of establishing a regional branch. On the other hand, if the application does not require long-term commitment and is not a critical function, a better choice is to have a contractual agreement with a business partner in a low-cost country. Although the latter is more captivating in terms of cost savings, it may not always be feasible. Management needs to determine which way to go depending on the objective and limitations. Once a final decision is reached, the time and place are identified based on the economic, sociologic, and political environment, as well as on the related business structure and availability of resources.

Short-term Conceptualization. In this stage, the outsourcing idea has already been conceived of by management, which, in turn, assigns a project team and project manager(s) to bring the idea to paper. The project team can apply the following measures to reduce the uncertainty the organization faces during the initial phases:

- Detailed market analysis and an investigation of the company's status in terms of the external environment
- A business survey to determine the standards of the market
- Benchmarking to provide a general view
- Proposals from vendors located in different regions of the world

Planning. The final work in the conceptual phase is determination of the timeline and budget constraints. The project team reports a preliminary schedule to senior management for approval before proceeding to the next stage. Given their strategic importance, the outsourcing decisions are structured on senior-management approval. Even though the essential part of success comes from the highest levels of the organization, effective communication through the organization is also crucial. If direct and unambiguous information is not provided, a chaotic environment may be slowly formed by employees who perceive the outsourcing motion from very different points of views, where some see it as a career opportunity and others fear it from the point of view of job insecurity. To mitigate the adverse effects, management should initiate face-to-face communication to create interteam cooperation and trust. The frequency and quality of communication are major factors that facilitate the development of mutual understanding of goals.[7]

Design Phase

The conceptual phase is the initiation point where the outsourcing decision is evaluated in terms of its strategic fit, whereas the design phase is a long and challenging stage where the decision is structured into operational boundaries. In the medium-range conceptualization, senior management reviews the location and contract/invest options and reaches a decision on whether or not to invest depending on the market transaction costs. There are various situations where a company may prefer direct investment:

- For some operations and industries, the transaction costs such as negotiation, contract, and monitoring costs are higher than the administrative costs. If the transaction costs associated with organizing across markets are greater than the administrative costs of organizing within firms, we can expect the coordination of productive activity to be internalized within firms.[8]
- Investment may be the only alternative because of extreme intellectual property security concerns.
- If the company wants to outsource some of its key functionalities, management will require long-term commitments.

The business conditions and company objectives determine the scope of outsourcing. Linder divides outsourcing into two categories, conventional and transformational.[9]

Conventional outsourcing involves transferring noncore, simple interfaces to another entity, whereas *transformational* outsourcing is outsourcing to achieve a rapid, sustainable step-change improvement in enterprise-level performance. Conventional outsourcing has little flexibility and involves well-understood processes, whereas transformational outsourcing involves outsourcing ongoing services that are critical to the performance of the business. Transformational outsourcing is operated through by partnering or investments (i.e., do it yourself, merge/acquire, or joint venture). Following is a case for the conventional outsourcing performed by Hewlett-Packard. In this case, the primary benefit of outsourcing is the cost savings obtained from reduced labor costs.

Case: Hewlett-Packard. Hewlett-Packard was able to reduce total cost, increase cash flow, conserve capital, and access markets by outsourcing its test-equipment products.[10] By doing so, management was able to focus on core capabilities, such as product design and marketing.

In early 1980s, the South Queensferry site had many manufacturing processes, such as cables, transformers, plastic molding, sheet-metal fabrication, precision machining, printed circuit board fabrication, printed circuit board assembly, subassembly build, and final assembly and test. As a result of a growing market, reduced life cycles, and cost competitiveness, it became difficult for Hewlett-Packard to continue to maintain a competitive advantage on all its processes for a long period of time. As a result, Hewlett-Packard started to subcontract these activities one by one.

Activity Subcontracted	Year
Cables	1987
Wound components	1985
Plastics	1986
Sheet metal	1987
PCBs	1993
PCAs	1994
Subassembly	1997

In ten years, Hewlett-Packard was able to shift from vertical integration to horizontal integration. Many important lessons have been learned along the way:

The decision to outsource a manufacturing process is fundamentally a business decision that affects a company's core business. Such a decision must be taken fully supported by senior management.

The company must ensure that a competitive advantage should not be lost as a result of the outsourcing decision. The competitive advantage may be in logistics, supply-chain management, or new product introduction.

Contract-Invest Decision. If a company chooses to invest in a low-cost country, the size of the investment should be determined in line with the scope of operational functions that will be outsourced. The extent of investment is a key element that must be considered in the design stage, where alternatives are analyzed in detail. On the other hand, if the company chooses contractual outsourcing, the type of contract is a determining factor for the outsourcing relationship. Figure 14.2 shows the content of four types of contractual outsourcing proposed by Nam et al.[10] depending on the strategic impact and contract duration:

- *Support.* Noncore activities are outsourced with small short-term contracts. *Example:* Contract programming, hardware maintenance.

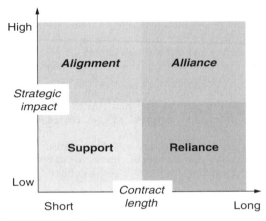

FIGURE 14.2   Contract types.

- *Reliance.* Noncore activities are outsourced with large substitution. These are longer-term contracts. *Example:* Contract programming with longer term contracts.
- *Alignment.* There is a low extent of substitution. The contracts are smaller with short-term scopes. The strategic impact is considerable. *Examples:* Consulting, technical supervision.
- *Alliance.* There is a high extent of substitution. These are large contracts with important strategic impact. *Example:* Complete transfer of information systems activities.

Location Decision.   Typically, analysis of location, time, and format of an outsourcing relation is performed concurrently. The objective is to find the optimal combination that will maximize the value and opportunities and minimize the risks and threats.

The "Global Outsourcing Report 2005"[11] assesses countries in terms of two indices: the global outsourcing index (GOI) and the future outsourcing rank (FOR). According to this report, India and China are the two distinct low-cost-labor countries that come first in the list of locations for almost every U.S. company considering outsourcing. China is mostly known for low-cost manual labor in manufacturing, whereas India has the advantage of English-speaking population and thus attracts a large amount of business process outsourcing (BPO) contracts. Alternatively, Taiwan and Korea are known as the centers of the semiconductor industry. Besides these big players, countries such as Indonesia, the Philippines, and Malaysia also take their places in the outsourcing business.

The number of location alternatives for outsourcing is limited by constraints specific to each business. For instance, for the food processing industry, only certain regions with certain climate conditions may be an option for outsourcing. The technical expertise and cultural environment also restrict the choices for a company determining the appropriate place to transfer operations.

Once the location alternatives are determined, systematic analysis is needed to identify the optimal place that encompasses the biggest cost reduction with as minimal risk as possible. Figure 14.3 shows the structure of a decision-support method for such an analysis.

The figure is an example of a decision matrix created for a perishable food company[12] where six countries are evaluated according to their costs, benefits, opportunities, risks, and threats. The alternatives represent the cells of the decision matrix, where the columns specify the country options and the rows are the outsourcing forms considered by the

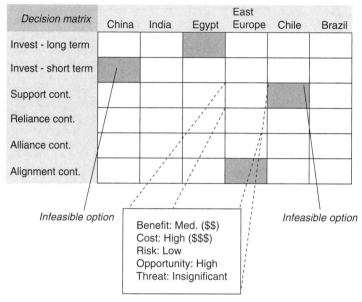

FIGURE 14.3 Decision matrix.

company. In case any of the combinations is economically infeasible, it is eliminated from further deliberation. The analyst first gathers data about different alternatives, such as labor rates, energy prices, tax and duties, raw materials prices, and transportation costs, that are relevant for a monetary comparison of countries in consideration. Using the quantitative data, the project team is able to examine the financial outcomes by performing benefit/cost analysis and return-on-asset calculations. According to the outcomes of the financial analysis, the decision matrix is continuously updated. The decision matrix also can be used as a tool for what-if analysis in the proceeding stages of the outsourcing project.

The challenge is that the real results are not based solely on financial outcomes because the business environment is complex. The interactions between economic and sociologic elements must be reflected in the dynamics of outsourcing. Cultural differences, language capabilities, and time zones are some of the qualitative variables that determine the productivity of outsourcing processes.[13] There may as well be tradeoffs among decision variables such as cost, quality, ease of communication, transportation, and reliability. For instance, the cost of manufacturing may be low in one country, but if there is no technology that can support efficient production, desired level of quality and sustainability may not be achieved. By the same token, in the software industry, the infrastructure of the country is as important as the technical skills and labor costs. Risk is another facet of the problem. Uncertainty must be considered explicit from the financial outcomes. Currency fluctuations, political transitions, flexibility, and cultural fit have substantial impact on the success of future operations.

The analyst's goal is to choose the best alternative—the optimum—but finding the optimum is not straightforward in such a complex environment where everything cannot

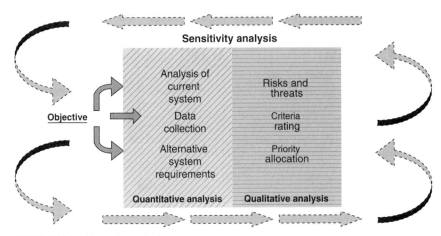

FIGURE 14.4   Alternative analysis process.

be denoted by mathematical equations. The monetary values such as cost can be expressed in terms of quantitative variables, but intangible values such as risks cannot be structured in numeric notations. For system analysis, Fisher suggests that quantitative analysis should be used as much as possible but must be supplemented by qualitative analysis as well.[14] The key point is to use the quantitative analysis as a support for the final decision maker. Figure 14.4 shows a systematic approach to the integration of quantitative and qualitative elements where sensitivity analysis is performed as a feedback mechanism to control uncertainties.

Uncertainty is unavoidable in the global environment involving countries with different economies and politics. An explicit solution is to identify the risks associated with the uncertainties and mitigate their effects as much as possible. There are several risk identification methodologies that have been used in the literature, such as research, structured interviews, and checklists. *Risk registration* is one of the practical tools to identify and control the uncertainties as part of a risk management effort. The same tool can be used for the purposes of outsourcing decision, too.[15] Risks are first listed in a risk registration form that stores information such as risk number, risk description, ownership, probability, impact, risk factor, response, and status. According to their features, risks are divided into categories. Then the severity of impact and probability of occurrence are examined based on the categories the risks are in. Response strategies follow the quantitative and qualitative uncertainty analyses thereafter. The response strategies can be used as a feedback mechanism during the analyses of alternatives for outsourcing while the behavior of outcomes is observed against a changing risk variable.

Implementation Phase

In the implementation phase, the outsourcing decision is brought to life. Essential elements for a successful implementation are a comprehensive contract, efficient relationship management, and a structural transition stage. Four basic management

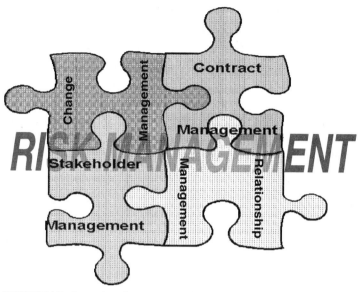

FIGURE 14.5   Integration of management principles.

principles are applied: change management, contract management, stakeholder management, and relationship management (Fig. 14.5).

Change Management.   Change management principles are applied during the formation of contractual relationships and while controlling ongoing activities such as training and testing. For organizational change management, there are few critical principles[16]:

- Determining barriers to implementing change
- Change management planning and strategies
- Managing employee/customer resistance
- Building executive sponsorship
- Creating communication plans
- Creating training and educational programs
- Maintaining business continuity

Change begins with the multinational transition of operations in the form of contracts, investment, acquire, or merge. In this section we will talk mainly about contractual relationships. Nevertheless, the basic elements can be practiced for "transformational outsourcing" types, where the company precedes with partnering or investment.

Contract Management.   There are two parties in an outsourcing contract, the outsourcing company and the vendor. A contract consists of several documents[17]:

- *Contract agreement.* Identifies the parties, defines the scope of work, and declares the price and schedule.

- *General specification and scope of work.* Describes the scope of work, the technical standards required, and administrative procedures to control.
- *General conditions of the contract.* Includes details about the agreement and related issues such as bonds, safety, risks, and disputes.
- *Special conditions of the contract.* Additions required by any of the parties.
- *Administrative and coordination procedures.* Includes the procedural aspects.

The baseline of an outsourcing contract is quality and productivity. The contract must include a definition of objectives, the structure of technology, historical data, scheduling, and all the other factors that may affect implementation of the project. It should reflect the size and time frame of the application and define standards as clearly as possible to prevent ambiguity. The contract should be comprehensive in determining the specification of the payment terms and responsibilities, revealing the perspectives of multiple parties. It is important that all the parties should play a role and understand how changes in the contract can affect their business processes. In addition to these basic principles, international contracts need to state explicitly which country's law will apply and specify the language of communication.

Stakeholder Management.   Outsourcing does not affect only the company; rather, the society as a whole is affected. The primary stakeholders, such as employees, employers, customers, and shareholders, experience the direct impact, whereas the entire national economy is involved as well. In most cases, each party's benefit is contradictory to each other. Julius[18] studied the stakeholder conflicts in globalizing businesses and categorized the stakeholders into four diverse groups: customers, employees, communities, and shareholders.

Customers.   The customers are always the primary stakeholders affected by changes in a business structure. The consequences of an outsourcing initiation are promptly reflected on the products as discount prices. However, outsourcing may not always result in higher customer satisfaction. While customers use the benefits of low-priced products and services, they also may face lower quality in products and inadequate service levels. A quality discrepancy will result in disappointment and force the customer change the product or shift to a different service. Thus it is important for a company to be in contact with customers throughout the outsourcing process to assure the customers about the continuation of the quality in the products and services.

Employees.   During the implementation stage, a company should not expect a truthful support from all its employees. While employees understand the benefits of outsourcing for shareholders and customers, they see their jobs being sent to low-cost countries. The staff will not be willing to share knowledge if they know that their jobs will be outsourced to another country. This prejudice may create problems during operational transfer, hindering the applications. A company can have a less painful transition by creating a more trustful environment for its employees. Training and education will ensure an opportunity for existing employees to have more strategic positions, for control and regulation of the future activities. If management can facilitate the realization of such outcomes, the employees will be more enthusiastic about the transfer period.

Communities.   As unemployment rates rise, outsourcing is subject to more arguments in the United States. On one side, consumers cherish the increasing purchasing power resulting from lower prices; on the other side, a growing percentage of the population is losing job and social security. Many fear the rise of China. In order to avoid dispute, companies are reluctant to announce their outsourcing decisions, whose consequence in many cases include loss of goodwill and trust.

Shareholders.   Shareholders are perhaps the largest group favoring outsourcing decisions. Cost reductions make profit expectations higher, and downsizing the company, without decreasing revenue, adds value to the company. In most cases, stock prices go up with the announcement of an outsourcing decision, reflecting the anticipation of an increasing return in the future. In reality, shareholder satisfaction is one of the biggest drivers behind outsourcing decisions. Even though shareholder pressure cannot be neglected, it is important for company management to remain objective and not take unnecessary risks in their decisions.

Relationship Management.   Four fundamental characteristics give shape to an outsourcing relationship[19]:

- *Depth of the relationship.* Depends on the criticality of the outsourced job. As the job gets closer to the core business process, greater depth is required.

- *Scope of the relationship.* Depends on the nature of the work outsourced.

- *Choice of asset to use.* Depends on the firms' ability to invest in asset development.

- *Choice of business culture to adopt and exploit.* Depends on which culture will enable a better and faster achievement of the objectives.

In order for an outsourcing process to survive, the relationship characteristics should be defined before the transition starts in lower organizational levels. Trust and communication are needed from the very beginning. Differences in style and culture are unavoidable, but as long as the parties recognize such differences, they can agree on common approaches. As part of the collaboration, both the outsourcer and the vendor should share responsibilities for the transition stage while setting goals and standards. A strong relationship will support the changes that company will face in the next stages, and it is also an essential element for a long-term and productive business process where all of the parties get the maximum value through a win-win situation.

Problems during the implementation stage should not be neglected in view of the fact that even the smallest disagreements may grow into serious crises in the long run. The project team should treat these problems in an organized manner with confidence and reliability. Cheung presents a dispute-resolution approach consisting of six steps[20]: prevention, negotiation, standing neutral, nonbinding resolution, binding resolution, and litigation. These steps should be followed in order such that binding resolution and litigation are used only if the previous methods fail because they are harsher applications.

Clear and exhaustive documentation prevents ambiguity and serves as a reference for management of future relationships, minimizing miscommunication between parties. All processes through the process need to be documented in every detail. Comprehensive documentation not only supports a tight communication between vendors but also helps to resolve disagreements that are likely to occur.

Smooth transition is vital for the success of an outsourcing project. Involvement of many stakeholders makes it more complex and fragile. While the changes are actually implemented, every stakeholder is concerned about his or her own situation. Some employees feel one minute away from losing their jobs and resist the change, whereas executives and shareholders see it as a cost-reduction effort and favor the change. Studies show that the reason behind most failed change projects is inadequate consideration of people and communication.[21] Miscommunication and lack of employee support cause prolonged training and testing phases. Today, a major proportion of American workers are oversensitive to any kind of decision process that may lead an outsourcing decision. Job security was a governing issue in the 2004 elections and continues to be overriding in media. As a result, employees who are in the process of transferring their jobs overseas are more reactive to the change and can resist one-to-one training. Overcoming the resistance barrier is not easy but can be achieved by communicating with people and ensuring retraining programs and career-development opportunities. During the outsourcing activities, employees may go through several change management classes. Managers also should be encouraged to hold meetings with their people to keep in touch. Having employee counseling services available is also helpful.

A structured planning will lead to a structured transition. *Studies show that when asked what they would do differently in structuring their outsourcing relationships, both buyers and service providers respond that they would do more upfront planning for the transition phase.* A white paper published by SourceNet groups the pitfalls during the transition phase into five categories[22]:

Pitfall 1: Inadequate knowledge transfer. During the transfer of operations, as soon as the provider vendor comes into play, a drop-off in service levels is inevitable, even if the provider performs the work correctly and efficiently. There are valuable aspects beyond the mechanical transformation. Outsourcing undermines some of the informal relationships that were built with customers by the outsourcing company. A partial remedy to this pitfall is adequate transfer of knowledge. The first step is documentation of the business structure of the organization, including the protocols and procedures. Especially in large organizations, the actual process of jobs may not be exactly the same as the documentations. In this case, the best approach is to insert a validation step into the documentation, where the provider vendor's employees are trained in the physical environment in which the business is conducted. By one-to-one training, knowledge transfer can be performed in a collaborative environment.

Pitfall 2: Inadequate measurement of service-level performance. The company may encounter problems with its customers when the provider vendor falls short in the performance levels that the company used to provide before the process was outsourced. The vendor may be meeting the contractual service-level specifications but does not concentrate on specific metrics. To prevent lack of satisfaction among customers, the company needs to provide a baseline of performance during the transition phase.

Pitfall 3: Lack of response-scenario planning. Going into the transition with the assumption that everything is planned is a pitfall. Contingency plans must exist against potential disruptive events that possibly can appear during the transition phase. A scenario-response plan, similar to a disaster-recovery plan, is the best approach. The company should know where to look if extra resources are required during the transition phase and should designate who will be in charge of updating the organization and resolving pressures. A scenario-response plan is beneficial to avoid chaos in case an adverse event happens.

Pitfall 4: Lack of executive sponsorship and staying the course. A pitfall that organizations run into is lack of sponsorship from senior management. As a result, the transition stage is either hindered or ends with a breakdown owing to the loud noise that comes from the parties that disagree with the outsourcing decision. Sometimes the decision-making executive announces the decision and leaves the organization thereafter. An effective approach is to have the chief executives lead the strategic changes, not the division or department managers. The executive should stress the commitment and responsibility toward the achievement of the objective. Weekly performance reviews by the executives and the people who are responsible for tactical execution strengthen the process.

Pitfall 5: Lack of flexibility. Occasionally, the service-level specifications and operating definitions in the contracts are based on assumptions. These assumptions may be wrong, and recalibration may be needed. Flexibility can be ensured by a review and tightening phase around the contractual service-level specifications that lasts for a predefined period of time during the transition state. If recalibration is needed, the contractual commitments can be refined on mutual agreement.

Case: Infoworld Media Group.   InfoWorld Media Group is a division of International Data Group (IDG), a technology, media, research, and event company.[24] The company supports its customers by providing them with IT news, technology comparisons, and focused research information. InfoWorld is not just a provider of technology but also a user of technology. In April 2001, InfoWorld hired a new chief technology officer (CTO). The CTO was faced with a broken IT infrastructure and dissatisfied users. InfoWorld started to consider business process virtualization to improve the current services. The CTO expressed his skepticism: "I wasn't a fan of outsourcing at all before this particular experience. When your back is against the wall and you have *x* amount of dollars to accomplish a particular goal, then you just have to look at it differently and see what else is possible."

Prior to startup of the outsourcing processing, for six weeks InfoWorld evaluated its network to understand its operational structure. After the network evaluation, the company performed testing for an additional four weeks. The company conducted actual rollout in weekends owing to the highly geographically distributed nature of the network environment.

Barriers to Implementation.   The biggest barrier was nonexistence of physical support. Employees had to solve the system problems via telephone calls without a physical contact.

Lessons Learned in the Testing Phase.   They found a lot of people running applications that were not supposed to be supported on a corporate network, such as music applications and file-sharing applications. During the testing phase, there were some legacy problems with Windows XP, which were solved afterwards. There were shortcomings in some of the services and lack of monitoring in areas such as finance, where the credit cards are cleared. The company was able to realize such shortcomings and put in better processes. In general, the testing phase was an opportunity to review the company's business processes.

Unforeseen Benefits of Implementation.   At the end of the implementation, InfoWorld realized that the services it got actually were better than the expectations. Secondary benefits were application awareness across the company and standardization of the applications.

Unforeseen Barriers of Implementation.   InfoWorld did not experience any unforeseen technical barriers to its desktop and server management virtualization. However, there were difficulties in persuading people to accept a change. It was hard to convince people of the benefits of the virtualization.

As a result, InfoWorld saved at least 30 percent on support costs in the first 12 months. It enabled flexibility toward changes in the business. If the company gets smaller, the cost is reduced directly by the provider.

Finalization Phase

Once the transition phase is completed, resources become redundant. The idle resources may be monetary assets as well as the human workforce. An organized plan for the relocation or elimination of idle resources is an important factor for the ongoing success of the outsourcing project. In most cases, major alterations in the organizational structure are inevitable to cope with the new operational requirements.

The business environment goes through many changes, and employees of the outsourcing firm no longer perform the same jobs. Responsibilities and roles do not stay the same either. As an example of role changes, Nextel's transfer of IT operations can be given. Jerry Brace was Nextel's vice president of customer billing services, which has grown since Nextel expanded its outsourcing relationship with Amdocs in 2000.[23] Before outsourcing, Brace led a group of 20 technicians who wrote the code for the billing system and eventually had the responsibility for technical assistance. They took orders from Nextel's business units. After outsourcing, the vendor, Amdocs, took over management of the technology side of billing services. Brace and his staff's job became monitoring and controlling Amdocs service levels. Brace had only 20 people to manage, but after the job was outsourced, he began to manage a 330-person organization for provision, messaging, and data management. At the same time, many employees were transferred to the vendors while Nextel outsourced its IT management. A total of 4500 employees were transferred to IBM as a result of their eight-year contract for the management of customer care services.

Unfortunately, many managers believe that the company is safe as long as the accounting book looks good. However, in the long run, the dynamics of an organization do not depend solely on monetary values. Without employee motivation, it is not possible to maintain efficient work. During an outsourcing process, organizational change is unavoidable, given that new employees will be hired, and some old employees will lose their jobs. These revolutionary changes may create a depressed psychology among employees. Reorganization programs are very important to minimize the adverse effects and to assist in the continual success of an outsourcing project. Necessary time and effort should be given to such programs.

An example is Hewlett Packard's successful reorganization programs that were initiated by a proactive management.[10] When the outsourcing trend in manufacturing started, Hewlett-Packard was quick to realize the trend and outsource PCA and PCB activities. In the following years, when a lot of competitors were forced by the changes to deal with inertia, Hewlett-Packard's management was able to grow another business while closing one. The proactive movement of Hewlett-Packard gave the company the time and opportunity to structure reorganization programs for its employees. During the finalization phase, Hewlett-Packard managers were measured on the success of the reorganization programs. This was done through project milestones and employment satisfaction surveys. As a result of shifting jobs overseas, a considerable number of employees became redundant. These people needed to be retrained. In Hewlett-Packard's case, the outsourcing of manufacturing processes meant that there were fewer production labor jobs and more desk jobs. Hewlett-Packard recognized this and made a significant investment in retraining, including career-development education. Employees that were affected by the reorganization were given priority for the open jobs. In case a person from the reorganized area was not hired for the new position, the hiring manager had to justify the reason and the company also arranged early retirement programs and voluntary services for employees who did not want to change their career paths.

Another natural consequence of outsourcing is exposure to new cultures and business styles. It is important to train both organizations' employees about the cultural differences in order to prevent misperceptions of one another. In a workshop held by B. Hurn and M. Jernkins at a large multinational company, Foseco, employees were asked to examine the cross-cultural issues involved in building and sustaining multinational teams and the problems of participating in multicultural meetings.[24] The major areas identified as part of the "cultural minefield" were greetings, degree of politeness, showing agreement and disagreement, use of interpreters, different approaches to time, gifts, the status of women, and body language. Linguistic barriers such as the use of complicated and idiomatic English also were mentioned. There also was discussion about different communication priorities in different cultures. For instance, American relationship building is based on direct communication, whereas in Asia and Latin America, the "getting to know you" phase is more emphasized. The authors agreed that top-management commitment is an essential prerequisite to developing the trust-building process. A technique for creating cultural synergy is adapted from a model by Adler.[25] In this technique, first, the situation is described from one's own cultural perspective. The next stage is to determine the underlying cultural assumptions behind these situations. Then the cultural overlap is assessed by discovering the similarities. Then the participants identify culturally synergic alternatives based on the overlaps and differences. Finally, a culturally synergic solution is implemented by selecting the best alternative.

Control Phase

An outsourcing project does not end until the outsourced operations are terminated. Experts suggest a continuous governance process to determine actual benefits derived from the joint work. Jim Leto, president and CEO of Robbins-Gioia, LLC, a leading program management consulting firm, states: "Just because you outsource something, it doesn't mean you can abdicate responsibility for it. The quality of management provided by the client is one of the most important factors in whether the relationship succeeds or not."[26] A successful start does not always mean that anticipated benefits will continue all the way through. Loss of direct interactions, distributed supply networks, and cultural differences challenge achievement of the objective. The complexity of the environment necessitates continuous monitoring of performance specifications. Any economic, sociologic, or political alteration in the world can affect the business. Hidden costs behind the operations, such as logistics and communication costs, are likely to be elevated by a global distortion. Reevaluation of the outsourcing decision should be performed periodically based on industry changes. There is always a possibility that cost-saving expectations may turn into negative incomes owing to cost increases or performance reductions.

Periodic evaluation of performance by customers is also important, as well as an internal review process. The customers in this case are the people who are in direct contact with the vendor. For instance, if a call-center unit is outsourced to India, the satisfaction of consumers can be assessed by surveys and interviews. If an IT operation is outsourced, direct feedback from employees is of use. The results of these evaluations will confirm the present condition in the outsourcing relationship. Not only negative outcome but also positive feedback should be discussed with the parties. The process is under everyone's responsibility, and common solutions can be derived in the presence of both parties. The assessment of drivers and consequences of the outcomes leads to reliability in the future.

For instance, costumer feedback changed the outsourcing practice of the computer giant Dell, which employs about 44,300 people, about 54 percent abroad. Just as with many other U.S. companies, its technical support center is in Bangalore, India. Some time after the full transfer of operations, Dell found out that many U.S. costumers complained about the thick accents and scripted responses of Indian technical support representatives. As a result, the company stopped using the technical support center in India to handle calls from its corporate customers, which accounted for 85 percent of Dell's businesses. Since home PC owners are not a big chunk of the business and individual miscommunication cannot cause massive losses, calls from home PC owners continue to be directed to India.[27]

There should be continual improvements even after the outsourcing project is completed. It is also important to provide a continuing support system for employees. Keys to success include[28]

- The right applications
- Strong project management
- Smooth/planned transition
- Ongoing support
- Deliverables and scope that are agreed to by both parties

Risks exist as long as outsourcing relations continue. The challenge of controlling and managing risks is much bigger than the challenges faced in implementation. In the 2004 issue of the Marsh & McLennan Companies journal (*Viewpoint*), risk factors were classified by giving examples from company cases[29]:

Loss of strategic control. JPMorgan Chase announced that it would bring back a major set of IT activities it had outsourced to IBM in a seven-year contract. After some experience period, the managers realized that it was critical to manage and control IT directly to gain competitive advantage.

Hidden costs. An AMR research study showed that 80 percent of outsourcing deals did not meet targeted return on investment. Another study of by Gartner found that one-sixth of companies outsourcing IT activities did not save any money.

Service quality problems. Lehman Brothers, Conseco, Capital One, and Dell all have experienced customer service disappointment from Indian call centers.

Lack of scalability. A major airline found that its outsourced maintenance provider could not meet its needs for innovation and expansion.

Brand damage. Nike was blamed for its outsourcing relationships with China and Central America.

Weak governance. At a leading high-tech company, a major function had been outsourced to the same provider independently by three different divisions via eight contracts worth $100 million annually. Management realized the situation only when one of the divisions expressed its dissatisfaction.

An ability to notice the risks and react timely can be ensured by constant monitoring and documentation. As a general rule, a person or a team, depending on the size of the outsourced application, can be formed to monitor and evaluate the changes throughout the relationship. The three critical factors that require measurement and monitoring are reduced costs, rapid cycle times, and responsiveness (three R's).[30] Companies can expect cost savings starting in the first three months of an outsourcing relationship. Costs adjusted for productivity need to be measured. New project initiatives normally should take shorter time periods as the relationship gets stronger. An alarming indicator is delayed operations and inability to meet deadlines. Reduced costs and rapid cycle times cannot be realized without a rapid response time. In addition to the three R's, evaluation of performance specifications and customer surveys should be included in periodic feedback reports to ensure continuous control over the outsourcing relationship.

CONCLUSION

Siff competition, short product life cycles, and increasing complexity of business structures drive the rise of outsourcing trend that started with manufacturing more than a decade ago. Recently, outsourcing began to receive attention for core competences such as design and research and development (R&D). Improvements in technological infrastructure and educational enhancements in developing countries usually drive globalization efforts. While "cost reduction" is a worthy outcome, often being the initial reason that organizations are attracted towards outsourcing, the procedures and results differ depending on the objective, operational structure. and the market. The steps toward an outsourcing initiative are not the same and should not be the same for every company. For this reason, a carefully planned project management approach is an effective tool in identifying, analyzing, and assessing the actions needed to be taken throughout the decision-making and implementation stages.

Basic project management principles apply to outsourcing decisions as well. The project life-cycle phases of an outsourcing decision are analogous to a classic project management structure. Scope and time objectives establish the basic structure of an outsourcing decision. The drivers and results are examined according to their priorities in the conceptual, design, implementation, finalization, and control phases. There are several aspects that influence the decisions and consequently the outcomes of the outsourcing project. Cost is considered to be the major aspect, but it is only one of the factors. Risk is also an important element that determines the fate of the project, and is an inevitable challenge that has to be mitigated throughout the course of this project. (Fig. 14.6).

The success of an outsourcing project depends on a number of critical factors. The support of executive team and user community has the foremost criticality. Morale and productivity are hard to measure but play an important role. Without support from higher levels, the organization cannot achieve the targeted productivity. Long-range planning cannot be effective if there is weak or no support from the chief executive that is not visible to each level of the organization. Style of management determines the actions of the executive in assuring the organization of the importance of the project. The executive must perceive the primary responsibility with an involvement starting from setting objectives and continuing with approval of strategies that lead to those objectives.

The skills of the project manager and the executives play an important part in the success of an outsourcing project. The project manager and the executive should have a basic knowledge of change management and risk management, as well as contract management,

FIGURE 14.6   Aspects of outsourcing decisions.[31]

because the outcome of an outsourcing project relies heavily on the contract structure and its implementation. If the contracts are made with good standards, outsourcing can be a win-win situation for both the outsourcing company and the vendor. Moreover, communication and detailed documentation add to the probability of success by ensuring an effective transition period. During the transition period, the first step is the transfer of intellectual capital from the client's organization to the outsourcing firm. Ideally, this process should be done one-on-one. Effective personnel communication and the development of an atmosphere of trust are also key elements in the success of the project.

An outsourcing project does not end when the operation transfer is completed. A frequent failure is to discontinue the assessment of the outsourcing decision once the process is on track. An outsourcing relationship is exposed to every economic, political, and sociologic alteration in the global environment. Key performance indicators must be monitored on a continuous basis to avoid the hidden costs. Periodic feedback from both the internal employees and participating customers is useful to review the success of the outsourcing relationship.

Outsourcing is an important decision that determines a company's operations and strategies. The outsourcing decision and execution constitute an extensive project that affects the major strategies of a company. Today, a growing number of U.S. companies move to the outsourcing model either to remain competitive or to maintain their existence in the market. A dangerous rationale is to decide and execute an outsourcing initiative without a long term vision. Thorough analyses of all factors should be performed by a systematic approach within a project management framework. The goals can be achieved only if all project phases are accomplished successfully.

REFERENCES

1. *PBS Frontline,* "Is Wal-Mart Good for America?" 2004.

2. Cleland ID, Ireland LR. 2002. *Project Management: Strategic Design and Implementation.* NewYork: McGraw-Hill.

3. Woody J. 2001. Business process outsourcing: The new market trend. Morgen Group White Paper Series on Outsourcing and Business Process Outsourcing; available at www.themorleygroup.com.

4. Overby S. 2004. One outsources, The other doesn't. *CIO Magazine,* November 1; available at www.cio.com.

5. Steiner GA. 1969. The critical role of top management in long-range planning, in ID Cleland, RW King (eds.), *Systems, Organizations, Analysis, Management: A Book of Readings.,* New York: McGraw-Hill pp. 132–139.

6. Balakrishnan J, Cheng C-H. 2005. The theory of constraints and the make-or-buy decision: An update and review. *J Supply Chain,* Winter: pp. 40–67.

7. Parker DW, Russel KA. 2004. Outsourcing and inter/intra supply chain dynamics: Strategic management issues. *J Supply Chain Manag,* Fall: pp. 56–68.

8. Grant RM. 2002 *Contemporary Strategy Analysis: Concepts, Techniques, Applications,* 4th ed. Massachusetts: Blackwell p. 390.

9. Linder JC. 2004. *Outsourcing for Radical Change.* NewYork: AMACOM. p. 28.

10. Reid D. 1998. Outsourcing for competitive advantage, in US Bitici, AS Carrie (eds.), *Strategic Management of the Manufacturing Value Chain.* Massachusetts: Kluwer Academic Publishers pp. 631–643.

11. Nam K, Rajagopalan S, Rao R, Chaudhury A. 1996. A two level investigation of information systems outsourcing. *Commun ACM.*39(7) pp. 36–44.

12. Minevich MD, Richter F-J. 2005. The global outsourcing report. *CIO Insight Whiteboard* 55, pp. 55–56.

13. Arisoy O, Bidanda B. 2005. The logistics of growing and processing tomatoes. Presented at the IIE Annual Conference, Atlanta.

14. Wood M. 2003. Don't be sunk offshore. *Electronics Weekly,* Sept 17, p. 4.

15. Fisher GH. 1969 The analytical bases of systems analysis, in ID Cleland, RW King (eds.), *Systems, Organizations, Analysis, Management: A Book of Readings.* NewYork: McGraw-Hill. p. 206–215.

16. Simister SJ. 2004. Qualitative and quantitative risk management, in PWG Morris, JK Pinto (eds.), *Wiley Guide to Managing Projects.* Hoboken, NJ: Wiley, pp. 30–46.

17. An Overview of Change Management, 20; available at http://www.change-management.com.

18. Lowe D. 2004. "Contract management," in PWG Morris, JK Pinto (eds.), *Wiley Guide to Managing Projects.* Hoboken, NJ: Wiley, pp. 678–707.

19. Julius D. 1997 Globalization and stakeholder conflicts: a corporate perspective. *International Affairs* (Royal Institute of International Affairs 1944–) 73(3):453–468.

20. Click RL, Duening TN. 2004 *Business Process Outsourcing: The Competitive Advantage.* Hoboken, NewJersey: Wiley, p. 157.

21. Cheung S. 1999. Critical factors affecting the use of alternative dispute resolution processes in construction. *Int J Project Manag* 5(4):231–236.

22. Hammer M, Stanton SA. 1995. *The Reengineering Revolution: A Handbook.* New York: Harper Business.

23. Change without pain: An alternative model for year one of outsourcing agreements. White Papers, SourceNet Solutions, January 2003.

24. Young M, Jude M. 2004 *The Case for Virtual Business Processes: Reduce Costs, Improve Efficiencies, and Focus on Your Core Business.* Indiana: Cisco Press, pp. 132–139.

25. Levinson M. 2004. Life after outsourcing. *CIO,* May 15.

26. Hurn BJ, Jenkins M. 2004. International peer group development. *Industrial and Commercial Training* 32(4):128–131.

27. Adler NJ. 1991. *International Dimensions of Organizational Behavior,* 2d ed. Boston: PWS-Kent.

28. Santana J. 2004. Decision Support: II. Outsourcing Relationships Don't Stop at Negotiations; available at http://insight.zdnet.co.uk.

29. CNN, November 25, 2003.

30. Clark J. 1998. Successfully implementing a global applications outsourcing strategy. *DM Direct,* November; available at www.dmreview.com.

31. Bovet D, Chadwick-Jones A. 2004. Outsourced but not out of mind: Turning contractors into strategic partners. *Viewpoint* (Marsh & McLennan Companies Journal) 33(2) pp. 19–29.

32. Chelikani S, Polineni VK. 2001. The 3 R's of Offshore Outsourcing, Saven Technologies, Inc.; available at www.saventech.com.

33. Naughton IE. 2005. Outsourcing: Project Management Role, Institute of Project Management, Ireland; available at www.projectmanagement.ie/articles/outsourcing.htm.

CHAPTER 15
PROJECT QUALITY MANAGEMENT IN INTERNATIONAL PROJECTS

Lewis R. Ireland

President, American Society for the Advancement of Project Management
Clarksville, Tennessee

Lewis R. Ireland has more than 30 years of project experience and 16 years of work with quality aspects of projects. He is an executive project management consultant and author of a number of quality and project management books. He served as the 1998 president and chair of the Project Management Institute (PMI) and as the president of the American Society for the Advancement of Project Management (*asapm*) since 2003.

Dr. Ireland's achievements in volunteer work have been recognized by the PMI through the Distinguished Contribution Award, the Person of the Year, and being made a fellow of PMI. He continues to contribute time and energy to the advancement of project management around the world through professional exchanges of information on the practice and theory of project management.

According to the *Oxford English Dictionary, quality* initially referred to the honesty and integrity of a person. It was not uncommon during the nineteenth century to hear "that is a person of quality," meaning that the person could be trusted, held high standards of integrity and honesty, and was well respected in the community. From this original definition of quality, there has been an evolution of the term and its application to situations.

The term *quality* subsequently took on the meaning of a product that possesses the characteristics, attributes, and functions that could satisfy the needs of a buyer, consumer, or other type of customer. The attributes included product durability, reliability, and maintainability. This led the manufacturer of such products to focus on the design to meet customer needs, workmanship to ensure proper assembly or construction of the product, and the use of appropriate materials in the construction. There was a high reliability on inspection of the product during construction and after final assembly.

Contemporary definitions of *quality*—and there are several—center on a prevention approach to avoiding defects in products during the design and construction phases. This approach focuses on process application and control with a significantly reduced inspection function. Well-designed products that are produced through a proven process have lower costs and achieve greater customer satisfaction—or in the current terminology used for many projects, such products have been made "faster, better, and cheaper."

Most recently, organizations have developed, adopted, or modified existing quality programs to meet their specific needs with a goal of improving product grade at lower cost to meet customer requirements. These quality programs include policies, procedures, and practices that avoid product defects through more of a preventative approach than the former "inspect and fix" mentality. Some of the titles of the more widely adopted programs are *total quality management, total quality control, total customer satisfaction,* and *Six Sigma quality.*

Project organizations are typically an extension of a parent organization and its quality program. Human resources are trained by the parent organization in quality practices and procedures, which are continued at the project level. Any shortfall in quality practices in the parent organization may adversely affect project quality functions. Both good and bad practices may be transferred to a project, as well as erroneous procedures. It is particularly important that the project manager, the quality leader for the project, understand the quality program, set the quality standards for the project, and apply good quality practices.

Project quality practices also may be challenged when there are temporary employees or consultants who are not indoctrinated in the parent organization's quality program. A lack of knowledge and application of the organization's quality practices can have an adverse impact on product quality. Thus any new personnel must be trained in quality for the project to ensure consistent, valid quality practices.

International projects—projects with two or more national entities participating—can present quality challenges that have adverse impacts on products and drive the cost and schedule to extremes. The key to successful international projects is qualification of participants and detailed planning. There is no substitute for planning while factoring in the potential variances in culture, language, business acumen, work practices, workmanship, and other practices that differ from the lead project organization.

INTERNATIONAL PROJECT QUALITY CHARACTERISTICS

Quality practices may vary from those of the organization leading the project and can pose some significant challenges to a project manager who is trying to design, develop, and deliver a project's product in such a manner that it gives value to the customer. While there may be good reasons for involving several organizations located in different countries, such as these countries constitute the market for the project's product, caution should be exercised in the selection of project partners or vendors.

Selection of partners or vendors that are qualified to perform the work is an important aspect to developing a project team that will meet the project's objectives. Every team member of the international project contributes to the success of the project through understanding and working toward the objectives in all dimensions of the project. Failure of one team member can have disastrous results.

Different quality practices typically are based on the needs of product consumers. Many countries have lower expectations for product functions and features that include reliability, durability, and maintainability. These expectations may result from the inability of a country to produce high-grade products for such reasons as inadequate materials, low-skilled workers, lack of modern equipment, and unsophisticated designs.

When products are manufactured to meet the requirements of a consumer in another country, the levels of product function and the product's features must match or exceed the expectations of the customer. One must understand the customer's expectations and get agreement with the customer as to the requirements, such as features, functions, characteristics, and form.

Services that are a part of the project or services that support the project need to be considered in planning an international project. Training in the operation or use of equipment is an example of where services may be required. Translation of documents or translations of an individual's oral report could be another area for consideration in the service-support area.

PLANNING FOR QUALITY IN INTERNATIONAL PROJECTS

Because modern quality management is a prevention-oriented function that calls for anticipating requirements, planning is a major consideration. Planning requires that a person define the future product and visualize how it will be built. As in all environments, the project manager as the primary quality leader must set the standards for quality and ensure they are met through both comprehensive plans and follow-through on the actual build and testing of the products.

Planning for quality takes on many aspects of defining the product in terms that are understood by the performing parties and that these parties have the capability to meet the specified levels of workmanship. Some examples and areas for consideration in international project quality are detailed here with brief explanations.

- Specifications for precision of measurements must consider the difference between the host organization of the project and those of all participants. In the United States, it is common practice to use inches, feet, and yards in describing the length parameters of products. Many countries use the metric system that has the meter (millimeter, centimeter, meter, or kilometer) as the basis for all linear measures. A comparison of some measures used in the United States versus the International Standard (metric) System is shown in the Table 15.1.

TABLE 15.1   Table of Measures*

Unit type	United States	International standard (metric) system
Length	inch, foot, yard, mile	meter
Area	Square inch, foot, yard, or mile (acre for land)	Square meter (hectare for land)
Weight	Pound, ton	Gram, kilogram
Volume	Cubic inch, foot, or yard	Cubic meter
Capacity (liquid)	Pint, quart, gallon, cubic inch, cubic foot	Liter
Capacity (dry)	Pint, quart, peck, bushel, cubic inch, cubic foot	liter
Velocity	Feet per second, miles per hour	Meters per second
Temperature	Fahrenheit (water freezes at 32 degrees and boils at 212 degrees)	Celsius (water freezes at one and boils at 100 degrees)
Force or Pressure	Poundal	Newton

Source: The World Almanac and Book of Facts, 2000.
*This information is a sample that may change over time and by usage.

- Measures used in specifications and contracts for international projects may use one system that would need to be converted to the general practice of the organization performing the work. Conversions are problematic and can lead to confusion and error. For example, 1 inch equals 0.0254 meter or 2.54 centimeters. Conversion of the values between different standards may pose problems. For example, when Canada converted to the metric system, an airplane was fueled in liters rather than in gallons. The airplane had less than 30 percent of the required refuel amount to fly from Toronto to Vancouver and had to make an emergency landing in Winnipeg.

- Numerical specifications may need to be expressed in two forms to convey the correct values. For example, rounding values may cause loss of the needed precision for constructed parts. Of particular importance is an interface between two or more parts. The question is whether the different builders have considered the other builder's use of measures.

SPECIFICATIONS PRACTICES

In developing the requirements and product design, it is essential that the specification accurately communicate what is needed in a precise language that cannot be misunderstood. This is a challenge when using one language, such as American English, and there is often a high reliance on descriptive terms. Specifications should tell what is to be accomplished and how it is to be accomplished. Under certain circumstances, one also may tell how something is not to be accomplished; for example, do not use a specific procedure or process.

Well-communicated specifications are essential if a quality product is to be designed, constructed, and delivered. The method of constructing the specification and the details included will be supportive of working under different environmental conditions that vary from country to country. Communicating the requirements for the product is essential, and a combination of media should be used ranging from words and notations to mathematics and numbers to graphics and illustrations.

DRAWINGS

Drawings are typically a part of the specifications for products. These graphic representations can be helpful in communicating requirements. Some difficulty may be encountered when two different measurement systems are used. This may require the drawings to be specifically prepared in the International System of Measures, that is, metric form, in addition to the U.S. measures.

When drawings comprise the specifications, it is best to determine whether the performing activity has the competence to be able to read and correctly interpret them. Caution needs to be exercised in assuming the drawings can be clearly and unambiguously understood. It may be helpful to review both the specification and the drawings with the performing contractor during early stages of the project.

Graphic presentations of requirements may offer many advantages in communicating product requirements. An illustration can overcome many of the disadvantages of text in describing relationships of parts and the sizes of components. Text, however, can be used to supplement the illustrations.

WORKMANSHIP AND WORKER QUALIFICATION

Different countries have a variety of workmanship capabilities. Some countries will have welders, for example, who are certified to perform welding operations that meet "country" needs but may not meet the requirements for either precision or high-pressure-vessel welding. During a visit to a country that was just emerging into high-technology operations, printed circuit boards often were found to have open connections. The repair operator was taking great pride in soldering the breaks in continuity by piling solder on top of the open circuit. The result was a *cold solder joint,* one that does not properly fuse the materials together, and the joint would open again under stress or extreme environmental conditions.

Another example of workmanship was when foreign welders were brought to the United States under a cooperative agreement to employ the excess labor. The task was to weld high-pressure pipes to withstand pressures as high as 1000 pounds per square inch and used to transport natural gas over long distances. A leak in a welded joint has the potential to ignite and cause severe damage to the surrounding area, as well as injure individuals in the vicinity. The welders were qualified to perform the welding operations but did not understand the need for precision in their welding. Once a defect was identified, the foreign welders were threatened with immediate return to their native country. This corrected the contractor's error in failing to inform the foreign welders of the standard and how the standard would be enforced.

Anticipating different levels of worker skill and qualifications permits one to assess and compare the existing capabilities against the required competence. Variances between the actual and required will require such solutions as training, bringing in external resources, and performing part of the work elsewhere.

WORK HABITS

Considering and accommodating the work habits and customs of a country is critical to successful project completion. Using a traditional model for employing indigenous labor may be counter to the country's custom. In one example, ships were being scraped cleaned of barnacles by local Ethiopian labor. The "project manager" attempted to hire individuals and was unsuccessful. The custom was that an entire village of males would be hired through the village leader. The village leader was paid for all labor and subsequently paid the workers. The accounting office was only accustomed to paying individuals and rejected the concept. All work was halted pending resolution of the matter, and the accounting office agreed to treating the village leader as a contractor.

In this same example of work habits in Ethiopia, the project manager brought a thermometer to the work place to record the temperature. The thermometer exploded when the temperature was significantly higher than 120°F. The workers, unfamiliar with a thermometer and having no idea of the actual temperature, stopped work until the project manager could persuade them to return to the tasks. (The actual temperature was 147°F on the metal dry dock.) Individuals were accustomed to working in the heat but suspected that something was wrong when the thermometer broke.

In a large Asian country, a large project was being completed without specific guidance from the project manager. Teams of workers were sent to the job site each day to perform whatever tasks were available. As the project manager explained the situation, "I just send people out to do work, and they choose the work they want to do. When they cannot find work, I send another team out to find work." Unfortunately, the rate of progress for completing the project was slow and randomly closing on completion objectives.

Typically, individuals in work environments do only what they are told to do. On a construction site, laborers were employed to dig a base for an equipment foundation. The requirement was that the earth be level and tamped to give it a base for pouring concrete footers. The supervisor was shouting at the laborers to move faster with the digging and leveling. It did not take long to observe the laborers shoveling dirt back and forth to please the supervisor. While work was being accomplished, the laborers were only moving dirt in different directions without making any noticeable progress.

Countries in tropical zones or having high temperatures during the day often will allow workers the opportunity to take a nap during the day. Work hours are modified to stop work during the hottest hours and to work in the mornings and evenings. For a project manager expecting continuous work on a project, this may be frustrating, and it also may have inefficiencies associated with interrupted workflow.

Religious customs also can change the manner in which work is scheduled and accomplished. Muslims, for example, have afternoon prayers that stop all work for some period of time while religious services are conducted. The work may or may not continue following the religious services. Other religions also can change the work hours and work environment.

Understanding work habits that may need to be accommodated rather than changed is important to obtain the desired results. There is perhaps no single model that one could use to avoid conflict with embedded work habits that have been cultivated over many years within a country. If it is a long-term project, it may be worth the effort to retrain the workforce. If the project is of short duration, it may be best to accept the work habits and any inefficiencies that accompany them.

TRAINING IN QUALITY PRACTICES

Often, a participating organization in another country will have no quality process in place. It may be that the level of sophistication in a process has not been documented to the level that the tasks can be deployed to the workforce. Training may be required prior to starting a project to raise the level of awareness in various workmanship practices such as assembly procedures or milling techniques. Also, the overall quality program needs to be deployed to the managers as well as to the workforce.

There was an example in a developing nation whereby a radio operator claimed to know the procedures for radio communications. There were indications that the radio operator was not using the prescribed procedures, and many mistakes were made in communicating information. On questioning, the individual thought that he understood the procedures, but the procedures were in English. His translation of the procedures into his native language was not precise, and errors were injected into the process. Instructions and training may be required to be given in the native language as well as in English.

Practices that have been used in the past may not meet the requirements for a new project. It may be necessary to retrain individuals in new practices that replace the existing ones. Identifying and establishing changes from old to new practices may be required to ensure the end state of the constructed product meets the criteria for quality, that is, meets the customer's requirements. Typically, the new practices will be in the technical fields that relate to design, fabrication, assembly, and testing. Some training may be required for managers and supervisors to indoctrinate them in the quality standards that must be achieved.

CERTIFICATION OF CAPABILITIES

Many different certifications are present for different tasks and organizational capabilities. These certifications typically meet the requirements of the country in which work is accomplished but do not necessarily translate to the quality requirements of the project. Certifications must be validated against the project's needs to ensure that the standards for quality of work are met.

An example of certification without the requisite capability was identified in a project where a foreign manufacturing company bid on a proposal to build bridges. The company showed a certificate from an audit agency attesting to the fact that the organization met all the requirements of ISO 9001. A check of the organization determined that there were no processes in place or instructions for fabrication of bridges. One of the fundamental requirements is to have instructions that describe the process for handling materials. No instruction was ever written, and therefore, the ISO 9001 certificate was invalid.

Individuals are often required to have certifications in various skills as well as the requirement to meet some basic knowledge and skill requirements. Several years ago a warehouse supervisor was charged with receiving and issuing parts for different projects. The basic skills were to be able to read, write, and speak in simple English so that the documents could be read and pieces counted on receipt and shipment. On payday, the warehouse supervisor was observed being paid, which required that he sign his name or alternatively place his thumbprint on a document indicating receipt of wages. He elected to use the thumbprint because he could neither read nor write in English. For several months this individual had copied numbers from one block on a form to another block without being able to read the document. This resulted in an inventory of the entire warehouse to reconcile the parts versus the records.

Certification of capabilities must be validated to give assurance that an individual or organization meets the certification requirements. Currency of certification and the certifying agency often build on the credibility of one's capabilities. It may be necessary to conduct an informal review to ensure that the individuals and organizations are actually conducting work processes in accordance with the certification criteria.

REVIEWING PARTNERS' QUALIFICATIONS

One way to ensure that the performing activity has the capability to perform the work is through a review of the operations. A visiting team may be used to validate processes, procedures, practices, and human competence in the required field. Identified weaknesses or shortfalls may be overcome through training or working with the partner to build on existing capabilities.

In addition to processes, procedures, practices, and human competence, there may be a need to assess tools and jigs, as well as the availability of materials. Tools should be matched to human skills to ensure proper use to achieve the desire results. Jigs may be unsophisticated and rough for one-time use or low usage, or there may be a need for technically complex jigs.

The availability of materials from local sources or by external purchase to meet the grade requirements must be ensured through evaluation of the planned use of specific types. The availability of materials in the proper quantity also can be critical to the success of the project, whether the materials are from local or from offshore suppliers.

Services that are an item for the contract or services that are required to support the project require special consideration because of the different cultural aspects of countries.

It is typical for a project partner to provide a number of services that either are a direct deliverable to the customer or a supporting element to building the project's product. Cultural expectations often bias how services are viewed and delivered.

On a major project in an African nation, the staff was housed and fed by the local nationals. The housing met acceptable standards, and housekeeping was above the requirement. However, each day the housekeeping staff would move personal objects of the project staff to a location nearer to the front door. If the occupant did not notice the relocation of the object for several days, it was assumed by the housekeeping staff that the occupant did not want the object because its migration toward the door was not noticed. Occupants cured the situation by moving objects back to their original location.

On this same project, the project staff ate their meals in a large dining facility. All waiters understood and spoke English—understanding American customs may have been something else. One morning a waiter patiently stood by while one of the staff reviewed the menu. It was obvious that the staff member was having difficulty in determining what to order. The young waiter said, "May I suggest something? How about a mushroom omelet?" The staff member responded, "Yes, bring me a mushroom omelet." It came as a surprise to the waiter that the staff member accepted his suggestion, and he backed away in confusion, saying, "We don't have. I just suggest." The waiter was just trying to help in the custom of his nation.

Reviews are helpful and build confidence in the capability of organizations. Conducting a review must focus on identifying both strengths and weaknesses—not just weaknesses to build on the existing capability. Any review should have the goal of "qualifying an organization as a partner" by overcoming any shortfalls that affect product quality. The review should not be used to assess business or other technical areas that are unrelated to the project.

CONTRACTUAL RELATIONSHIP

Contracts are similar in a fundamental way in that there is defined consideration for all parties. The terms and conditions define the specific requirements to be met for completing the contract to the mutual satisfaction of the parties. Contracts between parties in different countries pose special situations that can materially affect the results.

International contracts need to consider the following:

- Financial matters can have serious repercussions on contracts across international borders. First, the currency in which remuneration will be paid must be stated. Currency rate exchanges and inflation can change the profitability of project work. It is common for currency exchange rates to change as much as 20 percent over time. The variance in the exchange rates can be significant if, for example, payment is made in U.S. dollars rather than the currency of the country.

- The location or venue where any dispute resolution will be settled needs to be designated. If, for example, a contract would specify that all disputes are to be settled in the State of Delaware, all parties would need to agree to the jurisdiction and submission to the courts of that state. A Russian organization hired an English company to perform services, and the contract specified that all disputes were to be resolved in London. When the contract became very unfavorable to the Russian organization, payments were stopped, and the Russian organization refused to travel to London. Ultimately, the English company resolved the dispute by negotiating a new contract with significant differences.

- Wording of the contract may pose challenges when there are different denotations or connotations for terms used in the contract. This applies whether there are two or more languages involved or a single language such as English. Take, for example, the election of politicians to office. In the United Kingdom, politicians "stand" for office, and in the United States, politicians "run" for office.

- Any laws cited must be applicable to all parties for administration of the contract. It may be more appropriate to cite processes by which the parties will meet their respective obligations. An example is to cite the process for dispute resolution using the American Arbitration Association's rules rather than cite a venue for a court. Typically, the laws of a country apply only within the borders of that country.

A flawed contract affects the end result of a quality product when a performing contractor may not recognize the contractual requirements or that the contract fails for any number of reasons. A contract that is mutually beneficial to all parties gives the best chance for completing the work without resorting to enforcement means. The contract is the vehicle that "carries" quality to the product.

STABILITY OF A COUNTRY'S GOVERNING BODY

Developing countries can have unstable political organizations and governing bodies that cause major changes in how business is accomplished with external organizations. Unstable governments may cause new rules and regulations to be applied to performing contractors that may adversely affect the project. These new rules and regulations typically will be more restrictive and limiting for the performing contractor.

A risk assessment of the stability of a country's political situation and governing body should be accomplished prior to entering into a contract for products or services. This is especially important if a critical part of the project is to be performed in that country.

An example of the risk one might encounter was demonstrated when a water tower was constructed without consulting the local government. The water tower created an effect whereby a statue of the wife of the chief of state blended into the color of the water tower. Local officials demanded that the water tower be dismantled. The chief of state favorably ruled that if the water tower was painted a color that contrasted with the statue, the structure would not detract from the statue. The difference between the two solutions was several hundred thousands of dollars.

Projects in countries with stable governments have a greater chance of delivering a quality product than in an environment where dysfunctional government is present. Dysfunctional activities in the government typically flow over to businesses and any ongoing project. Interrupted work, labor strikes, vandalism, and the like can create a situation whereby a project cannot be completed to deliver a quality product to the customer.

TAXES AND TARIFFS

Levies of taxes and tariffs on goods produced in a country can add significantly to the overall burden on the project. Any additional costs that are typically outside the control of the supplier must be included in the profitability equation. For example, countries may charge taxes or tariffs on a product, whether whole or a part, for export to or import from another country.

Government-to-government agreements that specify transport of products across borders typically will include an exemption from taxes and tariffs. Private companies, however, do not always have the leverage to obtain concessions on taxes and tariffs. It may require research with the tax agency of a particular country to identify charges for products for export or for products imported to ensure factoring in any potential costs.

Additional costs to a project can affect the quality if a performing contractor is unable to complete the work under a cost-limited contract. Product quality may suffer if the additional cost burden imposed through taxes and tariffs causes the contractor to cut costs in materials or work practices.

PLANNING FOR INTERNATIONAL PROJECTS

There cannot be enough planning and anticipation of potential problems in international projects. Experience in one country may be helpful in assessing another country, but new situations always will emerge. The full range of potential challenges to projects probably will bring forth new challenges with each new environment.

Compiling a checklist and validating potential performing contractors are essential to be able to select the best contractor to conduct part of the project work. Checking on the governmental and cultural aspects of a country may reveal advantages or disadvantages for a project and an organization's ability to deliver a product that meets all the requirements of the customer.

International projects at first may appear to be simple and beneficial to all parties. There are pitfalls that can change a perceived highly beneficial project that has many identified advantages for all parties to one of catastrophic failure. Failure is often the result of operating in an unknown venue that does not have the capability to perform the project work.

When a project is conducted in a country other than that of the project's parent organization, one may need to plan for support services to accommodate all the project staff. Sleeping and eating accommodations are essential to meet the minimum needs of the staff to maintain morale. Project environments with extreme hot or cold temperatures will require some temperature conditioning to ensure the safety and comfort of the staff. A desert environment where temperatures during the day often exceed 110°F typically will require air conditioning for proper living temperatures. A project in Antarctica, for example, needs heat to ensure a workable situation from an outside temperature of perhaps −50°F.

SUMMARY

This chapter lists some of the areas to be considered and gives examples that may guide project managers in assessing the potential of partnering with an organization in another country. The examples show that many different factors may affect project and product quality. Some of these factors will be readily apparent, whereas others may be hidden at the start of the project. Weaknesses that are discovered must be dealt with as they occur.

Anticipating different practices that can affect product quality and planning to overcome any weaknesses will be helpful during project execution. Using the "defect prevention" approach can serve to preempt adverse situations that have a negative impact on quality. It is not sufficient to just state the requirements to a performing contractor, but the project manager must ensure that the contractor has the understanding and the capability to build a quality product for the project.

It is important to consider services required for the project whether they are part of the deliverable product or are supporting the project's work. Anticipating the unique nature of national customs and working to accommodate them are critical to project success. National customs, however honorable, may work counter to the project plan and the project's objectives.

CHAPTER 16

SUCCESS FACTORS IN VIRTUAL GLOBAL SOFTWARE PROJECTS

Dragan Milosevic

Maseeh College of Engineering and Computer Science,
Portland State University, Portland, Oregon

And Ozbay

Maseeh College of Engineering and Computer Science,
Portland State University, Portland, Oregon

Sabin Srivannaboon

Maseeh College of Engineering and Computer Science,
Portland State University, Portland, Oregon

A leading authority on program and project management, Dragan Milosevic earned his credentials as a project manager in the private sector managing large projects around the world. As associate professor of engineering management at Portland State University, he has developed practical tools and innovative approaches to the traditional and current challenges of project management. And as a consultant with Rapidinnovation, LLC, an executive consulting company, he helps leading companies streamline their project and program management models to ensure profitability. He has more than 25 years' experience in program and project management theory and practice. He has worked in this field at a wide range of blue-chip companies. He has managed projects worth more than $600 million with partners from over 50 countries. Dragan Milosevic has written extensively, and his work has been published in major academic and management publications around the world. His book, *Project Management Toolbox* (Wiley), received the Project Management Institute's (PMI's) the David I. Cleland Project Management Literature Award for 2004. Professor Milosevic holds a B.S., an MBA, and a Ph.D. in management, all from the University of Belgrade. He also conducted project management seminars for the PMI. He also holds PMP designation (#466).

And Ozbay holds a B.S. in industrial engineering and an M.S. in systems engineering from Bogazici University, Turkey. He is currently a Ph.D. candidate at Portland State University in the systems science/engineering management program. His Ph.D. research is focused on multi-organizational software projects. Ozbay has presented his research at international conferences. His recognitions include the best student paper award at the 5th Conference on Management Sciences and "Outstanding Graduate Student Award" from Maseeh College of Engineering and Computer Science of Portland State University. Ozbay has seven years of information technology (IT) project management experience. He currently works as a project manager, managing multi-organizational projects with IT and non-IT components.

Sabin Srivannaboon is currently a postdoctoral research associate faculty member at Portland State University, from which he received a Ph.D. in systems science/engineering management in mid-2005. His areas of interest include the strategic planning process, business strategy, project portfolio management, program/project management, and project strategy. Srivannaboon has presented his research at well-recognized international technology and project management conferences. Some of his articles have been published as chapters in books. In addition, Srivannaboon was a coinvestigator and participated in grant proposals (e.g., NASA, PMI) with one of the best project management research teams in the world. Aside from his research activities, Srivannaboon currently works as a new product introduction program manager for RadiSys Corporation, the leading supplier of advanced embedded systems used in commercial, enterprise and service provider markets. He will be listed in the upcoming 2005–2006 "Honors Edition" of the *United Who's Who Registry of Executives and Professionals*. He also won an "Outstanding Graduate Student Award" from Maseeh College of Engineering and Computer Science in the same year (2005).

THE UNIQUE WORLD OF GLOBAL SOFTWARE PROJECTS

The Importance of Software Development and How it Drives Other Industries

The importance of software development (SWD) has been increasing rapidly over the past few years (Baskerville and Pries-Heje, 1999; Hartman and Ashrafi, 2002; Hoch et al., 1999; Parzinger and Nath, 2000). Software is produced both as a product in itself and as an embedded component in hardware products. From the operational perspective, software enables and fuels growth across industries (Hoch et al., 1999). For example, in the service industries, many companies have been able to improve the speed and quality of their services with the integration of software. Additionally, in production industries, software is an essential component in almost every product, as well as in production processes (Nidumolu and Knotts, 1998).

From the strategic perspective, as different industries become more knowledge-driven, they become more akin to the software industry. Software is pure knowledge in a codified form (Hoch et al., 1999). Without software, it would not be possible for knowledge to be disseminated as quickly, and most businesses would not have experienced the rapid improvement that they have during the information age. Furthermore, in addition to industry, governments and the military benefit from software as a driving force for their operations (Nidumolu and Knotts, 1998).

Although the SWD industry offers immense opportunities for new and existing businesses, it presents equally big challenges. The majority of the ventures initiated by software companies in the last decade have been unsuccessful (Nambisan, 2001). Software companies face tremendous time pressures; in fact, most of the revenues generated in the SWD industry are from products that are less than two years old (Hoch et al., 1999). Moreover, the issues that are associated with this fast pace are coupled with historical problems that plague SWD efforts, for example, budget overruns and schedule delays. Even in today's connected world, these problems keep the SWD success rate at a lower level than in other industries. Several studies have reported failures in up to three-quarters of all software projects undertaken in the last decade (Berinato, 2001; Jiang and Klein, 2001; Nidumolu, 1996; Standish_Group, 1995). These failures are either total failures and cancellations or major slippages in cost, time, and quality targets.

What Makes SWD Projects Different

SWD projects are obviously big business with both strategic and tactical impact. But what is so special about them? Five project characteristics can to help answer this question in a comparison of SWD projects with new development and construction projects, two common types of projects in the business world (Fig. 16.1).

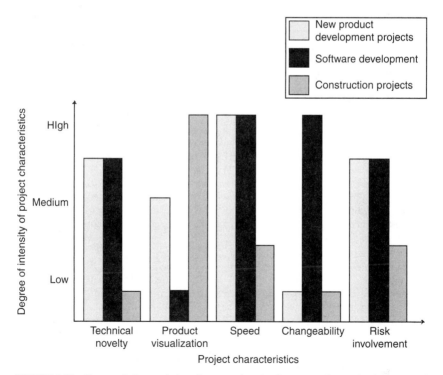

FIGURE 16.1 Compared characteristics of new product development, software development, and construction projects.

Technological Novelty.   Projects involving more novel technologies are considered to have a higher uncertainty than those with more mature technologies (Shenhar, 2001) For example, SWD projects that create new platforms have a higher level of technological novelty than projects based on reuse of old software. Since the essence of SWD and new project development (NPD) projects is an innovation advantage, a large number of these projects deal with a medium to high level of technological uncertainty. In comparison, construction projects deal with mature technologies and less technological uncertainty. Generally, projects with higher uncertainty require a more flexible project management style (Shenhar, 2001).

Product Visibility.   To what extent can one physically see or touch a project product? This question addresses the characteristic of product visibility (Brooks, 1987; McDonald, 2001). Software products, for example, have low visibility. In contrast, NPD products and constructed facilities have concrete visibility; in point of fact, construction projects have high concrete visibility, whereas NPD projects have a medium range of visibility. For this reason, it is easier for NPD and construction teams to transform this visibility into a tangible project scope (Clark and Wheelwright, 1993; Cooper, 1994). In contrast, it is much more difficult for an SWD team to visualize its product beyond a set of SWD requirements and specifications and to translate those into a tangible project scope (Findley, 1998).

Speed.   The ability to accelerate NPD and SWD projects is crucial to premium pricing, higher market share, and higher profits. However, speed may be detrimental. For example, many mistakes occur when skipping steps, a frequent approach to accelerating both SWD and NPD projects. In contrast, construction projects rarely face these high-speed pressures. Instead, their markets typically tolerate low to medium speed. Slower projects need a less flexible process, one that relies on sequential activities. Faster projects need a more flexible project management process, in which the activities are overlapped to accelerate their execution and shorten time to completion (Zirger and Hartley, 1996).

Changeability.   Changeability is the magnitude of the consequences of changing the project product design. For NPD projects, the level of changeability is low because of the high costs of change, including changes in interfaces, materials, etc., all resulting in the product being late to market (Brooks, 1987). The case of construction projects is similar. In contrast, if we characterize software as pure thought stuff, there are no tools, materials, or manufacturing process changes in SWD projects. Thus, changing the software is relatively easier. The differences in changeability in these classes of projects may result in different needs in managing the projects, for example, management of scope and customer involvement.

Risk Involvement.   For SWD or NPD projects, new technologies increase risks (Gupta and Wilemon, 1990; Raz, 1993). The risk level increases if the project involves many personnel, has a high product and application complexity, and suffers from a lack of sufficient resources and team expertise (Jiang and Klein, 2001, Tatikonda and Rosenthal, 2000). Consequently, many SWD and NPD projects face medium to high severity of risk. In contrast, risk is low to medium in construction projects and often is the by-product of new and untested architectural designs and construction techniques (Pinto and Govin, 1989). As a result, risk management has a more emphasized place in the management of SWD and NPD projects than in construction projects.

As discussed earlier, while SWD projects have similarities with other types of projects, they also have unique differences. These differences have prompted some experts to describe SWD projects as unique challenges. In particular, because SWD projects typically are implemented under severe speed and financial pressures, they tend to expose the strengths and weaknesses of a company, including its culture, management systems, organizational structure, and people. Therefore, SWD projects are a comprehensive real-time test of the whole corporation.

THE NATURE OF VIRTUAL GLOBAL SOFTWARE DEVELOPMENT

Virtual global software (VGS) development involves development teams across multiple countries collaborating and performing a variety of tasks, such as planning, controlling, coding, testing, implementing, and maintaining, in order to develop new software and achieve common project goals. Recently, many software companies have used VGS development instead of the usual centralized colocated form of development. U.S. spending for VGS projects, for example, is projected to grow at a compound annual rate of almost 26 percent, from approximately $10 billion in 2003 to $31 billion in 2008 (Behravesh, 2004). More than 50 other nations are also presently involved in VGS development.

Major benefits drive companies to make a transition to VGS development: VGS helps to reduce project completion time, reduce cost, make better use of scarce resources, and gain competitive advantage (Gorton and Motwani, 1996; Norbjerg et al., 1997; Carmel, 1999; Herbsleb & Moitra, 2001). In particular, Carmel (1999) claimed that the cycle time could be reduced by 20 to 35 percent using the around-the-clock or follow-the-sun development technique. In addition, King (2003) reported that low-cost programming development is the most important reason why U.S. organizations outsource to non-U.S. locations.

Despite a number of challenges (described below), VGS development will remain a vehicle for many companies to achieving success and will contribute to long-term business strategy as being of strategic importance.

WHAT MAKES VIRTUAL GLOBAL SOFTWARE PROJECTS DIFFERENT

VGS projects are conducted by internationally distributed groups of people—groups that are culturally diverse, geographically dispersed, and communicating electronically (Kristof et al., 1995). They have an organizational mandate to make or implement decisions with international components and implications (Maznevski and Chudoba, 2000). To execute the mandate, the teams in charge face projects that, in addition to the characteristics that differentiate software projects from other types of projects, as discussed earlier, display a new layer of characteristics that distinguish VGS projects from ones that are colocated. Here we describe this new layer of characteristics (summarized in Table 16.1), indicating their intermediate impact on projects. Then we will refer to the critical success factors described later in the text that reduce the impact of these characteristics. Finally, we will show the impact that the factors produce (ultimate impact).

TABLE 16.1   Summary of VGS Projects' Characteristics and Their Impacts, Critical Success Factor, and Ultimate Impact

Characteristic	Intermediate Impact/ Challenges	Critical Success Factor Addressing Characteristic	Ultimate Impact
Distance	Reduces communication frequency Reduces informal communication Lowers communication richness Impacts product architecture Impacts choice of process/ development strategy	1, 2, 4, 5, 6, 10, 11, 13, 14, 15, 16, 17, 18, 19, 20, 21, 22, 23, 24	Better control
Time separation	Inhibits the use of synchronous communication Affects the selection of communication media/types Affects task allocation	1, 2, 4, 5, 6, 10, 11 15, 16, 17, 18, 19 20, 21	
Language differences	Affects the selection of communication media/types Communication effectiveness	1, 2, 4, 10, 11, 16	Higher coordination efficiency and effectiveness
Cross-cultural differences	Affects group decision-making Team performance Communication effectiveness	1, 2, 4, 5, 7, 8, 9 10, 11, 12, 16, 17	Higher project performance
Multiple sites	Affects the type of technological infrastructure and communication Introduces human resource staff of different skill and productivity Increases management overhead Introduces the challenge of team building, especially establishing and maintaining trust	1, 2, 3, 4, 5, 6, 10, 11, 12, 16, 18, 19, 20, 21, 22, 23, 24	

Distance

An old rule goes that when team members are located more than 50 feet apart from each other, their frequency of communication decreases significantly (Allen, 1997). Imagine how much more the frequency declines between a software project manager in California and a programmer in India. For the same distance reason, other forms of communication also decrease: the informal, unplanned, and ad hoc communication so vital to supporting software team collaboration (Curtis et al., 1988; Perry et al., 1994; Herbsleb and Grinter, 1999). Worst of all, "rich" communication, defined as a two-way interaction involving more than one sensory channel, drops off because of the distance. For example, phone conversations, which occur frequently in VGS projects, are not as information-rich as face-to-face meetings, which are typical in colocated projects.

Why is this important to global SWD projects? These projects need a high level of coordination and control to be successful, which requires an exemplary quality of factors such as frequency of communication, both formal and informal communication, and the use of rich, high-efficiency communication media (Raffo and Setamanit, 2005).

When these factors decrease because of distance, the ultimate impact is lower coordination. Similarly, project control will suffer due to lack of information. Ultimately, project performance may slip. The product architecture needs to be adapted for multiple sites to create harmonious and parallel software development. In particular, proper architecture can develop modular design such that interdependence between modules, that is, between the sites responsible for them, is minimal, reducing coordination and control problems and increasing the likelihood of attaining the desired project performance.

The distance factor also dictates the process/development strategy. Specifically, when multiple sites are identified and product architecture developed, it is time to allocate tasks to the sites. There are three major process/development strategies (Fig. 16.2): module-based, phase-based, and integrated allocation (also called "follow-the-sun") (Carmel, 1999).

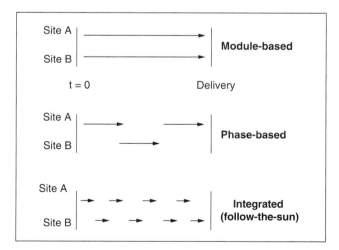

FIGURE 16.2 Three task-allocation strategies.

Time Separation

Differences between the time zones of multiple sites that are geographically dispersed are called *time separation*. Because of this temporal separation, the working hours of the sites may overlap, more or less. This difference in working hours, or *temporal distance* (Carmel and Agarwal, 2001), holds back the use of synchronous communication that is essential in collaborative SDW. Although the power of asynchronous communication (e.g., e-mail) is increasing continually, it pales in comparison with the ability to communicate synchronously (e.g., face-to-face meetings) to convey the speed and tone of voice, facial expressions, body language, etc. (Jarvenpaa, 1998). For example, in a project involving sites in Canada and Germany, an e-mail message took 16 hours to reach the destination, resulting in an increased coordination effort—and cost (Kogut and Meitu, 2000). For these reasons, synchronous communication can help to solve misunderstandings faster and prevent problems, thus having an impact on project coordination and control and, ultimately, project cycle time.

Temporal separation often determines the allocation of work across sites, that is, the task-allocation strategy (Carmel, 1999). The less overlap time (i.e., larger temporal separation) between the sites offers the advantage of longer development hours when deploying the follow-the-sun strategy. Ideally, the follow-the-sun approach can shrink the project-development cycle time by 50 percent (Carmel, 1999).

Language Differences

VGS teams are highly likely to have team members who speak different languages, which affects the selection of communication media and the effectiveness of communication. In particular, non-native English-speaking people prefer asynchronous communication (e.g., e-mail) to synchronous (e.g., videoconferencing) (see, for example, Carmel and Agarwal, 2001; Keil and Eng, 2003) because asynchronous communication allows them time to digest input and express their thoughts. However, asynchronous communication often results in delayed or complicated problems because it can take days for back-and-forth discussions (Carmel and Agarwal, 2001) as opposed to synchronous communication, where miscommunication and misunderstanding can be resolved quickly in real time. Moreover, miscommunication may occur easily in both asynchronous and synchronous types, reducing communication effectiveness and affecting project control, leading to project delays and other problems.

Cross-Cultural Differences

Two major roadblocks in VGS projects are differences in the corporate culture and in the ethnic cultures of team members. Corporate culture is a set of values shared by the organizational members, reflected in mechanisms such as management practices (e.g., project management methodologies, rewards, hiring, promotion, etc.). When the cultures of participating organizations in a project differ, there is a potential for culture clash, thereby decreasing coordination, control, and performance results. If different sites are parts of the same organization, of course, the impact of corporate culture lessens.

Ethnic culture is the collective mental program of the people in an environment and encompasses a number of instructions (Hofstede, 1984) that tell us what we should and should not do. They are also embodied in what we have created—our family structures, forms of social organizations, companies, laws, etc. (Hofstede, 1980) and even our project management practices.

Are there variables that permeate all cultures and help us to understand the root causes of the cultural differences of GSV team members? Yes, a set of such variables is termed a *cultural map*. One of the map's variables is *time orientation*, which we will use to point to the essence of cross-cultural project management. Specifically, cultures differ in how they value time. Some cultures emphasize a focus on the past, whereas others focus on the present or future. Americans, for example, focus primarily on the immediate effects of a challenge or action; they are present-time oriented. In contrast, the Japanese concentrate on long-term performance, or future time.

Let's take project scheduling as an example. Present-oriented schedulers are likely to develop a precise schedule for the near-future activities, and as information becomes available, the longer-term activities will be expanded in more detail following the "rolling wave" concept (Harrison and St. John, 1998). Everything will be done to preserve the deadlines because time is money. In contrast, the importance of deadlines is likely to be low to past-oriented project teams. In their minds, whether the deadlines will be met is God's will, something that human schedulers cannot dictate. The approach practiced by future-oriented schedulers is that schedules will focus on the long-term view and not be very detailed; to account for contingencies that life may deploy, any deadlines likely will be treated as tentative.

Similarly, cultural differences affect team members' perceptions of all areas of project management, from scope to resource allocation to project organization. The central point here is that these differences can play havoc in project communication, control, and performance. Simple strategies such as immersion, training, and more advanced techniques can help overcome these differences and their impact (Milosevic, 1999, 2001).

Multiple Sites

Multiple sites are often located in developing countries, which have different technological infrastructure and human resources. In particular, the cost, availability, and capability of data communication vary between these countries. In some countries with inadequate infrastructure, these lines are not available at all. Because of the lack of proper and dependable telecommunications, VGS teams are prevented from communicating effectively, and the coordination, control, and performance of the project are seriously affected.

Human resources in different countries vary as well. For example, the level of education, skill, and experience of developers depends on location. Availability of programmers also is location-specific. For example, some programmers, such as those in Japan, are willing to work longer overtime hours, whereas Scandinavians generally are not. All these factors influence productivity levels and project performance.

SYSTEM OF SUCCESS FACTORS

Success factors are those characteristics, conditions, or variables that, when sustained, maintained, or managed properly, can have a significant impact on the success of a project (Leidecker and Bruno, 1984). To increase the likelihood of a VGS project's success, senior and project managers need to address a specific group of success factors (Fig. 16.3). Should they address them individually or as a system?

There is no doubt that deploying success factors individually can improve VGS project performance incrementally. However, this approach hides a trap. Success factors are mostly interdependent, and building them individually without regard for the other factors

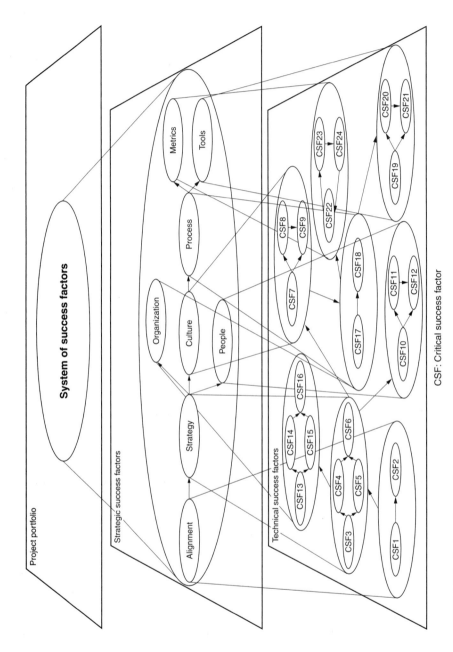

FIGURE 16.3 System of success factors.

may have a limited impact. For example, in Fig. 16.3, one of the strategic success factors is process. In deploying this success factor, a team will develop a clear project and product management process, including project phases, deliverables, and milestones. If this is not done, project tools will be used randomly instead of being used to support specific deliverables in the process. With no clear deliverables and no clear use of the tools, the basic purpose of the tools is missed. Therefore, for higher success of VGS projects, ideally you should treat success factors as a system and build that system. Together, the factors offer solutions to challenges that VGS project face (shown in Table 16.1) and support the accomplishment of project goals.

The system of success factors in general works at three levels. The first level includes a portfolio of all VGS projects, meaning that all VGS projects need one system of success factors. The second level includes strategic success factors. To provide the flexibility necessary to account for project specifics (size, market and technological novelty, and pace, for example), the factors may need to be customized. Each strategic success factor is at the highest level of VGS project makeup and contains multiple components or smaller success factors that we call *tactical success factors* (the lowest level). For a strategic factor to be deployed successfully, all its tactical factors have to work. Next, we will describe the strategic factors. Tactical factors are the focus of the next section.

There are eight strategic success factors—strategic alignment, project strategy, project culture, project people, project organization, project process, project tools, and project metrics—that, when deployed (level 2 in Fig. 16.3), may have a significant impact on project success. The strategic-alignment factor is how companies use VGS projects as vehicles to accomplish their business strategies. For this reason, the first condition for a successful VGS project is that senior management clearly defines the company's business strategy. No matter what the competitive attributes (more on this later under tactical success factors) that the business strategy is based on, a transparent strategic-alignment process, formal or informal, must be established.

The alignment process' job is to enable the business strategy to be communicated clearly to project managers and teams and to help VGS projects (through project planning) to be fully aligned with the chosen business strategy. Once the VGS project is in implementation, the strategic-alignment process should be able to maintain the alignment until project completion.

Once this process is in place and functioning, it will help to define and drive the makeup of the success factor we call *project strategy*. First, on the basis of the business strategy direction, project strategy characterizes the project-delivery approach. We find that the project-delivery model termed *rapid-release cycle* is crucial to success. This model favors frequent, smaller projects, each one implementing a small number of features. With such project anatomy in mind, project strategy helps to set corresponding project objectives and success measures. Also, harmoniously with the objectives and measures, project strategy defines clear software requirements (product definition) and project scope definition. Finally, project strategy spells out the strategic focus, a set of rules telling VGS project teams how to make decisions to accomplish the desired project objectives and hit the success measures. A properly defined project strategy helps to shape the next three strategic success factors—project culture, project people, and organization—which are next described in turn.

By deploying the project strategy success factor, senior management makes a statement: Develop project culture that will support our business strategy. For thist, performance-oriented values that are designed to direct project people first must be articulated clearly. In a way, this is a blueprint for developing the project management actions and behaviors to be *uniformly* practiced in the project. In plain terms, project culture is like the air we breathe: The cleaner the air, the healthier we are, and the more performance oriented the culture is, the more successful VGS projects are.

The project strategy also will drive the type of project people, probably the single most important strategic success factor for a project. Typically, the project will need its project manager and other team members to provide true leadership, overcoming all obstacles set by an environment of geographic, organizational, temporal, and cultural separation, and to rely, when possible, on face-to-face meetings. In this process, a VGS team needs to build a smooth communication flow, supported by trust among team members.

The project-strategy factor also sets the direction for what sort of project organization is needed to make the strategy work. The size and nature of the project determined by the strategy may well determine that a well-oiled matrix framework on the organizational level is needed to support all VGS projects. That the project relies on the matrix is very likely, considering that the rapid-release cycle favors small projects. Within the matrix, the cross-functional team structure is shaped, with clear avenues to identify and manage stakeholder expectations, primarily those of customers and the project sponsor, and fed by the matrix resources.

The factors of project culture, people, and organization transfer the message of project strategy and add their influence into the project process, shaping it to support them. This support will be offered through molding a process that is standard, to some degree, and flexible, to some degree, one that is able to produce the desired deliverables over project phases and at requested milestones. For this, the process needs planning but also a strong control to detect plan-versus-actual variances in performance targets and to identify corrective actions.

Project process dictates what project tools and metrics to employ. To begin with, the role of project tools is to support the process by providing procedures and techniques to solve the problems of the technical process of VGS development. This is what product management tools help to do. A second group of tools—project management tools—supports the managerial process of VGS development. Considering that team members in VGS projects are truly virtual, there is a vital need to share project information and deliverables and generally problem-solve across geographic and time separations. The third group of tools, the collaborative technology tools, facilitates this. It is important to understand that project process really has a decisive influence on the choice and nature of project tools. For example, if the project process is directed toward support of the project strategy of a speed-to-market nature, the major emphasis is on project tools that help to manage the VGS project schedule in a fast way.

Project metrics measure products of the project process. Therefore, the nature of the process dictates the metrics that are used. In essence, what is wanted is to control project efficiencies—Are we meeting our project schedule? for example—but also whether the process delivers to the customer what the customer expects. While these two might seem to be enough, the picture of project health metrics, as some call the metrics, is not complete unless we measure how well the project helps us to prepare for the future, that is, new VGS projects.

In the next section we will dissect each individual strategic success factor in order to uncover the substance of each: the individual tactical success factors (see Fig. 16.3).

TACTICAL SUCCESS FACTORS

Strategic Alignment

Two tactical factors are part of the strategic alignment, a key strategic success factor. The first one—*defining a clear business strategy*—is fundamental to sustaining competitive advantage over rivals in the global software business. For such a strategy to be executed, an *alignment process*—the second factor—should be established to help align priorities of the project with those of the strategy. With the business strategy and the alignment process in place, what remains is to achieve the alignment.

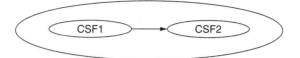

Critical Success Factor (CSF) 1: Defining a Clear Business Strategy. Companies in the virtual global software business should have a clear business strategy that reflects who they are and how they intend to outplay their rivals. Once formulated in this manner, the strategy must be turned into simple, understandable terms and communicated to project people, such as product roadmaps with the timeline for new software products. In addition, speed to market for each of the products must be defined, along with the product's feature set, customers to target, and expected revenue and profitability.

Accompanying this expression of the strategy is a clearly established set of priorities, whose implementation is expected to help the strategy's execution. Says one vice president of a global virtual software company in charge of the strategy:

> We want all project managers to understand our business strategy and to work on their projects to make it happen. Therefore, we translated our relatively high-level strategy and product roadmap into a set of strategic priorities for our business. In particular, these priorities are in four areas:
>
> *Customer expectations*
> Functionality
> Ease of use
> Service
> Customer support
> Time to market
>
> *Quality*
> Reliable products
> Integration
> Best-of-breed strategy
>
> *Business results*
> Sustainable competitive advantage
> Being the leader in the market
> Getting customers
>
> *Financial indicators*
> Return on investment (ROI)
> Market share
> Profitability
>
> We spend an enormous amount of time communicating these priorities to VGS project managers. Of course, we rate for them the importance of each priority, so they have a clear picture of what strategically matters to us.

CSF2: Achieving the Alignment. To ensure that the VGS projects are selected and executed in such a way that they support the business strategy, an alignment process— formal or informal—has to be established. Its purpose is straightforward: to help to align the VGS projects with the organization's business strategy and its priorities as described in the section "Defining a Clear Business Strategy" above. Each project is put through a planning process to achieve this alignment. As the project implementation unfolds, monitoring of the project continues throughout its life cycle to determine if there is misalignment and, if so, to take corrective actions. Depending on the operating conditions of projects, they may be required to adapt project management systems that include elements of project strategy, culture, organization, process, tools, and metrics. The goal is to accomplish project success and thus support organizational success.

Project Strategy

There are interrelated tactical success factors here. The first one—*rapid-release cycle*—portrays the project delivery mode, which helps to define and establish the second factor—*project objectives and success measure*—and the third factor—*product and project definitions*. Project strategy also makes clear what behavior rules to accomplish the fourth factor, which we term *strategic focus*.

CSF3: Using a Rapid-Release Cycle.   A rapid-release cycle refers to the project delivery mode in which are implemented frequent, smaller projects, each with a small number of features. This approach implies that the implementing company stays closely in touch with its customers. In doing so, for example, the customer requirements are identified and prioritized with the customers; the requirements with the higher priorities are executed first—in the first release. Then the lower-priority requirements are executed in the second and/or third release projects. Instead of having one large, long project, which is much more difficult to run, the rapid-release cycle enables the company to divide that project into a stream of smaller and shorter projects while at the same time constantly going back to the customers and communicating about their additional needs. In other words, the rapid-release cycle offers the ability to realign in order to match customer needs over time. Therefore, this flexibility is a key to the rapid-release cycle that is, in turn, key to delivering the projects on customer needs and on time. This flexibility is illustrated by a project executive working on VGS projects with India and Russia: "We constantly are having this conversation about what do you [the customer] really need and how've we gotten the latest of your needs. . . . Moving into this rapid-release model, building a tight relationship with customers and the flexible architecture are so important."

CSF4: Establishing Project Objectives and Success Measures.   Establishing clear project objectives is important to VGS teams. Given the unique characteristics of global software development, the project teams are dispersed across different locations. The lack of clear shared objectives may leave the team confused, jeopardizing team morale. To set project objectives, it is also important to link the project objectives to the organization's business strategy and needs that the project supports. This leads to a stronger alignment (CSF2).

By setting clear objectives, clear project success measures are set in advance. Clear success measures help VGS teams to stay focused not only on achieving the project objectives but also on contributing to the organization's success. Since success means different things to different people, defining the objectives must consider the different dimensions (e.g., project efficiency, direct commercial or organizational success, impact on users, etc.) that are specific, measurable, attainable, relevant, and timely. One such example, what it is called a *bounding box,* from a real company is given in Fig. 16.4. This company defines the target value for the objective and also defines threshold control limits for each objective, which represents the upper or lower limit of success for a particular objective. Status of each objective is reported monthly using the status lights (green—progressing well; yellow—warning/heads up; and red—stop/needs management intervention).

CSF5: Product and Project Definitions.   Clear product definition helps the VGS teams to avoid surprises during execution. It should begin by defining the target customers and their needs, as well as the features of the software product. Here, customer involvement is key. Requirements from customers should be well identified, under-stood, and translated to the software specifications. Many software companies employ a use-case analysis at this stage to capture how the user uses the software. Moreover, it is important that the prototype get developed and sent to users for the feedback loop: "The prototype should include all key functions of the product, although sometimes it may not be user-friendly."

Clear project definition—defining objectives, major deliverables, and activities—helps the VGS teams to focus on their tasks. This definition should be of an across-site nature, indicating which sites produce which deliverable, and be based on the defined product architecture and task-allocation strategy. Hopefully, the VGS project team is flexible enough to adjust to allocated tasks, or replanning and redefining the scope will occur.

CSF6: Having a Clear Strategic Focus.   Strategic focus refers to the rules that guide the behavior of the project team and direct them to accomplish the project objectives. It should be incorporated into—and be relevant to—the objectives of the organization's business strategy. For example, if the business sets its position to be that of a

Bounding box			
Project objectives/ success measures	**Box**		**Status**
Value proposition:	*Target*	*Threshold*	
• Increase market share in software segment			
➢ Order growth within 6 months of introduction	10%	5%	◉
➢ Market share increase one year after introduction	5%	0%	○
Schedule:			
• Project initiation approval	1/3/2000	1/15/2000	◉
• Software proposal approval	6/1/2000	6/30/2000	◉
• Engineering release approval	11/1/2000	11/30/2000	◉
• Software release to customers	12/1/2000	12/15/2000	○
Financials:			
• Project budget	100% of plan	105% of plan	◉
• Profitability index	2.0	1.8	◉

FIGURE 16.4   Bounding box.

fast time-to-market leader in software development, general rules for VGS team behavior may include allowing overlapping phases, combining milestones, and spending additional money to speed up the project: "You are using a process as a tool to get the desired results, not as a weight around your neck to slow you down."

Here, having a checks-and-balances system is important. The system should provide a mechanism to ensure that any of the defined behaviors—and the actions stemming from them—are not over the limit set by the checks-and-balance system (e.g., additional money can be spent up to 5 percent of initial requested budget).

Project Culture

There are three tactical success factors in this group. The first one—*building a high-performance project culture*—is an enabler of the second factor—*creating awareness of cross-cultural differences.* When such awareness exists, it is possible to recognize how big or small cross-cultural distances among cultural groups in a VGS team are. The existence of the awareness and the distances that are understood and recognized drive the development of *culturally responsive strategies to deal with potential problems* (the third factor).

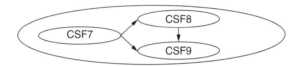

CSF7: Building a High-performance Project Culture.   Projects exist to deliver results that support organizational goals. Therefore, a parent company must build a high-performance culture and ethic that gives people both the confidence and capabilities to visualize the best way to deliver the results. The discipline with which such companies define and pursue their goals serves as a beacon to their employees as to how to behave. Such companies offer fertile ground for the growth of high-performance projects and teams not only by creating performance challenges but also by setting clear performance expectations and sending a message that results matter. It is for these reasons that it is of vital importance that senior management creates a high-performance corporate culture. How strongly this type of culture is ingrained in the minds of team members in a world-class company can be seen in a statement from an American project manager doing a VGS project in England: "In the world of our company, you know, we are very results-driven. If you can't demonstrate your success, then you have not accomplished anything."

Taking over from there, the VGS project manager should build a specific project culture, expressed as a set of clearly articulated performance-oriented values that are designed into project management practices/behaviors and then *uniformly* practiced in the project. For example, one such value is "being proactive," where team members practice a behavior of periodic progress reporting that includes predicting the schedule and budget at completion of their tasks. The intention here is that project team members have a sense of identity with the cultural values and accept the need to invest both materially and emotionally in their project. This should make them more engaged, committed, enthusiastic, and willing to support each other in accomplishing the project goals. As a result, they should work harder and be more effective, thereby increasing success.

CSF8: Create Awareness of Cross-Cultural Differences.   One of the toughest challenges in cross-cultural interactions is to learn that "they" (e.g., developers in Russia) are different from "us" (e.g., project managers from the United States). To overcome this challenge, one has to avoid the self-reference trap, a trap of interpreting the actions and behaviors of team members from another culture by means of one's own cultural values. The first step is creating awareness of the existence of cross-cultural differences. Some ways for this include understanding your own culture first and then understanding the culture of culturally different team members. Training can help in this. For example, on an American-Russian VGS team, the project manager said, "We've taken cross-cultural training to try to understand Russians, and they've also taken classes on how to understand how to work with the United States. How tough could that be? Well, we have our own prejudiced views of the world, so I'm sure we're tough people to deal with, to work with. So, you learn about some of the things, some of the barriers that you are going to be facing—and that helped."

A great way to reach this state of cultural awareness is via immersion, that is, living in the foreign culture. "I spent two times in Russia, three months each time," the executive sponsor of this project told us. The net result of these investments is faster and better communication, higher productivity, and shorter cycle time with, of course, good quality being a given.

CSF9: Build a Menu of Culturally Responsive Strategies. Once cross-cultural awareness is created, conditions are in place to develop a menu of strategies to predict and prevent potential problems or to reconcile cross-cultural project management distances. The choice of strategy hinges on the competency level in the counterpart's culture. Competency implies both a knowledge of cultural values and the ability to apply the knowledge in a project management interaction. For example, when the American project manager's competence in the counterpart's culture is low, the first option is to hire an independent facilitator to direct the parties' interactions throughout the course of the project. The second option—the *dominance approach*—is to impose American culturally defined project management practices, perhaps because of its technological superiority or dominant bargaining position. Here is how an American project manager exercised this approach softly in an American-Russian VGS project:

> They [the Russians] can't brainstorm with their superior. Because they have been in a country [Russia] with the big power distance [e.g., the difference in power between the boss and subordinate] for so long, they are just used to people telling them what to do. So, when you ask them to brainstorm and suggest new ideas, they won't. Because this is a crucial value in my company, I had them learn to brainstorm. I used all kind of tricks; I trained them, brought them to the United States for a few weeks, and paid them monetary incentives, and managed to get them to brainstorm.

Another approach offers mutual adjustment, in which project management practices of all team members are mixed, using the strengths of their cultures. When cross-cultural competency of the American project manager is high, he or she can either embrace the counterpart's culturally defined project management, which happened on a recent American-English VGS team, or use a synergistic approach that "recognizes and transcends the individual" elements of the cultures involved. It is worth noting that in some project situations, there may be a need to select a single strategy, whereas in others, all of them may be used.

Project People

This easily may be the top strategic factor given the separations brought about by VGS projects. As noted by a veteran of virtual projects, there are really only three major success factors in a virtual project: "people, people, and people." That is, no matter how good other factors are—such as the project management process or strategic alignment—project success is all about good people. Similarly, we believe that the people are the crux in VGS projects, especially three tactical factors related to these employees. *True leadership* (the first factor) on VGS teams dictates the *communication* (the second factor), whereas the first two factors enable a *drive toward trust building* (the third factor).

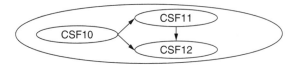

CSF10: Provide True VGS Team Leadership.   True team leaders forge the vision for the team, evangelically communicate it, and inspire and motivate team members to follow them. All this is typically associated with the face-to-face influence characteristic of colocated teams. On such teams, project managers exploit every second of their team time in every project activity to preach their leadership message continuously. Thus the question is: Is it possible build true leadership in VGS teams? Says a project manager of a project including Oregon, Massachusetts, Germany, and Italy:

> Leadership for a VGS team is possible, but it takes a special effort of many members. It was much easier before the traveling freeze, because we could take advantage of face-to-face meetings. Our VGS team had an assigned project leader—myself—but leadership roles can be expressed by anyone within the team and in fact may need to be in order to carry the team forward. Leadership roles included motivation, information or opinion seeking, mediation, facilitating communication, removing barriers, lubricating interfaces, and making each conflict functional so it could be used to improve the quality of our decisions. All these aspects are important for building team spirit. Now, after the freeze, only I am allowed to travel. And frankly, I am on the road all the time, trying to constantly link all team pieces and do all the roles. Yes, I think I am doing a good job, but it's too difficult, and sometimes it doesn't work. Why? Simply because sometimes I don't get to see some team members face to face for months, and other team members don't get to do their portion of leadership.

Obviously, true leadership in successful VGS teams is possible with true leaders and face-to-face meetings.

CSF11: Use All Communication Channels at All Times.   Remember, these are VGS projects fraught with communication barriers stemming from the geographic, temporal, cultural, and organizational separations (Zigurs, 2003). Therefore, management of communication is the foremost enabler of the successful execution of the rest of the VGS project management activities. With effective tools (see that strategic factor) and consciously designed effort, including simple and more complex issues, some project managers are able to alleviate the effects of all these separations, even linguistic separation. A very simple example from an executive who sponsored a VGS between Oregon and Russia will demonstrate: "We tend to emphasize a lot of written communication. So, there is lots of room for misunderstandings, and there is room for language issues to come up, and we emphasize creating some opportunities for face-to-face discussions." When it is not possible to provide opportunities for VGS team members to meet face to face, one company uses a "diplomat," who can speak the technical and business languages and who is bicultural, to travel between sites or it has on-site contact persons who regularly have face-to-face meetings. Furthermore, even clear milestones may provide simple *synchronization points for all sites*, according to an experienced VGS project manager.

To better understand the application of communication on a working level, consider a more complex issue of VGS team members who lack a shared understanding of project issues, solutions, and processes, a frequent problem in VGS environments. Successful VGS projects resolve this issue by scheduling periodic face-to-face meetings by rotation in different locations, focusing on trust building and conflict resolution during the meetings. They return to the regular, technology tools–based communication when shared understanding is established.

CSF12: Work Hard to Build Trust.   Trusting team members is a precondition to a healthy team atmosphere, which itself contributes to successful projects. Trust requires cooperation and interdependence, commitment and follow-through. To make it simple, we trust a team member we work with (cooperation) and whom we depend on (interdependence) when he or she delivers (follow-through) on what he or she promises (commitment). Spending more time together, such as in face-to-face situations, teams have an easier time building a stronger sense of team identity, spirit, and trust. Once trust is established, maintaining it faces the same obstacle—getting team members together. While this sounds like a simple team proposition, the trouble is that having multiple sites—and geographic, temporal, organizational, and cultural separation—does not support those face-to-face situations because they are costly and often not allowed by the parent company. Certainly communicating through collaborative tools—for example, e-mail or phone and videoconferences—helps, but these will not alleviate the issue of building and maintaining trust but rather aggravate the opposite. In conclusion, to avoid facing lack of trust and paying the price in lower performance, successful VGS projects invest in face-to-face project kick-off meetings in order to ensure the benefits of trust among team members: better project coordination, control, and performance.

Project Organization

Four interdependent tactical factors (see Fig. 16.3) support the strategic success factor project organization. The first tactical success factor—*the matrix structure*—provides the necessary infrastructure for the functioning of the second factor—*creating a cross-functional team*—and the third factor—*managing stakeholder expectations.* When a successful team is in place and stakeholders are treated properly, conditions exist to *use the available resources* effectively in order to make the most of this strategic success factor.

CSF13: Build a Well-Oiled Matrix Structure.   Very few VGS projects are large enough to warrant a full-time dedicated team. Rather, organizations pursue multiple concurrent projects that are smaller in size and are managed by project teams, the majority of whose members are part time, typically sitting on multiple teams that report simultaneously to multiple project leaders in addition to reporting to their functional manager. This condition is described as the *matrix structure*. To competently support a continuous delivery of quality projects, the matrix has to be well oiled. This means designing and smoothly executing the triad of power sharing, clear decision making, and continuous resource support.

The matrix often features the power struggles between the project and functional managers. The key to solving this problem, or *pathology,* as some experts call it, is to choose a clear power-sharing mechanism between the two managers, train them to deploy it, and constantly reinforce it from the top of the organization. This mechanism has an impacts, therefore, on the decision making and resource support. For example, in one organization, the choice was made to have project managers own the VGS project and major project decisions about the project strategy, whereas the functional managers were seen as the providers of resources to support those strategies in multiple concurrent projects, which is quite a challenge. Choices about the triad may be different—which depends largely on the organizational culture and strategy—but once made, and whatever they are, their success will, to a great degree, hinge on how well they are deployed by the players and oiled by the top management.

CSF14: Create a Cross-Functional Team Structure.   VGS projects are inherently cross-functional, involving collaboration of dispersed decision-making units. However, in order for all the interdependent modules developed by different sites to function as a seamless final product, a certain degree of centralization is also necessary. Success of VGS project depends on finding the balance between centralization and dispersion of the decision-making authority in the project. Therefore, clear roles of dispersed units and individual members are vital to VGS projects, as are good decision making and skill sets of team members.

It is crucial that decision-making protocols are clear. For that matter, the sixth strategic factor—the *process*—provides the mode for executing decisions among VGS sites, including the chain of command among the dispersed decision-making units. As one experienced VGS project manager noted: "Chain of command is a core principle, especially in large projects. We need to know who is responsible for making various decisions. I think collaborative decision making is a great thing, but you still have to have chain of command and a person who is responsible for seeing the decisions get made." Based on the nature of the VGS project and the choice of management, the decision-making authority may be centralized, or balanced, or dispersed among sites. The choice made must be consistently deployed and unambiguously communicated to the VGS team.

As for the members' skill sets, having competent VGS team members is one of the key enablers of their success. Some of these skills are worth mentioning. For example, the team members have to have more than the needed technical knowledge. Given the separation that exists between the sites, team members also need to be excellent communicators. They need to be aware of the ways that details can fall between the cracks and be very detail oriented to prevent that from happening. An experienced VGS project manager observed that "alignment of roles with personal qualities is important." This stresses the importance of having the right people for the job.

CSF15: Manage Stakeholder Expectations.   To be successful, VGS teams need to aptly manage their stakeholders—customers and the project sponsor primarily—and their expectations. First, the VGS team must know what customers want; this is of paramount importance. Note that assuming to know is unacceptable. If the team does not know the customer's requirements, the project may be in danger, as the project manager of a VGS project noticed: "The offsite team was simply too separated from the customer. That is why what they came up with did not exactly reflect what the customer wanted. They failed to capture these wants in the requirements document, elevating our risks." However, capturing the right customer requirements is not enough. The requirements may change during project execution for any number of reasons; therefore, staying in constant touch with the customer during that execution phase is a necessary practice.

Some organizations use the mechanism of project sponsors from the executive ranks in the case of strategically important projects or middle-management ranks if the project is not of top importance. In both cases, the project sponsor acts as the project advocate, removing higher obstacles to the project and helping to solve problems that the project manager alone cannot resolve. To fully use the sponsor's capacity, the VGS team should identify what information the project sponsor needs and when and make sure that the information flows smoothly. If the sponsor does not exist, the VGS team should identify who in the executive ranks is willing to act as the project champion and do all it takes to make that approach function.

CSF16: Use the Available Resources Effectively.   Another enabling factor for the organization that executes VGS projects is the effective use of human resources. One executive noted, "It is very easy for the remote teams to feel unimportant and left out." The VGS project team needs to expend extra effort to prevent this from happening. Some of the best practices are (1) senior team members spending time with teams on all sites, (2) recognition of the work done by all sites, and (3) enforcing team cohesion through team-building activities.

Especially when different sites are not parts of the same organization, *alignment of goals and roles* becomes very important. If the ultimate objectives of different sites are naturally in alignment with what is expected of them within the context of the VGS project, it has a positive impact on the effectiveness of the site.

Another important factor for increasing the effectiveness of the team is training. One project manager reported, "We made sure that everybody was up to speed on the development environment that we were going to use, and that made a big difference."

Process

Two interdependent tactical factors (see Fig. 16.3) support the strategic success factor of process. The first one—*building a relatively standard but flexible and customized project management process*—is essentially a roadmap for all VGS projects on how to create a predictable process but retain flexibility in situations where the projects are unique. Such a standard but flexible process drives the second tactical factor—*planning for and control of the project and its software product.*

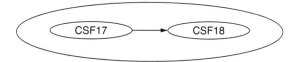

CSF17: Build a Relatively Standard But Flexible and Customized Project Management Process.   Project management process is a sequence of project activities that culminates in project deliverables. In successful VGS projects, the project management process is a delivery mechanism for project strategy (Kerzner, 2000), including several elements:

- Project life-cycle phases
- Managerial and technical activities
- Deliverables
- Milestones

Project life cycle is viewed as a collection of project phases determined by the control needs of the organizations involved in the project. Consequently, a variety of project life-cycle models are in use in corporations today, from traditional models such as the waterfall model to the spiral model to agile models. Project life-cycle phases are composed of logically related project activities that can be divided into two groups: managerial and technical activities. The former are activities by which we manage a project; *developing the project scope* and *constructing the project schedule* are typical examples. Technical activities (often referred to as *product management activities*) include *beta testing,* for example. They are project type–specific and reflect the nature of the project product.

Both managerial and technical activities usually culminate in completion of deliverables—in the tangible product. Managerial activities produce managerial deliverables (also called *project management deliverables*) such as *project schedule* (often referred to as the *product management process*). Technical activities lead to technical deliverables, for example, a requirements document.

The project management process in successful VGS projects tends to be relatively standard, with built-in flexibility, and often customized. *Relatively standard* means that some structured process is in place to provide a certain level of predictability, to make the project process to some extent repeatable, and to prevent project management activities from differing completely from project to project and from project manager to project manager. Said a VGS project manager, ". . . we had a reasonably mature implementation of the PLC process. So . . . depending on the size of the team, you can apply [this process] to a 500-person project; you can apply to a 5-person project. But you have to scale." If so, the parts of the project management process that are not standard should be made flexible to account for the project specifics. Also, often the process is customized to solve a specific problem, as in the following case. A project lead mentioned:

> There is so much involved with getting the development started and working efficiently. . . . So I'd say [communication] is most important . . . during low level design and development kick-off. We had releases where we [had] someone there to coordinate that initial kick-off of the development cycle. It really saves time, and it gets them productive much quicker. After that, [we] come back to the United States and work with them [remotely]. But that face-to-face time at the beginning of the development cycle is critical.

CSF18: Plan for and Control Project and Its Product.   In successful VGS projects, the project management process is used to do the planning and control of the projects, as well as product management. In particular, such planning and control mostly focus on project scope, quality, schedule, and risk. Simply put, when the project scope (i.e., deliverables) is planned and defined in detail, its quality is possible to determine, becoming the foundation for developing the schedule and planning for risk reduction. This becomes the baseline project plan. Against it is compared the actual status of the project, establishing the difference or variation, finding why it occurs, devising corrective actions to bring the project back to the baseline plan, and reporting project progress. An example of the widely popular type of project progress report called the *dashboard* is shown in Fig. 16.5. Over all, this is the classic process that all good VGS projects follow. While there is not much new about it, some of its details deserve attention.

Many successful VGS projects tend to minimize the interdependency of the tasks assigned to different sites to enable the sites to work as independently as possible. However, this is often hard to accomplish. One way to reach this task independence is to use work sites with module-based or phase-based development responsibility and to commit upfront to defining interfaces between the different modules. Prototype development is a valuable tool that can be used for this purpose.

Successful VGS project organizations often insist on knowing the skill sets of resources upfront before allocating tasks to the resources. Says an executive who was

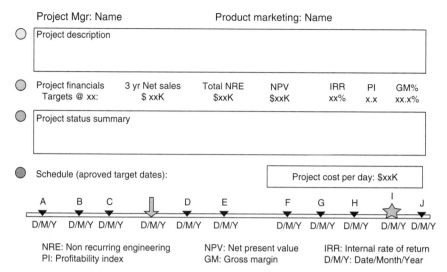

FIGURE 16.5 Dashboard.

involved in a VGS between Oregon and Iowa, "It is easier to allocate tasks to resources once you know the people and their skill sets." One way for the executives and project managers to expedite the process of leveraging the strengths of the offsite team is to establish history with the same team. In successful VGS projects, generally more iterative life-cycle models (such as the spiral model) provide better results owing to the abundance of synchronization points (milestones). The exception to this is when tasks assigned to different sites are highly independent.

Project Tools

Three interdependent tactical factors (see Fig. 16.3) support the strategic success factor of project tools: product management tools, project management tools, and collaborative technology tools. The first success factor—*product management tools*—is the underlying factor in that its purpose is to support the foundation stone of the software development: the technical process of the development. The nature of the technical process influences the choice and makeup of the second success factor—*project management tools*. When there is a clear selection of the product and project management tools, the challenge is to enable the VGS project team members to share them. This is where the third success factor—*collaborative technology tools*—comes in, providing the sharing capability.

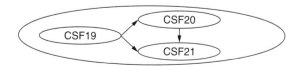

CSF19: Develop and Deploy the Product Management Toolbox. Product management tools include procedures and techniques by which a technical deliverable is produced. A typical example is a tool called a *requirements document form*, which supports a deliverable termed *software requirements defined.* Product management tools may be manual or in a software package format and also may be a success factor in a VGS project when standardized, integrated, simple, and few in number.

The point of standardization and integration is illustrated in a comment of a project manager in the Oregon-Iowa VSG project, "We finally decided to standardize Clear Case, an enterprise configuration management tool, and use Clear Quest as a defect/issue-tracking tool. That enabled all developers to look in Clear Quest, pick up the defects, fix them, and then the actual QA person would then get an e-mail notifying him [of] what build that fix was in, so we'd know what to retest then."

The most frequently used product management tools are for development (e.g., Visual Studio), a source control system (e.g., CVS), an enterprise-based configuration management system, a defect/issue tracking, a test-case tracking spreadsheets (Excel), and a document storage solution for sharing documents. While each tool has a specific function, the overall purpose is to ensure a more efficient support of the software production, thus contributing to success of the VGS project.

CSF20: Build and Deploy the Project Management Toolbox. Project management tools include procedures and techniques by which a managerial deliverable is produced. For example, if the project management deliverable is *project scope defined*, the tools that support it are a scope statement and a work-breakdown structure (WBS). These tools may be manual or in a software package format. In whatever format, project management tools are a success factor in VGS projects only if they are standardized, integrated, simple, and few in number.

Standardized project management tools means the degree to which the tools used in a project vary across the VGS team. To be successful, a VGS project needs very standardized tools in the form of templates shared by team members. As one project manager put it, "We have a complete process and the tools to support that process, and we have half of our engineering team in Russia, half over here, and it works pretty well—one reason is using templates." Project management tools are integrated with the project management process and metrics, and they are consistently used to enforce the project management process on a daily basis.

Project management tools used by successful VGS teams are simple, and there are only a few of them. For example, favorite tools are a WBS, a Gantt chart (with or without dependencies), a probability-impact matrix (risk tool), a status scorecard (called *dashboard*), a checklist, various types of the milestone charts, and postmortem review. An example is the milestone prediction chart (Fig. 16.6) that predicts major project events: milestones and project completion. The vertical axis shows the team's predicted baseline of milestones at the time of the finished planning. After the project work is kicked off, the team reviews progress regularly (once a week, as shown in Fig. 16.6) and makes new milestone predictions. The point is to be proactive in managing the schedule.

CSF21: Design and Deploy the Collaborative Technology Toolbox. *Collaborative technology tools* are any tools used by VGS team members to communicate when geographically and/or time separated. While they vary widely in complexity and information richness and offer different grades of efficiency, the crucial point is to devise standard communication guidelines for the tools' use. In one company, for example, the rule is to use mostly e-mail for daily communication, although it is an information-poor medium that has its own problems, as this team member observed: "Sometimes e-mail

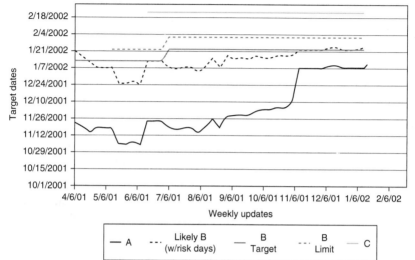

Note: Milestones are marked as A, B, and C because of the company confidential information.

FIGURE 16.6   The milestone prediction chart.

has a one-day lag. A Romanian person is going to send us e-mail, and we are going to read it the next morning. By the time we send back the reply, we have wasted a day on that."

For this, help can come from exchanging instant messages, as in the case of another VGS team: "We use instant messaging very heavily. It is installed on all our laptops and desktops. It will show you who is online and who is not. Obviously, during the day we do not expect the Russian team to be online, but a lot of times they are." If more information richness is needed, companies use phone conference calls such as weekly teleconferences (e.g., to report progress status). When even richer information is to be communicated, VGS teams use teleconferences and net meetings. Before even thinking about specific collaborative technologies, however, companies first resolve the issue of the infrastructure, as one project manager pointed out: "I've made sure that everyone on the team both in India and in the United States has the right office setup at home, so everyone has DSL or cable modem access; mobile headsets so they don't have to have a phone cradled to their ear for three hours if they're working on a long call; and we'll pay for such an office." While these issues do occupy the attention of VGS teams, other issues are also addressed. For example, one collaborative technology helps with a very important issue of documentation sharing, as in this example: "We have a public drive on one of our servers where all the minutes of all the meetings are kept. Also, we use a document storage solution where we can share documents."

This approach to product management, project management, and collaborative technology tools—insisting on standardized, integrated, simple, and relatively few tools—not only provides a high communication potential but also helps with all components of project success: more punctual schedules, more satisfied customers, better cost-effectiveness, and higher quality accomplishments. If this approach is not offered to the VGS team, the team members end up struggling to find the right tools and how to use them, introducing variability into the project management process. This may lead to subpar project performance. Therefore, mother companies should provide the approach, and VGS teams should get trained to use and understand such tools.

Metrics

Three interdependent tactical factors (see Fig. 16.3) support the strategic success factor metrics. These tactical success factors enable the management team not only to track where the project is but also to know if progress is being made and where the project is headed. Using the first tactical success factor—*project efficiency metrics*—provides the project manager with the ability to react in a timely fashion to deviations from cost, time, and quality targets. However, a project that is managed only with these success factors in mind still can fail to deliver to the expectations of the customer. It is also necessary to define and track metrics that proxy the *impact of the project on the customer*—tactical success factor number two. Finally, projects also need to be the means of carrying the organization toward its own objectives for the future. This is why selecting projects that score high in *future preparation metrics,* the third tactical success factor, is important.

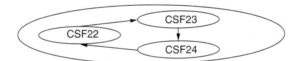

CSF22: Define and Use Project Efficiency Metrics.   Lacking major efficiency measures or metrics in VGS projects, such as the efficiency metrics of schedule, cost, and quality performance, makes the projects very vulnerable, and deploying them takes that vulnerability away, as a VGS project manager noted: "We have actually lived without metrics, and we got burned. It was really hard, and we were more vulnerable. Big slips, more unknowns. . . . When you are just hearing things, you are just hearing guesses. With metrics, now we know exactly what the right things are to look at." Especially in VGS, the efficiency metrics facilitate communication between the dispersed teams by specifying uniform targets across the board and measuring them.

In successful VGS projects, there are metrics that adhere to the overall project, such as if the team is in time with respect to the milestones. A useful tool for tracking this metric is a *project dashboard* (see Fig. 16.5), which uses color codes to show if a milestone is on time. A performance-to-commitment metric compares how much time was allocated upfront for each task and how much was used.

Good efficiency metrics also may be specific to the different stages of the project. For example, during the integration testing and validation, bug find and fix trends, bug severity, number of known bugs in the product, and releasing time are some of the metrics that are used. Process efficiency metrics also can act as a source of motivation for the team. A project manager who was in charge of an Oregon-Russia project said: "We track the number of bugs as well as their severity by developer and publish them. At the end of the day, the developers can say, this person had very few bugs, I had quite a few. And they will aim for that."

CSF23: Define and Use Customer Impact Metrics.   Successful VGS projects also feature customer impact metrics that can be measured after the product is shipped and the customer starts to use the product. Says an executive: "We not only need to be successful but also demonstrably successful." Unless there are metrics that quantify the impact of the product on the customer, the perceptions will be subjective and will fail to reflect the actual success. Customer impact metrics generally are harder to define. Return on investment (ROI) is the best known of these metrics. However, improvements generally result from a number of different reasons, and it may be hard to define ROI metrics. Customer satisfaction is the ultimate objective in all projects, VGS included. Impact metrics that can proxy customer satisfaction should be a part of the metrics used. In the words of an executive: "I call the key customers every now and then and do informal surveys." Customer satisfaction survey results not only can indicate where the product stands, but they also can provide ideas as to how to improve the product. These surveys can be informal as per the executive or can be more formalized. Other metrics can be based on interviews with customers, with the number of ideas, thoughts, and problems conveyed regarding the product considered.

In the context of VGS, especially when several consecutive releases of a software product are developed, customer impact metrics can provide valuable information to the team for identifying the most influential features and prioritizing tasks. Some of example metrics include reported problems, comparison of different releases by the customer, trend in the number of problems that require team intervention, and the cost of handling customer-reported problems.

CSF24: Define and Use Future Preparation Metrics.   Successful VGS projects tend to include future preparation metrics. These are key to gauging how well the project serves as a vehicle to carry the organization forward and prepare it for future assignments. Also, for the project team, they can serve as a way to gain executive buy-in to committing resources to the project.

Note that some metrics in this group are quantitative, whereas others are more qualitative. Says one executive about the quantitative ones: "I look at key results. Do we execute against them? What percentage of the planned features did we achieve? How many releases do we do? How many people per release? How many dollars per release? And for every release, is it going out, is it going through our whole process, the release cycle, in less than 10 days?" Another key metric is rather qualitative: the lessons learned from a project that help to solve problems in other projects.

CONCLUSION

Software development is a big business and a major driving force of growth across industries. Several factors contribute to software development's unique nature—technological novelty, product visibility, speed to market, changeability, and risk level—and the complexity of its management. These factors and the new ones make management of VGS projects, an increasingly important new mode of software development for companies in a global environment, even more complex. VGS development includes the endeavor where the development teams across multiple countries collaborate and perform a variety of tasks, such as planning, controlling, coding, testing, implementing, and maintaining, to develop new software and achieve common project goals. The new factors are characteristics of VGS projects, including the distance, time separation, language and cultural differences, and multiple sites. They tend to reduce coordination efficiency and effectiveness, control, and performance in VGS projects.

One effective way to overcome these problems and produce successful VGS projects is to build a system of critical success factors that is sufficiently flexible to account for the specifics of the various projects. This system consists of eight interdependent strategic success factors, each of them including several tactical factors. The point of the strategic factors is that in successful VGS projects one needs to perform the alignment (strategic factor one) of VGS projects with the business strategy, which will direct the shaping of the project strategy (strategic factor two), which, then, will drive the project organization, people, and culture (strategic factors three, four, and five). These three dictate the design of the project process (strategic factor six) that shapes up the use of project tools and metrics (strategic factors seven and eight). Together these eight strategic success factors, supported by 20+ tactical success factors, deliver successful VGS projects.

REFERENCES

Allen TJ. 1997. *Managing the Flow of Technology*. Cambridge, MA: MIT Press.

Baskerville R, Pries-Heje J. 1999. Knowledge capability and maturity in software management. *Database Adv Inform Syst* 30(2):26–43.

Battin RD, Crocker R. Kreidler J. et al. 2001. Leveraging resources in global software development. *IEEE Software* 18(2):70–77.

Behravesh N. 2004. *The Impact of Offshore IT Software and Services Outsourcing on the U.S. Economy and the IT Industry*. Information Technology Association of America (ITAA). Arlington, Virginia.

Berinato S. 2001. The secret to software success. *CIO* 14(18):76–82.

Bowen S, Maurer F. 2002. *Using Peer-to-peer Technology to Support Global Software Development: Some Initial Thoughts*. Orlando, FL: International Workshop on Global Software Development.

Brooks FP. 1987. No silver bullet: essence and accidents of software engineering. *IEEE Computer* 20(4):10–19.

Carmel E. 1999. *Global Software Teams*. Upper Saddle River, NJ: Prentice-Hall.

Carmel E, Agarwal R. 2001. Tactical approaches for alleviating distance in global software development. *IEEE Software* 18(2):22–29.

Clark KB, Wheelwright SC. 1993. *Managing New Product and Process Development Text and Cases*. San Francisco: Free Press.

Cooper RG. 1994. Debunking the myths of new product development. *Res Technol Manag* 37(4):40–50.

Curtis B, Krasner H, Iscoe N. 1988. A field study of the software design process for large systems. *Commun ACM* 31(11):1268–1287.

Damian D. 2002. *The Study of Requirements Engineering in Global Software Development: As Challenging as Important*. Orlando, FL: International Workshop on Global Software Development.

Dow Jones & Co., Inc. 2003. High-tech sector reduced work force by 10 percent in 2001–2002. *Wall Street Journal,* March 19, p. 1.

Findley DA. 1998. *Controlling Costs for a Software Development Project* (No. PC.04). Morgantown, WV: AACE International.

Gorton I, Motwani s. 1996. Issues in co-operative software engineering using globally distributed teams. *Inform Software Technol* 38:647–655.

Gupta AK, Wilemon DL. 1990. Accelerating the development of technology-based new products. *Calif Manag Rev* Winter:24–44.

Harrison JS, St John CH. 1998. *Strategic Management of Organizations and Stakeholders,* 2d ed. Cincinnati, OH: South-Western College Publishing.

Hartman F Ashrafi RA. 2002. Project management in the information systems and information technologies industries. *Project Manag J* 33(3):5–15.

Herbsleb JD, Grinter RE. 1999. *Splitting the Organization and Integrating the Code: Conway's Law Revisited.* International Conference on Software Engineering (ICSE'99). Los Angeles, CA: ACM Press.

Herbsleb JD, Moitra D. 2001. Global software development. *IEEE Software* 18(2):16–20.

Hoch DJ, Roeding CR, Purkert G, Lindner SK. 1999. *Secrets of Software Success.* Boston, MA: Harvard Business School Press.

Hofstede G. 1980. *Culture's Consequences.* Beverly Hills, CA: Sage.

Hofstede G. 1984. *Culture's Consequences: International Differences in Work-Related Values.* Newbury Park, CA, Sage.

Jarvenpaa SL. 1998. Communication and trust in global virtual teams. *J Comput Mediat Commun* 3(4).

Jiang JJ, Klein G. 2001. Software project risks and development focus. *Project Manag J* 32(1):4–9.

Kerzner H. 2000. *Applied Project Management.* New York: Wiley.

Keil L, Eng P. 2003. *Experiences in Distributed Development: A Case Study.* International Workshop on Global Software Development, Portland, OR.

King J. 2003. *IT's Global Itinerary: Offshore Outsourcing Is Inevitable.* Computerworld.

Kobylinski R, Creighton O, Dutoit AH, Bruegge B. 2002. *Building Awareness in Global Software Engineering: Using Issues as Context.* Orlando, FL: International Workshop on Global Software Development.

Kogut B, Meitu A. 2000. *The Emergence of E-Innovation: Insights from Open Source Software Development.* Philadephia: Wharton School, University of Pennsylvannia, pp. 1–32.

Kotlarsky JM, Kumar K, Van Hillegersberg J. 2002. *Coordination and Collaboration for Globally Distributed Teams: The Case of Component-based/object-oriented Software Development.* Orlando, FL: International Workshop on Global Software Development.

Kristof AL, Brown KG, Sims HP Jr, Smith KA. 1995. The virtual team: A case study and inductive model, in MM Beyerlein, DA Johnson, ST Beyerlein (eds.), *Advances in Interdisciplinary Studies of Work Teams: Knowledge Work in Teams.* Greenwich, CT: JAI Press, pp. 229–253.

Leidecker JK, Bruno AV. 1984. Identifying and using critical success factors. *Long Range Planning* 17:23–32.

MacCormack A. 2001. How internet companies build software. *Sloan Manag Rev* 42(2):75–84.

Maidantchik C, Da Rocha A. 2002. *Managing a Worldwide Software Process.* Orlando, FL: International Workshop on Global Software Development.

Maznevski ML, Chudoba KM. 2000. Bridging space over time: global virtual team dynamics and effectiveness. *Organ Sci* 11(5):473–492.

McDonald J. 2001. Why is software project management difficult? And what that implies for teaching software project management? *Comput Sci Educ* 11(1):55–71.

Milosevic DZ. 1999. *Project Management Standardization and its Effects on Project Effectiveness.* Portland, OR, Portland International Conference on Management of Engineering and Technology (PICMET).

Milosevic DZ, Inman L, Ozbay A. 2001. Impact of project management standardization on project effectiveness. *Eng Manag J* 13(4):9–16.

Nambisan S. 2001. Why service business are not product businesses. *Sloan Manag Rev* 42(4):72–80.

Nidumolu SR. 1996. A comparison of the structural contingency and risk-based perspectives on coordination in software development projects. *J Manag Inform Syst* 13(2):77–113.

Nidumolu SR, Knotts GW. 1998. The effects of customizability on perceived process and competitive performance of software firms. *MIS Q* 22(2):105–128.

Norbjerg J, Havn EC, Bansler JP. 1997. *Global Production: The Case of Offshore Programming.* Wirtschaftsinformatik '97. Berlin: Physica-Verlag.

Oppenheimer HL. 2002. *Project Management Issues in Globally Distributed Development.* Orlando, FL: International Workshop on Global Software Development.

Parzinger MJ, Nath R. 2000. A study of the relationship between total quality management implementation factors and software quality. *Total Quality Manag* 11(3):353–371.

Perry DE, Staudenmayer NA, Votta LG. 1994. People, organizations, and process improvements. *IEEE Software* 11(4):36–45.

Pinto JK, Govin JG. 1989. Critical factors in project implementation: A comparison of construction and R&D projects. *Technovation* 9:49–62.

Raffo DM, Setamanit S. 2005. *A Simulation Model for Global Software Development Project.* St Louis, MO: International Workshop on Software Process Simulation and Modeling.

Raz T. 1993. Introduction of the project management discipline in a software development organization. *IBM Syst J* 32(2):265–277.

Shenhar AJ. 2001. One size does not fit all projects: Exploring classical contingency domains. *Manag Sci* 47(3):394–414.

Snow CC, Davison SC, Snell SA, Hambrick DC. 1996. Use transnational teams to globalize your company. *Organ Dyn* 24(4):50–67.

Souza C, Basaveswara S, Redmiles DF. 2002. *Supporting Global Software Development with Event Notification Servers.* Orlando, FL: International Workshop on Global Software Development.

Standish_Group. 1995. *Chaos. West Yarmouth, MA* Standish Group International, Inc.

Tatikonda MV, Rosenthal SR. 2000. Technology novelty, project complexity, and product development project execution success: A deeper look at task uncertainty in product innovation. *IEEE Transn Eng Manag* 47:74–87.

Whitehead J. 1999. The future of distributed software development on the Internet. *Web Tech* 4:57–63.

Zigurs I. 2003. Leadership in virtual teams: Oxymoron or opportunity? *Organizational Dynamics* 31(4):339–351.

Zirger BJ, Hartley JL. 1996. The effect of acceleration techniques on product development time. *IEEE Trans Eng Manag* 43(2):143–152.

CHAPTER 17
MANAGING GLOBAL PROJECTS OVER A COLLABORATIVE KNOWLEDGE FRAMEWORK

Suhwe Lee

Singapore

Suhwe Lee has been a project manager with IBM Singapore to support global banking and supply-chain application systems since 1999. Before joining IBM, she was a project director of Acer Computer International based in Singapore. From 1991 to 1997, she was a department manager of the Computer and Communication Research Laboratories at the Industrial Technology Research Institute in Taiwan. During the same period, she also served as a project adviser in the Science and Technology Advisory Office of Taiwan. From 1984 to 1991, she was a project leader of AT&T Bell Laboratories in New Jersey in the development of applications for communication and operational support systems.

Lee has extensive planning, development, deployment, and production-support experience for global projects. In addition, she owns a patent for a global trading process named "Network-Based Virtual Commodity Exchange" and has published many articles in conferences proceedings and professional publications. Lee holds an M.S. degree in computer science from City University of New York and an M.S. degree in philosophy from Kent State University, Ohio. Currently, she lives in Singapore.

THE GARDEN OF EDEN: THE FIRST PROJECT

The first project on earth is documented in the Bible's Old Testament, Book of Genesis.[1] (The sponsor was the Lord God, the project manager was the man, and the project team members were the woman and a serpent.)

The Lord God formed the man from the dust of the ground. He took the man and put him in the Garden of Eden to work it and take care of it. And the Lord commanded the man, "You are free to eat from any tree in the garden; but you must not eat from the tree of the knowledge of good and evil, for when you eat of it you will surely die."

The serpent said to the woman, "Did God really say 'you must not eat from any tree in the garden'?" The woman said to the serpent, "We may eat fruit from the trees in the garden, but God did say 'you must not eat fruit from the tree that is in the middle of the garden, and you must not touch it, or you will die.'" The serpent said to the woman, "You will not surely die."

During the project review, the Lord God called to the man, "Where are you? . . . Have you eaten from the tree that I commanded you not to eat from?" The man said, "The woman you put here with me—she gave me some fruit from the tree and I ate it." The Lord God said to the woman, "What is this you have done?" The woman said, "The serpent deceived me and I ate."

The Lord God said, "By the sweat of your brow, you will eat your food until you return to the ground, since from it you were taken; for dust you are and to dust you will return."

Owing to the lack of communication and collaboration with stakeholders, the first simple project on earth failed to meet a simple requirement from the Lord God. The penalty was so high that all the offspring of the man have to suffer on earth until they die.

OUT OF EDEN

In the past, organizations had well-defined structures and missions. They had the responsibility to reward and protect their employees in return for their services. But the world has changed after globalization. Many organizational functions used to be long-term programs. They are now being operated like projects. With this change in what is managed (from programs to projects or at least large chunks of functional programs as projects), the functional manager's roles have been taken over by project mangers. Using projects to replace functional programs has become a trend for organizations to improve their productivity and efficiency.

According to *A Guide to the Project Management Body of Knowledge* (*PMBOK Guide*), by the Project Management Institute (PMI), project management is the application of knowledge, skills, tools, and techniques to project activities to meet project requirements.[2] The project activities may include (1) identifying requirements, (2) establishing clear and achievable objectives, (3) balancing the completing demands for quality, scope, time, and cost, and (4) adapting the specifications, plans, and approach to the different concerns and expectations of the various stakeholders, etc. These activities are accomplished through the application and integration of the project management processes for initiating, planning, executing, monitoring, controlling, and closing phases. The person responsible for accomplishing the overall project objectives is the project manager.

In general, a project manager's role is accomplished in two ways: (1) in communicating with project team members and stakeholders so as to collect and distribute project information in a timely manner and (2) in providing the critical links among people, ideas, and information for day-to-day operation and decision making. In the past, the focus of a project manager was on the first role, namely, generating reports and analyses to inform stakeholders about the progress and status of the project. Then the project manager will devote the rest of the time to the second role by walking around the office premises and calling meetings for discussion, review, and decision making.

To support global operations, the project manager, project team members, business partners, and other stakeholders may work remotely from many parts of the world through clusters of collaborative infrastructure. This new form of project workplace may include different types of online communication and community facilities. In most cases, a project will take advantage of its existing infrastructure that connects its internal network with its upstream and downstream business partners. It is foreseeable that future projects will adopt new technology as needed to further expand their business involvement globally.

As a result, we have seen that the same old human communication problems, from pure ignorance, to timing delays, to misinterpretations, to speculation, to distrust, to conflicts of interest, to hidden agendas, to cross-culture misunderstandings, to inadequate information sharing, and to skill mismatches have been transformed to new formats and reintroduced to the new project workplaces. The compound effects of solving global problems in a complex working environment complicate the new project workplaces even further. In the end, a project manager may find himself or herself in a situation that is mission-critical, yet he or she has no clue about what will happen next and how the risks should be managed.

GLOBAL BUSINESS AND ITS CHALLENGES

In the traditional business environment, a project is started with a well-defined charter and clearly specified requirements. All the project team members are physically located in nearby buildings. A project manager just follows through the project plan rigorously to ensure on-time delivery with quality under the allocated budget.

However, today's global project is so complex that it can no longer operate under a concrete structure from a designated location. For instance, the business model, which serves as the foundation of the project charter, is being challenged daily under global competition; the underlining technology, international standards, government policies, regional economies, and customer awareness are not always moving in the same direction as the project anticipates. To respond to the changes in the marketplace and working environment, a project may need to be regrouped, and the working environment may need to be reconfigured to support the changes. The following sections further elaborate the key contributors to the global business challenges along with proposed solutions.

Worldwide Competition with Local Incentive

A global project may include many teams and team members from different countries. Each country may have different regulations governing its business entities and organizational structures. The global project team members are supposed to share the same project mission and resources all over the world under slightly different circumstances. Yet culture, infrastructure, regulations, and support are different from country to country. Sometimes, to increase earnings, a global project may operate differently from country to country to take advantage of regional pricing or local government incentives. Even though general practices may be compromised by local exceptions, this adds value to the overall business results. Hence, to build a project management system that is able to capture all the project information from different sources and share it across the project team with a consistent point of view will help to sustain the company's global positioning.

From time to time, owing to worldwide market competitions, a global project may not be able to stay on the same path as its original scope would suggest. In some cases, it may require radical changes in business processes and organizational structure to cope with new business alliances and upcoming opportunities. The dynamics of a global business operation in search of new market opportunities demands a better project management system, one that provides real-time intelligence to guide the overall progress rather than the ones built around physically closed environments.

Virtual Team Supported by New Technology

In the past, project team members were able to meet face to face during a project kick-off meeting or workshop to become acquainted with each other. Under global competition, a project may need to be reorganized from time to time and relocated from place to place to support its worldwide operation. For instance, the organization may go through business transformations to streamline its worldwide operation. Or, owing to strategic alliances or partnerships through mergers or joint ventures, the organization may change its business model or operational processes to take a new direction. All these changes will have significant impacts on the structure and working environment of a global project. However, with intense competition and slim profit margins, it becomes too expensive to move people around the world just to meet each other.

Depending on project demands and service availability, new technology can be used to provide for information exchange through real-time or online interactive methods. Each method of information exchange may have its limitation. To meet the global business challenges and to proactively manage recurring changes, a project manager needs to continuously monitor the technology, process, and working environment through a global project management system.

Dynamic Workforce through Global Sourcing

Day after day, the boundaries of nations and the barriers of geographic distance are being removed under the rapid interchange of information on the Internet. Through the collaboration of global business units, standardization of industry segments, and regional trade agreements, work can be assigned to any country and region. To cope with these changes in business, human resources may be allocated and reallocated on demand to meet market needs. With the high availability of global resources, the workforce may be created dynamically through talent grids under worldwide skills matching. Regional specialty in a given subject matter may provide unique talent for the global workforce. To manage the human resources effectively and to shorten the learning curve of team members, a project manager needs to plan and coordinate resource allocation dynamically through a global project management system.

COMPLEX ENVIRONMENT AND ITS CHALLENGES

Besides global business challenges, there are also project management–related challenges owing to the increasing complexity of global operations. The following areas are the major concerns:

- Changing requirements owing to changing customers or customer expectations
- Managing global contract for multiple nations
- Maintaining a virtual workplace for the project teams
- Encouraging innovation and reusing intellectual property
- Managing total risk for global operations

Changing Requirements

A global project may overlook some country-specific detailed requirements. Sometimes the global project manager may not be aware of the amendment of local economic, political, and security policies and regulations until the user acceptance tests or project deployment. Owing to culture differences and diversity, a global project team may fail to reach a common understanding of requirements and completion criteria for the proposed solution. Ineffective communication and relationship management by global project teams may fail to capture the changing customers and their expectations, which may jeopardize final project delivery.

Global Contract

In the multinational context, it is not easy to define the statement of works that will get customer sign-off to establish a contractual baseline. It is even harder to track the change requests and revision enhancements from country to country during project execution. On the other hand, inadequate business partnership agreements internally with subcontractors through global sourcing also may contribute to the uncertainty and instability of service and delivery quality.

Virtual Workplace

For a global project, team members are working from remote locations through different communication methods to form a virtual workplace. If the project manager fails to establish proper management disciplines, execution processes, team structure, and a project management system, then he or she will have difficulties in planning, executing, monitoring, controlling, and closing the global project with all team members located worldwide. How a project manager creates a command, control, and communication center to manage a virtual workplace will determine the effectiveness and final results of the project.

Innovation and Reuse of Intellectual Property

Technology is changing every day. The project is only a temporary endeavor for a defined charter. Project team members come and go as expected. It is critical to the success of a global project to encourage innovation and reuse of intellectual property. The ability to increase the efficiency and productivity of a project through constant innovation and reuse of existing intellectual property has become a core competency of a project. Hence, creating intellectual property, managing it efficiently, and reusing it frequently have demanded an intelligent project management system.

Total Risk Management

In general, it is highly recommended to manage a project by closely monitoring all the risks and open issues throughout the project life cycle. For a global project, it is good practice to collect and consolidate all the known risks and manage them globally. Very often, issues and risks in one region may become a global phenomenon over time, especially in the area of security, e-commerce law, currency exchange, and taxation across country boundaries. In practice, global project management is a worldwide risk management. It is a big help to the project manager to have a project management system that allows him or her to follow through on all the issues and risks.

PROJECT MANAGEMENT SYSTEM

After globalization, a project may involve many activities around several geographic regions, across different time zones, and supported by global resources. The physical separation of the project team, timing delay, and resource mismatch can easily trigger the chain reactions of miscommunication. A global project team may lose its team consensus and consistent views during execution of the project. Furthermore, during the project life cycle, a project team needs to share, collaborate, and innovate to produce all milestone deliverables effectively. To overcome distance separation and time delay and facilitate information sharing and message processing, a project management system can be used to provide a set of tools, techniques, methodologies, resources, and procedures for a project manager to manage a project team in guiding a project to completion.

COLLABORATIVE KNOWLEDGE FRAMEWORK

The proposed project management system is based on a *collaborative knowledge framework*[3] that consists of following five modules. A *framework* is an extensible structure for describing a set of methods, technologies, and processes to organize a complex system logically. A project manger can base his or her project's need to customize the project management system based on the given framework.

Figure 17.1 describes the collaborative knowledge framework. It consists of five modules: (1) collaboration platform module, (2) knowledge portal module, (3) project center module, (4) project workplace module, and (5) connectivity map module. These modules can be described as follows:

1. *Collaboration platform module.* This provides configurable methods for real-time meetings, instant messaging, e-mail, online communities, and real-time data interchange.
2. *Knowledge portal module.* This personalizes knowledge management functions for news update, smart search, intellectual property sharing, online learning, and

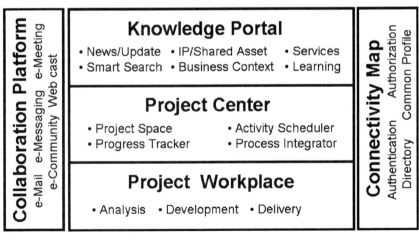

FIGURE 17.1   Collaborative knowledge framework.

on-demand services from the organizational knowledge portal. This module also creates a business context that consists of domain-specific resource links that provide external resource linkages and information repositories that collect business-related information to create a knowledge warehouse for reference.

3. *Project center module.* This serves as the command, control, communication, and collaboration center for projects and portfolio(s) of project(s).

4. *Project workplace module.* This is composed of a cluster of function-specific information repositories, tools, and workbenches to support project-specific activities. This module also provides records and data for project manager to generate reports from the project center.

5. *Connectivity map module.* This connects the knowledge portal, project center, and project workplace and modules into a configurable workplace protected by different levels of access security, authorization, and authentication depending on the roles and responsibilities in the project.

A project or a group of portfolio projects can be based on their missions and needs to create a project management system using the proposed collaborative knowledge framework. This framework is hardware-independent. The system can be built using Web services along with other information integrators to exchange all the project-related data among application systems through the organization's information technology (IT) infrastructure. Project team members and stakeholders can access the system through Web browsers or rich client software for additional functions.

Collaboration Platform Module

Project communication can be presented in the form of a meeting, project report, or some combination of both. Project meetings can be event-driven, informal, or formal. The formal project meeting can be for information gathering, decision making, or problem solving. Project reporting can be for review(s), status presentations, performance evaluations, or analyses. The reporting methods can be online, offline, or interactive. Depending on the nature of the activities, a project may require wired as well as wireless connection. Both wired and/or wireless connectivity requires equipment and services from service providers.

The typical collaboration platform supports e-mail, instant messaging, e-meetings, and online community and Web casting functions across the organization. The project team members can use e-meetings or Web conferencing facilities to update project status, to solve problems, and to make decisions in real time. To facilitate online interaction, a project team will need to create information repositories and workbenches for collaborating day-to-day planning, design, and implementation activities. To meet the market challenges under global competition, a project needs to have the capability to reconfigure the virtual workplace dynamically. For productivity improvement, the team members also can customize their individual workplace by personalizing the organization's knowledge portal to include news, directories, smart search, market intelligence, training, services, and other support functions.

All the collaborative features should be connected through the organizational network. This collaboration platform should integrate with the knowledge portal, project center, and project workplace to provide users with Internet (or just intranet) access for general information and service requests, as well as for project-specific information and activities. A simple scenario can be for a team member or a project manager to schedule an e-meeting to conduct a conference call by voice and video through Web conferencing services. Then the attendees will receive an e-mail notification or a meeting invitation or broadcast announcement in their messaging system. Before the meeting, the attendees may need to access the organization knowledge portal to refer to historical data and lessons learned from the past to prepare for the meeting. After the meeting, all the meeting-related materials and discussion are captured and stored in the project center and project workplace. Those who are not able to participate in the discussion can replay and view all the materials in the information repositories at any time.

To build a sustainable infrastructure for worldwide connection, a project manager needs to estimate the expected network utilization in terms of traffic volume, capacity bandwidth, response time, and throughput in advance through simulation or past experience and then allocate the budget and resources in the project plan. In fact, the connection method determines how fast the information will flow through the process, as well as the bottom line of project efficiency. Thus it is a good practice for a project manager to revisit the organizational IT strategy and existing availability during project initiation so that additional resources may be allocated adequately to support the project-specific needs. However, a collaboration platform need not be set up for each project independently. It should be part of organizational business transformation through the leadership of the organizational IT office.

Knowledge Portal Module

Most of the organizational intranet portal is in some form of knowledge management. This knowledge management module facilitates the following general functions through a single entrance:

1. News, press releases, and latest updates
2. Smart search and skills matching
3. Intellectual asset sharing and mining, allowing users to contribute and reuse project results
4. Online tutorial, learning, and personal development for job-related training and skills development
5. On-demand services such as online help and human resources–related services
6. Business context. The business context is organized and represented by a group of information repositories and resource links through the customized knowledge portal and further linked to external Web sites with e-mail notification and/or update alerts by subscription. As depicted in Fig. 17.2, the business context may include the following information and resource links:

   - Government-related regulations and policies updates
   - Business-related trade agreements and market research updates
   - Industry-related development of standards, standards body activities, and the latest technology trends
   - Consumer-related protection, safety reports, focus-group activities, and forecasts
   - Organization-related business control, instructions, and security guidelines

Some of the information repositories provide only the resource links to external Web sites for the news and intelligence gathering. Most of the information repositories are structured data such as organizational instructions, business control guidelines, market information, and recent developments in special interest group activities. In general, the business context is for information only, since its activities are beyond the project scope.

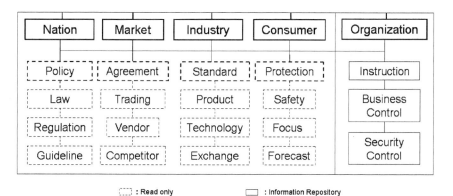

FIGURE 17.2   Business context.

During project initiation, the project manager should identify the business context based on the needs of the project. Some information in the business context that may not have been in the project manager's top priority list later may turn into a major threat to survival of the project. Hence it is important for a project manager to work with domain experts and sponsors to identify the crucial business context and constantly validate its latest update through the connection from the project workplace.

The knowledge portal is capable of integrating with other tools/services to provide online communication, collaboration, and community functions in a single look and feel. The portal also provides personalizing functions to let users customize their individual workplace according to their jobs and responsibilities. In addition, the portal also can provides resource links to subscribed intelligence services, publications (such as books or journals), online tutorials, courses, and mentoring guidance for personal development. Very often the project manager and team members are so caught up in the day-to-day work that they may not know all the latest technology, market, and consumer trends. With all the useful information available in one place, the knowledge management portal will be able to turn project members into knowledge workers and productive employees.

The knowledge portal module mainly takes advantage of portal middleware to tap into the organization's structured contents and services. By customizing the knowledge portal at the project level, the project team can easily access the organization's intellectual property, shared assets, lessons learned, and best practices. However, owing to performance concerns and compatibility among tools, the project-specific information repositories and workbenches are grouped under the project workplace and managed through the project center.

In order to get the expected benefits from the organizational portal, the project manager needs to communicate with the IT office to propose the requested services. Without proper planning and support, the value of the knowledge portal may diminish. As part of its business transformation, the organization needs to define its portal strategy for long-term planning and support through the leadership of the organization's IT office.

Project Center Module

In the past, projects have been managed individually. Now, many organizations manage projects by portfolio(s). According to the *PMBOK Guide,* a *portfolio* is a collection of projects or programs and other works that are grouped together to facilitate effective management of the work to meet strategic business objectives. Organizations as such, portfolios usually are managed based on specific goals. A project management office is an organizational unit to centralize and coordinate all the projects under its portfolios. A project management office also can be referred to as *project office*. The projects or programs supported or administrated by the same project office may not be related other than by being managed together. Under the current trend, more and more organizations manage projects by portfolios based on their business goals. The project office also has been used to manage a portfolio of projects.

In the proposed collaborative knowledge framework, the project center is a conceptual/logical structure for managing project(s). The same structure can be adopted by the project management office for managing portfolios as well. The proposed project center has the following four major functions to plan and manage project(s) based on the organization's processes:

- Creating and managing the project space
- Monitoring and scheduling activities
- Controlling and tracking progress
- Optimizing and integrating processes

The project center allows the project manager to manage the project life cycle from initiation, planning, and execution to closure. All the project data are provided by the project team members through the project management tools, information repositories, and workbenches from the project workplace. The project center operates on top of the project workplace connected by the connectivity map on the collaboration platform. The infrastructure support of the collaboration platform for each project center function will depend on it communication and collaboration methods. Figure 17.3 shows the layout of the project center and describes four major functions of a project center: (1) project creation, (2) project monitoring, (3) project control, and (4) process optimization.

Creating and Managing the Project Space.   To initiate a project, a project manager needs to identify the goals of the project and then define the scope and make the estimation based on the given project charter and mission. According to the scope and estimation, the project manager will break the work down further into an executable plan. In general, a project plan consists of a work-breakdown structure (WBS), schedule, budget, and required resources. Quality goals, risks, and project-related assumptions and constraints are also stated in the plan. If outsourcing, procurement, and additional service activities are required, all these work items also should be identified upfront and included in the WBS. This overall project plan creates a project space for the project manager and team members to work together as an organic entity.

For a global project, the project team members may be pulled together from different geographic locations. To maintain a unified view of the project, all the project members are required to update their progress regularly into the project space. Through this unified view, the project manger then manages the schedule, budget, and resources according to the tasks defined in the WBS. Most of the project management tools provide a dashboard viewer, traffic lights, scorecards, and reports for the project council to conduct routine project review. The project council is a committee represented by stakeholders, domain experts, and the project manager.

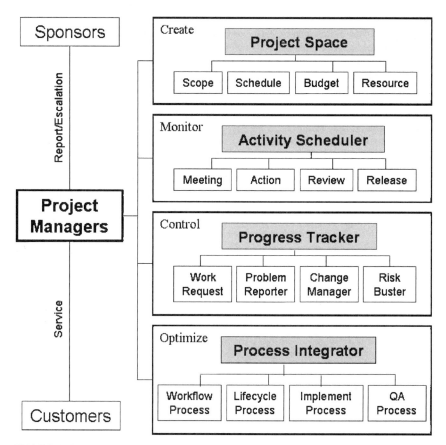

FIGURE 17.3 Project center module.

Monitoring and Scheduling Activity. During project execution, the project manager and team members will need to get together occasionally to discuss the work items, problems, issues, and new actions related to the project. In the project center, an activity scheduler can be used to schedule meetings, working sessions, reviews, and milestone releases through the tools used in the project workplace. In general, the activity scheduler should be able to schedule the requests and send out invitations with agendas and supplemental information to the members. An activity may be conducted offline, online, or in real time depending on the nature of the needs. The meeting minutes and action results will be recorded in text, audio, or video format in the project workplace, and the relevant project members will be notified after the activities for further reference. All the problem reports, change requests, or work requests resulting from the activity scheduler will be tracked and monitored under the project control function in the project center.

Controlling and Tracking Progress. Project control consists of four major types of activities: (1) detecting work results, (2) reporting problems, (3) requesting changes, and (4) managing risks. During project execution, the progress tracker first will detect the creation of work results such as software code, design documents, reports, and records through the approval of work requests. Most of the repository and workbench tools provide notification capability after each creation of work results in the workflow process.

According to the project management process, all work results generated from the collaboration environment should go through the workflow process for approval. Any changes, problems, or risks found during execution also should go through the progress tracker to evaluate the impact and obtain approval for further actions. All the approved actions will be stored in the repository in the project workplace and updated into the project space. During the scheduled review meetings, the project manager will generate progress reports for review with the project team members.

Optimizing and Integrating Processes.   The project life cycle from initiation, planning, execution, and control to closure involves many processes. In addition to the life-cycle processes, there are workflow control process to determine the procedure for reviewing and approving actions and results. Most organizations have their own control, audit, and quality assurance processes to cater to their specific needs.

Under global competition, many projects adapt agile or extreme project management methods. In order to be responsive to the market and business challenges, the process integrator plays an important role in safeguarding the project, as well as in providing efficient ways to improve output quality and productivity. Without the process integrator guiding the project with precision, the project may lose its focus.

The proposed project center is just an example of how to integrate project space, schedule works, track progress, and improve processes through the project life cycle. There are different types of projects for different business initiatives. There are also different tools and environments available commercially to support different industry segments and organizations. Decisions concerning the project center should be part of organization's transformation and strategic planning according to its global positioning and future growth.

Project Workplace Module

Based on the organization's structure, the project manager creates project-specific information repositories and workbenches for the project team. All the individual information repositories and workbenches should be integrated under the collaboration platform and managed by the project center. It can use the knowledge portal as an entrance to access the project center and project workplace.

The information repository is an IT tool that provides remote and mobile team members with a shared space in which they can work together—where they can write proposals, develop strategies, store project plans, and make decisions. Team members can navigate inside the information repository, share information, collaborate on work, create personal profiles, and set customized options. It also helps in organizing information to improve team effectiveness. In addition, the repository can be used for sharing premeeting materials, planning collaborative agendas, creating discussion threads, and tracking meeting outcomes to make the meetings more productive, focused, and shorter.

The workbench is a computer-based tool that provides an application/domain-specific facility for online design and development collaboration. There are many application-specific workbenches that can be configured to streamline the work process. The knowledge portal also can use its client management utility to support rich client functions to make the online collaboration even more effective.

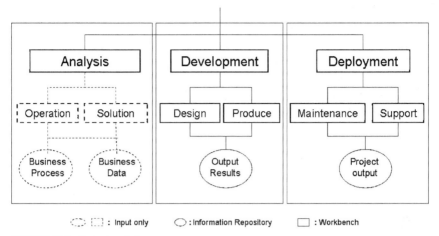

FIGURE 17.4   Project workplace.

Owing to the separation of duties and checks and balances between project and organizational functions, the information repositories and workbenches need to be laid out as depicted in Fig. 17.4 to represent the three different types of activities from project requirements or concept analysis, to project development, to solution deployment. For instance, the repositories for project analysis that support operations also may include business process and business data that contain trade secrets in doing business and specific requirements for the solution. The repositories and workbenches for project development may contain project results such as design details, intellectual property, and quality control records. The repositories for production deployment may contain project information such as hosting setup information, customer data, and production problems. If some project functions are sharing the same repository, proper access control rights need to be assigned to protect privacy and confidentiality.

All the project team members and stakeholders should be able to access the repositories in the project workplace according to their roles and responsibilities. The project manager needs to review and audit the access control lists and application system logs routinely through the connectivity map. All the repositories in the project workplace are vital organizational assets that should be hosted under a secure IT environment with online and offline information backup for disaster recovery.

Connectivity Map Module

The knowledge portal, project center, and project workplace modules are integrated through the connectivity map module for easy access and navigation. In general, the connectivity map provides mapping information to organizational directories and the common profiles system. It also defines access security level. For all the access requests to the project management system, the connectivity map will govern access based on the requester's role and responsibilities and his or her access permission level to perform proper authentication and authorization.

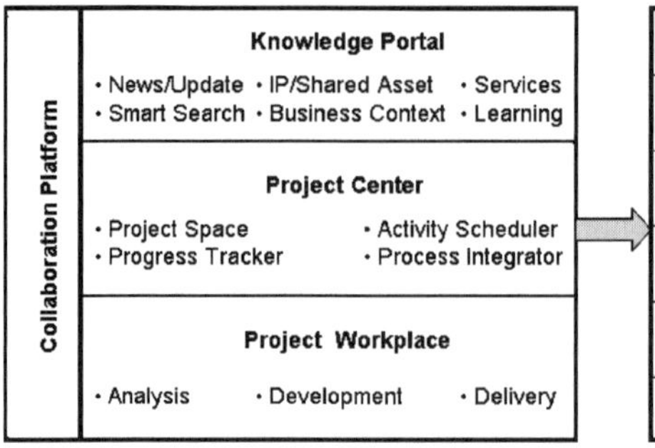

	Knowledge Portal			
Collaboration Platform	• News/Update • IP/Shared Asset • Services • Smart Search • Business Context • Learning			
	Project Center			
	• Project Space • Activity Scheduler • Progress Tracker • Process Integrator			
	Project Workplace			
	• Analysis • Development • Delivery			

Role	Responsibility	Access	Name
Project Manager	Knowledge Portal Project Center	R R/W	X
Team Lead	Knowledge Portal Project Workplace	R R/W	Y
Team Member	Knowledge Portal Project Workplace	R R/W	Z
Manager	Knowledge Portal Project Center	R/W R	A
End User		N	B

FIGURE 17.5   Connectivity map module.

Access to the project workplace is based on the individual's role and responsibilities. The project uses the organization's common profile under the organizational directory database to provide single sign-on and a unique look and feel for navigation. The project manager needs to monitor the integrity of the map routinely under business control and security audit guidelines. The project member's user identification and user profile registered under the organizational directory system will be used for access control. There may be different security levels for access restrictions to the proprietary information in the information repositories. The project manager needs to audit the connectivity map routinely to ensure integrity of project center and project workplace. Access to the knowledge portal and collaboration framework will be organization's responsibility. Figure 17.5 displays a sample connectivity map.

BENEFITS

Physical separation and timing delay can easily trigger the chain reactions of miscommunication and result in loss of team consensus and project focus. By adopting the collaborative knowledge framework, a project manager will be able to connect the project knowledge portal, project center, and project workplace by the connectivity map through the collaboration platform during project initiation to establish a project management system. Throughout project execution, a project manager can further refine processes to adjust the course of actions for performance, throughput, and productivity improvement. As a result, the project management system improves the effectiveness of the project management function, and it also gives the project manager more time to understand the business, market, and technology trends.

NEXT MILLENNIUM

Personal Witness: One Click Away from Each Other

In any working day, I am reachable from any part of the world through my company's intranet. My working hours are no longer 9 A.M. to 5 P.M. during the week days. Instead, I am available 24 hours a day 7 days a week through the virtual private network.

During work hours, all the employees and project team members are required to log onto the instant messaging system that sits on top of the corporate directory. By making every one connected online within the company, this creates a working environment in which everyone is one keystroke away from everyone else. In addition, individuals are required to update their personal profile in the corporate directory to include their latest experience and skill development. Sitting on top of this huge directory and corporate profile is a knowledge portal that allows individuals to configure their personal on-demand workplace. All the projects are gradually consolidated into a few key portfolio management systems under the project center. Based on the personal profiles in the corporate directory, human resources can be allocated and reallocated dynamically as in a talent grid.

Online learning and on-demand services have become the way of life. Skill transfer and new-technology adaptation happen in the background with e-mail notification or broadcasting messages through the corporate online community. Besides routine use of the online system for training and knowledge sharing, individuals also can conduct instant polls or participate in forums. There are so many community broadcasting channels for different types of activities in the company that on one occasion when someone accidentally used a wrong messaging system and asked, "Ajoy, when are you going home?" instantaneously, there were tens of responses asking, "Who is Ajoy?" Even more surprisingly, there were more than half dozen Ajoys worldwide, replying, "I am not going home yet." It is so real and so powerful that the collaborative knowledge framework has become a corporate core competence to compete in the global market.

However, everything that happened on the collaborative knowledge framework has left footprints, logs, and records that will be tracked and measured for quality and productivity improvement. Privacy protection and access security to this shared infrastructure need to conform with the code of conduct within the corporation.

The Future: Leading to the Next Industrial Revolution

The interests of global project management have grown from building and maintaining a project management system to new areas as process overhaul, life-cycle refinement, virtual team building, and leadership skill development. It is a good sign to see such awareness and change from a corporate "big brother" approach to a focus on the project team and its individuals. As I have seen, a new set of corporate values including customer and service focus, creativity and innovation, and personal trustworthiness such as integrity, accountability, commitment, adaptability, flexibility, and team spirit has been reemphasized for the success of global projects.

This has become a trend toward the next industrial revolution triggered by the challenges of global project management. In the future, the collaborative knowledge framework will be adopted to create more results in an even shorter time frame to benefit more people in the originations and global villages. I am very glad to see that it is still our responsibility and under our own control to manage the work/life balance for ourselves. Our fitness, emotional stability, and attitude will determine the final success of a global project and the future world.

CONCLUSION

A global project will be highly market-driven with technology leadership through global sourcing. It will require a guided process and a configurable working environment to support the project life cycle. Most of the existing global projects do have a defined process, an organizational structure, and some automated tools. However, they may not have been integrated to facilitate a global project management system. This chapter has proposed a collaborative knowledge framework for the creation of project management systems for global projects. After implementing this project management system, a company will transform its capability to the next level of efficiency, which will lead to the next industrial revolution.

REFERENCES

1. *The Holy Bible,* New International Version, Book of Genesis, Chapters 2 and 3.

2. Project Manadement Institute. 2004. *A Guide to the Project Management Body of Knowledge (PMBOK Guide)*, 3d ed. ANSI/PMI 99-001-2004. Project Management Institute., Pennsylvania

3. Suhwe Lee. 2002. Communication research for managing global e-business projects over a knowledge management infrastructure in today's e-world, in *PMI Research Conference 2002, (2002: Seattle, Washington) Frontiers of project management and research and application:preceeding of PMI Research Conference 2002 ISBN 1-880410-99-0, Published by Project Management Institute, Inc.*, Pennsylvania. pp. 309–317.

P · A · R · T · 4

MANAGEMENT OF THE PROJECT-ORIENTED COMPANY

In Chapter 18, Roland Gareis introduces the model of the project-oriented company. Its specific strategies, structures and cultures are described. In order to integrate the multitude of projects and programs performed simultaneously, the PM Office and the Project Portfolio Group as well as project and program management procedures and templates are presented as integrative structure of the project-oriented company.

In Chapter 19, the concept of a Project Portfolio Score Card (PPSC) is introduced as a useful instrument for controlling a project-oriented company by visualizing the progress of any given project. Methods for PPSC's use are given by Jankulik and Piff, along with multiple examples to familiarize the reader with its use in a project-oriented company.

In Chapter 20, Turner discusses partnering as a form of communication between client and contractor in a project. Turner shows how partnering is different from other forms of communication, when and how it can be effective, and what the different types of partnering are. Finally, methods for achieving partnering are discussed.

In Chapter 21, Roland Gareis and Michael Stummer introduce business process management as a maturity dimension of the project-oriented company. Business process management contributes to the professional performances of business processes in repetitive projects, such as contracting projects. Consequences for the organization and for personnel management of the project-oriented company are presented.

CHAPTER 18

MANAGEMENT OF THE PROJECT-ORIENTED COMPANY*

Roland Gareis

*Vienna University of Economics and Business Administration,
Vienna, Austria*

Roland Gareis holds an MBA and a Ph.D. He was a Fullbright scholar at the University of California, Los Angeles, in 1976, professor for construction management at the Georgia Institute of Technology, Atlanta, and visiting professor at the Georgia State University, ETH, in Zürich, Switzerland, and the University of Quebec in Montreal, Canada. Since 1983, he has been the director of the postgraduate program "International Project Management" at the Vienna University of Business Administration. For 15 years he was president of Project Management Austria, the Austrian project management association, he was project manager of the 10th Internet World Congress on Project Management, and manager of the research program "Crisis Management."

Currently, he is professor of project management at the Vienna University of Economics and Business Administration, manager of the global research program "Project Orientation (International)," and owner of Roland Gareis Consulting. He has published several books and papers on management of the project-oriented company.

ABSTRACT

Companies and parts of companies, such as divisions, business units, and profit centers, that use projects and programs as temporary organizations to fulfill relatively unique business processes of medium to large scope can be defined as *project-oriented companies*. Project-oriented companies have specific strategies, specific organizational structures, and specific cultures for managing projects, programs, and project portfolios. They apply "management by projects" as an organizational strategy; they have specific integrative organizational structures such as expert pools, a project portfolio group, and a project management office; and they perform specific business processes such as project and program management, project portfolio management, etc.

*Parts of this chapter are based on texts of the book "Happy Projects!" by Roland Gareis (Vienna: Manz, 2005).

THE PROJECT-ORIENTED COMPANY: A CONSTRUCT

In order to identify a company as a project-oriented company, the management of projects and programs within the organization and the strategic, structural, and cultural prerequisites for their performance are considered. Of course, a company also can be viewed from other perspectives. However, the *project-orientation view* provides a possibility for constructing a new organizational reality. By viewing an organization as a project-oriented organization, new possibilities for management intervention can be created by which the potential for the successful performance of projects and programs can be increased.

Project-oriented companies are characterized by projects and programs. At any given time, a number of projects can be started, performed, closed down, or stopped. In this way, a state of balance is created that should ensure the continuous development of the company and its survival.

The more varied the projects and programs of a project-oriented company are, the more complex the management of the organization will be. This depends on the dynamics and complexity of the individual projects, as well as on the relationships between the projects.

The project-oriented company has the following characteristics:

- Management by projects is an explicit organizational strategy.
- Projects and programs are used as temporary organizations.
- Networks of projects, chains of projects, and project portfolios are objects of consideration for the management.
- Project management, program management, and project portfolio management are specific business processes.
- Know-how provision and assurance takes place in expert pools.
- Project management competence is ensured by a project management office and a project portfolio group.
- A new management paradigm is applied that is characterized by teamwork, process orientation, and empowerment.

Not only companies but also subsystems of companies, such as divisions, business units, and profit centers, can be viewed as project-oriented organizations. Therefore, the terms *project-oriented company* and *project-oriented organization* can be used synonymously.

A project-oriented company is a company that has at its disposal specific strategies, structures, and cultures for the professional management of projects, programs, and project portfolios. The creation of the requisite "organizational fit" between these strategies, structures, and cultures poses a particular management challenge (Fig. 18.1).

"MANAGEMENT BY PROJECTS" AS AN ORGANIZATIONAL STRATEGY

The engineering organization Fluor Daniel views projects ". . . as a way of conducting its business and, of late, as a way of improving its internal tasks. . . . Fluor Daniel is able to conduct its business effectively in a decentralized, networked organizational atmosphere" (Thatcher, 1990).

The project-oriented company simultaneously performs projects for internal and external customers, small projects as well as projects of medium or large scope, and projects with different objectives. Project-oriented companies view projects and programs as a strategic

FIGURE 18.1 Requirement for an organizational fit in the project-oriented company.

option for designing the organizational structure. Companies have the choice of designing their organizations with or without projects and programs. By applying "management by projects" as a strategy, it is possible to realize the following organizational objectives:

- Creating organizational flexibility by using temporary organizations in addition to the permanent organization
- Delegating management responsibility to projects and programs
- Ensuring goal-oriented work by defining project and program objectives
- Ensuring organizational learning through the monitoring potential of projects and programs

Personnel management goals also can be realized through management by projects. In projects, it is possible to operationalize and integrate the often isolated or competing leadership models of management by objectives, management by delegation, management by motivation, etc. Management by projects uses as leadership strategy the motivational and personnel development functions of projects. Working in projects is attractive for many employees because projects

- Usually contain new business processes
- Are socially challenging and integrative because of teamwork
- Provide freedom of movement and promote creativity
- Are limited in time and therefore require feedback and new options after the end of the project

Individual learning in projects is promoted through the complexity of the problem situations. The marketing relevance of management by projects results from

- The effects of projects on relevant environments
- The application of project management as a sales instrument
- The possible marketing of project management as a service for internal and/or external organization markets

Through the more frequent definition and performance of projects, many companies apply management by projects implicitly. To create the benefits described above, an explicit application of management by projects and an explicit provision of the corresponding structural and cultural prerequisites are required.

ORGANIZATIONAL STRUCTURE OF THE PROJECT-ORIENTED COMPANY

The permanent organization of a company is designed to perform repetitive business processes. The organizational structures and business processes should provide orientation for employees through clear definitions of tasks and responsibilities. Furthermore, the organization should guarantee continuity in the relationships of the company with its relevant environments.

For the most part, these organizational objectives can be met by a stable, hierarchical line organization. However, a company that continuously performs new projects of different contents and degrees of complexity requires a more flexible, networked organizational structure. Companies can be positioned on a continuum between extreme steep hierarchical organizations and flat, network-type organizations. The amount of routine work in relation to the amount of project work determines the positioning of an organization on the continuum. There is no clearly optimal position for an organization, but a trend toward flatter, networked structures is observable.

In companies with little project orientation, projects are used in addition to the hierarchical line organization. Through the use of projects, this type of organization becomes flatter and more flexible (Fig. 18.2). Flattening comes about through an enlargement of the communications span and a (partial) reduction in the number of levels in the hierarchy. Flexibility is achieved through the possibility of using (project) organizations and then dissolving them after the objectives have been achieved.

In flat, networked organizations, the most important business processes will be performed within projects. An example of a flexible, networked structure is depicted in the organizational chart of the Gore Company (Fig. 18.3). The main characteristic of this organizational structure is that roles, lines of communication, and boundaries between teams, projects, and departments are depicted, but not the hierarchical relationships.

Project-oriented companies perform a number of different projects and programs at the same time. This high number of temporary organizations requires a high level of synchronization. In order to fulfill this integration function, projects (and programs) can be clustered into chains or clusters of projects, project portfolios, and networks of projects

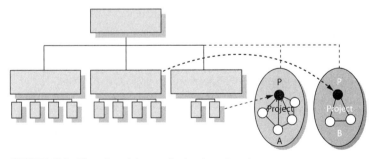

FIGURE 18.2   Flattening of the organization through projects.

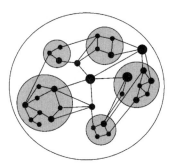

FIGURE 18.3 Organizational chart of Gore Company.

(Fig. 18.4; see also Chapter 7). Project portfolios and networks of projects are additional management objects of the project-oriented company. To manage them requires specific integrative organizations, such as the project portfolio groups and project management offices. It is their task to guarantee that the relatively autonomous projects and programs comply with the general objectives and rules of the project-oriented company.

A chain or cluster of projects is a number of sequential projects for the performance of several business processes. A project portfolio is the set of all the projects of a project-oriented company at a particular point in time. A network of projects is a set of several closely coupled projects at a given point in time. Grouping projects into networks requires different criteria, such as the use of a particular technology in all the projects, performance of the projects in the same geographic region, or performance of the projects for a common customer.

The organizational structure of a project-oriented company can be visualized in an organizational chart. An example of an organization chart of a project-oriented company is given in Fig. 18.5. The objectives, the position in the organization, the tasks, the environment relationships, and the formal authorities of expert pools, the project portfolio group, and the project management office are described in the following.

Since projects and programs have a high strategic importance for the project-oriented company, they also should be depicted symbolically in the organizational chart. It is not necessary to present each individual project but rather groups of projects (e.g., arranged according to types of projects) and programs.

When it comes to designing the organizational chart of a project-oriented organization, there are design options regarding the use of symbols for distinguishing between permanent and temporary organizations, regarding the terminology used for the organizational units,

Relationships between projects		
A set of sequential projects	All projects of a project-oriented organization	A set of closely-coupled projects
Over a period of time	At a point in time	At a point in time
Chain of projects	Project portfolio	Network of projects
Cluster		

FIGURE 18.4 Clustering of projects.

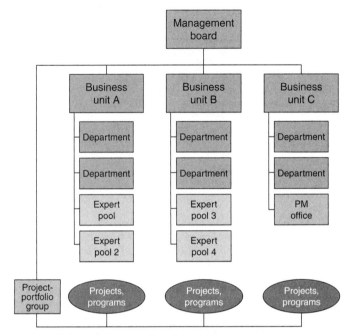

FIGURE 18.5   Organizational chart of the project-oriented company according to Roland Gareis' *Management of the Project-Oriented Company.*

and regarding the organizational incorporation of the expert pools, the project portfolio group, and the project management office. Boxes and ellipses can be used to depict permanent and temporary organizations, for example. The committee for coordinating the project portfolio can be referred to as the *project portfolio group* or as the *project portfolio steering committee*. In practice, the *project management office* is also referred to as *project management service* or *project management support*.

The organizational incorporation of the expert pools, the project portfolio group, and the project management office depends mainly on the size of the project-oriented organization. Basically, there are no right or wrong solutions.

EXPERT POOLS, PROJECT PORTFOLIO GROUP, AND PROJECT MANAGEMENT OFFICE

Expert Pools

Experts from various expert pools of the project-oriented organization perform the business processes in projects and programs. (Instead of *expert pool,* in practice, other labels such as *resource pool* and *center of excellence* are also used.) It is the objective of expert pools to provide sufficient, appropriately qualified experts for projects and programs. It is a further objective to ensure the prerequisites for efficient implementation of the business processes in the projects by means of professional process management.

The tasks to be fulfilled in the expert pool are personnel management, process management, and knowledge management tasks. Project-related tasks and their qualitative control are not performed in the expert pool but rather in the projects. In accordance with the model of the "empowered" project organization, the project team members and the project contributors are personally responsible for the manner and method of the performance—within the defined guidelines and standards—and for the quality of the performance of the work packages.

Depending on the business operations of a project-oriented company, several types of expert pools can be differentiated. In an engineering construction company, for example, there are various technical expert pools (e.g., mechanical engineering, electrical engineering, etc.), an expert pool "procurement," an expert pool "installation," etc. Also, in an information technology (IT) company, various expert pools can be differentiated, such as designers, programmers, testers, etc.

However, it is not only a sensible measure to organize expert pools just in contracting companies. Persons qualified to work in projects should be allocated to expert pools for internal projects, too. Not all employees in the marketing department of a bank, for example, are qualified for project work. However, people who also can represent their department's interests in projects, who also have specialized knowledge and sufficient project management competencies to work as project team members, should be assigned to an expert pool "marketing," possibly only in a virtual form.

A project-oriented company always should have an expert pool "project management." In larger organizations, an expert pool of project management trainers and project management consultants also can be defined.

Various different roles are performed in an expert pool. A distinction should be made between the pool manager and pool members. The members of an expert pool can represent various qualifications. A distinction between junior experts, experts, and senior experts enables the establishment of a career path as an expert in a project-oriented company.

The difference between an expert pool and a "traditional" department lies in the "empowerment" of the experts and in the perception of the management role of the expert pool manager. The "traditional" department manager considers himself or herself above all as an expert responsible for his or her employees' performance with regard to content. The expert pool manager considers himself or herself above all as the manager of the pool with personnel and organization responsibilities, not as a content expert. In this way, the expert pool manager sees himself or herself as undertaking expert tasks in projects. However, he or she is not responsible for the work performed by the other experts that make up the pool.

The expert pool manager should be assessed according to the performance of his or her management tasks in the expert pool and not according to the project and program results. The role of the expert pool manager is described in Table 18.1.

Project Portfolio Group

The project portfolio group presents a specific, permanent communication structure of medium-sized and large project-oriented companies. Only organizations with at least 200 to 300 employees that perform at least 15 to 20 projects simultaneously achieve a complexity that makes a separate communication structure for project portfolio management a sensible measure. It is only then that the management of a project portfolio should be given appropriate attention by means of establishing a project portfolio group. In smaller project-oriented companies, these tasks can be performed by management in the course of management meetings.

In the case of larger project-oriented companies, the project portfolio group should be responsible for the assignment of a project or a program and for project portfolio

TABLE 18.1   Description of the Role: Expert Pool Manager

Objectives
- Lead the expert pool members
- Assess the availability of resources for performing a project or a program (in the assignment process)
- Provide qualified employees for the projects and programs
- Provide guidelines and standards for performing the business processes of the expert pool
- Knowledge management in the expert pool

Position in the organization
- Reports to the manager of the profit center the expert pool belongs to
- Manages various qualification groups in the expert pool: junior experts, experts, and senior experts
- Contributes to the process of assigning a project or a program, to the start process and to the close-down process of a project or a program

Tasks
- Recruit and develop the expert pool personnel
- Dispose the expert pool personnel (into a project or a program)
- Develop and ensure know-how (methods, tools)
- Maintain a knowledge database with information regarding the business processes of the expert pool
- Obtain and provide the infrastructure necessary for performing the business processes of the expert pool
- Develop and provide guidelines and standards for performing the business processes of the expert pool
- Ensure compliance with the guidelines and standards for performing the business processes of the expert pool (e.g., by means of exchange of experience, supervision, audits, etc.)
- Define ethical standards and ensure professional ethics

Nontasks
- Perform project-related work packages
- Project-related quality control of the performance of the work packages

Environment relationships
- Members of the expert pool
- Other expert pools, PM office
- Management, managers of the profit centers
- Projects and programs
- Customers, partners, and suppliers

Formal authority
- Decisions regarding the organization, infrastructure, and budget of the PM office
- Decisions regarding the recruitment and the development of personnel for the expert pool
- Decisions regarding the disposition of expert pool members into a project or a program
- Approval of guidelines and standards for performing business processes
- Initialization of supervision or audits regarding the business processes of the expert pool

coordination. The project portfolio group is authorized to take decisions and thus is not to be considered a staff unit.

Although integrative structures, such as the management circle of a company, are frequently not depicted in the organizational charts of organizations, their strategic significance makes it advisable to depict the project portfolio group in the organizational chart. Members of the project portfolio group should be managers of the project-oriented company with holistic responsibility and strategic orientation. Typical members of the project portfolio group are, for example, the heads of marketing, finance, IT, and organization. In medium-sized project-oriented companies, members of the management board also may belong to the project portfolio group. One member is to be nominated as the spokesperson for the group.

A project portfolio group of an Austrian telecommunications company, for example, consists of five managers from those divisions particularly active in projects (finance, network setup, marketing, IT, and call center) and the project management office manager. The spokesperson for the project portfolio group is the manager of the finance division. This project portfolio group meets once a week for two to four hours for project portfolio management.

Depending on the number and the complexity of the projects to be coordinated, several project portfolio groups may be required in a project-oriented organization. At most, project portfolios with about 50 to 70 projects can be managed by one project portfolio group. Project portfolio groups can be differentiated according to company divisions (or profit centers) and types of projects.

An Austrian engineering construction company, for example, distinguishes among three project portfolio groups: one for offer projects and contracting projects, one for product-development projects, and one for personnel, organizational, and marketing projects. In order to ensure that the decisions taken by these three project portfolio groups are coordinated, individual managers are members of several project portfolio groups. A description of the role of the project portfolio group is given in Table 18.2.

Project Management Office

The project management office supports the project portfolio group in its preparation, performance, and follow-up of coordination meetings. In particular, the project management office can develop the project portfolio reports. Project management offices therefore perform services regarding not only the project and program management but also project portfolio management.

With the increasing importance of projects and programs in organizations, there arises a need to standardize the practices in projects and programs and to ensure the quality of project and program management. There also arises the need for a project portfolio point of view and for project portfolio reports. A project management office is frequently established in the course of the formal introduction of project and program management. The project management office represents the institutionalized competencies in project, program, and project portfolio management.

The objective of a project management office is to ensure professional project, program, and project portfolio management in the project-oriented organization. In this context, appropriate individual, collective, and organizational competencies should be developed by the project management office.

By providing tools for project and program management and by providing management support, the project management office contributes to achieving project and program objectives. By means of regular maintenance of the project portfolio database and the development of project portfolio reports and their adequate communication, a contribution is also made toward optimizing the project portfolio. Nonobjectives of the project management office are the performance of project owner team roles and project manager roles in projects.

The project management office sees itself as a service provider, not as a controller. The services of the project management office are listed in Table 18.3. The catalog presents the maximum amount of possible services by the project management office. Various tools can be provided in virtual form.

The management support for projects and programs can contain the following services:

- Providing support in the use of project management software for the development of project plans
- Moderating and recording project meetings

TABLE 18.2   Description of the Role: Project Portfolio Group

Objectives
- Optimize the project portfolio results and the project portfolio risk
- Design the project portfolio structures
- Implement the personnel and organization strategies in the project portfolio
- Contribute to the optimization of the results of networks of projects
- Contribute to the optimization of the management of chains of projects

Position in the organization
- Reports to the management of the project-oriented organization
- Members are managers of the project-oriented organization (e.g., managers of profit centers, managers of IT, organization, marketing and finance divisions) and the PM office manager
- Meetings: Approx. twice per month, 3–4 hours each

Tasks
Tasks in assigning a project or a program
- Possibly: Decide on investments to be selected (if no independent investment decision committee exists)
- Coordinate the project objectives with the strategic objectives of the project-oriented organization
- Decide on the organization form for initializing an investment (program, project, small project, permanent organization)
- Nominate the project owner team
Tasks in project portfolio coordination and networking of projects
- Coordinate both internal and external resources used in the project, determine project priorities
- Determine strategies for designing the relationships to project environments
- Brief analysis of selected (critical) projects
- Decide on the stopping or interruption of projects (for strategic reasons)
- Organize the learning of and between projects, the use of synergies
- Nominate the project owner team in chains of projects

Environment relationships
- Management, profit centers, PM office, etc.
- Project proposal teams, project owner teams and project manager
- Employees of the project-oriented organization
- Customers, partners and suppliers

Formal authority
- Decisions regarding the designing of project portfolios
- Possibly: Decision regarding investment proposals
- Decision regarding project proposals
- Nomination of the project owner team
- Stopping and interruption of projects
- Initialization of the networking of projects

- Developing project progress and project close-down reports
- Developing a project homepage, etc.

Differentiated according to types of project, the project management knowledge database should contain the actual project management documentation of closed-down projects, project progress and project close-down reports, and lessons learned from individual projects for project management.

The project management office can use various instruments for performing services. Table 18.4 provides an overview of possible instruments for project and program management and for project portfolio management.

TABLE 18.3   Catalog of Possible Services of the PM Office

Services for project and program management
Provision of project management instruments
• Providing instruments for project and program management (guidelines, forms, etc.)
Management support and ensuring management quality
• Management support for projects and programs
• Organizing management consulting, management auditing, and possibly evaluating of projects and programs
Individual and collective project management learning
• Organizing training and further training in project and program management and coaching of project and program managers
• Organizing the exchange of experience between project and program managers
Organizational project management learning
• Maintaining a knowledge database for project management
• Benchmarking the competencies for project and program management
Project management marketing
• Marketing the project and program management in the organization
• Developing and maintaining a PM office homepage

Services for project portfolio management
Provision of instruments for project portfolio management
• Providing instruments for project portfolio management (guidelines, forms, etc.)
Assignment of a project or a program
• Review of the quality of investment and project proposals
Project portfolio coordination
• Maintaining the project portfolio database
• Developing project portfolio reports
• Participating in and recording the coordination meetings of the project portfolio group
Networking of projects
• Initializing the networking and contributing to the networking of projects
• Ensuring continuity in the management of chains of projects

TABLE 18.4   Possible instruments of the PM Office

Instruments for project and program management
• Guidelines and forms for project and program management
• Standard project plans
• Guidelines and forms for management consulting and management auditing of a project or a program
• Career path in project and program management
• Standard training programs in project management
• IT infrastructure (project management software, project portals) and moderation tools
• PM Office homepage
• Project management reference cards

Instruments for project portfolio management
• Guidelines and forms for project portfolio management
• Standards for investment and project proposals
• IT infrastructure for project portfolio management (software for project portfolio management)
• Standard project portfolio reports

TABLE 18.5   Differences between PM Office and Project Office/Program Office

PM Office	Project Office, Program Office
• Permanent services for project-oriented organizations • For all projects and for the project portfolio • Integrated in the permanent organization	• Temporary, various life-cycle durations • Services for a project/program • Integrated in the project/program organization

A distinction should be made between the permanent project management office and temporary project and program offices. As a new, integrated organizational unit, the project management office performs services for the project-oriented company as a whole, whereas the project office/program office only performs services for one project/ program (see Chapter 7). The differences between the project management office and individual project offices/program offices are summarized in Table 18.5.

Depending on the size of the project-oriented organization and the scope of the project portfolio and the services on offer, the project management office can be made up of only one person or several people. A medium-sized production and trading firm with around 350 employees and a project portfolio averaging 25 projects, for example, employs two part-time employees for the project management office.

The basic organizational structure of a project management office is depicted in Fig. 18.6. The role of the project management office manager is illustrated in Table 18.6. Essential to the organizational chart of the project management office is the differentiation of positions that perform services for project and program management and positions that perform services for project portfolio management. The expert pools "project management" and "project management trainers/project management consultants" may belong to the project management office but also may belong to other organizational units of the project-oriented organization.

There are various options regarding the organizational incorporation of the project management office into the project-oriented company. The possible incorporation options into a business segment, into a service center, and as a staff unit next to the management board are depicted in Fig. 18.7.

Should there be several project management offices alongside each other in several business segments, they have to be coordinated formally or informally to ensure a standardized course of action in the projects in which several business segments cooperate. In large international concerns, for example, at Ericsson, there is sometimes a project management office at concern level whose operational implementation is supported by regional project management offices in various different countries.

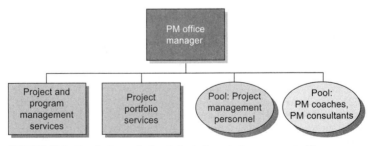

FIGURE 18.6   Standard organizational chart of a project management office.

TABLE 18.6 Description of the Role: PM Office Manager

Objectives
- Ensure the professional project, program, and project portfolio management
- Owner of the business processes of project and program management and of project portfolio management
- Lead the PM office employees

Position in the organization
- Reports to the profit center manager or the service division the PM office belongs to
- PM office employees report to the PM office manager
- Is a member of the project portfolio group

Tasks
Tasks in project and program management, quality assurance
- Work as an expert in project and program management (management support, consulting, auditing)

Tasks in assigning a project or a program
- Review the quality of investment and project proposals

Tasks in project portfolio coordination
- Develop project portfolio reports
- Participate in coordination meetings of the project portfolio group

Tasks in the networking of projects
- Initialize the networking of projects
- Ensure continuity in the management of chains of projects

Tasks in organizational design
- Further develop the instruments for project, program, and project portfolio management

Tasks in personnel management
- Coach project and program managers and project and program owners

Tasks in managing the PM Office
- Organize the PM office
- Manage the PM office personnel
- Manage the PM office budget
- Possibly lead the expert pools "project management" and "project management training and project management consulting"

Environment relationships
- PM office employees
- Project portfolio group
- Management, managers of profit centers, of expert pools
- Project proposal teams, project owner teams, and project managers
- Employees of the project-oriented organization
- Customers, partners and suppliers

Formal authority
- Approval of guidelines and standards for project and program management and project portfolio management
- Initialization of supervision or audits for project and program management
- Initialization of the networking of projects
- Decisions regarding the organization, personnel, infrastructure, and budget in the PM office

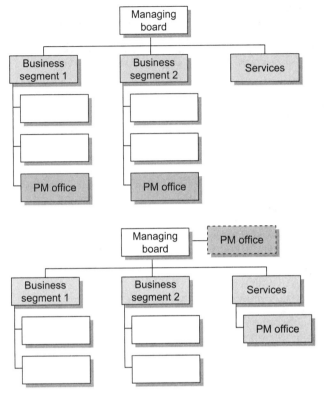

FIGURE 18.7 Options for the organizational incorporation of the project management office.

SPECIFIC BUSINESS PROCESSES OF THE PROJECT-ORIENTED COMPANY

The project-oriented company is characterized by the following specific business processes:

- Project management
- Program management
- Ensuring management quality in a project or a program
- Assignment of a project or a program
- Project portfolio coordination
- Networking between projects
- Personnel management in the project-oriented organization
- Organizational design of the project-oriented organization

In the process of assigning, the decision of whether or not a project or a program is to be performed is made. When the decision to perform the project has been made, the project can be assigned to a project team.

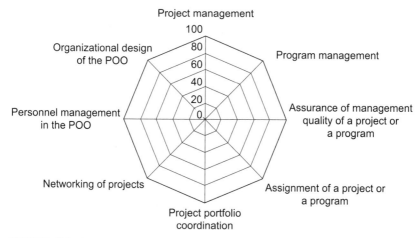

FIGURE 18.8 Maturity model of the project-oriented company according to Roland Gareis' *Management of the Project-oriented Company.*

The project management process begins with the project assignment and ends with the final approval of the project by the project owner. The process is made up of the sub-processes project start, project coordination, project control, possibly resolving a project discontinuity, and project close-down. Analogous to these are the program management subprocesses program start, program coordination, program control, possibly resolving a program discontinuity, and program close-down. To ensure management quality in a project or a program, the processes of management consulting and management auditing can be performed.

In the process of project portfolio coordination, the priorities between projects are set, and internal and external resources are coordinated. The process of networking of projects contributes to the assurance of synergies in the network.

Personnel management in a project-oriented organization includes the recruiting, disposition, and (continuous) development of project personnel. Employees of the project-oriented company who have the role of project or program owner, project or program manager, project team member, project contributor, etc. should be understood as project personnel.

The organizational design of a project-oriented organization includes the establishment of a project management office, a project portfolio group, and expert pools; the establishment of guidelines for project and program management and for project portfolio management; and the development of standard project plans. These specific processes can be depicted graphically in a maturity model of a project-oriented company (Fig. 18.8).

INTEGRATIVE METHODS OF THE PROJECT-ORIENTED COMPANY

Methods to integrate the different projects and programs performed simultaneously by the project-oriented company are

- Guidelines for project and program management
- Templates for project and program management

- Guidelines for management consulting and management auditing of projects or programs
- Guidelines for project portfolio management
- Standard project plans

Guidelines for Project and Program Management

In order to standardize the course of action and to ensure the quality in project and program management, project-oriented companies develop guidelines for project and program management. These guidelines are to provide employees with orientation for the management of projects and programs and to ensure the efficiency of the performance. Guidelines for project and progam management are an instrument to develop the organizational maturity of the project-oriented company.

The guidelines for project and program management define when a business process is to be organized as a project or as a program, which methods are to be used for their management, and which roles are to be performed in a project or a program. The guidelines exclusively contain descriptions of management tasks and do not contain any descriptions of the contents-related business processes for performing a project, such as purchasing, testing, etc. Sample documentations of projects and standard project plans can be provided in order to support the use of guidelines for project and program management. An extract of a table of contents of guidelines for project and program management of a public administration organization is given in Table 18.7.

Guidelines for project and program management should be kept as brief as possible (approximately 30 to 40 pages, excluding appendix). They should not be designed as training documentation. Special training tools are necessary to communicate information regarding project and program management.

The use of the business processes and methods described in the guidelines for project and program management should be binding. The guidelines should form part of any possible quality management documentation certified according to the International Standards Organization (ISO) of the project-oriented organization.

Guidelines for project and program management can apply to only one, several, or all types of projects of a project-oriented company. In addition to organization-specific guidelines, there are also guidelines used for several project-oriented companies and generic guidelines that can be used for all types of projects and all types of companies. Generic guidelines need to be adapted to be used by a company.

Templates for Project and Program Management

As a rule, the guidelines for project and program management also contain a set of templates that support the application of project and program management methods. These templates can be provided in electronic form by the project management office.

Guidelines for Management Consulting and Management Auditing of Projects or Programs

Since management consulting and auditing are becoming increasingly important for ensuring the quality of projects and programs in project-oriented companies, guidelines and methods for consulting and auditing must be provided.

TABLE 18.7   Table of Contents of the Guidelines for Project and Program Management

---

Table of Contents: Guidelines for Project and Program Management

1	**Introduction**
1.1.	Objectives, content of the guidelines for project and program management
1.2.	Updating of the guidelines
2	**Definitions**
2.1	Definition: Program, project, small project
2.4	Definition: Types of programs and projects
2.5	Definition: Project discontinuity
3	**Project management**
3.1.	Project management process
3.2.	Project management, subprocesses: Project start, project control, project coordination, resolution of a project discontinuity, project close-down
3.3.	Use of methods for project management
3.4.	Organization of projects
3.5.	Tools for project management
4	**Program management**
4.1	Program management process
4.2.	Program management, subprocesses: Program start, program control, program coordination, program monitoring, resolution of a program discontinuity, program close-down
4.3.	Use of methods for program management
4.4.	Organization of programs
4.5.	Tools for program management
5	**Appendix**
5.1.	Templates for project management
5.2.	Templates for program management
5.3.	Glossary
5.4.	Links to standard project plans and sample project documentations

---

Guidelines for Project Portfolio Management

The objective of the guidelines for project portfolio management is to further develop the organizational maturity of the project-oriented company. The business processes of project portfolio management and the roles and methods used for project portfolio management are described in the guidelines for project portfolio management.

Business processes of project portfolio management are the assignment of a project or of a program, project portfolio coordination, and the networking of projects. Roles of project portfolio management are investment proposal teams, the project portfolio group, the project management office, and expert pools. Essential methods used for project portfolio management are the investment portfolio score card, the business case analysis, the project definition, the project portfolio database, and the project portfolio reports. An example of the table of contents of guidelines for project portfolio management is given in Table 18.8.

Standard Project Plans

Standard project plans can be developed for performing repetitive projects, such as offer-development projects, contracting projects, product-development projects, event organization projects, etc. Standard work-breakdown structures, standard milestone plans, standard

TABLE 18.8   Table of Contents of the Guidelines for Project Portfolio Management

work-package specifications, standard responsibility matrices, and standard organizational charts, for example, can be used as standards for performing such projects.

The use of standard plans reduces the amount of planning at the start of a new project and makes it possible to revert to former experiences. The international IT concern Oracle, for example, provides its projects with standard plans for contracting projects, differentiated according to the implementation of various information technologies.

The use of standard project plans involves a risk owing to its "linear" application, without appropriately considering the specifics of a new project. Attention therefore must be paid to the adequate adaptation of the standard project plans in order to account for the specifics of a project.

INFRASTRUCTURES OF THE PROJECT-ORIENTED COMPANY

The infrastructure of a project-oriented organization can be differentiated into IT, telecommunications, and spatial infrastructure. These three dimensions of the infrastructure are treated differently in the following and yet are also considered in their relationships with each other. The implementation of cabling in order to implement an IT network, for example, depends on the spatial infrastructure. To implement temporary organizations, project-oriented companies need these infrastructures to be as flexible as possible.

IT Infrastructure of the Project-Oriented Company

Essential elements of the IT infrastructure of the project-oriented company are the system platform, the IT network, and the application software. The *system platform* of a project-oriented company consists of the basic hardware solution and the operating systems. The demands made by a project-oriented company on a system platform comply with the needs of conventional organizations. However, a specific demand is made in that the system platform needs to be flexible in order to be able to comply with the dynamics of the project-oriented company. Problems may occur, for example, should IT incompatibilities arise when cooperating with other project-oriented companies.

In order to avoid this risk, the design of the system platform should consider the use of open standards and flexible, easily scalable components. Thus the system platform can be adapted relatively easily to new demands. Web-based applications based on widespread standards and that can use Web browsers as universal user interfaces simplify cooperation between companies.

An efficient IT network is an essential prerequisite for efficient communication of the project-oriented company. The network architectures for data communication can be depicted in a layer model (Fig. 18.9). An opening takes place from the inside to the outside and requires the use of various technologies.

During implementation of the IT network, a sufficiently dimensioned, flexible, and easily extendible network architecture should be aimed at, for example, using flexible cabling and a wireless local-area network (LAN). This offers members of a project organization an efficient network connection irrespective of their location.

By providing employees with notebooks, the flexibility of the IT network can be used. Project contributors therefore can work both at their workstations and at the customer's site. The use of software for project management and project portfolio management, as well as groupware and project portals, is specific to project-oriented companies.

Project management software supports project planning and control. The standard software supports the planning and control of project scope, project schedule, project resources, and project costs. The tasks of designing the project organization and the project environment relations essentially cannot be performed using the project management software. Standard products available in the market are, for example, MS Project, Primavera Project Planner, Super Project, Project Scheduler, Open Plan, and SAP PS. Additions to the project management software are offered, on the one hand, in the form of graphics software, for example, Graneda or WBS Chart Pro, and, on the other hand, in the form of software for supporting special project management tasks.

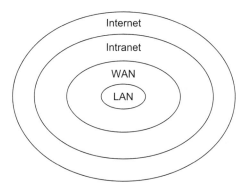

FIGURE 18.9 Layer model of the network architectures. (*From Grimm R, Kozok B, Lafos F. Kommunikationsinfrastruktur, Berlin : Springer Verlag, 2001 p. 199.*)

Software for project portfolio management supports the project-oriented company in the maintenance of a project portfolio database and in the development of project portfolio reports. Products available on the market that also cover project portfolio management are, for example, Primavera, Planview, Artemis, OPX2, Planta PPMS, and Niku Portfolio Manager.

Groupware supports communication and cooperation within projects. A relatively new aspect is the use of project portals for promoting Internet-based cooperation and communication within projects. A distinction should be made between general "collaboration" portals, such as community zero, same-page, and teamspace, and specific project portals, such as WelcomeHom, Primavera Teamplay, Pacific Edge Project Office, and MS Project Central. These specific applications of project-oriented companies also must be compatible with the organization's other applications in order to enable standardized flows of data without media discontinuities. Therefore, interfaces between the project management software and, for example, frequently used Enterprise Resource Planning (ERP)software (e.g., SAP or Oracle i-Business Suite) need to be defined.

In addition to groupware, a Web browser and video communication software also should be installed on the notebooks of members of virtual teams. The notebooks therefore also require appropriate peripheral devices, such as cameras, speakers, and microphones, in order to enable multimedia communication. It is possible to equip either each notebook or just individual machines located in special multimedia rooms with peripheral devices.

Telecommunications Infrastructure of the Project-Oriented Company

The term *telecommunications* encompasses the transmission of speech, data, and images by means of telephone, fax, e-mail, the Internet, and videoconferences. By using an appropriate telecommunications infrastructure, project-oriented companies can ensure both their organizational flexibility and their customer orientation. The use of a modern telecommunications infrastructure presents competitive advantages in the form of

- *Savings in time and costs.* Members of project organizations employed at different locations cooperate increasingly virtually. With regard to the communication technology, this cooperation can be supported by means of corporate networks that can run quickly and cheaply via speech, data, video, or multimedia communications.

- *Efficient flow of information.* Members of project organizations spend a major part of their working hours obtaining and forwarding information. Efficient networking of the computers and the telephone system ensures optimal organization of the communication.

- *Fast feedback.* Fast feedback on recommended solutions and intermediary results is important to ensure that appropriate progress is made on projects. The availability of the addressees can be supported by means of communication solutions, such as "call back on engaged tone," cordless and mobile communication, voice mail, e-mail, video, and multimedia communications.

Spatial Infrastructure of the Project-Oriented Company

Architecture is a central element of the organizational culture. The architectural design of the offices influences the levels of satisfaction, creativity, effectiveness, and productivity of employees. Flexible interior design options promote the project orientation of organizations. It should be possible to adapt the offices to the requirements of the current development phase of a project. Efficient communication in a project or a program is only enabled with the appropriate architecture and interior design.

If possible, the members of project teams should work together in open-plan offices even if the project is of a relatively short duration (e.g., three to four months). Communication between project teams working together in an open-plan office is more efficient than between project teams whose members work in several different office booths.

Both formal and informal communication is to be organized in a project or a program. Appropriately sized and equipped meeting rooms should be provided for project meetings and project workshops. However, the potential informal communication provided by jointly usable cafeterias, break rooms, smoking rooms, etc. also contributes to the success of a project or a program.

Communication within projects is further promoted by means of the furniture, for example, transparent walls, light tables and chairs, and low-level cupboards that enable eye contact between the employees. Mobile, height-adjustable tables enable the organization of brief standup project meetings.

When working on a project or a program, many employees spend a large part of their working hours not at any one fixed workplace. It is possible to provide such employees with workplaces based on the desk-sharing principle. These workplaces can be occupied flexibly. Representatives of relevant project environments also could use these workplaces.

For project workshops, rooms should be provided that can be adapted flexibly to various numbers of participants and that have the appropriate medial equipment, such as video beamers, flipcharts, overhead projectors, pin boards, etc. The use of flexible partition elements enables the room to be adapted to different numbers of participants.

CULTURES OF AND IN THE PROJECT-ORIENTED COMPANY

An *organizational culture* can be seen as the totality of the values, norms, behavioral patterns, and artefacts that are jointly developed and used by the members of an organization. The culture of an organization is not directly tangible. It can be observed by means of symbols, skills, and tools employed.

Specific values and norms characterize the culture of the project-oriented company and enable a differentiation between the project-oriented company and the non-project-oriented company. The way a project-oriented company sees itself can be documented in a mission statement (Fig. 18.10). Characteristics of a non-project-oriented company are described in Table 18.9. Non-project-oriented companies also can perform projects, yet they do not have any explicit culture and identity as a project-oriented company.

The values, norms, and behavioral patterns of an organization can be categorized by its management paradigm. A traditional management paradigm is characterized by hierarchy as a central integration instrument, by cooperation based on interface definitions, and by operations performed in functional organizational units. Organizations with a traditional management paradigm cannot fully use the organizational potentials of projects and programs.

---

2. We are a project-oriented company
We use projects for business processes of small, medium and large scope. We continually develop our project management culture. We apply project management methods differently according to the project requirements.

FIGURE 18.10   Extract of a mission statement of a project-oriented company.

TABLE 18.9   Characteristics of a Non-Project-Oriented Organization

- The term *project* is used for many different things, including routine tasks. A project inflation arises. Projects are not awarded adequate management attention.
- The project boundaries are defined according to the divisions and departments of the company. This results in too many small projects, which leads to suboptimizations. The integrative work must be performed by the permanent organization, which is, however, overtaxed by it.
- Nobody knows which and how many projects are being performed at any time. No information regarding the project portfolio exists. Projects arise informally, parallel projects with the same objectives are performed, and resources required for projects cannot be controlled.
- No project management methods are used in projects. This means that the transparency and the chance for efficient communication in projects are lost. This does not increase creativity; it reduces it.
- Individuals leave their mark on the working forms in projects. This means "reinventing the wheel" for each project. The professionalism in project management depends exclusively on the qualifications of individual persons.
- The objectives and the tasks are always agreed from one project meeting to the next. The lack of a "big project picture" means that the members of the project organization lack orientation.

A new management paradigm is required for the successful, efficient management of projects and programs. This new management paradigm can be characterized on the basis of

- Customer orientation
- Perception of the organization as a competitive factor
- Process orientation and team orientation
- Empowerment of employees
- Networking with customers, partners, and suppliers
- (Dis)continuous change

This new management paradigm is influenced by the model of the learning organization, by lean management, and by total quality management (Table 18.10).

TABLE 18.10   Influences of the "New Management Paradigm"

Influences of the learning organization (Senge, 1998)
- Distinction between individual, collective, and organizational learning
- Perception of the organization as a competitive factor
- Necessity of learning and delearning
- Continuous and discontinuous learning

Influences of lean management (Womack, 1992)
- Process orientation
- Concentration on core competencies
- Flat, lean organizational structures
- Team work
- Networks and cooperations
- Continuous improvement

Influences of total quality management (Juran, 1991)
- Customerorientation
- Product and process quality
- Quality control, quality assurance and quality management

TABLE 18.11   Relationship between the Management Paradigm and the Project Management Approach

	Traditional Management Paradigm	New Management Paradigm
Traditional project management	• Fitting culture • Inefficient projects • Dominance of the line organization	• Cultural combination is hardly conceivable • High potential for conflicts
Systemic project management	• Cultural differences • Efficient projects are possible, yet... • High potential for conflicts	• Fitting culture • Efficient projects • "Empowerment" of the projects

The management paradigm existing within a company creates a cultural framework for the performance of projects and programs. Even though a traditional management paradigm suits a traditional, method-oriented project management approach, it results in inefficient projects. Efficient projects based on a systemic, process-oriented project management approach are promoted by a new management paradigm. The relationships between the management paradigm of a project-oriented company and the practiced project management approach are depicted in Table 18.11.

Subcultures in the Project-Oriented Organization

By applying project and program organizations, subcultures are developed in the project-oriented company. This development of project- and program-specific cultures contributes to the success of projects and programs; that is, it is functional for the project-oriented company.

As a subsystem of an organization, a project can be distinguished from other subsystems, such as departments or other projects. Basically, the cultural division process into subcultures can be performed as far as desired. However, it is a prerequisite that the relevant cultures be characterized by their own values, rules, and behavior patterns, which can be learned and shared by the members.

REFERENCES

Grimm R, Kozok B, Lafos F. 2001. *Kommunikationsinfrastruktur für virtuelle Organisationen.* Berlin: Springer-Verlag.

Juran JM. 1991. *Handbuch der Qualitätsplanung.* Landsberg am Lech; Germany: Verlag Moderne Industrie.

Senge P. 1998. *The Fifth Discipline: The Art and Practice of the Learning Organization.* London: Century Business.

Thatcher JR. 1990. *New Age Managers for Projects.* Drexel Hill, PA: Project Management Institute.

Womack J. 1992. *Autoindustrie—Die zweite Revolution in der Autoindustrie.* Frankfurt:Campus Verlag.

CHAPTER 19
PROJECT PORTFOLIO SCORE CARD

Ernst Jankulik

Siemens AG Austria, Building Technologies,
1230 Vienna, Austria

Roland Piff

MCE AG, Vienna, Austria

Ernst Jankulik holds an M.Sc. and a MAS degree. He started his career with an apprenticeship as an electrical technician and was further educated as a measurement and control engineer, a university course in professional project management at the Vienna University of Economics, and a university course in process and quality management (business excellence) at the Danube University Krems. He received additional education as an EOQ quality systems manager, EOQ quality auditor, a senior project manager certification from IPMA and conducted train the trainer course in project management.

Professional experience includes work as an installer, supervisor, site manager, product manager, project manager, project coach, portfolio manager, process and quality manager, and coach and trainer. In addition, he spent five years as managing director of a bureau for electrical engineering. In all, he has 34 years total work and business experience, 18 years in foreign countries. Currently, he is responsible for project, process, and quality management for Siemens Building Technologies (SBT), Austria and Central and Eastern Europe (CEE) and is manager of business development for the same regions.

Roland Piff holds an M.Sc., an MAS, and an engineering degree. He started his career as a supervising engineer in a plant construction company; further occupational qualifications include experience in management systems for quality, safety, and the environment, a project manager certification (IPMA), and a university course in process and quality management (business excellence) at the Danube University Krems. He received additional education as an EOQ quality systems manager and an EOQ quality auditor.

Professional experience includes work as a supervisor, product manager, project manager, project coach, quality, safety, and process manager, coach and trainer, and facility manager. Currently, he is responsible for project, process, and quality management and internal auditing for MCE AG.

They have published a book entitled, Project Management and Process Measurement. (Erlangen, Publicis, 2005)

This chapter describes a further development of the project portfolio score card (PPSC) as a control instrument for project-oriented organizations. The goal of this development was to take into consideration the structures of the European Foundation of Quality Management (EFQM) model, as well as to incorporate into the project portfolio score card the evaluation of quality in the fulfilment of the business processes within a project-oriented organization. In this manner, the PPSC becomes a strategic control instrument.

The newly developed model of the PPSC will be explained, its criteria and units of measure described, and the results of use of the PPSC will be shown through a concrete example. In closing, the results of a case study in two organizations will be compared in a quality Shewhart control chart.

SCORE CARDS IN PROJECT-ORIENTED ORGANIZATIONS

Score cards for various applications have been developed on the basis of the balanced score card, such as the investment score card, the project score card, the project portfolio score card, and the risk score card. The origin of the score card can be found in the description of the evaluation and management system "balanced score card" by Kaplan and Norton[1] that was developed to provide managers with a comprehensive tool for evaluating the development of an organization.

Balanced Score Card

The balanced score card was conceived by the Norton Institute in 1990 under contract from corporate consultants KPMG as "measuring performance in the organization of the future" and has been further developed over time. The evaluation systems of various organizations in various industries were studied, out of which a uniform evaluation scheme was developed. *Balanced* means that the focus was not strictly on finance but that other perspectives that make a fundamental contribution to the success of the organization also are taken into consideration. The results were four balanced score card perspectives:

- Finance
- Customers and market
- Internal processes
- Learning and development

Only the combination of all four perspectives creates a complete picture of the organization. In order to gather the many indicators from an organization and seek out those which also provide key information for the fulfilment of the organization's strategic goals, it is necessary to recognize the relationships between the indicators and their interconnected influences. Out of these, the strategically important success factors can be compiled and defined as drivers for the achievement of the strategic goals.

An essential success factor in the balanced score card is its relationship to the future, whereas, for example, the DuPont[2] method deals only with the past. With the score card, a communication and control instrument becomes anchored in the organization, which makes the permanent verification of goals in every area of the organization possible.[3]

Project Score Card

The project score card (described earlier in this book) represents a project information system and serves as an aid for visualizing the current status of a project.

Project Portfolio Score Card

The project portfolio score card (PPSC) (as explained earlier in this book) is a control tool for the project-oriented organization. The PPSC is the "control center" of a project-oriented organization and provides for the operationalization of project-relevant strategic goals. The PPSC therefore is an instrument in which the strategic success factors of a project-oriented organization can be brought together and visualized.

The EFQM Model as Basis for the Further Development of the PPSC

The European Foundation of Quality Management (EFQM) model defines nine criteria, each of which plays a part in the evaluation of the progress of an organization on the way to top performance. Each of the criteria represents, in some respect, a building block of the organization. If each of the points addressed by the individual criteria were fulfilled to 100 percent, the result would be the "ideal organization." The criteria are built up on one another, are interconnected, and are weighted differently. This is reflected in the various numbers of points for each of the criteria. These points make it possible to determine the position of an organization on the way to "excellence" (Fig. 19.1).

Within the model, there are two types of criteria: the so-called enabler criteria and the results criteria. The term *enabler* also can be called *ways and means* or *potential factors* and *use factors*. Ways and means are more self-evident because they better express that

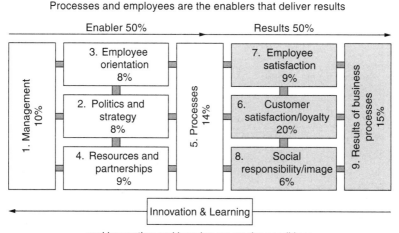

Processes and employees are the enablers that deliver results

and innovation and learning create the conditions

FIGURE 19.1 EFQM model.

this is about methods, procedures, and processes. One of the most important enabler criteria is therefore always defined directly as *process*. In the results, the actual financial and nonfinancial data will be evaluated and, with them, the quality of the results achieved by the organization.

Comparison of Various Score Card Models

Table 19.1 provides a summary of the score card models described.

FURTHER DEVELOPMENT OF THE PPSC

For further development of the PPSC from Roland Gareis, reference is given to the EFQM model. With the conventional perspectives of the PPSC, the business processes of the project-oriented organization were not taken into sufficient consideration. In order to realize the holistic approach of the EFQM model, the PPSC can be enlarged to include the additional criteria of the *excellence model*. With this holistic approach, the project-oriented organization can develop further in the direction of excellence (Fig. 19.2).

Integration of the philosophy of the EFQM model leads to extension of the Balanced Score Card to the PPSC to include the criteria of internal processes, partnerships/internal resources, and society. The criteria of the new PPSC are described through the questions in Fig. 19.3.

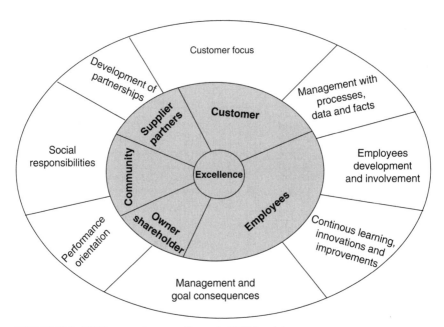

FIGURE 19.2   PPSC perspectives according to the EFQM model.

TABLE 19.1 Comparison of Score Cards

Criteria	Balanced Score Card	Project Score Card	Project Portfolio Score Card	European Foundation of Quality Management
Purpose	Strategic management of the organization	Establishing interfaces, defining priorities, coordination of plans, optimizing individual projects	Project portfolio controlling	Evaluation of organizational excellence
Derived goal	Organizational strategy	Project planning and project strategy	Project portfolio strategy	Organizational strategy
Controlling level	Strategic levels	Operative project level	Operative and strategic levels	Strategic levels
Object of consideration	Organization	Project and context	Project portfolio	Organization
Period of consideration	Quarter	Every 2–4 weeks	Every 2–4 weeks	Year
Responsible for the evaluation	Management team	Project manager, project controller	Project portfolio group	External or internal assessors

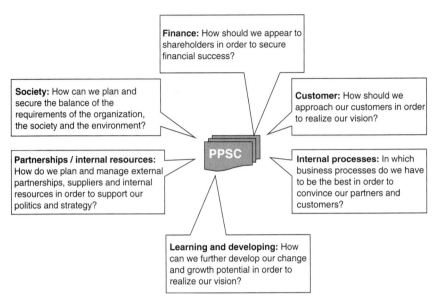

Finance: How should we appear to shareholders in order to secure financial success?

Society: How can we plan and secure the balance of the requirements of the organization, the society and the environment?

Customer: How should we approach our customers in order to realize our vision?

Partnerships / internal resources: How do we plan and manage external partnerships, suppliers and internal resources in order to support our politics and strategy?

PPSC

Internal processes: In which business processes do we have to be the best in order to convince our partners and customers?

Learning and developing: How can we further develop our change and growth potential in order to realize our vision?

FIGURE 19.3   Short description of the PPSC criteria.

Conception of the Criteria and Measuring Points of the PPSC

One goal of the PPSC is to balance financial success factors and nonfinancial performance drivers. Nonfinancial performance drivers are those criteria from which the cause of success or failure can be derived. The goal of this concept is to fill the gaps that all too often exist between the strategic goals and the instructions for concrete actions.[4]

Process measuring points make it possible to evaluate processes. One possibility for differentiation with regard to evaluation is given through the viewpoint of the observer. Traditionally, the processes are evaluated from the viewpoint of the process owner or the quality manager. In the new model the emphasis is put on the point of view of the project manager. This means that processes that may be running excellently from the point of view of the process owner can be examined from the point of view of process fitness by the executing project manager. In this way, for example, a procurement process may receive a positive result from the viewpoint of the process owner because of excellent purchasing conditions (e.g., favorable prices, fast, and flexible) but a negative result from the viewpoint of the project manager because of more difficult assembly conditions, poor assembly instructions, multiple partial deliveries, and so on. The internal process customer in the business process, the project manager, must be as satisfied as the external customer. By using this method of consideration, quality management in the internal processes becomes integrated, and the goals set for the processes are in line with the strategic orientation of the organization.

The combination of the simultaneous evaluations from the process and project viewpoints makes it possible to optimize the processes for the success of the entire organization. One necessary step is to weigh the individual and often diametrically opposed evaluation results against each other in order to reach an overall evaluation of the processes.

Regarding the availability of data, one should keep in mind that nonfinancial data are not always easy to acquire. The process owner should be defined as the person responsible for the provision of appropriate data. Table 19.2 contains an exemplary summary of the

TABLE 19.2 PPSC Criteria and Measuring Points

Criterion	Measuring Point	Data Source	Responsible	
Learning and Developing Perspective				
Lessons learned from project close down	Number of improvement measures implemented	Closing report	Project management office	In order to realize innovation, the use of the knowledge competencies of employees in each area must be increased. The strategy must first be reviewed to determine whether the existing competencies and knowledge are sufficient for achieving the goals. In this way, qualification and innovation play a determining role in the success of the organization (Vollmuth, 2001). The criteria of this perspective are also called *driver indicators* for the project portfolio score card.
Multirole deployment of team members	Number of roles per employee	Project personnel planning	Project management office	
Building up competence	Training status/requirements profile	Personnel file	Human resources	
Employee satisfaction	Survey	Evaluation of employee survey	Human resources	
Continuous Improvement	Savings	Improvement protocol	Quality management office	
Partnerships/Internal Resources Perspective				
Partner relationships	Increasing value through partnerships	Survey	Project management office	The *performance indicators* for partnerships/internal resources should indicate how the project-oriented organization interacts with its partners and resources. The questions "How do partners perceive the project-oriented organization?" "What does the partner contribute to the increasing value of the project-oriented organization?" "How carefully are internal resources used?" must be answered.
Supplier relationships	Continuity of the relationship	Supplier file	Purchasing	
Project management resources	Level of utilization	Personnel accounting program	Human resources	
Standardization through the use of electronic data processing	Level of use	Electronic data processing statistics	Electronic data processing support	
Social Perspective				
Social relationship	Acceptance in the society	Opinion surveys	Public relations	With the *early warning indicators* of the social perspective, the emphasis is on how society (meaning people in general) perceives the actions of the project-oriented organization.
Relationship to administrative bodies	Duration of approval proceedings	Approval proceedings	Project management	
Environmental compatibility	Pending environmental proceedings	Database of legal suits	Legal support	
Relationship to local residents	Number of complaints	Rate of complaints	Customer service	

(Continued)

TABLE 19.2 PPSC Criteria and Measuring Points (*Continued*)

Criterion	Measuring Point	Data Source	Responsible	
		Internal Process Perspective, Variation 1		Continual improvement is especially important in achieving internal process goals. They are, therefore, referred to as *performance indicators*. The measuring points are, however, only to be evaluated via "soft facts" and are therefore not exact. As a result, there are two variations to be considered. The first variation summarizes all content processes in one indicator.
Project quality	Number of warranty cases	Electronic data warehouse	Controlling	
Project management	Audit results, maturity model	Audit reports	Project management office	
Use of PM procedures	Audit results, level of use of electronic data processing tools	Audit reports/electronic data processing evaluation	Project management office	
Projects per cluster	Number of projects/ cluster	Project portfolio	Project management office	
Content processes	Survey	Questionnaire	Project management office	
		Internal Process Perspective, Variation 2		The second variation considers each process as its own indicator. The advantage of this is that the results of the measurements have a stronger effect on the entire project portfolio score card. In our further research, we chose this variation.
Project management	Survey	Questionnaire	Project management office	
Engineering	Survey	Questionnaire	Project management office	
Purchasing/logistics	Survey	Questionnaire	Project management office	
Assembly/supervision	Survey	Questionnaire	Project management office	
Initial operation/training	Survey	Questionnaire	Project management office	
Pilot operation	Survey	Questionnaire	Project management office	

Customer Perspective

Customer satisfaction	Customer satisfaction survey	Evaluation of customer satisfaction survey	Marketing
Customer loyalty	Rate of repeat contracts	Customer relationship management	Sales
Market share in project business	Turnover/turnover by market	Market analysis	Marketing
Image as project-oriented organization	Customer satisfaction survey	Evaluation of customer satisfaction survey	Marketing
Customer acquisition	Number of new customers	Customer relationship management	Sales

The customer-oriented *early warning indicators* are increasing in significance. In many organizations, quality awareness is already linked to customer requirements.

Finance Perspective

Project portfolio costs	Sum of all project costs	Electronic data warehouse	Controlling
Project portfolio results	Earnings before interest and tax (EBIT)	Electronic data warehouse	Controlling
Project portfolio budget	Planned budget/actual budget	Electronic data warehouse	Project management office
Project portfolio risk	Risk/turnover	Electronic data warehouse	Controlling
Project portfolio turnover increase	Net turnover	Electronic data warehouse	Controlling

The finance-oriented indicators are generally taken over from accounting. These indicators are "hard indicators" and evaluate the project-oriented organization in retrospect. These indicators are not particularly suitable for future planning. They serve a plan versus actual comparison of the project-oriented organization. They are therefore referred to as *late warning indicators*.

possible criteria and measuring points, as well as the data sources and those responsible for the provision of data used in the various perspectives of the PPSC.

Connecting the Perspectives of the PPSC

Process-oriented performance criteria help to interpret the results obtained correctly and make it possible to determine cause-and-effect relationships. An important aspect of the evaluation of the results is formulation of the question of who profits from the results and how the evaluation turns out from the viewpoint of the process customer.

It is primarily the strategic goals of the project-oriented organization that should be defined. In the framework of strategy/goal workshops, the criteria for achieving the strategic goals are identified and substantiated. The relationships between criteria are established after their identification.

These relationships make it possible to identify the connections between perspectives. This chain of effects begins with the learning and development perspective (long-term business success is not possible without employee competencies or potential and innovation) and moves through the partner/internal resources and internal process perspectives and on to the society and customer perspectives. The accumulated results are reflected in the finance perspective.

The essential drivers for business success can be found in the learning and development perspective. Early recognition of trends is possible through the customer and society perspectives. The performance indicators show which condition the internal processes and the partner/internal resource perspectives are in. The business results can be found in the finance perspective.

The Extended Model of the PPSC

The extended model of the PPSC is shown in Fig. 19.4 a, b, c.

A questionnaire has been developed to carry out a measurement of "internal processes" from the viewpoint of the project manager. An excerpt of this questionnaire is given in Table 19.3.

The evaluation criteria shown in Table 19.4 have been used to define each status when answering the questionnaire.

CASE STUDY

Measurement of the PPSC perspective "internal processes" was carried out in a plant construction as well as in a systems engineering organization. The following are examples of the results of one organization. The results of both organizations are compared in the next section.

Project Management Results

Table 19.5 shows the example answers to two questions on project management processes from 11 project managers surveyed.

In the bubble diagram in Fig. 19.5, the strengths and weaknesses in project management are presented in graphic form. This can be seen from the position of the individual bubbles. The numbers in or on the bubbles correspond to the number of the questions in the questionnaire.

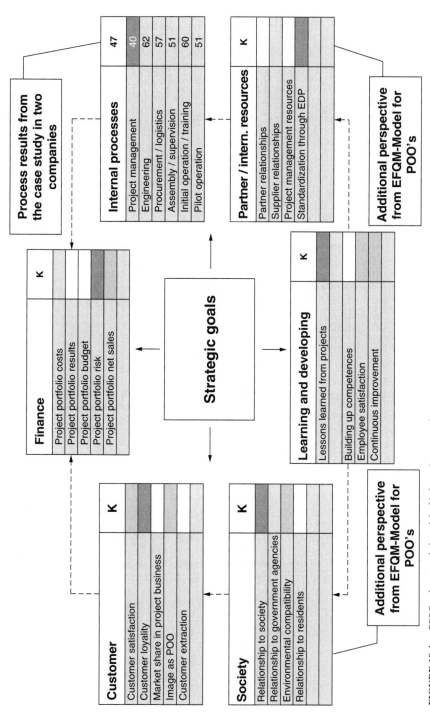

FIGURE 19.4a PPSC—the extended model of balanced score card.

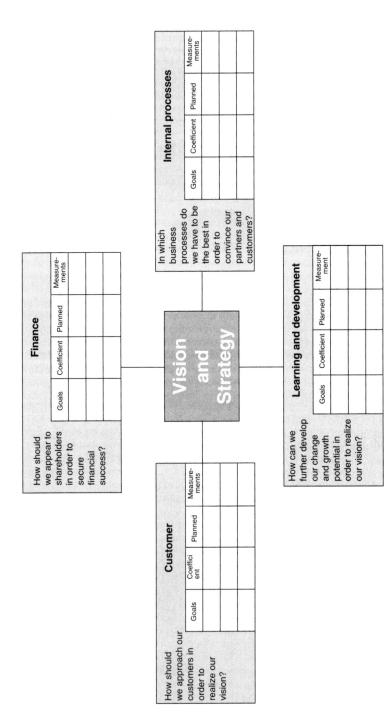

FIGURE 19.4b Bianced score card model.

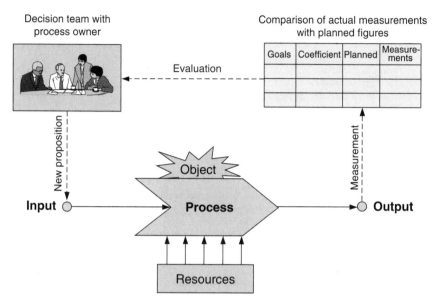

FIGURE 19.4c   Process measurement loop.

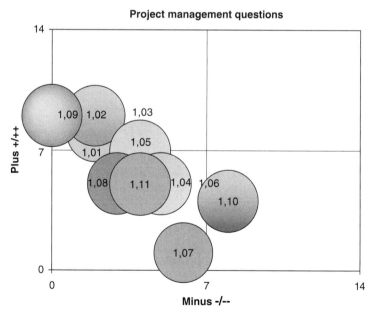

FIGURE 19.5   Results of the questionnaire.

TABLE 19.3   Excerpt from Questionnaire

Questions	Score
1 Project management	-- - 0 + ++
1.1 Has the project manager been given the necessary authority to make decisions during the project assignment?	
1.2 Was a formal project assignment given during the assignment process?	
1.3 Will a project-start workshop be carried out with the project owner and the project team?	
1.4 Will the results of the project-start workshop be made into a project handbook and will this be signed off by the project owner?	
1.5 Will a periodic project controlling process with documented results and progress reports be established?	
1.6 Will a project close-down workshop be held and will lessons learned be documented and made available to other participants to the project?	
1.7 Does the project manager have adequate resources available throughout the performance of the project?	
1.8 Will quality attributes be continually monitored in the project management process (such as review meetings)?	
1.9 Will project coordination be promoted through permanent communication with project team members (meetings, individual discussions, e-mail)?	
1.10 Will risk management be carried out and documented in the project controlling process?	
1.11 Will claim management (changes) be promoted and documented in the project controlling process?	
2 Engineering	-- - 0 + ++
2.1 Are the technical plans and documentation understandable (for example, short training time for assembly personnel)?	
2.2 Are the technical plans and documentation usable without corrections (for example complexity)?	
2.3 Is there enough technical know-how in the project pool around the project manager to provide support?	
2.4 Will the plans and documentation be prepared in such a way that few inquiries are needed?	
2.5 Are the facility and system completed without many changes in the technical customer specification?	
2.6 Are design review meetings in the project planning and are they carried out (such as milestones)?	
2.7 Are plans made in such a way that new customer wishes or necessary changes can be easily and quickly implemented?	
2.8 Are requests for planning changes carried out on time by the responsible members of the project pool?	
2.9 Are economic aspects of the on site assembly work adequately taken into consideration during project planning?	
2.10 Are requests for later acceptance tests considered during project planning?	

TABLE 19.4   Evaluation Criteria for Questionnaire

Symbol	Status	Evaluation Criteria
Dark green	++	Result is >65%
Light green	+	Result is between 65 and 50%
Yellow		Result is between 50 and 40%
Orange	–	Result is between 40 and 30%
Red	– –	Result is <30%

In the priority grid (Fig. 19.6), the recommended actions for dealing with the results are given.

Results of the Internal Processes

The results of the analysis of the internal processes of project management, engineering, procurement, assembly, initial operation, and pilot operation are shown in both a spider diagram (Fig. 19.7) and a bar chart (Fig. 19.8). The level of performance of the processes is shown in the diagrams. At the same time, the potential for improvement becomes visible. The dark areas represent the level of performance as a portion of the total area. The larger this area is, the greater the "excellence" of the project-oriented organization.

Target values for each process can be defined on the basis of the results of the analysis in Table 19.6. The target values for each period of observation can be defined jointly by the project management office and the process owner and recommended to management. The corresponding actions for achieving the target values are also to be defined.

BENCHMARKING THE INTERNAL PROCESSES

The quality of the fulfilment of internal processes from the two organizations in which the authors are active were compared. The instrument used was the Shewhart control chart (Fig. 19.9).

Two limits were entered into the Shewhart control chart: the lower limit and the upper limit of interference. If the quality of process fulfilment is lower than the lower limit (LL), which was set at 40 percent, immediate actions are necessary. Under the lower limit of interference (LLI), which was set at 50 percent, corrective actions are to be agreed.

TABLE 19.5   Excerpt from One of the Completed Questionnaires

Project Management	– –	–	0	+	++
Has the project manager been given the necessary authority to make decisions during the project assignment?		2	2	6	1
Was a formal project assignment given during the assignment process?	1		4	3	3

++	++/--
Good to very good performance. Very positive influence on the project results. **Priority 4**	Critical. Can lead to strong fluctuations in individual projects. Action required. **Priority 2**
+/-	--
Not critical. Average results, therefore little influence to be expected on the project results. **Priority 3**	Very critical. Negative influence on the overall results. Immediate action required. **Priority 1**

FIGURE 19.6   Priority grid.

The results were interpreted as follows:

- *Project management.* In this process, organization 2 (O2) was 10 percent better than organization 1 (O1). O1 was far under the lower limit of interference (LLI) and just under the lower limit (LL). This shows that a systems engineering company is inferior in this important process when compared with a classic engineering company.

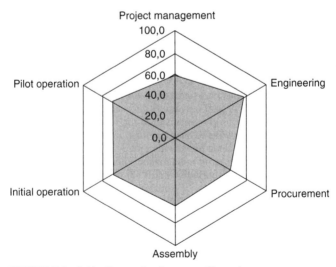

FIGURE 19.7   Spider diagram showing status of internal processes.

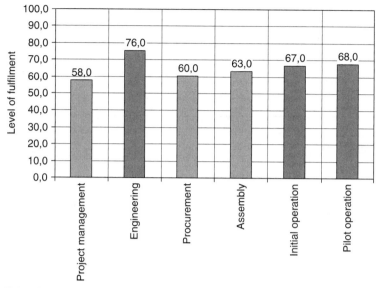

FIGURE 19.8   Bar graph showing the status of internal processes.

TABLE 19.6   Target Values and Actions for Each Process

Process	Score	Target Value	Actions
Project management	57,8	60	Further training, create project handbook, moderate project start workshop, moderate project close-down workshop
Engineering	75,9	80	Set and check quality gates for design review
Procurement/logistics	60,3	65	Integrate logistics process into commercial process
Assembly/supervision	63,2	65	Include construction-site management in the assembly calculation
Initial operation/ training	66,5	70	Keep an online construction diary
Pilot operation	67,8	70	Set and check quality gate before planing the performance of work package
TOTAL	64,9	68	

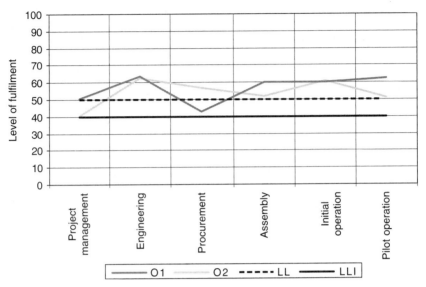

FIGURE 19.9   Benchmarking the internal processes of two organizations.

- *Engineering.* Both organizations have well-developed processes in this area.
- *Procurement.* O1 is less than the LLI for this process. O2 is far less and is just at the LL.
- *Assembly.* For this process, O1 is just under the LLI. O2 had very good results.
- *Initial operation.* Both organizations show a good result in this process.
- *Pilot operation.* In this process, O1 again was just under the LLI. O2 had very good results.
- *Overall status.* The overall processes of both organizations are not stable because some processes are under the LLI.

In terms of continuous improvement (CI), as soon as the level of fulfilment exceeds 65 percent, the limits will be pushed upward. A process can be considered to be stable or under control when its results always lie above the LLI.

Fundamentally, the results from both organizations represent starting levels for further measurements. A minimum of three measurements over a period of three years are necessary for obtaining relevant values. It is essential that the method of measurement and the questions are not, or only marginally, changed in order to ensure the comparability of the results.

CONCLUSION

Inclusion of the viewpoint of the project manager in the evaluation of processes of the project-oriented organization leads to new definitions of process goals. This can be demonstrated in the example of the procurement process: It must be the goal of the procurement process not only to purchase at the lowest price (viewpoint of central purchasing) but also to contribute to the minimization of the overall cost of the project (viewpoint of the project manager). By optimizing procurement, it is possible, for instance, to lower assembly costs, simplify the initial operation, and spend less time on documentation.

Only with a combination of viewpoints of both project and process management can a symbiosis of the two be realized in the alignment of the goals of the internal processes and with it support the alignment of the project-oriented organization in the direction of "project excellence."

REFERENCES

1. Kaplan R, Norton D. 1997. *Balanced Score Card.*, Stuttgart, Schäffer-Pöschl p. 21.

2. The classification system of financial control was developed in 1919 by the chemical company of the same name; see., DuPont, France.

3. Hillmar J. 2001. *Vollmuth: Führungsinstrument Controlling.*, Planegg, WRS Publisher p. 216.

4. Weber M. 2002. Kennzahlen, Unternehmen mit Erfolg führen, das Entscheidende erkennen und richtig reagieren, 3. Auflage, Freibung, Haufe Publisher p. 48.

5. Gareis, R. 2005. *Happy Projects!* Vienna, Mary Verlag.

CHAPTER 20
PARTNERING IN PROJECTS

J. Rodney Turner

The Lille School of Management, France, and University of Limerick, Ireland

Rodney Turner is professor of project management at the Lille Graduate School of Management and the Kemmy Business School at the University of Limerick. He is also an adjunct professor at the University of Technology Sydney, adjunct professor at Educatis University, Zurich, and visiting professor at Henley Management College, United Kingdom.

He studied engineering at Auckland University and did his doctorate at Oxford University, where he was also for two years a postdoctoral research fellow. He worked for six years for ICI as a mechanical engineer and project manager on the design, construction, and maintenance of a heavy process plant and for three years with Coopers and Lybrand as a management consultant.

Professor Turner is the author or editor of nine books, including *The Handbook of Project-based Management*, the best-selling book published by McGraw-Hill, and the *Gower Handbook of Project Management*. He is editor of the *International Journal of Project Management* (since May 1993) and has written articles for journals, conferences, and magazines. He lectures on and teaches project management worldwide.

From 1991 to 2004, Professor Turner was a member of council of the United Kingdom's Association for Project Management (APM), with two years as treasurer and two as chairman. He is now a vice president. From 1999 to 2002, he was president and then chairman of the International Project Management Association (IPMA), the global federation of national associations in project management, of which APM is the largest member. He has also helped to establish the Benelux Region of the European Construction Institute as foundation operations director. Professor Turner is director of several small to medium enterprises (SMEs) and a member of the Institute of Directors. Professor Turner is also a fellow of the Institution of Mechanical Engineers and a member of the Institute of Directors.

Turner and Müller (2004) have shown that better performance is obtained on projects if the client and contractor work together in a spirit of partnership, whereby they cooperate to achieve a mutually beneficial outcome, rather than each try to do better at the other's expense. The best results are obtained if the project is organized so that the goals of all parties are aligned and thus can work together rationally to achieve mutually consistent results. This is good practice on all projects, but where a formal contract exists between the client and the contractor, a form of contract is needed that encourages cooperative working. An approach called *partnering* is suggested to achieve this (Scott, 2001; ECI, 2003). Partnering is not appropriate on all projects, only on those where the client and contractor can both influence risk on a project and where the project involves some complexity (Turner, 2003). In other circumstances, more traditional forms are appropriate, but the parties to the contract still should work together cooperatively. This chapter describes partnering as a form of project contract management to encourage cooperative working between the client and the contractor.

I start by considering the need for cooperative working on projects but reflect how the norm has been to treat the project as a competition between client and contractor. I then discuss different attitudes toward risk sharing. Building on recent research by the European Construction Institute, I describe partnering as a form of contract to achieve cooperation where a formal contract exists between the parties. I describe the problems with traditional forms of contract and how partnering attempts to overcome those, but I also consider where partnering is appropriate or where others forms are appropriate. There are two forms of partnering, single-project partnering or alliancing and long-term or multiproject partnering. The former is where two or more parties agree to cooperate on a single project to achieve the best outcome for all on that project. The latter is where two or more parties agree to cooperate over an extended period of time to achieve performance improvements over several projects. Both forms of partnering are discussed. I define single-project partnering and describe how to establish and manage such a relationship. I then define long-term partnering and describe how to establish and manage that form of relationship. I also describe how to work toward a spirit of partnership using traditional forms of contract.

COOPERATIVE WORKING ON PROJECTS

There are two ways of viewing a project organization, what I would consider to be the correct way and the normal way, respectively:

- A temporary organization through which the owner assembles resources and motivates them in a climate of cooperation to achieve the owner's objectives
- A marketplace in which the owner tries to buy the project's outputs at the cheapest possible price in a climate of conflict with the owner's contractors and in which one is going to win and the other lose

In the more common approach, the client adopts the mind-set that he or she is going out to buy the project's outputs in the local bazaar, and he or she must negotiate hard to achieve the lowest possible price from the vendor (contractor). The negotiation is viewed as a win-lose game, in which one will gain the greatest share of a fixed cake. Therefore, a climate of conflict develops where the client and contractor try to outdo each other, and this spills over into project delivery, where the climate of mistrust continues. The client mistrusts the contractor throughout, assuming that the contractor is trying to claw back money through the project's delivery. This usually leads to a lose-lose outcome.

Turner and Müller (2003) viewed the project as a temporary organization through which a client tries to assemble resources to achieve the client's development objectives. As in any organization, the owner should view the resources working for him or her as his or her employees (albeit this will be a temporary employment relationship) and motivate the employees to achieve his or her objectives. Because it is a temporary employment relationship, the owner often will employ resources from an agency and will ask the agency (contractor) to do the work on his or her behalf. Effectively, the "employees" will be a company (contractor) rather than a person, what the Dutch would call a "legal person" rather than a "natural person." However, the owner should view these legal persons as much as his or her employees as natural persons and motivate them to achieve their project objectives.

Levitt and March (1995) say the following about the purpose of organizing:

> The problem of organizing [is] seen as one of transforming a conflict (political) system into a cooperative (rational) one. A conflict system is one in which individuals have objectives that are not jointly consistent. It organizes through exchanges and other interactions between strategic actors. A cooperative system is one in which individuals act rationally in the name of a common objective.

The aim of project organization should be to create a cooperative system in which individuals, legal persons and natural persons, work together in a rational way to achieve a common (the owner's) objective. The owner should try to motivate the contractors to achieve his or her objectives, and it is widely recognized that this is best done through a win-win game. Turner and Müller (2004) actually have shown that cooperative working on projects improves project performance; cooperative working is a necessary condition for project success. They defined cooperative working on projects as

- Having common, well-defined objectives
- Working together in a spirit of cooperation and partnership

Unfortunately, throughout the latter half of the twentieth century, the norm has been the alternative approach—to view the project as a competition in which only one party can be the victor, the contractor or the client. I can speculate why this might be. One reason is almost certainly that the client and project manager are in a principal-agent relationship (Turner and Müller, 2004; Jensen, 2000), in which the project manager has more information about project progress and the factors influencing project performance than does the client, leading to discomfort and mistrust on the latter's part. Turner and Müller (2004) have suggested communication mechanisms to reduce this discomfort. Another reason is the result of bounded rationality. Even though the project manager might like to achieve the client's objectives, through human frailty, he or she cannot do so perfectly because

- The project manager does not have perfect information about the client's requirements of project performance.
- The information the project manager does have he or she cannot process perfectly.
- The project manager cannot foretell the future and so cannot forecast all the risks and issues that will be encountered.

This leads the project manager to "satisfice"—to do what is adequate in the circumstances, not what is perfect.

Thus the aim of the project organization should be to develop a cooperative working relationship between the client and the project manager or between the client and the contractor. Where the client and project manager work for separate legal entities, the project contract is a key governance mechanism for project organization. Thus, to achieve cooperative working, we need forms of contracts that encourage it, and project partnering is one such form. However, before describing project partnering, I wish to consider how attitudes toward risk sharing on project contracts changed throughout the last two decades of the twentieth century.

RISK SHARING ON CONTRACTS

Back in the 1980s, the attitude on projects was to dump risk down the contract chain. The client dumped risk on the contractor, the contractor on the subcontractors, and the subcontractors on the material suppliers. The consequence often was that the client took risk that he or she could do something about reducing and gave it to the contractor, who would only be able to allow a contingency for it and add a profit margin on that contingency. This would contribute to the competitive project environment and conflict between client and contractor described earlier. The result was that the project usually ended up costing more than the target (Fig. 20.1, *left*). The contractor would argue that the scope of the project and risk were not perfectly defined and add variations to cover the unknowns. It was in the contractor's interest to make the variations as large as possible to increase his or her profit; the contractor's objectives were in direct conflict with those of the owner, which was to achieve the lowest possible price.

In the 1990s, the received wisdom came to be that risk should be assigned to the party best able to deal with it. This was reflected in the New Engineering Contract published in the United Kingdom by the Institution of Civil Engineers (1995). This sounded like a nice idea; each party could take responsibility for risk within its control and work to minimize it. The problem is that projects are coupled, nonlinear systems. A risk may be primarily within one party's control, but as that party tries to reduce the risk, he or she creates a bigger risk for another party (Fig. 20.2). As the client reduces his or her risk, he or she increases contractor A's risk; as contractor A reduces his or her risk, he or she increases contractor B's; and as contractor B reduces his or her risk, he or she increases the client's risk. Although each risk is primarily within one party's control, the risks are coupled and cannot be reduced independently. Thus this approach also led to conflict as each different party separately and independently tried to reduce his or her risk, often having a deleterious effect on other parties.

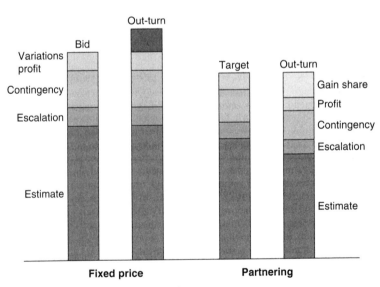

FIGURE 20.1   Project out-turn to target.

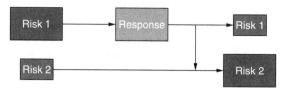

FIGURE 20.2   Coupled risks on projects.

Thus project partnering was adopted, whereby the various parties to a project form a partnership to work together to reduce the risk and overall cost of the project, sharing together in the benefit of doing this. This is illustrated in Fig. 20.1 (*right*). It is assumed that the target cost of the project is made up of several components:

- The estimate of the cost of works
- An allowance for known escalations such as inflation
- An allowance for risk contingency
- The contractor's profit as a percentage of the preceding three

The client and contractors work together in partnership to reduce these four items and thereby produce a saving, called the *gain-share pot*. This gain-share pot is then shared among all the parties, client and contractors, in proportion to their contribution. Thus, although a contractor's profit as a percentage of the estimate, escalation, and risk contingency is reduced, their overall profit is increased through the contractor's share of the gain-share pot. Thus the contractor's objectives are aligned with those of the client. If the cost to the client is reduced, the contractor's profit is increased, and vice versa. It is in everybody's interest to work together to their mutual benefit. This is the idea behind *partnering*.

TYPES OF PARTNERING

There are two types of partnering on projects:

1. *Single-project partnering* (sometimes called *alliancing*), whereby a client and one or more contractors form a partnership to undertake a single project. They work together to reduce the cost of that project. Although the focus is on the current project, a client may work with the same contractors over a sequence of projects and carry learning from one to the next to achieve improving performance over that sequence. For instance, in the United Kingdom, BAA, operator of the United Kingdom's major airports, and the oil company BP have achieved improving performance in this way.

2. *Multiproject or long-term partnering,* whereby a client enters into a preferred contractor relationship with one or more contractors to work together on the client's projects of a certain type over an extended but defined period of time (often five years) with the express aim of learning how to improve performance on that type of project.

Scott (2001) defines *single-project partnering* as

. . . a relationship between two or more companies or organizations formed with the express intent of improving performance in the delivery of projects.

The European Construction Institute (2003) defines *long-term partnering* as

> . . . the development of sustainable relationships between two or more organizations, to work in cooperation for their mutual benefit in the requisition and delivery of works, goods and/or services over a specified period to achieve continuous performance improvement.

In the next two sections I consider each of these forms of partnering in turn.

SINGLE-PROJECT PARTNERING

Why and When to Adopt Partnering

As we have already seen, partnering is adopted to overcome limitations in traditional contracting. Two of these limitations have been discussed already:

- Misalignment between the client's and the contractor's objectives
- Misalignment between the various contractors objectives

Another reason is to gain early access to contractor expertise. A problem with traditional contracting is that the construction contractor is only appointed when construction is about to start, which means that the contractor's construction expertise is not available to the design team to improve the constructability of the plant. Improving constructability can help to reduce construction costs. Under traditional contracting, the construction contractor is not appointed until the design is complete, but then it is too late to gain access to that contractor's expertise. Under a traditional contract, if the construction contractor is appointed before design is complete, during construction, the contractor will be seeking variations (see Fig. 20.1, *left*) to cover the uncertainties in the design that existed when the contractor was appointed. Under alliancing, the contractor is appointed early to help reduce the cost of construction, and the contractor's share of the gain-share pot covers the uncertainties in design that exist when the contractor is appointed.

Scott (2001) illustrates what can be achieved with partnering and alliancing (Table 20.1). The first column is the forecast cost of the project at concept stage, when most of the contractors are appointed. The second column is the estimated cost at sanction, and the third column is the outturn cost. The difference between the first and second column is primarily reductions in the cost of works from early access to contractor expertise,

TABLE 20.1   Savings from Project Partnering

Project	Concept Estimate	Sanction Value	Out-turn
Off-shore oil platform	£450 million	£373 million	£290 million
Refinery revamp		$295 million	$269 million
Plant addition	$175 million	$149 million	$133 million
Onshore terminal	£123 million	£119 million	£92 million
Off shore pipeline	£348 million	£319 million	£242 million
Hydrocracker revamp		£41 million	£39 million
FCCU revamp		£54 million	£47 million

and the difference between the second and third columns is primarily savings from reducing and eliminating risks. It is more difficult to achieve reductions in the cost of works after design freeze and sanction.

Partnering is not appropriate on every project, only where the client and the contractor can jointly control risk. In such cases, the risk usually lies both in the design of the plant and in the method of construction. Where the risk lies in the method of construction only, usually only the contractor can control that risk, and the appropriate form of contract is typically a fixed-price design-and-build type of contract. Where the risk lies in the design only, the appropriate form of contract is separate design-and-build contracts, with remeasurement payments for the build phase (Turner, 2003). Partnering also should be adopted only on projects worth more than about $15 million or £10 million. There are substantial setup costs, and the relationship requires careful management, increasing project management costs. This is only worthwhile if the potential savings are sufficiently large to cover these larger transaction costs.

Legal Considerations

Some people suggest that partnering is in violation of laws on competition. The client enters into a relationship with a construction contractor before design is complete, not giving other contractors a chance to bid fairly for the work. However, the usual interpretation is that as long as the process for appointing the contractors is fair and open, it falls within the law. In the circumstance, however, it is probably best that the appointment process be adhered to rigorously. A four-stage coached award procedure is recommended by the European Union:

Step 1: The job is widely advertised in the trade press, and a long list of potential contractors is formed.

Step 2: Those contractors are asked to submit information to judge their suitability for the work. This will cover their technical capability and financial strength but also can include their commitment to alliance working and problem-solving skills. Based on this information, a short list of prequalified contractors is formed.

Step 3: Problem-solving workshops are conducted with the contractors to brief them on the technical requirements of the work, the targets for cost reduction, and the implications for cooperative working. Contractors without the right attitude and approach may be eliminated at this stage. Contractors not willing to work in this way also may choose to withdraw from the process.

Step 4: The remaining contractors are asked to submit full proposals for the work. Workshops are held with the contractors individually to further coach them on the need for cooperative working and problem solving to achieve cost reductions and to judge their ability to do so. The contract is awarded based on this round.

Establishing and Managing the Alliance

Scott (2001) suggests a three-stage process for establishing and managing the alliance (Table 20.2). I just wish to emphasize four points:

1. *Client strategy.* Before starting the project, the client must determine that an alliance is the right approach for this project. I discussed earlier when it is appropriate. The client also must ensure that the right attitude to cooperative working exists throughout the

TABLE 20.2 Establishing and Managing an Alliance

Stage	Steps	Key issues
1. Project definition and partner selection	• Client strategy	Client decides to alliance and achieves internal alignment
	• Conceptual studies	Client conducts initial design studies
	• Appoint main design contractor	The main contractor is appointed against the conceptual studies using the coached award procedure
	• Write statement of requirements	The client and chosen contractor together write the statement of requirements
	• Appoint construction contractors and key subcontractors	Construction contractors and key subcontractors to join the alliance are appointed against the statement of requirements using the coached award procedure
	• Start systems design	The systems design is started while contractors are being appointed
2. Business case	• Complete design	The systems design is completed. The input of construction contractors is obtained.
	• Prepare sanction estimate	The sanction estimate is prepared. This also forms the basis of the target estimate from which the gain share will be calculated.
	• Obtain sanction approval	Approval to progress with the projects is obtained from the relevant authorities.
	• Finalize works contracts and alliance agreement	The works contract with each contractor and the ovrall alliance agreement are finalized.
3. Alliance	• Manage the alliance	Proceed with implementation of the project and management of the alliance.

client organization. Senior management must not say to clients, "We want to alliance," and then have junior engineers adopt traditional, confrontational approaches.

2. *Works contracts and alliance agreements.* Contractors will be appointed initially against a draft works contract and alliance agreement. This agreement cannot be finalized until sanction because the target cost cannot be agreed until sanction, and the target cost will include performance data provided by the contractors.

3. *Target cost.* The target cost against which the gain share will be calculated will be less than the sanction value by 5 to 10 percent. The difference is client contingency.

4. *Project management.* Some people think that partnering contracts will be easier to manage than traditional contracts. The client and contractors are working together in happy harmony, so it is not necessary to manage the relationship. Wrong! Maintaining the happy harmony and cooperative working requires more intensive project management than in a traditional contract.

Contracts

On an partnering project, two types of contracts are required:

1. The works contract
2. The alliance agreement

With each contractor, design contractor, construction contractor, and subcontractor, there will be a conventional works contract defining what they will do on the project. This will just be a standard works contract.

Then there will bee an alliance agreement between the client and all the contractors. They all must be covered by just one alliance agreement. This will be in the form of a charter partnership that will define

1. The objectives of the partnership
2. The gain-share agreement
3. The partnering relationships, including

   - Principles governing working relationships
   - Integrated project management
   - The partnership board
   - Dispute resolution

People may think that dispute resolution may be unnecessary, but it is very necessary to solve problems quickly to maintain the harmonious working relationships.

I have just shown how the gain share can reward contractors for cost reductions. It may be extended to cover other key performance indicators such as

- Schedule
- Safety
- First-year output from the facility or asset delivered by the project
- Availability, reliability, and maintainability of the asset

Sometimes the client and contractors form a joint-venture company to undertake the project. The joint-venture company is paid a fixed price by the client to design and construct the project, and client and contractors then share any profits according to their shareholdings. This approach was adopted for a small but highly complex part of the construction of the Betouweroute, a freight line in the Netherlands from the Port of Rotterdam to Germany.

LONG-TERM PARTNERING

Why Adopt Long-Term Partnering

The motivation behind long-term partnering is slightly different, reflecting a different genesis. Until the mid-1980s, many large companies in the process plant industry, oil companies and chemical giants, did all their own work:

- They designed and built their own plants.
- They operated their plants.
- They maintained their plants.
- They marketed and sold the products produced.

As is common with many large companies, their staff adopted restrictive and inefficient working practices.

In the late 1980s, many of these companies began to adopt the attitude that they should keep to their core business. Their core business is to make, market, and sell petroleum products or chemicals, and some went as far as saying that their core business is just to market the petroleum products or chemicals. Thus they began to outsource much of their traditional operations:

1. The design and construction of new plants were the first to be outsourced.
2. Then maintenance of plants and small retrofit projects were outsourced.
3. Then operation of the plants (under build-own-operate arrangements the company does not even need to own the plant) was outsourced.
4. And the oil giants often outsourced the operation of their filling stations.

The design and construction of a large new plant is now done using alliancing arrangements as described earlier. But this is inefficient for small retrofit projects and maintenance work. It is inefficient to go through the substantial setup costs for a single alliance on every small design job, maintenance job, or retrofit project. For very similar reasons, however, clients want to avoid confrontational working arrangements, perhaps more so on what is to be a long-term working relationship. Further, clients want to work with their contractors to achieve continual performance improvement on these small jobs. Thus long-term partnering is adopted.

The benefits the client hopes to obtain from long-term partnering are

- *Cost reduction*—lower rates, higher productivity
- *Profitability*—better returns for the contractor
- *Schedule*—better coordination of projects/work packages
- *Quality*—optimized design solutions, better reliability
- *Service*—better contractor response times
- *Safety*—better safety planning and performance
- *Reduced risk*—shared risks, better management

But there are also benefits to the contractors through stability of their turnover, allowing workforce stability and investment in improved working conditions for their staff. With predictable workload, contractors also can make more investment for the future in improved technology and staff training, delivering additional benefits to the client (win-win). Thus the reasons for adopting long-term partnering are similar but not identical to single-project partnering.

Note that long-term partnering is used both on routine work and on project work. Routine work where it is used is plant operation under build-operate-transfer (BOT) types of arrangements and online maintenance. Project work, where it is used, can be preferred contractor arrangements for small design projects, retrofit and small works–based construction projects, and scheduled shutdown maintenance and turnaround. Indeed, with retrofit projects, much of the construction will be done with the plant online, which is complex enough. However, some of the work, especially break-ins to operating plant, must be done during scheduled shutdown maintenance and turnaround, during very tight time windows, increasing risk and complexity and increasing the need for cooperative working between client and contractor. We are interested here in long-term partnering for project work.

Establishing and Managing the Partnership

There is a four-step process for establishing a long-term partnering arrangement:

Step 1: Process appraisal
Step 2: Partner selection
Step 3: Alignment
Step 4: Deployment

Process Appraisal. At this step, the client needs to understand that partnering is right for his or her business. The client needs to consider if he or she understands

- The business objectives and potential benefits
- The opportunities and threats from the environment
- The leadership and commitment required

The client also needs to ensure there is sufficient future workload to maintain the partnering arrangement.

Partner Selection. The process of partner selection is very similar to that described earlier, following the same four-step process. Key risks in this process are

- People are not committed.
- They do not understand the process.
- Threats come from the environment.

Alignment. The main aim of this step is to achieve alignment between the client and the contractors. This requires

- Alignment of objectives
- Reorganization of cultural and procedural differences
- Alignment of policy for risk management and problem solving

- Alignment of project management processes
- Agreement on the performance measures and targets

There are often two or three contracting companies as part of a long-term partnering arrangement, and this requires alignment of all of them. The client's processes will form a benchmark against which the others will be measured, but an enlightened client will recognize the need to move some way toward the contractor's current practices and not just insist that they all fall in with the client's current practices. The partnership often can form a culture of its own independent of all the participants' cultures.

Deployment.   Once the partnering arrangement is underway, several things can cause a breakdown in the relationship, including

- A focus on short-term cost reduction
- An inability to deal with setbacks
- Lack of continuity of support and participation
- Lack of meaningful feedback
- Becoming complacent with the existing relationship
- Failure of the client to deliver his or her input, leading to lack of performance by the contractors

In order to avoid this breakdown, the working of the partnering arrangement needs to be monitored. The following questions can help in this process:

1. Is the process of bringing people together into the wider organization working?
2. Are processes for measuring and monitoring in place?
3. Are the leaders of the partnering arrangement taking an interest and setting aside time to deal with specific issues?
4. Is the infrastructure managed in a way that is consistent with the partners?
5. Is an environment for learning and innovation encouraged?

COOPERATIVE WORKING WITH OTHER FORMS OF CONTRACT

Partnering arrangement are a specific form of contract to encourage cooperative working on projects between the client and the contractor, where both can make a contribution to reducing risk. As I said earlier, this will be the case where the risk is in both the design of the facility or asset to be delivered by the project and in the method of its delivery. Other, more traditional forms of contracts are appropriate on other types of projects (Turner, 2003), where either the contractor or the client alone controls the risk. However, although more traditional forms of contracts are used, this does not mean that there needs to be a return to the old, confrontational contractual relationships. The aim still should be to achieve cooperative working with shared objectives. However, this will work differently, as I shall try to explain briefly. Turner (2003) suggests that there are two dimensions to a project contract to encourage cooperative working:

1. The *ex ante* incentive arrangements to incentivize the contractor to deliver the client's objectives, appropriately compensating the contractor for the risk he or she bears. If the contractor bears little risk, then he or she needs little additional reward. However, if the

contractor bears higher risk, he or she should be rewarded appropriately, though this can be reduced if the client builds in a safeguard.

2. The *ex post* governance arrangements to encourage cooperative working and joint problem solving to deal with risks, both foreseen and unforeseen, as they occur. Additional rewards may be required to deal with unforeseen risks, but if cooperative working is encouraged, these can be agreed on in a way that rewards the contractor appropriately but encourages him or her to continue to achieve the client's objectives.

Contractor Controls the Risk

The contractor alone will control the risk if the risk lies mainly in the method of delivering the project. In this case, a fixed-price design-and-build type of contract is appropriate. The contractor should be left alone to solve the problems on the project. In this case, the client often can get a cheaper price than with a cost-plus or remeasurement type of contract, but if the contractor is left alone to solve the problems, he or she can reduce the cost of the project to achieve good profit margins. However, safeguards should be built in to compensate the contractor if any totally unforeseen risks occur. Unforeseen risks remain the client's responsibility. Also, although the client should leave the contractor to solve his or her own problems and not interfere, the client should maintain an open-door policy so that he or she is available if the contractor needs to speak to him or her. The contractor may have two equally preferred options and want to see which suits the client better, or some risks may occur that the client is better able to deal with.

If there is more than one contractor involved in the project, then the contractors should form a joint venture, consortium, or partnership so that they can share the risk and work together to eliminate it.

Client Controls the Risk

The client will control the risk if it mainly lies in the design of the asset to be delivered by the project. In this case, it is best to divide the project into a design and construction phases. The design project will be undertaken by a design consultant on a time-and-materials or target-price basis. The construction contract should start only when the design is complete, or else the risk becomes shared, and a partnering arrangement should be adopted. The construction work typically is done on a remeasurement basis, but this is effectively fixed price if the design is complete when construction starts. As mentioned earlier, safeguards should be built into the contract to deal with any unforeseen risks, and although joint problem solving should not be necessary during construction, processes should be built into the contract should they be needed.

CONCLUDING REMARK

In this chapter I have mainly discussed projects where the project work is done by an external contractor. On all projects, however, whether done by an external contractor or internal staff, you should encourage cooperative working between the client or sponsor and contractor or project manager. Cooperative working on projects is a *necessary condition* for project success. Without it, the project *will fail.* Every project should be viewed as a partnership between all the project participants, where they work together rationally to achieve mutually consistent objectives. Project partnering is a form of contract that helps to achieve this where the client and an external contractor both control the risk and must work together to reduce it.

REFERENCES

European Construction Iinstitute (ECI). 2003. *Long-Term Partnering: Achieving Continuous Improvement and Value.* Loughborough, UK: European Construction Institute.

Institution of Civil Engineers. 1995. *The Engineering and Construction Contract,* 2d ed. London: Thomas Telford.

Jensen MC. 2000. *The Theory of the Firm: Governance, Residual Claims, and Organizational Forms.* Cambridge, MA: Harvard University Press.

Levitt B, March JG. 1995. Chester I Barnard and the intelligence of learning, in OE Williamson (ed.), *Organization Theory: From Chester Barnard to the Present and Beyond,* exp. ed. New York: Oxford University Press.

Scott R (ed.). 2001. *Partnering in Europe: Incentive-Based Alliancing for Projects.* London: Thomas Telford.

Turner JR. 2003. Farsighted project contract management, in JR Turner (ed.), *Contracting for Project Management.* Aldershott, UK: Gower.

Turner JR, Müller R. 2003. On the nature of projects as temporary organizations. *Int J Project Manag* 21(1):1–8.

Turner JR, Müller R. 2004. Communication and cooperation on projects between the project owner as principal and the project manager as agent. *Eur Manag J* 22(3):327–336.

CHAPTER 21

BUSINESS PROCESS MANAGEMENT IN THE PROJECT-ORIENTED COMPANY

Roland Gareis

Vienna University of Economics and Business Administration, Vienna, Austria

Michael Stummer

Roland Gareis Consulting, Vienna, Austria

Roland Gareis holds an MBA and a Ph.D. He was a Fullbright scholar at the University of California, Los Angeles, in 1976, professor for construction management at the Georgia Institute of Technology, Atlanta, and visiting professor at the Georgia State University, ETH in Zürich, Switzerland, and the University of Quebec in Montreal, Canada. Since 1983, he has been the director of the postgraduate program "International Project Management" at the Vienna University of Business Administration. For 15 years he was president of Project Management Austria, the Austrian project management association; he was project manager of the 10th Internet World Congress on Project Management and manager of the research program "Crisis Management." Currently, he is professor of project management at the Vienna University of Economics and Business Administration, manager of the global research program "Project Orientation (International)," and owner of Roland Gareis Consulting. He has published several books and papers on management of the project-oriented company.

Michael Stummer is trainer and consultant in project and program management, business process management, and organization for Roland Gareis Consulting and is trainer in the postgraduate program "International Project Management" at the University of Economics and Business Administration and the Technical University Vienna. He is an authorized representative and responsible for controlling of Roland Gareis Consulting. Since 2002, he has been a board member of Project Management Austria. He graduated from the University of Economics and Business Administration, Vienna, and the postgraduate program "International Project Management" at the University of Economics and Business Administration and the Technical University Vienna. He is certified as a project manager through Project Management Austria, and he has experience as a project manager of information technology (IT), organization, research, and product development projects.

ABSTRACT

A *business process* is a sequence of tasks with defined objectives and a defined start and end event. The success of a project not only depends on performing project management professionally but also on fulfilling the contents-related business processes of the project successfully. Therefore, professional macro and micro business process management is required in the project-oriented company.

The quality of important business processes can be considered explicitly in the project portfolio score card. Business process management should become an additional dimension in the maturity model of the project-oriented (and process-oriented) company.

Business processes are objects of consideration in projects and programs. Therefore, competencies to design the organizational structures and the business processes are required in projects and programs.

BUSINESS PROCESSES AND ORGANIZATIONS FOR THEIR FULFILMENT

Business Process: Definition

A *business process* is a sequence of tasks with defined objectives and a defined start and end event. Elements of a business process are tasks, decisions, and their relations. It is fulfilled by different roles of one or more organizations. A business process runs "horizontally" through organizations (Fig. 21.1).

Business processes can be differentiated into primary, secondary, and tertiary processes. *Primary* business processes are those which contribute primarily to fulfilment of the purpose of the company. Primary business processes are characterized by direct relations to the clients, for example, when developing an offer or processing an order. *Secondary* business processes, such as launching a new product, provide direct support for the primary processes. *Tertiary* business processes, such as strategic planning, have no direct relations

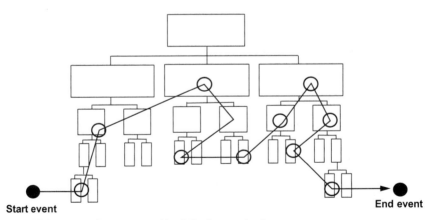

Start event

End event

FIGURE 21.1   A business process with a defined start and end event.

to the clients. "The distinction between the business processes is fluid. Depending on the nature and services/products of an organization, a specific business process can be a primary process in one company and a secondary process in another company" (Schmelzer, 2004, p. 52).

Also, a differentiation criterion for business processes is the degree of repetition. It is possible to distinguish between unique and repetitive business processes. Examples of unique business processes are the merging of two companies, developing a new market, etc. Examples of repetitive business processes are preparing a standard quotation, issuing an invoice, etc.

Organizations for the Fulfillment of Business Processes

The fulfillment of routine business processes of a company is carried out by the roles of the permanent organization or by working groups. For unique business processes of large scope, temporary organizations are required in addition to the permanent structures. A *project* is a temporary organization for the performance of a relatively unique, short- to medium-term, strategically important business process of medium or large scope. A *program* is a temporary organization to fulfill a unique and long-term business process of large scope (Fig. 21.2).

Investments are long-term capital commitments in assets, for example, in machines or buildings, but also in customer relations, in products, in the organization, or in personnel. Several business processes are combined in an investment life cycle. For example, an investment in an industrial plant combines the business processes "preparation of a feasibility study," "preparation of a concept," "engineering, procurement, and construction," "use of the plant," "maintenance," and "decommissioning."

Characteristics of business processes	Scale		
Frequency	continuously	uniquely	uniquely
Duration	short term	short, medium term	medium-, long term
Importance	low	medium – high	high
Scope	small	medium – large	large
Resource demand	low	medium	high
Costs	low – medium	medium – high	high
Companies involved	few	several - many	many
	↓	↓	↓
Organisation form	Permanent organisation / Working group	Project	Programme
	↓	↓	↓
Management approach	Business process management	Project management	Programme management

FIGURE 21.2 Organizations for the fulfillment of different business processes.

FIGURE 21.3   Segmenting an investment through projects.

Investments can be initialized by a project or by a program. If several projects or programs are to be performed, they segment the investment life cycle (Fig. 21.3).

BUSINESS PROCESS MANAGEMENT (BPM): AN OVERVIEW

Business Process Management: Objectives

The history of business process management is closely linked to a new management paradigm that manifests itself in relatively new management approaches such as quality management, lean management, continuous improvement, and business process reengineering. This "new" management paradigm has the following characteristics:

- Organization considered as a competitive advantage
- Concentration on core competencies
- Process orientation
- Teamwork
- Empowerment
- Customer orientation
- Networking
- (Dis)continuous change

In addition to the professionalism in fulfilling project management, the success of projects is influenced by the "maturity" in the fulfillment of the business processes required to achieve the project objectives. Thus the results of the project "plant construction" depend on the fulfillment of the business processes "engineering," "procurement," "installation," etc. The basis for the professional fulfillment of these business processes is created through business process management.

Business process management focuses on repetitive business processes. The objectives of business process management are to increase the organizational efficiency, to promote organizational learning, and to promote personnel development.

Macro Business Process Management

The tasks of business process management can be divided up into macro business process management and micro business process management. The objectives of *macro* business process management are the identification of business processes, the determination of interrelations between the business processes, and the definition of strategies for the management of the interrelations. In addition, the organization for business processes management is defined. Business process owners are identified, and business process management standards (e.g., methods, templates, IT support, etc. for business process management) are defined.

Methods applied in the macro business process management are the business process map, chains of business processes, and networks of business processes. Macro business process management provides the basis for micro business process management.

An example of a business process map of a training and consulting company is presented in Fig. 21.4. The business processes represented by boxes with dark frames (e.g., performing a consulting service or organizing an event) might require a project organization for their performance.

Micro Business Process Management

The objective of micro business management is the description of single business processes. The start and the end events of the business process are defined, its context is described, the tasks of the process are identified and structured, the process flow is illustrated, and the organization for the fulfillment of the business process is designed. Business process ratios in terms of time, quality, and costs are defined as the basis for the controlling of the business process.

Methods applied in micro business process management are process structure plans, process flowcharts, process responsibility charts, and process ratios. Examples of the definition of the objectives of a business process, of a business process structure, and of a business process responsibility chart for the business process "organizing a seminar" are shown in Fig. 21.5 and Tables 21.1 and 21.2.

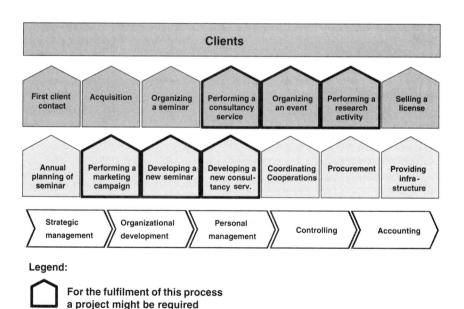

FIGURE 21.4 Business process map of a training and consulting company.

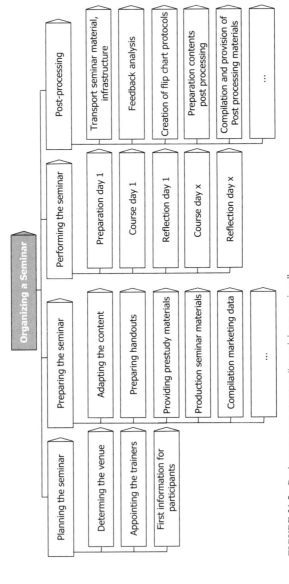

FIGURE 21.5 Business process structure "organizing a seminar."

TABLE 21.1 Objectives of the Business Process "Organizing a Seminar "

Start	Decision to Perform the Seminar	End	Seminar Documentation Filed	Duration	5–6 Weeks
Objectives	Professional seminar organization				
	Positive feedback by seminar participants				
	Generation of a profit				
	Information to participants about additional services, products				
Non-Objectives					
Results	Seminar documentation filed				

IDENTIFICATION AND DESCRIPTION OF BUSINESS PROCESSES IN THE PROJECT-ORIENTED COMPANY

In macro business process management, the business processes of the project-oriented company have to be identified. Overall business processes that might require a project or even a program for their fulfilment have to be further broken down into single business processes, which then can be described. The primary business processes that can be identified depend on the line of business the company is in. The secondary and tertiary business processes are similar for many companies because all of them have to perform such management processes as strategic planning, personnel management, etc.

There are business processes at different levels of detail. *Overall* or *major* business processes include several single business processes. Because of different start and end events, different objectives, and different organizational responsibilities of the single

TABLE 21.2 Business Process Responsibility Chart "Organizing a Seminar"

	RGC Seminar Management	RGC Back Office	RGC Accounting	RGC Trainers	Seminar Participants	Hotel/Catering	Courier Service
1.1 Planning the seminar							
1.1.1 Determing the venue	P					C	
1.1.2 Appointing the trainers	P			C			
1.1.3 First information for participants	M	Pr		I	I		
1.2 Preparing the seminar							
1.2.1 Adapting the content	I			P			
1.2.2 Preparing handouts	M	P		C			
1.2.3 Provide pre-study materials	M	P			I		
... ...							

Note: p = performin; c = cooperatin; m = managin; i = informe business processes, the description should be done at the level of single business processes. As an example, the *overall* business process of an IT company "implementing an IT application" may include the single business processes of analyzing, designing, programming, testing, and going live with an IT application.

By standardizing each of theses single business processes, that is, defining the sequence of the tasks, the responsibilities for the performance, and the methods to be applied, the efficiency in projects can be improved. The way of performing these processes does not have to be defined in each project again and again. The wheel is invented only once.

BUSINESS PROCESS MANAGEMENT, PROJECT AND PROGRAM MANAGEMENT

Project Management and Program Management: Business Processes of the Project-Oriented Company

Project management and program management are specific business processes of the project-oriented company (see Chaps. 2 and 7). Both processes are divided into the subprocesses start, continuous coordination, controlling, resolution of a discontinuity, and closedown.

The processes overall, as well as the subprocesses, are to be described. The advantage of applying business process management to the project management and the program management processes is the explicit definition of the objectives, tasks and responsibilities of these processes, and definition of the methods to be used for project and program management.

Business Processes as Objects of Consideration in Projects and Programs

Traditionally, project management is applied for technical projects in the construction, engineering, and IT industries. Recently, new types of projects and programs, such as organizational projects and marketing projects, have gained importance. Examples of organizational projects are the founding of a company or the reorganization of a division. For these project types, the organizational structures (i.e., roles, organizational chart, organizational rules, responsibilities matrices, and communication structures) and the business processes become objects of consideration. Therefore, competencies to design the organizational structures and the business processes are required.

To ensure integrated solutions, it is also necessary to consider business processes as objects of consideration in traditional projects and programs. There are no "pure" technical projects, but in any construction, engineering, and IT project organizational design measures also are required. Thus, for example, the successful completion of an industrial plant construction project presupposes not only the technical solution but also organizational solutions, such as definition of the operation and maintenance business processes.

Process-Oriented Structuring of Projects

The work-breakdown structures (WBS) and consequently the schedules and cost plan of projects should be structured in a process-oriented way—not in an object-oriented way.

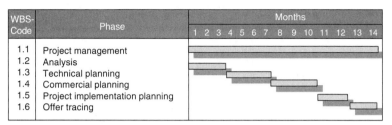

WBS-Code	Phase	Months 1 2 3 4 5 6 7 8 9 10 11 12 13 14
1.1	Project management	
1.2	Analysis	
1.3	Technical planning	
1.4	Commercial planning	
1.5	Project implementation planning	
1.6	Offer tracing	

FIGURE 21.6   Bar chart based on a process-oriented structuring of an offer-development project.

A bar chart based on a process-oriented structuring of an offer-development project is shown in Fig. 21.6.

The process-oriented structuring of projects contributes to professional project management by

- Ensuring an integrated perception of projects that involves different organizations of one or more companies
- Ensuring the completeness of the work breakdown structure because of the application of a chronological way of thinking when structuring the project
- Providing a basis for the comparison of planned versus actual data in project control because the actual data, for example, the cost data, occur according to the process of performing work packages
- Providing a possibility for standardizing project plans according to a common process-oriented structure because the processes in, for example, a construction project are constant and the objects of consideration are changing (e.g., in a school building project versus an office building project).

Standard project plans contribute to the organizational learning of the project-oriented company. Project plans that are capable of standardization are, for example, work breakdown structures, work package specifications, and milestone plans.

Definition of Program-Specific Business Processes

Because of the uniqueness of programs, some business processes to be performed are not defined and described yet. The definition and description of these business processes therefore must be done within the program. Often these business processes are applied more than once in the program. Therefore, corresponding standards can be created. The development of standards contributes to organizational learning in the program. These standards also constitute a central instrument for the integration of the projects in the program.

For program-specific business processes, temporary business process owners must be defined. As a member of the program team, the process owners are responsible for the design and implementation of the business processes in the program and for quality control regarding performance of the business processes. Figure 21.7 shows the role of the business process owner in the program organization.

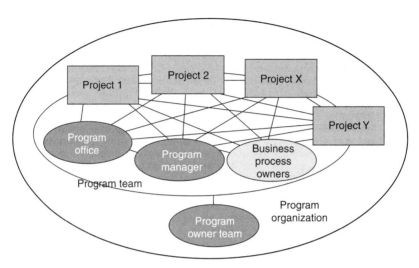

FIGURE 21.7   The role of the business process owners in the program organization.

BUSINESS PROCESS MANAGEMENT AND PROJECT PORTFOLIO MANAGEMENT

Business processes of project portfolio management include assignment of a project or a program, coordination of the project portfolio, and networking between projects (see Chap. 7). These project portfolio management processes, as well as the control of an investment (initiated through a project or a program), are the context of the project management and program management processes. The relationships between these business processes are shown in Fig. 21.8. This graphic presentation of chains of business processes promotes appropriate management of the relationships between the business processes (e.g., transfer of knowledge from the assignment process into the project start process).

A central instrument for project portfolio coordination is the project portfolio score card (see Chap. 7). Based on the aggregated view of all projects and programs held by the project-oriented company at any point in time, it is possible to draw conclusions regarding the quality of the underlying business processes. If, for example, the relationships to suppliers do not score favorably, the underlying procurement process might not be fulfilled appropriately. If required, optimization measures can be defined for the business process.

An explicit consideration of the quality of business processes of a project-oriented company is possible if the project portfolio score card of Jankulik and Piff is applied (see Chap. 19). In this model, the business processes "project management," "engineering," "procurement/logistics," "assembly/supervision," "initial operation/training," and "pilot operation of contracting projects" of an engineering construction company are scored (Fig. 21.9). Interventions by the project portfolio group for the improvement of single business processes are possible.

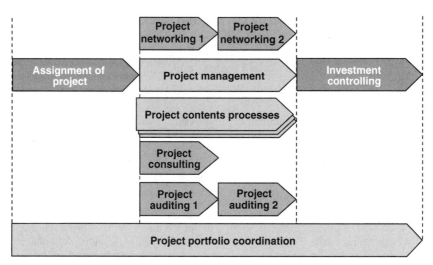

FIGURE 21.8   The project portfolio management processes as context of the project management and program management processes.

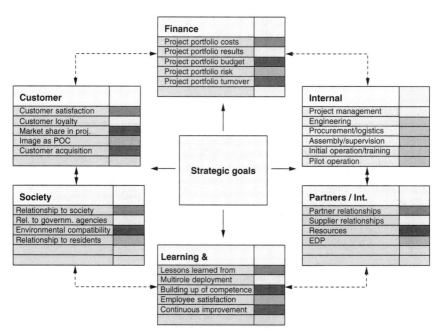

FIGURE 21.9   Project portfolio score card of an engineering construction company.

ORGANIZATIONAL DESIGN OF THE PROCESS- AND PROJECT-ORIENTED COMPANY

Organizational Structure of the Process- and Project-Oriented Company

In the process- and project-oriented company, both the process orientation and the project orientation have consequences in the organizational structure. Permanent roles for business process management are the business process owners and the business process management office. Business process management teams can be defined temporarily to support the business process owners in defining and controlling the business processes. The business process management office basically performs the tasks of macro business process management; that is, it provides standards for the definition and control of single business processes, develops the map of business processes, etc.

A central role in the management of a business process is that of the process owner (Table 21.3). The process owner is responsible for the micro business process management of his or her business process. This includes tasks such as the initial definition and structuring as well as the control and optimization of the business process.

A business process management office is a service organization in the process-oriented company and is responsible for the macro business process management, as well as for supporting the process owner in the micro business process management. Concrete duties of the business process management office are

- Identification and delimitation of business processes
- Preparation of a business process map
- Establishing of standards for micro business process management
- Organizing for training in business process management
- Supporting the process owners through coaching

The business process management office is also responsible for the infrastructure (e.g., IT tools) for business process management.

TABLE 21.3   Role Description of the Business Process Owner

Objectives
- Responsible for process organization (process documentation, process improvement)
- Coordination with other processes
- Nonobjective: Performance of a process

Organizational position
- Reports to the managing director

Tasks
- Process documentation
- Analysis of improvement potential in processes (together with the employees responsible for process execution)
- Accomplishment of optimizations
- Integration of the optimized process into the organization handbook
- Communication of change to the employee responsible for process execution

Authority
- Decision for process design (together with the managing director)

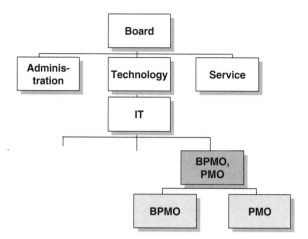

FIGURE 21.10 Integration of the business process management office and the project management office in an Austrian telecommunications company.

Permanent roles in order to ensure quality regarding the project orientation in a company are the expert pools, the project portfolio group, and the project management office (see Chap. 18). The projects and programs constitute temporary organizations.

In order to integrate the tasks of the business process management office and the project management office, these two permanent organizations can be merged. An integrated business process management/project management office bundles the competencies and responsibilities for both management dimensions. In this way, it can be ensured that the interrelations between the business process management and project and program management are given sufficient consideration and are managed in an optimal form. An example of such an integrated office is shown in Fig. 21.10, representing a part of an organizational chart of an Austrian telecommunications company.

CONSEQUENCES FOR PERSONNEL MANAGEMENT IN THE PROCESS- AND PROJECT-ORIENTED COMPANY

In addition to the organizational consequences, personnel consequences also result from perceiving a company as being process and project oriented. The consideration of business processes in projects and programs requires additional competences of project and program managers in business process management. This requirement leads to adaptions of the role descriptions and job profiles of project and program managers.

In order to develop the process management competencies of project personnel, the training programs and certification programs of process- and project-oriented companies have to be adapted.

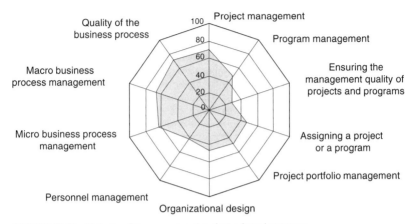

FIGURE 21.11   Maturity of the process- and project-oriented company.

MATURITY MODEL OF THE PROCESS- AND PROJECT-ORIENTED COMPANY

In Chap. 18 and 22, the maturity model of the project-oriented company is introduced. This model can be further developed in order to consider dimensions of business process management in addition to the dimensions of project, program, and project portfolio management. The dimensions representing the project orientation of the company are project management, program management, ensuring the management quality of projects and programs, assigning a project or a program, and project portfolio management. Additional dimensions representing the process orientation of the company are macro business process management, micro business process management, and the quality of the business processes. Dimensions that relate to the project orientation as well as to the process orientation are the organizational design and personnel management.

In the spiderweb presentation of the maturity model of the process- and project-oriented company, the maturities of each dimension, as well as the overall maturity visualized by the area in the spiderweb, can be seen (Fig. 21.11). Thus the maturity of the process- and project-oriented company is measurable. The maturity at an analysis date can be used as a basis for the definition of further development measures.

BIBLIOGRAPHY

Gareis, R. 2004. *Happy Projects!* Vienna: Manz.

Gareis R, Stummer M. 2006. *Geschäftsprozessmanagement: Projekt- und prozessorientiertes Unternehmen.* Vienna: Manz.

Jankulik E, Kuhlang P, Piff R. 2005. *Projektmanagement und Prozessmessung.* Erlanger: Publicis Corporate Publishing.

Schmelzer H, Sesselmann W. 2004. *Geschäftsprozessmanagement in der Praxis.* Munich: Hanser Wirtschaft.

Stummer M. 2000. *Organisational Learning by Documentations.* London: IPMA.

Willke H. 1996. *Systemtheorie II: Interventionstheorie.* Stuttgart: Lucius and Lucius.

P · A · R · T · 5

NATIONAL PROJECT MANAGEMENT

In Chapter 22, Roland Gareis and Claudia Gruber analyze Austria as a project-oriented nation. The results of a recent research project regarding the practices of some 60 Austrian project-oriented companies in project management, program management and project portfolio management as well as the project management related services of education, research and marketing institutions are described.

In Chapter 23, Dong, Chuah and Zhai introduce the reader to the state of project management and project management practices in China. Comparisons are drawn between China's and the United States' management styles, and show how project management is more important than ever in China. The results of a large-scale empirical study of information system management in China are also presented.

In Chapter 24, Kooyman details the rise of project management in Australia, from its birth and development to the present day state. Several recent major projects in Australia are presented, along with an analysis of projects within the construction and IT industries. Finally, Kooyman offers suggestions for the future of project management in Australia.

In Chapter 25, the political, economic and business sectors of Romania, along with their relation to Romania's project management industry, are discussed. Bodea also presents industry-specific limitations to growth that exist in Romania. The increasing importance of projects within Romania is discussed, along with possibilities for the future of projects and project management in Romania.

Chapter 26 outlines global project management in Japan. An overview of the status of global projects is given, along with a summary of the differences between Japanese and Western styles of project management. Tanaka places emphasis on engineering and construction projects in Japan, and ways of incorporating multicultural viewpoints of project management are also discussed.

CHAPTER 22

PROJECT MANAGEMENT IN AUSTRIA: ANALYSIS OF THE MATURITY OF AUSTRIA AS A PROJECT-ORIENTED NATION

Roland Gareis

Vienna University of Economics and Business Administration,
Vienna, Austria

Claudia Gruber

Vienna University of Economics and Business Administration,
Vienna, Austria

Roland Gareis holds an MBA and a Ph.D. He was a Fullbright scholar at the University of California, Los Angeles, in 1976, professor for construction management at the Georgia Institute of Technology, Atlanta, and visiting professor at the Georgia State University, ETH in Zürich, Switzerland, and the University of Quebec in Montreal, Canada. Since 1983, he has been the director of the postgraduate program "International Project Management" at the Vienna University of Business Administration. For 15 years he was president of Project Management Austria, the Austrian project management association, and he was project manager of the 10th Internet World Congress on Project Management and manager of the research program "Crisis Management." Currently, he is professor of project management at the Vienna University of Economics and Business Administration, manager of the global research program "Project Orientation (International)," and owner of Roland Gareis Consulting. He has published several books and papers on management of the project-oriented company.

Claudia Gruber studied at the Vienna University of Economics and Business Administration and holds a graduate degree. After her studies, she completed the postgraduate program "International Project Management" (Vienna) and the CEMS MIM Post-Graduate Program (Barcelona, Vienna). Between September 2002 and August 2005, she worked as a research assistant at the Projektmanagement Group (Vienna University of Economics and Business Administration). There she got experience as a project manager on various marketing and research projects. Between January 2004 and August 2005, she was project manager of the research project "Project Orientation (Austria)." In 2005, she worked as an assessor for the IPMA International Project Management Award. Currently, she is writing her Ph.D. thesis on the topic "Maturity Models in the Context of Project Management" in Barcelona and working as a network partner for the Roland Gareis Consulting.

ABSTRACT

A nation that applies projects and programs as temporary organizations to perform relatively unique processes of medium or large scope can be perceived as a project-oriented nation (PON). The maturity of a project-oriented nation can be analyzed by considering the practices of its project-oriented companies and industries, as well as by examining its project management-related services such as education, consulting, research, and marketing institutions. For analyzing and benchmarking the maturities of companies, industries, and nations, a "family" of project-orientation maturity models developed by the Projektmanagement Group was used. In the research project "Project Orientation (Austria)," which was conducted from January 2004 to July 2005, sixty Austrian project-oriented companies in six project-oriented industries were analyzed and benchmarked, and a final analysis of Austria as a project-oriented nation was carried out. Based on the results, strategies for the further development of the maturities of project-oriented companies, project-oriented industries, and Austria as a project-oriented nation were developed.

THE RESEARCH PROJECT "PROJECT ORIENTATION (AUSTRIA)"

Context of the Research Project

Between 1999 and 2002, the Projektmanagement Group of the University of Economics and Business Administration, Vienna, and the International Project Management Association (IPMA) conducted the research initiative "Project-Oriented Society (POS)," with the objectives to develop a maturity model of the POS, to analyze the competences of POSs, and to develop strategies for the further development of POSs. The research emphasis was on the generation of hypotheses and the development of models regarding the POS.

In the "POS Conception Project," the model of the POS was constructed, and dimensions for the description of a POS were defined. Based on these conceptual results, the project "POS Benchmarking" was performed. The objectives of this project were to analyze and benchmark the competencies of Austria, Denmark, Hungary, Ireland, Latvia, the Moscow region, Norway, Romania, Sweden, and the United Kingdom.

Structures of the Research Project "Project Orientation (Austria)"

The objectives of the research project "Project Orientation (Austria)" that was conducted from January 2004 to July 2005 were

- To analyze and benchmark the maturities of about 60 Austrian project-oriented companies (POCs)
- To analyze and benchmark the maturities of about five project-oriented industries
- To analyze the maturity of Austria as a project-oriented nation
- To develop strategies and measures for further development of the maturities of the project-oriented companies and of Austria as a project-oriented nation
- To present and publish the research results at conferences and in journals

The project was partly financed by the Jubiläumsfonds of the Austrian National Bank.

General Information about Austria

Austria is a federal state with a total area of 32,368 square miles (83,858 sqare kilometers) and is situated in south central Europe. It has a population of about 8 million, and 98 percent of Austria's population is German-speaking. Austria has a well-developed market economy and a high standard of living and is closely tied to other European Union economies, mainly Germany's. The Austrian's economy features up-to-date industrial and agricultural sectors. Timber is a key industry, 47 percent of the land being forested. Membership in the European Union has drawn an influence on foreign investors attracted by Austria's access to the single European market and its proximity to the new EU economies. Austria is the fourth richest country within the European Union, having a gross domestic product (GDP) per capita of approximately US$33,000, with Luxemburg, Ireland, and Denmark leading the list (see www.austria.org or www. nationmaster.com/country/au/economy).

Analyzing and Benchmarking Process

The process of analyzing project-oriented companies and project-oriented industries is shown in Fig. 22.1. At the beginning of the analysis, a briefing workshop with representatives of project-oriented companies (head of a project management office, project managers, project owners, etc.) took place. There the analyzing process, the maturity model of the project-oriented company, and the questionnaire were explained by the research team. Then at least five representatives of each project-oriented company carried out a self-analysis. The questionnaires were filled out in groups in moderated analysis workshops. In an external analysis, relevant documents, such as project management templates, project and program management guidelines, project management documents of two to three projects, etc., were analyzed by the research team.

In order to analyze and benchmark project-oriented industries, the average maturities of the companies belonging to different project-oriented industries were calculated. In a workshop "Benchmarking Project-Oriented Industries," representatives of the analyzed

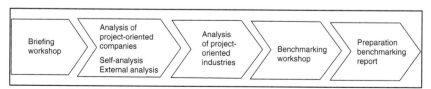

FIGURE 22.1   Analyzing and benchmarking process.

companies benchmarked the industry results. Based on these analyses and benchmarking activities, benchmarking reports were written for each project-oriented company analyzed. More detailed project results are described later in this chapter.

MATURITY MODEL OF THE PROJECT-ORIENTED COMPANY (MM-POC)

A company or a part of a company, such as a division or a profit center, that applies projects and programs as temporary organizations to perform relatively unique business processes of medium or large scope can be perceived as a *project-oriented company*. Project-oriented companies have specific strategies, specific organizational structures, and specific cultures for managing projects, programs, and project portfolios. The organizational competencies of the project-oriented company can be analyzed with the maturity model of the project-oriented company.

To analyze a project-oriented company, the maturity model includes the following dimensions:

- Project management
- Program management
- Assurance of the management quality of projects and programs
- Assignment of a project or program
- Project portfolio coordination and networking between projects
- Organizational design of the POC
- Personnel management in the POC
- Business process management in the POC

These dimensions are described briefly below:

Project management. A *project* is a temporary organization for the performance of a relatively unique, short- to medium-term, strategically important business process of medium or large scope. Project management is a business process of the project-oriented company. The project management process starts with project assignment and ends with project approval by the project owner. It consists of the subprocesses project start, project coordination, project control, project closedown, and possibly the resolution of a project discontinuity.

Program management. A *program* is a temporary organization for the fulfillment of a unique business process of large scope. In a program, a set of projects and tasks is closely coupled by common objectives. Programs are limited as to time and budget. Program management is a business process of the project-oriented organization. The program management process consists of the subprocesses program start, program coordination, program control, program close-down, and possibly the resolution of a program discontinuity.

Assurance of the management quality of projects and programs. Management consulting and management auditing can be performed in order to ensure the management quality of projects and programs.

Assignment of a project or program. In the process of assigning, the decisions as to whether or not an investment is undertaken and what is the appropriate organization to initialize the investment (project or program) are made.

Project portfolio coordination and networking between projects. A project portfolio is a set of projects (and programs) that is performed by a project-oriented company at a certain point in time. A project portfolio is more than the sum of its projects because it also considers the relationships between the projects. A project portfolio database is the basis for project portfolio management. Project portfolio reports can be used to decide if new projects should be started and to establish priorities among projects. The objective of project portfolio coordination is to optimize the results of the project portfolio. In project portfolio coordination, priorities between projects are set, and a coordination of the internal and external resources is made.

Organizational design of the POC. In order to integrate different projects and programs performed simultaneously, a POC has specific integrative organizational structures, such as project management offices, project portfolio groups, and expert pools. Further specific integrative tools such as project and program management procedures and standard project plans exist. In the organizational chart of a project-oriented company, the specific permanent organizations, as well as temporary organizations, can be visualized.

Personnel management in the POC. This dimension includes the recruiting, disposition, and (continuous) development of project personnel, such as the project or program owner, the project or program manager, project team members, project contributors, etc. In a project-oriented company, a project management career path and project management certification might exist.

Business process management. A business process is a clearly defined sequence of tasks in which several roles of one or more organizations are involved. Primary processes, secondary processes, and tertiary processes can be differentiated.

The maturity model of the project-oriented company describes each of the dimensions and operationalizes them through a set of questions. The number of questions per dimension is shown in the graphic presentation of the maturity model as a spiderweb in Figure 22.2. In total, the questionnaire consists of 74 questions and is based on Roland Gareis' *Management of the Project-oriented Company.*

Examples of questions to analyze the maturity of the POC are shown in Tables 22.1 and 22.2. The following assumptions have to be made:

Always	90–100%
Often	60–90%
Sometimes	30–60%
Seldom	10–30%
Never	0–10%

A POC maturity ratio can be calculated. It is a weighted sum of the maturities of the different dimensions. Since "project management" is considered to be the most important dimension, this dimension has a weight of 20 percent. The dimensions "assignment of a project or program" and "organizational design of the POC" are weighted at 15 percent, and the rest, at 10 percent.

The single questions in each dimension are equally weighted. If, for example, a question block consists of five questions, each question will be weighted at 20 percent.

MATURITY MODEL OF THE PROJECT-ORIENTED NATION (MM-PON)

Nations that use projects and programs regularly as temporary organizations can be perceived as *project-oriented nations* (PONs). The perception of a nation as a PON is a construction; it requires the observation of a nation with a specific "pair of glasses"—the glasses of project orientation.

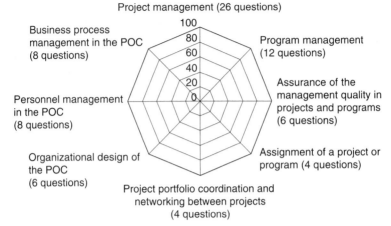

FIGURE 22.2   Number of questions for each dimension of the maturity model of the project-oriented company (POC).

Nations are becoming more project-oriented. Projects and programs are applied by different industries but also by new areas such as nonprofit organizations, associations, small municipalities, schools, and even families. Project and program management are not just a microeconomic but also a macroeconomic concern (Gareis, 2002 p. 28).

The maturity model of the project-oriented nation is based on the maturity model of the project-oriented company. The model considers the practice dimensions of project-oriented companies (practices in project management, program management, etc.), where the practice dimensions "assignment of a project or program" and "project portfolio coordination and networking between projects" are summarized in the dimension "project portfolio management." Further dimensions of project management–related services offered by education, consulting, research, and marketing institutions are considered.

Figure 22.3 shows the maturity model of the project-oriented nation with the dimensions of the practices of project-oriented companies and the project management–related services. The dimensions referring to the project management–related services of institutions are described briefly below:

Project management education and consulting services. Formal project management education programs are provided by different institutions, such as colleges, universities, and

TABLE 22.1   Example of a Question of the Dimension "Project Management"

A 1.1. In the project start process the following methods are used for project planning		
	External Projects	Internal Projects
Project objectives plan		
Work-breakdown structure		
Work package specifications		
Project milestone plan		
Project bar chart		
CPM schedule		

1 = always; 2 = often; 3 = sometimes; 4 = seldom; 5 = never.

TABLE 22.2   Example of a Question of the Dimension "Organizational Design of the POC"

F 2. Organizational processes of the project-oriented company

Mentioning the "project orientation" in the mission statement of the project-oriented company
Formal description of the business processes "project management" and "program management"
Formal description of the business process "assignment of a project or program"
Formal description of the business processes "project portfolio coordination" and "networking of
  projects"
Project and program management templates
Project portfolio coordination templates
Standard project plans for different project types
Project and program management marketing instruments (project management brochure, PM office
  homepage)

1 = continually optimized; 2 = very relevant; 3 = limited relevance; 4 = existing informally; 5 = not existing.

consulting organizations, and might lead to academic degrees in project management. The project management approach taught and the number of courses offered vary in different programs.

Project management research services. Project management–related research projects and programs, project management–related publications, and research events are services provided by research institutions. There might be specific national funds dedicated to project management research.

Project management marketing services. Project management marketing institutions in a project-oriented nation are universities, colleges, and national project management associations. Services such as membership, certification of project managers, project management events, provision of project management standards, etc. are provided by these associations. Further standardization services, such as provision of project management norms and formal project management requirements for public tenders, can be provided by standardization institutions.

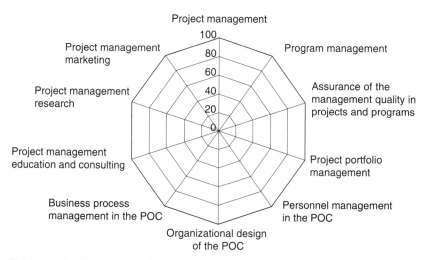

FIGURE 22.3   The maturity model of the project-oriented nation.

TABLE 22.3   Example of a Question of the Dimension "Project Management Education and Consulting"

A1.1) How many of the following institutions are offering formal project management education programs?*

Elementary schools
Secondary schools (such as high schools, trade schools), colleges
Universities of applied science
Universities
Postgraduate education institutions, adult education

1 = all of them (more than 30%); 2 = many of them (20–29%); 3 = some of them (10–19%), 4 = few of them (5–9%); 5 = none of them (less than 5%).
*Formal project management education program: project and/or program management as emphasis (at least six hours per term).

The questionnaire for the analysis of project management–related services of institutions includes 21 questions. Tables 22.3 and 22.4 provide examples of these questions.

The analysis of the project management–related services was performed by analyzing relevant documents of education, consulting, marketing, and research institutions, such as education curricula, Web pages, publications, etc. Interviews with representatives of these institutions were conducted in order to get additional information.

ANALYZING AND BENCHMARKING PROJECT-ORIENTED COMPANIES IN AUSTRIA

Average Results of 60 Austrian Project-Oriented Companies

The average results of the 60 Austrian companies analyzed are shown in the spiderweb presentation of the maturity model of the project-oriented company in Fig. 22.4. The 60 Austrian project-oriented companies have an average maturity of 49 percent. The dimensions "project management," "assignment of a project or program," and "organizational design of a

TABLE 22.4   Example of a Question of the Dimension "Project Management Marketing"

B3.6) Which of the following services are offered by the national IPMA association and the national PMI Chapter?

	IPMA Association	PMI Chapter
Certification of project managers		
Promotion of project management research		
Project management events		
Project management seminars		
Development of project management standards		
Project management–related awards		
Project management–related publications, newsletter		
Project management–related networks		
Specific project management–related interest groups		

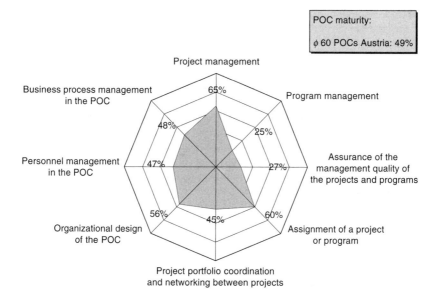

FIGURE 22.4   Maturity of the average of 60 project-oriented companies.

Maturity ratio	49%
Project management	65%
Program management	25%
Assurance of the management quality of projects and programs	27%
Assignment of a project or program	60%
Project portfolio coordination and networking between projects	45%
Organizational design of the POC	56%
Personnel management in the POC	47%
Business process management in the POC	48%

POC" have the highest maturities. The lowest maturities show the dimensions "assurance of the management quality of a project or program" and "program management." The maturity area is relatively homogeneous, with the exception of the drop in "program management" and the "assurance of the management quality of a project or program."

The average maturity of the 60 project-oriented companies and the results of the "best POC" and the "worst POC" are listed in the following tables. "Best" and "worst" refer to the maturity ratio of these companies overall and not to the "best" and "worst" for each dimension. "Best" and "worst" should show the spread of the maturities. The basis for the following interpretations is the average maturity of the 60 POCs.

Project Management.   Sixty-five percent of the 60 Austrian companies show a high maturity in the dimension "project management"(Table 22.5). The good results relate basically to external projects.

- Companies have the highest maturity to perform the subprocess "project coordination" in comparison with the other subprocesses such as "project start," "project control," and "project closedown."

TABLE 22.5   Project Management Maturity

	Worst POC	Best POC	Ø 60 POCs
Part A: Project management	**28%**	**87%**	**65%**
A 1. Project start	3,87	1,42	2,39
A 2. Project coordination	2,50	1,00	1,92
A 3. Project controlling	4,15	1,79	2,52
A 4. Project close-down	4,75	2,42	3,14
A 5. Resolving a project discontinuity	3,53	1,33	2,38
A 6. Project management process and project results	3,35	1,39	2,12
A 7. Small projects	5,00	1,40	2,27

1 = always; 2 = often; 3 = sometimes; 4 = seldom; 5 = never.
1 = very good; 2 = good; 3 = ok; 4 = bad; 5 = very bad.

- The quality of the project results achieved is evaluated to be "good" by the 60 companies.
- A differentiated management of small projects is performed "often" in the 60 companies.

  Table 22.6 presents the next level of detail of the questionnaire.

- In the project start process, most of the project management methods are used "often." Exceptions are the methods for considering the project context relationships, such as

TABLE 22.6   Project Start Maturity

	Worst POC	Best POC	Ø 60 POCs
A 1. Project start	3,87	1,42	2,39
A 1.1. In the project start process methods are used for project planning I (e.g. project objectives plan, project milestone plan, ...)	3,50	1,00	2,07
A 1.2. In the project start process methods are used for project planning II (e.g. project resource plan, project cost plan, ...)	4,50	1,33	2,24
A 1.3. In the project start process methods are used for considering the project context relationship (e.g. project environment analysis, ...)	4,00	1,33	2,77
A 1.4. In the project start process methods are used for designing the project organization (e.g. project organization chart, ...)	4,86	1,14	2,37
A 1.5. Consideration of representatives of "external companies" as project team members (e.g. representatives of customers, ...)	3,20	2,60	2,22
A 1.6. In the project start process methods are used for developing a project culture (e.g. project logo, "social" start event, ...)	4,00	1,50	2,67
A 1.7. In the project start process methods are used for project marketing (e.g. project presentations, project newsletters, ...)	3,00	1,00	2,41

1 = always; 2 = often; 3 = sometimes; 4 = seldom; 5 = never.

project environment analysis, and the methods for the development of a project culture, such as a project logo and a "social" start event. These are used "sometimes."

Program Management. Table 22.7 shows the program management maturity. Overall, the maturity of the 60 POCs in program management is only 25 percent.

- Program management is hardly established. This leads to relatively bad program management results.

Assurance of the Management Quality of a Project or Program. The average maturity for the dimension "assurance of the management quality of a project or program" is 27 percent (Table 22.8).

- Management consulting, as well as management auditing of projects and programs, "seldom" exists in the 60 POCs.

Assignment of a Project or Program. The average maturity for the dimension "assignment of a project or program" is 60 percent (Table 22.9).

- Methods for the assignment of a project or program, such as an investment proposal, project or program proposal, project or program assignment, analysis of alternative project portfolios, etc., are used "sometimes." Regarding design of the assignment process, design measures such as decisions about the appropriate organizational form for the initialization of the investment are made "often" by the project portfolio group.

TABLE 22.7   Program Management Maturity

	Worst POC	Best POC	Ø 60 POCs
Part B: Program management	**0%**	**94%**	**25%**
B 1. Use of program management methods in the program start	5,00	1,00	3,96
B 1.1. Use of methods for the program planning, the design of the program context and the program organization	5,00	1,00	3,91
B 1.2. Roles in the program organization	5,00	1,00	3,96
B 1.3. Developing the program culture	5,00	1,00	4,02
B 1.4. Program marketing	5,00	1,00	3,96
B 2. Other program management processes	5,00	1,36	3,98
B 2.1. Program coordination	5,00	1,00	3,91
B 2.2. Program controlling process	5,00	2,14	3,98
B 2.3. Program close-down	5,00	1,29	3,88
B 2.4. Methods for resolving a program discontinuity	5,00	1,00	3,90
B 3. Design of the program management process	5,00	1,32	4,06
B 3.1. Duration and frequency of the program management sub-processes	5,00	1,50	4,11
B 3.2. Performance of roles in program management	5,00	1,50	4,02
B 3.3. Quality of the program environment relationships	5,00	1,00	4,02
B 3.4. Quality of the program results	5,00	1,33	3,90

1 = always; 2 = often; 3 = sometimes; 4 = seldom; 5 = never.
1 = very good; 2 = good; 3 = ok; 4 = bad; 5 = very bad.

TABLE 22.8   Maturity in Ensuring of Management Quality of Projects and Programs

	Worst POC	Best POC	Ø 60 POCs
Part C: Assurance of management quality of projects and programs	**4%**	**95%**	**27%**
C 1. Management consulting of projects and programs	4,69	1,20	3,75
C 2. Management auditing of projects and programs	5,00	1,20	3,97

1 = always; 2 = often; 3 = sometimes; 4 = seldom; 5 = never.

Project Portfolio Coordination and Networking between Projects.   The average maturity for the dimension "project portfolio coordination and networking between projects" is 45 percent (Table 22.10).

- Methods for project portfolio coordination and networking between projects are used "sometimes" on average, although use of a project portfolio database, project portfolio reports, and project/program progress reports is higher than the methods of project networking, such as a network-of-projects graph or to do-lists, to ensure synergies between projects.
- Chains of projects are explicitly managed only "sometimes."
- Regarding design of the processes "project portfolio coordination" and "networking between projects," decisions by the project portfolio group and a promotion of networking between projects by the project management office occur "sometimes."

Organizational Design of the POC.   The average maturity regarding the dimension "organizational design of the POC" is 56 percent (Table 22.11).

- Expert pools or a project management office exist "with limited relevance." Formal structures, such as formal description of the business processes "project management" and "program management," project and program management templates, etc., exist "with limited relevance." Infrastructure, such as project management software and moderation tools, exists "with limited relevance." The culture of the POC shows here the highest maturity ratio. Teamwork, empowerment, customer orientation, etc. exist and are "very relevant." The further development of the organization as a POC has "limited relevance."

Personnel Management in the POC.   The average maturity regarding the dimension "personnel management" in the POC is 47 percent (Table 22.12).

TABLE 22.9   Maturity in Assigning a Project or Program

	Worst POC	Best POC	Ø 60 POCs
Part D: Assignment of a project or a program	**13%**	**83%**	**60%**
D 1. Methods for assigning a project or a program I	4,00	2,33	3,29
D 2. Methods for assigning a project or a program II	5,00	2,33	2,50
D 3. Design of the assignment process I	5,00	1,00	2,40
D 4. Design of the assignment process II	4,00	1,00	2,29

1 = always; 2 = often; 3 = sometimes; 4 = seldom; 5 = never.

TABLE 22.10 Maturity in Project Portfolio Coordination and in Networking between Projects

	Worst POC	Best POC	Ø 60 POCs
Part E: Project portfolio coordination and networking between projects	**0%**	**89%**	**45%**
E 1. Methods for project portfolio coordination and networking between projects	5,00	2,83	3,34
E 2. Management of chains of projects	5,00	1,00	3,22
E 3. Design of the project portfolio coordination	5,00	1,00	2,55
E 4. Design of networking between projects	5,00	1,00	3,35

1 = always; 2 = often; 3 = sometimes; 4 = seldom; 5 = never.

- "Project manager" as a profession, for example, having descriptions for the roles in the project-oriented company and having a career path in project management, exists "with limited relevance." Means for recruiting project and program managers "exist informally." Leading project and program management personnel by performance of temporary leadership tasks in projects/programs, as well as by incentive systems, and the development of project and program management personnel exist "with limited relevance." Regarding project management competencies (knowledge and experience in comparison with IPMA or PMI standards), the competencies of executives of the POC are higher than those of project and program management personnel.

Business Process Management. The average maturity of the dimension "business process management" is 48 percent (Table 22.13).

- Business process definitions and different types of business processes exist "with high relevance." The methods for macro and micro business process management, as well as the methods for optimization of the business processes, exist "with limited relevance." Moreover, the information technology (IT) infrastructure, as well as the organization for business process management, exists "with limited relevance."

TABLE 22.11 Maturity in the Organizational Design of the Project-Oriented Company

	Worst POC	Best POC	Ø 60 POCs
Part F: Organizational design of the project-oriented company	**11%**	**93%**	**56%**
F 1. Organizational structure of the project-oriented company	5,00	1,50	3,17
F 2. Organizational processes of the project-oriented company I	5,00	1,75	2,87
F 3. Organizational processes of the project-oriented company II	5,00	1,50	2,98
F 4. Infrastructure of the project-oriented company	3,86	1,00	2,54
F 5. Culture of the project-oriented company	3,50	1,00	2,16
F 6. Further development of the project-oriented company	5,00	1,00	2,87

1 = continually optimized; 2 = existing-very relevant; 3 = existing-limited relevance; 4 = existing informally; 5 = not existing.

TABLE 22.12   Maturity in Personnel Management in the Project-Oriented Company

	Worst POC	Best POC	Ø 60 POCs
Part G: Personnel management in the project-oriented company	**7%**	**86%**	**47%**
G 1. The 'project manager' as a profession	5,00	1,00	3,26
G 2. Recruiting project and program managers	5,00	2,00	3,61
G 3. Leading project and program management personnel	4,67	1,00	2,52
G 4. Incentive systems in the project-oriented company	3,50	3,25	3,48
G 5. Development of project and program management personnel	4,83	1,00	3,24
G 8. Design of the personnel management processes	5,00	1,25	3,68
G 6. Project management competencies (knowledge and experience) of the project and program management personnel	4,67	1,25	2,58
G 7. Project management competencies (knowledge and experience) of executives of the project-oriented company	5,00	1,75	2,45

1 = continually optimized; 2 = existing-very relevant; 3 = existing-limited relevance; 4 = existing informally; 5 = not existing.
1 = very high; 2 = high; 3 = average; 4 = low; 5 = very low.

Personnel management for business process management, such as a career path, exists "informally." Business process management competencies (knowledge and experience) are "average."

- Considering the correlation between project results and business process management, one can see that the higher the maturity of the dimension "business process management," the higher is the quality of the project results (Table 22.14).

Table 22.13   Maturity in Business Process Management in the Project-Oriented Company

	Worst POC	Best POC	Ø 60 POCs
Part H: Business process management in the project-oriented company	**58%**	**88%**	**48%**
H 1. Definitions and types of business processes	3,40	1,00	2,33
H 2. Macro-business process management	2,75	1,00	2,96
H 3. Micro-business process management	1,87	1,37	2,68
H 4. Optimization of the business processes	3,25	2,75	2,91
H 5. IT-infrastructure for business process management	1,67	1,00	2,98
H 6. Organization for business process management	1,50	1,00	3,17
H 7. Personnel management for business process management	4,00	2,00	3,81
H 8. Business process management competencies (knowledge and experience) in relation to national and international standards	3,00	1,60	2,73

1 = continually optimized; 2 = existing-very relevant; 3 = existing-limited relevance; 4 = existing informally; 5 = not existing.
1 = very high; 2 = high; 3 = average; 4 = low; 5 = very low.

TABLE 22.14   Relation between the Quality of the Project Results and Business Process Management in the Project-Oriented Company

	Worst POC	Best POC	Ø 60 POCs
Part H: Business process management in the project-oriented company	**58%**	**88%**	**48%**
A 6.6. Quality of the project results	1,83	1,00	2,12

1 = very good; 2 = good; 3 = ok; 4 = bad; 5 = very bad.

Results of the 60 Austrian Project-Oriented Companies Differentiated by Size

Regarding the number of employees, the 60 project-oriented companies have been differentiated into

- Small POCs < 49: 14
- Medium POCs 50–249: 19
- Large POCs > 250: 27

The average results for small, medium, and large companies are shown in Fig. 22.5.

Large project-oriented companies have a higher overall maturity than small and medium ones. Large POCs carry out programs and formal processes of consulting and auditing to ensure the management quality of projects and programs. Large companies have more

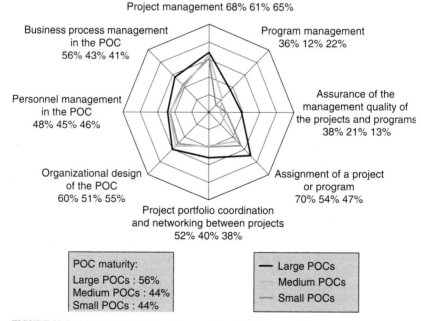

FIGURE 22.5   Maturities of small, medium, and large POCs.

possibilities regarding the organizational design of a POC, such as project management office, project portfolio group, etc., and take extensive measures regarding the development of employees.

Benchmarking Project-Oriented Industries

The 60 project-oriented companies were clustered into different industries. Given a minimum number of five POCs per industry, the following clusters resulted: Information and Communications Technology (ICT), research, engineering, consulting, and building construction, as well as nonprofit organization (NPO)/public sector.

It can be interpreted that the market situation influences the maturity of project-oriented industries. Thus, higher maturities result because of competition in the ICT industry or because of formal requirements by financing institutions in the research industry. Industries that mainly carry out customer-related projects (i.e., building construction and engineering) show a low maturity in the dimension of program management. This is so because most contracts are performed in projects and do not require program organizations.

Table 22.15 shows the results of the project-oriented industries differentiated by the dimensions of the maturity model. The ICT industry has the highest maturity ratio at 67 percent, and the NPO/public sector has the lowest maturity, at 39 percent.

MATURITY OF AUSTRIA AS A PROJECT-ORIENTED NATION (PON)

The maturity of Austria as a project-oriented nation can be determined by considering the average maturities of the 60 analyzed project-oriented companies and by analyzing their maturities regarding such project management-related services as education, consulting, research, and marketing institutions. The results of the analysis of the services provided by project management education and consulting institutions, project management marketing institutions, and project management research institutions are described below.

Project Management–Related Services of Education, Consulting, Research, and Marketing Institutions in Austria

Project Management Education and Consulting Services. *Formal project management education programs* are defined as programs in which project and program management is taught at least six hours per week per term. In Austria, project management is not taught in elementary schools. Curricula in Austria's high schools do not include project management yet. Because recently it has been possible for general high schools to choose their teaching subjects more freely, it can be expected that soon some of these schools will include project management in their curricula.

Austria's 108 trade schools offer already formal project management education programs. Also, institutions with higher technical education offer project management courses. Nine of 73 existing colleges offer six or more hours of project management courses per term. More than 50 percent of the universities of applied science analyzed (9 of 19) offer a formal project management education program, whereas only few universities offer project management-related courses. This can be explained by the fact that universities of applied science were introduced to the Austrian education sector only a few years ago and therefore are more likely to adapt their curricula to recent trends. Universities known

TABLE 22.15 Benchmarking the Maturities of Different Project-Oriented Industries

	Ø 6 POCs NPO/ Public Sector	Ø 7 POCs Building Construction	Ø 5 POCs Consulting	Ø 11 POCs Engineering	Ø 60 POCs	Ø 5 POCs Research	Ø 11 POCs ICT
Maturity ratio	39%	40%	46%	48%	49%	60%	67%
Project management	58%	66%	70%	60%	65%	71%	77%
Program management	25%	13%	14%	2%	25%	49%	52%
Assurance of the managment quality of project or programs	21%	9%	14%	27%	27%	29%	54%
Assignment of a project or program	65%	49%	38%	53%	60%	67%	75%
Project portfolio coordination and networking between projects	22%	25%	47%	47%	45%	69%	62%
Organizational design in the POC	39%	47%	66%	56%	56%	65%	72%
Personnel management in the POC	33%	40%	54%	50%	47%	60%	62%
Business process management in the POC	18%	37%	30%	65%	48%	56%	63%

for their less flexible structures often react more slowly to changes. Sixteen of 30 universities analyzed do not even offer project management-related subjects. Only the Vienna University of Economics and Business Administration and the University of Vienna offer formal project management education programs.

The trend to a more intensive project management education can be seen in the postgraduate and adult education sector. An academic degree in project management is provided by some universities of applied science. Until today, it has not been possible to obtain an academic degree in project management at an Austrian university. In postgraduate education, an MBA in project and process management and a master's of science in project management construction can be obtained.

All formal project management programs offer project management in their education programs. Program management and project portfolio management are not offered as frequently. Business process management is taught at universities on a regular basis only. Austrian consulting companies focus on project management–related education and consulting services. Project Management Austria (PMA) is the Austrian project management association, and it offers certification programs for project managers based on the International Project Management Association (IPMA) certification model. Table 22.16 shows the number of certified and recertified persons in 2003 and 2004.

In Austria in the years 2003–2004, 1153 people (of 8.2 million inhabitants in Austria) were certified by Project Management Austria (PMA). In comparison with Austria, in Sweden, only 260 people (of 8.9 million inhabitants) were certified by the IPMA. This shows that Austria is very active in the field of project management certifications (Schmehr et al., 2004, pp. 14ff).

The Project Management Institute (PMI) offers two different levels of certification: for professionals, the Project Management Professional (PMP), and for persons with less experience, the Certified Associate in Project Management (CAPM). In the years 2003–2004, 84 PMPs and no CAPMs were certified by Austrian PMI chapters (Table 22.17).

Project Management Research in Austria.   Universities are mainly responsible for project management–related research. In addition, universities of applied science, as well as consulting companies, perform some project management related–research, often cooperating with universities.

The analysis shows that in Austria many project management–related research projects have been conducted in the last two years. For instance, the research program "Program I Austria" was carried out by the Projektmanagement Group at the Vienna University of Economics and Business Administration to further develop project management in Austrian's companies, schools, municipalities, etc. between March 2000 and December 2003. The number of Austrian project management publications in the years 2003–2005 is shown in Fig. 22.6.

TABLE 22.16   Number of Certified Persons by the Austrian IPMA in 2003 and 2004

PMA	2003	2004	Sum
IPMA, Level A	2	0	2
IPMA, Level B	83 (+18)	66 (+17)	149
IPMA, Level C	211 (+8)	300 (+40)	511
IPMA, Level D	177	314	491
Sum	473	680	1153

Source: Schmehr et al. (2004).

TABLE 22.17   Number of Certified Persons by the PMI in 2003 and 2004

PMI	2003	2004	Sum
PMP	35	49	84
CAPM	0	0	0
Sum	35	49	84

Diploma theses were the most used form of project management publication in the last two years. In the years 2003–2005, nine books with project management content were published.

Few project management–related research events were carried out during the last two years. Each year, project management days (www.pmtage.at) are organized in Austria as an international research event.

Project Management Marketing in Austria.   Besides the national IPMA, there are three PMI chapters located in Austria (Styria, West Austria, and Vienna). Both organizations—PMA and PMI chapters—have about 350 members each. They offer a number of services, such as certification of project managers, promotion of project management research, project management events, development of project management standards, project management–related publications, newsletters, and project management–related networks. It is also one of the main objectives of the project management associations to promote the project manager as a profession.

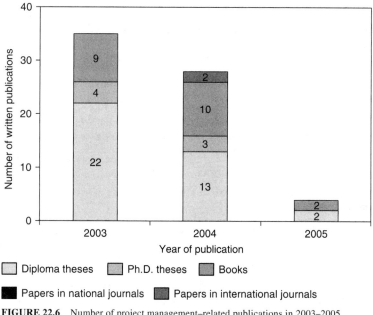

FIGURE 22.6   Number of project management–related publications in 2003–2005.

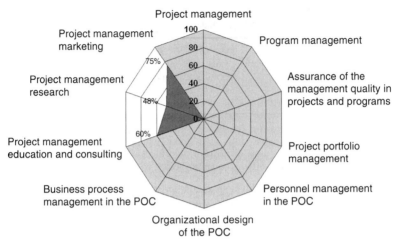

FIGURE 22.7   Maturities of project management–related services in Austria.

The project management baseline by the PMA and the *PMBOK Guide* by the PMI are the most important project management–related standards in Austria. There are also some special norms (ÖeNORM, DIN) for the standardization of applied project management.

Given the defined weighting scheme for project management–related service dimensions, the maturities of the service dimensions can be calculated and visualized in the maturity model of the project-oriented nation (Fig. 22.7).

Maturity of Austria as a Project-Oriented Nation (PON)

The maturity of Austria as a project-oriented nation in the year 2005 is presented in Fig. 22.8. Considering the maturity ratios of the 10 dimensions of the maturity model, Austria as a project-oriented nation has an overall maturity ratio of 50 percent.

The area in the maturity model is relatively homogenous and shows major strengths in the service dimension "project management marketing" and in the practice dimension "project management." Weaknesses are obvious in the practice dimensions "program management" and "assurance of the management quality of a project or program," as well as in the service dimension "project management-related research."

Development of the Maturity of Austria as a Project-Oriented Nation since 2000

In 2000, Austria was analyzed within the research project "POS—Benchmarking" together with other nations (see above). The result of the analysis of Austria of the year 2000 is shown in Fig. 22.9. The results for the year 2000 cannot be compared directly with the results for the year 2005. In recent years, the maturity model of the project-oriented nation, as well as the analyzing process, was developed further. Two dimensions, "assurance of the management quality of a project or program" and "business process management,"

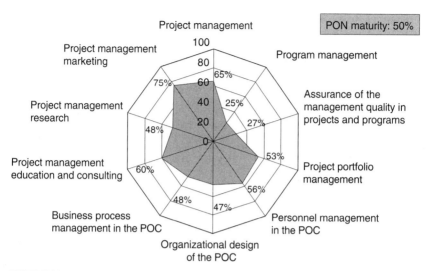

FIGURE 22.8 Maturity model of Austria as a PON in 2005.

were added to the model. In 2000, the analysis of the project management practices of project-oriented companies was done during a workshop by a panel of project management experts from different industries. During the workshop, the questionnaire was discussed and answered. The participants agreed on scores and defined the competencies of the project-oriented nation directly. No detailed analysis of project-oriented companies took place. Nevertheless, the results for 2000 can be taken as an orientation.

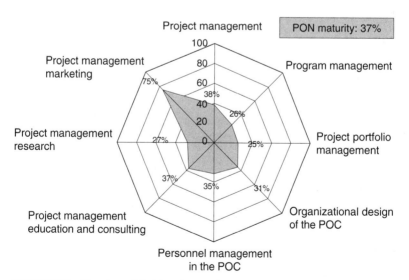

FIGURE 22.9 Maturity model of Austria as a PON in 2000.

Regarding the project management practices, improvements in the dimensions "project management," "project portfolio management," "organizational design," and "personnel management" can be seen. The dimension "project management education and consulting" also has improved significantly.

Strategies for the Further Development of Austria as Project-Oriented Nation

Based on the results of the research project "Project Orientation (Austria)," the following strategies for further development of Austria as project-oriented nation were defined:

- The consciousness of managers regarding the application of project management in companies has to be increased. "Projects" cannot be used only for external customer-related business processes but should be used as well for internal business processes, such as reorganizations, marketing campaigns, etc.
- For the fulfillment of a unique business process of a large scope and high strategic importance, such as a merger or the establishment of a new IT architecture, programs can be used as an adequate organizational form.
- The assurance of management quality by consulting and auditing of relatively autonomous projects and programs contributes to the success of the projects or programs.
- Strategies for further development of the maturities of project-oriented companies have to be differentiated by industry and by company size.
- Further project management education programs have to be developed. Existing education programs should be further developed. Project management should be integrated into the management curricula of universities.
- Project management research has to be promoted.
- Project management–related marketing activities have to be maintained. The promotion of project management certification programs can be seen as promotion of project management as a profession. A broad promotion of project management in schools, families, municipalities, regions, etc. is possible.

CONCLUSION

The research project "Project Orientation (Austria)" contributed to project management marketing in Austria. A follow-up research project, "Project Orientation (Austria) II," is being performed with the objectives of

- Analyzing and benchmarking project-oriented companies of different sizes and in different Austrian regions
- Benchmarking Austria with other project-oriented countries such as Australia, Croatia, Finland, Germany, Latvia, Norwegia, Slovakia, and South Africa.

This research project is part of the research program "Project Orientation (International)." In this program, some 15 nations will be analyzed and benchmarked (please see www.pmgroup.at/poi).

REFERENCES

Gareis R. 2002. Management in the project-oriented society, in *Proceedings of PMI Research Conference 2002, Moskau: Project Management Institute.*

Gareis R, Gruber C. 2005. *Final Research Report: Analysis of Austria as a Project-Oriented Nation (Bewertung Österreichs als projektorientierte Gesellschaft anhand eines Maturity-Modells). Vienna:* Projektmanagement Group, Vienna University of Economics and Business Administration.

Hallemann M. 2005. Analysis of project management-related services in Austria (Analyse projektmanagement-bezogener Dienstleistungen in Öesterreich). diploma thesis, Vienna: Projektmanagement Group, Vienna University of Economics and Business Administration.

Schmehr W, Knoepfel H, Gilles C. 2004. *IPMA Certification Yearbook 2004.* International Project Management Association.

CHAPTER 23
A BRIEF INSIGHT OF PROJECT MANAGEMENT IN THE MAINLAND OF CHINA

Dong Chao

Ph.D, Department of Manufacturing Engineering and Engineering Management,
City University of Hong Kong

K. B. Chuah

Associate Professor,
Department of Manufacturing Engineering and Engineering Management,
City University of Hong Kong

Li Zhai

Associate Professor, Fudan University, Shanghai, China

Dong Chao majored in management information systems for his B.Sc. and master's degree studies. After receiving his master's degree from the School of Management at Fudan University, Shanghai, he continued his research from the project management perspective. He received his Ph.D degree in the MEEM Department of City University of Hong Kong in 2006. His major research direction is project management in mainland China. Before he enrolled in the City University, he had directed and was involved in a few project management consulting projects for big companies in Shanghai. He had one of his papers published at the Project Management Institute (PMI) research conference in London in 2004. This contributed paper also was selected as a book chapter of in *Innovations: Project Management Research 2004,* edited by D. P. Slevin, D. I. Cleland and J.K.Pinto. (Project Management Institute)

Dr. Chuah is an associate professor in the Department of Manufacturing Engineering and Engineering Management at City University of Hong Kong. He has a bachelor of technology degree in mechanical engineering from Loughborough University, United Kingdom. His Ph.D. was awarded for his work on a U.S. Navy-sponsored project on roughness and hydrodynamic drag. He obtained his postgraduate diploma in management studies while working as a senior research coordinator managing a multidisciplinary Computer Integrated Manufacturing (CEM) research team at the University of Teesside, United Kingdom. He started lecturing at the University of Teesside in 1988 and later joined City University of Hong Kong in 1990. He is now a core faculty member in both the undergraduate and postgraduate programs and an active supervisor of M.Phil and Ph.D research studies.

Dr. Zhai is currently an associate professor in the Department of Management Science at the School of Management of Fudan University. She received her Ph.D. in management science in 1998 from Fudan University. She has a master's degree in management science and a bachelor's degree in operations research. She has served as a visiting scholar at the Sloan School of Management of the Massachusetts Institute of Technology in 2002 and the Olin Business School at Washington University in St. Louis in 1998. She worked as a research fellow in the MEEM Department of the City University of Hong Kong in 2000. Her major research interests are project management, new product development management, and innovation and technology management.

Striding into the twenty-first century, globalization is the main trend in the world business. Global business growth has spurred many effective management disciplines, including project management, to go beyond the boundaries of nations. The 2003 annual report of the Project Management Institute (PMI) shows that PMI membership was more than 120,000 strong, with representation in 135 countries—a growth rate of 21.6 percent over 2002. This number appears to imply that the global application of project management is emerging, and its importance to economic development has been recognized increasingly worldwide. For China, the world's leading destination for foreign investment since 2002, project management has shown its critical role in driving the fast economic development as a result of the massive inflow of foreign investment that has helped to set up of numerous international projects there. However, a survey of the current literature finds little systematic research on China's project management environment and practices against this background of fast-paced economic development that has been propelled by enormous foreign investment. How project management is practiced in China largely has remained unknown by Westerners.

Many cross-cultural studies have shown that different cultures support different sets of management beliefs and practices, particularly when those cultures reflect fundamentally different conceptions of reality.[1] Previous research has proved that Western project management theories do not translate easily into practice in the Middle East, which has a vastly different Arab culture from major Western countries.[2] Similarly, can these project management theories and practices based on North American and primarily U.S. research and experience[3] be translated into the practices in China with traditional dominant culture? Thus it is essential to recognize that national culture may affect project management practices and that one should take into account the implications of cultural differences when dealing with international projects involving project stakeholders from different cultures.

In the face of an increasing number of foreign investors entering the Chinese market, this chapter is written principally to present a general description of the current practices of project management in China and attempts to provide some pragmatic guidelines for handling cultural barriers by foreign stakeholders involved in projects in China.

The development of project management in China is described first. This is followed by a brief introduction to the application of project management in industries, with special attention paid to project-based software companies in China. A review of these Chinese project management practices is given next. Following this part, a large-scale empirical study of management of information systems (IS) projects in China is reported briefly. Some practical implications for foreign stakeholders in China's projects are discussed at the end of the chapter.

A CLOSE LOOK AT MAINLAND OF CHINA

The People's Republic of China (PRC), a country with a population that makes up approximately one-fifth of the world's total population, has been in transition and developing rapidly since the end of 1970s. Over the past two decades, China has gone through a tremendous amount of economic reform with the adoption of a market economy and an open-door policy. The long-established, centrally planned economic system has been replaced gradually; the influence of market forces on the economy has increased rapidly. The current socialist market economy, defined with Chinese characteristics, is turning China into one of the largest and fastest growing economies in the world. In past 10 years, the Chinese gross national product increased annually by nearly 9 percent on average.[4] At this amazing rate of growth, China could—on paper—surpass the United States within two decades to become the world's largest economy. China's foreign direct investment (FDI) inflows surpassed those of the United States in 2002, making China the world's leading destination for foreign funds. The FDI has contributed greatly to China's spectacular economic growth in past two decades, which brought not only the massive funds that China required but also a great number of modern management theories and technologies into China, including project management.

Although China has been on its way to quick globalization since its accession into World Trade Organization (WTO) in 2001, from the point of view of Westerners, it is still a country that has a different culture, different management practices, and a different business environment than the developed countries.[5–9] According to the research by Hofstede—alone and with Bond[5,6]—on the five dimensions of culture, Confucian dynamism is uniquely Chinese, and there are marked differences on the dimensions of power distance and individualism/collectivism between Chinese and Westerners. The other dominant culture model examined by Schwartz[10] explicitly categorized Chinese culture as kind of relationship culture that mainly adopts conservative values and accommodates value tensions between hierarchy and harmony. It is distinctly different from the culture of the United States, which is categorized as a contractual culture that adopts autonomous values along with value tensions between mastery and egalitarian commitment/harmony.

The deep-rooted traditional Chinese culture has perpetuated its profound influence to almost every aspect of the society, including, of course, management practices, and has created a singular business environment. Chinese tend to be more hierarchical, collectivistic, and context-oriented[8] when compared with Westerners, which implies that differing communication styles are used in Chinese society. Another striking feature of the Chinese business environment—one that is likely to be apparent to Westerners, with different culture values—is the importance of interpersonal relationships. The most important element of interpersonal relationship values is *guanxi*. The Chinese word "guanxi" can be broadly translated as "personal relationship" or "personal connection, that describes the basic force that holds the personalised networks of influence". *Guanxi* is not unique feature of Chinese society. It exists to some extent in every human society. What is special about Chinese society is the fact that *guanxi* is ubiquitous and plays a crucial role in daily life. *Guanxi* is a dominant cultural and social element in Chinese society that has a significant effect on almost every aspect of life in modern China.[11–14] It is a product of Confucian values and contemporary political and socioeconomic systems.[14] Without *guanxi,* one simply cannot get anything done.[11] Meanwhile, the deep-seated culture has a strong influence on the way the Chinese manage and are managed as well, which leads to substantial differences between managerial practices in the West and in China.[15] Chinese managers tend to put more emphasis on a subjective, intuitive, and implicit approach, whereas their Western counterparts prefer an analytical, logical, linear, orderly, and

explicit mind-set in management.[16] Western managers pay much attention to written contracts and procedures, whereas the Chinese prefer personal relationships and trust.[7]

PROJECT MANAGEMENT IN CHINA

Project Management Development in China

One of the earliest large projects in China was construction of the Great Wall, one of the
greatest wonders of the world, built more than 2000 years ago. In addition to the Great
Wall, numerous grand palaces, temples, and even canals were built in glorious history of
China. However, the concept of modern project management did not emerge in China until
the 1960s when the well-known Chinese mathematician Hua Luogeng came back to young
China from the United States. In 1964, Professor Hua Luogeng began devoting himself to
advocating and promoting an "overall planning method" in China, a set of systematic
methods of project management that were specially developed for Chinese practices. After
nearly two decades of application and improvement, the methods have been applied successfully in the management of a few megaprojects since the beginning of 1980s.

Meanwhile, since implementation of the open-door policy at the end of 1970s, the
booming economy of China has been spurring an increasing number of projects in various
industries. However, modern project management discipline was not officially introduced
into China to meet the intensive management requirement of countless projects until 1980s
with the help of the World Bank. The first successful project that was managed following
international project management practices in China was construction of the Lubuge
hydropower station in Yunnan Province in 1984, which was funded by the World Bank.
This project was widely considered a milestone of the application of modern project management in China. Then this project management experience was translated successfully to
the Ertan hydropower station project, which also was funded by the World Bank and was
the biggest hydropower dam before construction of the Three Gorges Dam.

In the two decades since this turning point, the Chinese government's proactive
financing policy has boosted domestic demand, stimulated economic development, and
generated an annual project investment of RMB 1 trillion. Investment in the construction
industry by the state-owned sector has increased from RMB 69.9 billion in 1979 to RMB
1700 billion in 1995,[17] which represents a nearly 25-fold increase in 16 years.[18] In addition, a large number of projects that were funded by foreign investors, including the
World Bank and the Asia Development Bank, were required to be managed following
international practices, and this has further promoted the development of project management in China.

In the late 1990s, the Chinese government began attaching greater importance to the
promotion of project management and published the *Essentials of China's Project
Management System and Standards of Qualification* with the intent of adapting China's
project management practices to international practices.[19] In addition, more than 1000
leaders and project managers of large state-owned enterprises received relevant training
on the international project management practices.

Project management is widely reported to have a bright future in China. The success
of the 2008 Olympic Games bid and its WTO accession, as well as implementation of
Western development strategy, no doubt will usher in a new round of investment upsurge
in China. The importance of project management in China now has being realized in a
rich range of fields, including industry, universities and research associations, and governmental institutes. The demand for the practices of project management will increase
rapidly in many economic sectors of China.

Booming Requirements of Project Management Training

Some investment bankers described China as an unparalleled construction site for an enormous number of projects. *Fortune Magazine* predicted that "project management professionals will be among the top careers in the twenty-first century." Accordingly, there is a great need for the Chinese to learn the knowledge and best practices of project management and to translate them into practice quickly.

A relatively early effort to meet the needs of trainers and the facilities of project management in China to improve project delivery in all sectors of the economy was a program entitled, "Training of Trainers," funded by the World Bank and launched at the end of 1994 and the beginning of 1995.[20] The program's objective was to develop a number of core trainers who would disperse to various regions of China to set up centers for the training of practitioners. In addition to this, there are hundreds of thousands of people in China who have been taking part in training programs on project management recently that are provided by renowned bodies such as the PMI, the International Project Management Association (IPMA), and domestic training companies that take initiative to gain the lion's share of the market. With the PMI alone, more than 10,000 people have taken the Project Management Professional (PMP) examinations, and more than 5000 of them have being issued the PMP certificate since 2000.[21] This number will continue to grow in the foreseeable future. PMI's annual report indicates that growth of PMP certification in China in 2003 was 155 percent compared with 2002; this is the fastest growth in the world.[22] Reliable statistics also demonstrate that China will need nearly 600,000 well-trained project management practitioners and some 100,000 certified PMPs in the coming three years in order to meet the huge demand for talent in this regard.[23]

PROJECT ORGANIZATIONS IN CHINA

In present-day China, in addition to a number of commercial training companies, such as BMMTEC International Education Group, the first and one of the largest registered education providers (REPs) certified by the PMI in China and founded to meet the booming training requirements of project management, the other important advocate of project management in China is the Project Management Research Committee, China (PMRCC). It was instituted in 1991 as a nationwide cross-industry and not-for-profit research association for project management and supervised by the Northwestern Polytechnic University. It is one of the national associations of IMPA and serves primarily to promote the education, academic study, and widespread application of project management in China. The other long-term objective of this association is to promote project management professionalism in the unique practices of China. To fulfill these goals, the PMRCC began systematic development of the *Chinese Project Management Body of Knowledge* (*C-PMBOK*) in 1993 and presented the first edition of *C-PMBOK* in May 2001. Meanwhile, the PMRCC also has been actively involved in introduction and promotion of the IPMA's four-level international certification program for project managers, which is called the *International Project Management Professional* (IPMP) in China to differentiate it from the PMP certification of the PMI.

Besides the PMRCC, the Institute of Beijing ZK Project Management is another newly established research-based institute by a few Chinese project management scholars and practitioners with purpose is to introduce international project management theory into China and to develop project management concepts, tools, and techniques based on Chinese practices. Meanwhile, a few government administrative and industrial institutes in China also have begun to introduce the concept of project management into their fields to promote wider recognition and application of project management, and these include the Institute of Policy and Management (Chinese Academy of Sciences), the Construction Project Contracting and Management Institute (China Exploration & Design Association), the China National Association of Engineering Consultants, and so on.

In addition, sponsored by the State Economic and Trade Commission of China, the Chinese Academy of Sciences, and the United Nations Industrial Development Organization, two international conferences on project management in China (ICPM China) were held in Beijing in 2002 and 2004 to show the government's attempt to advocate the use of project management in China. These two conferences are reported to have served as a platform to provide an opportunity for decision makers from China's central and local governments, representatives from international financial institutions and investors, specialists engaged in project management, and entrepreneurs in China to exchange their research and experience in project management and to seek workable approaches with common interests existing in project management so as to make project management in China international and standardized and at the same time explore the possibilities of international cooperation in project investment financing and management. Some milestone publications about the Chinese project management system, including "The Outline of the Project Management Knowledge System of China" and "Qualification Criteria for Project Management Professionals," were released at ICPM China in 2004. Another governmental endeavor to attach greater importance to project management and better serve the increasing needs of project management professionals in China has been the partnership between the PMI and the Administration of Foreign Experts Affairs (SAFEA), which is the chief governmental administration in charge of introducing overseas intellectuals.[23]

GOVERNMENT'S MEGAPROJECTS

Since the first successful trial of modern project management in China in 1984, it has gained increasing popularity in Chinese construction, aerospace, and military fields, especially in government-sponsored megaprojects such as the Three Gorges Dam, the Xiaolangdi Multipurpose Dam, the Ertan Hydropower Station, the Beijing Olympic Stadium, the Shenzhou spaceships, and so on. Project management has shown itself to be an effective management method, especially international project management practices, and has contributed significantly to the success of these monumental projects in China.

China's Three Gorges Dam project is the largest construction project in China since the Great Wall. Started in December 1994, the project is expected to take an estimated 250,000 workers about 17 years to finish. Extensive preparation and detailed, consistent, and unified project planning are needed. Primavera Project Planner for Windows, a professional planning software, has been used intensively in project planning. A computer concrete construction simulation system was used to provide reliable data as input to the detailed project planning process. A computer-based notes system also was employed for daily reporting and to closely monitor construction progress of contractors on the site. By far most of the preset milestones in the first two periods of the project (1994–2004) have been achieved successfully ahead of schedule.

The Xiaolangdi Multipurpose Dam Project, which is called one of the most challenging projects in the world by international experts, was completed successfully in 2001. As with others projects financed by the World Bank, one of the managerial factors that contributed greatly to the success of this difficult project was successful introduction of international competitive bidding procedures, namely, the International Federation of Consulting Engineers' (FIDIC's) international contracts and business practices, to this project, which provided scientific methods to choose the most competent contractors from all over the world to work on this project and to have them managed by professional practices.

PROJECTS IN OTHER INDUSTRIES

Apart from these huge projects that have been completed successfully as a result of national effort and substantive international support as the first field of project management introduction, still, a large number of domestic construction projects in China have suffered significantly from delays and overrun budgets. Although it is claimed that theses are mainly the result of government intervention, a tedious project approval process, and immature traditional practices, a lack of knowledge of construction management practices such as project planning, time management, and risk management is also regarded as one of weakest areas that needs extra effort in the Chinese construction industry.[18]

In addition to these fields, project management in governmental, social organizations, and other industries in China is said to be on the path of correct development in recent years. The importance of project management in Chinese business was not widely recognized until 1990s. Only in recent years has project management begun to emerge as necessary knowledge for a number of pioneer Chinese organizations to manage their projects. However, most projects in organizations are currently managed by some core of project participants rather than organizational effort to get them done. Even operation on the level of individual projects with project success depending greatly on certain "star" participants' competency, the benefit of employing project management has been recognized increasingly by Chinese organizations for various purposes, such as research and development (R&D), production development, infrastructure maintenance and update, technology transformation and improvement, outsourcing, and so on. Being adopted as a useful management method, project management theories and techniques have been applied in projects in Chinese educational, governmental institutes, and a range of other industries, including information technology (IT), manufacturing, petroleum, chemicals, telecommunications, and finance.

PROJECT-BASED SOFTWARE COMPANIES IN CHINA

The IT industry is one of China's pillar industries at present.[24] The average annual output of the IT industry grew 32.1 percent from 1990 through 1999, and strong growth has continued in recent years. IT projects also are reported as one of the fastest growing project types around the world. As a type of relatively young project for most countries, whether developed or developing countries, how their project-based software companies performed and how their IT projects are managed largely can reveal the national capability of practicing project management.

China's software industry is said to be still in its infancy and remains the weakest link in China's IT sector.[25] International Data Corporation (IDC) forecasts that the Chinese software market will continue to grow at a compound annual growth rate of over 30 percent between 2000 and 2005. However, industry output of $7.2 billion in 2000 remains small relative to the booming IT hardware manufacturing industry, and China even lags behind its neighboring countries siuch as India and Korea in software output.

Although China opened its doors to world in 1978, the Chinese software industry barely existed before the 1990s. The IDC estimated that by the end of 2000, there were more than 2000 registered software companies in China and another 3000 IT companies involved in the Chinese software business. The domestic software industry in China is extremely fragmented, with thousands of very small enterprises with fewer than 50 employees that lack economies of scale and have distinctive competence. In contrast to India's mature software industry, which has grown up to serve extremely sophisticated foreign corporations (such as Fortune 100 companies), the immaturity of the business market in China makes it difficult for Chinese software firms to develop successful new products or achieve economies of scale. Renowned international corporations such as Microsoft, IBM, Oracle, and SAP have dominated the software product market in China—accounting for over 65 percent of packaged software sales, including ERP (enterprise resource planning), because of their established brands and products.

The lack of management know-how, managerial experience, and models for software development is reported as one of the most significant weaknesses of China's software industry.[25,26] Quite a few Chinese scholars and practitioners even plainly pointed out the biggest gap in the software industry between China and India is the lack of project management capability in Chinese software companies.[27] Faced with fierce global competition, especially from China's close neighbor, the Indian software industry, Chinese software companies have realized these difficulties and have embarked on setting up their strategies to improve the situation by introducing quality management and process management systems and the project management practices of developed countries.

Most mainstream software enterprises in China received ISO 9000 certification several years ago. The next target is a Carnegie-Mellon Capability Maturity Model (CMM)–based capability maturity evaluation. A number of firms have started to apply for CMM certification to improve their capability of managing projects successfully and delivering products effectively. Right now, CMM and project management certification are the hottest topics in China's software community. To lead the direction of industry, government agencies are also beginning to provide financial incentives for software companies to engage in these CMM-based evaluations. The Shanghai Software Quality Consortium was established in 2000, for example, to promote software process improvement. In December 2002, Neusoft Co. became the first Chinese enterprise certified CMM Level 5. Only five Chinese companies have passed CMM Level 5 evaluation compared with 42 companies in India. The number of companies that passed CMM Level 2 evaluation is less than 50 in all of China.[28]

It seems that these facts lend evidence to the fact that most Chinese firms dramatically underestimate the extensive resources and commitment required to achieve these quality management standard and project management maturity—and the industry as a whole is likely to remain behind India and the West in the short run. As a sort of core competency for software companies, the lack of project management capability of most Chinese firms has weakened their global competitiveness substantially. The limited capabilities of Chinese software developers suggest that most firms will have difficulty competing with foreign companies in global software markets and that the main market opportunity for these enterprises, at least in the near term, will remain systems integration for domestic customers.[25]

THE THIRD EYE ON PROJECT MANAGEMENT OF CHINA

Presenting a striking contrast to the rapid growth of project management in China over the past two decades, an abundant literature survey has ferreted out only few studies that specifically address the issues of project management in China. At the end of 1980s, two studies had uncovered part of the whole about project management practices in mainland China from a Western perspective. U.S. researchers Cogal and Ireland participated in two project management delegations to China and mainly received briefings and observed projects in China, and they concluded that modern project management practices that had originated from developed countries had met great challenges in the unique environment of China.[29] They saw some distinct problems unique to the cultural requirements of Chinese society and human resources that were not solved by tried and true practices. Two other scholars, Graham and Sun, through a survey in Shenyang, presented a better grasp of project management in China by exposing and commenting on its areas of weakness.[30] One of the weak areas they pointed out is the lack of sufficient skilled personnel, which they thought would be developed through project management training. The other critical problematic areas probably resulted from the existing economical and financial system, an immature infrastructure, and a deep-rooted traditional culture could not be easily resolved in a short term and was somewhat out of the control of Chinese project managers. Both studies seem to suggest that modern project management theories from developed countries have encountered difficulties in translation into the unique practices of China.

Nearly 10 years later, despite widespread recognition and application of project management in China, research in one of most important economic development regions of China, Pudong, Shanghai, further revealed that project management in China was still in some ways behind that in the West, and this was shown empirically by the fact that more sophisticated project management techniques and computer-based tools are used rarely in China.[31] In addition, the official press in China also has confirmed very recently that it still has some way to go in the development of project management in China compared with its industrialized counterparts.[19]

Vice director of the Institute of Beijing ZK Project Management, Professor Xu Chengji, in a paper presented at the Second International Conference of Project Management in China (ICPM2004) in May of 2004 in Beijing, said

> During past two decades, in spite of over 100,000 people in China having received various project management training, there is still a huge gape between the shortage of professional project management personnel and the enormous requirements of the booming economy. Application of project management could only be found in a few pioneer organizations at the level of managing individual projects rather than organizational projects. The main causes that result in schedule delays, budget overages, and the failure of a large number of projects in modern China are still largely due to poor project planning and control in the area of sophisticated technical issues.
>
> Project management in China is currently still at a very early stage of its development compared with some developed countries, which is likely to turn into a roadblock that hinders further economic development in China. It seems that government has not realized the problem and still relies considerably on nongovernmental effort to advance the further development of project management. So far we are still heavily engaged in learning international project management theories and practices, attempting to absorb and apply them under Chinese practices and working hard on the promotion and advancement of project management in China.

China is still transitioning to modernization and globalization, and time and effort are needed for project management to fit into China's unique environment and distinctive economic organizational system and deep-rooted traditional culture. Over the past two decades, application of project management in China has revealed some critical problems in employing this modern management method in Chinese practice. Traditional organizational structures and management awareness inherited from the centrally planned system, shortages of relevant laws and regulations of project management to standardize project management implementation in industries, and a lack of skilled project management professionals are some of the most crucial problems that have considerably slackened the development of project management in China.[32] Evidence can be obtained easily from public media that some projects have suffered from these obstructions. One exemplary project that has been hotly debated recently is the National Grand Theater, which should be finished in the next year or so and will be one of the greatest architectural projects in modern China. However, some fundamental problems, such as who will be the manager of this megatheater and how it is going to operate, still remain open to discussion. Another such project is the magnetic levitation train in Shanghai, which is widely reported to be a source of much pride for the local people and their government officials. However, it has been suggested that this is "prestigious" project that focuses only "image" and "showing off" instead of economics. The train is very inconvenient to take, and tickets are too expensive for regular passengers. This has resulted in very little traffic since its opening, which seems to indicate the failure of this "proud" project.

Apart from these specific examples, cultural differences also are regarded as one of barriers to project management development in China. Project managers cultivated in the unique practices of China usually have a strong technical background and tend to be good at dealing with interpersonal and governmental relationships, and this makes them quite different from Western project managers, who generally require professional knowledge in project management, strong communication skills, and team spirit[33] to manage their projects effectively. Chinese cultural emphasis on a subjective, implicit, and middle-of-the-road philosophy is said to present a great challenge to project managers, who, it is said, need a strong analytical and logical mind-set, open-mindedness, and a confrontational approach to conflicts.

EMPIRICAL STUDY OF PROJECT MANAGEMENT IN CHINA

The preceding anecdotal descriptions have provided the basis to outline a profile of the project management environment and practices in China. We now turn to academic research to find out how project management is practiced in China. Unfortunately, a survey of the literature on project management finds no empirical effort to expose the real practices of current project management in the unique environment of the mainland China. In an effort to close this gap, the authors and a research team from Fudan University in Shanghai and supervised by Professor Zhai Li launched a large-scale empirical study to explore the project management practices of information systems (IS) in China from the perspective of critical success factors (CSFs). This three-year study was designed in two parts and was accompanied by two large-scale questionnaire surveys in mainland of China. The first questionnaire survey that accompanied stage one of the study was designed to collect empirical evidence to support a set of proposed CSFs relevant to contemporary China's IS projects. Grounded on the CSF findings of the first survey, the main focus of the second questionnaire survey in stage two of the study was to reveal real practices of Chinese project management by exploring how well these CSFs are performed in Chinese IS projects.

First Stage of the Study

The general introduction to mainland of China at the beginning of this chapter let us to believe that the CSFs identified in the developed countries of the West might not be completely applicable in the same manner to the Chinese IS project management environment and practices. Thus, based on an extensive literature review of project management, a set of CSFs that was generic enough to cover most of the concerns of Chinese IS project managers was compiled. These commonly cited CSFs are postulated as the conceptual list of CSFs for the research.[34] The proposed 12 factors are

- Effective communication
- Top-management support
- User involvement
- Competent project manager
- Competent project team members
- Project definition
- Project planning
- Project control and change management
- Technology support
- Relationship management (*guanxi*)
- Project organization
- Project management software and techniques

Among this proposed CSF list for Chinese projects, most items are suggested and upheld by most researchers. Only relationship management (*guanxi*) is newly proposed and uniquely Chinese. We believe that it will be particularly important for Chinese IS management practices. The importance of *guanxi* in Chinese daily life and business has been stressed repeatedly by numerous scholars.[5,12,35–37] As an important element of deep-rooted Chinese culture, *guanxi* is reported to have a profound influence on life and the work behavior of Chinese professionals.[37] Relationship management in this study addresses the question, "Do *guanxi*-based relationships have a significant influence on Chinese IS projects?"

Questionnaire Design and Data Collection.   The 12 CSFs and a total of 65 associated CSF statements were defined in the first questionnaire. Multivariate analysis was employed to assess the CSF concepts. Between three and eight different statements were elicited from each of the 12 CSFs to represent differing aspects of the CSFs. All these CSFs and most of the associated statements generally were based on the previous CSF studies discussed. Only a few of them are adapted or newly proposed to better suit this study of Chinese practices. A numerical scale of 1 to 7, ranging from "very unimportant" to "very important," was used to measure a survey respondent's perceived importance of the 65 CSF statements.

Three different sources of survey respondents were used at this stage of the research. The first is a randomly compiled list of firms from Web sites and the Yellow Pages of a telephone directory. The second is compiled from the list of MBA programs at Shanghai's Fudan University and IS project professional training courses sponsored by the Shanghai city government. Meanwhile, in order to increase the generalizability of the research findings, the questionnaire also was posted on two project management Web sites in the mainland China to acquire more respondents of diverse background. From early July to the middle of November 2003, 780 questionnaires were distributed to the first two sources of respondents. Data collection in mainland China proved to be difficult. It took us nearly five months to reach the sample size we wanted. The detailed distribution of questionnaires and the usable return rate are shown in Table 23.1. After data screening and "cleaning," a total of 247 usable and completed questionnaires were reserved for data analysis.

TABLE 23.1   Distributed and Returned Usable Questionnaires of the First Survey

Respondent Sources	Distributed Questionnaires	Returned Usable Questionnaires	Usable Return Rate
Randomly selected firms	488	96	19.67%
MBA students/IT training practitioners	292	81	27.74%
PM Web sites	—	70	—

Data Analysis.   To begin the data analysis, the nonresponse bias was examined first using the SPSS program. A one-way multivariate analysis of variance (MANOVA) was performed to investigate sample-source differences in CSF statements. The result of the MANOVA analysis gave us a Wilks' lambda value of 0.51, with a significance value of 0.22. The result shows that there is no statistically significant difference among the three different sample sources,[38] which means that there is no significant nonresponse bias. Therefore, it is acceptable to regard these three sample sources as one in the subsequent data analysis.

The scale of reliability and validity of the combined data set then was analyzed. We assessed the internal consistency for multi-item scales by computing Cronbach's alpha value. The 12 CSFs with different numbers of items have a composite scale reliability value ranging from 0.75 to 0.91, thus meeting the requirements for exploratory research.[39]

In addition, we examined the construct validity of the measures by using confirmatory factor analysis (CFA). Because of sample size restrictions, four separate tests were performed using the SAS CALIS procedure, each having three CSF constructs. The result shows that 60 of 65 CSF statements have a standardized factor loading of more than 0.60 corresponding to their respective CSFs. The average factor-loading coefficient for all 65 items is 0.70. Meanwhile, all questionnaire items have significant t values with a confidence interval at $p < 0.001$. The mean value of each CSF also was computed. The results are shown in Table 23.2.

TABLE 23.2   CSF Mean Ranking and Reliabilities of Measures of the First Survey

Rank	CSF	Mean	Cronbach's Alpha
1	Effective communication	5.92	0.88
2	Clear project definition	5.87	0.80
3	Top management support	5.86	0.77
4	Competent project manager	5.76	0.84
5	User involvement	5.68	0.81
6	Relationship management	5.66	0.91
7	Project control and change management	5.66	0.91
8	Project planning	5.61	0.84
9	Competent project team members	5.56	0.85
10	Project organization	5.46	0.75
11	Technology and expertise support	5.37	0.83
12	Project management software and techniques	4.88	0.87

Research Findings.   The results of the first questionnaire survey have, for the most part, supported the research findings of similar studies done in the West. One of the key findings in this preliminary analysis is that relationship management is first viewed as an important CSF for Chinese IS projects. Relationship management as a kind of distinctive Chinese phenomenon has been studied intensively in social and culture fields but rarely as a CSF in project management. This study result has ranked it in the middle, higher than a few other CSFs that have been studied more frequently. It is a clear manifestation of the significant influence of Chinese traditional beliefs and culture on Chinese organization and management practices today. *Guanxi* is still very critical to dealings among the Chinese, whether they are in a social or a job-related context. The IS project environment is evidently no different.

Based on the CFA results, the three lowest ranked CSFs in Table 23.2 and a few CSF statements were deleted to refine the CSF list. The modified CSF list consists of nine CSFs with 45 CSF statements. The CFA's output of the modified CSF list yields a result that shows not only high reliability and construct validity of the exploratory study but also relatively better goodness-of-fit indices for the whole of model.

Second Stage of the Study

Questionnaire Design.   The questionnaire that was used in the second stage was designed mainly to collect respondents' self-evaluations of project performance measured through different CSFs and detailed CSF statements. Nine CSFs and 45 associated CSF statements were defined in this questionnaire, which is based primarily on the CSF list that had been modified and refined empirically in the first survey. A Likert scale of 1 to 7, ranging from "very unsuccessful" to "very successful," was adopted to ask survey participants to indicate their perception of the degree of success with which the project had performed the task that each CSF statement proposed.

Sample and Data Collection.   Two different sources of surveyed projects were employed in the second stage of the study. One source was a randomly compiled list of organizations from Web sites and the Yellow Pages of a telephone directory. Date from 129 valid projects were collected from this source. The other source of survey date was a sampling of projects. Some of these source project data was collected from the class lists of MBA programs at Shanghai's Fudan University and IS project professional training courses sponsored by the Shanghai city government. The rest of these source project data was collected from organizations that have connections with our research team at Fudan University in Shanghai. From this source, usable data on 85 projects was collected by mail or e-mail. Data on a total of 214 valid projects were collected from these two sources.

Data Analysis.   The two sources projects were merged for subsequent data analysis after being examined by MANOVA that showed no significant difference between the two sources. Based on merged project data, surveyed IS projects were first grouped by industry and district, and the results are summarized in Table 23.3.

The industry classifications show responding projects are evenly distributed in a wide range of industries for the most part. This fact could be regarded as an indication that IS projects have been widely implemented in various types of organizations in mainland China at present.

The district distribution data reveal that responding IS projects come from widely distributed areas of mainland China. More than 40 percent of the responding projects are from Shanghai, the largest city and economic center of modern China.

TABLE 23.3   **Project Profile of the Second Survey**

Characteristic	Number of Responses	Percentage (%)
Industry distribution		
Education and research	31	13.84
Government and administration	31	13.84
Banking and finance	30	13.39
Telecommunication	30	13.39
Computer service and software	25	11.16
Manufacturing	20	8.93
Retail sales and business service	19	8.48
Insurance	10	4.46
Transportation	8	3.57
Other industries	20	8.94
District distribution		
Shanghai	96	42.86
Beijing	20	8.93
Shanxi	16	7.14
Guandong	11	4.91
Fujian	10	4.46
Other districts	56	25.00
Missing	15	6.70

The nine CSFs, with five measurement items under each of them, have a composite scale reliability value ranging from 0.81 to 0.91. The means of the CSFs also were calculated and are shown in Table 23.4.

Findings and Discussion

The newly added factor relationship management surprisingly scored highest among the nine CSFs, as shown in Table 23.4. The ranking shows this factor has been given enough attention by most project participants in the Chinese business environment. At the same time, *guanxi* or various other relationships among project participants also have been handled satisfactorily in most projects.

Apart from relationship management, the ranking also indicates that respondents generally agree that they have performed well in the area of project definition, communication, and enlisting top-management support. Clear project definition was ranked next to the top, which is in accordance with the preceding findings that reveal the expectation of clearly defined objectives for the Chinese.[40] The other factor that may help in interpreting this finding lies in Chinese culture. Quite a few studies have stressed repeatedly that the Chinese tend to be more long-term oriented than Westerners.[8] Effective communication was ranked third in the nine CSFs. This ranking probably could find close correlation with the top-ranked factor relationship management. For Chinese project personnel, effective communication is not only needed to resolve problems during project implementation but also is essential to maintain good personal relationships.

Viewing from the bottom of the ranking, most Chinese IS project practitioners admit that they have done poorly in staffing the project team with competent members, project control and change management, and project planning, especially the latter two CSFs.

TABLE 23.4   **Mean of CSF of the Second Survey**

Mean Rank	CSF	Mean
1	Relationship management	5.57
2	Clear project definition	5.39
3	Effective communication	5.15
4	Top management support	5.11
5	User involvement	5.11
6	Competent project manager	5.04
7	Competent project team members	5.03
8	Project control and change management	4.83
9	Project planning	4.77

Project planning was ranked as the lowest in the nine CSFs, which conveys the implicit message that the Chinese still have serious problems in using this most essential element of project management effectively. This is likely to be a manifestation of the fact that project management is still a fashionable term that appears frequently in textbooks rather than a workable method that can be applied in practices in most contemporary Chinese organizations. The next to the lowest ranked factor, project control and change management, is thought to be the logical consequence of poor project planning.

Consistent with the remarks based on anecdotal evidence mentioned earlier, although project management is being recognized increasingly in various industries in modern China, it is still a rather budding discipline that is too new for most Chinese organizations to adopt in the short run. These CSFs ranking lend support to the idea that most of Chinese organizations and their project participants have just started their learning curve on the pursuit of successful project management based on Chinese practices. This provides strong evidence to support the idea that Chinese project management is still in its infancy and is focused primarily on learning, promoting, and advancing project management. The prevailing trend of project management training and certification in China implies that a small community of project management practitioners and scholars is only just beginning to form in China as a widely accepted profession and that it still needs a long time to build. This is probably the reason why research-based institutes such as PMRCC and the Institute of Beijing ZK Project Management have been established and popularized in contemporary China rather than project management organizations such as the Project Management Institute (PMI) in the United States.

IMPLICATIONS FOR WESTERN PROJECT STAKEHOLDERS

Our empirical study has suggested explicitly that relationship management and other traditional Chinese cultural factors still have significant influence on the success of Chinese projects at present. Therefore, for project stakeholders from Western countries, it is believed that one of the greatest barriers to project success in China is the one that is presented by culture. Although a large amount of new technology, management theories, and experience have been introduced into China by the developed countries in recent years, including theories of project management, it is argued that it is much easier to introduce "hard" elements than their "soft" counterparts into Chinese practice.[15] An example of a "soft" element is is culture, which it is argued tends to change at a slower pace than political and economic structures. The relatively "hard" things, such as new knowledge, tools, and techniques in project management, can be introduced and adopted without much hesitation because they have demonstrated their superior effectiveness from the point of view of development of China's economy, but culture-based behaviors are not as easily changed. Although some scholars have pointed out that it is more than likely that the role of *guanxi* in business will diminish eventually as China moves toward an open-market system,[14] it also has been suggested that traditional Chinese culture will prevail and will remain the basis of Chinese organizational behavior and management style for some time.[1,12,15]

Thus foreign project stakeholders need to understand the unique culture of China and attempt to adapt to it to get their projects in China done. Two noticeable cultural differences deserve their attention so as to smooth their interaction with Chinese project partners. One involves the different languages and communication styles used in China; the other is the building and maintaining of interpersonal relationships.

Most Chinese can speak the standardized national language known as Mandarin (or Putonghua), whereas only a small number of people are able to speak English fluently. Therefore, being able to speak the native language will demonstrate your honor of and adaptation to Chinese culture and readily bring with it the trust and respect of your Chinese partners. For the most part, Chinese culture is a high-context culture.[5,6] The Chinese have a saying: "Westerners are very superficial—they believe what you say." This saying clearly reveals that the highly collectivistic culture of China leads Chinese to communicate in a very indirect manner. The messages that Chinese people send and receive are usually based as much on the context of the messages as on the actual words. Chinese people rarely say "No" directly; they only hint at difficulties. For instance, after receiving a request, a Chinese worker may reply, "This is very difficult, and I need to think about it" or "It is not convenient." This is actually an ambiguous way of informing that supplicant that "It is impossible." That Westerners need to learn to be able to discern the meaning of apparently ambiguous phrases is another managerial implication.

The other singular feature derived from Chinese collectivism is Chinese interpersonal relationship values with a core element of *guanxi,* which is widely reported to have a significant influence on China's international business. To have their projects completed successfully, Western stakeholders of projects in China must pay sufficient attention to develop and maintain business *guanxi* with their Chinese counterparts, especially with those in crucial positions. The Chinese have a tendency to develop personal relationships with their business partners first, before getting down to the details of business, which is quite the opposite of the way that Westerners usually work. For projects in a Chinese environment, relationship building usually comes first—before launching the specifics of the project. Offering a formal banquet followed by entertainment is a common way of taking the first step to showing your courtesy and respect in Chinese business culture. Then, by bestowing favors and honor through considerate and appropriate giving of chosen gifts and hosting appreciation dinners, a foreign project stakeholder can demonstrate the good faith to form the basis of short-term business *guanxi* with Chinese partners. Furthermore, if needed, paying enough personal attention to cultivate personal relationship and trust and nurturing mutual benefits are both useful approaches to establishing a long-term business *guanxi*.

Face (*mianzi*) is another key element in the development and maintenance of business relationships with the Chinese. Face is essentially the recognition by others of one's social standing, position, respect, and moral reputation in Chinese society.[41] Chinese people generally attempt to avoid direct confrontation and pursue harmony and consensus to keep face for others. Certainly, losing face is more important to a Chinese manager than to a Western one and is felt more deeply. Causing someone important among your Chinese partners in project to lose face, publicly or in front of other project participants, through criticizing, failing to treat with respect, losing your temper, or other insulting behavior may result in a loss of cooperation. Therefore, it is advisable for Westerners to avoid any public embarrassment and criticism of their Chinese partners as they may do in the West and try to discuss any issues in private so as to allow others to keep face. Of course, much can be gained by helping Chinese partners to gain face through certain considerate behaviors, such as praising the person to their Chinese colleagues in public or complimenting the person in front of his or her superior.

Consistent with face, conflict resolution is another sensitive cultural difference that deserves the attention of foreign project participants. The Chinese relationship culture heavily emphasizes hierarchy and the need to maintain harmony and values long-term cooperation for mutual benefits, which may have implications for the manner in which Chinese project participants experience and resolve conflicts.[1] Different from their Western counterparts, who may encourage open discussion on disagreements and conflicts to solve problems quickly and effectively, Chinese project personnel would try to avoid direct debate or confrontation and always attempt to get through conflicts quietly and as harmoniously as possible. They are likely to pay to try to maintain group harmony and face and to preserve relationships with everyone involved in projects when resolving conflicts. Therefore, it is worth remembering for Westerners not to talk about problems directly with their Chinese colleagues in public so as not to embarrass them or degrade their status.

In addition, in a high-power-distance culture such as China's, people incline to defer to authority and age,[42] which is quite different from Western countries. Westerners frequently see no differences in status, seniority, and age. However, most managers in China are expected to be treated differently from their subordinates. Thus it is recommended for foreign project stakeholders to adjust their attitudes and social behaviors to deal with their Chinese project partners at different hierarchical levels appropriately, especially for those decision makers who have significant influence on project outcome in Chinese organizations. On the other hand, project team members in China generally do not challenge their superiors or bosses in public and simply accept the orders they are given to show their respect. Thus, for Western project stakeholders, talking with your Chinese team members in private face to face instead of in public is a wise approach to collect their personal feedback and ideas.

CONCLUSION

This chapter first presented a general description on the current practices of project management in China. Various anecdotal evidence provided strong support to the idea that although there are significant requirements for project management in contemporary China, it is just at the beginning of its development and requires much learning, localization, and promotion in China.

A two-stage empirical study on the management of IS projects in China was then reported to show how project management is practiced in contemporary China. The empirical findings of the first stage of the study suggested an interesting ranking of 12 postulated CSFs, with the rarely studied factor of relationship management ranked in the middle. The findings of the second stage of the study not only further validated Chinese culture's significant influence on project success but also provided solid evidence of the immaturity of project management in modern China to prove the findings of the anecdotal analysis. Nevertheless, project management practices revealed in this chapter only represent a transient status of fast development of project management in China. No one can foresee precisely what project management will be like in China in the near future given its current rate of development. It is suggested that the Chinese old saying, "The future is bright, but the way is tough and long," would aptly describe the current practice of project management development in China.

The research findings of this empirical study emphasize the significant impact of traditional culture on Chinese project management practices for foreign project participants. To address this "soft" side of projects in China, some practical tips on effective communication and building and maintaining good business relationships with Chinese partners are given to Western project stakeholders to minimize the cultural clash and deal with Chinese culture effectively.

REFERENCES

1. Chen P, Partington D. 2004. An interpretive comparison of Chinese and Western conceptions of relationship in construction project management work. *Int J Project Manag* 22:394–406.

2. Chapman JD. 2004. A critical analysis of the application of Western project management theories in the Middle East, in *PMI Research Conference 2004 Proceedings*. Newtown Square, PA: Project Management Institute.

3. Forsberg K, Mooz H, Cotterman H. 2000. *Visualizing Project Management*, 2d ed. Hoboken, NJ: Wiley.

4. National Bureau of Statistics of China. 2004. *Statistic Year Book of China (2004)*. Beijing: National Bureau of Statistics Press.

5. Hofstede G, Bond MH. 1988. Confucius and economic growth: New trends into culture's consequences. *Organ Dyn* 16(4):4–21.

6. Hofstede G. 1991. *Cultures and Organizations: Software of the Mind*. New York: McGraw-Hill.

7. MacInnes P. 1993. *Guanxi* or contract: A way to understand and predict conflict between Chinese and Western senior manager in China-based joint ventures, in D MacCarty, S Hille (eds.), *Research on Multinational Business Management and Internationalization of Chinese Enterprises*. Nanjing: Nanjing University, pp. 345–351.

8. Stück JM. 1999. Cross-cultural management in China: An application of Hofstede's model, in N Campbell, C Jayachandran, Guijin Lin (eds.), *Advances in Chinese Industrial Studies: The Managerial Process and Impact of Foreign Investment in Great China*, Vol. 6. Stamford, CT: Jai Press, pp. 277–294.

9. Ambler T, Witzel M. 2000. *Doing Business in China*. London: Routledge.

10. Schwartz SH. 1994. Beyond individualism/collectivism: New cultural dimensions of values, in U Kim, HC Triandis, C Choi, et al (eds.), *Individualism and Collectivism: Theory, Method, and Applications*. Thousand Oaks, CA: Sage.

11. Davies H, Leung TKP, Luk STK, Wong YH. 1995. The benefits of *guanxi:* The value of relationships in developing the Chinese market. *Ind Market Manag* 24:207–214.

12. Yeung YM, Tung RL. 1996. Achieving business success in Confucian societies: The importance of *guanxi* (connections). *Organ Dyn* 25(2):54–65.

13. Yadong L. 2000. *Guanxi and Business*. Singapore: World Scientific.

14. Ying F. 2002. Questioning *guanxi:* Definition, classification and implications. *Int Bus Rev* 11:543–561.

15. Selmer J. 1997. *Cross-Cultural Management in China: Current Issues and Emerging Trends*. Hong Kong: Hong Kong Baptist University.

16. Xing F. 1995. The Chinese culture system: Implication for cross-culture management. *SAM Adv Manag J* 60(1):14–20.

17. National Bureau of Statistics of China. 1996. *Statistic Year Book of China (1996)*. Beijing: National Bureau of Statistics Press.

18. Chan WKL, Wong FKW, Scott D. 1999. Managing construction projects in China: The transitional period in the millennium. *Int J Project Manag* 17(4):257–263.

19. Xinhuanet. 2001. Project management to be promoted in China; retrieved January 2005 from http://english.enorth.com.cn/system/2001/11/29/000203176.shtml.

20. Myers C, Wu ZM. 1997. Project manager training of trainers program for China. *Project Manag J* 28(1):12–18.

21. *People's Daily Online.* 2002. Project management popular in China; retrieved January 2005 from http://english.people.com.cn/200409/10/eng20040910_156630.html.

22. Project Management Institute. 2004. PMI Annual Report 2003; retrieved January 2005 from www.pmi.org.

23. Project Management Institute. 2004. PMI and SAFEA jointly accelerating China's project management development; retrieved January 2005 from www.pmi.org/prod/groups/public/documents/info/ap_news-safea.asp.

24. ChinaOnline. 2000. China: IT industry continues strong growth; retrieved August 2004 from www.chinaonline.com/industry/infotech/NewsArchive/cs-protected/2000/december/C00120113.asp.

25. Saxenian A. 2003. Government and *guanxi:* The Chinese software industry in transition; retrieved March 2005 from www.sims.berkeley.edu/~anno/papers/softwareinchina.pdf.

26. Dehua Ju. 2001. China's budding software industry. *IEEE Software,* May–June:92–95.

27. Xinhai Jing. 2002. The only gap of software industry between China and India: Project management; retrieved March 2005 from www.ccw.com.cn/htm/work/handlers/jlrjs/02_4_12_2.asp.

28. Sun W. 2005. Grow up, software industry in China; retrieved March 2005 from http://tech.sina.com.cn/it/2005-03-02/1138539970.shtml.

29. Cogal HC, Ireland LR. 1988. Project management: Meeting China's challenge. *Project Manag J* 19(1):61–66.

30. Graham RG, Sun MH. 1988. An empirical analysis of project management in a selected industrial area in the People's Republic of China. *Project Manag J* 19(3):59–64.

31. Yang ML, Chuah KB, Rao VM, et al. 1997. Project management practices in Pudong: A new economic development area of Shanghai, China. *Int J Project Manag* 15(5):313–319.

32. HexiaoYang, Xiao Huang. 2003. Problems and suggestions of project management in China. *China Venture Capital High-Tech*, August:58–59.

33. Qishan Yuan. 2004. Culture differences of project management between China and Western countries. *Organ Culture*, February:52–53.

34. Chao Dong, Chuah KB, Li Zhai. 2004. A study of critical success factors of information system projects in China, in DP Slevin, DI Cleland, JK Pinto (eds.), *Innovations: Project Management Research 2004.* Newtown Square, PA: Project Management Institute.

35. Pye L. 1986. The China trade: Making the deal. *Harvard Bus Rev*, July–August:74–80.

36. Redding GS. 1993. *The Spirit of Chinese Capitalism.* Berlin: de Gruyter.

37. Wright P, Szeto R, Cheng LTW. 2002. *Guanxi* and professional conduct in China: A management development perspective. *Int J Hum Res Manag* 13(1):156–182.

38. Pallant J. 2001. *SPSS Survival Guide: A Step-by-Step Guide to Data Analysis Using SPSS.* North Sydney, NSW, Australia: Allen & Unwin.

39. Hair JF, Anderson RE, Tatham RL, Black WC. 1998. *Multivariate Data Analysis,* 5th ed. Englewood Cliffs, NJ: Prentice-Hall.

40. Andersen ES, Dyrhaug QLX, Jessen SA. 2002. Evaluation of Chinese projects and comparison with Norwegian projects. *Int J Project Manag* 20(8):601–609.

41. Wong YH, Leung TKP. 2001. *Guanxi: Relationship Marketing in a Chinese Context.* New York: International Business Press.

42. Osland GE. 1999. Doing business in China: A framework for cross-culture understanding. *Market Intell Plan* 8(4):4–14.

CHAPTER 24

PROJECT MANAGEMENT IN AUSTRALIA

Brian R. Kooyman

Managing Director, Tracey, Brunstrom & Hammond Group,
Offices in Sydney, Brisbane, Melbourne, Perth and Canberra, Australia

Brian Kooyman graduated as an architect in 1972 and has worked in the architectural and project management fields of the Australian construction industry. He is the Managing Director of the Tracey, Brunstrom & Hammond Group and has gained extensive experience in the management and planning of the design and construction phases of construction projects, as well as a range of information technology (IT) and telecommunications projects. He has worked on major projects such as the Sydney 2000 Olympics, Federation Square and the redevelopment of Darling Harbour (Sydney). Experience has been gained both in the resolution of contractual disputes and as an expert witness in construction disputes.

Kooyman has held positions as a founding director and national president of the Australian Institute of Project Management (AIPM), and he has chaired a number of committees for the Project Management Institute (PMI). He was the recipient of the 2003 Australian Council of PMI Chapters Distinguished Contribution award and is currently an Adjunct Professor to the School of Business (CURTIN University, Western Australia), an Adjunct Professor of project management (University of Technology, Sydney), and an Honorary Associate of the Graduate School of Government (University of Sydney).

This chapter looks at three particular aspects of project management in Australia—the genesis and development of Australian project management, developments in Australian project delivery methods, and two significant recent projects: the Sydney 2000 Olympic Games and the Qantas Airbus A330 Program. It also offers some thought on future directions for Australian project management. There is a bias toward project management in the Australian engineering/construction industry first because this was, for some decades, the main application area for project management development and practice in Australia and second because much of my experience in the past three decades has been in this industry. It also could be remarked that my increasing involvement in telecommunications/information technology (IT) projects in the past decade can be seen as reflecting the more general spread of project management into an ever-widening range of application areas in Australia.

THE GENESIS AND DEVELOPMENT OF PROJECT MANAGEMENT IN AUSTRALIA

Over the years, a number of books and articles have been written about the development of project management in North America and Europe. In particular, a very detailed history is given in Morris (1994). However, no such history of project management in Australia has been written to date. The following is very much a summary rather than a history. In order to draw a parallel, the format used is to briefly summarize international developments and then those in Australia to help to clarify the context of the latter.

The 1950s

There is general agreement nowadays that what is called *modern project management* began in this decade, some of the more relevant international developments being

- Bechtel's initiative in developing embryo project management approaches in the early 1950s, initially on the transmountain oil pipeline in Canada (Bechtel, 1989)

- The widespread use of joint-project offices in the U.S. Air Force from the early 1950s (Morris, 1994)

- Perhaps most significantly, the development of the critical path method (CPM) (Kelly and Walker, 1989) and the program evaluation and review technique (PERT) (Fazar, 1962) and subsequent publicizing of both in the late 1950s

The history of Australian project management has a parallel with what was occurring around the world. Particularly in the Australian construction industry, there was one initiative broadly parallel to Bechtel's.

In 1954–1955, an Australian company, Civil & Civic, initiated an embryo project management approach to its own major subdivision development, where, by persistent analysis and investigation of design alternatives by a "project engineer," the project was converted from a marginal development to a successful venture (Civil & Civic, 1969). From that point, Civil & Civic appointed its own "project engineers" to manage the design phases of all its own development projects and quality control of construction. By 1958, Civil & Civic began to market this service to external clients and later offered the natural extension of this, namely, full responsibility for all the phases of a construction project from inception to completion, which came to be described as its "Project Management Service." Initial market penetration was slow, but it had become quite substantial by the mid-1960s (Stretton, 1993).

No other comparable Australian project management initiatives in the 1950s are known of.

The 1960s

Internationally, the 1960s saw the development of the majority of tools and techniques that became central to project management. A very incomplete listing includes

- CPM (using arrow diagramming) and PERT were being used increasingly for time management, notably in construction and defence. Fondahl published what later came to be known as the *precedence diagramming method* (PDM) in 1961 (Fondahl, 1987).

These three time planning and management approaches are generically described as *network techniques.*

- Project management was closely identified with the use of network techniques for project planning, scheduling, and control.

- Project cost management was added to project time management as a distinctive technique (e.g., PERT/cost, C/SCSC), as was resource scheduling.

- Project management was still identified primarily with the construction, defence, and aerospace industries.

- Professional project management bodies were formed in Europe (Internet, now IPMA) in 1965 and in North America (PMI) in 1969.

In Australia, some of the overseas developments were adopted by varying degrees. The first known commercial use of CPM was by Civil & Civic in 1962. By mid-1963, that company had adopted PDM, which came to be generally used as a standard on its projects.

My company, now Tracey, Brunstrom & Hammond (the TBH Group), originated in the United States, came to Australia with the U.S. defence forces, and started practicing in Australia in 1965, specializing in CPM and time-control techniques. It was the first of several independent specialized project management companies that began establishing in the construction industry in the middle to late 1960s.

In the 1960s, contractors in the Australian building and construction industry were more reticent than their northern hemisphere counterparts in fully adopting network techniques. This undoubtedly contributed to a number of developments.

From the mid-1960s, there was an increasingly urgent push by many government agencies and authorities to require contractors in the building and construction industry to produce and upgrade CPM networks on government-funded projects. Contractually, they were intended for monitoring project progress and support for entitlement for extension to time claims.

As had happened internationally, project management in Australia in the 1960s came to be associated very strongly with network techniques. This had some positive aspects because it helped to increase the awareness of clients for the need and value of project time-control techniques.

The addition of cost management and resources scheduling techniques to time management, although starting, was slow to take off in Australia during the 1960s, but the techniques were used increasingly in the 1970s. The formation of a distinctively Australian professional project management body did not eventuate until the 1970s.

The 1970s

Internationally, this decade experienced developments in the following areas:

- Project management applications spread from construction, aerospace, and defence into virtually every industry (Kerzner, 1979).

- Application of a much wider range of tools and techniques (originally developed in the 1960s), such as work-breakdown structure (WBS), organizational breakdown structures (OBS), responsibility assignment matrices, and earned value, increased greatly.

- Interest in organizational forms to support project management increased.

- There was a greater concern with management of conflict on projects.

- There was a significant increase in "how to do project management" in the literature based on experience in practice. This appears to have led to what some have called the "professional definition" period.

In Australia, developments in project management began to obtain a wider acceptance and momentum. In the construction industry, project management spread beyond its more traditional areas into the vast emerging mining industry, which became a vitally important lynch-pin in Australia's economic progress as it moved from an agricultural to a mining economy. The construction of major mining infrastructure brought substantial overseas project experience to Australia.

The requirement for contractors in the building and construction industry to produce and upgrade CPM networks on government-funded projects became common practice and often was required contractually. During the 1970s, most Australian government capital works were procured through the federal government's Department of Works, which strongly promoted project management and time-control techniques.

This approach extended to many (but by no means all) state government departments. Included were the NSW Government Architect, the Victorian Department of Public Works, and the WA Department of Works.

The defence industry had strong associations with peer organizations in the United Kingdom and the United States and continued to place increasing emphasis on project management approaches.

There was a dramatic increase in inflation and financial interest rates in Australia in the mid-1970s, which focused attention on the escalating costs of delays in project completion. This further increased the perceived importance of time management and its integral impact on cost "blowouts" and led to additional attention directed toward contractual conflicts and their resolution. In addition, from the late 1970s, much greater attention came to be paid to the detailed planning and management of the design and documentation process to control time and cost issues in this project phase. A range of advanced techniques, including management by milestone objectives, already was being applied practically.

As mentioned earlier, the formation of a distinctively Australian professional project management body did not eventuate until the 1970s. In 1976, a group of project management practitioners in NSW formed the project managers forum (PMF), with the objective of providing a forum or network of individuals and organizations to compare experience and thinking on the application of project management in the Australian context. The PMF evidently fulfilled a latent need and rapidly expanded to develop chapters in most Australian states and territories.

The 1980s

Internationally, a number of significant developments in project management occurred, including

- Publication of the Project Management Institute's *Project Management Body of Knowledge (PMBOK)* (PMI, 1987), which can be seen as an effort to represent project management as a structured discipline and approach
- A movement toward looking at projects in their broader context, including "product" (verses project) life-cycle costing
- An emerging emphasis on managing the "front end" of projects, including client needs determination, feasibility studies, value analysis, risk management, and project start-up generally
- Increased focus on factors external to the project, particularly stakeholders and other interested parties, as well as environmental constraints
- Project management increasingly seen as a means of response to and initiation of change
- Initiation of certification/registration programs for project managers

In Australia, project practitioners were becoming increasingly aware of overseas developments, particularly from the mid-1980s onward, so there was less delay in opportunities to learn lessons from overseas. However, there was also a catch-up period. Australia followed the northern hemisphere in developing increased emphasis on the "front end" of projects, on looking toward product life-cycle costing, on awareness of factors external to the project, and on the importance of projects in facilitating change. As a natural development from the financial constraints of the 1970s, during the 1980s there was a significant focus on the management of cost and its relationship to the management of time. Cash flows and cost-control systems became a more common feature on major and more complex projects.

A significant local development was the establishment of the Warren Centre at the University of Sydney with the support of industry, government, and alumni. Its objective was to advance excellence and innovation in Australian engineering and to stimulate closer interchange between industry and academe. In 1985, the Warren Centre issued a report entitled, "Macroprojects, Strategy Planning and Implementation Project Report." The broad objectives of this study were to

- Specify the factors and problems associated with the synthesis and management of macroprojects
- Study and report on the characteristics of multidisciplinary teams and organizations capable of undertaking macroprojects
- Provide a guideline for the Australian macroproject engineering future

Specifically the study concentrated on

- The conceptual phase and the appraisal of macroprojects, including marketing and organizational structure
- Legal, contractual, and financial aspects and social, economic, political, and environmental considerations
- Project management strategies
- Engineering design, procurement, construction scheduling, and project control
- The characteristics of organizations involved in the process at the sponsor level
- The involvement of Australian organizations in future macroprojects

This forward-thinking report highlighted the need for specialized project management skills and a closer working relationship among universities, industry, and engineering and project management practitioners. The emergence of PMI's *PMBOK* and its Project Management Professional (PMP) credential persuaded the PMF that there was a need to establish a local recognition of project management as a distinctive profession and thus to develop appropriate quality methodologies and standards.

In February 1989 (in Adelaide), the PMF restructured and formally became the Australian Institute of Project Management (AIPM) by membership vote. The immediate priorities in the late 1980s and early 1990s were to establish

- A code of ethics (in 1990)
- Membership criteria as follows (from 1991 to 1992):
  - Associate member
  - Member of AIPM—M.A.I.P.M.
  - Fellow of the AIPM—F.A.I.P.M.
  - Honorary life fellow of the AIPM

Assessment processes related to membership were developed in the early 1990s.

The 1990s to 2005

Internationally, the 1990s saw the movement of project management toward a broader approach of being "a way to do business." New concepts on the potential application of project management began to emerge:

- Projects being used increasingly to implement corporate strategies
- An increased focus on balancing the needs of all stakeholders
- The incorporation of total quality management (TQM) approaches and ISO quality assurance standards into project management
- More cooperative alliances between organizations through "partnering" or "strategic alliances" to manage large contracts
- Increasing application of project management methodologies into "soft" projects from the traditional "hard" engineering-type projects
- New project management tools and techniques associated with computer technology and accessibility through PCs
- Increased project team empowerment for project team members to make decisions
- An increasing use of "simultaneous" or "concurrent" engineering
- An increasing move toward management by projects or project-based management
- Developments in multi-project management techniques leading to the development of program and portfolio management concepts and techniques

In Australia, developments in project management were by now running virtually parallel with international developments. Australian developments included the following:

- There was substantial adoption of many of the new international concepts of project management summarized earlier, particularly the first six.
- The concepts of "management by projects" and "project-based management" were spreading into the financial and telecommunications industries.
- Risk management and a more evenly distributed allocation of risk through different project delivery methods were being actively explored. This was particularly so for governments who were struggling with increasing demands for infrastructure with limited financial resources.
- Project management was firmly established as an important element in the construction industry and was being recognized in a generic format for financial projects.
- During the 1990s, the demand increased for recognition and certification of project managers, but this had to be established in the framework of the Australian National Competency Standards as set out by the Australian federal government.
  - Thus through the AIPM, the concept of the Registered Project Manager was developed within the government's framework for competency assessment in Australia. A stringent requirement for the establishment of competencies was that it must be done in conjunction with the relevant industry representatives. AIPM also was advised that no other institute at that stage (i.e., in 1993) had endeavoured to undertake preparation of competency standards for its profession.
  - AIPM then prepared a strategy paper and proposal seeking and obtaining funds from the government to establish an Industry Reference Group and to undertake the development of what are now known as the National Australian Competency Standards for Project Management. These standards were prepared between 1992 and 1995 and were endorsed by the Australian government in 1996. This is an area where Australia has led other international project management organizations.

- Toward the late 1990s, the Project Management Institute (PMI) established chapters in Australia, instigated by project managers who were employed primarily in the information technology (IT) industry. Although AIPM derived primarily from the construction industry, the competency standards had been developed on a "generic" project management basis. However, many in the IT industry worked for larger multinational organizations that recognized PMI's PMP certification, and therefore, the Registered Project Manager classification was not seen as appropriately relevant in the IT industry.

- It is hoped that one day in the near future this "cultural" discrepancy can be reconciled to the benefit of Australian project management at large.

DEVELOPMENTS IN AUSTRALIAN PROJECT DELIVERY METHODS

The history of the development of project management in Australia is closely linked to economic changes and to the onset of more demanding and complex projects, resulting in the development of a variety of project delivery methods. These different delivery methods are reflected in the variety of contractual arrangements prepared and entered into by principals and contractors over the last 50 years. It is understandable that although this observation is made based on my experience in the Australian construction industry, I suspect that a similar development is occurring in other industries, particularly in the telecommunications and IT industries.

Traditional Contractual Methods

If we look at the general economic cycles of Australia, in the 1950s and 1960s, Australia's export industry was dominated by agriculture through wool and wheat. During these two decades, the predominant project delivery methods were what I refer to as *traditional contractual methods.*

However, with changing market conditions and increasing financial and complex technical demands, pressures started mounting to reduce overall project delivery times. Additionally, clients increasingly sought to move risk away from themselves to others better able to manage that risk. The traditional lump-sum approach was becoming too time-consuming, and other forms of contract delivery began to appear.

Thus *design development, document, and construct approaches* and then the *design and construct approach* typically allowed construction to commence earlier than in the traditional lump-sum contract, leading to earlier overall project completion. Additionally, the earlier awarding of a contract moved the risk away from the principal at an earlier stage.

Hybrid Contractual Methods

The 1970s and 1980s saw the major export business of Australia move from agriculture to exploration and mining and the export of major minerals—particularly iron ore and coal. Additionally, oil and natural gas were discovered in Bass Strait and Western Australia. These changes increased the volume of heavy engineering/construction projects dramatically, which also had more complex technological requirements. This, in turn, stimulated changes in project delivery methods.

The mid-1970s also bought a sudden increase in inflation and significantly increased interest rates. This resulted in a rapid increase in project costs, and project feasibility became even more "time sensitive" to project delivery times.

In an effort to deliver projects more effectively (or what were called "fast-track projects"), there was a move away from the traditional lump-sum contracts to a range of hybrid contractual methods such as *managing contractor, construction management, partnering,* and *alliance contracts.* A summary review of these contractual methods follows.

Managing Contractor. This form of contract was one response to the increasing need to undertake and complete projects in a more rapid time frame. The concept is to award a contract to a contractor at a very early stage in the process so that the contractor takes on the role of managing the design, documentation, construction, and commissioning. Although this is similar to the design and construct contract referred to previously, this approach keeps the principal involved and controlling what he or she wants designed. The managing contractor's role is to manage the complete project process from sketch design through to commissioning. This approach allows the client various advantages, the main ones being

- Control of the design without the responsibility and risk of managing and integrating the design process.
- The contractor taking more of the risk but providing "buildability" advice and input into the design. Although the risk is moved into the contractor's realm of responsibility, he or she is probably better experienced and can manage that risk.
- A more rapid commencement to construction by overlapping design and documentation with the construction, that is, earlier award of trade subcontracts and earlier overall project completion.
- A "one-stop shop" for the client.
- Tenders for a managing contractor were often called on *preliminaries, overheads,* and *fixed profit.*

Construction Manager. This form of contract was similar to the managing contractor role except that the contractor is essentially responsible for managing the construction phase of the project. The concept remains of an early appointment of the construction manager who becomes part of the project team and is responsible for collation of the documents into trade packages, for calling tenders and awarding trade subcontracts, and for managing the construction work. This restricts the contractor's risk to the construction process but provides for the contractor to give advice on appropriate construction techniques and to integrate and assemble the documents for an efficient management of the trade subcontracts.
   This approach provides

- The client with greater design control, but the client assumes responsibility for managing the design to achieve the construction manager's program.
- Construction advice to assist the integrity of the documentation.
- The ability to commence construction earlier and thus fast-track project completion.
- Tenders for a construction manager are usually called on fixed price and completion date (subject to extensions of time in accordance with the contract).

Partnering. Partnering was a concept that came to Australia from the United States in the 1990s and was used briefly by some government organizations, but it was not a concept embraced by the private sector. The essence of partnering is a cooperative management style of work intent on overcoming traditional adversarial and litigious relationships and directed toward achieving the project objectives of all parties.

However, because in practice partnering may involve principal and contractor jointly assessing actual or potential non-conformances, it can give rise to significant legal issues for project managers in areas such as authority, delegation of powers, and establishment and documentation of on-site procedures.

The New South Wales government partnering guidelines state, "Partnering is not a contractual agreement, nor does it create any legally enforceable rights or duties. It is the contract that provides the legal relationship, with partnering establishing the working relationships among the stakeholders. . . . "

Essentially, partnering involves a commitment on behalf of the principal, attendance by all relevant parties (and stakeholders) at a workshop to identify common goals, the drafting and signing of a partnering charter that expresses those goals, and subsequently, the establishment and maintenance of communication links and procedures through the course of the project to ensure that the goals are achieved.

However, it has proved difficult to have, on the one hand, a "moral contract" and a charter that will "bind" each party to certain objectives without considering, on the other hand, whether that process creates any legitimate legal expectations and rights. In commercial relationships, much of the conduct between parties is regulated by general legal principles rather than by the terms of their contract.

This goes to the very heart of the partnering debate: "Whilst partnering as a process must be commended for the efficiencies and objectives it has achieved, many of its users fear that the process leaves some established contractual rights and remedies uncertain."

As a result, Australia appears to be heading away from the partnering concept.

Alliance Contracting.   This form of contract was originally more common in the mining and the oil and gas industries in Australia, but in the late 1990s, it began to be used in some areas of the construction industry, a notable building project being the recent National Museum of Australia in Canberra. This form of contract is usually a joint-venture arrangement between the principal, the major contractor, the major subcontractors, and the designers. Each stakeholder has shared objectives, each contributes in a significant way to the project, and each takes a risk on the success or failure of the project achieving the shared objectives. Profits are taken by bonus, and equally, losses are shared. Great care needs to be taken with the establishment and methodology of measuring the shared objectives, or the parties may feel disadvantaged. This style of contracting can be adopted where the actual scope of the project is not clearly defined at the outset of the project or significant change or variation is likely to occur as the project proceeds.

Engineering, Procurement, Construction Management (EPCM) Contracts.   This form of contract has been used virtually exclusively in the mining and oil and gas industries, where the client is seeking specialized experience in technical design and delivery skills. An example may be a mining company that is good at exploration and at finding markets for its product, has found a commercially viable discovery, and seeks to construct a processing plant for its minerals. Many processing methods have a proprietary processing system, and so the client seeks to have an EPCM contractor obtain the proprietary system or process; design, document, and construct the facility; and then achieve the required performance output for the processing plant, which means a "fully operational" facility where the client takes over an operational facility and only has to concern itself with finding and delivering the product to its markets.

This form of delivery usually requires an extremely large (often an international) project management and engineering company that can take on the associated risks and financially support such a large-scale financial investment.

Public-Private Partnerships (The Alliance of Government and Private Enterprise)

The 1990s and turn of the century came to be increasingly difficult for governments in Australia because of the increasing size, complexity, and cost of their projects and significantly increased environmental demands. Infrastructure projects in particular began to exceed the financial and capability resources of both state governments (responsible for health, transport, education, and primary services) and the Australian federal government (responsible for national defence and national rail projects).

Thus Australian governments, particularly state governments, are shying away from the "direct involvement" contractual methods and are moving toward what is called *public-private partnerships* (PPPs). In this type of arrangement, the current most common categories are called the *build, own, operate, and transfer* (BOOT) and the *build, own, and operate* (BOO), where the government grants a concession to a consortium through a tendering process.

The BOOT Scheme. A consortium (which usually consists of financiers, designers, and contractors) bids for the right to construct a facility, to then operate and own the facility for a period of time (often 30 years), and then to transfer the facility at minimal cost back to the relevant government. Thus the returns on the consortium's investment have to be achieved in that period, but the community has the use of that facility earlier than if it had to be funded from government revenue. An interesting example of a BOOT scheme is described in the Sydney 2000 Olympic Games project included in this chapter, namely, the Stadium Australia delivery structure.

The BOO Scheme. This approach is virtually the same as the BOOT scheme process except that the facility is not transferred back to the government, but ownership is retained by the consortium. An example of a BOO scheme is also described in the Sydney 2000 Olympic Games project, namely, the delivery structure for the athletes' village.

There are some other forms of PPPs, whose use depends on the facility being proposed and related circumstances. These include

- *Contracting out.* The private sector provides a service without assuming any financial risk.
- *Joint ventures.* Financing, owning, and operating responsibilities are shared between the two sectors.
- *Leasing.* The private sector funds, develops, and operates and maintains a facility, and the public sector leases it.

Such schemes involve large amounts of finance and long payback periods. As with any form of project finance, a sophisticated approach to risk management is an important aspect. The main risk categories are

- *Completion risk.* The risk that the project will not be completed or will be completed sufficiently late to affect the viability of the project.
- *Market risk.* The risk that sufficient cash flow will not be generated by the completed facility.
- *Operating risk.* The risk that the facility will not operate within design specification.
- *Political risk.* The risk that a change in government or in taxation legislation will affect the return on the investment.
- *Force majeure.* The risk that events entirely outside the control of the consortium will prevent completion of the project.

Some examples of major infrastructure projects undertaken on the basis of private finance include a number of elements of the Sydney 2000 Olympic Games; the Sydney Harbour Tunnel; the M2, M4, and M5 motorways in NSW; the Melbourne City Link Motorway; and a number of other projects currently underway or planned in the near future.

The main advantages of private-sector involvement over traditional public-sector procurement are that

- More infrastructure projects can be built.

- Projects can be built faster because they are not subject to the constraints of government handouts.

- Such projects encourage a "user pays" approach to services that results in greater efficiencies on the part of users. This, in turn, reduces the need for expensive new infrastructure.

- Having part of the utility privatized allows "competition by comparison" to arise. This results in a general improvement in the efficiency of the utility.

- Maintenance of facilities also may be higher owing to the requirements set by lenders.

The main disadvantages are that

- The public sector can borrow funds more cheaply than the private sector.

- Such projects generally involve difficult and expensive tender processes.

- The long-term nature of the investment, which generally involves low cash flows in the early years and a lack of liquidity, can make the investment unattractive.

- The full risks of long-term contracts (generally between 20 and 30 years) are not known.

- There is a possibility that "inefficient" projects are developed that will need to be heavily subsidized by governments.

Even at this time, there is significant social and political discussion regarding the commitment of state and federal governments to PPPs and the long-term benefits for the Australian public. The demand for substantial infrastructure development is ever-increasing in a large geographic country with a limited human and financial resource base.

TWO MAJOR AUSTRALIAN PROJECTS

The Sydney 2000 Olympic Games

Winning the Games. In late 1993, the International Olympic Committee (IOC) made the announcement that Sydney had won the right to stage the 2000 Summer Olympic Games. Over four years had been spent with a dedicated group appointed by the New South Wales state government preparing the Sydney 2000 bid for the Olympic Games. This bid was submitted to the IOC in late 1992.

The commitment made in the Sydney bid was to provide a games venue.

- With new facilities that meet the needs of competitors
- That provided a long-term legacy
- That involved the private sector
- That respected the principles of ecologically sustainable development (ESD)

The Sydney bid, in fact, was dubbed "The Green Games." The main site at Homebush Bay was an old industrial site that was significantly polluted, so the title "The Green Games" also meant a strong commitment to remediation of the site under the watchful eyes of Greenpeace, the community, and environmental specialists and experts—a critical audience with very high expectations.

The Sydney 2000 Bid Committee ceased to exist after the right to hold the games had been won—that project had been completed successfully.

Preparing for the Games.   When Sydney won the right to hold the games, some environmental remediation work was already under way on the site, and there was an international sports arena, a warm-up arena, and an aquatic centre already built and functioning on the site. However, there was a lot more required in the way of facilities on the Homebush Bay site, as well as in other locations around Sydney.

Although everyone had high expectations that Sydney would win the bid, when it was won, many parties were vying to be part of the process for both commercial and prestigious reasons. The first thing that had to be done was to restructure the government organizations that were to be involved in the delivery of the games in seven years' time.

The New South Wales government's first priority was to set up the main organization, which was called the Sydney Organising Committee for the Olympic Games (SOCOG). However, many existing government organizations wanted responsibility for delivery of facilities and infrastructure. Thus the confusing structure that began to develop was as shown in Fig. 24.1. This structure was a recipe for confusion, and the figure does not even include SOCOG, which sat to the side of this structure.

In 1995, the New South Wales government created a single authority for the delivery and coordination of the capital works and infrastructure. This organization was called the Olympic Coordination Authority (OCA), and its role was quite separate from that of the SOCOG, which was to concentrate on the organizing and actual running of the games and for raising sponsorship funds. The new organization is shown in Fig. 24.2. The government created a cabinet position of the Minister for the Olympics and a single leader, who was also a politician, was in charge of the OCA and SOCOG. This proved to be an excellent move.

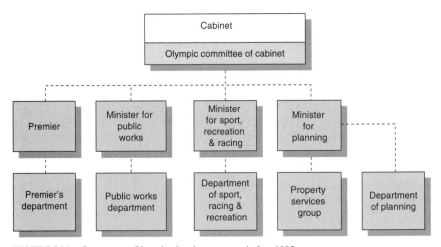

FIGURE 24.1   Government Olympic planning structure before 1995.

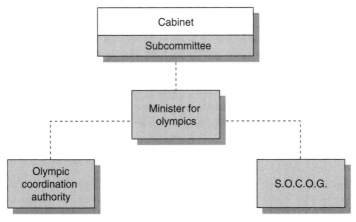

FIGURE 24.2   Government Olympic planning structure after 1995.

The Proposed Facilities.   One of the attractions of the Sydney bid was that all the events (at least the finals) for all Olympic sports could be held within 20 to 30 minutes travel time from the main site. Also, the Homebush Bay site was within 14 kilometres of the central business district (CBD) of Sydney. This was an unusual opportunity for a Summer Olympics when you consider the sports involved—sports including sailing, equestrian, track and field, beach volleyball, football, hockey, mountain bike riding, rowing, and white water rafting—and the list goes on.

The main facilities, both existing and new, and their location (either within the main Homebush Bay site or external to the site) are listed in Table 24.1.

Budget and Cost.   The original bid budget for facilities was on the order of Aus$1.5 billion, but when adjusted to 1996 dollars, this budget for facilities had escalated to Aus$1.7 billion, and the revised forecast construction cost at that time was Aus$2.3 billion—a variance of Aus$600 million. The budget was approved by the government at Aus$1.9 billion, leaving an OCA controlled contingency of Aus$400 million. The final end construction cost was Aus$2.241 billion.

The major reason for the variance in the cost estimates was a decision to relocate the Sydney Showgrounds from Moore Park to the Homebush Bay site. This was a strategic decision to provide a future function on the Homebush Bay site other than sport and would continue after the Olympics. The Sydney Showgrounds are the home of the annual Royal Easter Show, and they host over 1 to 1.5 million visitors over the Easter period each year.

Timetable.   Figure 24.3 indicates the planned timing and actual timing for the delivery of the main facilities required for the Olympics.

There were more facilities than just the main facilities indicated in Fig. 24.2, and it is important to note the six-month period required to install what was called the "Olympic overlay." This period was required to allow the construction of temporary walkways, barriers, seating, toilet facilities, public large-screen TV viewing areas, food and drink outlets, and the many requirements of such a large public event.

The new Showgrounds commenced construction in September 1996 and were completed in March 1998, in 19 months—only one day was lost in construction time. The strategy behind the early construction of the Showground was to allow the Easter Show in March 1998 to be held at Homebush Bay so that the new rail and public transport systems built for the Olympic site could be tested in a live situation. This strategy

TABLE 24.1   Main Facilities and Their Locations

Located within the Main Homebush Bay Site	Located outside the Main Homebush Bay Site
Existing Facilities • Aquatic Centre • Warm-up arena • State Hockey Centre	• Darling Harbour (upgrading for some indoor sports)—in the Sydney CBD. • Sydney Entertainment Centre (also for some indoor sports). • Rose Bay Yacht Club (new facilities adjacent to extend capacity for sailing events. These events were held predominantly in Sydney Harbour)—4 km from the Sydney CBD. • Sydney Football Stadium—5 km from the Sydney CBD, an existing facility capable of holding over 40,000 spectators and used for the football.
New Facilities • Main Stadium • Indoor Arena • Main Hockey Stadium • Showgrounds Site— including Baseball Stadium/Showring and a number of covered Pavilions • Archery • Tennis Centre • Rail Loop and Station • International Broadcasting Centre • Athletes Village on the adjacent site (known as Newington) • A Hotel • Millenium Parklands	• Equestrian Centre at Horsley Park—21 km west of Homebush Bay. • Softball Centre at Blacktown—22 km from Homebush Bay; one competition field and two training diamonds, 1000 permanent seats and a capacity to hold 8000 in Olympic mode. • Sydney International Regatta Centre—44 km from Homebush Bay; a venue for rowing and canoeing, a 2.3 km course with warm-up lake and foreshores, a permanent capacity of 1000 permanent seats and 30,000 for the Games mode. • A Shooting Centre at Cecil Park—33 km from Homebush Bay; 10 m 25 m 50 m indoor ranges; three trap and skeet ranges, a capacity to seat 10,000 spectators in games mode. • Velodrome at Bankstown—20 km from Homebush Bay. • Beach Volleyball at Bondi—8 km from the Sydney CBD (and 22 km from the Homebush Bay site).

allowed a well-developed transport system that had been substantially tested to be in place before the games in September 2000.

This strategy was further extended to virtually all aspects of the delivery of facilities such that all major sporting venues and the transportation and security systems were in place and had been used by the public for one to two years prior to the actual games. This strategy was possibly one of the most significant contributing factors to a secure, safe, and well-run Olympic Games. The repercussions of the strategy meant that all the facilities had to be completed well in advance of the games.

The Delivery Processes.   Some clever and innovative delivery strategies were developed, resulting in the contribution of Aus$1.1 billion from the private-sector involvement for a number of the main facilities, two of which are particularly worth understanding.

Three key areas of risk for the Olympic Games were identified by the New South Wales government, and these were

• The main Olympic stadium
• The athletes' village
• The multipurpose indoor arena

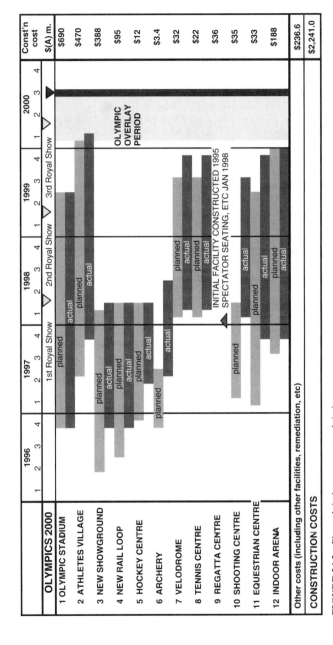

FIGURE 24.3 Planned timing versus actual timing.

It was considered that the people best able to manage these large areas of risk were those in the private sector. The government was prepared to underwrite the games but did not want the full cost exposure and the potential of being "held to ransom" over industrial disputes and delays. The key was to create an investment opportunity that would be attractive to the private sector to invest in. Two of the major facilities constructed by the private sector were the main Olympic stadium and the athletes village.

Main Olympic Stadium (Stadium Australia).　　Called Stadium Australia, the New South Wales government called for expressions of interest and tenders to construct a 110,000-seat stadium for the 2000 Olympic Games as an investment proposition and at no cost to the government. The consortium that won this bid consisted of a contractor, a developer, a financier/banker, and a facility manager.

As indicated in Fig. 24.4, this was a private consortium that put together a design and prospectus to invite investors by floating the consortium/investment vehicle on the Australian Stock Exchange—as a public company financed by the public.

The investment deal was for the Stadium Australia Consortium to build, own, operate, and transfer (BOOT). On this basis, the consortium owns and operates this facility for all events for the next 25 years. At the end of that period, the facility's ownership is transferred back to the New South Wales government (and therefore the Australian people) at a "peppercorn" cost.

A condition of the agreement was that the site for the stadium was freely available to the consortium, but the New South Wales government (through SOCOG) had the exclusive use of the facility for a six- to eight-week period. This period included the September 2000 Olympic Games period and the October 2000 Paralympic Games period.

All other profits for the facility, over the 25-year period, are to be retained by the Stadium Australia Consortium.

The Athletes' Village (Newington).　　An old armament depot was located adjacent to the Homebush Bay site, which was fortuitously a large area of wooded land that was seen strategically as a future garden suburb for Sydney. This suburb is now called Newington, and the New South Wales government's decision was to provide the land

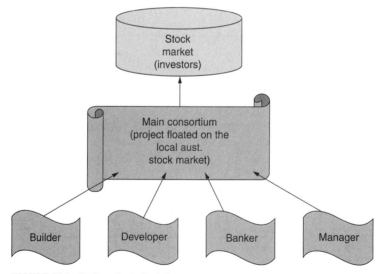

FIGURE 24.4　Stadium Australia delivery structure.

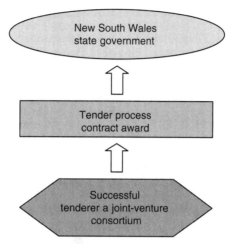

FIGURE 24.5   Olympic Athletes Village delivery structure.

to the private sector. The private sector would be given the opportunity to develop this land by building the infrastructure, shopping centres, schools, hospital, and residential facilities that could be used as an athletes' village during the Olympics and progressively sold as future housing for the new suburb.

Expressions of interest and tenders were called from private enterprise. A contract eventually was awarded to a consortium including a large residential developer and a large construction company. The contract structure was as shown in Fig. 24.5.

The arrangement finally entered into by the New South Wales government was a contract where all costs were borne by the private consortium other than the land supplied by the government. The village was available during the Olympic Games period to house over 15,000 athletes. The consortium took all risk on cost, receiving the first 15 percent of profit (after all costs) from the sale of the houses. After this, the profit was shared 50-50 between the consortium and the New South Wales government.

The Lessons and Legacy

- It is clear that the tight and efficient management structures introduced by government to manage the games delivery and operational requirements, together with the interface and contribution of the private sector, were a major contributor to the success of the games.

- The decision to outsource to the private sector the delivery of many of the games' facilities was highly successful.

- Timely and early completion is essential to allow extensive testing of facilities and infrastructure prior to the games commencing.

- A massive contaminated site was remediated and reclaimed, providing the legacy of a sporting and recreational precinct for the people of New South Wales.

- The games have been paid for (in fact, a profit was reported), and Sydney has enhanced its reputation as a tourist destination.

The Qantas Airbus A330 Program

This project not only was one of significance but also was the New South Wales state chapter's and the National Australian Institute of Project Management's (AIPM) winner of the Project Management Achievement Award for 2003.

Summary of the Project.   Founded in 1920, Qantas has built a reputation for excellence in safety, operational reliability, engineering and maintenance, and customer service. Today, Qantas is Australia's national airline and operates a fleet of 187 aircraft and a number of subsidiary business, including other airlines and businesses in specialist markets, such as Qantas Holidays and Qantas Flight Catering.

In November 2000, the board of directors approved the purchase of thirteen A330 aircraft for delivery between 2002 and 2005 with a total program cost of $4.1 billion. The A330 was a new-technology twin-engine aircraft designed for short- to medium-range routes.

The magnitude of the program was large and complex, as represented by the sheer scale and diversity of activities. Qantas is a large organization operating a complex, logistically intensive business. The A330 program had an impact on the processes of every business area, with over 2000 activities being actively managed. Over 4000 individuals required specific training. Certain functions such as aircraft engineers and pilots required several weeks of training supplemented with "line" operational experience with the aircraft. This involved working with other airlines overseas for extended periods to develop a core pool of experience within Qantas. The magnitude of the program drove a large number of risks, with over 200 significant risks actively managed throughout the program.

Qantas has a very strong functional structure with very different cultures. Multiple teams were used and managed as virtual teams. The core team of 20 included, at the peak, only seven full-time members. Approximately 150 team members were heavily involved in the team activities. The broader team, however, involved 4000 people. Setting up a workable matrix structure and communications was one of the many challenges.

Infrastructure, Startup, and Safety.   A significant portion of the program activity was infrastructure construction and set-up and start-up activities, such as

- New aircraft parking layouts and relocation of departure gates at Sydney, Melbourne, Brisbane, and Perth domestic terminals, including a total review of domestic terminal facilities and capacities.
- A comprehensive cabin-crew training package covering all aircraft systems and service procedures.
- Introduction of a new A330 maintenance system. A secondary objective was introduction of step-change business processes in conjunction with this.
- Avionics and mechanical specifications for flight-deck-related systems and equipment and development of flight and ground training courses and provisions.

Underlying this was a broad focus on the safety aspects.

The A330 program was positioned as a catalyst for major strategic change within Qantas' operations. Substantial transformational change strategies were integrated into the detailed work plans. The new Qantas-Airbus relationship was leveraged and brought about innovative change, including

- Latest flight-simulation technology (latest version using new cabin and avionics data)
- Custom-built cabin simulator (first breed for the new enhanced design)

- Dual aerobridges (first of type in the Australian domestic market)
- ULD freight container upgrade
- Highly complex first of type technologies and associated business processes implemented (For example, the A330 was a first of type for Airbus involving new cockpit avionics and enhanced cabin technologies.)
- Introduction of cutting-edge technologies, for example, e-management and workflow tools for engineering major enhancements to legacy systems in operations rostering
- New in-hold system designed (first for Airbus aircraft)
- A new supplier relationship with Airbus, based in France, presenting cultural challenges (This involved a huge change management task as well as understanding new operating concepts, from the flight deck to the cargo hold, and dealing with a new inventory of 11,000 spare parts.)

Successful Program that Delivered on Time and under Budget. The program was very successful, meeting the owner's and numerous stakeholders' expectations. It delivered on time and under budget notwithstanding unprecedented change in the aviation industry, including the terrorist attacks of September 11 in the United States, the collapse of Ansett Airways, the commencement of competition from low-cost airlines, and the Iraq war. This gave rise to many unexpected factors. Strategy alignment, scope management, cultural change, risk management, innovation management, and a massive logistics exercise were key challenges. Managing the complexity and the interfaces between a changing internal and external project environment was a major achievement. There were several success factors in management of the project complexities.

The program schedule was considered extremely tight based on historical fleet introductions. Detailed planning and milestone management at the macro and micro levels drove schedule achievement. Additional resources were provided to ensure a continued planning focus.

Senior management buy-in and involvement were high. The program structure provided coordination, communication, and visibility. Escalation paths were clear. Teaming was fostered and supported by a strong communication strategy.

Introduction of cutting-edge technologies was managed through tight application of project disciplines and integration of change management activities. Technical review groups to ensure quality and compatibility supported the teams. Vendor management techniques also were critical. In addition, broad communication throughout the program was a key to success.

A number of integration interfaces required management:

- Multiple stakeholder expectations on the detailed scope of each project
- Over 15 key cross-divisional interfaces
- Major strategic change activity, including major fleet and network changes
- Other major programs of activity, such as a new reservation system
- Consolidated program-level financial reporting with individual project reporting and corporate finance group accounting and budgeting
- Multiple interdependent deliverables between project teams

The key to integration success was broad stakeholder involvement throughout all key stages of the program with specific schedule management focus on these key integration interfaces.

Project management disciplines were applied through a number of project teams using a phased approach. This included a strong focus on scope and change management, risk, key performance indicators (KPIs), reporting, and human resources. Strong vendor and quality management and financial controls were implemented. Specific cultural change initiatives including communication, teaming, and collaboration underwrote this. A broad range of management skills was required to deliver the program.

FUTURE DIRECTIONS FOR AUSTRALIAN PROJECT MANAGEMENT

The development of project management in Australia has occurred at a rapid rate over the last two decades and is perceived as a potentially effective way to manage ever-increasing community demands for services and infrastructure with limited financial and personnel resources. However, project management still has to "prove" its real value as a methodology and become integral to the way in which business is done. Project management's challenge is to provide value to the "bottom line" of private organizations and government.

Current trends in Australia indicate that

- Traditional areas of project management are leading the way in maturity development. Universities are embracing project management as a formal area of education (although there is still debate as to whether the teaching should be in an engineering faculty or perhaps in a business school), but project management across industries is still uncoordinated.

- Project management in Australia is represented by two institutes that seem to serve the needs of project managers rather than the needs and promotion of project management as a professional skill. This must send a "mixed message" to industry and the community.

- Program management and portfolio management are being strongly promoted in the Australian environment, which hopefully can begin to provide tangible benefits to corporate and government needs and objectives.

Crystal ball gazing is always a difficult exercise, but a personal view of a way ahead may be

- Can project management develop as a traditional profession? The message to business and the community needs to be cohesive and unambiguous, and project management needs to identify itself clearly as a profession. It should be represented by a single professional body that has an alignment with international standards and maturity levels. Competency or certification standards may be "culturally local," but they must have relevance to international parity. This will become increasingly important for multinational organizations and can only benefit project managers themselves.

- Can outcomes of project management improve further? Project management must improve if it is to survive. More effort needs to be applied to the development of project initiatives and creative solutions. The current efforts seem to be focused more on process rather than on encouraging lateral thinking. It is my personal view that if this direction is not addressed, project management will be its own demise.

- What is meant by the *maturity* of project management? Is it a more strategic application? Recent developments toward project-based and enterprise management indicate that current thinking toward business applications for project management has potential. Strategic thinking is different depending on the level of business operation. The overall objectives of a company are different from the strategic thinking at an individual project level. The continued development of project and portfolio management concepts provides the opportunity to address these concepts.

- Can project management have a value-added benefit to business and the board room? Yes, but will it still be called project management?

ACKNOWLEDGMENTS

I would like to thank the many people who have contributed to my thinking and the preparation of this chapter both by their written contribution and by the stimulating discussions while I was preparing this chapter. Particular thanks go to Adjunct Professor Alan Stretton for his lecture notes entitled, "A Short History of Project Management," and for his help in editing this chapter. Also to Mr. Rob Sharp of QANTAS, who provided the information for the Airbus A330 Program case study.

REFERENCES

Bechtel SR Jr. 1989. Project management: Yesterday, today and tomorrow. *PMNETwork* 3(1):6–8.

Civil & Civic. 1969. Project engineer seminar, 18–19 September: Notes on proceedings. Sydney: Civil & Civic Pty Limited (mimeo).

Fazar W. 1962. The Origins of PERT. *The Controller*, December:598–621; quoted in Kelly JE, Walker MR. 1989. The origins of CPM: A personal history. *PMNETwork* 3(2):7–22.

Fondahl JW. 1987. Precedence diagramming methods: Origins and early development. *Project Manag J* 18(2):33–36.

Kelly JE Jr, Walker MR. 1989. "The origins of CPM: A personal history. *PMNETwork* 3(2):7–22.

Kerzner H. 1979. *Project Management: A Systems Approach to Planning, Scheduling and Controlling.* New York: Van Nostrand Reinhold.

Morris PWG. 1994. *The Management of Projects.* London: Thomas Telford.

Project Management Institute (PMI). 1987. *Project Management Body of Knowledge (PMBOK).* Drexel Hill, PA: Project Management Institute.

Stretton A. 1993. A short history of modern project management. Sydney: Master of project management course notes (mimeo).

Warren Centre. 1985. Macroprojects, strategy planning implementation project report. Warren Centre for Advanced Engineering, Sydney University.

CHAPTER 25
PROJECT MANAGEMENT IN ROMANIA

Constanta-Nicoleta Bodea

Academy of Economic Studies, Bucharest, Romania

Constanta Bodea gratuated the Academy of Economic Studies in 1982. She holds a Ph.D. in economics. Currently, she is professor of project management and artificial intelligence at the Academy of Economic Studies, Bucharest. She has published several books and papers on project management. Since 2000, she has been director of the master's degree program on project management at the Academy of Economic Studies, Bucharest, and president of Project Management Romania, the Romanian project management association.

THE BUSINESS ENVIRONMENT IN ROMANIA: A SHORT OVERVIEW

Romania is situated in southeastern Europe. It borders on Ukraine and the Republic of Moldova to the north and northeast, on Bulgaria to the south, on Serbia to the southwest, and on Hungary to the northwest. With an area of 238,391 square kilometers (91,780 square miles), Romania is the second largest country in central and eastern Europe (Fig. 25.1).

The territory of Romania is subdivided into 41 counties plus Bucharest, the capital; these are the administrative units of local government.

Romania is a constitutional republic. The present constitution was adopted on November 21, 1991 and was amended subsequently and ratified by Law 429/2003, such amendment being effective as of October 29, 2003. Legislative power is vested in a bicameral parliament. The bicameral parliament is composed of the senate (137 seats) and the chamber of deputies (332 seats). Parliamentary elections are held every four years, whereas presidential elections are held every five years. The president nominates the prime minister. Cabinet ministers, selected by the prime minister, have to be approved by parliament before taking office.

Key Economic Indicators

Key economic indicators are shown in Table 25.1.

The economy has grown, with figures for 2004 showing over 8 percent increase in gross domestic product (GDP), outpacing 2003's growth rate of 4.9 percent . Inflation slipped to 9.3 percent at end of 2004 from 14 percent at the end of 2003. The unemployment rate also

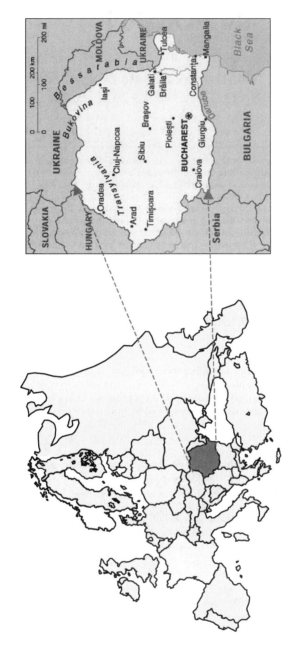

FIGURE 25.1 Romania, a southeastern European country.

TABLE 25.1 Key Economic Indicators

Indicator	2002	2003	2004
GDP (EUR billion)	48.4	50.3	58.9
GDP (% change against previous year)	4.9	4.9	8,3
GDP per capita (EUR)	2,230	2,318	2,714
Inflation (%)	17.9	14.1	9,3
Unemployment (%)	8.1	7.2	6.2
EUR/ROL exchange rate (average)	31,234	37,591	40,592
Foreign direct investment, FDI (EUR billion)	1.1	1.9	4.1
External debt (EUR billion)	14.6	15.24	17.5
Export FOB (EUR billion)	14.7	15.6	18.9
Imports CIF (EUR billion)	18.8	21.2	26.3
Credit rating:			
Standard & Poors	B+	BB	BB+
Moody's	B1	Ba3	Ba3
Fitch	BB	BB	BBB–

Source: National Institute of Statistics, NBR.

dropped, falling to 6.2 percent in 2004 as opposed to 7.2 percent at the end of 2003 ([Price Waterhouse Cooper 2005]).

The vigorous economic growth in the last five years, the continuous reduction of inflation, the progress in restructuring the economy, and the acceleration of the privatization process have determined the European Commission to acknowledge Romania as having a functioning market economy in its 2004 regular report.

The foreign direct investment stood at around EUR 4 billion, up 115 percent compared with 2003, according to data from the National Bank of Romania. The social capital subscribed by foreign investors in Romanian companies was EUR 25 billion in 2004, up 46 percent compared with 2003, according to the National Trade Register Office. The number of new companies established by foreign investors was of 10,169, having a subscribed social capital of EUR 160 million in 2004.

The privatization process began in 1990 with the creation of joint stock companies out of approximately 6200 state-owned entities. Of the shares in these companies, 70 percent were allocated to the state ownership fund (SOF) and 30 percent to one of the five private ownership funds (POFs). Following Emergency Ordinance No 296 (December 2000), the SOF became the Authority for Privatization and Management of State Ownership (APAPS), a public institution that operated under the authority of the Romanian government. In 2004, the Bank Asset Recovery Agency has merged through absorption with the Authority for Privatization and Management of State Ownership, resulting the Authority for State Assets Recovery.

The most significant privatization in the country's post-Communist history is the privatization of Petrom, the Romanian national integrated oil company and the largest Romanian company in terms of turnover (estimated EUR 2.3 billion for 2004) and market capitalization (EUR 6.2 billion as of the middle of June). The successful bidder was the Austrian OMV. Other privatization deals of 2004 included the privatization of the two electricity distribution companies, Electrica Banat and Electrica Dobrogea, with the Italian company Enel and the two gas distribution companies, Distrigaz Sud and Distrigaz Nord, with Gaz de France, respectively, the German E.ON Ruhrgas ([Ernst & Young Romania. 2004]) 2005, the government had finalized other two important privatizations in the energy sector. CEZ AS, the Czech Republic's biggest energy company, has taken over electricity distributor Electrica Oltenia SA, and E.ON AG, Europe's second-largest utility, acquired 51 percent of Electrica Moldova SA. The privatization process for Electrica Muntenia Sud is also scheduled to begin in 2005. Other electricity distribution companies also will be privatized, as well as the three power holdings: Craiova, Turceni, and Rovinari. In the financial sector, the two remaining large state banks are likely also to be sold in 2005–2006. In the telecom sector, the sale of the remaining state's shares of Romtelecom, as well as privatization of the Radio-communication National Company, is scheduled for 2006, whereas the privatization of the Romanian Post Office is schedule to be completed by 2008.

The main reasons ([Anca D., 2004]) for the foreign direct investment (FDI) increase in Romania are

- Romania represents the largest market in southeastern Europe.
- It is characterized by political stability and consensus for EU accession.
- It has a competitive location, bridging East and West and North and South.
- It has sustainable economic growth and declining inflation.
- It has the highest GDP growth rate in the region.
- It is committed to developing a modern economy.
- It was granted "market economy" status by the United States.
- It possesses a competitive, highly skilled labor force.
- It is granting incentives to foreign investors.

Doing Business in Romania

Starting-a-business indicators measure the procedures, time, cost, and minimum capital requirements to register a business formally. Table 25.2 presents the starting-a-business indicators for Romania and six other countries.

([International Bank for Reconstruction and Development, World Bank. 2004]) Two procedures—notification of existence and tax and social security registration—are usually sufficient for business registration. In reality, all countries impose additional requirements. Further, the regulation of business entry varies systematically across countries.

TABLE 25.2   Starting-a-Business Indicators

Country	Number of Procedures	Time (days)	Cost (US$)	Cost (% of Income per Capita)	Min. Capital (% of Income per Capita)
Romania	6	27	217	11.7	3.3
Australia	2	2	402	2.0	0.0
Austria	9	29	1534	6.6	140.8
France	10	53	663	3.0	32.1
Germany	9	45	1341	5.9	103.8
United Kingdom	6	18	264	1.0	0.0
United States	5	4	210	0.6	0.0

Source: Doing Business in 2004 (International Bank for Reconstruction and Development, World Bank , 2004).

Richer countries regulate less. So do countries in the common-law tradition. In poorer countries, market failures may be more severe and therefore may increase the desire to correct the failures by regulating entry.

Some developed economies also suffer from excessive regulation and pay the price. In France, the Ministry of Industry adopted the Loi d'Orientation du Commerce et de l'Artisanat in 1974 to protect small shopkeepers and craftsmen against competition from larger retail stores. The legislation created a zoning-permit requirement at the discretion of the local municipal council. These entry requirements weakened employment growth in the formal retail sector.

Closing-a-Business Indicators. These indicators measure the procedures, time, and cost to go through insolvency proceedings, as well as court powers in insolvency proceedings. In the United States, there are more than 55,000 corporate bankruptcy cases each year, 20 per 100,000 population. In the United Kingdom, there are some 40,000 a year, about 75 per 100,000 population. In contrast, about 500 bankruptcy cases were started in Spain, about 1 per 100,000 population. Nordic proceedings are the fastest, at around two years on average, and also the cheapest, at 4.5 percent of the estate value. Finland and Norway are among the world's top countries on time and cost. English-legal-origin countries are the second-fastest legal-origin group in resolving insolvency, at 2.7 years. In French-civil-law countries, insolvency lasts on average 3.7 years, and it costs 15 percent of the estate value. In transition countries, the process lasts around three years and costs 7 percent of the estate value. Table 25.3 presents the closing-a-business indicators for Romania and six other countries.

The Competitiveness of the Romania

In 2001, J. E. Austin Associates, Inc. (JAA), carried out a competitiveness benchmarking exercise to reflect how Romania ranks relative to the other countries in the southeastern Europe, the EU accession countries, and the EU countries themselves. The competitiveness benchmarking indicated that Romania shared some of the common problems of the southeastern Europe region.

The *Global Competitiveness Report 2005*, published by the World Economic Forum, ranked 117 countries based on the growth competitiveness index (GCI) and the business competitiveness index (BCI), a complement to the GCI. While GCI evaluates the macroeconomic and institutional factors influence, in a medium-term approach, BCI evaluates the underlying microeconomic conditions defining the current sustainable level of productivity.

TABLE 25.3   Closing-a-Business Indicators

Country	Time (years)	Cost (% of Estate)	Absolute Priority Preserved	Efficient Outcome Achieved	Goal of Insolvency Index	Court Powers Index
Romania	3.2	8	33	0	39	33
Australia	1	18	100	1	80	0
Austria	1.3	18	67	1	71	33
France	2.4	18	67	0	43	100
Germany	1.2	8	100	0	61	33
United Kingdom	1	8	100	1	86	0
United States	3	4	100	1	88	33

Source: Doing Business in 2004.

The underlying concept is that while macroeconomic and institutional factors are critical for national competitiveness, these are necessary but not sufficient factors for creating wealth. The wealth is actually created at the microeconomic level by the companies operating in each economy. The BCI evaluates two specific areas: the operating practices and the strategies of the companies and the quality of the microeconomic business environment in which a nation's companies compete.

According GCI, Romania had the sixty-seventh position (the sixty-third position in 2004). Romania was ranked 71 according the macroeconomic environment index in 2004, 74 after the public institution index and 47 after the technology index ([World Economic Forum. 2004], [World Economic Forum 2005]). According BCI, Romania's ranking in 2004 was 56 (61 after company operations and strategy subindex and 57 after the quality of the national business environment subindex).

The downward trend of ranking for Romania does not necessarily mean a downward trend of internal performance. As a positive trend we should consider the FDI, which had a gross growth of 45.6 percent as opposed to last year, an increase in GDP per inhabitant of 8.59 percent, and stability of the exchange rate.

The main competitiveness constraints in Romania are

- *Corruption and nontransparent procedures* in Romania are diminishing the country's competitiveness as they reduce its attractiveness as an investment destination.

- Romania's *relatively poor physical infrastructure* is a constraint on its economic development and its competitiveness.

- *Delayed engagement in higher-technology* and *higher-value-added economic activities* is wearing away Romania's competitiveness.

- The private sector's *lack of focus on international and domestic markets* is an issue.

- Romania has a cheap labor force but *lacks a market mentality and management system* as well as *access to information about both domestic and foreign markets* in order to compete better in a new global market context.

- The government's policy-making process *lacks private-sector consultation*, and policies fail to reflect the concerns of the private sector and hamper its competitiveness.

- *Lack of trust and bonds between the actors in civil society and between the government and different civil society actors* causes the formal nongovernment organizations (NGOs) to have only a marginal impact on influencing social and economic policy.

As in many other countries, Romanian industry has experienced an erosion of its competitiveness over the past decade. The following are some of the main factors that have contributed to this decline according to the JAA report:

- Delays in developing and securing a strong access to foreign markets

- Inadequate access to financing for domestic private firms

- Lack of product differentiation

- Relatively high transportation costs owing to Romania's insufficient infrastructure

- Inadequate recapitalization and restructuring efforts to infuse new technology into the industry and to establish industrial linkages that help Romania engage in high-value-added activities

- Lack of strong private-sector investment, which is considered a driving factor behind any country's sustained growth and employment generation

- Lack of strong individual companies that pioneer and lead the technological change and upgrade the processes in the industry

- Lack of market-oriented management and marketing skills that can improve efficiency in the industry, make Romanian brand names better known in the world markets, and proactively find new markets for Romanian products
- Lack of an overall industrial strategy and coordination/cooperation within the industry in order to acquire new technology and share market information or access new markets

Industry-Specific Constraints: Information and Communications Technology (ICT) and Tourism Examples. Since 1989, Romania has been trying to further develop the ICT sector, including gradual liberalization of the telecommunications sector and encouragement of foreign-investor participation. In recent years, attempts have been made to develop legislation that would address a number of e-commerce and e-business issues. However, the development of Romania's ICT remains limited. Major impediments include

- Limited availability and high-cost telecommunications access
- Lack of capital in the country to support expansion of existing businesses and formation of startup businesses
- Inadequate legal and regulatory framework to support the sector, particularly the export software trade
- Lack of reliable electric power supply and reliable and pervasive telecommunications infrastructure that links both domestically and internationally to support Romania's software exports
- Lack of a sizable or demanding domestic market that can stimulate the sector's development or attract information technology (IT) multinationals into collaborative relationships with local partners to serve such a market
- Loss of students graduating from universities who leave Romania for better-paying jobs in western Europe, the United States, and Canada
- Lack of information about both domestic and foreign markets
- Lack of entrepreneurship, marketing, and management skills that could bring more international exposure and experience to domestic firms
- Ineffective protection and enforcement of intellectual property rights
- Limited research and development (R&D) base and insufficient investment in R&D for new technologies and software
- Lack of private-sector consultation in policy formulation to support the industry as well as in R&D activities
- Need for more proactive policy support from the government to stimulate growth in the industry and make it internationally competitive

Romania's rich natural resource endowment offers many opportunities for strong tourism development. The sector so far has been following a low-end, low-price competition strategy and suffers from a lack of quality and strategy that could increase its competitiveness relative to other countries in the region. Major constraints on the tourism industry in Romania include

- A decline in low-cost advantage owing to price competition from other countries in the region
- Delayed engagement in high-end, more sophisticated tourism products
- Limited knowledge of outside markets and high-end product segments

- Degrading and inadequate infrastructure facilities, including roads, hotels, telecommunications, airports, and utilities
- Lack of quality market-oriented customer service
- Lack of management and marketing skills that can increase efficiency, attract more clients, and generate high-end demands for the sector
- Lack of strong private-sector investment in the sector
- Absence of an adequate legal and regulatory framework to support the sector

The Romanian government promotes the market economy for the purpose of Romania's durable economic development (Romanian Government, 2004). Private entrepreneurs and free initiative are stimulated. In order to achieve these objectives, the obstacles that hinder private initiative will be removed: corruption, heavy fiscality, and administrative barriers. A national action plan against corruption was adopted. Other measures for elimination of administrative barriers will be adopted, such as simplification of the procedures for market entrance and exit of companies and reduction of the administrative procedures related to obtaining authorizations, approvals, and notices.

The government's actions will aim to consolidate a stable and predictable business environment, eliminate state monopolies, consolidate free competition, and increase the transparency of the business environment. Ensuring the normative institutional conditions for the functioning of free competition will constitute a major objective of the government. To this purpose, the following objectives will be pursued: independence of the Council of Competition, efficient antitrust legislation, limitation of the state sector, and regulation of state support and other public interventions that damage the competitiveness of economic agents.

Building Romania's competitiveness requires a complex set of mutually reinforcing activities at the level of the firm and industry cluster reinforced by policy and institutional action at the national and local government levels. A key barrier to competitiveness is the mind-set of people combined with the ability to build the social capital of trust and cooperation. Learning from nations that have built prosperity quickly and aided by the foregoing analysis, one can formulate recommendations that deal with the private sector, with the public sector, and with the dialogue that connects them.

Competitiveness also requires the ability to cooperate as a cluster—no one firm can do it all. Competitiveness depends on the ability to form good alliances and partnerships. At the industry level, business associations can participate in efforts representing the business sector before government.

Business associations, working with the government of Romania, can develop international trade and investment linkages to get access to markets and technology. However, this undertaking requires greater communication and cooperation between the private sector and the public sector. Industry clusters also can implement workforce development and human resources and training initiatives by working with education and training providers so that the latter adapt their programs to industry needs. Another field of activity will be that of research, development, testing, and certification initiatives that can add value to the industry while adapting to ISO and similar standards.

ROMANIAN PARTICIPATION IN THE POS RESEARCH PROJECT

In 1999, the International Project Management Association (IPMA) started a research initiative to develop and apply the model of a project-oriented society (POS). The project started with the "POS Conception Project." The model of the POS was constructed, and criteria for the description of POSs were defined ([Gareis, 2001], [Gareis R, Huemann M. 2001])S model is described by specific processes performed by project-oriented companies and by specific services provided by project management–related institutions. These processes and services are illustrated in a POS spiderweb.

Following the "POS Conception Project," a second project, "POS Benchmarking," was started in April 2000. The objectives of this project were to assess and compare the maturities of the different POSs to analyze commonalties and differences between these POSs and to define strategies for further developing these maturities of the POSs. The project "POS Benchmarking" was performed as a cooperation among national project management associations.

Romania joined this project following an invitation by the Projektmanagement Group at the University of Economics and Business Administration in Vienna. Romania joined group 1, together with Denmark, Hungary, Sweden, and the United Kingdom. After one year, another three countries—Norway, Latvia, and Ireland—participated to the project as the group 2.

The objective of Romania's participation in the project was to get an assessment of project management practices and services currently available and to establish a strategy of improving the development of Romania as a POS, considering the similarities with other countries.

Activities Performed for Assessing and Benchmarking Romania as a POS

The main processes of assessing and benchmarking Romania as a POS were

- Establishment of the POS benchmarking team.
- Translation of the questionnaire into the Romanian language. The questionnaires were sent to different companies, especially primavera users, project management training and consulting companies, and big companies from different industries. There were no major problems with the terminology used by the questionnaire. Unhappily, we only few questionnaires were returned.
- Collection of the data regarding the economic competitiveness of Romania using the official sources. We have included these data in our assessment.
- Performance of the Internet-based investigation of project management institutions, especially those offering project management training programs.
- Consultation of 20 assessors in order to identify the project management practices used by some big companies. We met with the assessors weekly, and we made a pretty detailed assessment of the aspects related to
  - Project management practices
  - Portfolio management competences
  - Project personnel management competences
  - Competences to design the base organization

In November 2000 in Vienna, the Romanian team presented the first self-assessment results, and on March 2001 in Zurich, the final results were presented.

Self-Assessment Results

Importance of Projects in Romanian Society. Romania has passed through a rough economic restructuring process, implying projects for privatizing large state-owned enterprises, modernizing and updating strategic economic units, and creating new business units. For all industries and the nonprofit sector, projects are perceived as very important.

Between 2000 and 2004, Romania received important grants from the EU through the Phare, Ispa, and Sapard instruments that exceeded EUR 2.6 billion (Fig. 25.2). For 2005 and 2006, Romania is set to receive from the EU some EUR 1 billion per year as preaccession funds.

Other important projects are financed by the World Bank. For example, the Ministry of Commnunications and Information Technology in 2004 started preparation of the "Knowledge Economy Project" financed in part by the World Bank. The project aims to support knowledge-driven activities at the national level, as well as directy within local communities and in particular to accelerate the participation of knowledge-disadvantaged communities in the knowledge economy and society. The project will finance the establisment of local community e-networks (LCENs) through which communities will be offered access to knowledge via a number of services and technologies, including computers, the Internet, and communication services, with specific content provision for different target groups such as citizens, businesses, and pupils in rural and small urban communities.

The EU postaccession funds allocated to Romania (2007–2009) stand at EUR 11 billion, of which EUR 6 billion will be paid in this period (the rest of the payments to be made as the projects unfold). Romania's contribution to the EU budget will stand at some EUR 800 million in 2007, over EUR 800 million in 2008, and some EUR 900 million in 2009.

In order to execute these important projects, project management units have been set up. The external projects were used broadly in such industries as construction, energy, chemicals, and engineering. In the IT industry, the projects were internal and external. External companies that execute projects were specialized into a specific domain. Companies that offer consulting services for project management tend to cover a lot of project types from different areas.

As for program management, the programs developed in areas affected by restructuring processes were viewed as a strategic issue. For all industries and the nonprofit sector, programs are perceived as important. Demand for project and program management competencies is increasing.

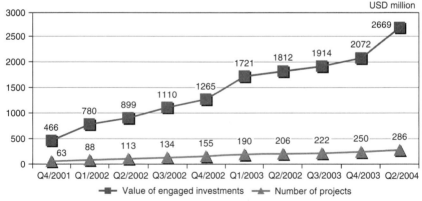

FIGURE 25.2   The number of projects and value of engaged investments over US$1 million, Q4/2001–Q2/2004. (*ARIS, Romanian Agency for Foreign Investment.*)

Maturity of Romania as a POS in 2000

Project Management–Related Services of Institutions. The project management–related services of education, research, and marketing institutions are listed in Table 25.4.

At the Academy of Economic Studies in Bucharest and at Ovidiu University Constanta, master's degree programs in project management were established in 2000. The curriculum of the master's program provided by the Academy of Economic Studies included from the beginning *compulsory subjects* such as fundamentals of project management, information technology, project financial management, project planning and control, project management software I (Microsoft Project) and II (Primavera), statistics for project management, project organization and human resource in projects, practice in project management, project-oriented companies, procurement in projects, project quality management, and dissertation elaboration/presentation, and *elective subjects* such as project management information systems, information management in projects, system engineering in project management, IT project management, construction project management, and public administration project management. The teaching approach is modern and comprehensive, based on different IT tools, such as project management software, software packages for quantitative methods and UML information modeling, statistics packages such as SPSS, and Web resources (course Web sites with forum, e-mail lists, and online resources).

In other Romanian universities, project management modules also have been included. No other formal project management education exists in Romania so far. Some consulting companies offer project management training.

Project Management Romania is a private professional association that is nonprofit, nongovernmental, and has no political influence. According to its charter, Project Management Romania initiates, supports, and organizes project management activities in all the economic and social fields. Project Management Romania has succeeded in obtaining formal recognition from the project manager profession in Romania by the Labor Ministry in the context of a wider effort to raise the awareness of the economic and academic communities regarding project management. As a result, the project manager profession has been included in the Romanian Occupation Classification Group 2419, code 241919. Project Management Romania represents Romania in the IPMA.

In 2000, the Attestation and Occupational Standards Committee (COSA) adopted the first Romanian Project Management Standard, code T-269. The standard defined the following seven competence units for project manager: requirements specification, resource estimation, scheduling, resource acquisition, contracts management, risk identification and control, project team management and implementation.

Project Management Practices. Romania shows low competencies in project and program management. Only a few project management methods are used. For instance, project management methods such as those for updating the project organization chart are never used. No project portfolio management exists yet. Only 2 percent of all companies are

TABLE 25.4 **Project Management–Related Services of Education, Research, and Marketing Institutions**

PM education	Some institutions offer formal PM education
	Two Masters degree programs are established, no other degrees, Ph.D. in PM not offered
	PM not included in secondary education
	No PM certification according to IPMA is offered
PM research	Little PM research activities
PM marketing	PM association (Project Management Romania) newly established

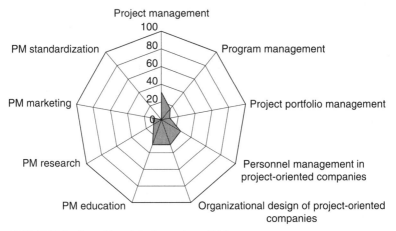

FIGURE 25.3 The spiderweb for Romania as a POS.

perceived as project-oriented, and their competencies in organizational design are low. The POS spiderweb for Romania is presented in Fig. 25.3, and the POS ratios for Romania are presented in Table 25.5 ([Gareis R, Huemann M, November 2001]). Table 25.6 shows the POS maturity ratios of the nations participating in the research project "POS Benchmarking."

In Romania, projects were only used in certain specific industries, such as construction, energy, chemicals, engineering, and IT. Romania is now passing through a rough economic restructuring process, applying projects for privatizing large state-owned enterprises, modernixing and updating strategic economic units, and creating new business units. For all industries and the nonprofit sector, projects are becoming very important. Companies that offer consulting services for project management tend to cover a lot of project types from different areas. Demand for the application of projects and programs to markets is increasing.

This discrepancy between project management being perceived as very important and the low project management practice ratio could have two major causes in my opinion.

TABLE 25.5 POS Ratios Calculated for Romania

Maturity Axis	Maturity per Axis	Overall Ratio
PM education	30	—
PM research	10	—
PM marketing	10	—
PM standardization	0	—
PM service ratio	—	17
Project management	31	—
Program management	17	—
Project portfolio management	10	—
Personnel management	26	—
Organizational design	30	—
PM practice ratio	—	25
POS ratio	—	23

TABLE 25.6 POS Benchmarking Results

	SWE	UK	NOR	IRL	DEN	AUT	HUN	ROM	LAT
POS ratio	56	55	46	45	42	37	34	23	22
Project management	63	56	51	54	46	39	42	31	28
Program management	70	30	55	44	37	26	37	17	16
Project portfolio management	57	30	45	39	43	25	37	10	0
Personnel management	62	58	47	46	50	35	46	26	25
Organizational design	65	40	45	45	55	31	35	30	22
PM practice ratio	63	47	46	46	46	33	40	25	21
PM education	40	80	30	34	30	36	30	30	11
PM research	40	70	44	16	30	28	20	10	11
PM marketing	40	70	38	67	40	71	15	10	50
PM service ratio	40	73	38	39	33	45	22	17	24

There are companies that recognize the importance of project management but do not have the knowledge to apply project management practices. They use unqualified personnel or people in an inadequate manner. For instance, one company we studied used the same person as project manager for 10 to 15 of the most important projects and as portfolio manager. In addition, there are also companies who recognize the importance of project management but do not intend to pay for project managers, who garner higher wages. They consider that managerial costs would rise if they use qualified project managers.

The project management support ratio is diminished by the lack of some important support issues such as project management standardization and insufficient development of project management marketing and research, although Romania obtained a satisfactory ratio for project management education.

Romania's score is very close to that of Hungary, also a transitional economy. It is not surprising that Romania has the lowest POS ratio at nearly 200. In the last two years, emphasis has be placed on the development of formal project management education programs, but there is not much competence in the other project management–related services such as research, marketing, or standardization. Nevertheless, Romanian project-oriented companies already show some project management competence (63 of 200), whereas program management and portfolio management are almost nonexistent.

Although Romania has the lowest score, it seems that there is a positive influence of support over practice, and the correlation between the two of them is similar to that of most countries. As a result, Romania intends to continue the development of support, hoping that this will have a good influence over practice.

Planned Maturity of Romania and the Strategy for Further Development of Romania as a POS

In the next 10 years, Romania has to further develop project management support services and sustain implementation of its existing project management practices. There are no studies in Romania to permit me to assess the impact of different services on the business environment. For example, the professional associations generally have a strong impact on business. The Romanian business environment does not promote professional associations as the most important potential for developing professionalism. This is why there is a low interest locally for professional associations. For the effectiveness of this type of support service, Romania needs research studies on the short-term impact of project management services and a strategy for long-term promotion of these services.

Project management practice improvement in the future cannot be estimated because Romania does not have enough information about the responsiveness of its business environment and its ability to improve its practices continuously by experience.

The POS model structures our strategy in two main directions:

1. Developing project management support through

   - Project management standardization (definition of a Romanian national competence baseline and adoption of other project management standards)
   - Project management research
   - Improvement in project management marketing activities, for example, organization of more project management events, better communication in the project management community, and more transparency in the activities of organizations involved in project management development
   - Development of international contacts, for example, affiliation of project management associations with different project management international bodies and participation in different international events

2. Improving project management practices. Project management practices must be improved in most companies because they are most likely to use empirical project management. It is also important for project management to be promoted in other new companies. This marketing activity should be based on scientific research that would demonstrate the efficiency of this type of management. Companies would be more responsive to a scientific study that proves that managerial costs are better controlled through project management and that even though these costs may rise, the economic growth will compensate for it.

CHANGES IN THE MATURITY OF ROMANIA AFTER THE POS PROJECT

Following this strategy for the development of Romania as a POS, some achievements were made in 2001–2004. Project Management Romania, the national association for project management, elaborated in 2002 the National Competence Baseline, which was adopted as Romanian Standard SR 13465:2002. Based on the National Competence Baseline, the Romanian association started the Project Management Certification Program. Project Management Romania—CERT, a unit of Project Management Romania, was designed as a certification body, and the association has nominated the first assessors. At the end of 2004, 35 Romanians were certified.

The national project management association promoted a common project management terminology by editing the first Romanian *Project Management Glossary.* As a result of this intense activity, the national association gained importance, having more than 100 members at present. A large number of the members of the association are involved in educational activities in the project management field through courses held at various universities and nongovernmental organizations oriented toward training and consultancy in Romania (Bucharest, Călăraşi, Craiova, Brasov, Constanta, Iasi, and Timişoara).

Project Management Romania has extended its activities. It does

- Take part in international actions (seminars, workshops, conferences, research projects, and publications) in the project management field in order to establish international collaboration and to promote international project management standards in Romania

- Develop its own research activities in the economic, technique, and environmental fields
- Distribute knowledge and research results, according to the law, by means of consultancy, assistance, and others similar tasks
- Support the integration of research results in the educational field
- Start and support projects performed in order to create new workplaces, improve working abilities, and introduce new technologies into current practice
- Disseminate its research results, as well as information from partner associations, by mass media and by editing and printing books, magazines, reports, recommendations, studies, and other kinds of specific materials
- Develop a documentation center with books, audio- and videotapes, and computer programs related to association purposes
- Start and take part into the implementation of new techniques to assess the impact of the projects according to national and international quality standards
- Give (by itself or in collaboration with other organizations) prizes and diplomas for special achievements related to the association purposes
- Support the development of a modern communication system among association members in order to have an efficient means of disseminating knowledge and information related to the project management field
- Support small and medium industries with regard to the initiation and development of evolution strategies in the specific competition environment

Following the example of Project Management Romania, other associations such as the Romanian Project Management Institute (PMI) chapter have become more active. It organized several courses for preparation for the certification examination so more than 20 Romanians obtained PMP certification in 2003–2004.

Having more interested people, more project management events have arisen. In 2004, the Project Management Forum was launched as an annual event, organized by Codecs. In 2005, another project management annual event was started, the Project Management Conference "All-inclusive Project Management." The conference was organized by BRM Business Consulting, the training and consulting division of the Romanian Commodities Exchange. Project Management Romania also organized several international project management seminars.

Project management research projects were financed by the Romanian Ministry of Education and Research. Some original books were written by Romanian specialists, and some important books were translated into the Romanian languages, such as *Happy Projects!* by R. Gareis; the *Gower Handbook of Project Management,* edited by J. Rodney Turner and Stephen J. Simister; and *Project Management,* by Dennis Lock.

Taking into consideration the rapid movement toward the maturization of project management approaches in Romania, we can expect this positive trend to continue.

REFERENCES

Anca D. 2004. *IT & C Sector: One of the Romanian Economy Priorities.* New York: Outsource World Techxny.

Ernst & Young Romania. 2004. *Doing Business in Romania* st & Young.

Gareis R. 2001. *Assessing and Benchmarking Project-Oriented Societies: Results of the POS Benchmarking Group1.* Projektmanagement Group, University of Economics and Business Administration, Vienna.

Benchmarking the project-oriented society. Presented at PM Days '01 Research Conference, Vienna.

Gareis R, Huemann M. 2001. Assessing and benchmarking project-oriented societies. *Int Project Manag J* 7(1):14–25.

JAA, E. Austin Associates, Inc., June 2001, *Romania: National Competitiveness Report—Executive Summary.*

PricewaterhouseCooper. 2005. *Business Guide to Romania 2005.* New York: PricewaterhouseCooper.

Project Management Romania. 2002. *Project Management Glossary.* Bucharest: Economic Printing House.

Romanian Agency for Forging Investment (ARIS). 2004. *Romania at a Glance* 4.

Romanian Government. 2004. *Government Program, 2005–2008.* Bucharest.

International Bank for Reconstruction and Development, World Bank. 2004. *Doing Business, Understanding Regulations.*

World Economic Forum. 2004. *The Global Competitiveness Report 2004.*

World Economic Forum. 2005. *Growth Competitiveness Index Rankings: 2005 and 2004 Comparisons;* www.weforum.org.

World Competitiveness of Romania, June 2005; www.roconsulboston.com.

CHAPTER 26

JAPANESE PROJECT MANAGEMENT PRACTICES ON GLOBAL PROJECTS

Hiroshi Tanaka

Yokohama, Japan

§Hiroshi (Hiro) Tanaka is the founder of the Japan Project Management Forum (JPMF), national president of the Project Management Association of Japan (PMAJ), fellow and global project management delegate of the Engineering Advancement Association of Japan (ENAA), and one of the distinguished leaders of the global project management community, currently serving as chair of the Global Project Management Forum (GPMF). Tanaka is also a member of the Project Management Institute (PMI), International Project Management Association (fellow of Project Management Associates, India and honorary member of Russian Project Management Association—SOVNET), Australian Institute of Project Management (AIPM), and Society of Project Management (SPM), Japan. He was an invited speaker in 15 countries and was conferred the PMI Distinguished Contribution Award 1998, Exxon Project Management Contribution Award, PMA India Global Fellowship awards, and Japanese engineering contribution awards. He wrote "Super Easy Project Management—Happy My Home Project," *PMBOK96*, Japanese edition (world's first translation), and dozens of papers on project management. Tanaka has 38 years of experience in the global engineering and construction industry with the JGC Corporation, Yokohama, Japan, for whom he is retired general manager of project services and board member of its division company JPS.

A CHARACTERISTIC PROFILE OF JAPANESE PROJECT MANAGEMENT

Japan excels in industrial project management on sizable capital investment and heavy infrastructure projects, as well as manufacturing technology transfer projects, that are carried out in Asia, the Middle East, Africa, Oceania, and Latin America, among other regions. Especially, the project management practiced in the engineering and construction (E&C) industry is the most advanced and typically embraces such characteristics as

- Mature state of project management fermented over the past five decades and forming a leading component of the global E&C project management sphere

- Management of the total cycle of a project encompassing business plans, project development and definition, engineering-procurement-construction (EPC), and operations and maintenance (O&M)

- Flexibility in project supply-chain arrangements in project-development formats and contracting strategies

- Transnational project management or integrative management of project operations components distributed globally and utilization of project resources procured from the global open market

This chapter discusses the basic structure and characteristic features of such Japanese total-cycle project management. The project management discussion in this chapter is based on the following premises:

- The Japanese project management dealt with in this chapter refers to the practice in the Japanese global E&C industry, in which Japanese contractor companies provide total project contracting services for global clients, referred to as owners, in the process industry, namely, the oil, natural gas, chemical, and petrochemical industry.

- Since the E&C industry companies are totally project-based entities, the term *project management* here may not be confined, depending on context, to a narrow project management discipline but may include a contractor's tiers of management functions as well.

- Living on the 80 to 70 percent of their turnovers from non-Japanese projects, the Japanese global E&C companies' project management is globally oriented and carries more than the stereotypical Japanese management characteristics, and as such, it does not depict an average profile of project management as practiced in the other branches of Japanese industry.

- The head of a project organization may be called the *project director* on major-sized projects or the *project manager* on projects of any size. In this chapter, the term *project director* is used representatively, which means heads of project organizations and may include its deputies.

LIFE CYCLE OF CAPITAL PROJECTS

Table 26.1 depicts the life cycle of a large capital investment project in the process industry as seen from an owner organization. Although there are slight differences in terminology used by owner or contractor companies, a typical project can be divided into four phases, namely, conception, definition, implementation, and completion. The approximate time required for each phase is indicated in the bottom column.

Conception Phase

During the conception phase, a sponsoring organization, in this case a plant owner, carries out basic data gathering, project needs screening, and feasibility studies for a potential project. This conception phase culminates in identification or confirmation of the goals

TABLE 26.1   Life Cycle of Capital Investment Projects

Conception	Definition	Implementation	Completion
6–18 Months once started	6–12 Months	2–5 Years	2–3 Months
Basic Data Gathering	Owner's Project Team	Owner/Contractor Project	Test and Inspection
Project Need Screening	Front-end Engineering	Teams	Precommissioning
Conceptual Project Scheme	Process Flow Diagram	Owner/Contractor Kick-off	Commissioning
Feasibility Studies	Equipment Datasheets	Project Execution Planning	Final Acceptance
Objectives of the Project	Instrument Datasheets	Follow-up on Project	Contract Close-out
Technical Studies	P&I Diagrams	Definition Package	Post-Project
Economic Analysis	Plot Plans	Planning/Analytical	Evaluation
Stakeholders Participating	Budgetary Cost Estimate	Engineering	
Preliminary Financing Plan	Key Project Execution Plans/	Production Engineering	
Risk Analysis	Contracting Strategy	Materials/Services	
Project Execution Scenario	Risk Analysis	Procurement	
Screening Cost Estimate	Project Definition Package	Construction (Erection)	
Project Proposal	Approval to Proceed	Project Management &	
Approval to Proceed	EPC Contractor Selection	Control	
	Firm Financing Plans	Project Administration	
	Project Management Involvement		
Limited	Considerable	Heavy	Heavy

and objectives of the project, preliminary plant scheme, economics, stakeholders participating in the project, risk level, and strategy for project development and execution. When the work for this phase is completed and there are good indications of project feasibility, the owner project team presents a project proposal to management of the sponsoring organization to obtain approval for proceeding to the next phase.

Definition Phase

The definition phase is a preamble to project implementation. It explores the feasibility in detail and further defines the project. Project definition work normally is undertaken with the owner employing a consulting firm or an international E&C company broadly experienced in this type of work for project development; such a company works in a joint team with the owner. The owner, assisted by a consultant, carries out front-end engineering, also called *basic engineering,* that produces a facility definition package. Based on this, the owner establishes budget and cash-flow forecasts and a project master execution plan, including contracting strategy for the implementation phase, which is also called in the industry the *EPC phase.* At the end of this phase, a prime EPC contractor is selected by the owner.

Implementation Phase

The implementation phase is the phase during which, based on the project basic planning and definition documents produced so far, the project gradually takes on physical shape in terms of engineering design documents, procured equipment and materials, and erected facilities. Most of the work in this phase is carried out by a prime contractor hired by the owner. Project management processes are deployed most intensively during this phase to direct the total project work, as well as to monitor, forecast, and control work scope, quality, project schedule, and costs.

Completion Phase

Now the project is around the final turn and into the home stretch, the completion phase. A project is not considered successful if it fails to attain the predetermined objectives. To complete a project smoothly, the contractor elaborately finalizes the project product, in this case a plant, so that the owner can accept the plant.

PROJECT MANAGEMENT INVOLVEMENT IN EARLY PROJECT DEVELOPMENT STAGES

Traditionally, the involvement of project management, especially that of contractor companies, has been mostly in the implementation phase. In this understanding, the role of project management exists in exerting efficient managerial efforts to complete the project to the plans laid down in the preceding project phases.

However, since both owners and E&C contractors in the process industry have tried to reap the benefits of combined expertise and experience to enhance project viability and optimize project plans, the chances of experienced contractors being involved in the project definition phase are increasing, and hence project management is afforded opportunities to expand into upstream project work.

The definition phase can be classified as a stand-alone subproject that produces a project definition package, project execution scenarios, and contractor selection, and thus project management in this phase is similar to that in the implementation phase, except that the former culminates in "soft" products and the latter in a "hard" product such as a plant or other built facility.

Further, project management in capital investment projects finds its application area more upstream, in the conception phase, if warranted by project development alternatives. This phase of a project usually is governed by a sponsor or owner company's strategic business management, but project management involvement is valued in the following alternatives:

- Contractor companies' broad project experience can contribute additional expertise to project development undertaken by owner companies with respect to comparative, country-to-country locating of production facilities, specific site selection, conceptual project scheme development, feasibility studies (referred to as *business cases* in other industry branches), project execution strategy development, and screening-cost estimate preparation.

- Owners who need financing for project materialization seek contractors' structured financing capabilities and brokerage capabilities for product marketing in association with their project development partners, including Japanese trading houses.

In particular, in the era of uneven distribution of funds required for project materialization, structured financing based on contractors' expert finance engineering techniques is an essential building block of project development. Such techniques support arranging for traditional financing, such as corporate financing and export credit agency (ECA) loans, and even open opportunities for project financing where traditional bank loans for projects are hard to be procured. Here, *project financing* means a scheme for raising project funds in which the repayment of loans is secured by the proceeds from the salable products from the plant built under the project in question.

Also characteristic of project planning during the definition phase is the technique called *front-end loading* (FEL). Project industry experience shows that consolidated and intensive cross-functional planning during the upfront phase of a project greatly enhances opportunities to optimize a project. This experience has led to the concept of the FEL exercise, in which owner and contractor key personnel responsible for the project planning, implementation, and utilization are gathered in an integrated team for some period during the definition or early execution planning phase and capitalize on their combined ability to influence a project in terms of facility configuration and performance, as well as to develop project execution alternatives.

PROJECT STRATEGY DEVELOPMENT

As a mature project management practitioner, Japanese E&C project management performs all the classic project planning functions based on the common methodologies available in the contemporary project management world. In addition, what characterizes Japanese E&C project management includes

- A broader project development strategy to maximize chances to win contracts using contractor business intelligence and capabilities
- A competitive supply-chain architecture design that crafts ever more innovative collaboration schemes among an owner, a contractor, and global projects interests
- Scenario analysis of project execution centering around use of cost-competitive project resources sourced globally on a project-to-project basis
- Contingency planning in provision for risk-intensive project environments on multi-hundred-million- to billion-dollar projects.

Project strategy and execution plans are compiled in an integrated project plan document and are shared by the project organization spread out across several countries.

PROJECT STAKEHOLDERS, CONTRACTING FORMATIONS, AND ORGANIZATIONS

One of the salient features of global E&C projects is a wide variety of project stakeholders, contracting formations and organizations. Figure 26.1 depicts the stakeholder structure of a major-sized refinery project in a developing country in which a project financing scheme was introduced. Project development schemes of this nature are becoming increasingly evident, where under the prevailing economic situation, the wisdom of raising project viability by way of unique commercialization routes proves to be a competitive edge.

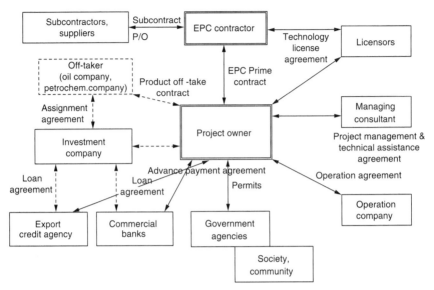

FIGURE 26.1   Stakeholder structure of a large E&C project.

The figure shows how major stakeholders ensuring the commercial viability of the project are involved in the project scheme, in addition to the usual project stakeholders in construction projects, such as an owner, a prime contractor, subcontractors, technology suppliers, materials suppliers, and society in general surrounding the project. Such stakeholders are investment companies supported by both export credit agencies (ECAs) and commercial banks, product off-taking companies, and plant operating companies.

Likewise, project delivery in the global E&C industry presents a variety of methods, reflecting the sets of owner companies' contracting philosophies and capital investment environments at the time. Alternatives in project delivery are shown in Fig. 26.2.

The once-through approach is such that a global E&C contractor is employed at an early stage of the project, namely, the definition phase, either from the detailed feasibility study (type I) or from the project definition work, in other words, front-end engineering work (type II). In the roll-over approach, a global E&C contractor is first assigned to the definition phase with the first-refusal right given to roll over the contract for the implementation phase (EPC phase); if the owner and the contractor come to terms at the end of the definition phase, such roll-over is realized.

The EPC turnkey route is the most common method of project delivery, in which international bidding for the EPC work is carried out based on the project definition package prepared by another consulting firm on behalf of the owner, and the successful bidder executes the total EPC work as the prime contractor. A variation on this delivery method is where the global contractor takes charge of the engineering and procurement work of the project, and the construction work is contracted out to an in-country erection contractor directly by the owner. The phase-to-phase contracting is piecemeal contracting by the owner for each, the engineering, procurement, and construction work; here, the global contractor's scope of work is mostly the engineering work, with an option for procurement assistance to the owner. This last route is not used on large-sized projects.

Figure 26.3 illustrates the E&C industry practice for contract compensation modes versus project delivery methods. Compensation modes are fixed lump sum (LS) or

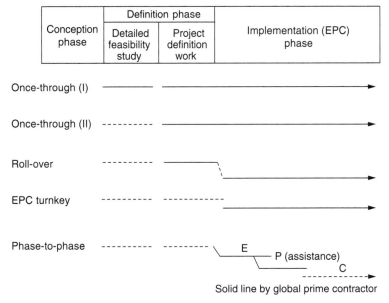

FIGURE 26.2   Project delivery method alternatives.

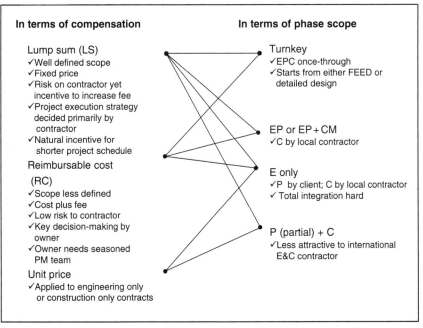

FIGURE 26.3   Prime contract format variations.

reimbursable cost (RC); rarely is the unit-price mode used for partial project phase contracts. Japanese and continental European global E&C contractors mainly operate under the LS system, whereas U.S. and U.K. contractors are more used to the RC system; such differences in operations are influenced by owners' and contractors' preferences.

In conjunction with the once-through or EPC turnkey project delivery alternatives, such unique variations as given below are introduced to take advantage of supply-chain innovation.

Strategic Alliances

An owner or owners and one or several prime contractors form an alliance for a specific project to reap benefits of the combined strengths of all the best aspects among the participating partners. The owners and the contractors form an entirely amalgamated project team for completely joint execution of the project and share the gains and losses of the project on an equal partner basis; this scheme is unique in turning the conventional, and often adversarial, client-contractor relationship on its head.

Partnering

Partnering is a special services agreement between an owner and a contractor for an extended period, typically from five to seven years, during which period the owner guarantees a certain annual amount of contracts and in return for that the contractor establishes and operates a dedicated division staffed with contractor technical employees satisfactory to the owner to work exclusively on an aggregate of the owners' projects. Partnering is used where an owner seeks consistent quality of work by a carefully selected contractor.

Joint-Venture/Consortium Prime Contractors

The increasing sizes of projects and associated large risks, the need to couple financing packages required to be brought in by prime contractors, the pursuit of combined strengths enhancing the chances to win a contract, and the preferences of the owner based on its contracting policy all encourage the formation of joint ventures or consortia of prime contractors from different countries. The term *joint venture* refers to an incorporated joint-venture company in many industries; however, in the E&C industry, the term is used more often for unincorporated joint contractor project organizations sharing both a single or significantly common financial fund and the project losses. Another collaboration format common among prime contractors is the consortium. In this scheme, a clear split of work for each member contractor is defined, and the consortium participants are individually responsible for their own defined scopes of work within the consortium. However, in both joint ventures and consortia, the partners are jointly and severally responsible to the owner for performance of the project.

Partners of a joint venture or consortium may vary between projects. E&C contractors may collaborate on one project and then turn around and compete with each other for other projects. This may sound contradictory, but E&C companies have proven that this flexibility of partnership has enhanced the overall capabilities of the total E&C industry.

PROJECT MANAGEMENT METHODS IN GLOBAL ENGINEERING AND CONSTRUCTION PROJECTS

The project management methods employed by the Japanese global E&C industry are basically similar to those used by its Western counterparts because they are rooted in the U.S. process industry, which is the cradle of project management, together with NASA and the U.S. defense industry. The top Japanese E&C contractors have 50 years of experience in practicing classic project management. This means that the cliché statement in many industry branches or public services that have lately entered the project management sphere that "project management is a core business competency" has been commonsense in the industry for decades. Also, the industry's project management is faced by ever-evolving challenges. One of the most crucial ones is how to manage global cooperative projects because no single corporation can thrive on its own resources in this borderless project industry scenario and tough economic situation. While Japanese project management tackles such emerging challenges, as discussed in the preceding section, its project management methods offer unique features in legacy project management areas as follows.

Enhanced Work-Breakdown Structure (WBS)

The WBS used by global E&C contractors, including the Japanese, is extensive in levels, even down to level 10 or more; is mostly standardized for uniform use on all company projects; and is structured for global collaboration of multiple parties involved in a single project. It facilitates communications between parties and allows quality definition of projects and a clearer split of work.

Multipillar Operations Management

Global E&C companies have developed methods and know-how to manage operations of a number of project components, called *operations centers,* distributed throughout the world on each project. The methods, among others, clarify the function of a project directorate and project operations centers. For efficiency, project management normally consists of two tiers: The project directorate manages the primary relationship with the owner project organization and undertakes the total management of the respective operations centers, and the day-to-day management of the respective project operations centers is left to the management of those under the guidelines agreed on between the project directorate and the management of the respective project operations centers. Scope splitting among operations centers depends on both technical and commercial parameters; the baseline is to choose the split of the work that is the best for the entire project. Usually, all project participants are aligned to the project and motivated to pursue harmonization because the success of the project will benefit all the participants; however, this cannot be expected without a well-thought-out communications system linking all operations centers.

Intensive Team Building

Since quite a few project members and other project stakeholders of many nationalities are involved in global projects, team building is an essential ingredient of project success, and it requires continuous attention by all the participants. Team-building sessions normally are hosted at the outset of the project and at one or two key project milestones, in which the owner project taskforce members and the contractor's key project members stay together at outside facilities for concentrated discussions and familiarization; a specialist team-building consultant and a total quality management (TQM) coordinator are assigned as required by contract terms or project specific consideration. Team-building sessions are intended to define or confirm—and positively agree on—the fundamental objectives and strategy of the project and understand how to work together in the most efficient and interactive way to achieve those objectives. Also, challenge targets, to improve project performance, are agreed on between the owner and the contractor.

Sophisticated Cost-Estimating Methods

The Japanese E&C companies, mostly operating on lump-sum turnkey (LSTK) contracts up to a billion dollars, have highly accurate cost-estimating capabilities, namely, a ± 2 to 3 percent accuracy from contracted fixed prices, which is necessary to stay in business. To sharpen this edge, contractor companies continuingly invest in cost-estimating methods and global cost databases. This capability, however, does not seem to be transportable to other industry branches because of differences in business structures and cost-estimating methods.

EDMS-Based Configuration Management

Multi-hundred-million- to billion-dollar-grade capital investment projects involve a huge number of document items. An electronic data management system (EDMS) enhances project work efficiency, especially in configuration management. Up-to-date design information and documents can be shared by project members concerned in all operations centers simultaneously. An EDMS also contributes to achieving the goal of "paperless" project operation.

Global Resources Management System

As discussed below, global project resources deployment is a vital ingredient for project success. To support this facet, proprietary resources management systems are used to track resources procurement and movement on a real-time basis.

Construction Planning to Design Using Multidimensional CAD

On-built facilities' projects, constructability assessment during the design stage is important. The current industry trend is to use three- or four-dimensional computer-aided design (CAD) to plan construction operations by means of CAD-assisted simulation techniques.

Cold-Eye Project Progress Review

For many years, the management of a project had been left to the project director, who was held accountable for project performance to the company management and who was required, therefore, to report project progress periodically. However, as projects have become increasingly more complex, project execution environments ever tighter, and the chances of substandard performance greater, owners and contractors alike now introduce structured project progress reviews, which are also called *cold-eye,* or *independent, project reviews.* In structured project reviews, project progress is evaluated at company-specified timing and according to given criteria by general managers of projects, chief project managers, heads of project management technology departments, or other seasoned experts who are not involved in the day-to-day management of the projects. The evaluation criteria include progress at company-selected milestones (e.g., major equipment orders committed, field erection started, peak construction, etc.) in the light of company standard data, cost expenditures, areas of concern, and remaining risk items. The review team offers to the project team constructive advice based on their cold-eye review. The project director not only benefits from the structured review but also uses the opportunity to secure commitments of support from upper management or functional department managers on areas of concern.

ENGINEERING MANAGEMENT

The engineering phase of capital investment projects consists of the front-end engineering stage, which defines a project's facility configuration, performance, and functionality and which are together referred to as the *basic facility design,* and the production engineering stage, which translates the basic design into detailed mechanical and structural designs through elaboration, with design data being made available gradually as the project progresses. In modern E&C project practice, project management is not involved in day-to-day technical management of engineering work, unlike those project managers in information technology (IT) and other technology projects. The engineering management is the role of the project engineering manager, reporting to project management, who carries out their function through project engineers or technical coordinators; the actual engineering work is done, under a matrix organizational system, by functional design engineering departments that specialize in particular engineering disciplines.

While the engineering phase does not involve serious uncertainties on projects using proven technology, such as familiar chemical processes, mechanical handling, or materials handling, projects face challenges posed by supply-chain strategy. Many global projects now use more than two production engineering offices, including those located outside Japan, to pursue lower engineering costs. This practice encourages project management to join engineering management in deciding on the most efficient production engineering formation under the project's given constraints; introducing quality assurance and time management plans for outsourced engineering work, as well as contingency plans, just in case; streamlining interfaces with downstream materials procurement work; and devising engineering logistics that support the use of home office engineering systems by remote production engineering offices and establishing a work flow for design products, routing them through design personnel at the various offices participating in the project.

GLOBAL PROCUREMENT MANAGEMENT

Large E&C projects source services, equipment, and materials required for projects from the worldwide open market wherever in the world the facilities are constructed, which literally characterizes global projects. Also, while front-end engineering is carried out normally at a contractor's home office in Japan, production engineering, or detailed engineering design, is performed mostly at the satellite engineering offices of the contractor's own or by associated engineering subcontractors both located in Asian countries or in Europe.

Site-erection work on facilities is sublet to erection contractors in the project host country or in surrounding countries, except for such trades that require highly sophisticated skills that can only be supplied by erection contractors in industrialized countries.

Procurement management practices in the global E&C industry are some of the most stringent and offer such features as

- Project procurement operations comprising project procurement planning, candidate vendor listing, inquiry, vendor selection and contracting, expediting (time management), quality control at source, traffic, and site delivery (Fig. 26.4)

- Procurement of all services and materials done to item-unique requirements and design specifications

- Procurement procedures both transparent and rigid to avoid unfair or sloppy procurement practices and requiring competitive bidding from sources in multiple countries, unless sole-source procurement is justified by a monopoly on a particular technology by a vendor

- Constantly variable procurement sources to take advantage of the changing competitiveness of vendors and service providers in a variety of countries and markets and depending on relative supplier workloads, exchange rates of the supplier countries, and commercial offerings in response to the inquiry at the time in question

- Consistent finding of low-cost vendors and service providers in developing countries to chase lower project costs in the face of stiff contractor market competition (This should be accompanied by contractor companies' secondment of personnel to low-cost suppliers to complement or reinforce their capabilities.)

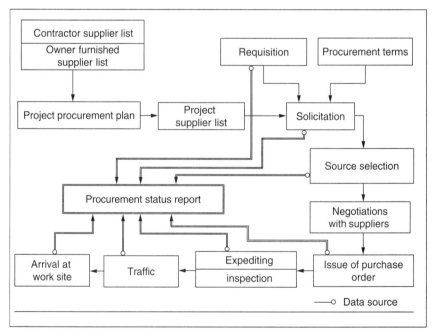

FIGURE 26.4   Flow of procurement operations.

Procurement operations alone are thus projects as well, and their management is project management in its own right.

Because of the vast U.S. dollar amounts and substantial work volume involved in procurement operations, E&C projects, without exception, rely on permanent procurement divisions or departments, although project procurement managers and buyers in the permanent procurement department are dedicated to sizable discrete projects. In such a modified project procurement system, the project director approves the nomination of a project procurement manager and a lead purchasing agent, project procurement strategy, and vendor evaluations for critical items that are costly or essential to ensure the operability of the built facilities. The primary project management role in the procurement phase includes ensuring that project procurement procedures comply with company rules, pursuing an optimal balance of competitive buying and securing the technical reliability of ordered items, ensuring that a self-sufficient procurement status reporting system is available that advises project management of the real-time movement of materials on order to avoid surprises, and integrating the procurement phase with the engineering and construction phases so that procurement operations do not proceed based solely on their own interests.

MANAGEMENT OF MULTICULTURAL SITE OPERATIONS

One of the salient features of project management on global E&C projects is the cross-cultural management of site project teams. Unlike the Japanese-managed projects a quarter century ago, one can probably not distinguish site operations managed by Japanese E&C companies from those managed by Western companies unless one notices the very few Japanese on site managing the project who are not found elsewhere. In fact, the number of Japanese managerial staff on site ranges from 5 to 20, even on projects in excess of several hundred million dollars in investment costs; instead, the site management team consists of Japanese, British, Korean, Indian, Pakistani, Filipino, American (few, except on a joint-venture project with a U.S. contractor), and project host country nationals.

In global E&C industry practice, the normal site project management representative is the site project manager, usually just called the *site manager,* who is delegated the authority by the project director to direct site operations. The project director, normally located at the home office, relocates to the site in those cases where the client's project director opts for being located at the site during the peak construction period. In any case, the total management of site operations is the responsibility of the site project manager, whereas the project director takes charge of overall project management integration.

The site project management is dedicated to the project management of the site construction phase, which includes the following unique functions:

- Be aware of the diversity of site human components and take proactive action toward integration of site management team members, who are diverse in nationality, ethnic group, culture, and project mind-set.

- Ensure that the contractor's site team maintains a win-win relationship with the owner site project team because both of them are locked day and night in the same neighborhood, unlike projects of other categories.

- Maintain a harm-free relationship with the surrounding communities, the interests of which are not always aligned with the construction project.

PROJECT MANAGEMENT INVOLVEMENT IN THE OPERATIONS AND MAINTENANCE OF BUILT FACILITIES

Years ago, E&C projects for built facilities, commercial, industrial, or public, ended basically when the completed facilities were accepted by owners and titles to built facilities were transferred from contractors to owners. This practice normally meant that owner and contractor project management for the EPC phase of the project had fulfilled its function when the project was accepted by the owner.

With the development of supply-chain and facility life-cycle management theories and strategies, however, an increasing number of public infrastructure or industrial production facilities are now developed with due consideration given to the maximization of life-cycle value or, conversely, the minimization of life-cycle costs of projects. On such projects, an E&C contractor's involvement in a project is expanded beyond the traditional project delivery point to additionally assume

- Facility operations and maintenance (O&M) services for a fee.
- Facility operation-in-hand under a concession from the sponsor for a fixed long term or under its own ownership, which are referred to as *build-operate-transfer* (BOT) and *build-own-operate* (BOO), respectively.
- Private-public partnership (PPP), in which commercial interests, including developers and contractors, finance, build, and operate built facilities on a public owner's behalf.

Because of the long-term engagement of contractor companies and differences in quality of project management expertise required in these project arrangements, it is unusual that project managers of the EPC phase are assigned to continue on to manage these extra phases. However, project directors are at least responsible for the following as part of total project management:

- Organize experts in total-cycle project management, including investment analysts and operations and maintenance management specialists.
- Ensure that project plans pursue life-cycle optimization of projects through front-end loading exercises.
- At an appropriate point in construction project progress, plan an organization and procedures to smoothly transition from the construction phase to the operation and maintenance phase.
- Carry out secure transfer of management responsibility to the operation and maintenance management.

PROJECT ICT INFRASTRUCTURE SUPPORTING GLOBAL PROJECT MANAGEMENT

Major-sized global E&C projects impose challenges on contractor project information and communication technology (ICT) infrastructure. The challenges are

- Robust systems structure that allows handling of the vast amount of data generated by multi-hundred-million- to billion-dollar projects
- Systems configuration that enables or facilitates data transfer from project execution to project management with a minimum of human intervention and synchronization of data among component project management information systems

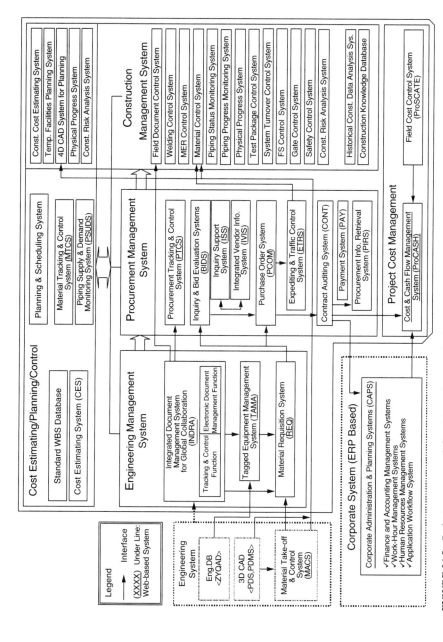

FIGURE 26.5 Project management information and communication system.

- High-speed transactions and data transfer for transnational project operations connecting multiple project operations centers distributed around the world
- Remote accessibility to home office systems, usually using Web technology, to support construction site teams and other distant participant offices
- Flexibility in tailoring output to absorb project-specific requirements (However, project managers should recognize that tailoring output to suit preferences or to satisfy technical curiosity is penalized by unjustifiable extra costs.)
- Connectivity with counterpart systems of partner contractor organizations under a joint-venture or consortium structure

Usually, contractor project management ICT systems for the E&C industry are built as a combination of commercial planning and scheduling software, commercial or home-built cost management software, and proprietary resource and cost-estimating and resource management systems based on the contractor's decades of experience and configured around relational database management systems (RDBMS). Figure 26.5 shows a typical structure of a Japanese global E&C contractor's project management system.

While project directors are not necessarily knowledgeable on the latest ICT, considering that reliable and efficient ITC use is vital for global projects, they should include a project ITC consultant in the project team during the planning and buildup phase to help the project director make informed decisions on the smart selection of project IT components used in the project and subsequent surveillance of systems functionality and troubleshooting.

INDEX

1

ABOUT THE EDITORS

DAVID I. CLELAND is a Fellow of the Project Management Institute and three-time recipient of the Institute's Distinguished Contribution to Project Management Award. The author/editor of 38 books on project management and engineering management, he has been described as the "Father of Project Management." The Project Management Institute's annual David I. Cleland Excellence in Project Management Literature Award is named in his honor.

ROLAND GAREIS is Professor of Project Management and Director of the post-graduate program on international project management at the Vienna University of Economics and Business Administration. He is also the owner of Roland Gareis Consulting. A recognized expert on project management, he is the author of *Happy Projects!* and other books.